SWORD & SHIELD REVISITED

A Practical Approach to Section 1983

Edited by Mary Massaron Ross

STATE AND LOCAL GOVERNMENT LAW SECTION

AMERICAN BAR ASSOCIATION

Cover design by Jim Colao.

Printed in the United States of America.

Library of Congress Catalog Card Number 97–80528
ISBN 1-57073-522-0

Discounts are available for books ordered in bulk. Special consideration is given to state bars, CLE programs, and other bar-related organizations. Inquire at ABA Publishing, Book Publishing, American Bar Association, 750 North Lake Shore Drive, Chicago, Illinois 60611.

02 01 00 99 98 5 4 3 2 1

Contents

Introduction
Mary Massaron Ross

In 1983, two preeminent civil rights lawyers edited *Section 1983: Sword and Shield*, an anthology that explored the expanding scope of 42 U.S.C. Section 1983 liability. In a series of articles, authors analyzed the history of § 1983, the scope of potential liability, available defenses, remedies, and policy implications after *Monell v. Department of Social Services*.[1] More than a decade has elapsed since then and much has changed. But practicing lawyers, academics, and judges are as hard-pressed to keep up with the twists and turns in this changing area of law as they were then. Whether tracing the lines of authority that set forth the parameters for an illegal search and seizure claim or examining the emerging retaliation theories brought by public employees, § 1983 claims are as legally and factually complex as ever. Grounded in the Constitution, this area of law affects every aspect of life in our constitutional democracy, from birth to death.[2]

Every official policy or conduct of a state or local government is potentially subject to a suit on some constitutional or statutory theory of liability. Every public employee, government official, citizen, or student in public and private schools is entitled to sue to vindicate his or her civil rights. A small town is forced to permit nude dancing in a local bar. A politician is prohibited from firing his political enemy when he takes office. A citizen's property development is limited due to government land use regulations. A jailer does not provide proper medical care to a prisoner or fails to protect him from other inmates who are threatening him. A police officer tries to arrest a suspected drug dealer or to search his house.

Alexis de Tocqueville recognized that there "is hardly a political question in the United States which does not sooner or later turn into a judicial one."[3] He might have expanded this to include social, economic, and cultural questions as well. Nowhere is the scope of the judiciary more apparent than in the area of § 1983.

---

1. 436 U.S. 658 (1978).
2. *See* Vacco V. Quill, 717 S. Ct. 2293 (1997); Cruzan v. Director, Missouri Dep't of Health, 497 U.S. 261 (1990); Webster v. Reproductive Health Service, 492 U.S. 490 (1989).
3. Alexis de Tocqueville, Democracy in America 270 (J.P. Mayer, ed., 1969).

With this new volume of *Sword and Shield Revisited: A Practical Approach to Section 1983*, the reader will see the framework for § 1983 as it has developed. Professor Sheldon Nahmod presents an overview of the *prima facie* § 1983 case through three hypotheticals. In a "cook's tour" of § 1983, Nahmod takes the reader through the concepts with an emphasis on the importance of the Fourteenth Amendment and its enforcement.

With that overview, the reader can learn the procedural intricacies of § 1983 litigation in federal court. Jane K. Swanson identifies important procedural issues including ripeness, forum choice, and removal. She discusses *Leatherman v. Tarrant County*[4] and its impact on the rules of pleading and the availability of motions to dismiss. Swanson's procedural guide sets forth considerations pertaining to damages, the jury charge, discovery, and waivable defenses.

Professor Steven Steinglass provides a comprehensive overview of § 1983 litigation in state court. Starting with its historical background, Steinglass provides a discussion of state court jurisdiction, forum choice considerations, the methodology of state court § 1983 litigation, and § 1983 remedial issues.

Professor Karen Blum describes the government's affirmative duties after *DeShaney v. Winnebago County Department of Social Services.*[5] She advocates a more expansive approach to substantive due process and suggests that the complexity of situations requires careful consideration of the level of culpability and the causal connection between the challenged conduct and the claimed injury.

Michael S. Bogren presents a more defense-oriented view of municipal liability, reviews the methods for showing that a municipality is liable, and explains recent Supreme Court decisions defining the critical proofs necessary to present a *prima facie* "failure to train" case.

Professor Kathryn R. Urbonya's article discusses police misconduct claims in the context of the continuum of force that police may use under a Fourth Amendment reasonableness analysis. Urging consideration of the gravity of the offense along with courts' traditional focus on danger to the police, Urbonya calls for increased judicial scrutiny of factors such as the suspect's movements and psychological condition.

---

4. 507 U.S. 163 (1993).
5. 489 U.S. 189 (1989).

In the chapter on the constitutional rights of public employees, I set forth the constitutional rights of public employees—rights that limit public employers substantially when dealing with their work force. Richard G. Carlisle discusses the § 1983 land use case from its inception to the Supreme Court's recent expansion of the rights of property owners.

David J. LaBrec and Katie Anderson discuss prison and jail litigation. They describe constitutional rights implicated by overcrowding, security, health and medical care, exercise, visitation, and numerous other aspects of prison life.

Margaret-Ann F. Howie tells us about the student's constitutional rights in the public school setting, a topic that demonstrates the reach of § 1983 into virtually every area of American life. Robert F. Brown provides an overview of the individual immunity defenses available for legislators, prosecutors, judges, and other public employees and officials sued under § 1983. Martin F. Schwartz provides a user's manual for the admissibility of investigatory reports in § 1983 civil rights actions. This evidence is often extremely significant to police misconduct claims. John W. Witt sets forth the principles of law that guide the collection of attorney's fees under 42 U.S.C. § 1988.

Since the 1960s, when the Warren Court expanded the reach of the courts, particularly in the area of constitutional law, there has been a resurgence of non-interventionist constitutional theories. These debates affect the hundreds of lawsuits filed in state and federal courts across this country litigating the rights and obligations of citizens and their governments. In this book, the authors provide a practical approach to this technically difficult and ever-evolving area of law.

About the Editor

Mary Massaron Ross, of Plunkett & Coooney, P.C., concentrates her practice on appellate law, civil rights, land use, and government liability. A former clerk for Justice Boyle on the Michigan Supreme Court, she has briefed and argued cases before the Michigan Supreme Court, the Michigan Court of Appeals, and the Sixth Circuit Court of Appeals. Notable cases that she has handled include *Mason v. Wayne County, Ortman v. Thomas, McBride v. Village of Michiana,* and *Kevorkian v. Thompson.*

Ms. Massaron Ross has chaired the Appellate Practice Section of the State Bar of Michigan. She also co-chairs the Michigan Appellate Bench Bar Conference Foundation, an organization of appellate lawyers and judges in Michigan. She has been active in the Appellate Advocacy Committee of the Tort and Insurance Practice Section of the ABA, serving as a past co-chair of its subcommittee on appellate rules of procedure. She was recently appointed by Chief Judge Corrigan to the Michigan Court of Appeals Internal Operating Procedures Task Force. Ms. Massaron Ross has served in the leadership of the State and Local Government Law Section of the ABA and now serves as a member of its governing council. She also chairs the Tort and Insurance Practice Section's Governmental Liability Committee.

Ms. Massaron Ross graduated second in her law school class from Wayne State University in 1990, where she served as an editor on the law review and was nominated to membership in the Order of the Coif. Ms. Massaron Ross has published numerous articles dealing with appeals, government law, zoning and land use, election law, and civil rights. She serves as an associate editor of the *Tort and Insurance Practice Law Journal.* A frequent lecturer, Ms. Massaron Ross has spoken at seminars around the country on such topics as preserving the record on appeal, the constitutional rights of public employees, and land use law. She is admitted to practice in all Michigan state courts, the United States Supreme Court, and the U.S. Court of Appeals for the Third, Sixth, and Seventh Circuits.

About the Contributors

Katie Anderson is a trial attorney and a member of the Strasburger & Price, L.L.P. law firm in Dallas, Texas, where she practices in the General Litigation Division and is a member of the Governmental Law and Litigation Practice Group. In addition to her practice in governmental law and litigation, she also handles litigation involving premises liability, products liability, and other related topics.

She recently authored a paper titled "Condition or Use of Tangible Personal Property Under the Texas Tort Claims Act" presented at the Governmental Law and Litigation Practice Group's 1996 Tort Litigation Seminar. Other papers include "What Private Investigators Can Do," presented at the Traveler's Insurance Seminar in 1996; "Medical Liens," presented at the ITT Hartford Seminar in 1997; and "A Case Study in Jail Condition Litigation," presented to the Texas Association of Counties' 1997 County Management Institute.

Ms. Anderson earned her B.B.A. from the University of Texas and her J.D. from Baylor University in Waco, Texas. While in law school, she was a member of the *Baylor Law Review* and took first place in the Moot Court Competition.

Karen M. Blum is a professor of law at Suffolk University Law School, where she teaches in the areas of civil procedure, civil rights, and police misconduct litigation. She received her B.A. in Philosophy from Wells College, her J.D. from Suffolk University Law School, and her LL.M. from Harvard University.

Professor Blum has been a regular faculty participant in Section 1983 civil rights programs and institutes sponsored by the ABA, the Massachusetts Bar Association, the Continuing Legal Education Division of Georgetown University Law Center, and the Illinois Institute for Continuing Legal Education. In addition, she has served as a faculty member for numerous workshops for federal judges and magistrate judges sponsored by the Federal Judicial Center.

Professor Blum has authored numerous articles on Section 1983 and is co-author with Michael Avery and David Rudovsky of *Police Misconduct, Law and Litigation* (3d ed., Clark Boardman Callaghan, 1996).

Michael S. Bogren is a shareholder in the Detroit-based firm Plunkett & Cooney, P.C., and is the managing shareholder of the firm's Kalamazoo, Michigan, office. He specializes in the representation of municipal defendants in civil rights litigation in both federal and state courts

Mr. Bogren is the author of several articles on civil rights litigation and constitutional law. He has lectured on civil rights litigation for the Michigan ICLE and also lectures for the Michigan Municipal League on civil rights issues.

Mr. Bogren is a member of the ABA, the Michigan Defense Trial Counsel, the Michigan Association of Municipal Attorneys, and the Kalamazoo County Bar Association. He earned his B.A. from Western Michigan University and his J.D. from the University of Detroit.

Robert F. Brown is a partner in the Dallas, Texas, firm of Vial, Hamilton, Koch & Knox, L.L.P., where he practices in the firm's State and Local Government Section. Mr. Brown specializes in litigation and appellate practice with an emphasis on municipal law, including constitutional law, civil rights, and zoning and land use matters.

In addition to his litigation practice, Mr. Brown acts as city attorney for a number of municipalities in the North Texas area. He is currently chair of the Federal Litigation Section of the Federal Bar Association and vice chair of the Government Liability Committee of the State and Local Government Law Section of the ABA.

Mr. Brown is a frequent author and speaker on civil rights and land use matters with over 25 articles and presentations to his credit, including co-authorship of *Seeking Terra Firma in Complex Zoning Litigation: The Defense Practitioner's Perspective,* published by Matthew Bender & Company in its 1994 Institute on Planning, Zoning and Eminent Domain.

Mr. Brown received his law degree from Texas Tech University School of Law and his B.B.A. from Texas A&M University in 1983.

Richard G. Carlisle is a partner in the Kansas City firm Freilich, Leitner & Carlisle. He has handled many of the nation's most complex cases in the fields of land use planning and environmental law. His experience ranges from resolving locational disputes regarding ski areas in Aspen and Eagle, Colorado, to negotiating the marina lease that led to the redevelopment of South Beach in Miami Beach, Florida. While Mr. Carlisle has argued appellate cases at all levels, including the U.S. Supreme Court, the emphasis in his practice has been on avoiding the high costs of litigation through use of mediation and other dispute resolution techniques.

Mr. Carlisle has published extensively and has served as either a faculty member or chair for various seminars and lectures, including presentations for the National Conference of State Legislators, ABA national institutes, various state bar planning associations, law schools including Georgetown, Duke and University of Missouri-Kansas City, the National College of District Attorneys, various state municipal leagues, ALI-ABA, and the National League of Cities.

Margaret-Ann F. Howie is counsel to the superintendent of the Baltimore County Public Schools. In this capacity, she advises the superintendent of schools and senior staff on a variety of issues involving employment, students' rights, and collective bargaining. She previously worked as director of Legal and Legislative Services for the Maryland Association of Boards of Education.

Ms. Howie is a member of the board of directors of the National School Boards Association's Council of School Attorneys and has served as chair of the council's Urban Law Committee. She has spoken and written nationally on legal issues related to student discipline and school violence.

Ms. Howie received her J.D. from Columbia University School of Law in 1988, her M.A. from Middlebury College, and her B.A. from Johns Hopkins University.

David J. LaBrec is a partner in the Dallas, Texas, law firm of Strasburger & Price, where he serves as the chief of the Governmental Law Practice Group. Mr. LaBrec has spent his entire legal career advising, representing, and defending local governmental entities, public officials, and employees.

Mr. LaBrec is a frequent speaker and noted author on local governmental and public official liability, insurance, and self-insurance. He was the recipient of the National Institute of Municipal Law Officers Outstanding National Public Service Award in 1986 while serving as First Assistant City Attorney for the city of Dallas, Texas. He served as general counsel for the Texas Municipal League and the Texas Municipal League Liability Self-Insurance Pool from 1980 to 1985.

Mr. LaBrec served as chair of the Governmental Liability Committee of the Defense Research Institute, Inc. (DRI) and is now on the DRI Board of Directors. He served as chair of the Governmental Liability Committee of the ABA, Tort and Insurance Practice Section, and on the boards of directors of the Southwestern Legal Foundation Municipal Legal Studies Center and the Southwestern Law Enforcement Institute. In addition, Mr. LaBrec served as chair of the State Bar of Texas Continuing Legal Education Institute on "Suing and Defending Governmental Entities and Public Officials" for a decade.

Mr. LaBrec received his B.A. from the University of Texas at El Paso and his J.D. from St. Mary's University School of Law.

Sheldon H. Nahmod is a distinguished professor of law at Chicago-Kent College of Law, Illinois Institute of Technology. In addition, he has argued civil rights cases before the U.S. Supreme Court and various federal courts of appeals.

Professor Nahmod has published extensively in the areas of constitutional law, the First Amendment, and civil rights, and is the author of the leading treatise on Section 1983, *Civil Rights and Civil Liberties Litigation: The Law of Section 1983*, a fourth edition of which will be published in late 1997. He is also co-author of the casebook *Constitutional Torts* (1995) and the editor of *A Section 1983 Civil Rights Anthology* (1994).

Professor Nahmod lectures regularly, not only to lawyers throughout the country on Section 1983, but also to federal judges under the auspices of the Federal Judicial Center in Washington, D.C.

Professor Nahmod has served as visiting professor at the University of Indiana, Bloomington; at the University of Cincinnati; and most recently at Boston College Law School.

A graduate of the University of Chicago (B.A.) and Harvard Law School (J.D. and LL.M.), Professor Nahmod received a Master's Degree in Religious Studies at the University of Chicago Divinity School in June 1996.

Martin A. Schwartz is a professor of law at Touro Law Center, Huntington, New York. He is the author of volumes 1A, 1B, and 1C, *Section 1983 Litigation Claims and Defenses* (3d ed., Wiley Law Publications, 1997) and *Section 1983 Litigation: Federal Evidence* (2d ed., 1995). He has written numerous articles on Section 1983 litigation. He is the author of a column in the *New York Law Journal* titled "Public Interest Law."

Professor Schwartz is co-chair of the Practicing Law Institute annual program on Section 1983 litigation. A legal services attorney from 1968 to 1984, Professor Schwartz has argued three cases before the U.S. Supreme Court.

Steven H. Steinglass is dean and professor of law at the Cleveland-Marshall College of Law, Cleveland State University, where he has taught since 1980. He teaches Civil Procedure, Federal Jurisdiction, and Section 1983 Litigation, and he lectures throughout the country on Section 1983 issues at continuing legal and judicial education programs.

Professor Steinglass, who writes frequently on Section 1983, is the author of *Section 1983 Litigation in State Courts,* a two-volume treatise published by Clark Boardman Callaghan.

Professor Steinglass, a member of the Ohio and Wisconsin bars, practiced in Wisconsin from 1969 to 1980 with Legal Action of Wisconsin, Inc., and its predecessor legal services organizations, and he has argued two Section 1983 cases in the U.S. Supreme Court, *Board of Regents v. Roth* and *Felder v. Casey.*

Jane K. Swanson practices in Woodlands, Texas, with the firm Johnson and Swanson. She is a former managing attorney and litigation director of East Texas Legal Services and a former project director of Wyandotte-Leavenworth Legal Services in Kansas City, Kansas.

In her legal services and private practice career, Ms. Swanson has litigated a wide variety of Section 1983 claims on behalf of indigent clients in both the federal and state court systems. She has been a frequent speaker on civil rights issues at seminars for legal services and other public interest attorneys, and has lectured on the topic "Procedural Issues in Section 1983 Litigation" for the ABA.

Ms. Swanson is 1977 graduate of the University of Houston Law Center.

Kathryn R. Urbonya, a professor at William and Mary School of Law, has written numerous articles about the use of force by governmental officials and the availability of the qualified immunity defense for constitutional torts. She has lectured at conferences sponsored by the ABA, Defense Research

Institute, Federal Judicial Center, Georgetown University Law Center, Practicing Law Institute, and the U.S. Information Agency.

Prior to teaching, Professor Urbonya was a law clerk for Justice Gerald W. VandeWalle of the North Dakota Supreme Court and Federal District Judge G. Ernest Tidwell in Atlanta. She is co-authoring a treatise on civil rights litigation to be published by West Publishing.

John W. Witt is special counsel in the San Diego, California, firm Lounsbery Ferguson Altona & Peak, L.L.P. He served as San Diego's city attorney from 1969 to 1996, as chief deputy city attorney from 1964 to 1969, and as deputy city attorney from 1961 to 1964.

Mr. Witt has served as chair of the ABA Section on State and Local Government Law and continues to serve in the Division Council of the Government and Public Sector Lawyers Division of the ABA. Mr. Witt has written numerous articles and is co-author of *Section 1983 Litigation Forms* (Wiley, 1994). He is a graduate of the University of Southern California, where he received his A.B. and J.D. degrees.

Acknowledgments

It is impossible to complete a project such as this without the help of a great many people. I wish to thank Professor Thomas Roberts of Wake Forest University, whose suggestions were invaluable and whose friendship and encouragement kept me going. I also wish to thank Richard Paszkiet, Donald Gecewicz, Holly Wehmeyer, and Carol Siedell of ABA Publishing and copy editor Sara Vlajcic for their expertise and guidance on this project.

Let me acknowledge the leadership of the State and Local Government Section of the ABA, especially Professor Patricia E. Salkin of Albany Law School and Larry C. Ethridge, who first talked to me about the project. I would also like to thank those at my law firm, Plunkett & Cooney, P.C., especially Elizabeth Logan, who helped with the proofreading and editing of this book; Tracey Beaudry, who helped with the typing; and the firm's librarians, Marianne Maher and Cindy Wadhams, for their research assistance.

The State and Local Government Law Section of the ABA is the preeminent bar organization for those interested in government law. Let me thank the section for the opportunity to work on this project, for patience during the delays in its completion, and for all the fun along the way.

Finally, let me thank the authors who gave of their time to complete this project. Writing in this area is particularly frustrating and difficult because the law changes so quickly, and because there are so many opinions it can seem overwhelming to keep up on emerging issues. The writers, without whom this book would not exist, are deserving of special thanks and gratitude for their knowledge, their patience, and their willingness to contribute to what we all hope will be a worthwhile and helpful publication in this important area of the law.

Mary Massaron Ross

Chapter One

The Prima Facie § 1983 Case

Sheldon H. Nahmod

This chapter provides a "cook's tour" of § 1983[1] and § 1983 damage actions. There is much, though, that cannot be covered, including § 1983 actions for injunctive relief,[2] so-called § 1983 "laws" actions,[3] and attorney's fees awards under 42 U.S.C. § 1988, the Civil Rights Attorney's Fees Awards Act of 1976.[4]

Section 1983 was enacted by the 42nd Congress in 1871. For the most part it remained dormant until 1961 when the Supreme Court decided *Monroe v. Pape,*[5] which held, among other things, that "color of law" includes misuse of authority.

---

1. 42 U.S.C. § 1983 (1976, Supp. Ill 1979) reads as follows:
   Every person who, under color of any statute, ordinance, regulation, custom, or usage, of any State or Territory or the District of Columbia, subjects, or causes to be subjected, any citizen of the United States or other person within the jurisdiction thereof to the deprivation of any rights, privileges, or immunities secured by the Constitution and laws, shall be liable to the party injured in an action at law, suit in equity, or other proper proceeding for redress. For the purposes of this section, any Act of Congress applicable exclusively to the District of Columbia shall be considered to be a statute of the District of Columbia.
2. *See* Sheldon H. Nahmod, Civil Rights and Civil Liberties Litigation: The Law of Section 1983 and its Annual Cumulative Supplement (3d. ed. 1991 and 1996). Every § 1983 issue discussed here is covered at length in the author's treatise [hereinafter referred to as Civil Rights and Civil Liberties Litigation]. This chapter is adapted and updated from an article published at 60 Chi.-Kent L. Rev. (1984) which was in turn based on a talk originally given at a program titled "What You Don't Know About Zoning Can Hurt You" at IIT/Chicago-Kent College of Law on January 14, 1983. That is the reason that the three hypotheticals in this chapter involve building inspections.
3. *See id.* at § 2.10, discussing Maine v. Thiboutot, 448 U.S. 1 (1980); and Middlesex County Sewerage Authority v. National Sea Clammers Assn., 453 U.S. 1 (1981).
4. *See id.* at § 1.17-1.20.
5. 365 U.S. 167 (1961).

Section 1983 is best understood as a federal statute that creates a Fourteenth Amendment action for damages. Its functions include the regulation of official conduct and the compensation of persons suffering constitutional deprivations.

The Supreme Court dramatically expanded the scope of liability under § 1983 and for a time, at least, made it much more pro-plaintiff than anyone imagined it would be.[6] On the other hand, as will be seen, the Supreme Court has subsequently handed down important pro-defendant decisions as well.[7] Three hypotheticals[8] will be used as a way of demonstrating the scope of § 1983 damage actions.

Hypothetical No. 1

Suppose that building inspectors are sued for damages in their individual capacities[9] by property owners under § 1983 for violations of their Fourth Amendment rights occurring in connection with certain inspections and causing the plaintiffs harm. The suit is brought in federal court. What are the elements of the prima facie case under § 1983?

The Prima Facie Case

At the outset, the federal court in the hypothetical has subject matter jurisdiction pursuant to 28 U.S.C. § 1343(3),[10] the jurisdictional counter-

---

6. As, for example, by holding that local governments are suable persons under § 1983, Monell v. Dept. of Social Services, 436 U.S. 658 (1978), and are not protected by any kind of immunity from compensatory damages liability, Owen v. City of Independence, 445 U.S. 622 (1980).
7. As, for example, in Harlow v. Fitzgerald, 102 S. Ct. 2727 (1982), by removing the subjective part of the qualified immunity test; and in Anderson v. Creighton, 483 U.S. 635 (1987), by making the objective reasonableness inquiry more fact-specific.
8. The first and second are the more important for purposes of this presentation. The third deals briefly with the issue of local legislator immunity.
9. If they had been sued in their official capacities, the legal effect would be the equivalent of a suit against their governmental employer, a topic discussed in connection with Hypothetical No. 2.
10. This provision reads as follows: (a) The district courts shall have original jurisdiction of any civil action authorized by law to be commenced by any person. . . .

part of § 1983. Also, the suit need not first be brought in state court. *Monroe v. Pape*[11] so held as a matter of § 1983 interpretation. In other words, there is no exhaustion of state judicial remedies required for a § 1983 plaintiff in federal court.

Similarly, as the Supreme Court reaffirmed, there is no need for a § 1983 plaintiff to exhaust his or her state administrative remedies before filing in federal court.[12] If in our hypothetical there were some sort of city procedure whereby property owners could assert their grievances against building inspectors, it would still be irrelevant for exhaustion purposes with respect to § 1983 damage actions brought in federal court.

The language of § 1983 refers to "[e]very person." The building inspectors in our hypothetical are suable persons, just as many state and local government officials acting under color of law are proper defendants under § 1983. However, some state and local government officials are protected by absolute immunity; this group includes state and regional legislators, judges, prosecutors[13] and local legislators as well.[14] In any event, our building inspectors are rather clearly defendants who are not protected by absolute immunity, but are instead protected by the affirmative defense of qualified immunity, discussed later.[15]

The next inquiry is whether the plaintiffs in the hypothetical have properly alleged a Fourteenth Amendment violation.[16] The Fourteenth Amendment-

---

(3) To redress the deprivation, under color of any State law, statute, ordinance, regulation, custom or usage, of any right, privilege or immunity secured by the Constitution of the United States . . . (b) For purposes of this section—

(1) the District of Columbia shall be considered to be a State; and

(2) any Act of Congress applicable exclusively to the District of Columbia shall be considered to be a statute of the District of Columbia.

11. 365 U.S. 167 (1961).
12. Patsy v. Florida Bd. of Regents, 457 U.S. 496 (1982).
13. Tenney v. Brandhove, 341 U.S. 367 (1951) (state legislators); Lake Country Estates, Inc. v. Tahoe Regional Planning Agency, 440 U.S. 391 (1979) (regional legislators); Pierson v. Ray, 386 U.S. 547 (1967) (judges); Imbler v. Pachtman, 424 U.S. 409 (1976) (prosecutors). *See generally* CIVIL RIGHTS AND CIVIL LIBERTIES LITIGATION, chapter 7.
14. Discussed later in connection with Hypothetical No. 3.
15. *See* chapter 11, "Individual Immunity Defenses Under § 1983."
16. The Fourteenth Amendment reads in relevant part as follows:
Section 1. All persons born or naturalized in the United States and subject to

ment applies to the states, while the various provisions of the Bill of Rights apply on their face only to the federal government. One gets from the alleged Fourth Amendment violations of these building inspectors to the Fourteenth Amendment and § 1983 through incorporation. The Fourteenth Amendment incorporates many of the provisions of the Bill of Rights, including specifically the Fourth Amendment in our hypothetical, and applies the Fourth Amendment to the states and local governments. The building inspectors are thereby governed by the Fourth Amendment, that is, they are required by the Fourteenth Amendment to comply with the provisions of the Fourth Amendment.

There is another aspect of incorporation that ties into the language of the Fourteenth Amendment and § 1983. The Fourteenth Amendment only applies to state action. It does not ordinarily apply to individuals acting in a private capacity. In order to have a Fourteenth Amendment violation, the building inspectors must have acted in a way which can be attributable to the state. This is another way of putting the state action requirement.[17]

In contrast, § 1983 speaks in terms of color of law, and not state action. It had been suggested that § 1983's color of law language might be narrower than the Fourteenth Amendment's state action requirement. However, the Supreme Court held in *Lugar v. Edmondson Oil Co.*[18] that where there is state action, there is also action under color of law. That is, whenever state action is present for purposes of the Fourteenth Amendment, the § 1983 color of law requirement is satisfied as well. Inasmuch as the building inspectors in our hypothetical allegedly violated the plaintiffs' Fourth Amendment rights in connection with their official conduct in inspecting buildings, there is no serious problem with either state action or color of law.

Another important prima facie case issue relates to what may be called the basis of liability or state of mind required for § 1983. The issue is

---

the jurisdiction thereof, are citizens of the United States and of the State wherein they reside. No State shall make or enforce any law which shall abridge the privileges or immunities of citizens of the United States; nor shall any State deprive any person of life, liberty, or property, without due process of law; nor deny to any person within its jurisdiction the equal protection of the laws.

17. On state action, *see* Civil Rights and Civil Liberties Litigation at § 2.04-2.09.

18. 102 S. Ct. 2744 (1982).

simply put: What did the Court mean when it said in *Monroe v. Pape* that § 1983 is to be interpreted against a "background of tort liability?" Some federal courts suggested that § 1983 had its own independent state of mind requirement, with the question of whether ordinary negligence was actionable under § 1983 becoming a subject of considerable controversy.

The Court twice granted certiorari to deal with the issue[19] but avoided it until *Parratt v. Taylor.*[20] *Parratt*, an important case, involved a prisoner who sued prison officials for damages under § 1983 because they allegedly were negligent and lost hobby materials that the prisoner had ordered through the mail. The theory of liability was that defendants had deprived plaintiff of a property interest without due process of law.

Parratt implicated two related, but different, issues. The first was whether § 1983 has its own independent state of mind requirement. The Supreme Court ruled that § 1983 does not have its own state of mind requirement. Whatever the state of mind requirement is for the particular constitutional violation, that is the extent of the § 1983 plaintiff's state of mind hurdle for the prima facie case.[21]

For example, in order to show an equal protection violation in a racial discrimination setting, a plaintiff must prove purposeful discrimination.[22] Consequently, where a § 1983 plaintiff alleges an equal protection violation and proves purposeful discrimination, that is enough to make out a prima facie case with respect to the state of mind requirement of the equal protection clause itself. There is no further need to worry about negligence, gross negligence, or recklessness with respect to § 1983. Supporting this result is the language of § 1983 itself, which on its face speaks only of causation; it says nothing about negligence or gross negligence.

The second issue in *Parratt* concerned the procedural due process merits. The Court reasoned as follows. First, there clearly was a property interest because the hobby materials were worth $ 23.50; de minimus, perhaps, during inflationary times, but a property interest nevertheless, especially for a prisoner. Second, in the now-overruled part of *Parratt*,

---

19. In Baker v. McCollan, 443 U.S. 137 (1979) and Procunier v. Navarette, 434 U.S. 555 (1978).
20. 451 U.S. 527 (1981).
21. I emphasize this because, as will be seen, objective reasonableness is a kind of state of mind requirement for the affirmative defense of qualified immunity.
22. Washington v. Davis, 426 U.S. 229 (1976).

there was a deprivation of that property interest: A property interest can be negligently deprived.[23]

However, the final procedural due process inquiry was in many respects the most important and the hardest: Was the appropriate process, the process which was due, given to plaintiff? The Supreme Court held that due process had been provided by the state because the plaintiff inmate had an adequate post-deprivation remedy: a cause of action under state law to recover the value of his lost property. Because the hobby materials were allegedly lost through the random acts of the defendants, no meaningful and workable pre-deprivation procedure could be set up by the state.

Consequently, *Parratt* held that a negligent deprivation of property does not violate procedural due process where there is an adequate post-deprivation remedy. However, Justices White and Blackmun emphasized in their concurring opinion that *Parratt* does not necessarily govern a situation where there is an intentional deprivation of property. Nor does *Parratt* govern where there is either a negligent or intentional deprivation of liberty. One can readily see that, depending on how broadly or narrowly it is read, *Parratt* had real implications, going well beyond the scope of this presentation, for procedural due process, substantive due process, and taking law.[24]

Following the constitutional violation, causation in fact is the next element of the prima facie case. For the building inspectors to be sued successfully for damages, the property owners must show that the building inspectors caused them some kind of harm. In this hypothetical there should be no serious problem with causation in fact; nor should there be any serious problem with that obscurantist tort concept called proximate

---

23. Thereafter, in Daniels v. Williams, 474 U.S. 327 (1986), the Court revisited this issue and held that more than negligence is necessary for any due process violation. Rather, an abuse of government power is required. The prevailing rule in the circuits is that deliberate indifference or reckless disregard is the minimum required for a due process violation. *See* CIVIL RIGHTS AND CIVIL LIBERTIES LITIGATION, ch. 3.
24. Examples in the circuits of broad readings of *Parratt* include: Rutledge v. Arizona Bd. of Regents, 660 F.2d 1345 (9th Cir. 1981), *aff'd on other grounds,* 103 S. Ct. 1483 (1983) (*Parratt* applies to deprivation of liberty); Johnson v. Miller, 680 F.2d 39 (7th Cir. 1982) (incorrectly stating that *Parratt* may apply to Fourth Amendment violation). *But see* Logan v. Zimmerman Brush Co., 455 U.S. 422, 435-36 (1982), holding that certain intentional deprivations of property by a state are not governed by *Parratt*.

cause. Proximate cause has bothered federal courts in some § 1983 cases,[25] but not here.

As to damages, the Supreme Court held in *Carey v. Piphus*[26] that damages may not be presumed in § 1983 procedural due process cases. Even though *Carey* was limited to procedural due process, any plaintiff's lawyer seeking damages would be foolish not to allege and attempt to prove actual damages in every § 1983 case. Actual damages include emotional distress, pain and suffering and the like. Punitive damages are also available against individuals under § 1983 where recklessness or deliberate indifference is shown.[27] However, they are not available against local governments.[28]

Section 1983 does not have its own statute of limitations. Pursuant to 42 U.S.C. § 1988, federal courts must apply the forum state's analogous statute of limitations, usually for personal injuries. Interestingly, the question of when a § 1983 cause of action accrues is an issue of federal law, but whether that § 1983 cause of action has tolled in a particular case is an issue of state law.[29]

Finally, there is no need on the part of the property owners, or any § 1983 plaintiff, to allege bad faith as part of the prima facie case. A plaintiff will allege bad faith in situations where he or she seeks punitive damages, but there is no need with respect to the prima facie case for compensatory damages to do so.[30]

---

25. *See, e.g.,* Duncan v. Nelson, 466 F.2d 939 (7th Cir.), cert. denied, 409 U.S. 894 (1972). Cf. Martinez v. California, 444 U.S. 277 (1980). The relationship between causation in fact and damages is more complex in procedural due process and First Amendment cases than it is in Hypothetical No. 1. *See* Mount Healthy City School Dist. v. Doyle, 429 U.S. 274 (1977) and Carey v. Piphus, 435 U.S. 247 (1978). *See generally* Civil Rights and Civil Liberties Litigation, ch. 3 on proximate cause and cause in fact.
26. 435 U.S. 247 (1978).
27. Smith v. Wade, 103 S. Ct. 1625 (1983).
28. City of Newport v. Fact Concerts, Inc., 435 U.S. 247 (1981).
29. Chardon v. Soto, 103 S. Ct. 2611 (1983); Delaware State College v. Ricks, 449 U.S. 250 (1980); Board of Regents v. Tomanio, 446 U.S. 478 (1980). *See* Civil Rights and Civil Liberties Litigation, at § 4.13.
30. Gomez v. Toledo, 446 U.S. 635 (1980).

The Affirmative Defense of Qualified Immunity

Suppose now that the plaintiffs' complaint survives a motion to dismiss and at trial the property owners make out a prima facie case against the building inspectors. Earlier, it was mentioned that the building inspectors are not absolutely immune defendants. Instead, they have the burdens of pleading and proving the affirmative defense of qualified immunity.[31]

Qualified immunity is designed to reflect a balance between the interest in Fourteenth Amendment compliance and the interest in fearless decisionmaking by officials. Until 1982, qualified immunity had two parts. There was, and still is, an objective part of the qualified immunity test, and there was, but no longer is, a subjective part of the qualified immunity test.

The objective part was put as follows: Did the defendant reasonably believe that he or she was acting constitutionally? The subjective part was at the time equally straightforward: Did the defendant honestly believe that he or she was acting constitutionally?[32] Both of these parts of the qualified immunity test saw considerable development after they were first set out. The subjective part was transformed for a time into the following: Did the defendant maliciously intend to harm the plaintiff?[33]

The objective part became considerably more complex than it had been earlier. In the landmark decision of *Wood v. Strickland*,[34] the Supreme Court said a rather remarkable thing about qualified immunity: In certain circumstances, governmental defendants have a duty to know settled, indisputable constitutional law. If they do not act in a manner consistent with settled law, they fail the objective part of the qualified immunity test as a matter of law. Since the qualified immunity test at the time *Wood* was decided had two parts, each of which a defendant had to overcome in order to prevail, a defendant who failed the objective part automatically lost on the issue of liability for compensatory damages.

There remain, even now, very troublesome aspects of the objective part of the qualified immunity test as developed in *Wood*. What does "settled law" mean? Does one need a Supreme Court decision on point? A circuit court of appeals decision? A federal district court decision? What about a

---

31. *See* Civil Rights and Civil Liberties Litigation, at § 8.13.
32. Scheuer v. Rhodes, 416 U.S. 232 (1974); Pierson v. Ray, 386 U.S. 547 (1967).
33. Wood v. Strickland, 420 U.S. 308 (1975).
34. *Id.*

federal court from another circuit or district? All kinds of problems are raised by this aspect of *Wood.*

"Settled law" gives a federal court considerable flexibility, if it is disposed to rule for the plaintiff, to find that there was, indeed, settled law in a particular case; such a federal court will freely extrapolate from existing law. In contrast, if a federal court is disposed to rule for the defendant, it will find no case on point at the time the defendant acted. Therefore, that defendant would not have breached his or her duty to know settled law.

The two-part qualified immunity test was in use until *Harlow v. Fitzgerald,*[35] decided in June of 1982. Fitzgerald, the plaintiff, sued the president of the United States,[36] his aides, and others because he allegedly lost his job as a result of "blowing the whistle" on the C5A transport cost overruns. He sued under a *Bivens*[37] theory of implying a cause of action directly under the Constitution. While the President was protected by absolute immunity,[38] his aides were found to be protected only by qualified immunity.

But the aides went on to argue that the two-part test should be changed. They noted that there were many situations where defendants showed through motions for summary judgment that they had in fact passed the objective part of the qualified immunity test as a matter of law. Nevertheless, in such cases, defense motions for summary judgment were regularly denied. These denials resulted from the use of the subjective part of the qualified immunity test, which focused upon a defendant's actual state of mind. Federal courts were treating this state of mind issue as appropriate only for a jury on the ground that it was a factual issue in dispute, precluding summary judgment. Yet, in almost all of these cases, the argument went, the defendants would ultimately prevail on the subjective part after going through a full-blown trial, and would therefore win on the merits.

The Supreme Court agreed with the defendants that the subjective part should be eliminated. The Court observed that it had hoped when it set out the two-part qualified immunity test for both *Bivens* actions and § 1983

---

35. 102 S. Ct. 2727 (1982).

36. *See* Nixon v. Fitzgerald, 102 S. Ct. 2690 (1982), *Harlow*'s companion case, holding that the President is absolutely immune from damage actions for executive acts.

37. Bivens v. Six Unknown Named Agents, 403 U.S. 388 (1971).

38. *See* note 35, *supra.*

actions that federal courts would readily be able to dismiss frivolous lawsuits. But this hope had not been realized. Consequently, the Court ruled, motions for summary judgment in appropriate cases may be granted by courts in favor of defendants based on the objective part alone.

Not only did the Court assert that defendants in these kinds of cases must be spared the costs, disruption, and aggravation of a trial, the Court insisted that there be no discovery until the plaintiff overcomes the qualified immunity test hurdle through summary judgment. Only when settled law is violated by a defendant in a § 1983 case will the plaintiff be allowed to obtain discovery. As a result of these developments, defense counsel will typically make use of *Harlow* in almost every § 1983 case involving individual damages liability.

Hypothetical No. 2

Suppose now that the property owners sue the city employing the building inspectors for damages under § 1983 for the unconstitutional inspections of its building inspectors.

Local Government Liability

Is the city a person? *Monroe v. Pape*[39] in its only pro-defendant aspect had held in 1961 that the city of Chicago and local governments in general were not persons.

However, in *Monell v. Dept. of Social Services*[40] the Supreme Court said that it had made a mistake in *Monroe*: A city is indeed a person and may be sued under § 1983. States are not proper § 1983 defendants, as it turns out, because they are protected by the Eleventh Amendment (for federal court purposes), and in any event are not persons within the meaning of § 1983.[41] But cities, counties, and local government entities in general are suable persons.

Respondeat superior cannot be used against a local government, or the city in the hypothetical, for § 1983 liability purposes. Just because the

---

39. 365 U.S. 167 (1961).
40. 436 U.S. 658 (1978).
41. Quern v. Jordan, 440 U.S. 332 (1979) (Eleventh Amendment); Will v. Michigan Dept. of State Police, 491 U.S. 58 (1989) (state not a person).

building inspectors are employed by the city, it does not follow that the city is liable for their unconstitutional conduct. According to *Monell*, there must instead be an actionable official policy or custom of the governmental body which, when implemented, causes the constitutional violation.

The easiest cases involving official policy are those in which the governmental body itself acts formally, for example, by passing an ordinance.[42] Moreover, there are situations in which high-ranking city officials can, in effect, bind the governmental body; such officials, denominated as policymakers, are thought to speak for the governmental entity.[43]

More difficult issues arise respecting custom, and those can only be dealt with very briefly here. Suppose it turns out that the building inspectors regularly, frequently, repeatedly, and customarily violate the Fourth Amendment when they make inspections. This, standing alone, is not enough to make the city liable. What is necessary in order to make the city liable is to attribute the inspectors' conduct to the city itself.

This might be done as follows: Either high city officials knew in fact what the building inspectors were frequently and customarily doing or, to stretch a bit, they should have known. The latter is a highly questionable kind of constructive notice approach to the use of custom as a basis of liability under § 1983.[44]

Once the plaintiffs make out a prima facie case against the city in our hypothetical, there is no affirmative defense.[45] The city might be liable even if, at the time the building inspectors acted, what they did was not considered to be unconstitutional. That is, there is local government liability even if a court holds after the fact that what the inspectors did earlier was unconstitutional. This should not be called strict liability, however,

---

42. *Monell* itself clearly involved an official policy promulgated by the defendant regarding forced unpaid leaves of absence for pregnant employees.
43. There is local government liability "when [the] execution of a government's policy or custom, whether made by its lawmakers or by those whose edicts or acts may fairly be said to represent official policy, inflicts the injury." *Monell*, 436 U.S. at 694 (emphasis added). On the policymaker issue *see* Praprotnik v. City of St. Louis, 485 U.S. 112 (1988). Local government liability for failure to train is also possible. City of Canton v. Harris, 489 U.S. 378 (1989). On local government liability generally *see* Civil Rights and Civil Liberties Litigation, ch. 6.
44. *See* cases collected in Civil Rights and Civil Liberties Litigation at § 6.07.
45. Owen v. City of Independence, 445 U.S. 622 (1980).

because an official policy or custom that causes constitutional injury is still required for government liability.

Thus, regardless of what the state of the law was at the time the challenged local government conduct occurred, if it turns out that a federal court later holds such conduct was unconstitutional, the local government may be liable. Of course, the building inspectors as individuals will not be liable under these circumstances because they will in all likelihood pass the objective reasonableness qualified immunity test as a matter of law.

It should be mentioned that the foregoing relates to a city's liability for compensatory damage. In *Newport v. Fact Concerts, Inc.*,[46] the Court held that local governments are not liable for punitive damages. In my view, the explanation for this decision is very simple: Enough is enough.

Hypothetical No. 3

Suppose that a city council and its members are sued for damages arising out of an ordinance setting out building inspection procedures which, when implemented by building inspectors, allegedly violate the Fourth Amendment rights of property owners.

Local Legislator Liability

It is clear with respect to the city, assuming there is a constitutional violation, that the city would be liable because the ordinance itself is formal action which surely constitutes an official policy. As to the city council members: Are local legislators absolutely immune defendants with respect to their legislative acts, or are they qualifiedly immune? Recall that state and regional legislators are absolutely immune from damages liability for their legislative acts.

The Supreme Court has increasingly moved from a status approach inquiry toward a functional approach to immunities which focuses on the nature of the challenged conduct. The Court applied such a functional approach to judges exercising legislative powers,[47] to regional legislators act-

---

46. 453 U.S. 247 (1981).
47. Supreme Court of Virginia v. Consumers Union, 446 U.S. 719 (1980).

ing legislatively,[48] and to police officers—ordinarily protected by qualified immunity—accused of perjuring themselves as witnesses at criminal trials.[49] It did the same to federal administrative agency officials acting in a judicial or prosecutorial capacity in agency adjudicatory proceedings.[50]

Consequently, when this issue finally reaches the Supreme Court, local legislators will almost surely be held to be protected by absolute legislative immunity for challenged legislative conduct. Indeed, this is the rule in the circuits.

Conclusion

The intellectual richness, technical complexity and practical importance of § 1983 have only been hinted at here. Nevertheless, it should be apparent that lawyers and others involved in state and local government matters who do not become familiar with this significant, century-old federal civil rights statute are at risk. It should also be evident that the overriding theme of § 1983 is the centrality of the Fourteenth Amendment and its enforcement.

---

48. Lake Country Estates, Inc. v. Tahoe Regional Planning Agency, 440 U.S. 391 (1979).
49. Briscoe v. LaHue, 103 S. Ct. 1108 (1983).
50. Butz v. Economou, 438 U.S. 478 (1978).

Chapter Two
Procedural Guide to § 1983 Litigation in Federal Court

Jane K. Swanson

The aim of this chapter is to identify and briefly examine some of the specialized procedural and tactical issues involved in the litigation of a § 1983 case, in the order in which these issues typically must be dealt with in the litigation process. As Chapter 3 focuses specifically on § 1983 litigation in state courts, this chapter will for the most part deal with § 1983 procedural issues as they occur in the federal court system, with some brief references to state court differences where applicable.

Pre-Litigation Considerations for Plaintiff's Counsel

Beyond the general "inquiry reasonable under the circumstances" minimally required in all cases pursuant to Federal Rule of Civil Procedure 11, an intelligent case acceptance decision in a potential § 1983 case requires an examination of more varied and complex factors than are immediately obvious.

Advisable Factual and Legal Investigation Prior to Case Acceptance

If the client's objective is money damages, counsel will need to consider how the doctrine of qualified immunity[1] can reasonably be expected to affect the client's likelihood of actually being able to impose liability on a defendant for damage claims. This in turn calls for a factually specific description of the defendant's (or defendants') conduct and a comparison of it to the standards set in similar cases by the Supreme Court and by the circuit court of the area in which the case would be filed.

Similarly, as § 1983 liability may not be imposed on a *respondeat superior* basis, a more particularized evaluation of the potential liability of the governmental unit on whose behalf the individual defendant(s) acted

---

1. *See* Chapter 11, "Individual Immunity Defenses Under § 1983 Actions."

will be required.[2] This may entail, for example, an examination of relevant state law to determine which officials had policymaking authority for which issues on behalf of the governmental unit in question. Then, counsel will need to evaluate if and how the policies set by these officials led to the client's damages. Most other possible bases of governmental unit liability require extensive factual development as to the policies, procedures, customs, and practices of the governmental unit in question and the ways in which they may have contributed to the deprivation of the client's constitutional and statutory rights.[3]

Although the Supreme Court's opinion in *Leatherman v. Tarrant County,*[4] discussed below, has eliminated the necessity for plaintiff's counsel to be able to plead a detailed factual basis for such governmental liability in the initial complaint without even the benefit of discovery, it has not changed the practical economic advisability of evaluating the potential liability of the governmental unit in question as carefully as possible, prior to deciding whether to accept the case and commit large amounts of time and other resources to it.

Typically, the prospective client will have almost none of the factual information which would bear on the issue of governmental unit liability. In order to develop such information, it is worthwhile to check at the courthouse and in available computer-accessible databanks for previous similar litigation filed against the same governmental unit, to review discovery materials if possible, and to confer with attorneys involved in such litigation. Additionally, the state equivalent of the Freedom of Information Act[5] (such as the Open Records Act[6] in Texas) can be very useful in obtaining documents concerning the history of the governmental unit with regard to the type of problem the client alleges.

Explanations to Client

A thorough examination of these factors will permit a better-reasoned decision regarding case acceptance, and a more realistic and thorough ex-

2. *See* Chapter 5, "Municipal Liability Under § 1983."
3. *Id.*
4. 113 S. Ct. 1160 (1993).
5. 5 U.S.C. § 552 (1989).
6. Texas Govt. Code ch. 552 (1994).

planation to the client of the difficulties, complexities, costs, and chances of success. Clients with potential § 1983 claims are unlikely to be familiar with any standard of employer or supervisory liability other than *respondeat superior*, and may therefore have unrealistic expectations if not given a basic explanation of what standards are in fact applicable to such a determination. Potential procedural complications, such as the possibility of an interlocutory appeal if qualified immunity is likely to be an issue, should be considered and explained at this stage as well. This will allow the accompanying delay and cost factors to be weighed together with other relevant considerations, and a realistic decision reached by both lawyer and client as to whether to make the necessary time and cost commitment to go forward with the case.

Fee Agreement with Client

Whatever fee agreement is reached with the client, § 1983 litigation is almost invariably done with the goal of ultimately collecting attorney's fees from the defendant(s), pursuant to 42 U.S.C. § 1988. The Supreme Court has held that the fee agreement between a plaintiff and her counsel is not determinative of the amount of the defendant's fee liability pursuant to § 1988, if the plaintiff prevails.[7] The converse is also true; i.e., if a plaintiff agrees to a fee contract with the attorney which would result in the payment of a higher fee amount than the court awards against the defendant, the plaintiff remains responsible for the higher fee amount if it is otherwise proper.[8]

Plaintiff's counsel should be aware that some local federal court rules enacted pursuant to the Civil Justice Reform Act require ultimate court approval of the fee to be charged the plaintiff by counsel, and specify how expenses are to be calculated in arriving at plaintiff's final fee liability amount on a contingent fee contract.[9] Thorough familiarity with the local rules of the jurisdiction in which the case is to be filed may avoid later embarrassment on this point.

If the sole or primary aim of the case is to obtain declaratory and/or injunctive relief, counsel should be aware at this stage of the *Evans v. Jeff*

---

7. Blanchard v. Bergeron, 489 U.S. 87, 95-96 (1989).
8. Venegas v. Mitchell, 495 U.S. 82, 90 (1990).
9. *See, e.g.,* United States Dist. Court for the E. Dist. of Texas, Civil Justice Expense and Delay Reduction Plan, Article Five.

D.[10] holding, and its implications for potential attorney's fee recovery in this situation. In *Jeff D.*, the Supreme Court, in effect, gave its stamp of approval to a defendant's tactic of offering to agree to the requested declaratory and injunctive relief, if and only if the plaintiff would waive all potential attorney's fee recovery from the defendant.[11]

While there is no easy solution to the potential problems raised by this scenario for the plaintiff and the plaintiff's counsel, a frank discussion about this possibility prior to filing the case provides a much greater possibility of an acceptable resolution than one which takes place only after such an offer has been made and after plaintiff's counsel has expended substantial time on the case. If dealing with a potential plaintiff who will not have the financial resources to pay a reasonable fee, and whose primary aim is injunctive and/or declaratory relief, counsel should consider reaching some agreement as to the handling of a potential future *Evans v. Jeff D.* situation, and incorporating the agreement into the written fee contract with the plaintiff.

Readiness of Claims for Court

While a complete exploration of readiness issues would be well beyond the scope of this chapter, some discussion is appropriate at this point because it may be possible, at this stage, to correct situations which could otherwise be stumbling blocks later in the litigation process.

Ripeness—This is not frequently a disputed issue in actions for damages outside the land use setting; however, it is always a requirement to consider when planning a suit for injunctive relief. The purpose of the ripeness requirement, theoretically, is to make certain that the constitutional Article 3 "case or controversy" requirement is met, and that the parties have a real, not merely a hypothetical, dispute, which will not be a waste of judicial resources.

Practically speaking, the ripeness requirement embodies the concern that the defendants' challenged action, or refusal to act, be definite and final, and therefore that the court process initiated to correct it is really needed.[12]

Frequently, plaintiff's counsel can avoid or minimize ripeness concern in lawsuits seeking declaratory and/or injunctive relief by postponing litigation until the litigant has made all reasonable attempts to obtain a defini-

10. 475 U.S. 717, 729-30 (1986).
11. *Id.* at 722.
12. *Cf.* Askins v. District of Columbia, 877 F.2d 94, 98-99 (D.C. Cir. 1989).

tive and clearly provable refusal by the defendants to provide the relief which the plaintiff is seeking.

For example, in an Eighth Circuit case, *Murphy v. Missouri Department of Corrections*,[13] inmates' First Amendment claims for recognition of their religious organization by prison officials were held not to be ripe for court review, because they had not complied, prior to filing their lawsuit, with the prison's requirement of making a written request in order to secure such recognition. The court saw this as a ripeness issue, not an impermissible exhaustion requirement, and plaintiffs were not successful in their argument that such a request should not be required because it would clearly have been futile.[14]

Although the plaintiffs in *Murphy* may well have been correct in thinking that the defendants' formal request requirement was a pro forma one with no realistic chance of success in their case, an attempt at using the procedure prior to filing suit would have been relatively simple to accomplish and might have saved a great deal of attorney time later. Consideration of this type of ripeness concern prior to filing suit for injunctive relief is not to be confused with a need to exhaust administrative remedies or to comply with locally created notice requirements for damage claims.

Plaintiffs in § 1983 land use litigation have encountered particularly complex and troublesome problems with ripeness issues.[15] One such doctrine amounts, in effect, to a requirement that state judicial remedies be exhausted prior to bringing a constitutionally-based damages claim through § 1983, although the courts have preferred to discuss and analyze this issue in terms of ripeness rather than exhaustion.[16]

First, plaintiffs wishing to assert constitutionally based claims for "taking" of their property without "just compensation," stemming from land use regulation, must obtain a final and definitive decision from the prospective governmental defendant prior to filing suit.[17] Very rarely may such plaintiffs effectively argue that the "mere enactment" of an ordi-

---

13. 814 F.2d 1252, 1257 (8th Cir. 1987).
14. *Id.* at 1257.
15. This topic is more fully addressed in chapter 8, "The § 1983 Land Use Case."
16. Williamson County Regional Planning Commission v. Hamilton Bank, 473 U.S. at 192-97.
17. Agins v. Tiburon, 447 U.S. at 259-62 (1980); Williamson County, 473 U.S. at 192-97.

nance or regulation affecting their land creates a ripe controversy for the court system.[18] Rather, the Supreme Court has required that "takings" plaintiffs first obtain an adverse decision from the defendant governmental body "regarding the application of the regulations to the property at issue," by submitting a proposed development plan.[19] Further, if their plan is denied, plaintiffs must use available procedures to attempt to obtain a waiver or variance from the prospective defendant, to permit the use they seek.[20] If plaintiffs fail to complete these steps before filing suit, their § 1983 claim based on the "taking" clause of the Fifth Amendment will be found not to present a ripe controversy and therefore dismissed, no doubt at great cost and frustration to them and to their counsel.[21] Futility is a recognized exception to these requirements, but a very narrowly construed one—invokable, for example, when the plaintiff is denied access to application or appeal procedures.[22]

The Supreme Court in *Williamson County Planning Commission v. Hamilton Bank*[23] carefully distinguished the above-referenced ripeness considerations from administrative exhaustion requirements, which may not properly be imposed on § 1983 land use plaintiffs. According to the Court, ripeness requires only that "the initial decisionmaker has arrived at a definitive position on the issue that inflicts an actual concrete injury. . . ."[24] Exhaustion, in contrast, refers to "procedures by which an injured party may seek review . . . of an adverse decision by a third party, in the hope of obtaining a remedy."[25]

In addition to the above-described contortions which land use plaintiffs, must perform in order to obtain a sufficiently final and definitive deci-

---

18. *See, e.g., Agins*, 447 U.S. at 259-62; Rent Stabilization Association v. Dinkins, 5 F.3d 591, 594-95 (2d Cir. 1993); Gilbert v. Cambridge, 932 F.2d 51, 55-57 (1st Cir. 1991), *cert. denied,* 502 U.S. 866.
19. *Williamson County*, 473 U.S. at 187-191. There is also authority indicating that to establish a final decision and therefore a "taking" the plaintiff must also try and fail to obtain approval for other potentially valuable and beneficial uses, even if denied one such use. MacDonald, Sommer & Grates v. County of Yolo, 477 U.S. 340, 346-53 (1986).
20. *See, e.g., Williamson County,* 473 U.S. at 200.
21. *See, e.g.*, Gilbert v. Cambridge, 932 F.2d at 60-63, and cases cited therein.
22. 473 U.S. at 192-94
23. 473 U.S. at 193.
24. *Id.*
25. *Id.*

sion as to what use of their property will be permitted, plaintiffs seeking damages for governmental "taking without just compensation" face an additional ripeness hurdle. That is, they must first attempt to obtain such compensation through any state-created judicial remedies available to provide it, such as inverse condemnation.[26] Reasoning that pre-deprivation compensation is not required by the "taking" clause, the Supreme Court has held that ". . . the State's action here is not 'complete' unless and until the State fails to provide adequate compensation for the taking through its available judicial procedures."[27] Section 1983 claims based on the denial of procedural or substantive due process in a land use context may be subject to somewhat different ripeness requirements, depending on the type of claim.[28]

Exhaustion requirements and related concerns—Exhaustion issues, in general terms, involve statutory or court-imposed requirements that other administrative or judicial remedies be pursued unsuccessfully to their conclusion, prior to filing a § 1983 claim in court. This chapter attempts only to mention the basic characteristics of the more commonly encountered exhaustion requirements and to alert counsel that further reading and research on this topic is required prior to proceeding with a § 1983 court action.

Requirements specified by statute—In a few instances, a specific federal statute controls the question of what, if any, alternate remedies must be pursued to their conclusion prior to seeking relief in federal court for violations of federal constitutional or statutory rights. This is the case, for example, with respect to the federal habeas corpus statute for prisoners, which requires prior exhaustion of state judicial remedies.[29] The Supreme Court has held that any prisoner action seeking declaratory and/or injunctive relief from the *fact* or *duration* of current confinement (as opposed to its conditions) is, however the plaintiff seeks to classify it, in effect a ha-

---

26. 473 U.S. at 194-97. It is very important to avoid inadvertently creating a res judicata effect on potential federal constitutional claims while so doing. *See* Fields v. Sarasota Manatee Airport Authority, 953 F.2d 1299, 1306-09 (11th Cir. 1992).
27. 473 U.S. at 195.
28. *See, e.g.*, Southview Associates v. Bongartz, 980 F.2d 84, 97 (2d Cir. 1992), *cert. denied*, 113 S. Ct. 1586 (1993).
29. 28 U.S.C. § 2254(b) - (c) (1992).

beas corpus action, requiring such exhaustion.[30] Additionally, potential § 1983 claims of adult inmates of state and local correctional facilities must, pursuant to the Civil Rights of Institutionalized Persons Act,[31] be first asserted through administrative grievance procedures available to inmates, if those procedures meet the minimum standards specified by the Attorney General for the resolution of such complaints.

Another example of a statutorily imposed exhaustion requirement applicable to claimed violations of federal constitutional and statutory rights is the 1986 amendment to the Individuals with Disabilities Education Act (IDEA). The statute addresses the circumstances under which students and their parents may assert alternate or additional causes of action (apparently including § 1983 actions) in fact situations to which the IDEA would apply.[32] This statute provides that nothing in the IDEA prevents the assertion of such alternate or additional claims. However, plaintiffs asserting them must exhaust the administrative remedies specified in the IDEA to the same extent as if their claims were based on its provisions.[33]

Even if no specific federal statutory exhaustion requirements are applicable, counsel should examine potential state judicial and administrative remedies before proceeding.

State judicial remedies—In 1961, the Supreme Court clearly indicated in *Monroe v. Pape*[34] that a § 1983 plaintiff need not either exhaust the possibilities of obtaining relief in state court nor demonstrate the inadequacy of available state court procedures as a prerequisite to filing a § 1983 action in federal court. (In fact, to attempt to do so would invite res judicata problems.)

This is still basically good law, but plaintiff's counsel should be aware of some circumstances in which the federal courts now impose something which sounds, on the surface, like an exhaustion requirement but is in fact something even worse. A § 1983 plaintiff seeking to use a federal constitutional due process theory to vindicate harm not brought about by the application of established state procedures will encounter the grow-

---

30. Preiser v. Rodriguez, 411 U.S. 475, 496-500 (1973).
31. 42 U.S.C. § 1997e (1989 and Supp. 1995).
32. 20 U.S.C. § 1415 (f) (Supp. 1995).
33. *Id.*
34. 365 U.S. 167, 173-80 (1961).

ing body of case law deferring, in effect, to state-created tort and other judicial remedies in this context. If these state-law-based remedies are theoretically available and at least minimally adequate for the purpose of providing compensation for the loss, a would-be § 1983 plaintiff cannot state a valid claim for deprivation of due process under color of state law.[35] This, of course, is not an exhaustion requirement, but instead a court-imposed mandatory detour away from constitutional law and toward state common law tort claims.

Another doctrine with a superficial resemblance to a judicial exhaustion requirement was announced by the Supreme Court in *Heck v. Humphrey*.[36] The Court held that a § 1983 damages action for harm caused by an allegedly unlawful criminal conviction or imprisonment requires, as a prerequisite, that the conviction have been previously either invalidated through reversal on appeal or expungement by executive order, or called into question by a federal court's issuance of a writ of habeas corpus.[37] The Court stated, however, "We do not engraft an exhaustion requirement upon § 1983, but rather deny the existence of a cause of action."[38]

As with the procedural due process case situation described above, such a plaintiff does not have a § 1983 claim, if these alternate remedies are pursued unsuccessfully to their conclusion.

Counsel should also be aware that a related state judicial proceeding pending at the time the plaintiff wishes to file a § 1983 action will probably create *Younger* problems, which should be thoroughly researched prior to any consideration of such filing.[39]

State administrative remedies—In the absence of a specific statutory requirement such as the examples mentioned above, a § 1983 plaintiff need not exhaust state administrative remedies prior to filing a § 1983 claim.[40]

---

35. Hudson v. Palmer, 468 U.S. 517, 533-36 (1984); Parratt v. Taylor, 451 U.S. 527, 543-44 (1981).
36. 114 S. Ct. 2364, 2372-74 (1994).
37. *Id.* at 2372.
38. *Id.* at 2373.
39. *See* Younger v. Harris, 401 U.S. 37 (1971), and the discussion of this doctrine in the sources listed in "Suggestions for Further Reading."
40. Patsy v. Board of Regents, 457 U.S. 496, 515-16 (1982).

A related state administrative proceeding pending at the time the plaintiff wishes to file a § 1983 action in court may create *Younger* problems similar to those created by pending state judicial proceedings, and this issue should likewise be researched, if such circumstances exist.[41]

"Notice of claim" requirements—Some state and local governmental entities have created an array of procedural notice requirements, frequently with very short time deadlines, which, according to the statute or regulation containing such provisions, must be satisfied by any person with a claim for damages against such entity, as a prerequisite to filing the claim in state court. In *Felder v. Casey*,[42] the Supreme Court held a state's application of such notice requirements to § 1983 claims filed in its courts to be violative of the Supremacy Clause, if they significantly burden § 1983 plaintiffs' right to seek redress for § 1983 violations through the state court system. The Court found it unacceptable, under the terms of the Supremacy Clause, that such restrictive procedural requirements would predictably cause different outcomes for § 1983 claims, depending on whether the claims were brought in federal or state court.[43] Further, the Court viewed the "notice of claim" prerequisite, as applied to § 1983 actions, to be an impermissible state imposition of an exhaustion requirement on a federally created cause of action as to which Congress has imposed no such requirement.[44]

Of course, such "notice of claim" requirements may still control the preservation and proper presentation of some state-created causes of action which a § 1983 plaintiff may wish to raise as pendent claims.

Structuring the Lawsuit

After reviewing the facts and legal issues thoroughly and deciding to proceed with the § 1983 claim, the next step is to determine how best to structure the lawsuit, taking into consideration potential defendants and whether they will be sued in their individual or official capacities.

---

41. *Cf.* Ohio Civil Rights Comm'n v. Dayton Christian Schs., 477 U.S. 619, 625-29 (1986).
42. 487 U.S. 131, 150-53 (1988).
43. *Id.* at 153.
44. *Id.* at 146-150.

"Every Person"

Section 1983 provides for the liability of "every person" who subjects the plaintiff or causes the plaintiff to be subjected to the deprivation of federal constitutional or statutory rights "under color of any statute, ordinance, regulation, custom, or usage, of any State or Territory or the District of Columbia...." With one important exception, both natural persons and entities such as corporations and governmental units are "persons" who are proper defendants in § 1983 cases. The state itself has been held not to be a "person" that may be named as a defendant in a § 1983 case, either in federal or in state court.[45] This holding also applies to specific agencies of the state.

If the plaintiff seeks injunctive relief against the state pursuant to § 1983, it is still possible to properly plead for such relief through the use of the "*Ex Parte Young* fiction," as reaffirmed by the Court in a footnote to the majority opinion in *Will*.[46] This involves naming as defendants the appropriate state officers in their official capacities, and pleading only for injunctive relief, not damages.[47] Such a device, according to the Supreme Court, permits the courts to effectuate the purpose of the Fourteenth Amendment by bringing the state into compliance with federal law, while simultaneously recognizing the state's specially protected status.[48] While the issue in *Ex Parte Young* was the effect of the Eleventh Amendment, not the definition of "person" as used in § 1983, the Court's approving reference to this pleading method in the *Will* opinion expressly signals its continued viability and applicability in connection with the latter issue as well.[49]

"Official Capacity" vs. "Individual Capacity"

A suit against a governmental officer or employee in his or her "official capacity" is, in effect, a suit against the governmental entity of which that person is an agent.[50] Suing an officer or employee in this manner for

---

45. Will v. Michigan Dep't of State Police, 491 U.S. 58, 69-71 (1989).
46. *Id.* at 71, n.10, citing Kentucky v. Graham, 473 U.S. at 167, n.14 (1985); and Ex Parte Young, 209 U.S. 123, 159-60 (1908).
47. *Cf.* Ex Parte Young, 209 U.S. at 154-56.
48. *Id.* at 149-50.
49. 491 U.S. at 71, n.10.
50. Kentucky v. Graham, 473 U.S. 159, 165 (1985), citing Monell v. Dep't of Social Servs., 436 U.S. 658, 690, n.55 (1978).

damages does not seek personal liability on the part of the individual, but rather seeks recovery from the funds of the governmental unit which that person represents.[51] Death or replacement of the named official-capacity defendant during the pendency of the action does not affect its status, as the successor will be automatically substituted as named defendant and the action continues, in effect, against the governmental unit.[52]

Other than the *Ex Parte Young* situation where official-capacity suits are necessary to obtain injunctive relief from violations of federal law by a state agency, it is probably less confusing to simply name the governmental unit itself as the defendant when seeking relief from it.

It is also important to understand that suing a governmental unit by naming an officer in his or her official capacity is merely a pleading device, not one that effects any substantive changes in the requirements for governmental liability, or the immunities therefrom. For example, suing a state officer in his or her official capacity for damages pursuant to § 1983 is not permissible, both because the state is not a "person" pursuant to § 1983 and because the Eleventh Amendment bars the federal courts from entertaining such a suit, if filed there. Naming a particular state officer in his or her official capacity as defendant does not cure either of these problems because the suit is still an impermissible attempt to obtain a monetary recovery against the state, and therefore is barred by the doctrines explained above.[53]

In contrast, a § 1983 claim against a governmental officer or employee in his or her "individual capacity" or "personal capacity" is not a suit against the governmental unit, but instead an action to impose personal liability against the individual for actions taken under color of state law.[54] Individual immunities will be applicable to such a claim, and not those liability requirements and immunities which would apply if the governmental unit on whose behalf the officer acted were the defendant.[55]

It is best for counsel to clearly state in the caption and in the body of the complaint the capacity in which each defendant is sued. Defendants may be sued in both their official and individual capacities, if the plaintiff can show an entitlement to both types of relief.

---

51. Kentucky v. Graham, 473 U.S. 159, 166 (1985).
52. *Id.* at 166, n.11.
53. *Cf.* Will v. Michigan Dep't of State Police, 491 U.S. 58, 71 (1989).
54. Kentucky v. Graham, 473 U.S. 159, 165-68 (1985).
55. *Id.* at 166-68.

The following includes an overview of the status of several types of individuals and entities as "persons" potentially subject to § 1983 liability.

State Officers and Employees

State officers and employees sued in their *individual capacities* for damages are still "persons" and therefore proper § 1983 defendants.[56] Although not protected from such claims by the Eleventh Amendment, these persons may be able to assert either absolute or qualified "individual" immunity for their challenged actions.[57]

Local Governmental Officers and Employees

Officers and employees of counties, municipalities, school districts, and other local governmental units are also "persons" for § 1983 purposes, and therefore proper § 1983 defendants. However, like state employees, they may be entitled to assert either absolute or qualified individual immunity.[58]

Occasionally, counsel is unaware or uncertain of the identity of one or more persons who should be sued as defendants in their individual capacities. For example, the plaintiff may have descriptions but not names of police officers who participated in an incident giving rise to an excessive force claim. In such an instance, it is possible to list these defendants as "John Does" in the complaint. The unknown defendants and the fact situation giving rise to their liability should be described in as much detail as possible in order to place counsel on notice to prepare a defense for such additional defendants. Counsel should then immediately commence discovery to ascertain their identities.

It is safest to amend and substitute the correct identities prior to the expiration of the statute of limitations if at all possible. If not, some courts have held that, if the above steps are diligently accomplished, pleading amendments adding named defendants who have previously been identified in the pleadings as "John Does" relate back to the original filing for statute of limitations purposes.[59]

---

56. Hafer v. Melo, 112 S. Ct. 358, 365 (1991).
57. *See* chapter 11, "Individual Immunity Defenses Under § 1983 Actions."
58. *Id.*
59. *See, e.g.*, Felix v. New York City Police Dep't, 811 F. Supp. 124, 126-29 (S.D.N.Y. 1992).

Local Governmental Units

Counties, municipalities, school districts, and other local governmental bodies are "persons" for § 1983 purposes, and therefore proper § 1983 defendants, although not liable for the actions of their officers and employees solely on the basis of *respondeat superior*.[60] (See chapter 5, "Municipal Liability Under § 1983," for a full discussion of the way in which the § 1983 causation standard is applied in connection with governmental unit liability.)

These governmental units do not have qualified immunity from compensatory damage claims, as do some individual defendants, but are absolutely immune from liability for punitive damages.[61]

Other Potential Defendants

Occasionally, individuals who are not governmental officers, agents, or employees have acted under color of state law to deprive the plaintiff of federally protected rights, either by conspiring with governmental actors to do so, or by using state-created procedures found to be violative of the plaintiff's federally protected rights. In such a situation, these individuals are appropriate § 1983 defendants, even if any governmental representative(s) with whom they acted are absolutely immune from such a suit.[62] These non-governmental actors are apparently not entitled to qualified immunity from suit for damages, but may be entitled to a "good faith" defense against such damage claims.[63]

Initial Selection of Forum

Section 1983 creates a cause of action which, in general, may properly be filed in either federal or state court. The Supreme Court has held that the Supremacy Clause prevents a state from using its sovereign immunity laws to block § 1983 claims from being litigated in its courts.[64] The related

---

60. Monell v. Dep't of Social Servs., 436 U.S. 658, 690-95 (1978).
61. Owen v. City of Independence, 445 U.S. 622, 650-58 (1980); City of Newport v. Fact Concerts, Inc., 453 U.S. 247, 258-71 (1981).
62. Dennis v. Sparks, 449 U.S. 24, 27-32 (1980).
63. Wyatt v. Cole, 112 S. Ct. 1827, 1834 (1992).
64. Howlett v. Rose, 496 U.S. 356, 375-83 (1990).

attorney's fee statute, 42 U.S.C. § 1988, is as applicable to § 1983 claims filed in state court as to those filed in federal court.[65]

Because § 1983 is a federally created remedy, its litigation in state court produces many thorny issues as to exactly how the extensive body of federal law interpreting and applying it interacts with the rules of the forum state in resolving disputed issues. This is the mirror image of the classic *Erie Railroad v. Tompkins*[66] issue, which arose in the context of the federal courts entertaining state-created causes of action through the exercise of their diversity jurisdiction.

As can be seen from *Felder v. Casey,*[67] it is not a simple matter of distinguishing between what is "substantive" and what is "procedural." A state-created "procedural" rule may still be impermissible to apply to § 1983 claims, if it substantially burdens or thwarts the assertion of these claims in a way which is inconsistent with the purpose of this federal statute.[68] Many of these "converse Erie" questions which arise in the context of the litigation of § 1983 claims in state court are examined in chapter 3 in this volume.

Limitations on § 1983 Plaintiff's Choice of Forum

The most significant limitation on the § 1983 plaintiff's opportunity to choose the forum for a § 1983 claim is the fact that, if the plaintiff chooses to file in state court, the defendants have a statutory right to remove the action to federal court.[69] This is because the § 1983 claim arises under the ". . . Constitution, treaties or laws of the United States . . ." and therefore falls within the "original jurisdiction" of the federal courts.[70] The mechanics of the defendants' exercise of this right are discussed below.

In looking ahead to the possibility of removal, plaintiff's counsel should be aware that, once an action is properly removed to federal court, there is no sure way of returning it to state court, even by voluntarily dismissing the § 1983 claim and retaining only state-law-based pendent

---

65. Maine v. Thiboutot, 448 U.S. 1, 8-11 (1980).
66. 304 U.S. 64 (1938).
67. 487 U.S. 131, 147-51 (1988).
68. *Id.*
69. 28 U.S.C. § 1441 (a) - (b) (1988).
70. *Id.*

claims.[71] The majority opinion of the Supreme Court in *Carnegie-Mellon University v. Cohill* holds that a federal court has discretion to remand a removed case to state court if all federal claims have been dismissed, but also indicates that one of the factors the court should consider as weighing against such possible remand is the presence of deliberate "forum manipulation" by the plaintiff's counsel.[72]

Therefore, if it would be considered a grave calamity to try a particular case in the federal court to which it would be removed, counsel should consider pleading only state law-based claims, such as parallel state constitutional provisions or individual rights statutes, or common law tort remedies. If this is done, defendants do not have a removal right, even though on the same facts the plaintiff *could* have pleaded a § 1983 claim or other federal remedy.[73]

The Pennhurst Situation

A plaintiff seeking declaratory and/or injunctive relief against state officials pursuant to § 1983 and also pursuant to pendent state law-based claims will have to either file the entire action in state court or bifurcate it, with all the attendant risks and complications. This issue was dealt with in the case of *Pennhurst State School and Hospital v. Halderman*.[74] There, the Court indicated that the rationale of the *Ex Parte Young* doctrine does not extend to the enforcement of *state-created* rights.

Therefore, the Court reasoned, the Eleventh Amendment bars federal courts from issuing injunctions against state officials for the enforcement of such state law-based rights even when they are asserted as pendent claims together with causes of action over which the federal court has primary jurisdiction.[75]

---

71. *See* Carnegie-Mellon Univ. v. Cohill, 484 U.S. 343, 357 (1988).
72. *Id.* at 357.
73. *See, e.g.,* Merrell Dow Pharmaceuticals v. Thompson, 478 U.S. 804, 809, n. 6 (1986), and cases cited therein.
74. 465 U.S. 89, 103-06 (1984).
75. *Id.* at 117-21; *see also* Silver v. Baggiano, 804 F.2d 1211, 1213-15 (11th Cir. 1986).

Abstention

While a substantive discussion of abstention issues is beyond the scope of this chapter, counsel should be aware that there are fact situations in which abstention is such a strong possibility that it is probably best to file in state court and avoid the probability of a time-consuming procedural battle on this topic.[76]

Factors to Consider in Forum Choice

Despite the fact that there are some exceptions, the general rule is that the § 1983 plaintiff has a choice, at least initially, as to the federal or the state court system. This choice should be exercised very thoughtfully because, even though removal is an option, if defendants either are unable to agree as to removal or do not act quickly enough to bring it about, the plaintiff's forum choice will be the final one.

Assuming that the plaintiff has a choice of forum, based on the substantive law applicable to the case, the following are examples of some practical factors to consider in making such a choice:

1. Federal court personnel still have much more familiarity with § 1983 claims. However, familiarity does not necessarily mean receptivity. The records of specific judges to whom the case may be assigned are always a consideration.
2. Increasingly, some state supreme courts interpret constitutional rights more broadly than do the federal appellate courts. It is advisable to investigate particular rulings on any constitutional issue which the case situation raises, prior to making a forum choice.
3. The breadth and volume of discovery available in each potential forum should be compared. In view of the 1993 modifications to the Federal Rules of Civil Procedure and the highly restrictive local rules enacted in many districts in connection with these changes, discovery will in many instances be more broadly available in state court.[77] However, early availability of the material that must be

---

76. *See* "Suggestions for Further Reading" at the end of this chapter.
77. *See, e.g.*, Fed. R. Civ. P. 33(a); United States Dist. Ct. for the E. Dist. of Texas, Civil Justice Expense and Delay Reduction Plan, Article One.

provided in initial disclosures in federal court can be critically important, if this provision is not modified by local rule and is actually stringently enforced in the local federal court system.[78]

4. If a jury trial is likely, counsel should consider such variables as geographical area from which the jury array will be summoned, voir dire procedures, likely time limits on final argument, and civil verdict requirements in both the federal and state forums; i.e., less than a unanimous verdict may be permitted in state court.
5. Docket congestion, and therefore the length of time required to get to trial, may vary markedly between the federal and the state forum. If preliminary injunctive relief is sought, availability of court time to schedule a hearing of reasonable length in the near future may be very different as well, and this may influence the probability of obtaining such relief.
6. If it appears likely that a temporary restraining order must be sought, counsel should investigate and consider the procedures and actual practices of both forums with respect to how such requests are handled, as the exact same request may be received very differently in each. Bond setting practices may also be very different. Since there tend to be many traditions and standard practices which are not official or even written, it is highly advisable for inexperienced counsel to consult at this point with one or more attorneys who have practiced for some time in the forums being considered.
7. Particularly in the case of small governmental entities which do not often have § 1983 claims raised against them, the choice of forum may actually determine the choice of counsel by defendants. Filing in a federal forum will almost always trigger the immediate hiring of counsel who are knowledgeable and experienced regarding § 1983 claims; filing in state court may not. Even if the case is subsequently transferred to counsel more experienced in defending against civil rights claims, some time-limited options, such as removal to federal court, may have been lost. On the other hand, the possibility of reaching a speedy, reasonable settlement of a well-founded claim because of the advice of a knowledgeable defense counsel may have been lost as well.

78. *See* Fed. R. Civ. P. 26(a)(1).

Jurisdiction and Venue in the Federal Forum

For § 1983 cases filed in federal court, the following are the basic jurisdictional and venue provisions which are applicable:

Primary Jurisdiction

Section 1983 cases always invoke general "federal question" jurisdiction, pursuant to 28 U.S.C. § 1331. The other jurisdictional statute commonly invoked for § 1983 actions is 28 U.S.C. § 1343(a)(3), which provides for federal jurisdiction over cases brought to:

> redress the deprivation, under color of any State law, statute, ordinance, regulation, custom or usage, of any right, privilege or immunity secured by the Constitution of the United States or by any Act of Congress providing for equal rights of citizens or of all persons within the jurisdiction of the United States. . .[79]

This statute covers all § 1983 actions based upon constitutional deprivations, and some § 1983 actions based upon statutory entitlements held to involve "equal rights." However, it has been construed not to be as broad as the § 1983 "laws" provision. Therefore, there are some statutory provisions, such as certain portions of the Social Security Act, which may be enforced through § 1983, but do not fit within § 1343(a)(3) jurisdiction.[80] However, this is not a barrier to access to federal court, because § 1331 "federal question" jurisdiction is always applicable and, since the Federal Question Jurisdictional Amendment Act of 1980, has no minimum jurisdictional amount requirement.[81]

Supplemental Jurisdiction

If a complaint properly invokes the jurisdiction of the federal court as to at least one claim raised therein, the next jurisdictional question involves "pendent" claims; i.e., what other claims may the complaint properly bring

---

79. 28 U.S.C. § 1343(a)(3) (1988).
80. *Compare* Maine v. Thiboutot, 448 U.S. 1, 4-8 (1980), with Chapman v. Houston Welfare Rights Org., 441 U.S. 600, 615-23 (1979).
81. 28 U.S.C. § 1331 (1986).

before the federal court, if these claims by themselves would not trigger federal jurisdictional provisions?

The supplemental or "pendent" jurisdiction of federal courts was markedly expanded by the Judicial Improvements Act of 1990, codified at 28 U.S.C. § 1367. Even prior to the enactment of this statute, the jurisdiction of a federal court over a "pendent" state law-based claim was invokable if such claim arose from the "same nucleus of operative fact" and was against the same defendant as the claim(s) over which the federal court had primary jurisdiction.[82] However, federal courts were much less likely to take jurisdiction in a "pendent party" situation, in which the plaintiff sought to include a defendant against whom *only* a state law-based claim existed, arising from the same factual nucleus as the federal claims against the other defendants.[83]

The Judicial Improvements Act of 1990 increased the range of circumstances in which a federal court must exercise its pendent or "supplemental" jurisdiction over both claims and parties.[84] As to "federal question" cases such as § 1983 actions, this Act mandates that, with only a few exceptions, a federal court with appropriate "primary" jurisdiction over one of a plaintiff's claims must also assume "supplemental" jurisdiction of all other claims that the plaintiff seeks to assert, if they form "part of the same case or controversy under Article III of the United States Constitution."[85] (This Article III "same case or controversy" standard has been interpreted to mean that the claims arise from a "common nucleus of operative fact" such that they would ordinarily be expected to be tried in the same proceeding.[86])

The only exceptions to the statutory presumption favoring the court's exercise of its "supplemental jurisdiction" are for claims raising a "novel or complex issue of State law," case situations in which a state claim "substantially predominates" over the federal claim(s) case situations in which all claims over which the court had primary jurisdiction have been dismissed, and "exceptional circumstances" in which there are "other compelling reasons for declining jurisdiction."[87]

---

82. United Mine Workers v. Gibbs, 383 U.S. 715, 724-25 (1966).
83. *Cf.* Aldinger v. Howard, 427 U.S. 1, 14-19 (1976).
84. 28 U.S.C. § 1367 (Supp. 1995).
85. 28 U.S.C. § 1367(a) (Supp. 1995).
86. Owen Equip. and Erection Co. v. Kroger, 437 U.S. 365, 371-72 (1978); United Mine Workers v. Gibbs, 383 U.S. 715, 724-25 (1966).
87. 28 U.S.C. § 1367(c) (Supp. 1995).

This expansion of the federal courts' supplemental jurisdiction to include most "pendent party" situations permits plaintiffs to include in their lawsuit as defendants persons and entities against whom a § 1983 claim could not be stated, if they are appropriate defendants in connection with a pendent state law-based claim arising from the same "case or controversy"; that is, a defendant's employer who has *respondeat superior* liability for the employee's tort pursuant to state law, but not enough culpability to trigger § 1983 liability. Further, it permits the inclusion of "pendent party plaintiffs" as well; e.g., spouses of § 1983 plaintiffs asserting state law-based claims for loss of consortium.[88]

Powerful though it is, the Judicial Improvements Act does not, of course, eliminate the Eleventh Amendment barrier that prevents pendent state law-based claims being raised in federal court lawsuits against state officials.[89]

Federal Venue

For "federal question" cases, such as those including § 1983 claims, venue options are set forth in 28 U.S.C. § 1391(b), which states that, "except as otherwise provided by law," the suit may be filed in the following locations:

1. If all defendants reside in the same state, then the suit may be filed in any judicial district in which a defendant resides.[90] (For venue purposes, a corporation "resides" in any judicial district with which it has sufficient contacts to be subject to personal jurisdiction at the time the action is commenced.[91])
2. Alternatively, the suit may be brought in any judicial district in which a "substantial part of the events or omissions giving rise to the claim occurred, or a substantial part of property that is the subject of the action is situated."[92] The Second Circuit case *Bates v.*

---

88. *Cf.* Niehus v. Liberio, 973 F.2d 526, 532 (7th Cir. 1992).
89. *See* Pennhurst v. Halderman, 465 U.S. 89, 117-21 (1984); Silver v. Baggiano, 804 F.2d 1211, 1213-15 (11th Cir. 1986).
90. 28 U.S.C. § 1391(b)(1) (Supp. 1995).
91. 28 U.S.C. § 1391(b)(c) (Supp. 1995).
92. 28 U.S.C. § 1391(b)(2) (Supp. 1995).

C&S Adjusters provides an instructive analysis of this provision and its history, interpreting it to authorize multiple venue possibilities—assuming that the defendant is subject to personal jurisdiction in each—and to indicate that the federal courts no longer must resolve venue disputes by attempting to select the location with the greatest "weight of contacts."[93]

3. If neither of the above provisions can be applied to authorize a filing location, then the suit may be filed in any judicial district "in which any defendant may be found" (again assuming that the defendant(s) may be subjected to personal jurisdiction there.)[94]

There are special provisions for the venue of suits against alien defendants, foreign countries, and United States agencies or their officers.[95]

Even if venue is proper in the district where the case is originally filed, the district court in which it is filed may exercise its sound discretion to transfer it to any other district in which it could have been brought, either on motion of a party or on the court's own initiative.[96] This consideration should be based largely on "the convenience of parties and witnesses," and there must be a showing of significantly greater convenience of the requested forum for the transfer to be appropriate.[97]

Pleading and Filing the § 1983 Lawsuit

A few cautionary considerations are appropriate here, particularly in reference to looking ahead to attorney's fee claims.

Drafting the Complaint

Although any substantive discussion of attorney's fee claims is beyond the scope of this chapter, there are a few basic principles of which plaintiff's counsel should be aware when he or she is drafting initial pleadings. The Supreme Court's decisions regarding attorney's fee awards make it clear that plaintiff's counsel is not well advised either to inflate damage claim

---

93. 980 F.2d 865, 866-68 (2d Cir. 1992).
94. 28 U.S.C. § 1391(b)(3) (Supp. 1995).
95. 28 U.S.C. § 1391(d)(f) (Supp. 1995).
96. 28 U.S.C. § 1404(a) (1988).
97. *See, e.g.*, Time, Inc. v. Manning, 366 F.2d 690, 698 (5th Cir. 1966).

amounts for dramatic effect or to use a shotgun-type approach in pleading causes of action and claims for relief. (This is not to suggest that such a strategy might be appropriate or effective for any other purpose. It simply means that the boomerang effect of such a course of action on later attorney's fee claims is particularly clear.)

The Supreme Court's holding in *Hensley v. Eckerhart*[98] is one precedent with which counsel should be familiar at the complaint drafting stage. This opinion indicates that, although the fee to a successful plaintiff's counsel should not be reduced simply because the court did not fully accept all contentions raised, neither should counsel ordinarily be compensated for time spent on unsuccessful claims that are not "substantially related" to the successful ones.[99] In practice, it may be very difficult to clearly distinguish such time, and the presence of several "unrelated" unsuccessful claims may result in a substantial overall discounting of plaintiff's counsel's fee. (See, for example, *Fair Housing Council v. Landow,*[100] in which fees were totally denied to a successful plaintiff's counsel by the Fourth Circuit in such a case situation.)

Another very instructive opinion for plaintiff's counsel at the complaint drafting stage is *Farrar v. Hobby.*[101] The Supreme Court held that, although a plaintiff who obtained only nominal damages, from one defendant, was a prevailing party, no attorney's fees were appropriate because of the lack of significance of the relief obtained.[102] The result might well have been the same if the plaintiff's counsel had not pleaded for seventeen million dollars from six defendants, but it is notable that this damage demand amount is mentioned four times in the six-page majority opinion.[103] (It is also a major focus of Justice O'Connor's concurrence.[104])

Whatever the substantive import of these cases, familiarity with them should have an impact on complaint drafting as well. What can reasonably be gathered from them is that, not surprisingly, plaintiff's own initial pleadings are a major factor in shaping the court's later view of the success of

---

98. 461 U.S. 424, 434-37 (1983).
99. *Id.*
100. 999 F.2d 92, 97-98 (4th Cir. 1993).
101. 113 S. Ct. 566, 574-78 (1992).
102. *Id.* at 574-75.
103. *Id.* at 570-75.
104. *Id.* at 575-79.

the litigation or lack thereof; and that, in the long run, caution is probably more advisable than exaggeration.

Heightened Pleading Requirements for § 1983 Complaints in Federal Court

Prior to the Supreme Court's 1993 holding in *Leatherman v. Tarrant County,*[105] the federal courts had been following a course of imposing increasingly stringent and demanding specificity requirements for plaintiffs' initial pleadings in § 1983 litigation, in a variety of particular situations. As further explained below, even after the unanimous and remarkably forceful *Leatherman* opinion, there remains uncertainty as to the scope of its applicability, and therefore uncertainty as to the circumstances in which "heightened" pleading requirements may still be imposed on § 1983 plaintiffs in case situations for which *Leatherman* is not directly on point.

*Pre-***Leatherman** *Background and Generally Applicable Law*

Federal Rule of Civil Procedure 8, which provides standard requirements for federal pleadings, calls for only "a short and plain statement of the claim showing that the pleader is entitled to relief"[106] and also states: "No technical forms of pleading or motions are required."[107] The Supreme Court has held that the appropriate test of the sufficiency of most federal pleadings is the "fair notice" standard; i.e., whether or not the action is pleaded with sufficient concreteness and clarity to give the opposing party fair notice of its basis and enable him or her to properly prepare a responsive pleading.[108] In *Conley v. Gibson* the Court stated:

> . . . we have no doubt that petitioners' complaint adequately set forth a claim and gave the respondents fair notice of its basis. The Federal Rules reject the approach that pleading is a game of skill in which one misstep by counsel may be decisive to the outcome. . . .[109]

---

105. 113 S. Ct. 1160, 1161-63 (1993).
106. Fed. R. Civ. P. 8(a)(2).
107. Fed. R. Civ. P. 8(e)(1).
108. Conley v. Gibson, 355 U.S. 41, 47-48 (1957); *cf.* McLain v. Real Estate Board, 444 U.S. 232, 246-47 (1980).
109. Conley v. Gibson, 355 U.S. 41, 48 (1957).

Despite these generally applicable principles, the approach expressly rejected by the Court in *Conley* was an excellent description of the prevailing situation in § 1983 cases prior to *Leatherman.* (As discussed below, in some respects it remains a good description.)

There has always been some tension between the pure "notice pleading" standard and the goal of eliminating, at a relatively early stage, cases in which the plaintiff will not be able to assert in good faith each essential element of the cause of action. The recurring tension between these competing goals has been the major underlying theme in the developing case law about pleading requirements for § 1983 litigation. In these cases, the policy considerations involved in protecting certain defendants from unfiltered exposure to the litigation process are at their strongest, but so are the values reflected in Rule 8, regarding the practical availability of the federal courts.

Prior to the *Leatherman* holding, the overall trend in § 1983 litigation was one of increasingly radical departure from the generally applicable federal notice pleading standard, in more and more specific case situations.

In cases against individual defendants who may be entitled to assert either absolute or qualified individual immunity, many circuits have required plaintiffs to plead in their complaints, prior to any opportunity for discovery, specific facts negating the applicability of such immunity.[110] Allegations of conspiracy also have triggered a heightened pleading requirement in some courts.[111]

Similarly, if an individual defendant's state of mind or motive is an element of plaintiff's cause of action (e.g., in a First Amendment retaliatory termination case), specific factual allegations supporting the claim of improper motive on the part of the defendant have been required by many courts.[112] The District of Columbia Circuit has carried this even further and required not only factually specific supporting evidence of improper motive but *direct*, not circumstantial, factually specific supporting evidence of same—a requirement not even present at final trial in a criminal case.[113]

---

110. *See, e.g.*, Sawyer v. County of Creek, 908 F.2d 663, 665-68 (10th Cir. 1990); Elliott v. Perez, 751 F.2d 1472, 1477-82 (5th Cir. 1985).

111. Streetman v. Jordan, 918 F.2d 555, 557 (5th Cir. 1990); Sooner Products Co. v. McBride, 708 F.2d 510, 512 (10th Cir. 1983).

112. *See, e.g.*, Branch v. Tunnell, 937 F.2d 1382, 1386-88 (9th Cir. 1991).

113. *See* Siegert v. Gilley, 895 F.2d 797, 800-05 (D.C. Cir. 1990), *aff'd on other grounds,* 111 S. Ct. 1789, 1793-94 (1991).

Section 1983 complaints asserting damage claims against municipalities or other governmental units were also exposed to very exacting pleading requirements in some circuits. That is, plaintiffs were required to set forth, without benefit of discovery, detailed factual allegations specifying the precise way in which the policies, established customs, or training deficiencies, etc., of the governmental unit defendant brought about the deprivation of the plaintiff's rights.[114]

Leatherman v. Tarrant County

The *Leatherman* case involved § 1983 plaintiffs' claims of municipal and county liability, based largely on alleged failure to properly train law enforcement officers. The trial court granted a motion to dismiss the complaints, based on lack of specificity in the plaintiffs' pleadings about alleged defects in the governmental units' training policies and procedures.[115] The Fifth Circuit affirmed, relying on its established heightened pleading standard for civil rights complaints against municipalities.[116]

In an opinion as striking for its forcefulness and its unanimity as for its actual holding, the Supreme Court reversed.[117] Indicating that it needed to "resolve a conflict among the Court of Appeals concerning the applicability of a heightened pleading standard to § 1983 actions alleging municipal liability," the Court struck down the Fifth Circuit's rigorous pleading standard for such claims.[118] In so ruling the Court held, in effect, that Rule 8 means what it says.[119]

The defendants argued that the degree of factual specificity called for by Rule 8 should be held to vary according to the complexity of the underlying substantive cause of action being asserted. However, the Supreme Court rejected this analysis of what it meant to "state a claim" pursuant to Rule 8(a)(2). Referencing its prior holdings requiring only "notice pleading" of claims, not factually detailed pleading, the Court reasoned that

---

114. *See, e.g.*, Palmer v. City of San Antonio, 810 F.2d 514, 516-17 (5th Cir. 1987); Strauss v. City of Chicago, 760 F.2d 765, 767-70 (7th Cir. 1985).
115. 755 F. Supp. 726, 729-31 (1991).
116. 954 F.2d 1054, 1057-58 (1992).
117. Leatherman v. Tarrant County, 113 S. Ct. 1160, 1163 (1993).
118. *Id.* at 1161-63.
119. *Id.* at 1163.

these general standards must also be applied to civil rights claims.[120] The Court also found it significant that the federal rules expressly listed a few types of claims which required more detailed pleadings, and took this to indicate that types of claims which were not so listed were not intended to have to meet such a requirement.[121]

The Court also considered and rejected the defendants' argument that more relaxed pleading standards would overburden governmental entities by requiring them to respond to discovery in every § 1983 case, whether or not well-founded.[122] The Court reasoned that a city's lack of susceptibility to *respondeat superior liability* under § 1983 is very different, for this purpose, from an individual defendant's immunity from *suit*, qualified or otherwise.[123] To ultimately establish liability, of course, the plaintiff must still prove how the "municipal policy or custom caused the constitutional injury."[124] As to initial pleading, however, broad, global allegations to this effect were found acceptable.[125]

The Court carefully noted that the case situation before it in *Leatherman* was not one involving claims against individual government employees, and that, therefore, it had no occasion to rule on the issue of heightened pleading requirements with respect to such claims.[126]

*Post-*Leatherman *Circuit Court Decisions*

Although the voice of the Court seemed unusually strong and clear in *Leatherman*, it has produced an amazing cacophony of responses.

Uncertainty as to scope—In many circuits, it is impossible to tell at this point to which particular § 1983 claims, if any, heightened pleading requirements will still be applied after *Leatherman*, either because there is no opinion which is clearly on point, or because existing opinions seem to demonstrate internal inconsistencies. See, for example, *Hill v. City of New York*, in which the Second Circuit gave lip service to applying *Leatherman*

---

120. *Id.*
121. *Id.*, citing Fed. R. Civ. P. 9 (b).
122. *Id.* at 1162.
123. *Id.*, citing Owen v. City of Independence, 445 U.S. 622, 650 (1980).
124. *Leatherman*, 113 S. Ct. at 1162-63.
125. *Id.*
126. *Id.* at 1162.

in connection with conspiracy allegations, but then proceeded to reverse the district court's decision not to dismiss such claims, holding that the plaintiff "has not alleged facts sufficient to support this charge. . . ."[127]

Not surprisingly, the Fourth Circuit has recently ruled that *Leatherman* is properly applicable to governmental unit liability claims in addition to those based on failure to train, and that it "constitute[d] a rejection of the specific requirement that a plaintiff plead multiple instances of similar constitutional violations to support an allegation of municipal policy or custom."[128] This Fourth Circuit panel did not take a position on whether a heightened pleading requirement could still be imposed in cases against individual defendants, but stated that the Supreme Court's reference to this question in *Leatherman* "seemed almost to suggest [it] might be answered in the affirmative. . . ."[129]

Broad or narrow application—In a few courts, *Leatherman* has been applied more broadly, to include § 1983 claims filed against individual defendants.[130]

In contrast, the Eighth and Ninth Circuits have stated that, unless and until the Supreme Court expressly extends *Leatherman* to suits against individual government employees, they will stand by their policies that heightened pleading standards are to be applied in this situation.[131]

The D.C. Circuit also persists in its highly demanding pre-Leatherman pleading requirements for plaintiffs raising claims against individual defendants, when improper motive or intent is an element of the cause of action.[132] *Kimberlin v. Quinlan* was a *Bivens* case, in which the defendants moved to dismiss prior to any substantial discovery. Because matters outside the pleadings were submitted by the parties and considered by the

---

127. Hill v. City of New York, 45 F.3d 653, 664 (2d Cir. 1995).

128. Jordan v. Jackson, 15 F.3d 333, 337-40 (4th Cir. 1994).

129. *Id.* at 339, n.5.

130. Black v. Lane, 22 F.3d 1395, 1399 (7th Cir. 1994); Matthews v. Peters, 818 F. Supp. 224, 226 (N.D. Ill. 1993); Reitz v. Persing, 831 F. Supp. 410, 415-16 (M.D. Pa. 1993).

131. Edgington v. Missouri Department of Corrections, 52 F.3d 777, 779, n.3 (8th Cir. 1995); Branch v. Tunnell, 14 F.3d 449, 455-57 (9th Cir. 1994), *cert. denied,* 114 S. Ct. 2704.

132. Kimberlin v. Quinlan, 6 F.3d 789, 794, n.9, and 797-98 (D.C. Cir. 1993), *rehearing en banc denied*, 17 F.3d 1525 (1994), *vacated and remanded on other grounds*, 115 S. Ct. 2552 (1995).

court, this was treated as a motion for summary judgment and denied in part by the trial court.[133] The defendants filed an interlocutory appeal on qualified immunity grounds, and the D.C. Circuit reversed, holding that the defendants' motion should have been granted in toto and all the plaintiff's claims dismissed.[134] The court took the opportunity to expressly reaffirm a heightened pleading requirement for cases against individual defendants, and to reiterate that plaintiffs with "improper motive" claims against such defendants had to come forward with direct, not circumstantial, evidence of such improper motive before being permitted to engage in standard discovery.[135] The Supreme Court granted certiorari and heard argument in this case, but vacated and remanded on jurisdictional grounds without reaching these issues.[136]

Creative resistance—Meanwhile, the Fifth Circuit, sitting en banc, has come forth with a particularly tenacious and innovative reconstruction of its pre-*Leatherman* heightened pleading requirement for cases involving individual defendants, changing its form but retaining its substance.[137] In *Schultea v. Wood*, the court dealt with a § 1983 complaint against city councilmen which the trial court had refused to dismiss on the defendants' motion, alleging that it failed to state a claim. A Fifth Circuit panel reversed in part, but remanded to give the plaintiff an opportunity to amend his pleading to better state the constitutional claims which he sought to raise through § 1983.[138] The Fifth Circuit granted rehearing en banc in order to prescribe the pleading standards to which the plaintiff should be held on remand. The court then used the occasion to retool and, in essence, reaffirm its heightened pleading requirement in cases in which qualified immunity is an issue.

Acknowledging that qualified immunity is a defense, and that the burden to raise this issue is on the defendant, the court shifted its focus away from Rules 8 and 9, pertaining to stating claims, and toward Rule 7, pertaining to replies to pleadings.[139] The majority opinion indicates

---

133. 774 F. Supp. 1, 7-8; 6 F.3d at 793, n.7; *see also* 17 F.3d at 1525, n.1.
134. 6 F.3d at 795-98.
135. *Id.* at 794, n.8, and 793-98.
136. 115 S. Ct. 2252 (1995).
137. Schultea v. Wood, 47 F.3d 1427 (5th Cir. 1995).
138. 27 F.3d 1112 (5th Cir. 1994).
139. *Schultea*, 47 F.3d at 1432-34.

that if a defendant pleads qualified immunity, the plaintiff should be required, either on the defendant's motion or on the court's own initiative, to reply in detail, refuting this defense.[140] Deftly manipulating the Supreme Court's analysis of the federal pleading rules in *Leatherman*, the majority found Rule 8(a)(2)'s "short and plain statement" standard inapplicable to Rule 7 replies, because Rule 8 does not expressly reference them.[141] (The more general rule governing the content of pleadings, Rule 8(e)(1), which the majority acknowledged to be applicable, prescribes "simple, concise, and direct" pleadings. This sounds a great deal like the same thing, but has the advantage of not yet having been construed by the Supreme Court in a manner directly adverse to the Fifth Circuit's creative interpretation of it.[142])

Throughout its analysis, the majority emphasized that it felt its procedural requirements were necessary to implement the substantive rights of defendants with well-founded claims of immunity from suit. The court, noting that this en banc opinion was "our answer to *Leatherman,*" then provided instructions for trial judges as to how to use available procedural devices to effectuate such rights.[143] These include requiring a complaint that "rests on more than conclusions alone," routinely requiring a detailed reply from the plaintiff if the defendant raises the defense of qualified immunity, either banning or limiting discovery until "sufficient precision and factual specificity" is present in the reply, and then "consider[ing]" summary judgment motions pursuant to Rule 56.[144]

The court also reaffirmed its precedents to the effect that a different, more demanding analysis could be applied to initial complaints filed in forma pauperis, as further discussed below.[145]

In a concurring opinion, several judges indicated that, in view of the fact that the Supreme Court had expressly reserved this issue in *Leatherman*, the majority was prematurely modifying the circuit's heightened pleading requirement for complaints.[146]

---

140. *Id.* at 1432-34, citing Fed. R. Civ. P. 7(a).
141. *Id.* at 1433.
142. *Id.*; Fed. R. Civ. P. 8(e)(1).
143. *Id.* at 1433-36.
144. *Id.* at 1433-34
145. *Id.* at 1434.
146. *Id.* at 1434-36.

Heightened Pleading Requirements in State Courts

It should be noted that pleading requirements, while classically considered "procedural" in nature, can quite obviously be outcome-determinative, as they were in many of the above-cited cases. This should mean, among other things, that state courts may not impose them more exactingly than federal courts, in a manner which significantly burdens the exercise of plaintiffs' right to file and pursue § 1983 claims in state court.[147] This and related topics are discussed in chapter 3.

In Forma Pauperis Filing

A case may be filed without payment or security for the costs of court if the plaintiff moves the court for permission to do so, and files an affidavit to the effect that he or she is unable, due to poverty, to make such payment or post such security.[148] This motion must be granted and the case be allowed to proceed, unless it appears to the court that the allegation of poverty is untrue, or the court is "satisfied that the action is frivolous or malicious."[149]

The primary effect of the in forma pauperis filing status is to permit the filing of the suit without prepayment of the filing fee, and to place a duty on the officers of the court to serve required legal process in the case without charge. It does not excuse the payment of witness fees and expenses or place the duty of such payment on the government.[150]

The Supreme Court has held that only natural persons, and not associations or other artificial entities, are eligible to file in forma pauperis.[151]

Nature and Standard of Review for Frivolousness

Filing in forma pauperis places the complaint in a position of having to clear an additional hurdle, although this should not ordinarily be a problem for well-founded claims. If the complaint clearly "lacks an arguable basis

---

147. *Cf.* Felder v. Casey, 487 U.S. 131, 150-53 (1988).
148. 28 U.S.C. § 1915(a) (1989).
149. 28 U.S.C. § 1915(d) (1989).
150. *See, e.g.,* Malik v. Lavalley, 994 F.2d 90 (2d Cir. 1993).
151. Rowland v. California Men's Colony, 113 S. Ct. 716, 720-26 (1993).

in law or fact," the trial court may dismiss it without requiring service on the defendant.[152] Unlike the scope of the trial court's review pursuant to a defendant's Rule 12(b)(6) motion to dismiss, in reviewing a complaint pursuant to § 1915(d), the trial court may "pierce the veil of the complaint's factual allegations" and dismiss complaints based upon "fantastic or delusional scenarios."[153] However, it is not appropriate for a trial court to dismiss simply because the complaint's allegations are unlikely or improbable.[154]

As noted above, the Fifth Circuit recently held en banc that *Leatherman* should have no effect on trial courts' review of complaints filed in forma pauperis, and that such review may include a consideration of whether or not ". . . it is clear that the defendants are immune from suit. . . ."[155]

Dismissal of a complaint pursuant to § 1915(d) does not have a res judicata effect precluding the filing of a paid complaint raising the same claims, but it may preclude subsequent consideration of the same allegations again raised in forma pauperis.[156]

Appellate review of a trial court's § 1915(d) dismissal is for abuse of discretion, not de novo.[157]

Defendant's Options

Defense counsel who have occasion to deal with in forma pauperis complaints should familiarize themselves with the Tenth Circuit's opinion in *Lemmons v. Morris and Morris*, wherein the court reviewed for abuse of discretion a trial judge's dismissal of an inmate's § 1983 complaint pursuant to § 1915(d).[158] As can be seen from this opinion, although the defendant is not required to make any response until the § 1915(d) issue is settled, or to file an appellate brief to aid an appellate court in reviewing it, should it reach that level, there are times when it may be wise to do so.[159]

---

152. 28 U.S.C. § 1915(d) (1989); Neitzke v. Williams, 490 U.S. 319, 325 (1989).
153. Neitzke v. Williams, 490 U.S. 319, 327-28 (1989); *see also* Denton v. Hernandez, 112 S. Ct. 1728, 1732-34 (1992).
154. *Denton*, 112 S. Ct. at 1733-34.
155. Schultea v. Wood, 47 F.3d 1427, 1434 (5th Cir. 1995), quoting Neitzke v. Williams, 490 U.S. 319, 327 (1989).
156. *Denton,* 112 S. Ct. 1728, 1734 (1992).
157. *Id.*
158. 39 F.3d 264, 268-69 (10th Cir. 1994).
159. *Cf. id.* at 268-69.

If a complaint survives scrutiny under § 1915(d), defendants are not, according to the Fifth Circuit, thereby precluded from moving for its dismissal for failure to state a claim, pursuant to Rule 12(b)(6).[160] The standards of review applicable to these two considerations are different, so that a complaint may be found not to be frivolous under the terms of § 1915(d) and still fail, in some respect, to state a claim pursuant to 12(b)(6).[161]

Initial Considerations for Defendant's Counsel

Conflicts of Interest in § 1983 Defense Work

All case situations in which counsel is asked to represent more than one defendant present at least some potential ethical problems, but such case acceptance decisions for defense counsel in § 1983 litigation can be particularly complex and troublesome. If, for example, an attorney is asked to defend both an individual governmental employee and the governmental entity which employs him against a suit for damages, there are many obvious and not so obvious ways in which the interests of these potential clients may diverge.

The interest of a governmental entity defendant may well be in showing that the defendant employee did not act in accordance with the established policies, procedures, and customs of the governmental unit, but instead acted erratically and unpredictably in such a manner that it would be unjustified to impose liability for his actions on the governmental unit. Conversely, the interest of the employee may be best served by showing that he followed an accepted, standard, approved course of conduct sanctioned by the policies of the governmental unit in question.

A less common but just as troublesome example is that of the governmental employee who has clearly committed an unlawful act for which the plaintiff seeks to impose liability on this individual's employer on "a failure to train" basis. One possible strategy for defending the governmental unit would be to attempt to defeat causation by establishing that the employee was so bent on committing misconduct that

---

160. Jackson v. City of Beaumont, 958 F.2d 616, 618 (5th Cir. 1992).
161. *Id.* at 618-19, citing Neitzke v. Williams, 490 U.S. 319, 326 (1989).

no amount of training would have made any difference.[162] Of course, such an argument could not be made by an attorney who also represents the individual employee.

There are several cases in which the courts, faced with disgruntled individual defendants at the conclusion of litigation in which defense counsel undertook multiple representation, have issued rulings on whether or not a new trial was required, or about whether or not the trial judge was obligated to warn individual defendants about the hazards of such joint representation.[163] The real significance of these cases for defense counsel, though, is not the trial court's finding in each as to whether or not enough supporting facts were shown to entitle the individual defendants to a retrial—rather, the significance lies in the extent of the troubles that accrued to defense counsel as a result of the joint representation.[164]

It may be possible to avoid the worst potential conflicts through governmental unit decisions to fully indemnify its individual employees in some types of case situations, or through stipulations as to some issues which could otherwise create conflicts.[165] However, even these situations may expose defense counsel to increased risks, and therefore call for careful communication and file documentation about such things as informing all clients of litigation risks and settlement offers, diligence in following up on evidentiary leads suggested by clients, etc.[166] It is clear that mere boilerplate, pro forma "disclosure" and "consent" are not enough.[167] In addition to exercising caution about the acceptance of joint representation in the first place, counsel should also remain on the alert as the case develops for unexpected circumstances that increase the seriousness of potential

---

162. E.g., would it have helped to send Mark Fuhrman to racial and gender diversity classes?
163. *Compare, e.g.*, Dunton v. County of Suffolk, 729 F.2d 903, 907-10 (2d Cir. 1984), *modified on other grounds,* 748 F.2d 69; *with* Rodick v. City of Schenectady, 1 F.3d 1341, 1349-50 (2d Cir. 1993); *see also* Gordon v. Norman, 788 F.2d 1194, 1198-99 (6th Cir. 1986).
164. *See, e.g.*, Gordon v. Norman, 788 F.2d 1194, 1198-99, nn. 4 and 5 (6th Cir. 1986).
165. *See, e.g., id.* at 1198; Manganella v. Keyes, 613 F. Supp. 795, 798-99 (D. Conn. 1985).
166. *See, e.g.*, Rodick v. City of Schenectady, 1 F.3d 1341, 1350-51 (2d Cir. 1993); Gordon v. Norman, 788 F.2d 1194, 1198 (6th Cir. 1986).
167. *See, e.g.*, Dunton v. County of Suffolk, 729 F.2d at 909.

conflicts, and that may mandate the hiring of separate counsel, even if it must be at the expense of the governmental unit.

Interestingly, the above-referenced practical problems in providing counsel for individual defendants in civil rights cases may have had an influence on the development of the law regarding such claims. In *Kimberlin v. Quinlan*, one D.C. Circuit judge stated:

> Of course, in *Bivens* cases, individual governmental officers are sued personally, and are sometimes obliged to pay attorneys' fees out of modest government salaries. That is why the court has recognized that early dismissal of all but the few obviously meritorious cases is desirable.[168]

Removal

After the decision as to whom to represent, the next decision which must be made is whether or not to remove to federal court, if the case is filed in state court. As noted above, defendants have the ultimate choice of forum in § 1983 cases, if they are aware of it and know how to exercise it.[169] Whether or not to do so should be governed by a similar type of analysis to that suggested above for plaintiffs' counsel determining where to file. While some governmental defendants feel more at home at the state courthouse and consider the federal courthouse to be foreign and dangerous territory, others may be more concerned about jury procedures or such factors as the availability of interlocutory appeal for immunity issues, which are not uniform among the states at this point.

The substance of defendants' removal right is governed by 28 U.S.C. § 1441—the procedure for its exercise by 28 U.S.C. § 1446. Section 1446 provides for the filing of a "notice of removal" in the federal district court for the district where the action is pending, together with copies of all the state court papers served on the defendant.[170] The notice should contain a "short and plain statement of the grounds for removal."[171] It is no longer

---

168. 17 F.3d 1525, 1526 (D.C. Cir. 1994). (Silberman, J., concurring in denial of rehearing *en banc*.)
169. 28 U.S.C. § 1441(a) (1988).
170. 28 U.S.C. § 1446(a) (1989).
171. *Id.*

necessary to file a bond, and the notice need not be verified—rather it must simply be "signed pursuant to Rule 11."[172]

The defendant then gives written notice of the removal to all adverse parties, and sends a copy of the removal notice to the clerk of the state court. No hearing or other consideration of the removal notice may take place in the state court; the removal is automatic upon compliance with the above-referenced steps. The state court then loses jurisdiction, and any consideration of remand must take place in the federal court.[173]

Pitfall Alert on Removal Procedures

Although § 1446 appears on the surface to be relatively simple to understand and comply with, this is cruelly deceptive and, in fact, various forms of technical peril lurk therein.[174] Further, it is strictly construed against removing defendants—and procedural defects, including failure to meet applicable time limits, will probably be held to waive the right to remove.[175]

The major traps for the unwary defense counsel are the computation of the time limit for filing the removal notice, especially in multiple defendant cases, and the standards for complying with the requirement that, ordinarily, all defendants must join in this notice.[176] As it would be impossible to cover all the potential complications of either, counsel unfamiliar with this area of law are simply warned to be wary of these issues and urged to familiarize themselves with the relevant Wright and Miller sections referenced in "Suggestions for Further Reading" and with the authorities cited above.

---

172. *Id.*
173. 28 U.S.C. § 1446(d) (Supp. 1995); *see, e.g.*, Libhart v. Santa Monica Dairy Co., 592 F.2d 1062, 1064 (9th Cir. 1979).
174. *See, e.g.*, Roe v. O'Donohue, 38 F.3d 298, 301, 303-04 (7th Cir. 1994), and authorities cited therein; *see also Defense Practitioners Slumber No More: Pennsylvania Courts Deliver an Unexpected Wake-Up Call Concerning the Section 1446(b) Removal Time Period.* 29 DUQ. L. REV. 601 (Spring 1991).
175. *Id.*
176. *Id.*

Waivable "Procedural" Defenses in Federal Court

If the case is to be litigated in federal court, defense counsel must next determine whether or not any potential defense is present which will be waived if not asserted very early in the litigation process. Pursuant to Federal Rule of Civil Procedure 12(h)(1), there are four such initial "procedural" defenses:

1. lack of personal jurisdiction over the defendant;
   (Note that a suggestion that the court lacks subject matter jurisdiction of the case, unlike a claim of lack of personal jurisdiction over the defendant, may be raised at any time during the litigation, even on appeal.[177])
2. improper venue;
3. insufficiency of process; and
4. insufficiency of service of process.[178] (Note that the defense of "insufficiency of service of process" includes objections to the timeliness of service, which objections will be held to have been waived unless raised at the time and in the manner described below.[179])

These four easily waivable procedural defenses may ordinarily be raised in either of two ways, through a pre-answer motion or in the original answer itself.[180] However, be aware that if counsel files a Rule 12 motion of any type at or before filing an answer, all the above-referenced procedural defenses which exist at that time *must* be included in it or they will be waived; i.e., they cannot be included either in a later motion or in the defendant's answer.[181]

Although the defendant may seek leave of court later in the case to amend an answer and assert additional defenses of most types, a later

---

177. Fed. R. Civ. P. 12 (h)(3); *see, e.g.,* Tongkook America, Inc. v. Shipton Sportswear Co., 14 F.3d 781, 786 (2d Cir. 1994).
178. Fed. R. Civ. P. 12 (h)(1).
179. Santos v. State Farm Fire and Casualty Co., 902 F.2d 1092, 1096 (2d Cir. 1990); Kersh v. Derozier, 851 F.2d 1509, 1511-12 (5th Cir. 1988).
180. Fed. R. Civ. P. 12 (b).
181. Fed. R. Civ. P. 12 (g) and (h)(1); Albany Insurance Co. v. Almacenadora Somex, 5 F.3d 907, 909-10 (5th Cir. 1993); Pardazi v. Cullman Medical Center, 896 F.2d 1313, 1314-17 (11th Cir. 1990).

amended answer may not be used to assert for the first time any of these four Rule 12(h)(1) defenses, unless the amendment is filed within the time for amendment as of right, pursuant to Rule 15(a).[182]

Requests to Dismiss

Federal Rule of Civil Procedure 12(b)(6) authorizes a defendant to seek the dismissal of a complaint which fails to state an actionable claim, or which reveals the presence of a bar to recovery, such as the statute of limitations. The target of such a motion is the pleading only, not the evidence which might or might not support the pleading. The distinction between a motion to dismiss and a motion for summary judgment does not depend on what title is used for the motion, but rather on whether or not the court considers materials outside the pleadings in connection with the motion.[183] That is, if matters outside the pleadings are submitted by either party and considered by the court, the motion must be treated as one for summary judgment and Rule 56 procedures must be followed, including giving all parties the opportunity to submit evidentiary materials in response. (See page 52 for a discussion of summary judgment motions in the § 1983 context.)

Requests to dismiss pursuant to Rule 12(b)(6) may be made either in the defendant's answer or by pre-answer motion.[184] However, the defendant does not waive the right to contend that the plaintiff has failed to state an actionable claim by not filing a pre-answer motion to this effect, or by omitting this contention from the original answer.[185] Although such issues are usually raised early in the case, Rule 12 expressly provides that a request to dismiss for failure to state an actionable claim may be made in any pleading, in a motion for judgment on the pleadings during the pendency of the case, or even at trial.[186] Not surprisingly, the Sixth Circuit has recently held that filing a pre-answer Rule 12 motion without

---

182. Fed. R. Civ. P. 12 (h)(1); *see, e.g.*, Konigsberg v. Shute, 435 F.2d 551, 552 (3d Cir. 1970).
183. Fed. R. Civ. P. 12 (b).
184. *Id.*
185. Fed. R. Civ. P. 12 (h)(2).
186. Fed. R. Civ. P. 12 (h)(3).

raising the issue of qualified immunity therein did not waive the defendant's right to seek dismissal on this ground in a later pleading or in a post-answer motion.[187]

Because of their focus on pleadings, the relative usefulness of Rule 12(b)(6) motions for defendants in § 1983 litigation has been reduced by the Supreme Court's *Leatherman* opinion, discussed previously. Although immunity defenses may be raised through such a motion, if this is done only the pleadings and no evidentiary materials are before the court, and the plaintiff's factual allegations must be taken as true for purposes of ruling on the motion.[188] For an example of use of a motion to dismiss to raise a qualified immunity claim, see the Seventh Circuit case *McMath v. City of Gary, Indiana*.[189]

Discovery and Summary Judgment Issues

Probably the most significant change in the federal rules pertaining to discovery is new Federal Rule 26(a)(1), effective December 1, 1993. It provides for automatic disclosure of basic witness and document information by all parties very early in the litigation, without even the requirement of a discovery request for same.

Although modified in many jurisdictions by local rules, in effect it requires that such information is to be provided about "disputed facts alleged with particularity in the pleadings."[190] This gives each side the opportunity to attempt to move the discovery process along faster by including more specific allegations in its pleadings than would otherwise be required, thereby placing opposing counsel under the obligation to disclose more witness and document information very early. However, whether or not more particularized pleadings are used, the same substantive standard for discoverable information (i.e., "relevant to the subject matter involved in the pending action") should ultimately be in effect.[191]

---

187. English v. Dyke, 23 F.3d 1086, 1089-91 (6th Cir. 1994).
188. *See, e.g.*, United States v. Mississippi, 380 U.S. 128, 143 (1965).
189. 976 F.2d 1026, 1031 (7th Cir. 1992).
190. Fed. R. Civ. P. 26 (a)(1).
191. Fed. R. Civ. P. 26 (b)(1).

Increased Importance of Discovery and Summary Judgment Issues after Leatherman

The Supreme Court in *Harlow v. Fitzgerald* expressed its abiding concern that governmental officers, sued personally for damages, will be substantially impaired in the performance of their job duties by the litigation process itself, whatever the outcome.[192] Of course, the major burden of the litigation process is the obligation to respond to discovery, referred to by the court in *Harlow* as potentially "wide-ranging, time-consuming, and not without considerable cost."[193]

Although the Supreme Court has repeatedly stated its support for the goal of protecting from the litigation process those governmental officials with well-founded claims of individual immunity, it has also recently given a strong indication that it will probably not permit this to be accomplished through the imposition of a heightened pleading standard.[194] Whatever the outcome of the heightened pleading issue regarding individual defendants, it is already indisputably clear that the goal of filtering out unsubstantiated claims against governmental units can no longer be accomplished through this means.[195]

The range of reasonable possibilities as to how it *is* to be accomplished now seems to be narrowed to two: control of discovery and effective use of summary judgment procedures. Indeed, in *Leatherman*, the Court expressly stated that ". . . federal courts and litigants must rely on summary judgment and control of discovery to weed out unmeritorious claims sooner rather than later."[196]

Summary Judgments in Federal Court

Rule 56 provides for either party to seek summary judgment on any issue as to which he or she claims no material fact is in dispute, and on which he or she claims to be entitled to judgment as a matter of law.[197] Summary

---

192. 457 U.S. 800, 815-18 (1982).
193. *Id.* at 817, n. 29, quoting Halperin v. Kissinger, 606 F.2d 1192, 1214 (1979).
194. *See* Leatherman v. Tarrant County, 113 S. Ct. 1160, 1162-63 (1993).
195. *Id.*
196. *Id.* at 1163.
197. Fed. R. Civ. P. 56 (a) and (b).

judgment is not a test of the sufficiency of the pleadings of the opposing party, but instead probes for the existence of some proof that an actual factual dispute is present and that, therefore, a trial on the merits is required.[198]

The aggressive use of summary judgment motions to test the sufficiency of litigants' claims has for many years been an important part of the federal judicial process for all types of cases. Although in many state court systems summary judgment is a disfavored device regarded with heavy skepticism by trial court judges, in the federal court system it is a well-respected tool for avoiding unnecessary trials and for narrowing the issues which will require trial on the merits.[199]

Celotex Corp. v. Catrett

Through its *Celotex* opinion in 1986, the Supreme Court clarified the analysis which is to be applied in ruling on summary judgment motions, and in doing so made these motions an even more powerful tool for defendants—or, more precisely, for parties who do not have the burden of proof with respect to the particular issue that is the subject of the motion.[200] The defendant in *Celotex* used a summary judgment motion, in effect, to test whether or not the plaintiff could come forward with some proof of each essential element of the cause of action. The defendant did not produce any definitive proof of its own negating any element of the plaintiff's case, but rather used the summary judgment motion as a device to force the plaintiff to come forward with proof in order to avoid summary judgment being granted for the defendant. The plaintiff was unable to provide acceptable proof of one essential element of the claim, and the court granted summary judgment for the defendant.[201]

The Supreme Court approved the granting of the defendant's summary judgment motion in these circumstances, although noting that the plaintiff need not necessarily have produced evidence that would be admissible at trial, but rather "some evidence," such as an affidavit.[202] (The plaintiff did

---

198. Fed. R. Civ. P. 56 (c) and (e); *see, e.g.*, Zweig v. Hearst Corp., 521 F.2d 1129, 1133 (9th Cir. 1975), *cert. denied*, 423 U.S. 1025.

199. *See, e.g.*, McEwen v. Delta Air Lines, 919 F.2d 58, 60 (7th Cir. 1990); Freeman v. Continental Gin Co., 381 F.2d 459, 467-70 (5th Cir. 1967).

200. Celotex Corp. v. Catrett, 477 U.S. 317, 322-23 (1986).

201. *Id.* at 320-21.

202. *Id.* at 324.

produce three documents which were discounted as not meeting the requirements of admissible materials as defined by Rule 56(c)and(e)).[203] The Court also recognized the potential problem with premature consideration of such motions, and pointed out that Rule 56(f) could be applied to prevent such premature disposition.[204] This subpart of Rule 56 provides that a summary judgment motion may be denied, or a hearing on the motion continued until after further discovery is made, if the responding party cannot "for reasons stated" present facts by affidavit at the time of first consideration of the motion.[205] The Court in *Celotex* interpreted this to indicate that such a ruling may be continued ". . . if the nonmoving party has not had an opportunity to make full discovery."[206]

Summary Judgment/Discovery Issues re: Governmental Entity Defendants

One of the most notable effects of the Supreme Court's *Leatherman* opinion is to move the first major battle between the civil rights plaintiff and the governmental entity defendant a bit further into the litigation process—i.e., at the discovery/summary judgment stage, rather than at the initial pleading/motion to dismiss stage.

Theoretically, plaintiffs should no longer be, in effect, forced to develop almost all aspects of their case through informal discovery prior to filing an initial pleading, in order to survive a motion to dismiss. However, trial courts will now be faced with increasing numbers of discovery battles between plaintiffs and governmental unit defendants as plaintiffs file broader, more general initial pleadings and then seek specific supporting evidence through extensive discovery.

Although governmental unit defendants clearly have no claim of immunity from the litigation process itself, as do some individual defendants, they can certainly make early and aggressive use of *Celotex*-type summary judgment motions in an attempt to weed out cases against them. This may be especially effective if the case development efforts of plaintiffs' counsel are not diligent, expeditious, and clearly focused, as discussed below.

---

203. *Id.* at 320-21.
204. *Id.* at 326.
205. Fed. R. Civ. P. 56 (f).
206. Celotex Corp. v. Catrett, 477 U.S. 317, 326 (1986).

The *Celotex* opinion refers to the provision of an "opportunity to make full discovery" on the part of the non-moving party, pursuant to Rule 56(f), prior to summary judgment consideration.[207] However, this subsection of Rule 56 provides a fairly amorphous guideline, and the trial court has been held to have a good deal of discretion as to how, exactly, it is to be applied.[208] Also, the Supreme Court's reference in *Leatherman* to "control of discovery" as a way to "weed out unmeritorious claims sooner rather than later" is a rather ominous one for plaintiffs in this context.[209] Courts which strongly supported the imposition of a heightened pleading requirement prior to *Leatherman* may seize on the technique of prematurely granting defendants' summary judgment motions, after little or no discovery, as a way to accomplish the same goal without directly flouting the *Leatherman* mandate.

In a somewhat different context, the D.C. Circuit attempted exactly this in the *Bivens* case *Kimberlin v. Quinlan*, in which the defendant's dispositive motion was considered and ruled on as one for summary judgment—although the court also took the opportunity to reaffirm its heightened pleading standard for cases against individual defendants in which improper motive is an issue.[210] In an opinion concurring in the denial of rehearing en banc, joined by two other judges, Judge Williams of the D.C. Circuit stated:

> Although our 'direct evidence' rule is a variation on what is often referred to as a 'heightened pleading' standard, in fact the 'standard' normally has nothing to do with pleading, but simply allows summary judgment to be granted before the plaintiff has had as great an opportunity to subject defendant to discovery as is conventionally available.[211]

---

207. *Id.*

208. *See* Sheinkopf v. Stone, 927 F.2d 1259, 1263-64 (1st Cir. 1991); Pittman v. Gaines, 905 F.2d 199, 201 (8th Cir. 1990); *but see* Dean v. Barber, 951 F.2d 1210, 1213-14 (11th Cir. 1992).

209. Leatherman v. Tarrant County, 113 S. Ct. 1160, 1163 (1993).

210. 6 F.3d at 794-95, nn. 8-10 (D.C. Cir. 1993), *rehearing en banc denied*, 17 F.3d 1525 (1994), *vacated and remanded on other grounds,* 115 S. Ct. 2552 (1995).

211. 17 F.3d at 1525, n. 1.

(As noted above, the Supreme Court granted certiorari in this case, but vacated and remanded on a jurisdictional point without reaching the above-referenced issues.[212])

Indeed, in terms of the effect on a civil rights plaintiff, there is very little practical difference between a motion to dismiss, based on the pleadings, that disposes of the case before there is opportunity to do discovery in order to plead more specifically, and a motion for summary judgment that disposes of the case before there is opportunity to do discovery in order to come forward with evidence to effectively oppose the motion.

Until the Supreme Court further clarifies the ground rules for this increasingly critical battlefield, there are several things plaintiffs' attorneys can do in anticipation of, and in response to, premature summary judgment motions by defense counsel, in order to preserve their clients' right to trial on the merits of their claims. First, because the availability of full, broad-based discovery can never be completely assured, counsel are still well advised to do as much informal discovery as possible prior to filing their complaints. This should assist both in responding to such motions without the benefit of extensive discovery, if necessary, and in providing a careful and specific focus for the discovery efforts that are made.

Second, many reported opinions have focused on the need for specificity in Rule 56(f) affidavits, and have rejected broad, global allegations to the effect that more time is needed for discovery, and that further discovery is expected to produce "relevant information."[213] If it is necessary for a plaintiff to file a Rule 56(f) affidavit, counsel should state as specifically as possible what further discovery he or she wishes to do, what information is expected to be developed through it, and how such information will be probative of a material fact issue in the case, so as to make the entry of summary judgment inappropriate.[214] Additionally, plaintiff's counsel should proceed with discovery as expeditiously as permitted by the local rules, and any unavoidable delays in doing so should be specifically explained to the court in the Rule 56(f) affidavit.[215]

---

212. 115 S. Ct. 2552 (1995).
213. *See, e.g.*, Lewis v. City of Ft. Collins, 903 F.2d 752, 758-59 (10th Cir. 1990).
214. *See, e.g.*, United States v. Leong Chinese Merchants Ass'n Bldg., 918 F.2d 1289, 1294-95 (7th Cir. 1990), *cert. denied,* 502 U.S. 809 (1991).
215. *See, e.g.*, Sofo v. Pan-American Life Ins. Co., 13 F.3d 239, 242 (7th Cir. 1994), in which the court held that ongoing settlement negotiations did not provide an effective excuse for plaintiff's failure to pursue discovery for ten months.

In summary, plaintiff's counsel should know as much as possible about the § 1983 case against a governmental unit prior to filing it in court, and should then proceed as quickly as possible with well-focused discovery which is not vulnerable to claims that it is a "fishing expedition." If defendant pursues a premature summary judgment motion, plaintiff's counsel should file an affidavit, pursuant to Rule 56(f), specifying what factual material counsel is still seeking to discover, from which sources, what indications there are that such material is actually available from these sources, and precisely how it will assist in developing a material fact issue necessary for the plaintiff's opposition to the motion. Defendant's counsel should be on the alert from the beginning of the case for any deviation from the above-referenced standards, and if one occurs, should make effective use of it in a Rule 56 motion.

Summary Judgment/Discovery Issues in Suits Against Individual Defendants

The general summary judgment principles outlined above are also applicable in cases involving individual defendants. Additionally, such cases involve policy issues further favoring the use of such motions and the imposition of limits on discovery. It should be noted that the standard-setting *Celotex* case involved an issue on which the non-movant, the plaintiff, would have had the burden of proof (apparently both persuasion and production) at trial. Therefore, the Court reasoned, it was fair to require the non-movant to come forward with some evidence prior to trial, even though the movant, the defendant, had not produced proof conclusively negating what the plaintiff needed to prove on the issue.[216] If the courts are to treat qualified immunity as a true affirmative defense, in which both the burden of persuasion and the burden of production remain with the defendant, then *Celotex* is not logically fully on point.[217]

The issue with respect to qualified immunity claims is whether the defendant violated "clearly settled law," which at first glance looks like a strictly legal question, easily lending itself to disposition by summary judg-

---

216. Celotex v. Catrett, 477 U.S. 317, 324 (1986).
217. *See id.* at 324; *compare* Elliott v. Thomas, 937 F.2d 338, 344-45 (7th Cir. 1991), *cert. denied*, 502 U.S. 1074 (1992), *with* Feliciano-Angulo v. Rivera-Cruz, 858 F.2d 40, 47-48 (1st Cir. 1988).

ment motion. Also, the early use of a summary judgment motion to resolve this issue furthers the important policy consideration of protecting governmental officer defendants whose claims of immunity are sound from the full hardships of the legal process.[218]

Such a procedure may sound logical in the abstract and be understandably favored by the Supreme Court on policy grounds, but in practice it has proven to be extraordinarily difficult for lower courts to implement in a consistent and fair manner. Many times disputed factual issues simply must be resolved in order for the trial court to rule properly on claims of qualified immunity. Although the issue of what law was clearly settled at the time of the defendant's challenged actions is always a legal matter for the court to determine, many times the actual actions the defendant took are hotly disputed. If, under the plaintiff's version of the facts, the defendant took actions which no reasonable official in the defendant's position could have believed to be lawful, and under the defendant's version of the facts the actions were ones which a reasonable official *could* have believed to be lawful, a genuine factual dispute exists which should preclude resolution by summary judgment.[219]

One of the Supreme Court's most strongly worded opinions about the use of the summary judgment procedure to resolve qualified immunity issues is the 1991 case *Hunter v. Bryant*.[220] This was a *Bivens* lawsuit in which Fourth Amendment damage claims were raised against Secret Service agents, who claimed qualified immunity for their actions in arresting the plaintiff.[221] After the trial court denied the defendants' summary judgment motion, the Ninth Circuit partially upheld this decision, indicating that the plaintiff's "arrest without probable cause" claim could properly be disposed of by summary judgment on qualified immunity grounds only if there were "only one reasonable conclusion a jury could reach" on this point.[222]

The Supreme Court reversed the Ninth Circuit on this issue, and discussed the analysis which should be applied to a qualified immunity summary judgment motion. Emphasizing that qualified immunity protects

---

218. *See, e.g.*, Harlow v. Fitzgerald, 457 U.S. 800, 814-18 (1982).
219. *See, e.g.*, Harper v. Harris County, 21 F.3d 597, 600-02 (5th Cir. 1994).
220. 112 S. Ct. 534 (1991).
221. *Id.* at 536.
222. *Id.* at 536-37.

governmental officers who could reasonably have thought they were not violating the law, the Court indicated that summary judgment should have been granted on the facts of the *Hunter* case.[223] The Court summarized by stating that "immunity ordinarily should be decided by the court long before trial."[224]

Despite this sweeping language, the Court failed to provide effective guidelines for the lower courts and for litigants as to how to effectuate such a goal. Surely, factual disputes on issues affecting the qualified immunity defenses of individual defendants are the norm rather than the exception in civil rights litigation, and such legitimate factual disputes cannot properly be resolved by summary judgment motion.[225]

Despite the current uncertainties as to the exact procedural implementation of their defense, individuals with well-founded defenses of absolute or qualified immunity from suit have a strong rationale for asserting same by way of a summary judgment motion early in the litigation process, simultaneously moving to stay all discovery, including the "automatic disclosure" obligation referenced above, until the determination of such motion.[226] Discovery against such a defendant should then be limited to those factual issues, if any, which must be further developed in order to rule on the legal issues raised by the defendant's qualified immunity claim.[227]

Rather than attempting to proceed at that point with broad-based discovery against the individual defendant, plaintiff's counsel faced with such a motion should respond by showing the court exactly what factual material, if any, is necessary to refute the defendant's qualified immunity claim, and how any discovery sought at that point particularly relates to such determination. A too broad discovery order at this stage may in some circumstances properly be subject to interlocutory appeal by an individual defendant.[228]

---

223. *Id.*
224. *Id.* at 537.
225. *See, e.g.*, Weaver v. Brenner, 40 F.3d 527, 537 (2d Cir. 1994); Harper v. Harris County, 21 F.3d 597 (5th Cir. 1994).
226. *Cf., e.g.*, Anderson v. Creighton, 483 U.S. 635, 646-47 (1987).
227. *See, e.g., id.* at 646-47, n. 6; Gaines v. Davis, 928 F.2d 705, 707 (5th Cir. 1991).
228. *See, e.g.*, Gaines v. Davis, 928 F.2d at 706-07.

Interlocutory Appeals

As chapter 3 deals with procedural issues in the litigation of § 1983 claims in state court, this section will focus exclusively on interlocutory appeal issues as they occur in the federal court system.

The issues of availability and scope of interlocutory appellate jurisdiction for defendants in § 1983 cases are among the most hotly disputed, heavily litigated matters in current civil rights law. The 1994-95 Supreme Court term produced two major opinions on these topics, *Swint v. Chambers County* and *Johnson v. Jones*, both of which are discussed below.[229]

Background and Rationale

Interlocutory appeals by defendants in § 1983 litigation are a judicially created exception to the rule that, except in certain statutorily enumerated circumstances, only final orders of trial courts are appealable.[230] This exception stems from the "collateral order" doctrine; i.e., the rationale that certain district court orders, although interlocutory, determine with finality important claims which are separate and independent from the claims on which the litigation is based, and which cannot or should not await appellate review at the conclusion of the entire litigation.[231] Individual defendants' claims of either qualified or absolute immunity seem to fit well within this rationale, because they are important claims of right, and—as this immunity is from *suit*, not just from liability—the right can never be effectively vindicated after the suit is over.[232] In *Mitchell v. Forsyth*, the Supreme Court held that trial courts' denials of individual defendants' summary judgment motions based on either absolute or qualified immunity are immediately appealable "collateral orders" for these reasons.[233]

The *Mitchell* Court, apparently reassuring itself that it was not creating a monster, reasoned that it would not be necessary for the appellate court to resolve disputed facts in this type of interlocutory appeal;

229. Swint v. Chambers County, 115 S. Ct. 1203 (1995); Johnson v. Jones, 115 S. Ct. 2151 (1995).
230. Mitchell v. Forsyth, 472 U.S. 511, 524-30 (1985).
231. Cohen v. Beneficial Indus. Loan Corp., 337 U.S. 541, 546 (1949).
232. Mitchell v. Forsyth, 472 U.S. 511, 526-27 (1985).
233. *Id.* at 530.

". . . on the contrary, all it need determine is an issue of law. . . ."[234] As with some of the Court's other pronouncements as to how individual immunities are to be implemented, this opinion led to uncertainty for litigants and chaos in the lower courts, some but not all of which has been resolved in the last Supreme Court term.

Issues Which May Be Reviewed on Interlocutory Appeal

In cases involving individual defendants claiming absolute or qualified immunity, interlocutory appeal is available to challenge how the law is to be applied to given facts.

For the reasons outlined above, an individual defendant whose dispositive motion based on qualified or absolute immunity is denied has a right to interlocutory appeal if the denial implicates a legal issue, as opposed to a purely factual dispute.[235] The difficulty, of course, is in sorting out what is really denial of a qualified immunity claim on legal grounds, and what is denial of a claim of "I didn't do it" or "I didn't do it like that" on the part of a defendant whose case situation involves qualified immunity issues.[236]

As described by the court in *Mitchell*, the issue on appeal is whether, accepting the plaintiff's version of the facts, ". . . the legal norms allegedly violated by the defendant were clearly established at the time of the challenged actions. . . ." If the trial court has denied summary judgment for the defendant on the ground that even under the defendant's version of the facts his conduct violated clearly established law, then the appellate issue is ". . . whether the law clearly proscribed the actions the defendant claims he took."[237]

But interlocutory appeal is not available to challenge the trial court's determination of what fact issues are "genuine."

In practice, many cases which involve individual defendants' claims of qualified immunity also involve hotly disputed facts as to what actions the defendant, in fact, took. These disputed fact issues are frequently closely intertwined with the issue of qualified immunity, if not nearly identical

234. *Id.* at 528.

235. Johnson v. Jones, 115 S. Ct. 2151, 2158-59 (1995); Mitchell v. Forsyth, 472 U.S. 511 (1985).

236. *See* Johnson v. Jones, 115 S. Ct. 2151, 2158-59 (1995).

237. Mitchell v. Forsyth, 472 U.S. 511, 528 (1985).

with it; e.g., in excessive force cases.[238] In these cases, defendants can move for summary judgment on various grounds, some of them involving the "clearly settled" law applicable to their conduct, some alleging that fact issues unrelated to qualified immunity must be resolved in their favor as a matter of law, and some of them raising harder-to-classify summary judgment claims, grounded in qualified immunity and also involving disputed facts. Many of these appellate situations are clearly far afield from the prescribed *Mitchell v. Forsyth* analysis set forth above.[239]

Prior to *Johnson v. Jones*, the circuits had reached varying results in their attempts to sort out the situations in which denials of individual defendants' summary judgment claims would trigger interlocutory appellate jurisdiction.[240] One major question was whether or not the interlocutory appellate jurisdiction of the circuit courts was properly invoked by individual defendants claiming qualified immunity, when their "evidence sufficiency" summary judgment motions were denied.[241] In *Johnson v. Jones*, the Supreme Court held that it was not.[242]

The facts in *Johnson v. Jones* centered on the summary judgment claims of three individual defendants in an excessive force case, to the effect that there was no evidence either of their involvement in the beating of the plaintiff, or of their observation of anyone else doing so.[243] The trial court denied the defendants' summary judgment motion, and the Seventh Circuit dismissed their appeal of same, holding that interlocutory appellate jurisdiction was not present to review this type of "evidence sufficiency" dispute.[244]

In reaching its ruling affirming the Seventh Circuit's jurisdictional decision, the Supreme Court reviewed and explained its views about the purposes and the boundaries of interlocutory appellate jurisdiction in civil rights cases. According to the court, this jurisdiction is properly usable not to determine what factual issues are "genuine," but instead only to

---

238. *Cf.* Johnson v. Jones, 115 S. Ct. 2151, 2157 (1995).

239. *Cf. id.* at 2156-58.

240. *Compare, e.g.,* Elliott v. Thomas, 937 F.2d 338, 341-42 (7th Cir. 1991), *cert. denied,* 502 U.S. 1074 (1992); *with* Kelly v. Bender, 23 F.3d 1328, 1330 (8th Cir. 1994).

241. *Id.*

242. 115 S. Ct. at 2151, 2156 (1995).

243. *Id.* at 2154.

244. *Id.*

determine what law was "clearly established" at the time of the defendant's actions, when this would control the outcome of a defendant's summary judgment motion.[245] To find otherwise, according to the Court, would not only be counter to the original rationale and purpose of the interlocutory appeal procedure as originally authorized in *Mitchell*, but would create an unnecessary and burdensome chore for the appellate courts—i.e., they would frequently be faced with a detailed examination of numerous evidentiary materials in order to rule on factual issues, a task for which trial courts were better suited.[246] In many cases, the appellate court would probably have to look at the same case's factual record twice, once on interlocutory appeal and later, in a more developed state, after trial on the merits.[247]

The main thrust of the Court's opinion in *Johnson* is a renewed emphasis on the literal language of *Mitchell v. Forsyth*, where the Court spoke of an interlocutory appellate procedure available for the resolution of legal, not purely factual, disputes. In effect, the Supreme Court ratified the view of the circuits, which contended all along that the interlocutory appellate process was not properly used to entertain claims of "We didn't do it."[248] The Court acknowledged that its relatively narrow view of the circumstances in which interlocutory appellate jurisdiction is available will serve to limit the practical enforceability of individual defendants' immunity from suit, but held that this was unavoidable.[249]

In response to the defendants' contention that the parties could manipulate the record in the trial court for the purpose of making the case look to be appealable or not appealable, the Court indicated that it felt its standard to be workable. The Court encouraged trial courts, when ruling on individual defendants' summary judgment motions, to include a listing of facts which they took to be established for the purpose of ruling on the motion, in order to aid the appellate court in its threshold determination of whether it has jurisdiction on interlocutory appeal.[250]

---

245. *Id.* at 2156-58.
246. *Id.* at 2158.
247. *Id.*
248. *See, e.g.*, Elliott v. Thomas, 937 F.2d 338, 342 (7th Cir. 1991), *cert. denied,* 502 U.S. 1074 (1992).
249. Johnson v. Jones, 115 S. Ct. 2151, 2158 (1995).
250. *Id.* at 2159.

In applying the *Johnson v. Jones* holding, most circuit courts have held that a trial court's characterization of its ruling denying a defendant's immunity claim as based on "legal" or "factual" issues does not control the appellate court's determination as to whether or not such ruling is properly subject to interlocutory appeal.[251] Rather, if in the view of the appellate court the outcome of a defendant's immunity claim is controlled by a legal issue, interlocutory appellate jurisdiction is properly invokable to decide such issue, whether or not the district court approached the case in this manner.[252] For example, in *Sanderfer v. Nichols*,[253] the district court denied a defendant's qualified immunity claim, on the stated basis that its examination of the facts of the case led it to the determination that "more than a scintilla" of evidence supported the plaintiff's version of events. The circuit court nevertheless found that it had interlocutory appellate jurisdiction to review the trial court's decision because, in the opinion of the appellate court, the plaintiff's version of the facts, even if true, failed to state a constitutional violation.[254] This appellate opinion therefore served to correct the district court's interpretation of applicable law, in a manner necessary to protect a defendant's correctly asserted right not to be subject to the litigation process—an appropriate use of interlocutory appellate jurisdiction, despite the district court's characterization of the matter as a factual dispute.

In summary, as the Sixth Circuit explained in *Christophel v. Kukulinsky*[255]: "A defendant's right to appeal the denial of qualified immunity does not turn on the phrasing of the district court's order. . . ."

The Supreme Court recently placed its stamp of approval on this reasoning in *Behrens v. Pelletier*,[256] holding that defendants may properly invoke the interlocutory appellate process to raise issues of law which they contend control their immunity claims, regardless of whether the district court characterized its ruling as based on legal grounds or factual grounds.

---

251. *See, e.g.*, Sanderfer v. Nichols, 62 F.3d 151, 153 and n. 2 (6th Cir. 1995); Rivera v. Senkowski, 62 F.3d 80, 83-84 (2d Cir. 1995); Christophel v. Kukulinsky, 61 F.3d 479, 485 (6th Cir. 1995).
252. *See, e.g.*, Christophel, 61 F.3d at 485.
253. 62 F.3d at 153, n. 2.
254. *Id.*
255. 61 F.3d at 485.
256. 116 S. Ct. 834, 842 (1996).

Interlocutory appeal is available to review denial of Eleventh Amendment sovereign immunity claims.

The Supreme Court has held that denial of a defendant's claim of Eleventh Amendment sovereign immunity is reviewable by interlocutory appeal.[257] In speaking of the boundaries of such interlocutory appellate jurisdiction, the Court declined to distinguish those cases in which the claimed Eleventh Amendment immunity was "bound up in factual complexities" from those in which the relevant facts were undisputed.[258]

Interlocutory appeal is not available to review denials of summary judgment motions asserting non-liability of local governmental units.

Local governmental units are not automatically liable for the unlawful conduct of their employees, but this does not mean that they have any type of immunity from suit, as do the state and some individual defendants—rather, they simply have a right not to be found liable unless and until certain facts are established.[259] Therefore, such defendants have no valid collateral entitlement which would be permanently defeated unless the appellate court acted to effectuate it during the pendency of the case.[260]

For this reason, the Supreme Court held in *Swint v. Chambers County* that a county was not entitled to invoke the interlocutory appellate jurisdiction of a circuit court to appeal denial of its summary judgment motion, contending that it could not properly be found liable because a particular official was not its policymaker.[261] Presumably, this reasoning would be applicable to denial of a summary judgment motion by such a governmental unit asserting its non-liability on any other grounds, as well.

Procedural Circumstances That Trigger the Right to Interlocutory Appeal

Assuming the presence of an appropriate legal issue as described above, what exactly does the trial court have to do, or fail to do, in order to trigger the defendant's right to invoke interlocutory appellate jurisdiction?

---

257. Puerto Rico Aqueduct & Sewer Auth. v. Metcalf & Eddy, Inc., 113 S. Ct. 684, 689 (1993).
258. *Id.* at 689.
259. Swint v. Chambers County, 115 S. Ct. 1203, 1208 (1995); Leatherman v. Tarrant County, 113 S. Ct. 1160, 1162 (1993).
260. *Id.; compare* Mitchell v. Forsyth, 472 U.S. 511, 526 (1985).
261. 115 S. Ct. 1203, 1208 (1995).

Denial of motion for summary judgment—As described above, this is the most common procedural scenario through which a defendant's immunity claim can properly reach the appellate court prior to the completion of the case.[262]

Denial of motion to dismiss—This also triggers interlocutory appellate jurisdiction, given the presence of an appropriate legal issue.[263] (The issue of whether more than one interlocutory appeal may be taken in the same case by the same defendant is discussed below.)

"De facto" denial of motion for summary judgment or to dismiss, permitting overly broad discovery—Defendants are entitled to rulings on their immunity claims, when presented through dispositive motions. Occasionally, rather than rule squarely on such claims, the trial court will defer the ruling until further discovery is accomplished, or indefinitely, or "until trial."[264] If the court's refusal to act on, or delay in acting on, such a motion has the effect of depriving a defendant of an asserted immunity of the type described above, the defendant may appropriately invoke interlocutory appellate jurisdiction to review it without relying on the extraordinary remedy of mandamus.[265]

However, if a defendant's immunity claim turns partially on a fact question, and the court permits further development of this particular fact question through specifically tailored discovery, such an order has been held not to trigger interlocutory appellate jurisdiction.[266] In contrast, if a court defers its ruling on such a motion until after broad-based discovery is completed, if such discovery is allowed to explore areas not necessary to rule on defendants' immunity claims, interlocutory appeal has been held to be available.[267]

---

262. *See, e.g.*, Anderson v. Creighton, 483 U.S. 635, 638 (1987).
263. Mitchell v. Forsyth, 472 U.S. 511, 527 (1985); *see also, e.g.*, McMath v. City of Gary, Indiana, 976 F.2d 1026, 1030-31 (7th Cir. 1992).
264. *See, e.g.*, Workman v. Jordan, 958 F.2d 332, 335-36 (10th Cir. 1992); Gaines v. Davis, 928 F.2d 705, 707 (5th Cir. 1991).
265. Workman v. Jordan, 958 F.2d at 334-36, and cases cited therein; *see also* Valiente v. Rivera, 966 F.2d 21, 23 (1st Cir. 1992), in which a trial court's refusal to permit a defendant to file a qualified immunity summary judgment motion was held to be an appealable event.
266. Lion Boulos v. Wilson, 834 F.2d 504, 507-10 (5th Cir. 1987); *see* Smith v. Reagan, 841 F.2d 28, 31 (2d Cir. 1988).
267. *See, e.g.*, Gaines v. Davis, 928 F.2d 705, 707-10 (5th Cir. 1991); Smith v. Reagan, 841 F.2d 28, 30-31 (2d Cir. 1988).

Denial of motion for summary judgment or to dismiss, as to damage claims, when claims for injunctive relief are also pending—Qualified immunity is, of course, qualified immunity from claims for damages, not from claims for injunctive relief. However, all circuits have now held that interlocutory appeal is available for the denial of a dispositive motion based on qualified immunity from damage claims, even if claims for injunctive relief against the same defendant remain pending.[268]

Scope of Review on Interlocutory Appeal

Assuming that the interlocutory appellate jurisdiction of a circuit court is properly invoked, exactly what issues in the case before it may the court appropriately consider?

Consideration of the background of this issue requires an examination of the *Siegert v. Gilley* case, which reached the Supreme Court on review of an interlocutory appellate decision by the D.C. Circuit.[269] The Court, in reviewing the D.C. Circuit's qualified immunity ruling, disposed of the case by holding that the plaintiff had not alleged the violation of a clearly established constitutional right; therefore, no further consideration of other legal issues was necessary.[270]

Although itself based on a clear "threshold issue" situation, the *Siegert* opinion, taken together with language in a few Supreme Court opinions in other types of cases, spawned a plethora of circuit court holdings taking broader and broader views of what issues could be considered on interlocutory appeal, once a case was properly before the appellate court.[271] The concept of "pendent appellate jurisdiction," furthering the goal of "judicial economy," was used to support these wide-ranging holdings.[272] The boundaries of this type of jurisdiction were seen as discretionary, with an emphasis on resolving as many issues as reasonably possible while the case was in the appellate court, in order to better direct the subsequent course of the

---

268. *See, e.g.*, Young v. Lynch, 846 F.2d 960, 961 (4th Cir. 1988); *see also* Acierno v. Cloutier, 40 F.3d 597, 607-09 (3d Cir. 1994) (*en banc*).
269. 111 S. Ct. 1789 (1991).
270. *Id.* at 1793-94.
271. *See, e.g.*, Schmelz v. Monroe County, 954 F.2d 1540, 1542-43 (11th Cir. 1992); O'Bar v. Pinion, 953 F.2d 74, 79-81 (4th Cir. 1991).
272. *Id.*

litigation.[273] Because of this, there were many instances in which an interlocutory appeal filed to assert a qualified immunity defense resulted in a decision on some grounds other than, or in addition to, qualified immunity. This trend continued unabated until the Supreme Court's 1995 holding in *Swint v. Chambers County*.[274]

In *Swint v. Chambers County*, the plaintiffs sued two individual police officers, a county sheriff, a city, and a county commission for alleged misconduct in connection with law enforcement raids on a nightclub.[275] All the defendants filed summary judgment motions—the individual defendants claiming qualified immunity from suit, and the county commission claiming, in effect, a lack of liability because the sheriff who authorized the raid was allegedly not the county's final law enforcement policymaker.[276] After the trial court denied all defendants' summary judgment motions, the individual defendants appealed, invoking classic *Mitchell v. Forsyth* interlocutory appellate jurisdiction.

The city and the county commission also appealed, contending that their alleged right not to be found liable for the actions of their sheriff entitled them to interlocutory appeal, after their summary judgment motion based on such defense was denied.[277] Alternatively, they argued that, based on "pendent appellate jurisdiction," the circuit court could entertain their appeals in the interest of "judicial economy," because the appeals of the individual defendants in the same case were already properly before the court.[278]

The Eleventh Circuit, although finding that the local governmental units would not by themselves have been within the court's interlocutory appellate jurisdiction, considered and ruled on the county's contention that it was not liable because the sheriff was not its law enforcement "policymaker." The Court held that to take jurisdiction of this issue was within its discretion and within the reach of its "pendent appellate jurisdiction."[279]

---

273. *Id.*; *see also, e.g.*, Stewart v. Baldwin County, 908 F.2d 1499, 1509 (11th Cir. 1990).
274. 115 S. Ct. 1203 (1995).
275. *Id.* at 1206.
276. *Id.*
277. *Id.* at 1207.
278. *Id.*
279. 5 F.3d 1435, 1448-52 (11th Cir. 1993), *modified,* 11 F.3d 1030, 1031-32 (1994).

As noted above, the Supreme Court dealt with this case first by determining that the county's summary judgment motion contending that the sheriff was not its "law enforcement policymaker" did not assert an immunity from suit but rather a "mere defense to liability." Therefore, it did not in itself trigger an entitlement to interlocutory appeal.[280]

The Court then held that the concept of "pendent party appellate jurisdiction," exercisable in the court's discretion if "judicial economy" warranted, simply did not exist in the manner that some appellate courts had previously thought.[281] Although recognizing that in some circumstances review of threshold issues or issues inextricably intertwined with immunity might be appropriate and, in fact, unavoidable, the Court indicated that it might reject any purported exercise of "pendent appellate jurisdiction" which went beyond these clearly necessary extensions of the court's examination of immunity issues on interlocutory appeal.[282] In the *Swint* case situation, the order which the county sought to appeal involved a clearly separate issue—in fact, a separate party; so the Court found it easy to determine that jurisdiction over the county's interlocutory appeal was absent.[283]

Although the *Swint* decision does not answer all questions about the circumstances in which appellate courts should resolve any issue other than the specific immunity claims before them on interlocutory appeal, it does significantly narrow the potential scope of such appellate review. Probably, the future guideline will be close to the following recommendation, which the Court quoted with approval:

> Only where essential to the resolution of properly appealed collateral orders should courts extend their *Cohen* jurisdiction to rulings that would not otherwise qualify for expedited consideration.[284]

Circuit courts' interpretations of this guidance from the Supreme Court have produced varied language but fairly consistent results. Not surpris-

---

280. Swint v. Chambers County, 115 S. Ct. 1203, 1207-08 (1995).
281. *Id.* at 1208-12.
282. *Id.* at 1212.
283. *Id.*
284. *Id.* at 1212, quoting Kanji, *The Proper Scope of Pendent Appellate Jurisdiction in the Collateral Order Context,* 100 Yale L.J. 511, 530 (1990).

ingly, circuit courts have continued to explicitly consider and rule on "threshold issues" in interlocutory appeals.

Effect of Interlocutory Appeal on Proceedings in the Trial Court

The filing of a notice of interlocutory appeal has been held to divest the trial court of jurisdiction to conduct further proceedings as to "those aspects of the case involved in the appeal."[285] How, exactly, is the trial court to distinguish between an aspect of the case which is so involved and one which is not? And what, if anything, can the trial court do to prevent this powerful defense tool from being used in a dilatory or manipulative manner?

Clearly, any continued trial court proceedings that would have the effect of thwarting the immunity claim which the defendant is asserting on appeal should not be permitted while such appellate review is pending.[286] As the Seventh Circuit stated in *Apostol v. Gallion*, "It makes no sense for trial to go forward while the court of appeals cogitates on whether there should be one."[287] Similarly, it would clearly make no sense for discovery against individual defendants to proceed while the court of appeals considers whether they should be immune from it.[288]

However, there are questions which are not so clearly answerable. What about discovery against other defendants not raising immunity defenses? What about the availability of preliminary injunctive relief from the trial court, while interlocutory appellate review of immunity from damage claims is pending? Ordinarily, the required separability of the issue raised in an interlocutory appeal is very helpful in the determination of what matters are "involved in the appeal"; but, as the Court acknowledged in *Johnson v. Jones*, separability has always been the weak link in attempting to bring immunity issues within the established analytical framework of interlocutory appellate jurisdiction.[289]

---

285. Griggs v. Provident Consumer Discount Co., 459 U.S. 56, 58 (1982); Stewart v. Donges, 915 F.2d 572, 574-76 (10th Cir. 1990); Apostol v. Gallion, 870 F.2d 1335, 1337-40 (7th Cir. 1989).
286. *Id.*
287. 870 F.2d 1335, 1338 (7th Cir. 1989).
288. *See, e.g.*, Gaines v. Davis, 928 F.2d 705, 707-10 (5th Cir. 1991).
289. 115 S. Ct. 2151, 2156-57 (1995).

While not all the above questions have definitive answers, there has been some useful guidance from the circuit courts as to what will and will not be permitted to take place in the trial court while an interlocutory appeal is pending. Further, recognizing the hazards of potential misuse of this type of interlocutory appeal, the circuit courts have established procedures which may assist in preventing some of the most problematical situations.

One of the most thorough examinations of these interlocutory appellate procedural issues occurred in *Stewart v. Donges*, a 1990 Tenth Circuit case.[290] In *Stewart*, a defendant police officer filed an interlocutory appeal from the denial of his summary judgment motion based on qualified immunity.[291] The trial court also denied the defendant's motion to vacate the trial setting date and stay further trial court proceedings, and the defendant did not seek a stay from the appellate court.[292] The plaintiff did not request the trial court to certify the defendant's appeal as frivolous, nor did the trial court so find on its own.[293] The case proceeded to trial during the pendency of the officer's interlocutory appeal, and a judgment for damages was rendered against him.[294] He then took a second appeal, which was consolidated with the still-pending interlocutory one.[295]

Upon consideration of this appeal, the Tenth Circuit held that the trial proceeding, conducted during the pendency of the defendant officer's interlocutory appeal, was "a nullity."[296] The court explained that, because the defendant's immunity claim constituted a claim of immunity from the *entire* proceeding against such defendant, the divestiture of trial court jurisdiction over the defendant during his appeal on immunity grounds was virtually total.[297] (This, of course, assumes that no claim for injunctive relief, from which the defendant could not claim immunity, remained pending.)

Recognizing that such a doctrine could potentially facilitate abuse of the interlocutory appellate process for purposes of delay or manipulation,

---

290. 915 F.2d 572 (10th Cir. 1990).
291. *Id.* at 574.
292. *Id.*
293. *Id.*
294. *Id.*
295. *Id.*
296. *Id.*
297. *Id.* at 576.

the Tenth Circuit indicated its approval of a procedure through which a trial court, believing an interlocutory appeal to be frivolous, may certify it as such and therefore retain jurisdiction over the case.[298] However, it is not effective for the district court simply to say later that it retained jurisdiction because the appeal was frivolous; rather, it must formally certify to the court of appeals that the appeal is frivolous or forfeited on procedural grounds (see below).[299] It is the plaintiff's burden to obtain such a determination from the trial court, if he wishes to continue with proceedings against a defendant who has filed a notice of interlocutory appeal.[300]

The defendant need not move for a stay in the trial court in order to effectively preserve this right; the stay is, in effect, automatic unless a trial court certification of "frivolousness or forfeiture" of the appeal is made to the court of appeals.[301] The certification must be made before any further proceedings take place in the trial court—it cannot be entered retroactively in order to validate proceedings which have already taken place.[302] Circuit courts which have addressed the issue have emphasized the need for district courts making such a certification both to use one of the key words "frivolous" or "forfeited" and to include findings supporting such conclusion on their part.[303]

In *Langley v. Adams County*,[304] the Tenth Circuit further developed its doctrine as to the effect of a trial court's certification of frivolousness of a defendant's interlocutory appeal. The *Langley* case situation involved an interlocutory appeal by several defendants, including one whose appeal had been certified as frivolous by the district court.[305] The Tenth Circuit held that this certification did not remove the defendant and the issues he raised on appeal from the appeal process or from the jurisdiction of the appellate court; rather, it created a "dual jurisdiction" situation in which the district court had

---

298. *Id.* at 576-77, citing United States v. Hines, 689 F.2d 934, 936-37 (10th Cir. 1982) (a double jeopardy case) and Apostol v. Gallion, 870 F.2d 1335, 1338 (7th Cir. 1989).
299. Stewart v. Donges, 915 F.2d 572, 577-79 (10th Cir. 1990).
300. *Id.* at 577-78.
301. *Id.* at 577-78 and n. 6.
302. *Id.* at 578, n. 8; *see also* Chuman v. Wright, 960 F.2d 104 (9th Cir. 1992).
303. Stewart v. Donges, 915 F.2d 572, 577-79 (10th Cir. 1990); *cf.* Apostol v. Gallion, 870 F.2d 1335, 1339-40 (7th Cir. 1989).
304. 987 F.2d 1473 (10th Cir. 1993).
305. *Id.* at 1477.

power to continue its proceedings, but the appellate court also had power to hear and rule on this defendant's appeal.[306]

According to other courts which have addressed the issue, the remedy for a defendant who wishes to avoid further trial court proceedings, and whose interlocutory appeal has been certified as frivolous, is to seek a stay of such proceedings first from the trial court and, if unsuccessful there, from the appellate court.[307]

Timing, Forfeiture, and Frequency Issues

Examining issues such as timing, forfeiture, and frequency in interlocutory appeals gives rise to the questions "How late is too late?" and "How often is too often?"

Timing and forfeiture of interlocutory appeals—Given the above-described ability of interlocutory appeals to bring trial court proceedings to a screeching halt, the courts have understandably been concerned that some defendants will use this important procedural right in a dilatory or manipulative manner. Indeed, it does appear to have been so used in several reported instances—for example, by defendants filing for summary judgment on immunity grounds five years after suit was filed and days before the trial setting, and then seeking interlocutory appellate review of the trial court's denial of same.[308]

Appellate courts seem to agree that there is a need to control such use of interlocutory appeals, and that the way to do so is to impose a forfeiture of the right to take such an appeal on defendants who attempt to make use of the right in a dilatory or manipulative manner.[309] The reported appellate cases on this topic leave the first-line responsibility for determining when such a forfeiture should be imposed with the trial

---

306. *Id.*, citing United States v. Hines, 689 F.2d 934, 937 (10th Cir. 1982).
307. Fed. R. App. P. 8; *see* Chuman v. Wright, 960 F.2d 104, 105, n. 1 (9th Cir. 1992) and Apostol v. Gallion, 870 F.2d 1335, 1339 (7th Cir. 1989).
308. Yates v. City of Cleveland, 941 F.2d 444, 448-49 (6th Cir. 1991); *see also* Spann v. Rainey, 987 F.2d 1110 (5th Cir. 1993).
309. *See, e.g.*, Yates, 941 F.2d 444, 449 (6th Cir. 1991); Apostol v. Gallion, 870 F.2d 1335, 1339-40 (7th Cir. 1989).

court.[310] While there are no bright-line rules at this point for such determination, the existing case law suggests that trial courts would be within the appropriate boundaries of their discretion to subject summary judgment motions based on qualified immunity to the same "motion deadlines" as all other similar motions in the case, and to certify interlocutory appeals of denials of subsequently filed motions as "forfeited."[311]

Also, the generally applicable rules of appellate procedure are not suspended in the case of interlocutory appeals. Therefore, the time limit prescribed by such rules, specifying how soon after the entry of the challenged trial court order the notice of appeal must be filed, is applicable.[312]

Finally, it is important to note, with respect to this point, that the "forfeiture" being discussed here is forfeiture of the right to take an interlocutory appeal, not forfeiture of the right to claim qualified immunity. If a defendant does not seek summary judgment on the qualified immunity claim, or seeks it so late in the case that the trial court certifies the interlocutory appeal from the denial of same as forfeited, what the defendant has forfeited is the right to take an interlocutory appeal, not the right to claim qualified immunity at trial, assuming he or she has pleaded this defense in a timely and adequate manner.[313]

Frequency of interlocutory appeals—Theoretically, if frequency of interlocutory appeals is not to be limited, a defendant claiming immunity could file an unlimited number of dispositive motions, perhaps with slightly varying contentions, and seek interlocutory appellate review of each, delaying the trial interminably and, in the process, bankrupting the plaintiff and/or his or her counsel. One approach to these concerns is for the trial court to weigh them as one factor in its consideration of whether the right to interlocutory appeal has been forfeited by being used manipulatively. However, some appellate courts, faced with successive interlocutory appeals in the

---

310. *Id.*

311. *See, e.g.*, Kennedy v. City of Cleveland, 797 F.2d 297, 300-301 and n. 6 (6th Cir. 1986), *cert. denied,* 479 U.S. 1103 (1987).

312. Fed. R. App. P. 4(a); *see, e.g.*, Taylor v. Carter, 960 F.2d 763, 764 (8th Cir. 1992); Kennedy v. City of Cleveland, 797 F.2d 297, 301 (6th Cir. 1986), *cert. denied,* 479 U.S. 1103 (1987).

313. *See, e.g.*, Taylor v. Carter, 960 F.2d 763, 764 (8th Cir. 1992); Apostol v. Gallion, 870 F.2d 1335, 1339 (7th Cir. 1989).

same case, responded with bright-line rules authorizing a particular number of such appeals and no more.[314]

Prior to the Supreme Court's decision in *Behrens v. Pelletier*,[315] the Ninth Circuit has been particularly emphatic in its holdings to the effect that a defendant seeking a ruling on immunity claims has only one chance per case at an interlocutory appeal on this issue.[316]

Summarizing Interlocutory Appeals Issues

Based on the above-described case law, defendants are well advised to use their powerful weapon of interlocutory appeal only when such use is within the limits currently prescribed by the Supreme Court. This area of law is in a stage of very active development, and may reasonably be expected to remain so for the next few years, so up-to-date research on this issue is particularly important.

Plaintiffs, on the other hand, should not assume that every interlocutory appeal filed by a defendant is properly before the appellate court, and proceed to briefing the merits. Rather, they should carefully consider whether the appeal, or part of it, may not be within the court's interlocutory appellate jurisdiction as discussed above; if not, they should file a motion to dismiss in the appellate court on these grounds. Further, they should consider whether the appeal may be appropriately considered "frivolous" or "forfeited" as described above; if so, they should file a motion in the trial court seeking to have it declared as such so that the case may continue to progress there during the pendency of the appeal.

Procedural Issues at Trial

At trial, the interwoven legal and factual issues pertaining to several commonly hard-fought issues, such as qualified immunity, raise a whole

---

314. *See, e.g.*, Pelletier v. Fed. Home Loan Bank, 968 F.2d 865, 870-71 (9th Cir. 1992) (one); Feliciano-Angulo v. Rivera-Cruz, 858 F.2d 40, 48, n. 8 (1st Cir. 1988) (one); Kennedy v. City of Cleveland, 797 F.2d 297, 299 (6th Cir. 1986), *cert. denied,* 479 U.S. 1103 (1987) (two).

315. 116 S. Ct. 834, 840-41 (1996).

316. *See* Nelson v. Silverman, 999 F.2d 417, 418 (9th Cir. 1993); Pelletier v. Fed. Home Loan Bank of San Francisco, 968 F.2d 865, 870-71 (9th Cir. 1992).

new set of procedural complexities, in terms of which issues are to be determined by the trial court judge, which must be submitted to a jury, and how they are to be submitted.

Who Are the Policymakers?

The question of who a governmental unit's "policymakers" are as to a particular matter has been held to be an issue of law, primarily state law, determinable by the trial court judge, not the jury.[317] The jury should be instructed as to these findings and then asked about causation, according to the Supreme Court in *Jett v. Dallas Independent School District*.[318]

The *Jett* opinion builds on the Court's previous plurality holding in *Praprotnik v. City of St. Louis*,[319] in which the Court emphasized the pivotal importance of state law to the identification of a local governmental unit's policymakers as to particular issues.

Policy, Custom, or Decision

The jury should be told in the charge who the governmental unit's policymakers have been found to be, and asked whether the plaintiff was deprived of federally protected rights as a proximate result of a ". . . custom, policy, ordinance, regulation or decision . . ." of either the lawmakers or the policymakers of the governmental unit in question.[320] For an interesting example of some more specific language for this type of instruction, see the Third Circuit case *Bielevicz v. Dubinon*.[321]

Failure to Train or Supervise

City of Canton v. Harris described the standard of liability for local governmental units' failure to train employees as "deliberate indifference

---

317. Jett v. Dallas Indep. Sch. Dist., 491 U.S. 701, 737 (1989).
318. *Id.*
319. 485 U.S. 112, 124-26 (1988).
320. *Id.*; *Jett*, 491 U.S. at 737; *see also* DEVITT, BLACKMAR AND WOLFF, FED. JURY PRACTICE AND INSTRUCTIONS §103.11 (1987 and Supp. 1995).
321. 915 F.2d 845, 851 (3d Cir. 1990).

to the rights of persons with whom the [employees] come into contact."[322] The plaintiff must further show that the identified training deficiency was the cause in fact of the violation of the plaintiff's constitutional rights.[323] These are fact questions about which the jury should be instructed, assuming some evidence in their support. The jury must be instructed substantially in accordance with *City of Canton.*

Supervisory Liability of an Individual Defendant

In *Doe v. Taylor Independent School District,*[324] the Fifth Circuit found that "deliberate indifference" toward the constitutional rights of the plaintiff, and resulting constitutional injury, were necessary for individual supervisory liability for constitutional violations.[325] "Deliberate indifference" also appears in the language of many other circuit court opinions setting the standard for this type of liability.

Qualified Immunity

The import of *Hunter v. Bryant,*[326] discussed above, may be to give the ultimate qualified immunity determination always to the trial court judge, on the basis that it is controlled by a question of law (i.e., what law was "clearly established" at the time of the defendant's actions). Some courts have reasoned that, if there are disputed facts which impact on the qualified immunity question, as frequently there will be, the court should present these to the jury in separate special interrogatories, obtain the jury's factual answer(s), and then apply the law to these factual determinations.[327] This sounds much more workable in the abstract than it actually is in practice. One appellate judge has referred to such handling of qualified immunity claims as "a fear-

---

322. 489 U.S. 378, 387 (1989).
323. *Id.* at 388.
324. *See, e.g.*, Slakan v. Porter, 737 F.2d 368, 373-76 (4th Cir. 1984), *cert. denied*, 470 U.S. 1035 (1985); Bolin v. Black, 875 F.2d 1343, 1347 (8th Cir. 1989), *cert. denied*, 493 U.S. 993.
325. 15 F.3d 443, 454 (5th Cir. 1994) (*en banc*), *cert. denied*, 115 S. Ct. 70.
326. 112 S. Ct. 534, 537 (1991).
327. *See, e.g.*, Stone v. Peacock, 968 F.2d 1163, 1166 (11th Cir. 1992); Warren v. Dwyer, 906 F.2d 70, 76 (2d Cir. 1990), *cert. denied*, 498 U.S. 967 (1990).

ful tangle" and another as "a way that will cause procedural nightmares."[328] However, alternate possibilities have complications as well.

The Fifth Circuit pattern jury instructions still provide, post-*Hunter*, for the jury to make the ultimate determination about qualified immunity if the underlying facts about the defendants' conduct are disputed, with the judge instructing them as to what relevant law was clearly settled at the time of the defendants' challenged actions.[329]

Compensatory Damages

Although state common law tort concepts have been said to be the "appropriate starting point" in determining the elements and prerequisites of compensatory damages which may be awarded pursuant to §1983, they are definitely not the final word on these topics.[330] Rather, the courts should effectuate the remedial purpose of § 1983 by applying damage standards which are broad and consistent, as opposed to varying from state to state, based on the idiosyncrasies of that state's tort law.[331]

The general analysis to be used in determining whether to apply federal or state rules in particular § 1983 case situations is found in 42 U.S.C. § 1988. Section 1988 provides that, in determining the rules of decision applicable to § 1983 claims, the courts should look first to federal laws "so far as such laws are suitable to carry [§ 1983] into effect."[332] If there is no suitable federal law, the court should look next to state "common law, as modified and changed by the constitution and statutes" of the forum state. However, courts are to apply state law only to the extent that it is "not inconsistent with the Constitution and laws of the United States."[333]

Some of the most complex applications of these principles in § 1983 cases have arisen in the context of survival and wrongful death damage

---

328. Mahoney v. Kesery, 976 F.2d 1054, 1059 (7th Cir. 1992); Act Up/Portland v. Bagley, 988 F.2d 868, 875 (9th Cir. 1993) (J. Norris, dissenting).
329. Pattern Jury Instructions—Civil Cases, U.S. Fifth Circuit Dist. Judges Ass'n, 1995 edition.
330. Carey v. Piphus, 435 U.S. 247, 257-59 (1978).
331. *Cf. id.* at 257-59; *see also, e.g.*, Bolden v. Southeastern Pennsylvania Transp. Auth., 21 F.3d 29, 35 (3d Cir. 1994).
332. 42 U.S.C. § 1988 (Supp. 1995).
333. *Id.*; *see* Burnett v. Grattan, 468 U.S. 42, 47-48 (1984).

claims. While an examination of these matters is beyond the scope of this article, counsel facing any such issues should be aware that further research is necessary, and that detailed information is available from the sources listed in "Suggestions for Further Reading" at the end of this chapter.

Specific Holdings on Compensatory Damage Issues

Joint and several liability for indivisible injuries—Several circuits have held that, pursuant to federal standards, each one of multiple defendants whose actions or omissions proximately cause indivisible harm to the plaintiff is jointly and severally liable for the full amount of such harm.[334] However, there are a few circuit-level cases in which the courts expressly reference state standards on this point to the same effect, find them not to be inconsistent with the remedial goals of § 1983, and apply them.[335]

Compensatory damages for emotional distress—In § 1983 cases, damages may be awarded for emotional distress, based on appropriate supporting testimony, without regard for the required elements of proof of such damages in the courts of the state where the action is tried.[336]

Prejudgment interest—Similarly, prejudgment interest has been held to be awardable to a § 1983 plaintiff, in appropriate circumstances, whether or not it would be awardable on a tort claim in the courts of the state in which the trial takes place.[337] The First Circuit has held that such a request must be submitted to the jury, while the Third Circuit has ruled that it is within the discretion of the trial court.[338]

Punitive Damages

With respect to punitive damages, the federally created standard expressed in *Smith v. Wade* is applicable—i.e., the trier of fact must find that

---

334. *See, e.g.*, Weeks v. Chaboudy, 984 F.2d 185, 188-89 (6th Cir. 1993); Watts v. Laurent, 774 F.2d 168, 179 (7th Cir. 1985), *cert. denied*, 475 U.S. 1085 (1986).
335. *See, e.g.*, Hinshaw v. Doffer, 785 F.2d 1260, 1268-69 (5th Cir. 1986).
336. Bolden v. Septa, 21 F.3d 29, 35 (3d Cir. 1994).
337. Savarese v. Agriss, 883 F.2d 1194, 1207 (3d Cir. 1989).
338. *Compare id.*, at 1207 *with* Cordero v. De Jesus-Mendez, 922 F.2d 11, 13 (1st Cir. 1990).

the defendant acted either with "evil motive or intent" or "reckless or callous indifference to the federally protected rights" of the plaintiff.[339] Punitive damages are available whether or not compensatory damages are awarded, and this does not vary based upon the law of the state in which the trial takes place.[340] Punitive damages are not awarded jointly and severally but must be specifically considered and awarded as to each defendant.[341] As noted above, local governmental units are immune from awards of punitive damages.[342]

"Excessiveness"—The federal appellate courts' approach to reviewing juries' punitive damages awards for excessiveness has varied considerably, based on the circuit involved and the facts of the particular case. Many appellate courts have reviewed, in a very deferential manner, for what they describe as "conscience-shocking" excessiveness, otherwise leaving the amount to the discretion of the fact-finder.[343] In contrast, in one recent case, the Second Circuit gave lip service to the "shock the conscience" standard, but then engaged in what it referred to as "a stringent standard of review ... an independent and detailed appraisal of the evidence bearing on damages."[344]

The relationship of the amount of the punitive damages award to the defendant's net worth is a commonly mentioned factor which should be taken into consideration, if evidence of same is in the record.[345] Most holdings are to the effect that it is the defendant's burden to put on such proof, if he wishes it to be considered.[346]

Constitutional due process considerations—Within the past few years, the Supreme Court has issued two major opinions in response to constitutional

---

339. 461 U.S. 30, 56 (1983).
340. *See, e.g.*, King v. Macri, 993 F.2d 294, 297-98 (2d Cir. 1993), and cases cited therein.
341. *See, e.g.*, McFadden v. Sanchez, 710 F.2d 907, 913 (2d Cir. 1983), *cert. denied*, 464 U.S. 961.
342. City of Newport v. Fact Concerts, Inc., 453 U.S. 247, 258-71 (1981).
343. *See, e.g.*, Keenan v. City of Philadelphia, 983 F.2d 459, 472 (3d Cir. 1992).
344. Vasbinder v. Scott, 976 F.2d 118, 121 (2d Cir. 1992), citations omitted.
345. *See, e.g.*, *id.*
346. *See, e.g.*, Hutchinson v. Stuckey, 952 F.2d 1418, 1422, n. 4 (D.C. Cir. 1992) and cases cited therein; Littlefield v. McGuffey, 954 F.2d 1337, 1349 (7th Cir. 1992).

due process challenges to punitive damage awards rendered by juries in state courts—*Pacific Mutual Life Insurance Co. v. Haslip*[347] and *TXO Production Corp. v. Alliance Resources Corp.*[348]

These opinions should be reviewed by counsel prior to the trial of any case in which a large punitive damages award is seen as a real possibility. Although both these cases involve state court decisions, there are no reasonable indications that the minimal requirements of due process, sufficient to insulate a punitive damages award against constitutional scrutiny, would be any less in the federal court system.[349]

The earlier opinion, *Haslip*, focused on minimal procedural guidelines which must be used in submitting punitive damages issues to juries, and in rendering and reviewing judgments based on the juries' verdicts. The *Haslip* opinion indicates that defendants' due process rights may be violated unless: 1) The jury instructions adequately inform the jury of the purposes of punitive damages; 2) there are adequate post-trial procedures for state trial court review of punitive damages awards; and 3) there are substantive state appellate review standards for such awards.[350]

In the later case, *TXO v. Alliance Resources Corp.*, the Court applied a seemingly more relaxed constitutional analysis in reviewing the verdict in a state court tort case, in which the jury awarded $19,000 in compensatory damages and $10 million in punitive damages.[351] First, a plurality of the court found that such a ratio of compensatory to punitive damages did not in itself create constitutional infirmity, despite its previous suggestion to the contrary in *Haslip*.[352] Second, the plurality approved the consideration of "likely or potential harm" which could have resulted from the defendant's conduct as a factor which could be argued to, and considered by, the jury in connection with a punitive damages issue.[353] Although the opinion contains some discussion regarding the potential constitutional implications

---

347. 499 U.S. 1 (1991).
348. 113 S. Ct. 2711 (1993).
349. *See* Morgan v. Woessner, 997 F.2d 1244 (9th Cir. 1993), *cert. dismissed*, 114 S. Ct. 671 (1994); *but see* Angarita v. St. Louis County, 981 F.2d 1537, 1548 (8th Cir. 1992).
350. Pacific Mutual Life Ins. Co., 499 U.S. at 17-24.
351. TXO Production Corp., 113 S. Ct. at 2714.
352. *Id.* at 2721-22.
353. *Id.*

of the emphasis on the defendant's wealth, which was apparent in the jury argument and the jury instructions, it contains no definitive ruling on same because of the Court's holding that this issue was waived by the defendant's counsel.[354]

As Justices Scalia and Thomas noted in their concurring opinion, *TXO* puts a stamp of approval on punitive damages procedures which are "far less detailed and restrictive than those upheld in *Haslip*."[355] While such opinion only deals with minimal constitutional requirements for punitive damage awards, it is still reassuring to plaintiff's counsel and disheartening to defendant's counsel after *Haslip*, with its indications that both damage ratios and post-trial review procedures might receive more exacting scrutiny on constitutional grounds.

Jury Charge Summary

Reported cases are replete with instances in which erroneous jury instructions or issues were submitted to the detriment of a party, but the error was waived through failure to object, or failure to object with appropriate clarity.[356] It is particularly important, well in advance of trial, to review the relevant law in the circuit in which the case is to be tried in order to be prepared to tender a proposed charge in substantially correct form, and to object appropriately on the record to any incorrect submissions.

If there is a published collection of model or pattern jury instructions for the circuit in which the case is tried, this should be the starting point for preparation of the jury charge. (See "Suggestions for Further Reading" at the end of this chapter.) The Devitt, Blackmar, and Wolff book on this topic, which is included in the reading list, is generally useful as well, but all of these materials will still require modification based on the specific case situation. If preparing to try a case before an unfamiliar judge, it is also a good idea to attempt to determine well in advance of trial whether he or she has particular "standard" instructions for use in the type of case to be tried, so that if counsel has strong objections to any of them, there will

354. *Id.* at 2723-24.

355. *Id.* at 2727.

356. *See, e.g.*, King v. Macri, 993 F.2d 294, 297-98 (2d Cir. 1993); Taken Alive v. Litzau, 551 F.2d 196, 199, n. 4 (8th Cir. 1977).

be the opportunity to compile the research and arguments to raise these objections effectively.

Conclusion

Section 1983 litigation has provided and continues to provide some of the most complex and hotly debated procedural issues present in the federal court system. In some situations, such as those involving court-imposed "heightened pleading requirements," procedural issues have definitely been outcome-determinative in large numbers of § 1983 cases. With its recent decisions in *Leatherman v. Tarrant County*, *Swint v. Chambers County*, and *Johnson v. Jones*, the Supreme Court has clearly acted in a manner which has eroded at least some of the procedural barriers to plaintiffs' prosecution of well-founded § 1983 claims. Just as clearly, the Court is still struggling to determine how, if at all, the promise of *Harlow v. Fitzgerald* and *Mitchell v. Forsyth* for defendants with well-founded qualified immunity claims can be made a workable reality, without a substantial rebuilding of those barriers.

The continued development of the law with regard to these and many of the other procedural issues discussed herein can be expected to be critical to the substantive rights and interests of § 1983 plaintiffs and defendants.

Suggestions for Further Reading

SHELDON H. NAHMOD, CIVIL RIGHTS AND CIVIL LIBERTIES LITIGATION, Shepard's McGraw-Hill, Inc. (1991 and Supp. 1995).

MARTIN A. SCHWARTZ and JOHN E. KIRKLIN, SECTION 1983 LITIGATION: CLAIMS, DEFENSES, AND FEES, John Wiley & Sons (1991 and Supp. 1994).

WRIGHT, MILLER & COOPER, FEDERAL PRACTICE AND PROCEDURE: JURISDICTION 2D §§ 3730-3740, West Publishing Co. (1985 and Supp. 1994).

DEVITT, BLACKMAR & WOLFF, FEDERAL JURY PRACTICE AND INSTRUCTIONS – CIVIL, PART VI, § 103, West Publishing Co. (1987 and Supp. 1994).

FIFTH CIRCUIT PATTERN JURY INSTRUCTIONS - CIVIL CASES, West Publishing Co. (1995).

EIGHTH CIRCUIT MODEL CIVIL JURY INSTRUCTIONS, West Publishing Co. (1995).

NINTH CIRCUIT MODEL CIVIL JURY INSTRUCTIONS, West Publishing Co. (1993).

Chapter Three
An Introduction to State Court § 1983 Litigation

Steven H. Steinglass

The federal cause of action contained in § 1983[1] permits persons whose federal rights are violated by defendants acting under color of state law to bring civil suits for both damages and injunctions. The statute is not a source of substantive rights, but it is the principal civil remedy for the private enforcement of the federal Constitution against state and local governments and their employees.

Most § 1983 litigation has taken place in federal courts since 1961 when the Supreme Court in *Monroe v. Pape*[2] resurrected this seldom used legacy of Reconstruction. Before *Monroe*, § 1983 suits against state and local governmental defendants were relatively rare because of the narrow construction given to § 1983 itself[3] and because of the existence of few

---

1. 42 U.S.C. § 1983 (1988), as amended by the Federal Courts Improvement Act of 1996, Pub. L. No. 104-317, § 309(c), 110 Stat. 3847 (1996). The statute, in its entirety, provides as follows:
   Every person who, under color of any statute, ordinance, regulation, custom or usage, of any State or Territory, or the District of Columbia, subjects, or causes to be subjected, any citizen of the United States or other person within the jurisdiction thereof to the deprivation of any rights, privileges, or immunities secured by the Constitution and laws, shall be liable to the party injured in an action at law, suit in equity, or other proper proceeding for redress, except that in any action brought against a judicial officer for an act or omission taken in such officer's judicial capacity, injunctive relief shall not be granted unless a declaratory decree was violated or declaratory relief was unavailable. For the purposes of this section, any Act of Congress applicable exclusively to the District of Columbia shall be considered to be a statute of the District of Columbia.
2. 365 U.S. 167 (1961).
3. *See* Michael G. Collins, *"Economic Rights," Implied Constitutional Actions and the Scope of Section 1983*, 77 Geo. L.J. 1493, 1499-1506 (1989).

constitutional limitations on the states.[4] *Monroe* established § 1983 as a supplementary federal remedy and refused to require § 1983 plaintiffs to first seek relief under even adequate state remedies.[5] Consequently, § 1983 plaintiffs may go directly to federal court,[6] and the volume of § 1983 litigation in the federal courts has increased more than one hundredfold in the last three decades.[7]

Under the presumption of concurrent jurisdiction, state courts may also exercise jurisdiction over § 1983 cases,[8] and in recent years there has been a sharp increase in the volume of state court § 1983 litigation throughout the country. The precise number of state court § 1983 cases is unclear because states do not collect this statistic,[9] but a review of appellate court decisions makes clear that for a variety of ad hominem, doctrinal, and tactical reasons, an increasing number of § 1983 plaintiffs are forsaking the federal courts and seeking relief in state courts.[10]

---

4. *See* LOUISE WEINBERG, *The Monroe Mystery Solved: Beyond the "Unhappy History" Theory of Civil Rights Litigation*, 1991 B.Y.U. L. Rev. 737, 745-57 ("The decade immediately following Monroe was marked by increasing absorption of the Bill of Rights into the fourteenth amendment.").
5. 365 U.S. at 183 ("The federal remedy is supplementary to the state remedy, and the latter need not first be sought and refused before the federal one is invoked.").
6. *See* Patsy v. Board of Regents, 457 U.S. 496, 504 (1982) (construing § 1983 as providing "immediate access to the federal courts notwithstanding any provision of state law to the contrary").
7. *See* STEVEN H. STEINGLASS, *Section 1983 Litigation in the Ohio Courts: An Introduction for Ohio Lawyers and Judges*, 41 CLEV. ST. L. REV. 407, 409 n.7 (1993) [hereinafter STEINGLASS, *Section 1983 Litigation in Ohio*]; *see also* STEVEN H. STEINGLASS, *The Emerging State Court § 1983 Action: A Procedural Review*, 38 U. MIAMI L. REV. 381, 393 n.52, 435 (1983) [hereinafter STEINGLASS, *Emerging State Court § 1983 Action*]; STEVEN H. STEINGLASS, SECTION 1983 LITIGATION IN STATE COURTS § 2.7 (rev. ed. 16th release, 1996) [hereinafter STEINGLASS, SECTION 1983 LITIGATION].
8. *See infra* notes 67-69 and accompanying text.
9. *See* STEINGLASS, SECTION 1983 LITIGATION IN OHIO, *supra* note 7, at 424 n.95.
10. For a discussion of choice of forum considerations, *see infra* notes 106-141 and accompanying text.

Commentators have recognized the importance of state court § 1983 litigation,[11] and the Supreme Court has begun to pay greater attention to state court § 1983 cases.[12] Nonetheless, most scholarly and practice-oriented writing on § 1983 focus on the federal courts. This chapter seeks to fill this void by providing judges and lawyers with an introduction to state court § 1983 litigation. This chapter also addresses a number of the unique procedural and remedial issues that have arisen, or are likely to arise, in § 1983 litigation in the state courts.

Reconstruction Background

Section 1983, which has its origins in the post-Civil War Reconstruction Era, is the current version of § 1 of the Civil Rights Act of 1871,[13] a statute adopted to enforce the Fourteenth Amendment.[14] Section One created a civil remedy to enforce federal constitutional provisions against state or local officials who violated the "rights, privileges, or immunities" of persons within the United States.[15] Ironically, in light of its current promi-

---

11. *See, e.g.*, Susan N. Herman, *Beyond Parity: Section 1983 and the State Courts,* 54 Brook. L. Rev. 1057, 1057 (1989) ("State court is the new frontier of civil rights litigation.").
12. *See, e.g.*, National Private Truck Council, Inc. v. Oklahoma Tax Comm'n 115 S.Ct. 2351 (1995); Dennis v. Higgins, 498 U.S. 439 (1991); Howlett v. Rose, 496 U.S. 356 (1990); National Collegiate Athletic Ass'n v. Tarkanian, 488 U.S. 179 (1988); Felder v. Casey, 487 U.S. 131 (1988); Maine v. Thiboutot, 448 U.S. 1 (1980); Martinez v. California, 444 U.S. 277 (1980).
13. Act of April 20, 1871, ch. 22, § 1, 17 Stat. 13 (current version at 42 U.S.C. § 1983 (1988)).
14. *See infra* note 41.
15. Civil Rights Act of 1871, § 1. This civil cause of action was patterned after the criminal provision contained in § 2 of the Civil Rights Act of 1866, ch. 31, 14 Stat. 27 (1866). *See* Briscoe v. LaHue, 460 U.S. 325, 360-61 (1983) (Marshall, J., dissenting). Section Two's modern equivalent can be found at 18 U.S.C. § 242 (1988). For discussions of this criminal provision, *see* Screws v. United States, 325 U.S. 91 (1945); United States v. Classic, 313 U.S. 299 (1941); *see also* United States v. Lanier, 73 F.3d 1380 (6th Cir.) (*en banc*), *cert. granted*, 116 S.Ct. 2522 (1996).

nence, § 1983 was a minor, and not heavily debated,[16] provision of a more far-reaching statute designed to restore federal supremacy in the face of a widespread breakdown of law and order in the southern and border states.[17] Known as the Ku Klux Klan Act, the act permitted the president to use the military to protect federal rights[18] and to suspend temporarily habeas corpus,[19] restricted federal jury participation by former confederate loyalists,[20] and created civil and criminal sanctions that reached the *private* conspiracies of the Ku Klux Klan and similar organizations.[21]

The predecessor to § 1983 was adopted during the period that marked the sharpest permanent expansion of federal court jurisdiction in the nation's history,[22] and the Supreme Court in *Mitchum v. Foster*[23] characterized § 1983 as

> a product of a vast transformation from the concepts of federalism that had prevailed in the late 18th century. . . . The very purpose of § 1983 was to interpose the federal courts between the States and the people, as guardians of the people's federal rights—to protect the people from unconstitutional action under color of state law, 'that action be executive, legislative, or judicial.'[24]

---

16. *See* Monell v. Department of Social Servs., 436 U.S. 658, 665 (1978); *see also* Briscoe, 460 U.S. at 361 (Marshall, J., dissenting).
17. *See generally* Monroe v. Pape, 365 U.S. 167, 174-83 (1961). For a further discussion of the events leading to the passage of the Civil Rights Act of 1871, *see Developments in the Law–Section 1983 and Federalism*, 90 HARV. L. REV. 1133, 1141-56 (1977).
18. Civil Rights Act of 1871, ch. 22, § 3, 17 Stat. 13, 14 (1871).
19. *Id.* at § 4, 17 Stat. 13, 14 (1871).
20. *Id.* at § 5, 17 Stat. 13, 15 (1871).
21. *Id.* § 2, 17 Stat. 13 (1871). Section Two of the act contained the precursor to the civil conspiracy causes of action in 42 U.S.C. § 1985 (1988), which, *inter alia,* authorizes a civil action for conspiracies to "depriv[e], either directly or indirectly, any person or class of persons of the equal protection of the laws, or of equal privileges or immunities under the laws. . . ." *See* 42 U.S.C. § 1985(3) (1988). The 1871 act also contained the precursor to 18 U.S.C. § 241 (1988), which provides a criminal sanction for such conspiracies.
22. *See* WILLIAM M. WIECEK, *The Reconstruction of Federal Judicial Power, 1863-1875*, 13 AM. J. LEGAL HIST. 333 (1969).
23. 407 U.S. 225 (1972).
24. *Id.* at 241 (quoting *Ex parte* Virginia 100 U.S. 339, 346 (1879)).

Given the origins of § 1983 in a period marked by a profound distrust of the state courts and by a major change in the relationship between state and federal courts, the emergence of state courts since the 1980s as the forum of choice for many persons who believed that their federal rights had been violated by state and local governmental defendants is ironic. It is even more ironic that many state court § 1983 defendants now take advantage of the liberal federal question removal statute to veto plaintiffs' choice of state courts and remove § 1983 cases to federal courts.[25] Nonetheless, despite the increasing importance of federal question removal in § 1983 litigation, a substantial number of § 1983 cases are litigated in the state courts.

The § 1983 Remedy

Section 1983 is a remedial statute that only authorizes a civil action against defendants who act under color of state law and violate rights secured by federal law. The Supreme Court has made clear that § 1983 confers no substantive rights,[26] and state courts have consistently recognized this principle.[27] Thus, for there to be a viable § 1983 claim, there must be a violation of a substantive or rights-conferring provision of federal law.

Nonetheless, courts and litigants often assert that defendants have or are alleged to have "violated § 1983."[28] There is no such thing as "violations of § 1983," however, and it is a misnomer to make such references. More important, this concern about inappropriate references to "violations of § 1983" is not simply a law professor's fetish about the aesthetics of pleading. Such references often mask serious analytical flaws on the part of judges and attorneys addressing § 1983 issues. For example, some plain-

---

25. *See generally infra* Part VIII (discusing removal).
26. *See* Chapman v. Houston Welfare Rights Org., 441 U.S. 600, 618 (1979). ("Standing alone, § 1983 clearly provides no protection for civil rights since, as we have just concluded, § 1983 does not provide any substantive rights at all.")
27. For state court cases recognizing this principle, see STEINGLASS, SECTION 1983 LITIGATION, *supra* note 7, at § 3.1 n.2.
28. *See, e.g.*, Schwarz v. Board of Trustees of the Ohio State Univ., 510 N.E.2d 808, 809 (Ohio 1987) (noting that "plaintiff alleged that defendants, acting under color of state law, denied her due process of law in violation of Section 1983").

tiffs' attorneys seem to believe that outrageous conduct *simpliciter* is actionable under § 1983, but such an approach deflects attention from the essential task of identifying the specific federal constitutional or statutory provisions that the defendants allegedly violated. Therefore, attorneys defending § 1983 cases (and judges hearing such cases) should press plaintiffs (and their attorneys) to identify with particularity the specific provisions of federal law that they claim the defendants violated.

On the other hand, some defendants' attorneys seem to believe that conduct in violation of state law also cannot be actionable under § 1983. While it is true that § 1983 is only available to remedy violations of federal law,[29] the same conduct may be actionable under *both* state law and § 1983.[30] Thus, § 1983 plaintiffs must be prepared to identify the specific provisions of federal law that they claim have been violated. Moreover, there is no exhaustion of judicial remedies requirement under § 1983, and plaintiffs may join both § 1983 and state law claims in the same action under the liberal joinder provisions that characterize state and federal rules of civil procedure.[31]

---

29. *See* Shirokey v. Marth, 585 N.E.2d 407, 410 (1992) ("Section 1983 does not cover official conduct that violates only state law."), *cert. denied*, 506 U.S. 864 (1992); *cf.* Davis v. Scherer, 468 U.S. 183 (1984) (violation of clearly established state law is not sufficient to deny a qualified immunity to a § 1983 defendant who also violated federal law).
30. *See* Monroe v. Pape, 365 U.S. 167, 196 (1961) (Harlan, J., concurring) ("[A] deprivation of a constitutional right is significantly different from and more serious than a violation of a state right and therefore deserves a different remedy even though the same act may constitute both a state tort and the deprivation of a constitutional right.")
31. The judge-made doctrine of pendent jurisdiction, *see generally* United Mine Workers v. Gibbs, 383 U.S. 715 (1966), was codified as "supplemental jurisdiction" in Title III of the Judicial Improvements Act of 1990, which contains the Federal Courts Study Committee Implementation Act of 1990. Pub. L. No. 101-650, 104 Stat. 5089 (1990) (creating 28 U.S.C. § 1367 (Supp. III. 1990). Under § 1367, plaintiffs may invoke the supplemental jurisdiction of the federal courts to join § 1983 and state law claims in a single civil action. *See generally* STEVEN H. STEINGLASS, *State Courts and Supplemental Jurisdiction Under the Civil Rights Act of 1991*, in THE CIVIL RIGHTS ACT OF 1991 93 (American Law Institute–American Bar Association Committee on Continuing Professional Education 1993).

Color of Law Requirement

The Supreme Court has broadly construed § 1983's color of law requirement to reach not only conduct that is authorized by state law but also conduct that is unauthorized (or even barred) by state law. Thus, in *Monroe v. Pape*,[32] the Court rejected the argument that § 1983 was only available as a remedy for officially sanctioned conduct[33] and held that police officers who conducted an unreasonable search and seizure in violation of state law also could be sued under § 1983 for violating the Fourth Amendment.

Most § 1983 cases are brought against governmental officials for acts taken as part of their official duties, and there is rarely a dispute about whether such defendants are acting under color of state law.[34] Nonetheless, the § 1983 "color of law" requirement reaches the conduct of private individuals who act not only in concert with governmental officials[35] but also pursuant to state authority.[36] On the other hand, the Court has been reluc-

---

32. 365 U.S. 167 (1961).
33. In his Monroe dissent, Justice Frankfurter argued that § 1983 was limited to official conduct. *See id.* at 202; *see also* Eric H. Zagrans, *"Under Color of" What Law: A Reconstructed Model of Section 1983 Liability*, 71 Va. L. Rev. 499 (1985) (defending the Frankfurter position). *But see* Steven L. Winter, *The Meaning of "Under Color of" Law*, 91 Mich. L. Rev. 323 (1992).
34. *See* West v. Atkins, 487 U.S. 42, 50 (1988) (noting that "generally, a public employee acts under color of state law while acting in his official capacity or while exercising his responsibilities pursuant to state law," and holding that a prison physician acts under color of state law). *But see* Polk County v. Dodson, 454 U.S. 312 (1981) (treating a public defender as not acting under color of state law in representing an indigent criminal defendant because public defenders are required to exercise independent professional judgment on behalf of their clients).
35. *See* Tower v. Glover, 467 U.S. 914 (1984) (public defender who conspires with public officials acts under color of state law); Dennis v. Sparks, 449 U.S. 24 (1980) (private person who conspires with a judge acts under color of state law despite the judge's absolute immunity).
36. *See* Lugar v. Edmondson Oil Co., 457 U.S. 922 (1982) (private party's use of statutory prejudgment attachment procedures is action under color of state law, but the misuse of such state procedures is not).

tant to extend § 1983 to private actors simply because they are performing public functions[37] or receiving significant state aid.[38]

Deprivations of Federal Rights

In addition to an act taken under color of state law, a proper § 1983 claim requires the existence of a "deprivation of . . . rights, privileges, or immunities secured by the Constitution and laws. . . ."[39] This formulation is quite broad, and the Supreme Court has not limited § 1983 to the types of conduct that led to the passage of the Civil Rights Act of 1871.

Constitutional Rights—Section 1983 had its origin in a broad proposal, introduced on March 28, 1871, by Representative Shellabarger at the request of the Grant Administration to address the state of lawlessness through-

---

37. *See* Flagg Bros., Inc. v. Brooks, 436 U.S. 149 (1978) (limiting the public function test to functions that have traditionally been the exclusive province of government and holding that the sale of goods under a warehouseman's lien is not action under color of state law, because such disputes are frequently resolved without governmental involvement). The Court has held that a wide range of government activities are not public functions for purposes of the state action/color of law inquiry. *See, e.g.*, National Collegiate Athletic Ass'n v. Tarkanian, 488 U.S. 179 (1988) (regulation of intercollegiate sports); Blum v. Yaretsky, 457 U.S. 991 (1982) (provision of nursing home services); Rendell-Baker v. Kohn, 457 U.S. 830 (1982) (education of maladjusted students); Jackson v. Metropolitan Edison Co., 419 U.S. 345 (1974) (provision of utility services). *But see* Edmonson v. Leesville Concrete Co., 500 U.S. 614 (1991) (finding state action in a challenge to the discriminatory use of peremptory challenges, in part, because jury selection involves a traditional government function).
38. *See, e.g.*, *Blum*, 457 U.S. at 1010-11 (discharge of patients by nursing home not action under color of state law despite substantial state funding); *Rendell-Baker*, 457 U.S. at 839-42 (governmental funding of private school not sufficient to make a claim challenging the discharge of teachers actionable under § 1983); *Jackson*, 419 U.S. at 358-59 (termination of utility services by heavily regulated private utility with a state-created partial monopoly not action under color of state law); Moose Lodge v. Irvis, 407 U.S. 163, 171-77 (1972) (possession of state liquor license not sufficient to make discriminatory refusal to serve blacks action under color of state law absent state-compelled discrimination).
39. 42 U.S.C. § 1983 (1988).

out much of the South[40] and to enforce the Fourteenth Amendment.[41] The debates on the Civil Rights Act of 1871 make clear the close nexus between § 1983 and the Fourteenth Amendment.[42] Nonetheless, the reference in § 1983 to "rights, privileges, or immunities secured by the Constitution" is not, by its terms, limited to Fourteenth Amendment rights, and the Supreme Court has not construed § 1983 so narrowly.[43]

Most § 1983 cases involve constitutional claims that are based directly or indirectly on the Fourteenth Amendment, and for many years it remained unclear whether § 1983 reached constitutional claims that were not grounded on the Fourteenth Amendment.[44] In *Dennis v. Higgins*,[45] however, the Supreme Court held that dormant Commerce Clause claims were actionable under § 1983. As a result, it is likely that § 1983 can also be used to enforce non-Fourteenth Amendment claims having their origin in the Obligation of Contracts Clause,[46] the Ex Post Facto Clause,[47] and the Article IV Privileges and Immunities Clause.[48]

Statutory Rights—As enacted in the Civil Rights Act of 1871, the cause of action that became § 1983 did not make any reference to deprivations of federal statutory rights.[49] In 1874, however, in the course of codifying the

---

40. *See* Cong. Globe, 42d Cong., 1st Sess. 236 (1871) (President Grant's message to Congress urgently recommended legislation to deal with "[a] condition of affairs . . . in some of the States of the Union rendering life and property insecure.").
41. *See Monroe*, 365 U.S. at 171 (noting that "the purpose [of § 1983] is plain from the title of the legislation, 'An Act to enforce the Provisions of the Fourteenth Amendment to the Constitution of the United States, and for other Purposes'").
42. *See generally Developments in the Law, supra* note 17, at 1153-56 (describing congressional concern about the abdication of law enforcement responsibilities).
43. *But see Collins, supra* note 3, at 1502-04 (describing the earlier use of a narrow definition of what rights are "secured" under § 1983).
44. *See* Steinglass, Section 1983 Litigation, *supra* note 7, § 2.5(b) (2).
45. 498 U.S. 439 (1991).
46. U.S. Const. art. I, § 10.
47. U.S. Const. art. I, § 9, cl. 2, § 10.
48. U.S. Const. art. IV.
49. *See* Civil Rights Act of 1871, ch. 22, § 1, 17 Stat. 13 (1871) (current version at 42 U.S.C. § 1983 (1988)).

federal statutes, Congress separated the cause of action in § 1 of the Civil Rights Act of 1871 from the jurisdictional counterpart in the same section and added the phrase "and laws" to the cause of action.[50] The significance of this change remained unclear for more than a century, but in *Maine v. Thiboutot*,[51] the Supreme Court construed the phrase "and laws" to reach all federal statutes.[52]

Despite the broad holding of *Thiboutot*, the Court has restricted the use of § 1983 to enforce federal statutes by defining narrowly when federal statutes contain judicially enforceable rights[53] and by implying limitations on the scope of § 1983 from the existence of private remedies.[54] Moreover, in *Suter v. Artist M.*,[55] the Court limited the availability of § 1983 in cases involving the "state plan" requirements of the Social Security Act, but Congress quickly adopted legislation to limit the impact of *Artist M.*[56] and restore the availability of § 1983 in such cases.[57]

---

50. *See* Chapman v. Houston Welfare Rights Org., 441 U.S. 600, 608-09 (1979).
51. 448 U.S. 1 (1980).
52. *See id.* at 6-8.
53. *See generally* Pennhurst State Sch. & Hosp. v. Halderman, 451 U.S. 1 (1981) (§ 1983 not available to enforce the Developmentally Disabled Assistance and Bill of Rights Act because the act does not create enforceable rights and obligations).
54. *See* Middlesex County Sewerage Auth. v. National Sea Clammers Ass'n, 453 U.S. 1, 20 (1981) ("When the remedial devices provided in a particular Act are sufficiently comprehensive, they may suffice to demonstrate congressional intent to preclude the remedy of suits under § 1983."). *But see* Wilder v. Virginia Hosp. Ass'n, 496 U.S. 498 (1990) (§ 1983 available to enforce the state obligation to provide reasonable and adequate Medicaid reimbursement rates); Golden State Transit Corp. v. City of Los Angeles, 493 U.S. 103 (1989) (§ 1983 available to enforce preemption claims under the National Labor Relations Act); Wright v. City of Roanoke Redevelopment & Hous. Auth., 479 U.S. 418 (1987) (§ 1983 available to enforce Brooke Amendment claims under the Housing Act).
55. 503 U.S. 347 (1992) (§ 1983 not available to enforce the "reasonable efforts" requirement of the Adoption Assistance and Child Welfare Act).
56. In Pub. L. 103-382, § 555(a), 108 Stat. 4057 (1994) (adopting 42 U.S.C. § 1320a-2), Congress overruled the rationale of *Artist M.* and restored the governing law that the Supreme Court had been following before *Artist M.*
57. *See* Harris v. James, 883 F.Supp. 1511 (M.D. Ala. 1995); Jeanine B. v. Thompson, 877 F. Supp. 1268 (E.D. Wis. 1995). *See generally* STEINGLASS, SECTION 1983 LITIGATION, *supra* note 7, at § 2.5.

State of Mind Requirement

In *Monroe v. Pape*,[58] the Supreme Court rejected the existence of a "specific intent" requirement in § 1983 and construed § 1983 against principles of tort law.[59] This use of tort principles raised the question of whether § 1983 was available in cases involving only negligent conduct, but in *Parratt v. Taylor*,[60] the Court held that § 1983 does not contain a state of mind requirement. Nonetheless, the federal rights that are actionable under § 1983 often contain state of mind requirements.[61] Thus, the defendant's state of mind is often a relevant issue in § 1983 litigation.[62]

State Court Jurisdiction

Unlike § 1983, which is only a cause of action, § 1 of the Civil Rights Act of 1871 contained both a cause of action and a jurisdictional provision.[63] The latter was necessary because in 1871 there was no general federal question jurisdictional provision for the federal courts.[64] In the 1874

---

58. 365 U.S. 167 (1961).
59. *Id.* at 187 (observing that the statute "should be read against the background of tort liability that makes a man responsible for the natural consequences of his actions"). The Monroe Court recognized that § 1983, unlike its criminal counterpart, *see supra* note 21, does not contain an explicit state of mind requirement.
60. 451 U.S. 527 (1981).
61. *See, e.g.*, Daniels v. Williams, 474 U.S. 327 (1986) (negligent conduct not sufficient to state a due process claim); Estelle v. Gamble, 429 U.S. 97 (1976) (negligent denial of medical care by prison officials not actionable under § 1983, but the Eighth Amendment is available for claims involving deliberate indifference to inmates' serious medical needs).
62. Although not directly relevant to the availability of either qualified or absolute immunities, *see infra* notes 202-21 and accompanying text, the defendant's state of mind is relevant to claims for punitive damages. *See infra* notes 329-30 and accompanying text.
63. The jurisdiction language provided that "such proceedings to be prosecuted in the several district or circuit courts of the United States, with and subject to the same rights of appeal, review upon error, and other remedies provided in like cases in such courts. . . ." Civil Rights Act of 1871, ch. 22, § 1, 17 Stat. 13 (1871).
64. The predecessor to 28 U.S.C. § 1331 (1988), the general federal question jurisdiction statute, was adopted in the Act of March 3, 1875, Ch. 137, § 1, 18 Stat. 470 (1875).

codification of the United States Statutes, however, Congress separated the jurisdictional provision from the cause of action,[65] and this pattern continues today. Thus, it is necessary to look someplace other than § 1983 to determine whether state or federal courts have jurisdiction over § 1983 actions.

Federal courts are courts of limited jurisdiction, and there must be an affirmative grant of subject matter jurisdiction before a federal court may entertain a civil action.[66] State courts, however, are courts of general jurisdiction,[67] and the Supreme Court has relied on the presumption of concurrent jurisdiction[68] that characterizes our system of judicial fed-

---

65. *See* Chapman v. Houston Welfare Rights Org., 441 U.S. 600, 608-09 (1979).
66. *See* Erwin Chemerinsky, Federal Jurisdiction § 5.1 (2d. ed. 1994); Charles Alan Wright, Law of Federal Courts 477-78 (5th ed. 1994). The Federal Rules of Civil Procedure recognize that federal courts are courts of limited jurisdiction and require the party seeking to invoke federal court jurisdiction to include in his or her pleading "a short and plain statement of the grounds upon which the court's jurisdiction depends." Fed. R. Civ. P. 8(a) (1).
67. Although some state courts are courts of limited jurisdiction, all states have courts of general jurisdiction. State pleading rules reflect the different status of state courts, and unlike their federal counterpart, generally do not require pleading the existence of subject matter jurisdiction for suits filed in courts of general jurisdiction. *See, e.g.*, Ala. R. Civ. P. 8(a); Colo R. Civ. P. 8(a); Minn. R. Civ. P. 8.01; Ohio R. Civ. P. 8(A); Wis. R. Civ. P. 802.02(1). *But see* Ariz. R. Civ. P. 8(a) (1); Fla. R. Civ. P. 1.110(b).
68. Under this presumption, state courts may exercise jurisdiction over federal causes of action as long as Congress has not explicitly or implicitly made federal court jurisdiction exclusive. An implied exclusivity can result from an "unmistakable implication from legislative history, or by a clear incompatibility between state-court jurisdiction and federal interests." Gulf Offshore Co. v. Mobile Oil Corp., 453 U.S. 473, 478 (1981) (citations omitted). The classic statement of the presumption of concurrent jurisdiction is contained in Claflin v. Houseman, 93 U.S. 130, 136 (1876) ("[W]here jurisdiction may be conferred on the United States courts, it may be made exclusive where not so by the Constitution itself; but, if exclusive jurisdiction be neither express nor implied, the State courts have concurrent jurisdiction whenever, by their own constitution, they are competent to take it."). *See generally* Martin H. Redish & John E. Muench, Adjudication of Federal Causes of Action in State Courts, 75 Mich. L. Rev. 311 (1976); Steinglass, Section 1983 Litigation, *supra* note 7, § 9.2. The Supreme Court has unanimously relied on the presumption to permit state court jurisdiction over Title VII and civil RICO actions, *see* Yellow Freight System, Inc. v. Donnelly, 494 U.S.

eralism to hold that state courts have concurrent jurisdiction over § 1983 actions.[69]

The Nondiscrimination Principle, Valid Excuses, and the Affirmative Duty to Entertain § 1983 Suits

The Supreme Court has provided only limited guidance as to whether state courts are obligated to exercise their concurrent jurisdiction over § 1983 suits. The Court has treated the nondiscrimination principle as preventing state courts from excluding § 1983 claims on a discriminatory basis, but it has not decided whether federal law requires states to create forums that can entertain § 1983 claims[70] or whether state courts are under an affirmative obligation to treat § 1983 suits more favorably than analogous state law claims.

The nondiscrimination principle has its roots in litigation in the earlier part of the century involving the refusal of state courts to entertain suits under the Federal Employers' Liability Act (FELA). State courts were reluctant to entertain FELA claims, but the Court relied upon the nondiscrimination principle to impose an obligation on state courts to entertain such federal causes of action.

In *Mondou v. New York, New Haven & Hartford Railroad*,[71] the Court held that the state courts of Connecticut could not refuse to exercise juris-

---

820 (1990) (Title VII employment discrimination actions); Tafflin v. Levitt, 493 U.S. 455 (1990) (civil RICO actions), and the only criticism from the Court of the presumption has come from justices who would strengthen it. *See Tafflin*, 493 U.S. at 469 (Scalia, J., concurring) (questioning whether concurrent state court jurisdiction can ever be rebutted by implication from legislative history or by findings of incompatibility).

69. *See* Maine v. Thiboutot, 448 U.S. 1, 3 n.1 (1980); Martinez v. California, 444 U.S. 277, 283 n.7 (1980); *see also* Felder v. Casey, 487 U.S. 131, 147 (1988) (reaffirming concurrent state court jurisdiction over § 1983 actions).
70. *See* Howlett v. Rose, 496 U.S. 356, 378 (1990) ("This case does not present the questions whether Congress can require the States to create a forum with the capacity to enforce federal statutory rights or to authorize service of process on parties who would not otherwise be subject to the court's jurisdiction."); *see also id.* at 378 n.20 ("We have no occasion to address in this case the contention[] . . . that the States need not establish courts competent to entertain § 1983 claims.").
71. 223 U.S. 1 (1912).

diction over FELA cases. Building on cases establishing the principle of concurrent jurisdiction, the Court stated that "[t]he existence of the jurisdiction creates an implication of duty to exercise it, and that its exercise may be onerous does not militate against that implication."[72]

In *McKnett v. St. Louis & San Francisco Railway*,[73] the Court elevated the principle of nondiscrimination from a rule of statutory construction to a constitutional principle in holding that Alabama could not refuse to hear transitory FELA actions between nonresidents on out-of-state accidents when it heard similar transitory actions under state law as well as non-transitory FELA actions. Thus, state courts of general jurisdiction may not refuse to hear claims solely because they are brought under federal law.

In *Testa v. Katt*,[74] the Rhode Island state courts refused to hear actions under the Federal Emergency Price Control Act because the actions included claims for treble damages. Previously, the Court had upheld the nondiscriminatory refusal to entertain a subclass of a federal cause of action when a state had a "valid excuse" for such partial exclusions.[75] The *Testa* court, however, held that the failure to enforce "penal" statutes of other jurisdictions, including those of the United States, was not a valid excuse when the state court entertained the "same type" of state law claims as well as double-damage claims under other federal statutes.

The Supreme Court has made clear that the nondiscrimination principle applies to state court § 1983 litigation.

In *Martinez v. California*,[76] the Court reserved the question of whether state courts are obligated to entertain § 1983 actions, but it relied on the nondiscrimination principle in observing that under certain circumstances state courts must hear federal claims.[77]

---

72. *Id.* at 58.
73. 292 U.S. 230 (1934).
74. 330 U.S. 386 (1947).
75. *See* Douglas v. New York, N.H. & H.R. Co., 279 U.S. 377, 387-88 (1929) (approving evenhanded exclusion of FELA actions by nonresidents on out-of-state accidents); *see also* Missouri *ex rel.* Southern Ry. v. Mayfield, 340 U.S. 1 (1950) (permitting the nondiscriminatory use of forum non conveniens to exclude FELA actions by nonresidents on out-of-state accidents).
76. 444 U.S. 277 (1980).
77. *Id.* at 283 n.7 ("We note that where the same type of claim, arising under state law, would be enforced in state courts, the state courts are generally not free to refuse enforcement of the federal claim.").

In *Howlett v. Rose*,[78] the Court applied the nondiscrimination principle to § 1983 actions and rejected an argument that sovereign immunity represented a jurisdictional limitation on the power of the Florida courts. Comparing § 1983 actions to the tort claims against state entities that Florida entertained in its courts of general jurisdiction, and looking at the exercise of jurisdiction by Florida courts over § 1983 actions against individuals, the Court held that federal law required the Florida courts to entertain § 1983 actions against local school boards.[79] In taking this position, the Court defined broadly the comparison to be made under the nondiscrimination principle and suggested that states that opened their courts to § 1983 actions may not pick and choose among the § 1983 actions they wished to entertain by classifying state policies as jurisdictional.[80]

Given the breadth of the nondiscrimination principle, state courts are, in effect, required to hear § 1983 actions. To exclude § 1983 cases, a state would have to close its courts to similar actions authorized by state and federal law against state and local governmental bodies and their employees. Although such wholesale exclusions of legal challenges to governmental action are theoretically possible, they are so implausible that one commentator has concluded that the nondiscrimination principle imposes a "de facto obligatory jurisdiction" on state courts.[81] Moreover, the Court has never approved a total exclusion of a particular federal cause of action by state courts.

The Supreme Court has not squarely decided whether state courts are under an affirmative duty to hear § 1983 causes of action where they exclude analogous state causes of action, but the Court in *Howlett* noted that "[v]irtually every state has expressly or by implication opened its courts to § 1983 actions and there are no state court systems that refuse to hear § 1983 cases."[82] This willingness of state courts to open their doors voluntarily to § 1983 claims has made it unlikely that the Court will have to address

---

78. 496 U.S. 356 (1990).
79. *Id.* at 379-80.
80. *See id.* at 381; *see also* Willbourn v. City of Tulsa, 721 P.2d 803, 805 (Okla. 1986) (relying on the nondiscrimination principle to hold that state courts must entertain § 1983 actions).
81. *See* Burt Neuborne, *Toward Procedural Parity in Constitutional Litigation,* 22 Wm. & Mary L. Rev. 725, 759 (1983).
82. *See Howlett*, 496 U.S. at 378 n.20 (citing Steinglass, Section 1983 Litigation, *supra* note 7, at 1-3 & App. E).

the ultimate question of whether a state may refuse to hear § 1983 actions.

Nonetheless, the Court has given state courts the theoretical option of refusing to entertain § 1983 and other federal causes of action when they have a "valid excuse."[83] In *Howlett*, the Court alluded to this possibility when it noted that "[a] state court may not deny a federal right, when the parties and controversy are properly before it, in the absence of 'valid excuse.'"[84] Although acknowledging that in some circumstances state courts may rely on neutral state policies to refuse to exercise jurisdiction over federal cases, the Court defined narrowly the type of jurisdictional and other rules that it would accept as "valid excuses."

> The fact that a rule is denominated jurisdictional does not provide a court an excuse to avoid the obligation to enforce federal law if the rule does not reflect the concerns of power over the person and competence over the subject matter that jurisdictional rules are designed to protect."[85]

The *Howlett* Court also noted that the cases in which it had found valid excuses for state court refusals to entertain federal causes of action involved neutral rules of judicial administration, including such matters as the state doctrine of forum non conveniens, the jurisdiction of state courts of limited jurisdiction, and access to state courts by nonresidents.[86] Finally, the Court concluded that it "is quite inadmissible" for states to decline jurisdiction over federally created causes of action because of disagreements with federal policy.[87]

Despite the strong support for the existence of a state court duty to entertain § 1983 actions, the Supreme Court in *National Private Truck Council, Inc. v. Oklahoma Tax Commission*[88] ignored *Howlett* and characterized the obligation of state courts to entertain § 1983 actions as an open issue, observing that "[w]e have never held that state courts must entertain § 1983 suits."[89]

---

83. *See supra* note 75.
84. 496 U.S. at 369 (quoting *Douglas*, 279 U.S. at 387-88).
85. *Howlett*, 496 U.S. at 381.
86. *See id.* at 374-75.
87. *Id.* at 371.
88. 115 S.Ct. 2351 (1995).
89. *Id.* at 2355 n.4.

Because the Court in *National Private Truck Council* held that § 1983 was not available in a suit seeking declaratory or injunctive relief against a state tax where the state provided an adequate legal remedy, it did not have to reach the jurisdictional issues the case posed. Nonetheless, the Court provided limited support for the proposition that, in some circumstances, the Supremacy Clause obligated state courts to entertain § 1983 and other federal causes of action. Referring to the period before the creation of federal-question jurisdiction, the Court observed that state courts were under an obligation to entertain federal claims.

> As petitioners note, it was not until 1875 that Congress provided any kind of general federal-question jurisdiction to the lower federal courts. . . . Until that time, the state courts provided the only forum for vindicating many important federal claims. Because of the Supremacy Clause, state courts could not have refused to hear cases arising under federal law merely to ensure uniformity between state and federal courts located within a particular state.[90]

Although state courts may not be obligated to entertain *every* § 1983 case that comes before them, the jurisdictional principles summarized in *Howlett* establish that state courts are obligated to do more than refrain from discriminating against federal causes of action. Even when state courts apply their policies evenhandedly to both state-created and § 1983 actions, states should only be able to deny § 1983 claimants a state forum when the states have a sufficiently strong interest in the administration of their judicial system to justify use of state policies. Despite the fact that the Supreme Court has upheld the use of state policies governing which federal actions will be heard based on the identity of parties and the relation of the parties and the cause of action to the forum, the existence of a strong state interest in such state policies does not *ipso facto* justify the refusal of state courts to entertain particular § 1983 actions,[91] especially where the state has already opened its courts to other § 1983 actions.

---

90. *Id.* at 2335 (quotations omitted).
91. *Cf.* Felder v. Casey, 487 U.S. 131 (1988) (state interest in notice of claim requirement does not support its application to § 1983 actions).

Selective Refusals to Exercise Jurisdiction

Although no state court system categorically excludes § 1983 cases from its courts, some states exclude subclasses of § 1983 cases. Such selective exclusions, however, are improper when they are not based on valid excuses and neutral rules of judicial administration.[92]

The most flagrant example of a state court system selectively excluding § 1983 cases is the refusal of the New York courts to entertain § 1983 actions against state correctional officials. Under state law,[93] state courts may not hear damage suits brought against correctional officers for acts taken within the scope of the latter's employment. In *Cepeda v. Coughlin*,[94] a case predating *Howlett*, the New York appellate court construed state law as denying the New York courts subject matter jurisdiction in such cases. The court then held that the evenhanded application of the exclusion both to state and federal claims made it proper.[95]

The New York courts have not revisited this issue in light of the Supreme Court's unanimous decision in *Howlett* holding that a refusal to entertain § 1983 cases could qualify as a "valid excuse" only if the exclusion was pursuant to a neutral rule of judicial administration. The New York policy of precluding suits against correctional officers is based on a substantive judgment that the state, as contrasted to state employees, should be liable for certain wrongful acts, and such a policy does not come close to being a neutral rule of judicial administration. Moreover, the willingness of New York to entertain other types of § 1983 suits, including individual capacity § 1983 suits against other state employees, is inconsistent with the suggestion in *Howlett* that a state that opens its courts to some § 1983 suits may not bar other § 1983 suits.

The proper approach to these jurisdictional issues is illustrated by the decision of the Ohio Court of Appeals in *Weinfurtner v. Nelsonville-York*

---

92. *See supra* note 70 and accompanying text.
93. *See* N.Y. Correction Law § 24(1) (McKinney 1987).
94. 513 N.Y.S.2d 528 (App. Div.), *appeal denied*, 512 N.E.2d 560 (N.Y. 1987).
95. *See also* Faulkner-King v. Wicks, 590 N.E.2d 511 (Ill.App. Ct.) (post-Howlett decision holding that Illinois courts lack subject matter jurisdiction over § 1983 employment discrimination claims), *appeal denied*, 602 N.E.2d 450 (Ill. 1992), *cert. denied*, 507 U.S. 960 (1993).

School District Board of Education.[96] Relying on *Howlett*, the court held that the state policy of providing the State Employment Relations Board with exclusive jurisdiction over disputes involving unfair labor practice charges was not a neutral jurisdictional rule and, thus, was not a valid excuse for divesting Ohio courts of subject matter jurisdiction over § 1983 claims arising out of such disputes.[97]

Courts of Limited Jurisdiction and Joinder of Claims

States have some leeway in determining which courts they will open to federal causes of action,[98] but states may not adopt jurisdictional policies that burden the litigation of § 1983 or other federal claims.[99]

Some § 1983 suits involving relatively small damage claims are appropriate for consideration by small claims courts, but state courts are split as to whether they must open their small claims courts to § 1983 suits. In *Terry v. Kolski*,[100] the Wisconsin Supreme Court, relying principally on state law, held that small claims courts in Wisconsin may entertain § 1983 claims. On the other hand, in *City of Cleveland v. A.A. Rose Manufacturing Company*,[101] the Ohio Court of Appeals concluded that the Cleveland Municipal Court could not entertain a § 1983 counterclaim because municipal courts were not courts of general jurisdiction.[102]

---

96. 602 N.E.2d 318 (Ohio Ct. App. 1991).
97. *Id.* at 321-22; *accord* Thomas v. Allen, 837 S.W.2d 631, 632-33 (Tex. 1992) (relying on *Howlett* and the absence of a neutral rule of judicial administration to reverse a trial court's discretionary refusal to assume jurisdiction over an inmate's § 1983 claim against correctional officers).
98. *Cf.* Herb v. Pitcairn, 324 U.S. 117 (city court of limited jurisdiction may decline to exercise jurisdiction over FELA actions on the ground that the action arose outside its territorial jurisdiction), *supplemental opinion*, 325 U.S. 77 (1945); Manning v. Ohio State Library Bd., 577 N.E.2d 650 (Ohio 1991) (holding that Ohio courts may entertain Title VII employment discrimination actions against the state but only in the Court of Claims).
99. *See generally* Steinglass, Section 1983 Litigation, *supra* note 7, § 11.2.
100. 254 N.W.2d 704 (Wis. 1977).
101. 624 N.E.2d 245, 249 (Ohio Ct. App. 1993).
102. For a discussion of this issue, see Steinglass, Section 1983 Litigation in Ohio, *supra* note 7, at 119-22; *see also* Steinglass, Section 1983 Litigation, *supra* note 7, § 11.2(a).

Related issues arise when plaintiffs join § 1983 claims with special state proceedings for judicial review of administrative decisions. Some states permit such joinders,[103] while others do not.[104]

In *Maisonet v. New Jersey Department of Human Services*,[105] the Appellate Division of the New Jersey Superior Court refused to exercise original jurisdiction over a § 1983 claim raised only in a notice of appeal by a party who also sought judicial review of a decision of a state administrative agency. Although upholding the Appellate Division's refusal to exercise original jurisdiction as based on a neutral rule of judicial administration, the New Jersey Supreme Court found a way to permit petitioners who elected to commence judicial proceedings without filing complaints in courts of general jurisdiction to pursue both their § 1983 and judicial review claims. Recognizing the importance of providing federal access to state forums that can adjudicate all claims, including federal claims, the court established a procedure under which New Jersey courts could entertain § 1983 claims arising out of decisions rendered by state and local administrative agencies. Without requiring the Appellate Division to exercise original jurisdiction over § 1983 claims, the court permitted the § 1983 portion of the claim to be heard by requiring the appellate court to transfer the § 1983 claim to a state trial court.

Choice of Forum Considerations

Most choice of forum discussions focus on plaintiffs because they are responsible for choosing the court in which to file a suit. Defendants, however, have an equal interest in which court will hear a case. Accordingly, the factors that convince some § 1983 plaintiffs to select state courts often

---

103. *See, e.g.*, Stratos v. Department of Pub. Welfare, 439 N.E.2d 778 (Mass. 1982); Thiboutot v. State, 405 A.2d 230 (Me. 1979), *aff'd on other grounds sub nom.*, Maine v. Thiboutot, 448 U.S. 1 (1980); Maldonado v. Nebraska Dep't of Pub. Welfare, 391 N.W.2d 105 (Neb. 1986).

104. *See, e.g.*, Orvis Co. Inc. v. Tax Appeals Tribunal, 612 N.Y.S.2d 503 (App. Div. 1994), *aff'd on other grounds*, 654 N.E.2d 954 (N.Y.), *cert. denied*, 116 S.Ct. 518 (1995); Spencer v. South Carolina Tax Comm'n, 316 S.E.2d 386 (S. C. 1984), *aff'd by an equally divided court*, 471 U.S. 82 (1985); *cf.* Human Development of Erie, Inc. v. Zoning Hearing Bd. of Millcreek Township, 600 A.2d 658 (Pa. Cmwlth. 1991).

105. 657 A.2d 1209 (N.J. 1995).

lead defendants to seek ways to avoid remaining in state courts. Given the liberal federal question removal statute, state court defendants who prefer to defend § 1983 claims in federal court can almost always remove such cases, and they are increasingly doing so.[106]

A full review of choice of forum considerations is beyond the scope of this chapter,[107] but some of the more important factors deserve mention. At first, however, a caveat: At best, any choice of forum discussion only identifies factors that should be considered. Which direction these factors point will vary based on the nature of the case, the identity and attitudes of the parties and attorneys, the relief sought, the identity of the judge, and the respective roles of the judge and the jury. In addition, the body of relevant precedents as well as a myriad of tactical considerations influence choice of forum decisions.

The Decisionmakers

The Judges—The identity of the judge who will hear a case is one of the more important choice of forum factors, but it is difficult to generalize as to how differences between state and federal judges influence choice of forum decisions in specific cases. Moreover, because it is not possible to know which judge in a multijudge district or division will be assigned to a particular case, initial judgments about the attractiveness of the state or federal benches are necessarily collective judgments.[108]

Federal judges clearly have better jobs than their state counterparts. They have higher wages, better working conditions, and greater job security, including a guarantee of life tenure that enables them to remain not

---

106. For a discussion of removal, *see infra*.
107. For a general review of choice of forum considerations and for a choice of forum checklist, *see* Steinglass, Section 1983 Litigation, *supra* note 7, Chs. 5-9 & App. G.
108. Unlike plaintiffs' attorneys, who rarely know which judge will be assigned to their case, state court defendants obviously know the identity of the state court judge to whom a case has been assigned and may effectively divest a particular state court judge of jurisdiction by removing the case to federal court. *But cf.* Rothner v. City of Chicago, 879 F.2d 1402, 1404 (7th Cir. 1989) ("The thought that Congress could have intended litigants to use § 1441 to 'test the waters' in state court before deciding whether to exercise their right to remove is simply absurd.").

only above partisan politics but also independent of the bar, the public, and the media.[109] But this guarantee of independence may also account for what some view as a federal judiciary that has lost touch. State court judges, on the other hand, lack the independence that characterizes the federal bench, especially in states that have rejected "merit selection" and have retained the tradition of a politicized and partisan state judiciary.[110]

Federal judges also have the institutional support to give their cases adequate attention. Their caseloads are significantly lighter than those of state trial judges, and their resources are invariably more substantial than those available to their state court counterparts.

These generalizations, however, do not do justice to the subtle forces that influence individual judges. Many state court judges, despite their lack of resources, efficiently manage their caseloads. Likewise, many federal court judges, despite their institutional advantages, do not.[111] Thus, like collective judgments about the competence or attitudes of the state or federal judiciary, generalizations about efficiency or capacity have little relevance to how individual judges act in specific cases.

The Juries—There are significant differences in the composition of juries in the state and federal courts as well as in their mode of selection and method of operation. State court juries are typically selected from a venire representing a single county, unlike multicounty federal juries.[112] Thus, state court juries more closely resemble the county in which a suit is filed. Attorneys in many state courts conduct the voir dire and, thus, play a greater role in selecting juries than do attorneys in the federal courts. Finally, juries in most state court systems decide civil cases by a non-unanimous vote

---

109. *See generally* RICHARD A. POSNER, THE FEDERAL COURTS: CRISIS AND REFORM 30-48 (1985).

110. This is not to suggest that all federal judges have left their political or partisan concerns behind after their confirmation. Nor does it suggest that all state court judges lack independence. Rather, it is easier for federal judges to remain independent.

111. The Judicial Improvements Act of 1990 attempted to improve the efficiency of the federal bench by requiring all federal districts to adopt "a civil justice expense and delay reduction plan." Pub. L. No. 101-650, § 103(a), 104 Stat. 5098 (1990) (creating 28 U.S.C. § 471 (Supp. III 1991)).

112. STEINGLASS, *Emerging State Court § 1983 Action*, *supra*, note 7 at 418-21.

rather than by the unanimous vote required in federal court under both the Seventh Amendment and the federal rules.[113]

Doctrinal Limitations

Federal courts are courts of limited jurisdiction, and federal practice is characterized by restrictive policies on such justiciability requirements as standing, mootness, and ripeness. Likewise, the various abstention doctrines limit the equitable power of federal courts. In addition, the Eleventh Amendment limits the ability of federal courts to enter decrees having an impact on the state treasury.[114]

Because state courts operate independently of federal constraints, state courts may hear federal claims that federal courts may not hear.[115] Thus, in *Texas Association of Business v. Texas Air Control Board*,[116] the Texas Supreme Court looked to state law as the source of a broader standing doctrine than that used in federal courts.[117]

> The differences between our Texas Constitution and the Federal Constitution not only justify, but also require, that citizen groups

---

113. *See* American Publishing Co. v. Fisher, 166 U.S. 464, 467-68 (1897); *see also* FED. R. CIV. P. 48.

114. *See generally* CHEMERINSKY, *supra* note 66, § 7.4.

115. *See* City of Los Angeles v. Lyons, 461 U.S. 95, 113 (1983) ("[T]he state courts need not impose the same standing or remedial requirements that govern federal-court proceedings. The individual states may permit their courts to use injunctions to oversee the conduct of law enforcement authorities on a continuing basis."); *see also* Langford v. Superior Court (Gates), 729 P.2d 822, 833 n.6 (Cal. Ct. App.) (noting that "California's [standing] requirements are less stringent than those imposed by federal law"), *cert. denied*, 484 U.S. 824 (1987); *but cf.* Girard v. Wagenmaker, 470 N.W.2d 372, 387 n.14 (Mich. 1991) (citing Supreme Court cases on standing based on Article III of the U.S. Constitution, but observing that "Michigan law embodies a similar requirement of an 'actual controversy'").

116. 852 S.W.2d 440 (Tex. 1993).

117. In ASARCO Inc. v. Kadish, 490 U.S. 605, 622-23 (1989), however, the Supreme Court held that it is not bound by the same justiciability requirements that apply in federal trial courts at the outset of litigation. In expanding its power to review state court judgments, the Court permitted losing state court defendants to rely on the state court judgment itself for the injury that meets the case or controversy requirement and, thus, permits Supreme Court review.

> be accorded a broader right of access to our state courts. The Texas Constitution contains no express limitation of courts' jurisdiction to "cases" or "controversies," as provided by the federal charter. . . . Instead, it affirmatively protects the rights of litigants to gain access to our judicial system.[118]

As a result, many state courts, unlike federal courts, make broad use of taxpayer standing.[119] Also, unlike federal courts, state courts have rejected the narrow federal mootness doctrine,[120] and have refused to apply the strict

---

118. 852 S.W.2d at 471-72.

119. *Compare* Streight v. Ragland, 655 S.W.2d 459 (Ark. 1983) (taxpayer has standing to challenge the constitutionality of state income tax exemptions on retirement income of state and federal pensioners); Mendoza v. Tulare County, 180 Cal. Rptr. 347 (Ct. App. 1982) (taxpayer has standing to challenge conditions of jail); Mandel v. Hodges, 127 Cal. Rptr. 244 (Ct. App. 1976) (taxpayer has standing to challenge released time given state employees for Good Friday observance); Noyola v. Board of Educ. of City of Chicago, 592 N.E.2d 165, 167 (Ill. App. Ct.) (concluding that "it would serve no useful purpose to further expand the concept of standing in Illinois beyond the present requirement that the plaintiff show an injury in fact to a legally cognizable interest"), *appeal denied*, 602 N.E.2d 458 (Ill. 1992); Doremus v. Board of Educ., 75 A.2d 880, 881-82 (N.J. 1950) (permitting taxpayers to challenge a state statute providing for daily Bible reading in the public schools), *appeal dismissed*, 342 U.S. 429 (1952) *with* United States v. Richardson, 418 U.S. 166 (1974) (denying taxpayer and citizen standing to challenge secrecy concerning expenditures of the Central Intelligence Agency as inconsistent with a federal constitutional provision requiring a regular statement and account of public funds).

120. *Compare* Duhon v. Gravett, 790 S.W.2d 155 (Ark. 1990) (relying on considerations of public interest and the prevention of future litigation to decide an otherwise moot § 1983 action challenging the constitutionality of the state postjudgment execution law); Shapiro v. Columbia Union Nat'l Bank & Trust Co., 576 S.W.2d 310 (Mo. 1978) (en banc) (permitting female student to challenge a charitable trust for "deserving boys" attending private universities despite her graduation, because the question was one of great public importance and involved public rights), *cert. denied*, 444 U.S. 831 (1979); Wickham v. Fisher, 629 P.2d 896, 899 (Utah 1981) (permitting courts to hear issues that are moot as to the litigant but are of wide concern, affect the public, and are likely to recur in a similar manner); Milwaukee Professional Firefighters Local 215 v. City of Milwaukee, 253 N.W.2d 481, 488 (Wis.

federal standing requirements involving third-party standing,[121] and causation and redressability.[122]

On the other hand, state courts may be limited in their ability to refuse to hear § 1983 claims that federal courts could hear. For example, a narrow state court interpretation of what controversies are justiciable may not be an adequate state ground on which to base a judgment and preclude Supreme Court review of a state court case rejecting a federal claim.[123]

Tactical Differences

State and federal courts often have different procedural policies governing civil litigation. Despite the widespread adoption by states of rules of civil procedure patterned after the Federal Rules of Civil Procedure, many of the most populous states retain systems of code pleading and reject the use of notice pleading.[124] Moreover, even states that follow the lead of the federal rules sometimes reject federal policies. Finally, some states that have adopted identical rules have construed the rules differently from the federal courts.

1977) (permitting decision of constitutional issues in otherwise moot actions) *with* Weinstein v. Bradford, 423 U.S. 147 (1975) (limiting capable of repetition yet evading review mootness exception to cases in which the named party may again be affected).

121. *See, e.g.*, Parrish v. Civil Serv. Comm'n, 425 P.2d 223 (Cal. 1967) (social worker terminated because of refusal to participate in early morning raids on homes of welfare recipients may raise rights of recipients in his own proceeding for reinstatement); State Bd. for Community Colleges and Occupational Educ. v. Olson, 687 P.2d 429, 434-36 & 440-41 (Colo. 1984) (faculty advisor to student-run newspaper has third-party standing to raise rights of students in challenging termination of funding); Right to Choose v. Byrne, 450 A.2d 925 (N.J. 1982) (plaintiffs challenging state restrictions on abortion funding permitted to raise free exercise claim under state constitution because New Jersey standing rules are more liberal than federal rules).

122. *See, e.g.*, Stocks v. City of Irvine, 170 Cal. Rptr. 724 (Ct. App. 1981); Southern Burlington County NAACP v. Township of Mount Laurel, 336 A.2d 713 (N.J. 1975).

123. *See infra* notes 163-71 and accompanying text [167-171].

124. This includes such states as California, Illinois, and New York. *See generally* John B. Oakley & Arthur F. Coon, *The Federal Rules in State Courts: A Survey of State Court Systems of Civil Procedure*, 61 WASH L. REV. 1367 (1986).

Rule 11 of the Federal Rules of Civil Procedure and the willingness of federal judges to use (or to threaten to use) Rule 11 and other sanctions may deter some plaintiffs from filing § 1983 cases in federal courts.[125] In state courts, however, the analogous rules generally have far fewer teeth.[126] Even more important, state trial court judges are often reluctant to use sanctions aggressively against attorneys whose support they may need to retain their jobs.

Federal case management procedures are also more demanding than analogous state procedures, especially in the age of "civil justice reform."[127] Because moving cases to trial quickly is one of plaintiffs' goals, one might think that plaintiffs would prefer judges who have both the tools and the inclination to accomplish this. Nonetheless, some plaintiffs resist what they believe to be overly demanding case management requirements, and they often have concerns about the interventionist approach of many federal judges.

Discovery rules in the state and federal courts are becoming less similar. The federal courts have made major changes in discovery, moving to a system of mandatory pretrial disclosure, but many federal courts have "opted out" of the disclosure procedures.[128] It is unclear, however, whether these disclosure procedures apply to § 1983 cases,[129] and whether states will follow the federal lead and move away from reliance on the traditional discovery devices.

---

125. The revision of Rule 11, which became effective on December 1, 1993, was intended to place "greater constraints on the imposition of sanctions." Advisory Committee on Civil Rules, comment (on proposed Rule 11).
126. *See generally* Byron C. Keeling, *Toward a Balanced Approach to "Frivolous" Litigation: A Critical Review of Federal Rule 11 and State Sanctions Provisions*, 21 Pepp. L. Rev. 1067 (1994).
127. *See generally* Judicial Improvements Act of 1990, Pub. L. No. 101-650, § 105, 104 Stat. 5098 (1990).
128. Under Fed. R. Civ. P. 26(a) (1), as amended, federal district courts may adopt local rules that make inapplicable or modify disclosure procedures, and half of the federal districts have adopted local rules opting out of mandatory disclosure. *See* Edward D. Cavanagh, *Congress' Failed Attempt to Spur Court Efficiency the Legacy of the Civil Justice Reform Act*, Legal Times 28 (Nov. 25, 1996).
129. *See* Shilpa Shah, *An Application of Federal Rule of Civil Procedure 26(a) (1) to Section 1983 Actions: Does Rule 26(a) (1) Violate the Rules Enabling Act?* 43 Clev. St. L. Rev. 115 (1995).

There are also different procedural tools available in state and federal courts. Some states expressly permit the use of Doe Defendants to allow the joinder of unknown defendants after the expiration of the statute of limitations.[130] In contrast, the availability of this practice in federal court is unclear.[131] The federal offer of judgment rule[132] also represents a difference between federal and state civil procedure. Though used only occasionally, this rule is a powerful weapon for federal court defendants. It provides leverage to force settlements by limiting their exposure to fee awards in § 1983 suits.[133] There is no analogous provision under the law of many states.[134] Finally, the clear availability of interlocutory appeals of § 1983 qualified immunity issues in the federal system, as contrasted to the uncertainty of such interlocutory review as of right in the state courts,[135] is another reason § 1983 plaintiffs may prefer state courts.

Differences between state and federal practice are often more than simply a question of comparing the text of the relevant rules. One of the most significant areas of difference for purposes of choice of forum decisions involves the availability of summary judgment. Some states have expressly rejected the federal model of summary judgment,[136] but even when states

---

130. *See, e.g.*, N.J. Civ. Prac. R. 4: 26-4; Ohio R. Civ. P. 3(A) & 15(D).
131. *See* Barrow v. Wethersfield Police Dep't, 66 F.3d 466 (2d Cir. 1995) (refusing to permit amendment substituting Doe Defendant to relate back when failure to name police officers was due to lack of knowledge of their identity); Worthington v. Wilson, 790 F. Supp. 829 (C.D. Ill. 1992) (refusing to permit relation back of amendment adding Doe Defendants under Fed. R. Civ. P. 15(c), as amended in 1991), *aff'd*, 8 F.3d 1253 (7th Cir. 1993). *But see* Wilson v. City of Atlantic City, 142 F.R.D. 603 (D. N.J. 1993) (permitting use of state relation back rules under Fed. R. Civ. P. 15(c), as amended in 1991). *Cf.* Cabrales v. Los Angeles County, 864 F.2d 1454 (9th Cir. 1988) (permitting use of state relation back rules under pre-1991 version of Fed. R. Civ. P. 15(c), *vacated on other grounds*, 490 U.S. 1087 (1989). For a further discussion of this issue, see Steinglass, Section 1983 Litigation, *supra* note 7, at § 8.2(c).
132. Fed. R. Civ. P. 68.
133. *See* Marek v. Chesny, 473 U.S. 1 (1985) (construing Fed. R. Civ. P. 68 to permit the use of rejected offers of judgment to limit awards of attorney fees to plaintiffs under 42 U.S.C. § 1988).
134. *See, e.g.*, Ohio R. Civ. P. 68 (barring the use of rejected offers of judgment to determine costs).
135. *See infra* notes 268-83 and accompanying text.
136. *See* Steinglass, Section 1983 Litigation, *supra* note 7, at § 8.2(d).

maintain summary judgment rules patterned after the federal model, federal judges are far more likely than state court judges to dismiss plaintiffs' § 1983 claims on summary judgment. In part, this is a result of recent Supreme Court decisions that encourage greater use of summary judgment,[137] especially in § 1983 cases,[138] but it also may be a function of the greater resources that federal courts can bring to the task of addressing complex, document-intensive motions for summary judgment. Independent of doctrine, it is often easier for state court judges to deny summary judgment and to set a case for trial rather than to produce a written opinion granting summary judgment. Federal judges, on the other hand, are more likely to refer the stack of depositions, affidavits, and briefs to a law clerk (or law student intern), a luxury available to few state trial courts.

Federal Law and the Law of the Circuit

State courts often look to the court of appeals for the federal circuit in which their state is located for guidance in construing § 1983. Even though the same body of federal law governs § 1983 actions in state and federal courts, state courts are not obligated to follow the law of their federal circuit.[139] Although somewhat surprising, this is consistent with the structure of the federal judicial system in which the U.S. Supreme Court is responsible for resolving conflicts between state and federal courts on the meaning of federal law.[140] Thus, when state and federal courts differ on their

---

137. *See* Celotex Corp. v. Catrett, 477 U.S. 317, 322 (1986) ("[T]he plain language of Rule 56(c) mandates the entry of summary judgment, after adequate time for discovery and upon motion, against a party who fails to make a showing sufficient to establish the existence of an element essential to that party's case, and on which that party will bear the burden of proof at trial."); *see also* Anderson v. Liberty Lobby, 477 U.S. 242 (1986); Matsushita Elec. Indus. Co. v. Zenith Radio Corp., 475 U.S. 574 (1986).

138. *Cf.* Harlow v. Fitzgerald, 457 U.S. 800 (1982) (adopting an almost exclusively objective qualified immunity standard).

139. *See* United States *ex rel.* Lawrence v. Woods, 432 F.2d 1072, 1075-76 (7th Cir. 1970), *cert. denied*, 402 U.S. 983 (1971).

140. *See generally* Steinglass, Section 1983 Litigation, *supra* note 7, § 5.4; *see also* Beason v. Harcleroad, 805 P.2d 700, 704 (Or. Ct. App. 1991) (noting that "in cases in which federal law is applied, Oregon courts are not bound by Ninth Circuit decisions. . . ."); Graham v. Scissor-Tail, Inc., 623 P.2d 165,

interpretations of important elements of the § 1983 remedy or the underlying substantive law enforceable through § 1983, both plaintiffs and defendants should consider the impact of such conflicts on their choice of forum decisions.[141]

Methodology of State Court § 1983 Litigation

As the volume of § 1983 state court litigation increases, state courts have had to address a number of novel issues. State courts that entertain § 1983 actions tend to apply familiar state policies, including state rules of practice and procedure. This application of state policies raises a number of discrete state and federal law issues, including whether the state policies apply to § 1983 claims as a matter of state law and, if so, whether such applications are consistent with federal law.

The Supreme Court requires state courts to use federal standards to define the elements of the § 1983 cause of action.[142] States may not go beneath this federal floor to reject federal policies on such matters as the available immunities, the absence of exhaustion requirements, and the availability of attorney fees to prevailing parties.[143] Nor may states adopt policies that discriminate against or burden § 1983 actions.[144] On the other hand, when the policies applicable to federal court § 1983 litigation are not derived from § 1983 itself, such as with the jury unanimity requirement of the Seventh Amendment or the case or controversy requirement of Article III, state courts are generally free to follow their own policies.[145]

---

179 (Cal. 1981) ("[T]his court is in any event under no obligation to follow federal lower court precedents interpreting acts of Congress when we find those precedents unpersuasive."); Gayety Books v. City of Baltimore, 369 A.2d 581, 585 (Md. 1977) ("The courts of this State . . . are not bound by the holdings of a federal district court or of a federal circuit court of appeals.").

141. For example, the Sixth Circuit has interpreted federal law as requiring the use of a two-year statute of limitations for § 1983 cases, but some Ohio courts of appeals have selected a four-year limitations period. *See* STEINGLASS, SECTION 1983 LITIGATION in Ohio, *supra* note 7, at 490-92.

142. *See infra* notes 151-55 and accompanying text.

143. *See infra* notes 196-221, 351-61, and 384-95 and accompanying text.

144. *See infra* notes 156-59 and accompanying text.

145. *See generally* STEINGLASS, SECTION 1983 LITIGATION, *supra* note 7, at § 10.3.

The Meaning of State Law

State courts must initially determine whether state law applies to § 1983 actions. By addressing this issue first, state courts can avoid reaching federal issues. For example, in *Terry v. Kolski*,[146] the Wisconsin Supreme Court relied on principles of state court jurisdiction to hold that state law required small claims courts to entertain § 1983 actions otherwise within their jurisdiction. The *Terry* court, therefore, had no reason to reach the ultimate question of whether federal law required the same result.[147]

In many cases, however, state statutes are not clear as to whether they apply to § 1983 actions, and this raises difficult issues of state statutory construction. In such cases, state courts often assume that state policies apply to § 1983 claims *as a matter of state law*.[148] An alternative approach to this initial state law issue is followed by the Supreme Judicial Court of Massachusetts. In *Mellinger v. Town of West Springfield*,[149] the court adopted a "clear statement rule" under which it refused to apply the Massachusetts notice of claim requirement to § 1983 claims "absent a clear legislative statement that § 1983 claimants must comply" with the state policy.[150] Because state legislators rarely have § 1983 or other federal causes of action in mind when they adopt policies to govern state court litigation, the Massachusetts rule of statutory construction seems more sound than a rule that presumptively applies state substantive policies (or state procedural policies that have a substantive impact) to federal causes of action.

A Federal Definition of § 1983

When states voluntarily open their courts to federal causes of action, they must give plaintiffs "the benefit of the full scope of these [federally created] rights."[151] This principle requires state courts to apply the federal

---

146. 254 N.W.2d 704 (Wis. 1977).
147. *See id.* at 713.
148. *See, e.g.*, Felder v. Casey, 408 N.W.2d 19 (Wis. 1987) (construing state statute providing that "no action may be brought . . . unless" a claimant complies with the state notice of claim requirement as applying to § 1983 actions), *rev'd on other grounds,* 487 U.S. 131 (1988).
149. 515 N.E.2d 584 (Mass. 1987).
150. *Id.* at 589.
151. Garrett v. Moore-McCormack Co., 317 U.S. 239, 249 (1942).

definition of the § 1983 cause of action.[152] In *Howlett v. Rose*,[153] the Supreme Court extended this principle and rejected the availability of state sovereign immunity as a defense to a § 1983 suit against a local school board. Noting that "[t]he elements of, and the defenses to, a federal cause of action are defined by federal law,"[154] the Court made clear the primacy of federal standards in defining § 1983.

> [A]s to persons that Congress subjected to liability, individual States may not exempt such persons from federal liability by relying on their own common-law heritage. If we were to uphold the immunity claim in this case, every State would have the same opportunity to extend the mantle of sovereign immunity to 'persons' who would otherwise be subject to § 1983 liability. States would then be free to nullify for their own people the legislative decisions that Congress has made on behalf of all the People.[155]

The Nondiscrimination Principle

The Supreme Court has relied on the nondiscrimination principle to limit the ability of state courts to exclude § 1983 actions from their courts.[156] This jurisdictional principle, however, also prevents states from singling out federal causes of action and applying policies not followed in analogous state-created actions.[157] Moreover, in *Felder v. Casey*,[158] the Court broadened the nondiscrimination principle by treating as discriminatory policies that the state imposed "only upon those who seek redress for injuries resulting from the use or misuse of governmental authority."[159]

---

152. *See generally* Steinglass, Section 1983 Litigation, *supra*, note 7, §§ 10.3, 15.2(c) (1); *see also* Martinez v. California, 444 U.S. 277, 284 n.8 (1980) (states may not narrow § 1983 cause of action by immunizing conduct wrongful under § 1983).
153. 496 U.S. 356 (1990).
154. *Id.* at 375.
155. *Id.* at 383.
156. *See supra* note 70 and accompanying text.
157. *See generally* Steinglass, Section 1983 Litigation, *supra* note 7, § 10.4.
158. 487 U.S. 131 (1988).
159. *Id.* at 141 (rejecting the application to § 1983 of a state notice of claim requirement that the state applied only on a specific class of plaintiffs—those who sue governmental defendants, the archetypical § 1983 defendant).

State Policies and Burdens on § 1983 Litigation

The purposes of § 1983 are compensation and deterrence.[160] State policies that are inconsistent with those purposes, or that burden the litigation of § 1983 claims, should be rejected in § 1983 litigation in both state and federal courts. Thus, federal law bars the use of state policies in state court § 1983 litigation even when state courts apply those policies evenhandedly to both state and federal causes of action.

In *Felder,* the Court gave content to the compensation purpose of § 1983 by holding that state policies that limited the right of recovery for the purpose of minimizing governmental liability were inconsistent with federal law.[161] In addition, the Court held that state policies applicable only to state court § 1983 actions must be rejected not only when they are inconsistent with federal policies concerning immunities, exhaustion and statutes of limitations but also when they burden state court § 1983 litigation.[162]

Although state court judgments based on state procedural doctrines are insulated from Supreme Court review under the adequate state ground doctrine,[163] the adequacy of the state ground is itself a federal question. For example, in FELA litigation, the Supreme Court observed that "the forms of local practices" cannot defeat the federal right,[164] and further stated that "[s]trict local rules of pleading cannot be used to impose unnecessary

---

160. *See generally* Robertson v. Wegmann, 436 U.S. 584, 590-91 (1978) ("The policies underlying § 1983 include compensation of persons injured by deprivation of federal rights and prevention of abuses of power by those acting under color of state law.").
161. 487 U.S. at 153.
162. *Id.* at 150 ("Federal law takes state courts as it finds them only insofar as those courts employ rules that do not 'impose unnecessary burdens upon rights of recovery authorized by federal laws.'") (quoting Brown v. Western Ry. of Ala., 338 U.S. 294, 298-99 (1949)).
163. Under the adequate state ground doctrine, the Supreme Court cannot review a decision resting on an adequate and independent state ground because the Court's review of the federal issue would not affect the state court judgment and, thus, would only be an advisory opinion. *See* Michigan v. Long, 463 U.S. 1032, 1040-41 (1983). For a discussion of the adequacy of state procedural doctrines grounds as a bar to Supreme Court review of state court § 1983 decisions, *see* STEINGLASS, SECTION 1983 LITIGATION, *supra* note 7, § 10.6.
164. *Brown*, 338 U.S. at 296.

burdens upon rights of recovery authorized by federal laws."[165] States may not use procedural doctrines that discriminate against federal causes of action to refuse to reach the merits of federal claims, nor may they give their courts unlimited discretion to determine when to overlook procedural defaults and reach federal issues.[166]

In *Howlett v. Rose*,[167] the Supreme Court explored the adequate state ground doctrine in the course of rejecting the use of the state-created doctrine of sovereign immunity to protect local school boards that would have been subject to suit under § 1983 in federal court. Noting "the concern that the state court may be evading federal law and discriminating against federal causes of action," the *Howlett* Court stated that "[t]he adequacy of the state law ground to support a judgment precluding litigation of the federal claim is itself a federal question which we review *de novo*."[168] The Court then stated that it "is within our province to inquire not only whether the [federal] right was denied in express terms, but also whether it was denied in substance and effect, as by putting forward nonfederal grounds of decision that were without any fair or substantial support."[169] For example, a state court that maintained a case or controversy requirement that was narrower than the federal counterpart may not apply the requirement to § 1983 claims.[170] Such an interpretation of what controversies are justiciable under state law is not an adequate state ground on which to base a judgment and deny Supreme Court review of otherwise reviewable federal issues.[171]

*Intrastate Uniformity and the "Reverse-*Erie*" Approach*

In *Felder*, the Court also rejected the use of "outcome determinative" state policies in state court § 1983 litigation.[172] In doing so, the Court relied

165. *Id.* at 298.
166. *See* Sullivan v. Little Hunting Park, Inc., 396 U.S. 229 (1969) (state rule concerning notice for reviewing a transcript on appeal deemed discretionary and not an adequate state ground to prevent Supreme Court review of federal issues in a § 1982 case).
167. 496 U.S. 356 (1990).
168. *Id.* at 366.
169. *Id.*
170. *Cf.* Liner v. Jafco, Inc., 375 U.S. 301 (1964) (treating a decision based on state mootness grounds as not resting on an adequate state ground).
171. *See generally* Steinglass, Section 1983 Litigation, *supra* note 7, §§ 10.6, 13.2.
172. 487 U.S. at 151-52.

heavily on the federal interest in "intrastate uniformity" and the principles developed in diversity cases under the *Erie* doctrine. "Just as federal courts are constitutionally obligated to apply state law to state claims, . . . so too he Supremacy Clause imposes on state courts a constitutional duty 'to proceed in such manner that all the substantial rights of the parties under controlling federal law [are] protected'.[173] Because the notice of claim requirement did not apply to § 1983 claims filed in the federal courts, the application of the requirement to § 1983 state court actions would permit the choice of forum to dictate the outcome and, thus, would encourage the type of forum shopping that the *Erie* doctrine was intended to limit.

Nonetheless, *Felder* gave states some room to adopt policies that differ from federal policies and are more congenial to § 1983 claims.[174] Thus, federal policies that are not derived from § 1983 itself, such as policies involving jury unanimity or the standing and other justiciability requirements applicable in federal courts, need not be followed by state courts in § 1983 actions.

Finally, in *National Private Truck Council, Inc. v. Oklahoma Tax Commission*,[175] the Court rejected the use of the principle of "intrastate uniformity" to bar state taxpayers from bringing a § 1983 case involving state taxes in state court because they could not bring a similar case in the federal court. Although construing § 1983 as not reaching challenges to the constitutionality of state taxes (whether in state or federal courts) where the state provided an adequate legal remedy, the Court stated that the principle of "intrastate uniformity" was not a basis for state court refusals to entertain federal causes of action.[176]

Therefore, when limitations on § 1983 are derived from the Court's interpretation of § 1983 itself, those limitations are equally applicable in state and federal courts. Thus, on issues such as the appropriate immuni-

---

173. *Id.* at 151 (quoting Garrett v. Moore-McCormack Co., 317 U.S. 239, 245 (1942)).

174. 487 U.S. at 151 ("States may make the litigation of federal rights as congenial as they see fit . . . because such congeniality does not stand as an obstacle to the accomplishment of Congress' goals.").

175. 115 S.Ct. 2351 (1995).

176. *Id.* at 2355 ("Nor can a desire for 'intrastate uniformity' permit state courts to refuse to award relief merely because a federal court could not grant such relief.").

ties, the no-exhaustion principle, the availability of attorney fees, and the availability of § 1983 in state tax cases, the Court has applied the same policies to state and federal court § 1983 litigation. When limitations on the § 1983 cause of action come not from the Court's interpretation of the cause of action but from jurisdictional and other limitations on the power of federal courts, such limitations should not *ex proprio vigore* apply to § 1983 actions in state courts.

Section 1983 Remedial Issues

Pleading

Plaintiffs in § 1983 cases need only plead that some person, acting under color of state law, deprived them of federal rights secured by § 1983. It is not necessary to allege that defendants acted in bad faith or abused their qualified immunities, and defendants must raise such "confession and avoidance" defenses affirmatively.[177] Despite this liberal approach to pleading, most federal courts, until recently, had applied a strict or heightened pleading requirement to § 1983 complaints.[178] This had been most common on immunity issues, but some federal courts had extended the heightened pleading requirement to nonimmunity issues such as municipal liability.[179] The Supreme Court, however, in *Leatherman v. Tarrant County Narcotics Intelligence and Coordination Unit*,[180] rejected the application of strict pleading requirements to § 1983 claims.

In *Leatherman*, the plaintiff alleged that a municipality engaged in a policy or custom of inadequate police training for which the municipality could be held liable.[181] The Fifth Circuit dismissed the § 1983 complaint

177. *See* Gomez v. Toledo, 446 U.S. 635, 640-41 (1980).
178. *See* Hobson v. Wilson, 737 F.2d 1, 30 n.87 (D.C. Cir. 1984), *cert. denied*, 470 U.S. 1084 (1985), and cases cited.
179. *See, e.g.*, Sivard v. Pulaski County 959 F.2d 662, 667 (7th Cir. 1992) ("This Court demands that plaintiffs suing a municipal body under § 1983 plead with greater specificity than might ordinarily be required."); *accord* Palmer v. City of San Antonio, 810 F.2d 514, 516-17 (5th Cir. 1987); Strauss v. City of Chicago, 760 F.2d 765, 767 (7th Cir. 1985).
180. 507 U.S. 163 (1993), *rev'g* 954 F.2d 1054 (5th Cir. 1992).
181. *See* 954 F.2d at 1058.

because it failed to allege with particularity all material facts establishing the plaintiff's right to recovery, including facts that supported the allegation.[182] In rejecting this heightened pleading standard, the Supreme Court relied on the normal pleading requirements of the federal rules and the failure of the drafters to extend the special pleading requirements of Rule 9(b) of the Federal Rules of Civil Procedure to § 1983 or other civil rights complaints.[183]

Before *Leatherman*, a number of state courts had relied on federal cases as authority for the use of strict pleading requirements.[184] *Leatherman* un-

---

182. *Id.*

183. *See* 507 U.S. at 168 (noting that FED. R. CIV. P. 9(b) imposes a particularized pleading requirement for averments of fraud and mistake). Nonetheless, the *Leatherman* Court expressly declined to consider the application of a heightened pleading requirement to § 1983 immunity issues. *Id.* at 166-67. For a discussion of this issue, *see infra* notes 237-41 and accompanying text; *see also* KAREN M. BLUM, *Heightened Pleading: Is There Life After Leatherman*? 44 CATH U. L. REV. 59 (1994).

184. *See, e.g.*, Kyle v. Civil Serv. Comm'n, 588 So. 2d 1154, 1160 (La. Ct. App. 1991) (expressing concern about permitting plaintiffs to state § 1983 claims with "vague, broadly worded complaints," and, relying on Fifth Circuit decisions, imposing a stringent pleading requirement under which "to commence a lawsuit against a public official for acts for which he is potentially immune, the complaint must allege with particularity all material facts on which [the claimant] contends . . . that the plea of immunity cannot be sustained") (internal quotations omitted), *writ denied*, 595 So. 2d 654 (La. 1992); Henschke v. Borough of Clayton, 598 A.2d 526, 530 (N.J. Super. Ct. App. Div. 1991) (relying on Third Circuit cases and stating that "a plaintiff is required to set forth specific conduct by the state or its officials which violated the constitutional rights of the plaintiff . . . [and] is required to establish with specificity that defendant deprived him of a right secured by the Constitution and that such a deprivation was caused by a person acting under color of state law"). *Cf.* Black v. Rouse, 587 So. 2d 1359, 1361 (Fla. Dist. Ct. App. 1991) (applying Florida strict pleading rules requiring the pleading of a "short and plain statement of the ultimate facts showing that the pleader is entitled to relief" to a § 1983 complaint), *review denied*, 598 So. 2d 75 (Fla. 1992); International Soc'y for Krishna Consciousness v. City of Evanston, 411 N.E.2d 1030 (Ill. App. Ct. 1980) (applying Illinois strict pleading rules to § 1983 complaints), *cert. denied*, 454 U.S. 878 (1981). *But cf.* Cunha v. City of Algoma, 334 N.W.2d 591, 596 (Iowa 1983) (rejecting strict pleading standard for § 1983 cases); Casteel v. Vaade, 481 N.W.2d 476 (Wis. 1992) (applying liberal pleading standards to pro se § 1983 complaints).

dercuts federal support for an across-the-board strict pleading requirement for § 1983 cases, but it does not answer whether states may independently, as a matter of state law, impose strict pleading requirements on § 1983 or other federal civil rights claims.

Under the nondiscrimination principle, a state may not impose heightened pleading requirements on federal claims, if it does not impose the same standards on state claims,[185] but a difficult question arises when a state evenhandedly applies strict state pleading rules to state and federal claims. The Supreme Court has not directly addressed this issue in § 1983 litigation, but in *Brown v. Western Railway of Alabama*,[186] a FELA case, the Court stated that "[s]trict local rules of pleading cannot be used to impose unnecessary burdens upon rights of recovery authorized by federal laws."[187] The *Brown* Court further observed that it would not "fail to protect federally created rights from dismissal because of over-exacting local requirements for meticulous pleadings. . . ."[188] Some state courts have relied on these federal principles to reject the application of state pleading requirements to § 1983 complaints,[189] and a number of state courts have relied on *Leatherman* to reject the application of strict pleading requirements to § 1983 cases.[190]

---

185. *See supra* notes 156-59 and accompanying text.
186. 338 U.S. 294 (1949).
187. *Id.* at 298.
188. *Id.* at 299.
189. *See, e.g.*, Bach v. County of Butte, 195 Cal. Rptr. 268, 272-74 (Ct. App. 1983) (relying on Brown and federal standards to determine the sufficiency of a § 1983 complaint); Kay v. David Douglas Sch. Dist., 719 P.2d 875 (Or. Ct. App. 1986) (holding state rule requiring specific pleading of attorney fees inapplicable to § 1983), *rev'd as moot,* 738 P.2d 1389 (Or. 1987), *cert. denied*, 484 U.S. 1032 (1988).
190. *See, e.g.*, Fulwood v. Porter, 639 A.2d 594, 598 n.7 (D.C. 1994) (noting similarity in language between state rule and Fed. R. Civ. P. 8(a) (2) and treating Leatherman as authoritative in the District of Columbia); Culver-Union Township Ambulance Service v. Steindler, 611 N.E.2d 698 (Ind. Ct. App. 1993), *rev'd on other grounds*, 629 N.E.2d 1231 (Ind. 1994); Ennis v. Dasovick, 506 N.W.2d 386, 390 (N.D. 1993) (rejecting application of heightened pleading standard to a prisoner's § 1983 claim alleging deliberate indifference to serious medical needs arising out of the state's refusal to provide him with free eyeglasses).

A recurring pleading issue in state court § 1983 litigation is whether plaintiffs must specifically plead that they are relying upon § 1983.[191] Federal courts have not imposed such a pleading requirement,[192] and state courts have generally taken the same position.[193] Although such courts generally look to the course of the litigation to determine whether a suit included a § 1983 claim, a number of state courts that have not required the pleading of § 1983 have nonetheless observed that the "better practice is to specifically plead" reliance on § 1983."[194]

Unlike the refusal of federal and state courts to require specific pleading of § 1983, some federal courts have strictly required plaintiffs to plead whether § 1983 claims are being brought against defendants in their individual or official capacities. The use of such a pleading standard, however, even if occasionally appropriate in federal courts of limited jurisdiction, seems inappropriate in state courts of general jurisdiction.[195]

Official Immunities

Section 1983, by its terms, is silent about the availability of any immunities for officials who violate federal law. Nonetheless, the Supreme Court has established an elaborate system of absolute and qualified immunities

---

191. Plaintiffs who prevail only on state law claims may sometimes recover attorney fees if the suit also included a § 1983 claim. *See infra* notes 393-94 and accompanying text. Thus, the issue of whether a claim was brought under § 1983 often arises at the end of litigation when a prevailing plaintiff seeks a fee award.
192. *See, e.g.*, Americans United for Separation of Church and State v. School Dist. of Grand Rapids, 835 F.2d 627, 635 (6th Cir. 1987).
193. *See, e.g.*, Gumbhir v. Kansas State Bd. of Pharmacy, 646 P.2d 1078 (Kan. 1982), *cert. denied*, 459 U.S. 1103 (1983); Rzeznik v. Chief of Police of Southampton, 373 N.E.2d 1128, 1134 n.8 (Mass. 1978); L.K. v. Gregg, 425 N.W.2d 813 (Minn. 1988); Marx v. Truck Renting and Leasing Ass'n, 520 So. 2d 1333 (Miss. 1987); Tarkanian v. National Collegiate Athletic Ass'n, 741 P.2d 1345 (Nev. 1987), *rev'd on other grounds*, 488 U.S. 179 (1988); Packard v. Gordon, 537 A.2d 140 (Vt. 1987); Boldt v. State, 305 N.W.2d 133 (Wis.), *cert. denied*, 454 U.S. 973 (1981).
194. *Gumbhir*, 646 P.2d at 1085; *accord* Rzeznik, 373 N.E.2d at 1134 n.8; *L.K.* 425 N.W.2d at 820.
195. This issue comes up most often in § 1983 suits against state officials. *See infra* notes 306-17 and accompanying text.

to protect government officials and employees from personal liability under § 1983. It has done this by reading § 1983 against the background of the common law that existed in 1871. When an immunity was well-established at that time, the Court has been unwilling to assume that Congress would have overridden the immunity without expressly providing so.[196]

The immunities applicable to federal court § 1983 claims also apply in state courts, and the Supreme Court, in *Martinez v. California*,[197] held that federal, not state, law governed their availability.

> Conduct by persons acting under color of state law which is wrongful under 42 U.S.C. § 1983 . . . cannot be immunized by state law. A construction of the federal statute which permitted a state immunity defense to have controlling effect would transmute a basic guarantee into an illusory promise; and the [S]upremacy [C]lause of the Constitution insures that the proper construction may be enforced. . . . The immunity claim raises a question of federal law.[198]

State courts have widely accepted the *Martinez* principle. For example, in *Cooperman v. University Surgical Associates*,[199] the Ohio Supreme Court noted that "[i]mmunity, for purpose of a federal claim, is clearly a question of federal law."[200] The Supreme Court, however, has not addressed the extent to which, or even whether, states may develop their own policies for the administration of federal immunities, and it is unclear whether state courts entertaining § 1983 claims are required to follow the lead of federal courts and limit discovery, make expanded use of summary judgment, restrict the role of the jury, and expand the availability of interlocutory appeals.

---

196. *See generally* Pierson v. Ray, 386 U.S. 547, 554-55 (1967); Tenney v. Brandhove, 341 U.S. 367, 376 (1951).
197. 444 U.S. 277 (1980).
198. *Id.* at 284 n.8 (citations and quotations omitted); *see also* Felder v. Casey, 487 U.S. at 139 ("[A] state law that immunizes government conduct otherwise subject to suit under § 1983 is preempted, even where the federal civil rights litigation takes place in state court, because the application of the state immunity law would thwart the congressional remedy, . . . which of course already provides certain immunities for state officials.").
199. 513 N.E.2d 288 (Ohio 1987).
200. *Id.* at 296.

Absolute Immunities—The Supreme Court maintains a presumption against absolute immunity and has been "'quite sparing'" in recognizing it.[201] Most governmental officials, including governors and executive branch officials, have only a qualified immunity from § 1983 damage suits,[202] but some § 1983 defendants may claim an absolute immunity from suit. For example, state legislators have absolute immunity from § 1983 damage suits for their legislative acts[203] as do regional[204] and local legislators.[205] Likewise, state court judges and prosecutors have absolute immunity from § 1983 damage claims involving their judicial or prosecutorial functions.

Absolute immunity, however, is limited. Judges only have an absolute immunity from § 1983 damage suits for judicial acts taken within their jurisdiction,[206] and they may be liable for damages under § 1983 for their

---

201. Burns v. Reed, 500 U.S. 478, 487 (1991) (quoting Forrester v. White, 484 U.S. 219, 224 (1988)); *accord* Antoine v. Byers & Anderson, 508 U.S. 429, 432 (1993) (stating that "[t]he proponent of a claim to absolute immunity bears the burden of establishing the justification for such immunity" in the course of rejecting absolute immunity for court reporters for the ministerial act of preparing verbatim transcripts of criminal trials).

202. *See* Scheuer v. Rhodes, 416 U.S. 232 (1974); *see also* Harlow v. Fitzgerald, 457 U.S. 800, 807 (1982) (observing that qualified immunity represents the norm for executive officials).

203. *See* Tenney v. Brandhove, 341 U.S. 367 (1951); *see also* Supreme Court of Virginia v. Consumers Union, 446 U.S. 719, 732 (1980) ("Although *Tenney* involved an action for damages under § 1983, its holding is equally applicable to § 1983 actions seeking declaratory or injunctive relief.").

204. *See* Lake Country Estates, Inc. v. Tahoe Regional Planning Agency, 440 U.S. 391 (1979).

205. The Supreme Court has not decided whether local legislators have absolute immunity from § 1983 damage claims, *but cf.* Spallone v. United States, 493 U.S. 265, 278-80 (1990) (relying on considerations developed in state legislative immunity cases to reverse contempt sanctions against city council members), but the federal circuits have consistently extended absolute immunity to local legislators for legislative acts. *See, e.g.*, Acevedo-Cordero v. Cordero-Santiago, 958 F.2d 20, 22-23 (1st Cir. 1992); Haskell v. Washington Township, 864 F.2d 1266, 1277 (6th Cir. 1988); Aitchison v. Raffiani, 708 F.2d 96, 98-100 (3d Cir. 1983).

206. *See* Stump v. Sparkman, 435 U.S. 349 (1978) (absolute judicial immunity for ordering sterilization of a "somewhat retarded" 15-year-old girl); Pierson v. Ray, 386 U.S. 547 (1967) (absolute judicial immunity for unconstitutionally

administrative decisions.[207] They may also be sued under § 1983 for injunctive relief (on claims for which they have an absolute immunity from damage suits), and they are subject to liability for attorney fees.[208]

Similarly, prosecutors have absolute quasi-judicial immunity when performing prosecutorial functions intimately associated with the judicial phase of the criminal process,[209] but they are not entitled to absolute immunity for

---

convicting persons challenging segregated interstate bus terminal facilities); *see also* Mireles v. Waco, 502 U.S. 9 (1991) (per curiam) (absolute judicial immunity for allegedly ordering a police officer to use excessive force to bring a public defender to the judge's courtroom); *cf.* Butz v. Economou, 438 U.S. 478 (1978) (hearing examiner and administrative law judge performing independent adjudicatory activities entitled to absolute immunity).

207. *See* Forrester v. White, 484 U.S. 219 (1988) (no absolute judicial immunity for the nonjudicial administrative act of demoting and dismissing a court-attached probation officer); Harris v. Harvey, 605 F.2d 330 (7th Cir. 1979) (denying absolute judicial immunity to a judge who used his political influence to have a police officer disciplined), *cert. denied*, 445 U.S. 938 (1980); Zarcone v. Perry, 572 F.2d 52 (2d Cir. 1978) (denying absolute judicial immunity to a judge who ordered a coffee vendor brought before him in handcuffs because of the poor quality of the coffee).

208. In Pulliam v. Allen, 466 U.S. 522 (1984), the Supreme Court held that the doctrine of judicial immunity did not preclude suits against state court judges for injunctive relief and the award of attorney fees to prevailing parties in such suits against state court judges. In the Federal Courts Improvement Act of 1996, Pub. L. No. 104-317, § 309(c), 110 Stat. 3847 (1996), Congress partially limited the availabaility of injunctive relief in § 1983 actions against judicial officers acting in their judicial capacity to those cases in which judicial officers either violated a declaratory judgment or in which declaratory relief was unavailable. This amendment, however, does not appear to alter the availability of injunctive relief in § 1983 suits against judicial officers acting in their administrative capacity. The Federal Courts Improvement Act of 1996, Pub. L. 104-317, § 309(b), 110 Stat. 3847 (1996), also overruled Pulliam by amended 42 U.S.C. § 1988(b) to provide that attorney fees are not available in actions against judicial officer for acts or omissions taken in a judicial capacity unless the judicial officer acted clearly in excess of the officer's jurisdiction. *See infra* note 385.

209. *See* Imbler v. Pachtman, 424 U.S. 409, 430 (1976); *see also* Butz v. Economou, 438 U.S. 478 (1978) (applying a functional test to extend absolute immunity to federal administrative officials responsible for initiating administrative proceedings). The Supreme Court has also extended absolute immunity to

either investigative or other nonprosecutorial activities. Thus, in *Burns v. Reed*,[210] the Court denied absolute immunity to a prosecutor for providing legal advice to police officers concerning the hypnotizing and questioning of a suspect. Likewise, in *Buckley v. Fitzsimmons*,[211] the Court held that prosecutors who were engaged in entirely investigative activities before there was probable cause to make an arrest were not entitled to absolute immunity either for fabricating evidence during the preliminary investigation of a crime or for making false statements at a press conference announcing the return of an indictment.

Qualified Immunities—The Supreme Court has held that public officials who are not entitled to absolute immunity may still be immune from § 1983 damage suits when their performance of discretionary functions violates federal law.[212] In 1975, in *Wood v. Strickland*,[213] the Supreme Court defined the § 1983 qualified immunity in both objective and subjective terms. Seven years later, however, in *Harlow v. Fitzgerald*,[214] a *Bivens* action,[215] the Court eliminated the subjective leg and defined qualified immunity in objective terms by asking whether the defendants violated clearly established federal law.

---

police witnesses sued as a result of their testimony. *See* Briscoe v. LaHue, 460 U.S. 325 (1983). *But see* White v. Frank, 855 F.2d 956 (2d Cir. 1988) (holding that complaining witnesses are not entitled to absolute immunity for testifying before a grand jury, although witnesses who merely testify before grand juries are protected by absolute immunity).

210. 500 U.S. 478 (1991).
211. 509 U.S. 259 (1993).
212. *See* Scheuer v. Rhodes, 416 U.S. 232, 246-49 (1974); Pierson v. Ray, 386 U.S. 547, 564 (1967); *cf.* Wyatt v. Cole, 504 U.S. 158 (1992) (holding that private defendants who relied on a state replevin statute subsequently declared unconstitutional were not entitled to an objectively defined qualified immunity).
213. 420 U.S. 308 (1975).
214. 457 U.S. 800 (1982).
215. Bivens actions are suits brought against federal officials directly under the federal constitution. *See* Bivens v. Six Unknown Named Agents, 403 U.S. 388 (1971). Many of the Court's most important qualified immunity decisions arose in Bivens, not § 1983, actions, but the Court has applied the same immunity policies to both actions. *See Harlow*, 457 U.S. at 818 n.30; Butz v. Economou, 438 U.S. 478, 504 (1978).

> [G]overnment officials performing discretionary functions generally are shielded from liability for civil damages insofar as their conduct does not violate clearly established statutory or constitutional rights of which a reasonable person would have known. . . . On summary judgment, the judge appropriately may determine, not only the currently applicable law, but whether that law was clearly established at the time the action occurred. If the law at that time was not clearly established, an official could not reasonably be expected to anticipate subsequent legal developments, nor could he fairly be said to 'know' that the law forbade conduct not previously identified as unlawful. . . . If the law was clearly established, the immunity defense ordinarily should fail, since a reasonably competent public official should know the law governing his conduct.[216]

In *Anderson v. Creighton*,[217] the Court held that the determination of whether the law was clearly established required a particularized definition of the issue of federal law that must be clearly established.

> [T]he right the official is alleged to have violated must have been 'clearly established' in a more particularized, and hence more relevant, sense: The contours of the right must be sufficiently clear that a reasonable official would understand that what he is doing violates that right. This is not to say that an official action is protected by qualified immunity unless the very action in question has previously been held unlawful, . . . but it is to say that in the light of pre-existing law the unlawfulness must be apparent.[218]

---

216. *Harlow*, 457 U.S. at 818-9; see also Davis v. Scherer, 468 U.S. 183 (1984) (holding that federal, not state, law must be clearly established to deny defendants a qualified immunity). The Harlow definition of qualified immunity also contained a small subjective component under which an official who violates clearly established federal law may still be entitled to qualified immunity if the official "claims extraordinary circumstances and can prove that he neither knew nor should have known of the relevant legal standard." 457 U.S. at 819.
217. 483 U.S. 635 (1987).
218. *Id.* at 640.

Anderson requires courts addressing qualified immunity issues to define the underlying right with a high degree of particularity, thus expanding the utility of qualified immunity for § 1983 defendants.[219] The Court, however, has not provided guidance as to where courts should look to determine whether federal law is clearly established,[220] and courts have disagreed as to where they should look to make this determination.[221]

Administering the § 1983 Qualified Immunity—In addition to the threshold question of whether a defendant is entitled to absolute or qualified immunity, difficult administrative issues arise in the area of immunities, especially qualified immunities. These issues have taken on even greater significance because the Court has relied on the breadth of qualified immunity to restrict the availability of absolute immunity in § 1983 litigation.[222]

Pleading

In *Gomez v. Toledo*,[223] the Supreme Court held that qualified immunity was an affirmative defense that § 1983 plaintiffs were not obligated to anticipate and rebut in their complaints. Until recently, however, the Court has provided little guidance on either the pleading standards applicable to § 1983 qualified immunity issues or on the proper approach to deciding such issues, but in 1991, the Court addressed these aspects of § 1983 litigation.

In *Siegert v. Gilley*,[224] a *Bivens* action by a former federal employee involving an alleged deprivation of a liberty interest without due process,[225] the Court required the plaintiff to plead the violation of a clearly

---

219. *Cf.* Elliott v. Thomas, 937 F.2d 338, 341 (7th Cir. 1991) ("By sleight of hand you can turn any defense on the merits into a defense of qualified immunity."), *cert. denied*, 502 U.S. 1121 & 1074 (1992).
220. *See* Kit Kinports, *Qualified Immunity in Section 1983 Cases: The Unanswered Questions*, 23 Ga. L. Rev. 597, 605 n.41 (1989).
221. *See* Karen M. Blum, *Qualified Immunity: A User's Manual*, 26 Ind. L. Rev. 187, 203-05 (1993). For a discussion of the role of state law in determining whether federal law is clearly established, *see* Richard B. Saphire, *Qualified Immunity in Section 1983 Cases and the Role of State Decisional Law*, 35 Ariz. L. Rev. 621 (1993).
222. *See* Burns v. Reed, 500 U.S. 478, 495 n.8 (1991).
223. 446 U.S. 635 (1980).
224. 500 U.S. 226 (1991).
225. The plaintiff in Siegert claimed that his supervisor's writing a defamatory letter deprived him of procedural due process.

established constitutional right.[226] Before *Siegert,* many federal courts would assume the existence of a violation of the underlying federal right but dispose of cases on qualified immunity grounds because the federal right was not clearly established.[227] *Siegert* rejected this approach. It held that the initial inquiry was not whether the plaintiff alleged a violation of federal law that was clearly established at the time of the defendant's action but whether the plaintiff alleged *any* violation of federal law as currently understood.[228]

In addition, *Siegert* provided guidance for the analysis of qualified immunity issues. Initially, the Court noted that "[q]ualified immunity is a defense that must be pleaded by a defendant official."[229] The Court then described the qualified immunity inquiry in terms of both current law and the law at the time the action occurred. "Once a defendant pleads a defense of qualified immunity, '[o]n summary judgment, the judge appropriately may determine, not only the currently applicable law, but whether that law was clearly established at the time an action occurred.... Until this threshold immunity question is resolved, discovery should not be allowed.'"[230]

Although *Siegert* makes an important clarification of the analytical approach to deciding qualified immunity issues, the Court did not reach the issue on which it had granted certiorari: namely, the application of strict or heightened pleading requirements to civil rights actions.[231] Most federal circuits had imposed such heightened pleading requirements,[232] and this had been most common on qualified immunity issues.[233] Nonetheless,

---

226. *Id.* at 231.
227. *See, e.g.*, Danese v. Asman, 875 F.2d 1239 (6th Cir. 1989) (not reaching the merits of a § 1983 jail suicide claim because the underlying law was not clearly established), *cert. denied*, 494 U.S. 1027 (1990).
228. *Siegert*, 500 U.S. at 231.
229. *Id.*
230. *Id.* (quoting *Harlow*, 457 U.S. at 818).
231. Siegert, 500 U.S. at 227.
232. *See supra* note 178.
233. *See* Elliott v. Thomas, 937 F.2d 338, 345 (7th Cir. 1991), *cert. denied*, 502 U.S. 1121 & 1074 (1992), and cases cited; *see also* Siegert v. Gilley, 895 F.2d 797, 802 (D.C. Cir. 1990), *aff'd on other grounds*, 500 U.S. 226 (1991); Elliott v. Perez, 751 F.2d 1472, 1477-78 (5th Cir. 1985). *But see* Bergquist v. County of Cochise, 806 F.2d 1364, 1367 (9th Cir. 1986) (rejecting the use of a strict pleading standard for § 1983 claims).

some federal judges had suggested that a heightened pleading standard was inconsistent with the notice pleading requirements of the federal rules,[234] and the Supreme Court in *Leatherman v. Tarrant County Narcotics Intelligence and Coordination Unit*[235] rejected the use of such a standard. The Court, however, expressly left open whether the use of a heightened pleading standard could be justified for § 1983 suits against individuals who could raise immunity defenses.[236]

Despite *Leatherman*, most federal circuits that have addressed the issue have adhered to earlier circuit precedent and continued to apply strict pleading requirements to § 1983 complaints implicating qualified immunity issues.[237] Some courts, however, have seen the logic of *Leatherman* as precluding all use of strict pleading requirements.[238]

The only Supreme Court discussion of this precise issue was by Justice Kennedy, who concluded in his concurring opinion in *Siegert* that the

---

234. *See* Elliott v. Perez, 751 F.2d at 1482-83 (Higginbotham, J., concurring); *see also* Elliott v. Thomas, 937 F.2d at 345.

235. 507 U.S. 163 (1993).

236. *Id.* at 166-67 ("We thus have no occasion to consider whether our qualified immunity jurisprudence would require a heightened pleading in cases involving individual government officials.").

237. *See, e.g.*, Edington v. Missouri Dep't of Corrections, 52 F.3d 777, 779 n.3 (8th Cir. 1995) (follow existing circuit precedent and requiring heightened pleading in individual capacity § 1983 suits); Moore v. Agency for Int'l Dev., 994 F.2d 874, 877 (D.C. Cir. 1993) (noting that *Leatherman* had not rejected the use of a heightened pleading requirement for individual defendants, and relying on circuit precedent to apply a heightened pleading standard); Kimberlin v. Quinlan, 6 F.3d 789, 794 n. 9 (D.C. Cir. 1993), *reh'g en banc denied*, 17 F.3d 1525 (D.C. Cir. 1994), *vacated*, 115 S.Ct. 2552 (1995); Branch v. Tunnell, 937 F.2d 1382, 1386-87 (9th Cir. 1991), *cert. denied*, 114 S.Ct. 2704 (1994).

238. *See* Triad Assocs., Inc. v. Robinson, 10 F.3d 492, 497 (7th Cir. 1993); *see also* Callaghan v. Congemi, No. CIV.A.91-1496, 1993 WL 114523, at *5-6 (E.D. La. Apr. 8, 1993) (treating *Leatherman* as "sound[ing] the death knell for . . . [the] requirement of heightened pleading in suits involving individual government officials" and noting "that *Leatherman* cannot be limited to its holding"). *But see* Veney v. Hogan, 70 F.3d 917 (6th Cir. 1995) (requiring the use of a heightened standard of pleading for § 1983 actions in which a defendant raises a qualified immunity defense). *But cf.* Schultea v. Wood, 47 F.3d 1427 (5th Cir 1995) (*en banc*) (requiring the use of a reply under FED. R. CIV. P. 7(a) to meet the heightened pleading goal).

substantive nature of the § 1983 qualified immunity justified the use of a heightened pleading requirement on § 1983 qualified immunity issues.

> There is a tension between the rationale of *Harlow* and the requirement[s] of malice, and it seems to me that the heightened pleading requirement is the most workable means to resolve it. The heightened pleading standard is a departure from the usual pleading requirements of Federal Rules of Civil Procedure 8 and 9(b), and departs also from the normal standard for summary judgment under Rule 56. But avoidance of disruptive discovery is one of the very purposes for the official immunity doctrine . . . [and] [t]he substantive defense of immunity controls.[239]

Given the Court's decision in *Leatherman*, federal courts would have difficulty imposing a heightened pleading requirement on § 1983 qualified immunity issues without taking the bold step of construing the immunity from suit as an element of substantive law that overrides the broad delegation of rule-making that Congress gave the Supreme Court in the Rules Enabling Act.[240]

---

239. *Siegert*, 500 U.S. at 235-36. Justice Kennedy also stated in his concurrence that "[t]he heightened pleading standard is a necessary and appropriate accommodation between the state of mind component of malice [in some substantive constitutional claims] and the objective test that prevails in qualified immunity as a general matter." *Id.* at 235.

240. 28 U.S.C. § 2072 (1988). Under § 2072(b), the Court may not adopt rules that "abridge, enlarge, or modify any substantive right," but the delegation of rule-making to the Court is quite broad. *See generally* Hanna v. Plummer, 380 U.S. 460 (1965). The Court has never rejected a federal rule because of a conflict with the substantive law. *See* Gene R. Shreve & Peter Raven-Hansen, Understanding Civil Procedure § 40[C][2] 159 (1989); *see also* Burlington N. R.R. v. Woods, 480 U.S. 1, 6 (1987) ("[T]he study and approval given each proposed Rule by the Advisory Committee, the Judicial Conference, and this Court, and the statutory requirement that the Rule be reported to Congress for a period of review before taking effect, . . . give the Rules presumptive validity under both the constitutional and statutory constraints."). The Court, however, has often construed a federal rule narrowly to avoid such a conflict. *See Hanna*, 380 U.S. at 472. Given the relatively recent characterization of the qualified immunity as an immunity from suit, *see* Harlow v. Fitzgerald, 457 U.S. 800 (1982), it is difficult to argue that the drafters of the federal rules did not intend the liberal pleading requirements

If the Supreme Court held that federal immunity law was substantive and overrode the liberal pleading requirements of the federal rules (and required the application of a heightened pleading requirement to § 1983 complaints against individuals), plaintiffs would not be able to resist the argument that federal law also overrode liberal state pleading requirements. On the other hand, if the Supreme Court rejected the application of a heightened pleading requirement to § 1983 suits against individuals, state courts that desired to continue to apply strict state pleading requirements could do so only if the state pleading rules did not burden § 1983.[241]

Discovery

In *Harlow v. Fitzgerald*,[242] the Court treated the existence of qualified immunity as a threshold legal issue based on whether the federal right in question was clearly established at the time of the alleged violation.[243] This analysis also led the *Harlow* Court to require courts to stay discovery until the threshold issue is resolved.[244]

Despite this preference for resolving qualified immunity issues early in the litigation, the Court, in *Anderson v. Creighton*,[245] opened the door to limited discovery, at least when the immunity issue is fact-specific. In *Anderson*, the Court recognized that "the determination whether it was objectively legally reasonable to conclude that [the alleged conduct was legal] . . . will often require an examination of the information possessed by" the defendants.[246] "The relevant question . . . is the objective (albeit fact-specific) question whether a reasonable officer could have believed [the defendant's conduct] . . . to be lawful, in light of clearly established law and the information the [defendant] . . . possessed. [The defendant's] . . . subjective beliefs . . . are

---

to apply to suits against public officials. *But see* Nixon v. Fitzgerald, 457 U.S. 731, 744 (1982) ("This Court consistently has recognized that government officials are entitled to some form of immunity from suit."). For a discussion of the potential conflict between the immunity from suit and the rules of civil procedure governing voluntary pretrial disclosure, *see Shah*, *supra* note 129.

241. *See supra* notes 160-71 and accompanying text.
242. 457 U.S. 800 (1982).
243. *Id.* at 817-19.
244. *Id.* at 818 ("Until this threshold immunity question is resolved, discovery should not be allowed.").
245. 483 U.S. 635 (1987).
246. *Id.* at 641.

irrelevant."[247] The *Anderson* Court also acknowledged that when the factual allegations of the parties differ, "discovery may be necessary before [the defendant's] . . . motion for summary judgment . . . can be resolved."[248]

It is unclear whether these limitations on discovery apply with equal force to state court § 1983 litigation. Even given the characterization of the § 1983 immunity as an immunity from suit, it is difficult to accept the proposition that federal law requires states to organize their judicial systems to mirror the federal model. Some state court systems might rely heavily on summary judgment and limit discovery, while others might downplay summary judgment, expand discovery, and rely more heavily on trials.[249] While a state that imposed cumulative burdens on the qualified immunity available to individual § 1983 defendants might violate federal law, the interest of states in the administration of their judicial systems may well outweigh the relevant federal interest and give state courts some leeway in managing discovery in § 1983 cases.[250]

Summary Judgment

In redefining qualified immunity, the *Harlow* Court expressly relied on its concern about the difficulty of resolving qualified immunity issues on summary judgment.[251] Although the Supreme Court has defined the qualified immunity in objective terms, the underlying constitutional rights enforceable through § 1983 often contain state of mind requirements.[252] Some federal courts, however, relying on the Court's desire to expand the use of summary judgment,[253] have refused to permit state of mind discovery even

---

247. *Id.*

248. *Id.* at 646 n.6.

249. States are involved in a number of experiments to make civil litigation more efficient. *See, e.g.*, Robert D. Myers, *MAD Track: An Experiment in Terror*, 25 Ariz. St. L.J. 11 (1993) (discussing Arizona's Mandatory Alternative Discovery Track program for reducing discovery costs and minimizing the time involved in getting civil cases through the system).

250. *But cf.* Felder v. Casey, 487 U.S. 131, 145 (1988) (rejecting the argument that sound notions of public administration justified the application of a state notice of claim requirement to state court § 1983 litigation).

251. *Harlow*, 457 U.S. at 815-18.

252. *See supra* note 61.

253. *See supra* note 137.

when motive or bad faith is an element of the underlying substantive federal standard unless the plaintiff comes forward with allegations of direct, not circumstantial, evidence of unconstitutional motive.[254] Justice Kennedy, who appears to be the Court's strongest proponent of a heightened pleading requirement,[255] has rejected the use of a direct evidence requirement and has taken the position that plaintiffs can meet their burden in cases involving unconstitutional motives by presenting circumstantial evidence.[256]

As with other issues involving the administration of § 1983 qualified immunities, it is unclear whether states must follow the federal model or

---

254. *See* Siegert v. Gilley, 895 F.2d 797, 803-04 (D.C. Cir. 1990), *aff'd on other grounds*, 500 U.S. 226 (1991); Whitacre v. Davey, 890 F.2d 1168, 1171 (D.C. Cir. 1989), *cert. denied*, 497 U.S. 1038 (1990); *accord* Moore v. Agency for Int'l Dev., 994 F.2d 874, 877 (D.C. Cir. 1993) (adhering to circuit's heightened pleading standard and requiring the plaintiff to "produce some direct evidence that the officials' actions were improperly motivated . . . if the case is to proceed to trial").

255. *See supra* note 239 and accompanying text. Judge Easterbrook of the Seventh Circuit has suggested that the debate over the use of a heightened pleading requirement on § 1983 qualified immunity issues does not really involve the pleadings but rather the timing of motions for summary judgment and the showing that a plaintiff must make to be permitted to conduct discovery when state of mind is an element of the underlying claim. *See* Elliott v. Thomas, 937 F.2d 338, 345 (7th Cir. 1991), *cert. denied*, 502 U.S. 1121 & 1074 (1992); *see also* Crawford-El v. Britton, 93 F.3d 813, 823 (D.C. Cir. 1996) (*en banc*) ("The label 'heightened pleading' for special requirements for constitutional torts involving improper motive was always a misnomer.").

256. *See Siegert*, 500 U.S. at 236 (Kennedy, J., concurring) ("Upon the assertion of a qualified immunity defense the plaintiff must put forward specific, nonconclusory factual allegations which establish malice, or face dismissal. I would reject, however, the . . . statement that a plaintiff must present direct, as opposed to circumstantial, evidence. . . . Circumstantial evidence may be as probative as testimonial evidence."); *see also id.* at 245 (Marshall, J., dissenting) (rejecting the refusal of the court of appeals to permit limited discovery of unconstitutional motive absent *direct* evidence, and noting that "[b]ecause evidence of such intent is peculiarly within the control of the defendant, the 'heightened pleading' rule . . . effectively precludes any *Bivens* action in which the defendant's state of mind is an element of the underlying claim").

whether they may apply summary judgment standards that place a greater burden on defendants' seeking to assert an immunity from suit. Although many state courts have embraced aspects of the federal summary judgment model, it is difficult to imagine federal law requiring state trial courts to make greater use of summary judgment on § 1983 qualified immunity issues than state law otherwise permits.

Role of the Jury

The Supreme Court's treatment of qualified immunity as raising an objective legal question in *Harlow* expanded the role of trial court judges at the expense of the jury, but there remains a great deal of confusion over the precise role of the judge and the jury on qualified immunity issues. In *Hunter v. Bryant*,[257] the Supreme Court summarily reversed a Ninth Circuit decision because the court framed the qualified immunity issue for the jury in terms of whether a reasonable officer could have believed there was probable cause to make a warrantless arrest. The Supreme Court concluded that this routinely placed the question of qualified immunity in the hands of the jury, whereas "[i]mmunity ordinarily should be decided by the court long before trial" by the court "ask[ing] whether the [defendants] acted reasonably under settled law in the circumstances. . . ."[258]

Before *Hunter*, federal courts had taken different positions on the role of the jury on qualified immunity issues,[259] and *Hunter*'s significance is

---

257. 502 U.S. 224 (1991) (per curiam).

258. *Id.* at 228.

259. *Compare* Finnegan v. Fountain, 915 F.2d 817 (2d Cir. 1990) (treating availability of qualified immunity as a legal question for the court); Warren v. Dwyer, 906 F.2d 70, 76 (2d Cir.) (treating qualified immunity as a legal question for the court but encouraging the use of special interrogatories to the jury on the underlying factual issues), *cert. denied*, 498 U.S. 967 (1990); Coffman v. Trickey, 884 F.2d 1057, 1063 (8th Cir. 1989) (reversible error to submit question of the availability of qualified immunity to the jury), *cert. denied*, 494 U.S. 1056 (1990) *with* Melear v. Spears, 862 F.2d 1177, 1184 (5th Cir. 1989) (requiring the "trier of fact . . . [to] determine the objective legal reasonableness of an officer's conduct by construing the facts in dispute"); Thorsted v. Kelly, 858 F.2d 571, 575 (9th Cir. 1988) (treating as a triable issue of fact "whether a reasonable [police] officer placed in the circumstances faced by . . . [the defendant] could reasonably believe that his conduct was legal. . .").

unclear. There is no disagreement that federal court judges are responsible for determining what is clearly established federal law for qualified immunity purposes. Most federal judges, however, view qualified immunity as involving a two-step analysis that requires the court to determine not only whether the law was clearly established but also the "objective legal reasonableness of the defendants' conduct."[260]

The most difficult qualified immunity issues arise when the legal standard itself contains a reasonableness requirement. In cases involving such standards, most federal courts have viewed the second step of the analysis as raising an issue for the judge. For example, in *Scott v Henrich*,[261] the Ninth Circuit treated the standard for analyzing excessive force claims as the same as the qualified immunity standard, but it noted that "even though reasonableness traditionally is a question of fact for the jury, . . . defendants can still win on summary judgment if the district court concludes, after resolving all factual disputes in favor of the plaintiff, that the officer's use of force was objectively reasonable under the circumstances."[262]

---

260. *See, e.g.*, Biddle v. Martin, 992 F.2d 673, 675 (7th Cir. 1993). The *Harlow* Court treated the qualified immunity inquiry as a single question and assumed that if the law was clearly established a reasonable public official would be aware of this and act accordingly. *See Harlow*, 457 U.S. at 818-9. ("If the law was clearly established, the immunity defense ordinarily should fail, since a reasonably competent public official should know the law governing his conduct."). Anderson required a more particularized definition of the clearly established federal right. *See supra* notes 217-221 and accompanying text.
261. 39 F.3d 912 (9th Cir. 1994), *cert. denied*, 115 S.Ct. 2612 (1995).
262. *Id.* at 915; *see also* ActUp!/Portland v. Bagley, 988 F.2d 868, 873 (9th Cir. 1993) (modified opinion) (interpreting Hunter "to hold that the question of whether a reasonable officer could have believed probable cause (or reasonable suspicion) existed to justify a search or an arrest is 'an essentially legal question,' that should be determined by the district court at the earliest possible point in the litigation"). *But see* Mahoney v. Kesery, 976 F.2d 1054, 1058 (7th Cir. 1992) (describing the problem that arises when the qualified immunity issue merges with the merits and noting "that *often* the question of immunity is one of law—specifically, it is the question: what was the clearly established rule of law when the officers committed the acts for which they are being sued?" but further noting that "where . . . the only contested issue bearing on immunity is whether a reasonable officer would have thought the defendant had committed a crime, there is no question of law—at least in the sense of a question reserved for judges, for the jury is going to decide the same question").

Even read broadly, however, *Hunter* does not eliminate the role for juries in performing the fact-finding that is relevant to qualified immunity issues. For example, in *Washington v. Newsom*,[263] a case involving the use of deadly force, the Sixth Circuit recognized the factual nature of the qualified immunity question by pointing out that the question of whether an objectively reasonable police officer would have known that the decedent was not armed depended upon the factual question of the precise information possessed by the officers.

Under the practices generally followed in state and federal courts, juries apply the law to the facts.[264] In the area of determining entitlement to qualified immunity, the Court has made clear that the judge, not the jury, is responsible for identifying the clearly established federal law, but the Court has not explained why it has deviated from the prevailing policies that typically govern whether the judge or the jury will be responsible for applying the law to the facts.[265] Nor has the Court explained how either the Seventh Amendment or sound principles of judicial administration support giving federal trial judges responsibility for determining whether § 1983 defendants acted reasonably in violating clearly established federal law.

Even assuming that federal court judges, not juries, are responsible for determining whether § 1983 defendants acted unreasonably in failing to follow federal law, states are not precluded by federal law from following their traditional practices in allocating decisionmaking authority between judges and juries,[266] and a number of state courts have treated the question

---

263. 977 F.2d 991 (6th Cir. 1992), *cert. denied*, 507 U.S. 1031 (1993).
264. *See generally* W. Page Keeton et al., Prosser and Keeton on the Law of Torts § 37, at 235-38 (5th ed. 1984) (discussing the functions of the court and the jury in negligence cases); *see also* Fleming James, Jr. et al., Civil Procedure § 7.18, at 353-56 (4th ed. 1992) (discussing the role of the jury in assessing the legal consequences of the facts).
265. *See Bagley*, 988 F.2d at 874 (Norris, J., dissenting) (dissenting from failure to rehear case en banc) (describing the panel opinion as "def[ying] our common law tradition, which since time immemorial has considered the reasonableness of human conduct to be a quintessential jury question").
266. *But cf.* Dice v. Akron, Canton & Youngstown R.R., 342 U.S. 359 (1952) (treating the allocation of responsibility between judge and jury as a matter of federal law in a state court FELA action).

of whether the defendant acted reasonably in light of the applicable legal principles as raising a factual issue for the jury.[267]

Interlocutory Appeals

Under the final judgment rule[268] federal appellate courts, with limited statutory exceptions not relevant here,[269] only have jurisdiction over appeals from final decisions of district courts. There is, however, a judicially developed collateral order exception to the final judgment rule, and in *Cohen v. Beneficial Industrial Loan Corporation*,[270] the Supreme Court permitted the immediate appeal of district court decisions that fall within "that small class which finally determine claims of right separable from, and collateral to, rights asserted in the action, too important to be denied review and too inde-

---

267. *See, e.g.*, Carroll v. Robinson, 874 P.2d 1010 (Ariz. Ct. App. 1994) (treating the question of whether the legal right allegedly violated was clearly established as a question of law, but treating the question of whether a reasonable official would know that he or she was violating that clearly established law as a question for the jury); Fulwood v. Porter, 639 A.2d 594, 599 (D.C. 1994) (noting that in cases where qualified immunity is asserted, the factual circumstances necessary to decide the immunity issue should be presented to the jury, but the court should decide the purely legal issue of whether a right was clearly established, but in "failure to act" cases, the issues are inseparable, and therefore, "the question . . . of whether [the defendant-police chief] violated clearly established rights of which he should have known—the immunity issue—and the question whether he exhibited deliberate indifference to the violation of constitutional rights by street level officers—the liability issue—are effectively the same"); Lee v. Greene, 442 S.E.2d 547 (N.C. Ct App. 1994) (holding that highway patrol officers did not violate clearly established rights in entering arrestee's house to make an arrest, but that genuine issues of historical fact respecting the officers' conduct or its reasonableness under the circumstances precluded summary judgment on the issue of whether highway patrol officers were entitled to qualified immunity on a § 1983 excessive force claim).
268. 28 U.S.C. § 1291 (1988) ("The courts of appeals . . . shall have jurisdiction of appeals from all final decisions of the district courts of the United States. . . .").
269. *See, e.g.*, 28 U.S.C. § 1292(a) (1) (1988) (permitting interlocutory appeals from orders granting or denying preliminary injunctions); 28 U.S.C. § 1292(b) (1988) (permitting interlocutory appeals from otherwise nonappealable orders certified as involving controlling questions of law).
270. 337 U.S. 541 (1949).

pendent of the cause itself to require that appellate consideration be deferred until the whole case is adjudicated."[271] The Supreme Court has applied this collateral order exception to the *immunity from suit* provided by absolute and qualified immunity,[272] and individual § 1983 defendants[273] may immediately appeal trial court decisions denying them either type of immunity.[274]

State courts throughout the country have taken different positions on the availability of immediate appeals of trial court decisions denying qualified or absolute immunity. Some state courts have followed the federal model and extended an appeal as of right to defendants who have been denied qualified immunity by trial courts.[275] On the other hand, some state courts have rejected the federal model and denied the availability of immediate qualified immunity appeals.[276] Finally, some state courts have rejected the availability of an appeal as of right while still providing an

---

271. *Id.* at 546.

272. *See* Mitchell v. Forsyth, 472 U.S. 511, 530 (1985) (construing 28 U.S.C. § 1291 to permit immediate appeals of the "denial of a claim of qualified immunity, to the extent that it turns on an issue of law"); *see also* Nixon v. Fitzgerald, 457 U.S. 731, 742-43 (1982) (permitting immediate appeal of denials of absolute immunity).

273. Municipalities, on the other hand, are not entitled to an immediate appeal of federal trial court decisions forcing them to go to trial. *See* Swint v. Chambers County Comm'n, 115 S.Ct. 1203, 1208 (1995). *But see* Puerto Rico Aqueduct and Sewer Auth. v. Metcalf & Eddy, Inc., 506 U.S. 139 (1993) (permitting immediate appeals by defendants claiming an eleventh amendment immunity from suit in federal court).

274. *Cf.* Johnson v. Jones, 115 S.Ct. 2151 (1995) (denying immediate appeals of fact-based decisions rejecting the availability of qualified immunity).

275. *See, e.g.*, Virden v. Roper, 788 S.W.2d 470 (Ark. 1990); Robinson v. Beaumont, 725 S.W.2d 839 (Ark. 1987); Tucker v. Resha, 648 So.2d 1187 (Fla. 1994); Lord v. Murphy, 561 A.2d 1013 (Me. 1989); Breault v. Chairman of the Bd. of Fire Comm'rs of Springfield, 513 N.E.2d 1277 (Mass. 1987), *cert. denied*, 485 U.S. 906 (1988); Anderson v. City of Hopkins, 393 N.W.2d 363 (Minn. 1986); Richardson v. Chevrefils, 552 A.2d 89 (N.H. 1988); Corum v. University of North Carolina, 413 S.E.2d 276 (N.C.), *cert. denied*, 506 U.S. 985 (1992); Lancie v. Giles, 572 A.2d 827 (Pa. Cmwlth Ct. 1990).

276. *See, e.g.*, Jaggers v. Zolliecoffer, 718 S.W.2d 441 (Ark. 1986); Pizzato's Inc. v. City of Berwyn, 523 N.E.2d 51 (Ill. App. Ct. 1988), *cert. denied*, 489 U.S. 1054 (1989); Klindtworth v. Burkett, 477 N.W.2d 176 (N.D. 1991); Ohio Civil Serv. Employees Ass'n v. Moritz, 529 N.E.2d 1290 (Ohio Ct. App. 1987); Noyola v. Flores, 740 S.W.2d 493 (Tex. Ct. App. 1987).

avenue for discretionary interlocutory appellate review in appropriate cases.[277] For example, in *Turner v. Giles*,[278] the Georgia Supreme Court relied on the right of Georgia to define the appellate jurisdiction of its courts and held that there was no right to an immediate appeal of a denial of § 1983 qualified immunity. Nonetheless, the court noted that discretionary appeals were available to seek review of decisions denying qualified immunity and that trial courts should generally permit such appeals.[279]

State courts have been sharply divided on whether federal law requires states to provide an immediate appeal of trial court denials of qualified or absolute immunity,[280] but in *Johnson v. Fankell*,[281] the court unanimously held that federal law did not require such immediate appeals. In so holding, the court treated the right to an immediate appeal in federal court as not derived from § 1983 but rather as a "federal procedural right that simply does not apply in a nonfederal forum."[282]

The *Fankell* court also made clear that the "outcome" it had in mind when it adapted the outcome-determinative test to § 1983 claims in *Felder v. Casey*[283] was the ultimate disposition of the case and not simply some aspect of the litigation. Thus, the court refused to require states to abandon their own neutral jurisdictional policies and permitted states to preclude immediate appellate review of trial court decisions rejecting immunity defenses.

---

277. *See, e.g.*, McLin v. Trimble, 795 P.2d 1035 (Okla. 1990) (permitting immediate review through an extraordinary writ filed in the Oklahoma Supreme Court under its original jurisdiction); Henke v. Superior Court, 775 P.2d 1160 (Ariz. Ct. App. 1989) (accepting jurisdiction on special-action petition and ordering the trial court to dismiss § 1983 claim); Carrillo v. Rostro, 845 P.2d 130 (N.M. 1992) (adopting the collateral order doctrine "as a matter of sound judicial administration" and holding that the writ of error is the proper procedural device for qualified immunity appeals).
278. 450 S.E.2d 421 (Ga. 1994), *cert. denied*, 115 S.Ct. 1959 (1995).
279. *See also* Arnison v. Jezwinski, 556 N.W.2d 721 (Wis. 1996) (not reaching whether a denials of qualified immunity is a final order subject to and immediate appeal as of right but holding that the Wisconsin Court of Appeals must grant a discretionary appeal of every denial of qualified immunity that turns on a legal issue).
280. *See* Steinglass, Section 1983 Litigation, *supra* note 7, § 8.11(b) (1).
281. 117 S. Ct. 1800 (1997).
282. *Id.* at 1802. *See also id.* at 1807 ("We have made it quite clear that it is a matter for each State to decide how to structure its judicial system.")
283. 487 U.S. 131 (1988).

Municipal Liability

In *Monroe v. Pape*,[284] the Supreme Court held that cities were not "persons" within the meaning of § 1983 and, thus, were not amenable to suit. In *Monell v. Department of Social Services*,[285] however, the Court reversed this aspect of *Monroe* and held that cities could be sued under § 1983, but the Court rejected *respondeat superior* as a basis for liability.[286] Nonetheless, municipalities and other units of local government may be liable under § 1983 for violations of federal rights when the challenged actions are 1) based on official policies made by the municipality's lawmakers,[287] 2) taken by other official policymakers,[288] 3) the result of inadequate training or other policies that reflect a deliberate indifference to the constitutional rights of persons with whom municipal employees come into contact,[289] or 4) part of

284. 365 U.S. 167 (1961).
285. 436 U.S. 658 (1978).
286. *Id.* at 691 ("[A] municipality cannot be held liable solely because it employs a tortfeasor—or, in other words, a municipality cannot be held liable under § 1983 on a *respondeat superior* theory.").
287. *Id.* at 694.
288. *See* Jett v. Dallas Indep. Sch. Dist., 491 U.S. 701, 737-38 (1989); *see also* City of St. Louis v. Praprotnik, 485 U.S. 112 (1988); Pembaur v. City of Cincinnati, 475 U.S. 469 (1986). The Supreme Court treats "the identification of those officials whose decisions represent the official policy of the local governmental unit . . . [as] a legal question to be resolved by the trial judge before the case is submitted to the jury." Jett, 491 U.S. at 737. The determination of who is an official policymaker may involve not only an analysis of "state and local positive law" but also "custom or usage having the force of law." *Id.* (internal quotations omitted) (quoting *Praprotnik*, 485 U.S. at 124 n.1. (Although the Supreme Court apparently expects federal judges to do whatever fact-finding is necessary to identify the official policymakers, state courts may have more authority to assign such fact-finding to the jury.
289. *See* City of Canton v. Harris, 489 U.S. 378 (1989). A single unconstitutional act by a municipal employee, standing alone, may not be the basis for inferring an improper training policy. *See* City of Oklahoma City v. Tuttle, 471 U.S. 808 (1985). However, when combined with sufficient evidence of inadequate policies of training or supervision, a single act may be the basis for imposing § 1983 liability on a municipality. *See* City of Oklahoma City, 471 U.S. at 821-22; *accord* Pembaur, 475 U.S at 480 ("[I]t is plain that [§ 1983] municipal liability may be imposed for a single decision by municipal policymakers under appropriate circumstances.").

the custom or practice of the municipality.[290] In all cases, however, there must be a causal connection between the action or inaction of the municipality and the resulting injury.[291]

Unlike individual governmental employees, municipalities and other political subdivisions cannot claim a qualified immunity under § 1983.[292] As a result, § 1983 plaintiffs often join municipalities or other governmental entities to assure the presence of a defendant that lacks an immunity and is capable of satisfying a judgment. The joinder of political subdivisions in § 1983 suits, however, can complicate § 1983 litigation, especially when entity liability is based either on inadequate training or supervision or on the existence of a custom.[293]

Plaintiffs may sometimes avoid these difficulties in states that permit suits to be brought directly against political subdivisions based on *respondeat superior* or that maintain liberal indemnification policies under which judgments against employees are paid by the governmental entity.[294]

Suits Against States

Cities and other units of local government are "persons" for purposes of suit under § 1983, but in *Will v. Michigan Department of State Po-*

---

290. *See* Bordanaro v. McLeod, 871 F.2d 1151, 1155-63 (1st Cir.), *cert. denied,* 493 U.S. 820 (1989); Leach v. Shelby County Sheriff, 891 F.2d 1241, 1246-48 (6th Cir. 1989), *cert. denied,* 495 U.S. 932 (1990).

291. *See Jett*, 491 U.S. at 737 ("Once those officials who have the power to make official policy on a particular issue have been identified, it is for the jury to determine whether *their* decisions have caused the deprivation of rights at issue. . . .").

292. *See* Owen v. City of Independence, 445 U.S. 622 (1980); *see also* Berkley v. Common Council of the City of Charleston, 63 F.3d 295 (4th Cir. 1995) (en banc) (rejecting argument that municipalities are immune from suit under § 1983 for legislative decisions), *cert. denied,* 116 S.Ct. 775 (1996).

293. Section 1983 claims against governmental entities often represent a case within a case and can significantly lengthen and complicate a trial. Thus, a number of federal judges bifurcate § 1983 claims and hear the claims against the individual defendants first. *See generally* Douglas L. Colbert, *Bifurcation of Civil Rights Defendants: Undermining Monell in Police Brutality Cases*, 44 Hastings L.J. 499 (1993).

294. *See generally* Steinglass, Section 1983 Litigation, *supra* note 7, at § 15.2(e).

lice,[295] the Supreme Court held that states are not. Thus, the Court immunized states from § 1983 suits in state courts.[296]

Federal, not state, law, however, governs whether a political subdivision must be considered the state for purposes of § 1983, and in *Howlett v. Rose*,[297] the Court held that local school boards in Florida were subject to suit under § 1983 in the Florida state courts.[298]

Even before *Will*, unconsenting states could not be sued in federal court under § 1983 because of the Eleventh Amendment.[299] State officials, however, have long been subject to § 1983 official capacity suits in federal court for prospective injunctive relief even though such relief really runs against the state.[300] *Will made clear* that § 1983 was equally available in state courts for suits against state officials for prospective injunctive relief,[301] and state courts have recognized this.[302]

Suits Against State Officials

In contrast to the availability of § 1983 suits seeking prospective injunctive relief against state officials, § 1983 is not available in official capacity damage actions against state officials. Nonetheless, in *Hafer v.*

---

295. 491 U.S. 58 (1989).

296. In rejecting the availability of § 1983 as a basis for obtaining relief against the state in state courts, the Court imported the distinctions used in federal court for purposes of the Eleventh Amendment into the definition of "person" under § 1983. *See Will,* 491 U.S. at 66-67 ("[I]n deciphering congressional intent as to the scope of § 1983, the scope of the Eleventh Amendment is a consideration, and we decline to adopt a reading of § 1983 that disregards it.").

297. 496 U.S. 356 (1990).

298. *See also* Blades v. Woods, 667 A.2d 917 (Md. Ct. App. 1995) (rejecting the argument that the Baltimore City Police Department is a state agency for purposes of § 1983).

299. *See* Quern v. Jordan, 440 U.S. 332 (1979).

300. *See generally* Edelman v. Jordan, 415 U.S. 651 (1974); *cf. Ex parte* Young, 209 U.S. 123 (1908) (creating a fiction under which state officers could be sued for injunctive relief directly under the constitution despite the Eleventh Amendment).

301. 491 U.S. at 71 n.10 ("Of course a state official in his or her official capacity, when sued for injunctive relief, would be a person under § 1983 because 'official-capacity actions for prospective relief are not treated as actions against the State.'").

302. *See generally* STEINGLASS, SECTION 1983 LITIGATION, *supra* note 7, at § 15.3.

Melo,[303] the Supreme Court held that state officials were subject to personal liability in individual capacity § 1983 damage claims for acts taken as part of their official duties.

The implications that flow from the characterization of a § 1983 damage suit against a state official as an individual or official capacity suit are significant. State officials have a potential qualified immunity in individual capacity damage suits, and neither state nor federal courts may entertain official capacity damage claims against state officials.[304] Therefore, a threshold question in any § 1983 suit naming a state official is the determination of the capacity in which the official is sued.[305] Unfortunately, plaintiffs often fail to state clearly the capacity in which they are suing governmental officials.

Federal courts are divided as to how to construe § 1983 complaints that seek damages against state officials but do not make clear whether the suits are being brought against the officials in their individual or official capacities. For example, some federal courts treat § 1983 complaints that fail to state expressly that governmental officials are being sued in their individual capacity as official capacity suits.[306] Moreover, even though

---

303. 502 U.S. 21 (1991).

304. In federal court, state officials can avoid such suits by relying on their Eleventh Amendment immunity from official capacity damage suits, while in state court they can rely on the Court's limited definition as to who is a "person" under § 1983.

305. Similar issues arise in § 1983 suits against local governmental officials. Such individual capacity defendants, like state officials, may assert a qualified or an absolute immunity, but local governments do not share that immunity. *See supra* note 292. Because an official capacity § 1983 suit against a local governmental official is really another way of naming the entity, *see* Brandon v. Holt, 469 U.S. 464 (1985), the entity may not claim an immunity. On the other hand, to prevail in an official capacity § 1983 damage suit against a local governmental official, a § 1983 plaintiff must meet *Monell* standards and prove that an official policy of the entity caused the deprivation of federal law. *See supra* notes 285-91 and accompanying text.

306. *See* Yeksigian v. Nappi, 900 F.2d 101, 104 (7th Cir. 1990) ("In the absence of any express statement that the parties are being sued in their individual capacities, an allegation that the defendants were acting under color of law generally is construed as a suit against the defendants in their official capacities only."); *see also* Wells v. Brown, 891 F.2d 591, 592 (6th Cir. 1989). *But see* Biggs v. Meadows, 66 F.3d 56 (4th Cir. 1995) (not requiring a § 1983 plaintiff to plead the capacity in which a state official is being sued).

issues of capacity are generally waivable, the Sixth Circuit treats this issue as jurisdictional because it implicates the Eleventh Amendment.[307]

The Supreme Court did not reach the pleading issue in *Hafer*[308] and, thus, did not decide whether the Third Circuit acted properly in looking to the proceedings below to determine whether the § 1983 damage suit was brought against the state official in her official or her personal capacity.[309] Nonetheless, the *Hafer* Court agreed with the Third Circuit's observation that "[i]t is obviously preferable for the plaintiff to be specific in the first instance to avoid any ambiguity."[310]

Despite the Supreme Court's failure to reach this issue and its obvious preference for clarity in pleading, the Court has approached the issue of determining the capacity in which a § 1983 suit has been brought by looking to the course of the proceedings.[311] Moreover, the Court's willingness to permit the *Hafer* suit to go forward suggests that the pleading of individual capacity is not jurisdictional.

A policy treating capacity as jurisdictional, even if proper for suits against state officials in federal court, is inapplicable to state court § 1983 claims. In *Carrillo v. State*,[312] the leading state court case addressing the construction of § 1983 complaints that are ambiguous as to the capacity in which individuals are being sued, the Arizona Court of Appeals recognized the "important repercussions" of treating a § 1983 suit as a personal capacity as contrasted to an official capacity suit.[313] Nonetheless,

---

307. *See Wells,* 891 F.2d at 593.

308. *See Hafer,* 502 U.S. at 24 n.*.

309. *See* Melo v. Hafer, 912 F.2d 628, 635-36 (3d Cir. 1990), *aff'd*, 502 U.S. 21 (1991). Other circuits following this approach and cited by the Court are: Conner v. Reinhard, 847 F.2d 384, 394 n.8 (7th Cir.), *cert. denied*, 488 U.S. 856 (1988); Houston v. Reich, 932 F.2d 883, 885 (10th Cir. 1991); Lundgren v. McDaniel, 814 F.2d 600, 603-04 (11th Cir. 1987). The Court cited the Sixth and Eighth Circuit decisions in *Wells* and Nix v. Norman, 879 F.2d 429, 431 (8th Cir. 1989), as imposing more rigid pleading requirements.

310. *See Hafer,* 502 U.S. at 24 n * (quoting 912 F.2d at 636 n.7).

311. *See* Kentucky v. Graham, 473 U.S. 159, 167 n.4 (1985) (observing that "[i]n many cases, the complaint will not clearly specify whether officials are sued personally, in their official capacity, or both. 'The course of proceedings' in such cases typically will indicate the nature of the liability sought to be imposed.") (quoting Brandon v. Holt, 469 U.S. 464, 469 (1985)).

312. 817 P.2d 493 (Ariz. Ct. App. 1991).

313. The court defined the "repercussions" as follows:

the court rejected a requirement that plaintiffs plead that they are suing a defendant in his or her personal or individual capacity.[314]

Viewing the strict pleading approach as derived, in part, from the jurisdictional requirements of the Eleventh Amendment, the Arizona court refused to impose a similar requirement on state court § 1983 plaintiffs.

> [A] plaintiff should allege specifically the capacity in which he is suing the official. Such specificity both relieves courts from the difficulty inherent in interpreting an ambiguous complaint and gives the defendant clear notice of his possible personal liability for damages. We decline to hold, however, that failure to allege specifically official or personal capacity will be the death knell of a § 1983 action or that an allegation of capacity, standing alone, is determinative of this issue. Such a conclusion would result in a harsh elevation of form over substance.[315]

Instead, the court applied an "interpretive" approach, which it found supported by the Supreme Court's decision in *Brandon v. Holt*.[316] Following this approach, the state court reviewed the pleadings and the course of the proceedings to determine that the case before it was a § 1983 personal capacity suit.[317]

> The plaintiff in a § 1983 action can recover monetary damages, including punitive damages, only against a defendant named in his personal capacity. Balanced against that right of recovery, however, is the right of a defendant named in his personal capacity to assert a defense of qualified or absolute immunity, a defense not available to one named in his official capacity.

Id. at 497 (citation omitted).

314. *Id.* at 497.

315. *Id.* The court also relied on Ariz. R. Civ. P. 9(a), which limits required allegations of capacity to those going to jurisdiction. *Id.* at 497 n.3. *But cf.* Ashton v. Brown, 660 A.2d 447, 468 (Md. 1995) (distinguishing *Hafer* from suits against local governmental officials, who cannot claim an Eleventh Amendment immunity from official capacity suits, and refusing to treat § 1983 claims against the latter as individual capacity claims when they relate to actions taken to implement governmental law, policy, or custom).

316. 469 U.S. 464, 469 (1985).

317. *Carrillo*, 817 P.2d at 497.

Damages

Compensatory Damages—In *Carey v. Piphus*,[318] the Supreme Court looked to the federal principle of compensation as the source of a uniform § 1983 damage policy that would not vary from state to state. The Court also made clear that § 1983 damages are not limited to those available in 1871, when the predecessor to § 1983 was enacted, but are based on evolving federal standards.[319] Finally, the Court rejected the availability of presumed damages for procedural due process violations.[320]

Under federal principles, a broad range of damages may be awarded in § 1983 cases,[321] including damages for mental and emotional distress.[322] In *Memphis Community School District v. Stachura*,[323] however, the Court rejected the availability of presumed damages to supplement § 1983 damage awards but permitted such damages as a substitute when traditional damages are difficult to prove.[324] Thus, in the typical § 1983 case, a plaintiff may not recover damages for the value of the constitutional right itself.

The damage policies in § 1983 actions are based on the common law but are not dependent upon the law of the forum state.[325] For example, the Sixth Circuit has held that the federal doctrine of joint and several liability

---

318. 435 U.S. 247 (1978).
319. *Id.* at 257-59.
320. *Id.* at 260-64.
321. State law, on the other hand, governs the survival of § 1983 claims, *see* Robertson v. Wegmann, 436 U.S. 584 (1978), and the damage policies applicable to § 1983 survival and wrongful death claims, unlike the typical § 1983 damages policies, involve a certain amount of borrowing from the law of the forum state. For a detailed discussion of § 1983 survival and wrongful death issues, *see* Steven H. Steinglass, *Wrongful Death Actions and Section 1983*, 60 Ind. L.J. 559 (1985) [hereinafter Steinglass, *Wrongful Death Actions*]; *see also* Steinglass, Section 1983 Litigation, *supra* note 7, ch. 21.
322. Carey, 435 U.S. at 263-64 & n.20.
323. 477 U.S. 299 (1986).
324. *Id.* at 310-11.
325. *See* Basista v. Weir, 340 F.2d 74, 86 (3d Cir. 1965) ("We believe that the benefits of the [Civil Rights] Acts were intended to be uniform throughout the United States, that the protection to the individual to be afforded by them was not intended by Congress to differ from state to state, and that the amount of damages to be recovered by the injured individual was not to vary because of the law of the state in which the federal court suit was brought.").

applies to § 1983 claims.[326] Likewise, most federal courts apply a federal, not a state, collateral source doctrine to determine whether reductions should be made to § 1983 damage awards.[327] State courts have generally followed federal policies to determine the damage policies applicable to § 1983 claims.[328]

Punitive Damages—Punitive damages are available in § 1983 litigation when defendants act intentionally or with reckless or callous disregard for plaintiffs' rights.[329] Furthermore, under federal common law principles, punitive damages are available against individual defendants even absent actual damages,[330] and it is the responsibility of the jury to determine eligibility for and amount of punitive damages under the traditional civil burden

---

326. Weeks v. Chaboudy, 984 F.2d 185, 188-89 (6th Cir. 1993) (holding that there is a federal rule of joint and several liability in § 1983 cases and reversing the apportionment of liability for compensatory damages among the defendant and other prison personnel who were not parties to the action).
327. *See* Linda L. House, *Section 1983 and the Collateral Source Rule*, 40 Clev. St. L. Rev. 101, 112-13 (1992).
328. *See, e.g.*, Sundholm v. City of Bettendorf, 389 N.W.2d 849 (Iowa 1986) (following federal law to permit punitive damages under § 1983 despite the absence of actual damages); Janda v. City of Detroit, 437 N.W.2d 326 (Mich. Ct. App. 1989) (applying federal standards to affirm a § 1983 award of punitive damages despite the unavailability of punitive damages for punishment under state law); Rogers v. Saylor, 760 P.2d 232 (Or. 1988) (rejecting the application of the $100,000 damage ceiling of the Oregon Tort Claims Act and the immunity of governmental employees from awards of punitive damages to § 1983 actions); Orr v. Crowder, 315 S.E.2d 593 (W. Va. 1983) (following federal law to uphold a § 1983 damages award for mental anguish absent physical injury), *cert. denied*, 469 U.S. 981 (1984); Thompson v. Village of Hales Corners, 340 N.W.2d 704 (Wis. 1983) (holding that the state's $25,000 damage ceiling on municipal liability does not apply to § 1983 actions under principles of federal law).
329. *See* Smith v. Wade, 461 U.S. 30, 51 (1983) ("[R]eckless or callous disregard for the plaintiff's rights, as well as intentional violations of federal law, should be sufficient to trigger a jury's consideration of the appropriateness of punitive damages.").
330. *See* King v. Macri, 993 F.2d 294, 297 (2d Cir. 1993); Erwin v. County of Manitowoc, 872 F.2d 1292, 1299 (7th Cir. 1989); Wilson v. Taylor, 658 F.2d 1021, 1023 (5th Cir. 1981); Basista v. Weir, 340 F.2d 74, 87-88 (3d Cir. 1965).

of proof: the preponderance of the evidence standard.[331] Municipalities, however, are not subject to § 1983 claims for punitive damages.[332]

A number of states have limited the availability of punitive damages by requiring the showing of actual malice[333] or by requiring the plaintiff to satisfy the state's clear and convincing standard of proof.[334] A few states have reduced the role of the jury by limiting the jury's function to determining whether the plaintiff is entitled to an award of punitive damages but leaving determination of the amount of such an award to the judge.[335]

There are substantial questions as to the validity of these state punitive damages policies under state law[336] and as to whether they apply to § 1983 and other federal causes of action as a matter of state law, but, assuming their validity and applicability, there are also substantial questions as to whether federal law permits states to apply such policies to § 1983 claims.

One relatively easy issue involves the standards for awarding punitive damages under § 1983. Although the Supreme Court has not directly addressed the issue, the damages available in § 1983 actions are part of

---

331. *See* Bird v. Figel, 725 F. Supp. 406 (N.D. Ind. 1989).
332. *See* City of Newport v. Fact Concerts, Inc., 453 U.S. 247 (1981). The Court in Fact Concerts left a small opening for the award of punitive damages against municipalities under § 1983 in an "extreme situation where the taxpayers are directly responsible for perpetuating an outrageous abuse of constitutional rights." *Id.* at 267 n.29. Courts have generally rejected the availability of § 1983 punitive damage awards against municipalities even in egregious circumstances. *See* STEINGLASS, SECTION 1983 LITIGATION, *supra* note 7, § 16.3(c) n.51.
333. *See, e.g.*, Ohio Rev. Code Ann. § 2315.21(C) (Anderson 1991).
334. *See* Pacific Mut. Life Ins. Co. v. Haslip, 499 U.S. 1, 23 n.11 (1991) (citing and speaking favorably of state statutes that require a higher burden of proof for punitive damages awards).
335. *See, e.g.*, Kan. Stat. Ann. § 60-3702 (Supp. 1992); Ohio Rev. Code Ann. § 2315.21(C) (Anderson 1991).
336. *See, e.g.*, Zoppo v. Homestead Ins. Co., 644 N.E.2d 397 (Ohio 1994) (holding that the Ohio statute giving the judge, not the jury, responsibility for determining the amount of punitive damages to be awarded violates the civil right to trial by jury guarantee of Art. I, § 5 of the Ohio Constitution), *cert. denied*, 116 S.Ct. 56 (1995). *But see* Smith v. Printup, 866 P.2d 985 (Kan. 1993) (upholding the validity under the state constitution of the statute that required the judge to determine the amount of punitive damages).

the federal definition of the § 1983 cause of action.[337] Consequently, state courts generally rely upon uniform federal, not state, policies to determine the damages available under § 1983, and state courts should apply federal punitive damages standards rather than the state statutory standards to § 1983 claims.

The more difficult federal issues involve the change in the burden of proof and the reduction in the role of the jury. Federal courts entertaining diversity actions treat the burden of proof as part of the definition of the element of damages and apply state policies under the *Erie* doctrine.[338] State courts, however, have been reluctant to abandon state punitive damages policies. For example, until recently, the Louisiana courts did not permit punitive damages in § 1983 cases,[339] while the Colorado Supreme Court has upheld the application of the state's unusual "beyond a reasonable doubt" burden of proof to § 1983 claims.[340] The better view, however, is that the available damages are part of the § 1983 remedy and that state courts entertaining § 1983 claims are required to provide the full range of damages that are available under federal standards. Because the burden of proof is bound up with the element of damages, state courts entertaining § 1983 claims should apply the traditional preponderance of the evidence burden of proof rather than the state clear and convincing standard to punitive damage claims.[341] Moreover, the use of "outcome determinative" state policies to govern the availability of punitive damages in state court § 1983 litigation is inconsistent with the federal interest in "intrastate uniformity" and the "reverse *Erie*" principle that the Supreme Court applied to state court § 1983 cases in *Felder v. Casey*.[342]

---

337. *See supra* note 151-55 and accompanying text.
338. *See, e.g.*, Galjour v. General American Tank Car Corp., 746 F. Supp. 1093 (E.D. La. 1991) (treating the burden of proof on punitive damages as a substantive issue governed by state law in diversity cases). *Cf.* Palmer v. Hoffman, 318 U.S. 109, 117 (1943) (holding that the burden of proof in diversity cases is allocated according to state law).
339. *See* Ricard v. State, 390 So. 2d 882 (La. 1980) (holding that punitive damages are not available in § 1983 actions in the Louisiana courts). *But see* Booze v. City of Alexandria, 637 So.2d 91 (La. 1994) (overruling *Ricard* and permitting punitive damages in § 1983 actions in the Louisiana courts).
340. *See* Boulder Valley Sch. Dist. R-2 v. Price, 805 P.2d 1085 (Colo. 1991).
341. *See* Steinglass, Section 1983 Litigation, *supra* note 7, § 16.3(c).
342. 487 U.S. 131 (1988); *see also supra* notes 172-76 and accompanying text.

The removal from the jury of the power to determine the amount of punitive damages would raise substantial Seventh Amendment issues in federal court,[343] but the Seventh Amendment is not applicable to state courts.[344] Nonetheless, federal statutory causes of action often have their own jury trial guarantees,[345] and the right to trial by jury in § 1983 cases may come from § 1983 itself.

Although there is no explicit trial by jury provision in § 1983, it is likely that the members of the 42d Congress, which enacted the predecessor to § 1983, contemplated that juries would hear such cases. The language in § 1 of the Civil Rights Act of 1871 providing that defendants shall "be liable to the party injured in any *action at law*"[346] suggests that Congress was thinking about legal actions to which the jury trial guarantee attached. Moreover, in response to a question about how to measure damages under a different section of the 1871 act, a member of the House responded as follows: "Precisely the same as you do in an action of tort. The question of damages is a question in the sound discretion of the jury."[347] Although this seems like slender support for finding a statutory right to jury in § 1983 itself, the Supreme Court has not required an

---

343. *See* McKinnon v. City of Berwyn, 750 F.2d 1383, 1392 (7th Cir. 1984) (reversing a district court's remittitur of punitive damages, without option of a new trial, in a § 1983 case, and noting that the "Seventh Amendment reserves the determination of damages, in jury trials within its scope, to the jury"); *cf.* Defender Indus., Inc. v. Northwestern Mut. Life Ins. Co., 938 F.2d 502, 507 (4th Cir. 1991) (*en banc*) ("An assessment by a jury of the amount of punitive damages is an inherent and fundamental element of the common-law right to trial by jury."). *But cf.* Tull v. United States, 481 U.S. 412 (1987) (holding that the Seventh Amendment does not guarantee a jury trial to assess civil penalties under a federal statute).

344. *See* Walker v. Sauvinet, 92 U.S. 90, 92-93 (1876).

345. For example, under the cause of action for intentional employment discrimination, 42 U.S.C. § 1981a (Supp. III 1991), created by the Civil Rights Act of 1991, Pub. L. No. 102-166, § 102, 105 Stat. 1071, 1072-73 (1991), the right to trial by jury extends to any party in a case in which "a complaining party seeks compensatory or punitive damages." *See* 42 U.S.C. § 1981a(c) (Supp. III 1991).

346. Civil Rights Act of 1871, ch. 22, § 1, 17 Stat. 13 (1871) (emphasis added) (current version at 42 U.S.C. § 1983 (1988)).

347. CONG. GLOBE, 42d Cong., 1st Sess. 804 (1871) (statement of Rep. Poland).

explicit statutory provision to extend the jury right to state court litigation of other federal causes of action.[348]

Even if a federal statutory right to trial by jury extended to state court § 1983 litigation, courts would have to determine which attributes of the federal right applied in state courts. The Supreme Court has not addressed these issues in the context of § 1983 actions, but it has provided some guidance in FELA litigation in which it has not required state courts to follow the federal jury unanimity policy[349] but has treated the allocation of responsibility between judge and jury as a matter of federal law.[350]

No-Exhaustion Policy

In *Patsy v. Board of Regents*,[351] the Supreme Court applied a general no-exhaustion policy to § 1983 actions and held that § 1983 plaintiffs need not exhaust state administrative remedies. A number of state courts, however, initially viewed the *Patsy* no-exhaustion policy as only applicable in federal courts,[352] but in *Felder v. Casey*,[353] the Court applied the no-exhaustion policy to state court § 1983 actions in the course of holding that state courts could not apply notice of claim requirements to § 1983 claims. Most state courts have recognized that *Felder* goes beyond notice of claim requirements and construed it to bar the use of exhaustion of administrative remedy requirements in state court § 1983 litigation.[354]

---

348. The right to trial by jury in state court FELA cases is not derived from an explicit provision of the federal statute but from the Court's conclusion that "the right to trial by jury . . . is part and parcel" of the FELA remedy. Bailey v. Central Vt. Ry., 319 U.S. 350, 354 (1943); *see also* Rogers v. Missouri Pacific R.R., 352 U.S. 500, 508-09 (1957) (discussing the history of the proposed FELA provision on the right to trial by jury and the congressional concern that the factual issue of employer fault be decided by juries not judges). The only statutory reference to the jury in the FELA statute is in 45 U.S.C. § 53 (1988), which deals with the role of the jury in reducing damage awards based on the comparative negligence of the employee. For a further discussion of these issues, *see* Steinglass, Section 1983 Litigation, *supra* note 7, ch. 14.
349. *See* Minneapolis & St. Louis R.R. v. Bombolis, 241 U.S. 211 (1916).
350. *See* Dice v. Akron, Canton & Youngstown R.R., 342 U.S. 359 (1952).
351. 457 U.S. 496 (1982).
352. *See* Steinglass, Section 1983 Litigation, *supra* note 7, § 17.3(b) n.34.
353. 487 U.S. 131 (1988).
354. *See* Steinglass, Section 1983 Litigation, *supra* note 7, § 17.3(b) n.51.10.

The *Patsy-Felder* no-exhaustion policy must be contrasted with *Parratt v. Taylor*[355] in which the Court held that in cases involving random and unauthorized actions, states can meet their obligation to provide procedural due process by having adequate postdeprivation remedies.[356] *Parratt*, however, does not impose an exhaustion requirement with which plaintiffs must comply before filing § 1983 suits. Rather, it is an interpretation of the requirements of procedural due process and a recognition that in limited circumstances in which it is not feasible to provide predeprivation remedies,[357] the state may meet its constitutional obligation by providing adequate postdeprivation remedies.

Despite the general no-exhaustion policy applicable to § 1983 claims, there are limited circumstances in which Congress has authorized exhaustion of administrative remedies requirements. For example, in § 1983 suits by prisoners, the Civil Rights of Institutionalized Persons Act, [358] as amended by the Violent Crime Control and Law Enforcement Act of 1994,[359] permits courts to stay judicial proceedings for up to 180 days while prisoners use prison grievance procedures that are "plain, speedy and effective."[360] The act does not expressly apply to state courts, but state courts have treated it as applicable.[361]

---

355. 451 U.S. 527 (1981).

356. *See also* Hudson v. Palmer, 468 U.S. 517 (1984) (applying the *Parratt* requirement to intentional acts). *But see* Logan v. Zimmerman Brush Co., 455 U.S. 422 (1982) (holding *Parratt* inapplicable to established state policies).

357. See Zinermon v. Burch, 494 U.S. 113 (1990) (limiting *Parratt* to cases in which it is not feasible to provide predeprivation remedies). *But see* Albright v. Oliver, 510 U.S. 266, 283-86 (1994) (Kennedy, J., concurring) (arguing that *Parratt* should not be limited to procedural due process cases).

358. Pub. L. No. 96-247, 94 Stat. 352 (1980) (current version at 42 U.S.C. § 1997 (1988)).

359. Pub. L. No. 103-322, 108 Stat. 1796, 1833-34, § 20416 (1994).

360. 42 U.S.C. § 1997e(a) (1).

361. *See* Casteel v. Vaade, 481 N.W.2d 476 (Wis. 1992) (rejecting a § 1983 exhaustion of administrative remedies requirement that does not comply with the standards of the Civil Rights of Institutionalized Persons Act). For a discussion of the applicability of this requirement to state court § 1983 litigation, *see* STEINGLASS, SECTION 1983 LITIGATION, *supra* note 7, § 17.4(a).

Statutes of Limitations

Section 1983 does not contain a statute of limitations, but the Supreme Court has applied the borrowing principles authorized by 42 U.S.C. § 1988,[362] the civil rights choice of law statute,[363] to fill this gap in federal law with state statutes of limitations. Under *Wilson v. Garcia*,[364] courts must select a single statute of limitations for § 1983 claims in each state, and this is the personal injury limitations period.[365] Some states, however, have multiple limitations periods for personal injury actions, but in *Owens v. Okure*,[366] the Supreme Court held that in such cases the relevant period is found in the "general or residual statute for personal injury actions."[367]

The Supreme Court has not addressed whether the same federal principles that apply to the selection of § 1983 statutes of limitations in federal

---

362. 42 U.S.C. § 1988 (1988). For a discussion of this complex statute, see STEINGLASS, *Wrongful Death Actions*, *supra* note 321, at 612-25.

363. Although § 1988, by its terms, appears to be addressed to federal courts, the Supreme Court has treated it as applicable to state courts. *See* Sullivan v. Little Hunting Park, Inc., 396 U.S. 229, 240-41 (1969); *see also* STEINGLASS, SECTION 1983 LITIGATION, *supra* note 7, § 10.5. *Cf.* Maine v. Thiboutot, 448 U.S. 1 (1980) (applying the attorney fees provision of 42 U.S.C. § 1988 to state court § 1983 litigation).

364. 471 U.S. 261 (1985).

365. *Id.* at 279-80.

366. 488 U.S. 235 (1989). The *Owens* Court also rejected the use of the statute of limitations for intentional torts. *Id.* at 249.

367. *Id.* at 250. The *Owens* Court, however, reaffirmed the Court's earlier rejection of the residual limitations periods, while allowing the use of the residual *personal injury* limitations period.

> Our decision today is fully consistent with *Wilson*'s rejection of a state residual, or "catch-all," limitations provision as the appropriate one for § 1983 actions. In *Wilson*, we rejected recourse to such provisions in the first instance, a position we continue to embrace. Courts should resort to residual statutes of limitations only where state law provides multiple statutes of limitations for personal injury actions and the residual one embraces, either explicitly or by judicial construction, unspecified personal injury actions.

Id. at 250 n.12.

court apply in state courts, but most state courts have assumed that they do,[368] and this position seems correct.[369]

Preclusion

Federal courts are required to give state court judgments the same preclusive effect that state courts give them,[370] and this principle is applicable to § 1983 litigation.[371] Thus, both state and federal courts entertaining § 1983 actions look to state law to determine the preclusive effect of prior state court judgments. When prior judgments are rendered by federal courts on the other hand, the relevant preclusion policies come from federal law. The principle that the court rendering a judgment determines the scope of the judgment has guided federal courts in developing a federal law of preclusion,[372] and federal law requires state courts to give federal judgments the same full faith and credit that federal courts give them.[373]

---

368. *See Felder*, 487 U.S. at 154 (White, J., concurring), and cases cited.
369. *Cf.* Engel v. Davenport, 271 U.S. 33 (1926) (barring states from applying shorter statutes of limitations to FELA claims). *But see* Susan N. Herman, *Beyond Parity: Section 1983 Actions and the State Courts*, 54 Brooklyn L. Rev. 1057, 1082 n. 106 (1989) (suggesting that § 1988 does not apply in state courts and that states may adopt longer statutes of limitations for § 1983 actions than those applicable in federal court).
370. *See* 28 U.S.C. § 1738 (1988).
371. *See* Migra v. Warren City Sch. Dist., 465 U.S. 75 (1984) (claim preclusion); Allen v. McCurry, 449 U.S. 90 (1980) (issue preclusion).
372. *See* Restatement (Second) of Judgments § 87 (1982) ("Federal law determines the effects under the rules of res judicata of a judgment of a federal court.") *See generally* Stephen B. Burbank, *Interjurisdictional Preclusion, Full Faith and Credit and Federal Common Law: A General Approach*, 71 Cornell L. Rev. 733 (1986).
373. *See* Limbach v. Hooven & Allison Co., 466 U.S. 353, 361-63 (1984) (treating the collateral estoppel effect of a prior federal court ruling in state court as governed by federal law); *see also* International Bd. of Electrical Workers v. Hawaiian Tel. Co., 713 P.2d 943, 955 n.17 (Haw. 1986) ("In a subsequent state court action, the collateral estoppel effect of a federal law ruling in a prior federal court adjudication is a question of federal law."); Veiser v. Armstrong, 688 P.2d 796, 799 (Okla. 1984) ("Federal law governs both the preclusive and res judicata effect of the prior federal-court judgment. . . .").

Some state courts, however, look to their own law of preclusion, rather than federal law, when determining the preclusive effect of prior federal court judgments. Usually, this does not result in different outcomes, but in states that define "claim" more narrowly than federal law, this difference can be significant.[374]

Preclusion issues often arise in § 1983 litigation when federal court plaintiffs fail to take full advantage of the doctrine of supplemental jurisdiction by not joining potential state law claims with their § 1983 claims.[375] When federal courts refuse to exercise jurisdiction over state law claims, most state courts entertain the state law claims.[376] On the other hand, when plaintiffs do not join state law claims that are within the supplemental jurisdiction of the federal courts, both state and federal doctrines of res judicata (or claim preclusion) generally bar state courts from hearing the state law claim.

---

374. *See, e.g.*, Lamartiniere v. Allstate Ins. Co., 415 So. 2d 499 (La. Ct. App.) (narrowly defining a "cause of action" for purposes of res judicata and permitting plaintiffs to bifurcate their state and federal claims), *writ denied*, 420 So. 2d 442 (La. 1982); Cranwill v. Donahue, 426 N.E.2d 337 (Ill. App. Ct. 1981) (relying on state definition of cause of action to permit litigation of pendent claims dismissed by federal court). *But see* Reeder v. Succession of Palmer, 623 So.2d 1268, 1271 (La. 1993) (relying on the *Restatement (Second) of Judgments* and recognizing that the preclusive effect of a federal court judgment rendered by a federal court exercising federal question jurisdiction is governed by the federal law of res judicata), *cert. denied*, 114 S.Ct. 1191 (1994).
375. *See supra* note 31.
376. *See, e.g.*, Terrell v. City of Bessemer, 406 So. 2d 337 (Ala. 1981); DeLaurentis v. City of New Haven, 597 A.2d 807 (Conn. 1991); *see also* Rennie v. Freeway Transp., 656 P.2d 919, 924 n.8 (Or. 1982), and cases cited. *Cf.* Toomey v. Blum, 426 N.E.2d 181 (N.Y. 1981) (entertaining claim after refusal of federal court to decide § 1983 claim based on the Eleventh Amendment). *But see* Mattson v. City of Costa Mesa, 164 Cal. Rptr. 913 (Ct. App. 1980) (barring a state court plaintiff who had earlier proceeded to trial in federal court on federal claims after the federal court declined to exercise pendent jurisdiction over a state law claim from bringing such state law claim in state court); City of Los Angeles v. Superior Court, 149 Cal. Rptr. 320, 324 (Ct. App. 1978) (observing that "a litigant cannot avoid the impact of the rule against splitting causes of action by choosing for his first foray a tribunal of limited jurisdiction").

When federal courts lack the power to exercise supplemental jurisdiction over state law claims, however, state courts should not refuse to entertain the state law claims. For example, federal courts may not exercise supplemental jurisdiction over certain state law claims as a result of the Supreme Court's decision in *Pennhurst State School and Hospital v. Halderman*[377] erecting an Eleventh Amendment bar to the litigation of state claims for injunctive relief against state officials. Accordingly, plaintiffs facing a potential *Pennhurst* problem in federal court sometimes bifurcate their claims and file their state claims in state court and their federal claims in federal court. In such circumstances, state courts should not require federal court litigants to go through the futile task of attempting to join their state law claims in federal court.

On the other hand, when federal courts have the power to entertain supplemental state law claims, state courts are generally (and appropriately) reluctant to assume that federal courts will exercise their discretion and decline to hear the state law claims. Thus, state courts in such cases will often require plaintiffs either to attempt to join the state law claims in federal court or to make a strong showing that it would have been futile to do so.[378] Although some state courts have excused plaintiffs who failed even to attempt to join state law claims in earlier federal court litigation by deciding that the federal court would not have exercised jurisdiction over the state law claims,[379] plaintiffs who wish to preserve access to a federal

377. 465 U.S. 89 (1984).

378. *See, e.g.*, Terrell v. City of Bessemer, 406 So. 2d 337 (Ala. 1981); Merry v. Coast Community College Dist., 158 Cal. Rptr. 603, 607-08 (Ct. App. 1979) (concluding that "since it clearly appears that the federal court would have declined to exercise its pendent jurisdiction to adjudicate plaintiff's state claims had they been raised, the . . . [federal court] summary judgment is not a bar to the maintenance of the instant action"); Anderson v. Phoenix Investment Counsel of Boston, Inc., 440 N.E.2d 1164, 1168-69 (Mass. 1982) (following the *Restatement (Second) of Judgments* § 25, comment e, illustration 10 (1982), and requiring state court to dismiss state law claim unless it is clear that the federal court would not have had pendent jurisdiction or, having jurisdiction, clearly would have declined to exercise it as a matter of discretion); Rennie v. Freeway Transp., 656 P.2d 919, 924 (Or. 1982).

379. *See, e.g.*, City and County of Denver v. Block 173 Assocs., 814 P.2d 824 (Colo. 1991) (relying on the consistent refusal of federal courts to exercise pendent jurisdiction over state law claims after the dismissal of federal claims to refuse to apply claim preclusion to bar a state law claim after a federal

forum without running the risk of losing their state law claims should attempt to join those claims in the federal court proceeding.

Federal courts do not adhere to the requirements of mutuality, and the Supreme Court has permitted both the offensive and defensive use of collateral estoppel (or issue preclusion).[380] Consequently, federal courts entertaining § 1983 actions have precluded permitted nonparties to earlier litigation to take advantage of issue preclusion and have precluded parties (to the earlier litigation) from relitigating issues that were resolved against them.[381]

In states that have not abandoned the doctrine of mutuality, nonparties to earlier litigation may not use findings of fact or conclusions of law against parties from earlier litigation in whose case both legal and factual issues were resolved.[382] When the earlier litigation was in federal court, however, state courts must give the federal court judgment the same preclusive effect that federal courts would give it. Thus, some state courts may be required by *federal* law to ignore their own preclusion policies and apply federal issue preclusion policies under which nonparties may take advantage of earlier judgments rendered against their adversaries.[383]

---

court dismissed factually identical federal claim at summary judgment); Pope v. City of Atlanta, 240 S.E.2d 241, 243 (Ga. 1977) (refusing to apply claim preclusion to state law claim after concluding that federal court would "most likely" not have exercised pendent jurisdiction), *cert. denied*, 440 U.S. 936 (1979).

380. *See* Parklane Hosiery Co. v. Shore, 439 U.S. 322 (1979) (permitting offensive use of issue preclusion); Blonder-Tongue Laboratories, Inc. v. University of Illinois Foundation, 402 U.S. 313 (1971) (permitting defensive use of issue preclusion).

381. *See, e.g.*, McDuffie v. Estelle, 935 F.2d 682 (5th Cir. 1991) (applying offensive collateral estoppel against prison officials on some, but not all, § 1983 claims).

382. *See generally* Michael J. Waggoner, *Fifty Years of Bernhard v. Bank of America Is Enough: Collateral Estoppel Should Require Mutuality But Res Judicata Should Not*, 12 Rev. Litig. 391 (1993); Janet Schmitt Ellis, *Nonmutuality: Taking the Fairness Out of Collateral Esptoppel*, 13 Ind. L.Rev 563 (1980).

383. *See, e.g.*, Edwards v. First Fed. Sav. & Loan Ass'n, 696 P.2d 484 (N.M. Ct. App. 1985) (permitting defensive use of collateral estoppel of a federal judgment despite state adherence to mutuality).

Attorney Fees

Prevailing plaintiffs in § 1983 actions are entitled to attorney fees as a result of the Civil Rights Attorney's Fees Awards Act of 1976,[384] which added fee-authorizing language to 42 U.S.C. § 1988.[385] The Fees Act was adopted to overrule *Alyeska Pipeline Service Co. v. Wilderness Society*,[386] a Supreme Court case which held that federal courts did not have an inherent power to award fees to prevailing parties under a private attorneys general theory. The language in the act, however, is not limited to federal court litigation, and in *Maine v. Thiboutot,*[387] the Supreme Court characterized the availability of attorney fees as an "integral" part of the § 1983 remedy[388] and applied the Fees Act to state court § 1983 litigation.[389]

State courts have recognized the applicability of the Fees Act to state court § 1983 litigation and have generally followed federal standards in applying the act.[390] Thus, in addressing the availability of fees, most state

---

384. Pub. L. No. 94-559, 90 Stat. 2641 (1976).
385. 42 U.S.C. § 1988(b) (Supp. 1994) ("In any action or proceeding to enforce a provision of sections 1981, 1981a, 1982, 1983, 1985, and 1986 of this title, title IX of Public Law 92-318, the Religious Freedom Restoration Act of 1993, title VI of the Civil Rights Act of 1964, or section 13981 of this title, the court, in its discretion, may allow the prevailing party, other than the United States, a reasonable attorney's fee as part of the costs, except that in any action brought against a judicial officer for an act or omission taken in such officer's judicial capacity such officer shall not be held liable for any costs, including attorney's fees, unless such action was clearly in excess of such officer's jurisdiction."). The Fees Act was amended by the Federal Courts Improvement Act of 1996, Pub. L. No. 104-317, § 309(c), 110 Stat. 3847 (1996), to limit the availability of attorney fees in cases against judicial officers.
386. 421 U.S. 240 (1975).
387. 448 U.S. 1 (1980).
388. *Id.* at 11.
389. For a discussion of the application of the Fees Act in state courts, *see* STEINGLASS, SECTION 1983 LITIGATION, *supra* note 7, §§ 22.3, 22.4.
390. *See, e.g.*, Ferdinand v. City of Fairbanks, 599 P.2d 122, 125 (Alaska 1979) (holding that "federal guidelines appl[y] in ascertaining an appropriate fee award"); International Soc'y for Krishna Consciousness v. Colorado State Fair and Indus. Exposition Comm'n, 673 P.2d 368 (Colo. 1983); Johnson v. Blum, 448 N.E.2d 449 (N.Y. 1983); Thompson v. Village of Hales Corners, 340 N.W.2d 704 (Wis. 1983).

courts have followed federal standards under which prevailing plaintiffs are presumptively entitled to fee awards, except in rare cases in which defendants can point to special circumstances that justify the denial of fees.[391] Likewise, state courts have generally followed federal standards in determining the amount of fee awards.[392]

State courts have also been willing to award fees to plaintiffs who prevailed on state law claims that were joined with substantial federal claims,[393] although some state courts have been uncomfortable with the prospect of doing so when state law does not authorize fee awards.[394]

---

391. *See, e.g.*, Henderson v. District of Columbia, 493 A.2d 982 (D.C. 1985); O'Connors v. Helfgott, 481 A.2d 388 (R.I. 1984); Jacobsen v. City of Seattle, 658 P.2d 653 (Wash. 1983).
392. *See, e.g.*, Henderson v. District of Columbia, *supra*; Holden Arboretum v. City of Kirtland, 483 N.E.2d 167 (Ohio Ct. App. 1984).
393. *See, e.g.*, Davis v. Everett, 443 So.2d 1232 (Ala. 1983); Allison v. Board of County Comm'rs of Johnson County, 737 P.2d 6 (Kan. 1987); Crane v. Commissioner of Pub. Welfare, 400 Mass. 46, 507 N.E.2d 751 (Mass. 1987); Stratos v. Department of Pub. Welfare, 439 N.E.2d 778 (Mass. 1982); Thomasel v. Perales, 585 N.E.2d 359 (N.Y. 1991); Doe v. Cuddy, 487 N.E.2d 914 (Ohio Ct. App. 1985); International Ass'n of Machinists v. Affleck, 504 A.2d 468 (R.I. 1986); Lorenc v. Call, 789 P.2d 46 (Utah Ct. App.), *cert. denied*, 795 P.2d 1138 (Utah 1990). *Cf.* Filipino Accountants v. State Bd. of Accounting, 204 Cal. Rptr. 913 (Ct. App. 1984) (applying federal standards to award fees in § 1981 action to party who prevailed on state grounds). For a discussion of the availability of fees to § 1983 plaintiffs who prevail on state law claims, *see* Steinglass, Section 1983 Litigation, *supra* note 7, ch. 23.
394. *See, e.g.*, Still v. Personnel Bd. of Jefferson Co., 406 So.2d 860 (Ala. 1981), *cert. denied*, 455 U.S. 1020 (1982); Gumbhir v. Kansas State Bd. of Pharmacy, 646 P.2d 1078 (Kan. 1982), *cert. denied*, 459 U.S. 1103 (1983); Jackson v. Inhabitants of the Town of Searsport, 456 A.2d 852 (Me. 1983), *cert. denied*, 464 U.S. 825 (1983); Oregon State Police Officers Ass'n, Inc. v. State of Oregon, 783 P.2d 7 (Or. 1989), *cert. denied*, 498 U.S. 810 (1990).

    State courts may refuse to award fees to plaintiffs who prevail on state law claims when the joined constitutional claims are wholly insubstantial, *see* County Executive of Prince George's County v. Doe, 479 A.2d 352 (Md. 1984), or when the particular constitutional claim cannot be raised under § 1983, *see* Dennis v. State of Nebraska, 451 N.W.2d 676 (Neb. 1990), *rev'd on other grounds*, 498 U.S. 439 (1991), but some state courts confuse the question of "substantiality" with the merits of the constitutionally based fee claim. *See, e.g.*, Slawik v. State, 480 A.2d 636 (Del. 1984).

State courts have approved fee awards in a number of circumstances in which federal courts either have abstained or probably would have applied an abstention or other door-closing doctrine.[395]

Removal

Given the liberal federal question removal statute,[396] state court defendants who prefer to defend § 1983 claims in federal court can almost always remove such cases, and they are increasingly doing so.[397]

Removal of state court § 1983 cases is not available when the state court defendant fails to meet the timeliness and other procedural require-

---

395. *See, e.g.*, Lucero v. Municipal Court, 19 Cal. Rptr.2d 143 (Ct. App. 1993) (affirming an award of attorney fees in a § 1983 suit for declaratory and injunctive relief successfully brought by the owner of adult movie theaters to enjoin criminal prosecutions under an ordinance limiting the location of adult entertainment businesses), *ordered not officially published* (Cal. Aug. 22, 1993), *cert. denied*, 510 U.S. 1045 (1994); Robinson v. City of Omaha, 495 N.W.2d 281 (Neb. 1993) (holding that a plaintiff who filed a state court suit presenting only a state law claim to the state courts after a federal court Pullman abstention is a prevailing party and entitled to a fee award under § 1988). *Cf.* Crane v. Commissioner of Pub. Welfare, 400 Mass. 46, 507 N.E.2d 751 (Mass. 1987); Stratos v. Department of Pub. Welfare, 439 N.E.2d 778 (Mass. 1982) (authorizing a fee award to plaintiffs who obtained prospective relief under § 1983 in federal court and retroactive relief under state law in state court).

396. 28 U.S.C. § 1441(a) (1988) (permitting defendants to remove federal question cases to federal court if the action could have originally been filed in federal court). *See generally* Dorsey v. City of Detroit, 858 F.2d 338 (6th Cir. 1988) (applying § 1441 to permit removal of § 1983 cases).

397. This conclusion about the increase in the removal of state court § 1983 actions is based on the author's analysis of raw statistical data from the Administrative Office of the United States Courts, from discussions with practicing attorneys throughout the country, from the increasingly frequent references to removal in federal court § 1983 opinions, and from the general increase in the number of state court cases removed under federal question removal. *Cf.* Neal Miller, *An Empirical Study of Forum Choices in Removal Cases Under Diversity and Federal Question Jurisdiction*, 41 Am. U. L. Rev. 369, 389 n.86 (1992) (documenting the increase in federal question removal).

ments of removal,[398] when less than all state court defendants join the removal petition,[399] when the defendant's conduct in the litigation constitutes a waiver of the right to remove,[400] or when the federal court "lacks subject matter jurisdiction" over the case.[401]

Because state courts are not required to follow the justiciability requirements of Article III of the United States Constitution, defendants may not remove § 1983 cases that meet state, but not federal, justiciability requirements.[402] Likewise, federal courts do not have removal jurisdiction over cases that are barred from federal court by the Eleventh Amendment.[403] When cases are removed to federal courts that lack subject matter jurisdiction, federal courts are required to remand the cases to state courts.[404]

---

398. Defendants wishing to remove state court § 1983 cases must file a notice of removal "within thirty days after receipt by the defendant, through service or otherwise, of a copy of the initial pleading . . . or within thirty days after service of summons. . . ." 28 U.S.C. § 1446(b) (1988). Under this requirement, the removal period can begin before formal service of the summons. *See* Roe v. O'Donohue, 38 F.3d 298, 304 (7th Cir. 1995) (holding that "the 30 day commences when the defendant, or its authorized agent, comes into possession of a copy of the complaint whether or not the delivery complies with the requirements of 'service.'"); *see also* ROBERT P. FAULKNER, *The Courtesy Copy Trap: Untimely Removal from State to Federal Court*, 52 MD. L. REV. 374 (1993).
399. *See* Hewitt v. City of Stanton 798 F.2d 1230, 1232 (9th Cir. 1986).
400. *See* Rothner v. City of Chicago, 879 F.2d 1402, 1412-16 (7th Cir. 1989) (discussing the waiver doctrine but expressing doubts about its status). *But see* Bullard v. American Airlines, Inc., 929 F. Supp. 1284 (W. D. Mo. 1996) (rejecting the "receipt" rule and calculating the period to remove as beginning with service of process).
401. *See* 28 U.S.C. § 1447(c) (1988).
402. *See* International Primate Protection League v. Administrators of Tulane Educ. Fund, 500 U.S. 72, 88-89 (1991) (noting that "plaintiff's lack of Article III standing would not necessarily defeat its standing in state court").
403. *See* McKay v. Boyd Constr. Co., 769 F.2d 1084, 1086-87 (5th Cir. 1985); David Nursing Home v. Michigan Dep't of Social Servs., 579 F. Supp. 285, 288 (E.D. Mich. 1984) (removal to federal court not a waiver of the Eleventh Amendment).
404. *See* 28 U.S.C. § 1447(c); *see also* Henry v. Metropolitan Sewer Dist., 922 F.2d 332 (6th Cir. 1990) (treating a § 1983 official capacity claim as a suit against the state that is barred by the Eleventh Amendment and ordering a

Conclusion

As this review of § 1983 litigation in the state courts suggests, § 1983 litigation is no longer exclusively the province of the federal courts. And that is how it should be in a system of judicial federalism. As former Supreme Court Justice William J. Brennan, Jr., himself a former state court judge, once observed, "One of the strengths of our federal system is that it provides a double source of protection for the rights of our citizens."[405] In part, this means that state courts should pay close attention to their own constitutions, but it also suggests the important role that state courts should play in enforcing federal law.

---

remand but retaining jurisdiction over the § 1983 individual capacity claim). *But see* Frances v. Wright, 19 F.3d 337 (7th Cir.) (rejecting Henry and interpreting § 1441(a) as denying a defendant the right to remove an action if it contains any claim that is barred by a state's sovereign immunity), *cert. denied*, 115 S.Ct. 204 (1994). For a further discussion of jurisdictional issues in removed § 1983 cases, *see* STEINGLASS, SECTION 1983 LITIGATION, *supra* note 7, § 24.4.

405. WILLIAM J. BRENNAN, JR., *State Constitutions and the Protection of Individual Rights*, 90 HARV. L. REV. 489, 503 (1977).

Chapter Four

Affirmative Duties of Government After *DeShaney**

Karen M. Blum

Since the Supreme Court's decision in *DeShaney v. Winnebago County Department of Social Services*,[1] a clear consensus has yet to emerge on the criteria for defining the circumstances that give rise to a constitutional duty of the state to provide protection to persons from acts of private violence. The *DeShaney* Court expressly rejected the argument

> that once the State learns that a third party poses a special danger to an identified victim, and indicates its willingness to protect the victim against that danger, a 'special relationship' arises between State and victim, giving rise to an affirmative duty, enforceable through the Due Process Clause, to render adequate protection.[2]

Although *DeShaney* may be narrowly read to limit any affirmative duty to protect to situations in which "the State takes a person into its custody and holds him there against his will,"[3] a number of lower federal courts

---

* This chapter is adapted from "DeShaney: Custody, Creation of Danger, and Culpability," which originally appeared in 27 Loy. L.A. L. Rev. 435 (1994).

1. 489 U.S. 189 (1989). Although most readers are probably familiar with the tragic facts of *DeShaney*, they bear repeating here. Four-year-old Joshua had been repeatedly beaten by his father. *Id.* at 192. The county child protection agency, which had been monitoring his case through social workers, failed to protect Joshua from his father's last beating, which left Joshua in a permanently brain-damaged state. *Id.* at 193. A majority of the Supreme Court held that nothing in the Due Process Clause of the Fourteenth Amendment creates an affirmative duty on the part of the state to "protect the life, liberty, and property of its citizens against invasion by private actors." *Id.*at 195. The Court concluded that "[a]s a general matter, . . . a State's failure to protect an individual against private violence simply does not constitute a violation of the Due Process Clause." *Id.* at 197.
2. *Id.* at 198 n.4.
3. *See, e.g.*, Youngberg v. Romeo, 457 U.S. 307 (1982) (substantive due process component of Fourteenth Amendment Due Process Clause imposes duty on state to provide for safety and medical needs of involuntarily committed

confronting the question have interpreted *DeShaney* to recognize a duty to protect outside the contexts of imprisonment and involuntary confinement in public institutions.

Plaintiffs who have successfully survived the *DeShaney* analysis have generally asserted substantive due process claims[4] based on a breach of the

---

mental patients); Estelle v. Gamble, 429 U.S. 97 (1976) (state has constitutional duty to provide adequate medical care to incarcerated prisoners); Foy v. City of Berea, 58 F.3d 227, 231 (6th Cir. 1995) ("When the state limits an individual's ability to care for himself by, for example, incarceration in a prison or involuntary confinement in a mental hospital, the Constitution does impose an affirmative duty of care and protection. There is no such affirmative duty, however, absent such restraint."); Garrett v. Gilless, 47 F.3d 1168 (Table), 1995 WL 16810, at *1 (6th Cir. Jan. 17, 1995) (holding defendants had no duty to provide police protection to victim of domestic violence and her children in absence of special relationship); Pinder v. Johnson, 54 F.3d 1169, 1175 (4th Cir. 1995) (*en banc*) ("Some sort of confinement of the injured party—incarceration, institutionalization, or the like—is needed to trigger the affirmative duty. . . . This Court has consistently read *DeShaney* to require a custodial context before any affirmative duty can arise under the Due Process Clause."); Lovins v. Lee, 53 F.3d 1208, 1210 (11th Cir. 1995) ("Attempting to escape the clear language of *DeShaney*, plaintiff argues that this case fits within the 'special relationship' exception to the general rule that the Due Process Clause does not entitle a citizen to be protected from violence at the hands of non-governmental actors. Unfortunately for plaintiff, that exception is limited to circumstances in which there is a special relationship between the government and the victim of violence or mistreatment, a circumstance that is lacking in the present case. Examples of special relationship cases include those involving incarcerated prisoners and involuntarily committed mental patients."); Souza v. Pina, 53 F.3d 423, 426 (1st Cir. 1995) ("Absent the kind of custodial relationship apparently contemplated by the Court [in *DeShaney*], the Due Process Clause does not require the state to protect citizens from 'private violence' in whatever form, including suicide.")

4. The Court has recognized three types of claims that may be asserted under the Fourteenth Amendment Due Process Clause. First, the Bill of Rights sets forth specific rights that are incorporated and made applicable to the states through the Fourteenth Amendment Due Process Clause. Zinermon v. Burch, 494 U.S. 113, 125 (1990). Second, rights exist to substantive due process and to be free from government action that is arbitrary, irrational, and wrongful, regardless of the procedure accompanying the conduct. *Id.* Third, a right to procedural fairness exists when the state acts to deprive a person of a constitutionally protected interest. *Id.*

duty to protect in one of two contexts: (1) The plaintiff was in the state's "functional custody" when harmed, or (2) the plaintiff was in a "snake-pit"[5] situation where the state created or increased the danger to which the plaintiff was exposed.[6]

This chapter examines post-*DeShaney* cases that have addressed the functional custody and snake-pit approaches to substantive due process claims. In a custody context, the examination exposes problems created by any requirement that involuntariness serve as a threshold that must be satisfied before the state has an affirmative constitutional duty to protect citizens from harm caused by private actors.[7] Although the nature of the custody may be relevant in determining the level of culpability that will be required to establish a due process claim for failure to protect, this chapter takes the position that the criterion of involuntariness should not serve as a talisman for either the duty owed or the standard of culpability applied.[8]

Separately, the noncustodial snake-pit or state-created danger cases reveal the difficulties inherent in any theory of affirmative duty based on a distinction between action and inaction.[9] It is suggested in this context that a duty to protect should be recognized when the state, by affirmative acts

5. In Bowers v. DeVito, 686 F.2d 616 (7th Cir. 1982), Judge Posner wrote that "[i]f the state puts a man in a position of danger from private persons and then fails to protect him . . . it is as much an active tortfeasor as if it had thrown him into a snake pit," *Id.* at 618.
6. Chief Justice Rehnquist, writing for the majority in *DeShaney*, suggested that the case might have been decided differently if the state had helped create the dangers that Joshua faced or had rendered Joshua more vulnerable to these dangers. *DeShaney*, 489 U.S. at 201.
7. *See infra* "The Functional Custody Case."
8. *See infra* "The Functional Custody Case."
9. Justice Brennan, dissenting in *DeShaney*, noted that "[i]n a constitutional setting that distinguishes sharply between action and inaction, one's characterization of the misconduct alleged under § 1983 may effectively decide the case." *DeShaney*, 489 U.S. at 204 (Brennan, J., dissenting). In the dissent's view, "inaction [could] be every bit as abusive of power as action. . . ." *Id.* at 212 (Brennan, J., dissenting). The distinction drawn between affirmative acts and omissions has received extensive criticism elsewhere. *See, e.g.*, Thomas A. Eaton & Michael Wells, *Governmental Inaction as a Constitutional Tort:* DeShaney *and Its Aftermath*, 66 Wash. L. Rev. 107, 109 n.9 (noting "the distinction between acts and omissions often turns on how one poses the question").

or sins of omission, creates or enhances the risk of harm confronting an individual.[10] In the snake-pit context, less emphasis should be placed on the affirmative nature of the state's acts, while rigorous scrutiny should be given to the factors of causation and culpability.[11] The latter factors better determine the ultimate finding of a breach of duty and the imposition of constitutional liability.

The Functional Custody Cases

Some plaintiffs have attempted to satisfy even the most uncompromising interpretation of *DeShaney*: that an affirmative duty to protect exists only in an involuntary custodial situation. These plaintiffs have urged the courts to expand the notion of what constitutes "custodial" beyond the strict confines of a prison or state-operated institution for the mentally ill.[12]

Foster Care Context

The most widely accepted scenario for extending the duty to protect beyond the prison or state hospital setting arises in the context of foster care. In *DeShaney,* the Court acknowledged that the situation in which the state removes a child from "free society" and places him or her in a foster home might be "sufficiently analogous to incarceration or institutionalization to give rise to an affirmative duty to protect."[13] Indeed, the lower federal courts that have ruled on this issue since *DeShaney* have uniformly recognized a constitutional right to protection from unnecessary harm on the part of foster children involuntarily placed by the state in a foster care situation.[14]

---

10. *See infra* "The Snake-Pit Cases."
11. *See infra* "The Snake-Pit Cases."
12. *See* White v. Rochford, 592 F.2d 381 (7th Cir. 1979).
13. DeShaney, 489 U.S. at 201 n.9. Prior to *DeShaney*, two circuit courts of appeals had recognized an affirmative duty under the Constitution to protect children placed by the state in foster care. *See* Taylor v. Ledbetter, 818 F.2d 791 (11th Cir. 1987) (*en banc*) (holding affirmative duty under substantive Due Process Clause to provide protection and supervision was created by the state in foster home and that duty was breached only by showing of "deliberate indifference"), *cert. denied*, 464 U.S. 864 (1983).
14. *See, e.g.,* Angela R. v. Clinton, 999 F.2d 320, 323-24 (8th Cir. 1993) (observing "class members who are foster children in the State's custody have stronger constitutional claims than abused or neglected children who have not

In *Norfleet v. Arkansas Department of Human Services,*[15] the plaintiff went on a two-day trip and left her two children with a neighbor.[16] The plaintiff's four-year-old son, who had a history of asthma problems, suffered an attack in his mother's absence.[17] A hospital treated him and gave him two different medications to take home.[18] Later, the caretaker neighbor was arrested, and the children were placed in the custody of a certified foster parent.[19] The foster parent failed to supervise or direct the taking of the medication, and the boy suffered another attack.[20] The foster parent ordered the child to bed, but several hours later called for emergency assis-

---

been placed in foster care"); Norfleet v. Arkansas Dep't of Human Servs., 989 F.2d 289, 293 (8th Cir. 1993) (recognizing "[c]ases from this and other circuits clearly demonstrate that imprisonment is not the only custodial relationship in which the state must safeguard an individual's civil rights"); Yvonne L. v. New Mexico Dep't of Human Servs., 959 F.2d 883, 893 (10th Cir. 1992) (denying qualified immunity to defendant officials as it was clearly established that "children in the custody of a state had a constitutional right to be reasonably safe from harm"); K.H. v. Morgan, 914 F.2d 846, 853 (7th Cir. 1990) (denying qualified immunity to extent or complaint asserted "prima facie right not to be placed with a foster parent who the state's caseworkers and supervisors know or suspect is likely to abuse or neglect the foster child"); Meador v. Cabinet for Human Resources, 902 F.2d 474, 476 (6th Cir.) (holding "due process extends the right to be free from the infliction of unnecessary harm to children in state-regulated foster homes"), *cert. denied*, 498 U.S. 867 (1990); Griffith v. Johnston, 899 F.2d 1427, 1439 (5th Cir.) (*en banc*) (recognizing creation of "special relationship" requiring provision of constitutionally adequate care when state removes child from natural home and placed under state supervision), *cert. denied*, 498 U.S. 1040 (1990); LaShawn A. v. Dixon, 762 F. Supp. 959, 992-93 (D.D.C. 1991) (finding rights of children in foster care analogous to rights of those involuntarily committed), *aff'd*, 990 F.2d 1319 (D.C. Cir. 1993). *But see* Wooten v. Campbell, 49 F.3d 696, 699-701 (11th Cir. 1995) (finding no "substantive due process right is implicated where a public agency is awarded legal custody of a child, but does not control that child's physical custody except to arrange court-ordered visitation with the non-custodial parent").

15. 989 F.2d 289 (8th Cir. 1993).
16. *Id.* at 290.
17. *Id.*
18. *Id.*
19. *Id.*
20. *Id.*

tance.[21] Tragically, the child died in the early hours of the morning.[22] The plaintiff, who returned home on the evening before her son's death, learned the whereabouts of her children from a department caseworker, was assured that her son was fine, and was told that she would be reunited with both children the next morning.[23] Early the next morning she was informed of her son's death.[24]

The Court of Appeals for the Eighth Circuit affirmed the district court's denial of qualified immunity to the Director of the Arkansas Department of Human Services and the department caseworker who had been involved in the circumstances that resulted in the death of the plaintiff's child.[25] Relying on both pre- and post-*DeShaney* decisions in the circuit,[26] the court concluded that it was clearly established at the time of the devastating occurrence that the state had a duty to provide for the safety and medical needs of the plaintiff's child.[27]

The court in *Norfleet* explained that a child placed in foster care, like a prisoner, is deprived of "freedom and ability to make decisions about his own welfare, and must rely on the state to take care of his needs."[28] Interestingly, however, the court proceeded to underscore that the reason the child was placed in foster care was precisely because the child was unable to care for himself without adult supervision and protection.[29]

Thus, the state's act of removing the child from free society was not the cause of the child's inability to provide for his own needs and protection and, therefore, was not the source of the duty to protect.[30] Rather, the

---

21. *Id.*
22. *Id.*
23. *Id.*
24. *Id.* at 293.
25. *Norfleet*, 989 F.2d at 290.
26. *See, e.g.,* Gregory v. City of Rogers, 974 F.2d 1006, 1010 (8th Cir. 1992) (*en banc*) (recognizing state's affirmative duty to protect citizens in custodial and other settings in which the state has limited the individuals' ability to care for themselves), *cert. denied*, 113 S. Ct. 1265 (1993); Freeman v. Ferguson, 911 F.2d 52, 55 (8th Cir. 1988) (extending circuit's previously narrow view of affirmative duty beyond strict confines of prison-like setting), *cert. denied*, 489 U.S. 1012 (1989).
27. *Norfleet*, 989 F.2d at 293.
28. *Id.*
29. *Id.*
30. *Id.* at 292.

state owed a duty to the child because the state had assumed control of the child's environment and responsibility for the child's welfare, replacing whatever private source of protection the child may have had in the "free" world.[31]

Although the result in *Norfleet* is to be commended, the rationale of the decision may be construed so as to belie the reality of what criteria are important in the affirmative duty cases. Fixation on the concept of custody, with attempts to characterize situations so that they are analogous to incarceration or institutionalization, have led plaintiffs to plead—and some courts to insist upon—a showing of state action that has caused the *involuntary* restriction of the plaintiff's freedom. If custody is to be a threshold requirement in affirmative-duty cases, the notion of custody should not only be viewed in more expansive terms, encompassing all situations where the state assumes responsibility for and control over an individual's environment, but also should be uncoupled from the requirement that custody be of an involuntary nature.

If Taureen Norfleet, the young boy who died from an asthma attack, had been "voluntarily" placed with the state by his mother, a number of courts would hold that the state owed him no affirmative duty under the Due Process Clause, even assuming that subsequent to his placement the same events that led to his death unfolded.[32] One of the first courts to interpret *DeShaney* to require a finding of involuntary custody before an affirmative duty of protection could be imposed, did so in the context of foster care. In *Milburn v. Anne Arundel County Department of Social Services*,[33] the Court of Appeals for the Fourth Circuit held under *DeShaney* that when parents voluntarily place their child in the foster care system, the state has no constitutional duty to protect the child against private violence.[34]

---

31. *Id.* at 293.
32. *See, e.g.*, Wilson v. Formigoni, 42 F.3d 1060, 1067 (7th Cir. 1994) ("Wilson does not complain that she was held at [Mental Health Center] against her will, and thus cannot maintain that the state did not do enough to ensure her safety while she was committed there.").
33. 871 F.2d 474 (4th Cir.), *cert. denied*, 493 U.S. 850 (1989). The facts and holding of *Milburn* received extensive treatment by Professor Laura Oren in her excellent article. *See* LAURA OREN, DeShaney*'s Unfinished Business: The Foster Child's Due Process Right to Safety*, 69 N.C. L. REV. 113, 133-47 (1990).
34. *Milburn*, 871 F.2d at 476-78.

Other courts have similarly focused on the involuntary nature of the plaintiff's relationship with the state as a predicate to the finding of a constitutional duty. In *Monahan v. Dorchester Counseling Center, Inc.*,[35] the plaintiff, a voluntarily committed mental health patient, sued several state officials who were charged with his care for serious injuries he sustained when he jumped out of a van while being transported between health facilities.[36] The First Circuit, relying on *DeShaney*, rejected the plaintiff's argument that his mental condition, "which may have made him functionally dependent on his caretakers,"[37] imposed upon the state a constitutional duty to provide for his safety and well-being.[38] As a voluntary patient, the plaintiff was not "in custody." Thus, the court concluded that "[b]ecause the state did not commit [the plaintiff] involuntarily, it did not take an 'affirmative act' of restraining his liberty, an act which may trigger a corresponding due process duty to assume a special responsibility for his protection."[39]

---

35. 961 F.2d 987 (1st Cir. 1992).
36. *Id.* at 989.
37. *Id.* at 992.
38. *Id.*
39. *Id.* at 991; *see also* Higgs v. Latham, 946 F.2d 895 (6th Cir. 1991) (text in WESTLAW) (If district court was correct in concluding that the plaintiff was a voluntary patient at the state hospital, then she had no constitutionally based right of action against any defendants under § 1983.); Fialkowski v. Greenwich Home for Children, Inc., 921 F.2d 459, 465 (3d Cir. 1990) (holding state acquires affirmative duty under Fourteenth Amendment to provide safe conditions only where mentally retarded person is taken into custody without consent); Martin v. Voinovich, 840 F. Supp. 1175, 1207 (S.D. Ohio 1993) (In a class action brought on behalf of people in Ohio with mental retardation or other developmental disabilities, the court, noting that it was bound by the Sixth Circuit's opinion in *Higgs, supra*, concluded "that only those members of the plaintiffs' class who are involuntarily institutionalized may assert a Youngberg claim."); Rogers v. City of Port Huron, 833 F. Supp. 1212, 1217 (E.D. Mich. 1993) ("[I]f a person's attendance at an event or area is voluntary, . . . and that person was not physically placed there by the state, the person cannot be considered to be in 'functional custody.'"); Baby Neal v. Casey, 821 F. Supp. 320, 334-35 (E.D. Pa. 1993) (noting that "[n]umerous courts have made this involuntary versus voluntary distinction," and concluding "that Plaintiffs who have been involuntarily placed in the custody of DHS may state a claim for violation of their substantive due process rights based upon their right to freedom from harm under the Fourteenth Amend-

The problem with emphasizing custody is the baggage that the concept has come to encompass since *DeShaney*. The notion that one is not "in custody" unless the state has taken some affirmative steps to hold the person against his or her will makes any substantive due process duty to protect turn on the status of an individual as a prisoner, an involuntarily committed mental patient, or an involuntarily placed foster child.

Custody, as a status rather than a situation, is an unsatisfactory indicator of when a constitutional duty is owed. An interpretation of *DeShaney* that would support treating two children in the same foster care situation differently under the Constitution because one child was voluntarily placed in the system is difficult to defend. Common sense and notions of basic fairness dictate that all children, whether placed voluntarily or involuntarily in the state's care, should be entitled to equal rights under the Constitution. The custody concept should be linked to the condition of being in an environment subject to the state's control and supervision, rather than to the process of how one got there.[40]

---

ment of the United States Constitution"); Jordan v. Tennessee, 738 F. Supp. 258, 259-60 (M.D. Tenn. 1990) (holding that mentally retarded child, *voluntarily* committed to state institution by parents, did not have substantive due process right to safe conditions).

40. *See, e.g.*, Walton v. Alexander, 44 F.3d 1297, 1308-09 (5th Cir. 1995) (*en banc*) (Parker, Robert. M., J., joined by Politz, C.J., and Stewart, J., concurring specially) ("The majority's holding that custody must be 'involuntary' and 'against [a person's] will' is so restrictive that it precludes any type of custody short of incarceration or institutionalization giving rise to the duty of protection . . . Such a narrow application of this duty clearly was not contemplated in *DeShaney*. . . . The question is not so much how the individual got into state custody, but to what extent the State exercises dominion and control over that individual."); Buffington v. Baltimore County, Maryland, 913 F.2d 113, 119 (4th Cir. 1990), *cert. denied*, 111 S. Ct. 1106 (1991) (refusing to find that affirmative duty owed to someone in custody turns on either the reason for taking custody or on whether a state or private actor brought the need for custody to the state's attention); Ringuette v. City of Fall River, 888 F. Supp. 258, 268 (D. Mass. 1995) (concluding that "the state has a duty under the constitution to protect persons who are taken into protective custody because of incapacitation and who lack the capacity to give knowing, intelligent and voluntary consent to protective custody"); Connecticut Traumatic Brain Injury Ass'n v. Hogan, 161 F.R.D. 8, 10 (D. Conn. 1995) (determining that "[t]he mechanism which brought the individuals to the

Public School Context

The compulsion to wed the concepts of custody and involuntariness, along with the emphasis upon restraint of freedom rather than assumption of control and responsibility by the state, have led the majority of courts to reject arguments that public schoolchildren should be viewed as in the "functional custody" of the state during school hours.[41] Thus, these courts have held that the state does not owe a duty of protection from harm inflicted by fellow students or other private actors.[42] An examination of four circuit court

---

various facilities, whether considered 'voluntary' or 'involuntary,' is not controlling; 'in either case they are entitled to safe conditions and freedom from undue restraint' [cite omitted]"); Clark v. Donahue, 885 F. Supp. 1159, 1162 (S.D. Ind. 1995) (recognizing that several courts have held that "institutionalization which originated voluntarily may at some point involve restraint of personal liberty sufficient to trigger the protections of the due process clause"); Estate of Cassara v. State of Illinois, 853 F. Supp. 273, 279 (N.D. Ill. 1994) ("[T]his court holds that voluntary institutionalization may involve a restraint of personal liberty sufficient to trigger the due process clause."); United States v. Commonwealth of Pennsylvania, 832 F. Supp. 122, 125 (E.D. Pa. 1993) (rejecting defendants' argument "that voluntarily confined patients are not entitled to the constitutional right to treatment and care by virtue of the 'voluntariness' of their initial confinement").

41. It is also worth noting the following dicta in Justice Scalia's opinion in Vernonia School District 47J v. Acton, 115 S. Ct. 2386, 2392 (U.S. 1995), the case upholding random drug testing of secondary school athletes:

> While we do not, of course, suggest that public schools as a general matter have such a degree of control over children as to give rise to a constitutional 'duty to protect,' see [*DeShaney*], we have acknowledged that for many purposes 'school authorities ac[t] *in loco parentis* [cite omitted], with the power and indeed the duty to 'inculcate the habits and manners of civility' [cite omitted].

42. It is well-settled that schoolchildren have a liberty interest in their bodily integrity that is protected by the Due Process Clause of the Fourteenth Amendment. *See, e.g.*, Ingraham v. Wright, 430 U.S. 651, 673-74 (1977). The school cases in which *DeShaney* is implicated must be distinguished from those in which the alleged harm is attributed to a state actor, generally a teacher or other school official. *See, e.g.*, Doe v. Taylor Independent School District, 15 F. 3d 443, 454 (5th Cir. 1994) (*en banc*) ("A supervisory school official can be held personally liable for a subordinate's violation of an elementary or secondary school student's constitutional right to bodily integrity in physical sexual abuse cases if the plaintiff establishes that: (1) the defendant learned

opinions, presenting very different factual contexts, underscores the difficulties inherent in an approach that concentrates on the elements of custody, involuntariness, and restraint of freedom, rather than control and culpability.

In *D.R. v. Middle Bucks Area Vocational Technical School,*[43] the Court of Appeals for the Third Circuit, sitting en banc, confronted a "classic case of constitutional line drawing in a most excruciating factual context."[44] The plaintiffs were two female students who attended a graphic arts occupation class at Middle Bucks School.[45] One of the plaintiffs, D.R., a hearing-impaired student with related communications problems, was sixteen at the time of the alleged conduct.[46] She asserted that over a five-month

---

of facts or a pattern of inappropriate sexual behavior by a subordinate pointing plainly toward the conclusion that the subordinate was sexually abusing the student; and (2) the defendant demonstrated deliberate indifference toward the constitutional rights of the student by failing to take action that was obviously necessary to prevent or stop the abuse; and (3) such failure caused a constitutional injury to the student."), *cert. denied sub nom* Lankford v. Doe, 115 S. Ct. 70 (1994); Stoneking v. Bradford Area Sch. Dist., 882 F.2d 720, 724 (3d Cir. 1989) (opinion on remand) (recognizing difference from DeShaney because injury, sexual molestation of plaintiff, resulted from conduct of state employee, not private actor), cert. denied, 493 U.S. 1044 (1990); K.L. v. Southeast Delco School District, 828 F. Supp. 1192, 1196 (E.D. Pa. 1993) (making clear that "[t]he holding [of C.M., *infra*] is limited to teachers, whom the state has placed in sensitive positions involving close, daily contact with children, and over whom school administrators have direct supervisory authority"); C.M. v. Southeast Delco School District, 828 F. Supp. 1179, 1189 (E.D. Pa. 1993) (Finding the identity of the alleged perpetrator as a state actor to be determinative, the court concluded that "the affirmative-duty line should be drawn at state action. That is, in light of Stoneking and D.R., *DeShaney* stands only for the proposition that states have no affirmative duty to protect people from private actors, rather than the broader proposition that states have no duty to protect people from actors who are the state's own.").

Compare D.T. by D.T. v. Independent School District No. 16, 894 F.2d 1176, 1192 (10th Cir. 1990) (school district not liable for child molestation committed by teacher, where teacher not acting under color of state law), *cert. denied*, 498 U.S. 879 (1990).

43. 972 F.2d 1364 (3d Cir. 1992) (*en banc*), *cert. denied*, 113 S. Ct. 1045 (1993).
44. *Id.* at 1365.
45. *Id.* at 1366.
46. *Id.* at 1366 n.5, 1370.

period she was sexually molested two to four times per week by several male students in a unisex bathroom and a darkroom, both of which were part of the graphic arts classroom in which she had an assigned class.[47] The other plaintiff, L.H., seventeen at the time in question, claimed to have been likewise molested two to three times per week over a similar period of time.[48] The molestation, which consisted of "offensive touching of their breasts and genitalia, sodomization and forced acts of fellatio,"[49] allegedly took place during school hours, when the student teacher "was or should have been in the classroom . . . and either heard or should have heard the incidents taking place."[50]

The plaintiffs sued the school defendants, asserting four different theories of constitutional liability.[51] The first theory claimed that a special relationship existed between the plaintiffs and the school defendants while the plaintiffs were in attendance at school, giving rise to an affirmative duty to protect the plaintiffs from the type of harm inflicted by the male students.[52] In an effort to meet a stringent reading of *DeShaney*, the plaintiffs argued that "Pennsylvania's scheme of compulsory attendance and the school defendants' exercise of *in loco parentis* authority over their pupils so restrain schoolchildren's liberty that plaintiffs can be considered to have been in state 'custody' during school hours for Fourteenth Amendment purposes."[53]

---

47. *Id.* at 1366.
48. *Id.*
49. *Id.*
50. *Id.*
51. *Id.* at 1368-77.
52. *Id.* at 1368. The second theory of liability was based on a snake-pit rationale, claiming that the defendants had created the danger that caused harm to the plaintiffs. *Id.* This theory is discussed *infra* part III. The third theory claimed the existence of an official policy, custom, or practice that caused the constitutional deprivations. *Id.* Finally, plaintiffs alleged a conspiracy by defendants to deprive plaintiffs of their constitutional rights. *Id.*
53. *Id.* at 1370. The district court had held that compulsory attendance laws created a custodial relationship between schoolchildren and the state, thereby mandating an affirmative constitutional duty to provide protection. *Id.* at 1367. The court concluded, however, that plaintiffs' allegations were insufficient to establish a breach of the duty through reckless indifference to plaintiffs' rights by the school defendants. D.R. v. Middle Bucks Area Vocational Technical Sch., Nos. CIV.A.90-3018, 90-3060, 1991 WL 14082, at *11 (E.D.

Grounding the argument for an affirmative duty in an analogy to involuntary institutionalization automatically excluded the plaintiff L.H. from the scope of any duty that might exist, since Pennsylvania's compulsory attendance law applied only until a child reached seventeen years of age.[54] As for the plaintiff D.R., the majority of the court rejected the analogy between compulsory school attendance and imprisonment or involuntary commitment, concluding that schoolchildren are not in the type of physical custody envisioned by *DeShaney*, in the sense of being subject to "full time severe and continuous state restriction of liberty."[55] The majority stressed that parents remain the primary caretakers responsible for meeting the basic needs of their children, and are free to remove their children from school if the welfare of their children is threatened.[56] This fact made the situation of schoolchildren unlike that of prisoners or involuntary mental patients.[57]

Pa. Feb. 1, 1991). A Third Circuit panel affirmed the decision but rejected the establishment of a special custodial relationship in the public school setting. D.R. v. Middle Bucks Area Vocational Sch., Nos. 91-1136, 91-1137, 1991 WL 276292 (3d Cir. Dec. 31, 1991).

54. *D.R.*, 972 F.2d at 1370.
55. *Id.* at 1371-72.
56. *Id.*
57. *Id.* at 1373. In so holding, the Third Circuit's opinion was in agreement with the only other court of appeals to have addressed the issue at that time. *See* J.O. v. Alton Community United Sch. Dist. 11, 909 F.2d 267, 272-73 (7th Cir. 1990) (rejecting argument that compulsory attendance laws made schoolchildren, like mental patients and prisoners, unable to provide for their own basic needs and are therefore owed affirmative duty of protection by state).

    Other circuits have since adopted views consistent with those of the Third and Seventh Circuits. *See, e.g.*, Wright v. Lovin, 32 F.3d 538, 540 (11th Cir. 1994) (observing that "[t]o date, every federal circuit court of appeal to address the question of whether compulsory school attendance laws create the necessary custodial relationship between school and student to give rise to a constitutional duty to protect students from harm by non-state actors has rejected the existence of any such duty. [citing cases]"); Graham v. Independent School District, 22 F.3d 991, 994 (10th Cir. 1994) (noting "we have clearly held compulsory school attendance laws do not spawn an affirmative duty to protect under the Fourteenth Amendment. [footnote omitted] Nonetheless, plaintiffs urge *Maldonado*'s holding does not foreclose the existence of a constitutional tort where a student is the victim of a foreseeable assault. . . . We hold foreseeability cannot create an affirmative duty to

Finally, in rejecting the custody basis for finding a duty of protection in these circumstances, the court distinguished the foster care context, concluding that any analogy to foster care was "not decisive."[58] The court explained that the relationship between the state and foster children exists by virtue of an affirmative act of the state in locating the children and placing them with foster families.[59] The state, through the foster family, assumes responsibility for the children's basic needs.[60] For the public school student, however, "required to spend only 180 six-hour days in the classroom

---

protect when plaintiff remains unable to allege a custodial relationship."); Dorothy J. v. Little Rock School District, 7 F.3d 729, 732 (8th Cir. 1993) (agreeing with Third, Seventh, and Tenth Circuits that "state-mandated school attendance does not entail so restrictive a custodial relationship as to impose upon the State the same duty to protect it owes to prison inmates . . . or to the involuntarily institutionalized"); Maldonado v. Josey, 975 F.2d 727, 732 (10th Cir. 1992) (determining that "compulsory attendance laws do not create an affirmative constitutional duty to protect students from the private actions of third parties while they attend school"), *cert. denied*, 113 S. Ct. 1266 (1993).

See also Walton v. Alexander, 44 F.3d 1297, 1305 (5th Cir. 1995) (*en banc*) (holding that where attendance at school was voluntary and there was a right to leave at will, child's "status as a resident student [did not place] him within the narrow class of persons who are entitled to claim from the state a constitutional duty of protection from harm at the hands of private parties"); Johnson v. Dallas Independent School District, 38 F.3d 198, 203 (5th Cir. 1994) (noting that, "while a persuasive argument can be made for applying a *DeShaney* 'special relationship' in some measure to public school students who are forced by compulsory education laws to attend school and have no choice among public schools [footnote omitted], even under such a legal regime the appellant's claim would not succeed. Andrew Gaston's death is attributable to the fortuity that an armed, violent non-student trespassed on campus. There can be no liability of state actors for this random criminal act unless the Fourteenth Amendment were to make the schools virtual guarantors of student safety—a rule never yet adopted even for those in society, such as prisoners or the mentally ill or handicapped, who are the beneficiaries of a 'special relationship' with the state.").

58. *D.R.*, 972 F.2d at 1372.
59. *Id.*
60. *Id.*

per year[,] . . . parents or others remain a child's primary caretakers and decisionmakers."[61]

Chief Judge Sloviter, in a persuasive dissent, criticized the majority's unwillingness to recognize any situation in which schoolchildren might be entitled to a substantive due process duty of protection by the state.[62] The dissent underscored the disingenuousness of much of the rationale supporting the majority opinion. Giving a more expansive reading to *DeShaney's* reference to "restraint of personal liberty"[63] as a predicate to any substantive due process duty to protect, the dissent disparaged the majority's holding "that the duty to protect can be triggered only by involuntary, round-the-clock legal custody."[64]

---

61. *Id.* In Black v. Indiana Area Sch. Dist., 985 F.2d 707 (3d Cir. 1993), the Third Circuit found *D.R.* controlling in a case that determined whether the superintendent of schools had a duty to protect six-, seven-, and eight-year-old girls from alleged sexual molestation by their school bus driver, *Id.* at 714. The plaintiffs looked to the superintendent's liability under *DeShaney* as the bus driver was found not to be a state actor because he was employed by a private entity under contract with the school district. *Id.* at 709-11. Because the students were not compelled to ride the school bus and their parents were "free" to arrange for other modes of transportation, the court determined that "the plaintiffs here were less affected by state restraints at the time of their alleged injuries than was *D.R.*" and concluded that no affirmative duty of protection existed under the Constitution. *Id.* at 714. Judge Scirica, concurring in the opinion, expressed some reservation about the situation being governed by *D.R.* Finding the facts "more compelling" than Judge Scirica made the following observation:

    I recognize we must draw lines to refine the state action requirement and the special relationship of care developed in [*DeShaney*]. But applied here, these principles lead to a result that belies the gravity of the constitutional claims involved. Denying these § 1983 claims also ignores the practical realities of this case—the necessity for small school districts to contract out bus service, the reliance of families in rural areas upon school buses, and the defenselessness of young girls riding a school bus. When claims like these fall through the cracks, § 1983 seems less than the powerful tool to vindicate constitutional rights it was designed to be.

    Id. at 715 (Scirica, J., concurring).

62. *D.R.*, 972 F.2d at 1377-84 (Sloviter, C.J., dissenting).
63. *DeShaney,* 489 U.S. at 200.
64. *D.R.*, 972 F.2d at 1379 (Sloviter, C.J., dissenting).

In an attempt to satisfy *DeShaney's* emphasis on the involuntariness of the constraint imposed on the individual's freedom to provide for his or her own needs, the dissent objected to the majority's refusal to acknowledge the real force of compulsory education laws.[65] The majority's conclusion that parents may choose to send their children to private schools, educate them at home, or remove them from the public school for certain reasons,[66] reflects an incredible lack of connection with life in the "real" world.[67] As the dissent noted, "For the vast majority of children of school age, this is no choice at all."[68]

The dissent obviously felt obligated to make the case for compulsory attendance laws satisfying any involuntary restraint requirement imposed by *DeShaney*. However, it is clear that the duty to protect recognized by the dissent was grounded more in the nature of the relationship that the state had with children who were in attendance at school than in any state laws compelling them to be there. Chief Judge Sloviter, writing in dissent, would have held

> that the state compulsion that students attend school, the status of most students as minors whose judgment is not fully mature, the discretion extended by the state to schools to control student behavior, and the pervasive control exercised by the schools over their students during the period of time they are in school, combine to create the type of special relationship which imposes a constitutional duty on the schools to protect the liberty interests of students while they are in the state's functional custody.[69]

The dissent appeared willing but unable to totally abandon the shackles of the involuntary restraint predicate to finding an affirmative duty. As

---

65. *Id.* at 1379-81 (Sloviter, C.J., dissenting).
66. *Id.* at 1371 (Sloviter, C.J., dissenting).
67. *Id.* (Sloviter, C.J., dissenting).
68. *Id.* at 1380 (Sloviter, C.J., dissenting).
69. *Id.* at 1377 (Sloviter, C.J., dissenting). Judge Becker, expressing agreement with most of Chief Judge Sloviter's analysis, resisted the adoption of any "bright-line rule," but would have held on the facts of this case that the school had a constitutional duty to protect the plaintiffs from the harm to which they were exposed. *Id.* at 1384 (Becker, J., dissenting).

Chief Judge Sloviter implied,[70] however, the technical, legal requirement of compulsory attendance makes little sense as the *sine qua non* for an affirmative duty owed to schoolchildren who are in fact, whether voluntarily or involuntarily, in the state's care and under the state's control while in attendance.[71] Any insistence that a legal compulsion to attend school be present before an affirmative duty to protect is recognized would result in the drawing of irrational and arbitrary classifications defining the circumstances and situations in which students are afforded constitutional protection.[72] The key to the duty owed should be the state's assumption of responsibility for the care and control of students while they are physically present in a state-created and controlled environment.[73]

Because the dissent concluded that the facts alleged were sufficient to establish that an affirmative duty of protection was owed, it also had to address the question of whether the facts, as they pertained to a breach of

---

70. Chief Judge Sloviter observed that "[a]lthough L.H. at seventeen may not have been compelled to attend school, I see no reason to draw an age distinction between students who, in fact, are attending a state school." *Id.* at 1379 n.3 (Sloviter, C.J., dissenting).
71. *Id.* at 1379 (Sloviter, C.J., dissenting).
72. For example, a constitutional duty linked to compulsory attendance would totally exclude any situations encompassed by after-school, extracurricular activities. *See, e.g.*, Leffall v. Dallas Independent School Dist., 28 F.3d 521, 529 (5th Cir. 1994) (holding "no [special] relationship exists during a school-sponsored dance held outside of the time during which students are required to attend school for non-voluntary activities"); Fenstermaker v. Nesfedder, 802 F. Supp. 1258, 1265 (E.D. Pa. 1992) (concluding that "*DeShaney* cannot be the basis for a federal cause of action against a coach when a wrestler, who is not obliged in any way to participate in an extracurricular wrestling program, alleges that he was injured during a bout"); Reeves v. Besonen, 754 F. Supp. 1135, 1140 (E.D. Mich. 1991) (concluding school owes no constitutional duty of protection to students against assault by other students inflicted during ride on school bus in connection with wholly voluntary participation on school football team). Nor would the duty apply to conduct occurring during the type of optional, "extended day" programs that more and more public school systems are offering.
73. *See* Stephen F. Huefner, Note, *Affirmative Duties in the Public Schools After* DeShaney, 90 Colum. L. Rev. 1940, 1957 (1990) (arguing that, in school context, courts should look to "implications of custodial control, rather than only to control itself, because it is the underlying dependency that actually obligates the state to act, not the state's legal status as custodian").

that duty, were adequate to withstand a motion to dismiss.[74] Given the allegations, which included assertions that the student teacher in charge of the classroom witnessed some of the offensive conduct and that other school officials knew about the problems in the graphic arts classroom, the dissent found that the complaint "sufficiently allege[d] deliberate and reckless indifference by school officials to the safety and physical well-being of the students while they were in the functional custody of the school."[75]

In *Maldonado v. Josey*,[76] the Court of Appeals for the Tenth Circuit joined the Third[77] and Seventh[78] Circuits in holding that "compulsory attendance laws do not create an affirmative constitutional duty to protect students from the private actions of third parties while they attend school."[79] The facts of *Maldonado* were very different from the facts of *D.R.* as Mark Maldonado, an eleven-year-old fifth grader, died of strangulation when he became caught on his bandanna in a cloakroom next to his classroom.[80]

This was not a case that required a decision based on arbitrary line drawing concerning the scope of any affirmative duty the state may have toward schoolchildren after *DeShaney*. It was not necessary to categorically reject a constitutional duty to protect schoolchildren to conclude that the plaintiffs had stated no constitutional claim upon which relief could be granted. Judge Seymour, in a concurring opinion, concluded that the court should recognize "*some* affirmative duty on the part of public school teachers to protect students who are in the total care of the school during the period of their compulsory attendance."[81]

---

74. *D.R.*, 972 F.2d at 1378 (Sloviter, C.J., dissenting).
75. *Id.* (Sloviter, C.J., dissenting).
76. 975 F.2d 727 (10th Cir. 1992).
77. *D.R.*, 972 F.2d at 1372 (holding "school defendants' authority over *D.R.* during the school day cannot be said to create the type of physical custody necessary to bring it within the special relationship noted in *DeShaney*").
78. J.O. v. Alton Community United Sch. Dist. 11, 909 F.2d 267, 272-73 (7th Cir. 1990) (concluding "[s]chool children are not like mental patients and prisoners such that the state has an affirmative duty to protect them").
79. *Maldonado*, 975 F.2d at 732 (footnote omitted).
80. *Maldonado*, 975 F.2d at 728. The facts indicated that the boy had been in the cloakroom unsupervised for approximately 20 minutes, though no reason was provided for his having been sent there. *See id.*
81. *Id.* at 735 (Seymour, J., concurring).

Even though she acknowledged that a duty was owed, Judge Seymour would have affirmed the district court's grant of summary judgment on behalf of the defendant teacher based on the plaintiff's failure to raise a material fact with respect to the issue of breach of that duty since there were no facts alleged from which a jury could have found that the teacher had been deliberately indifferent to Mark Maldonado's exposure to potential danger.[82]

The concurrence in *Maldonado*, like the dissent in *D.R.*, appeared to be much more in tune with the reality of the situation confronting both schoolchildren and parents vis-à-vis their relationship with the state in the matter of public education.

Judge Seymour addressed the argument that a schoolchild—unlike a prisoner, involuntarily committed mental patient, or child involuntarily placed in the state's foster care system—is not in "custody" because the child's parents remain responsible for providing the child's basic needs. She commented:

> Obviously, a parent does not lose all control over, nor all responsibility for, satisfying a child's basic needs simply as a result of school attendance laws. But younger children are incapable of providing for their own basic needs; they depend on parents or other caretakers to provide for them. Even older children may be forced by school disciplinary procedures and rules to rely on authority figures at school to protect them from harm. I cannot fathom who, other than a teacher or other school staff member, is capable of ensuring the 'reasonable safety' of schoolchildren during the school day and class periods.[83]

In two recent cases, the Fifth Circuit has implicitly rejected the existence of an affirmative duty based upon a notion of custody stemming from compulsory attendance laws and has explicitly rejected the concept of a special relationship founded on a state-controlled environment. In *Johnson*

---

82. *Id.* (Seymour, J., concurring). As Judge Seymour explained: "I do not believe the Constitution requires an elementary school teacher to protect her students from unknown and unforeseen harms, or to follow the minute-by-minute progress of her eleven-year-old charges." *Id.* (Seymour, J., concurring).

83. *Id.* at 734-35 (Seymour, J., concurring) (footnote omitted).

v. Dallas Independent School District,[84] a fifteen-year-old boy was shot in the head and killed by a nonstudent who had taken a school bus to the high school, entered without a required ID badge, and fired the fatal shot in the hall of the high school during school hours. The concealed handgun had not been detected because the school's metal detectors were not being used.

The victim's father filed suit against the school district and the principal of the high school, asserting two theories of liability under § 1983. One theory was grounded on an affirmative duty arising from the state's compulsory attendance laws, while the second theory set forth the state-created danger argument.[85] The district court dismissed the complaint for failure to state a claim and an appeal was taken.

The court of appeals in *Johnson* found it unnecessary to decide whether compulsory attendance laws created a special relationship between the school and students, giving rise to an affirmative duty to protect. Rather, the court concluded that "even under such a legal regime the appellant's claim would not succeed . . . [because] [t]here can be no liability of state actors for this random criminal act unless the Fourteenth Amendment were to make the schools virtual guarantors of student safety."[86] In short, even if a duty were owed in this setting, the plaintiff failed to make out the requisite level of culpability on the part of the defendants and failed to establish the necessary causal link between the injury and the defendants' conduct.

In a footnote, the court made some interesting observations about the "custody" argument in the public school context. The court noted that even with compulsory attendance laws, attendance at public schools is generally considered to be voluntary because parents are free to withdraw their children from public schools and parents remain the primary caretakers.[87] The court went on to note, however, the fact that "[s]chools may be said to control children's environments to the same or even greater degree than state-sponsored foster care services, which have been held, post-*DeShaney*, to bear affirmative obligations to their client children."[88] The court, clearly uncomfortable with "the deficiencies of governing circuit caselaw" in this area, acknowledged that rejection of the "custody" rationale in the school

84. 38 F.3d 198 (5th Cir. 1994).
85. *Id.* at 200.
86. *Id.* at 203.
87. *Id.* at 203 n.7.
88. *Id.*

context "appears to derive less from logic than from a pragmatic desire to limit [the schools'] legal liability."[89]

In *Walton v. Alexander*,[90] a resident student at the Mississippi School for the Deaf was sexually assaulted by the same classmate on two occasions. Christopher Walton brought suit under § 1983, asserting that the superintendent of the school, defendant Alexander, violated his substantive due process right to bodily integrity by not protecting him from sexual assaults by another student. Alexander raised the defense of qualified immunity, arguing that even if there was a constitutional right of one student to be protected from harm inflicted by another student, such a right was not clearly established at the time of the sexual assaults. The district court denied qualified immunity and an interlocutory appeal followed.[91]

A majority of the panel hearing the appeal held that a special relationship existed between Walton and the school by virtue of his being in the school's "custody," and, thus, an affirmative duty existed to provide for protection from the violent acts of private persons.[92] The panel reversed the

89. *Id.* Indeed, the court suggested that there was a good argument for placing upon school officials "an obligation to protect students at least from certain kinds of foreseeably dangerous harm during regular school hours." *Id.*
90. 44 F.3d 1297 (5th Cir. 1995) (*en banc*).
91. A denial of qualified immunity, to the extent it turns on a question of law, is immediately appealable as a collateral order. Mitchell v. Forsyth, 472 U.S. 511, 530 (1985).
92. The panel opinion is reported at 20 F.3d 1350 (5th Cir. 1994). In a case factually similar to *Walton*, a panel of the Eleventh Circuit had held that an affirmative duty of protection was owed to a full-time resident student who was sexually assaulted by a classmate at the Georgia School of the Deaf. The individual defendants, however, were granted qualified immunity because the law was not clearly established at the time of the incident. Spivey v. Elliott, 29 F.3d 1522, 1525-27 (11th Cir. 1994). The opinion was subsequently withdrawn to the extent that it had determined the existence of a substantive due process right to protection in the residential state school setting. Spivey v. Elliott, 41 F.3d 1497, 1499 (11th Cir. 1995) ("[I]n the interest of efficiency and collegiality on this Court, where there are differing views as to the substantive right, this panel has chosen to withdraw all of its prior opinion which relates to whether the complaint alleges a constitutional right so that the opinion will serve as no precedent on that issue. The opinion is fully reaffirmed, however, on the holding that there was no constitutional duty clearly established at the time of the sexual assault, so the defendant officials were properly entitled to qualified immunity.").

district court's denial of qualified immunity, however, because Alexander could not be found to have been deliberately indifferent to Walton's due process rights.

In reviewing the denial of qualified immunity, the en banc court followed the structural analysis suggested by the Supreme Court in *Siegert v. Gilley*.[93] The Fifth Circuit has interpreted *Siegert* as requiring an initial inquiry into whether the plaintiff has stated a constitutional violation at all before deciding whether the alleged right was clearly established at the time.[94] Thus, the en banc court addressed the issue of whether there existed a "special relationship" between the school and Walton by virtue of his being a resident student committed to the full-time custody of the state institution, such that Superintendent Alexander owed him an affirmative duty under the Constitution to protect him from harm inflicted by third-party private actors.[95]

Concluding that "*DeShaney* stands for the proposition that the state creates a 'special relationship' with a person only when the person is involuntarily taken into state custody and held against his will through the affirmative power of the state[,]"[96] the court proceeded to analyze the nature of the relationship that existed between the school and Walton. The court found sufficient support in the record to sustain assertions that Walton's daily activities were completely controlled by the school, that he slept and ate his meals there, that he was totally dependent upon the school for his basic needs. More important, however, was the determination "that Walton attended the school through his own free will (or that of his parents) without any coercion by the state."[97]

The exercise of control over someone in the full-time custody of the school was not a sufficient basis for the creation of a "special relationship" under *DeShaney*. The key factor in establishing the affirmative duty to protect is the state's affirmative act of taking an individual's liberty "under terms that provide no realistic means of voluntarily terminating the state's custody *and* which thus deprives the [individual] of the ability to provide

93. 500 U.S. 226 (1991).
94. White v. Taylor, 959 F.2d 539, 545 (5th Cir. 1992).
95. 44 F.3d at 1300-01.
96. *Id.* at 1304.
97. *Id.* at 1305.

for his own care and safety."[98] Absent the state's affirmative exercise of power and absent any involuntary confinement of Walton, the court concluded there could be no constitutional duty owed by Superintendent Alexander to protect Walton from the sexual assaults of his classmate.[99] Thus, the district court's denial of qualified immunity was reversed.

In a special concurrence, Judge Robert M. Parker criticized the majority of the en banc court for adopting "a bright line rule that represents an extreme constitutional viewpoint," and one which would confine the duty to protect to those incarcerated or involuntarily institutionalized.[100] Noting criticism of the adoption of "involuntary" custody as a threshold requirement for establishing an affirmative duty in the public schools context,[101] Judge Parker observed that "[t]he question is not so much *how* the individual got into state custody, but to what extent the State exercises dominion and control over that individual."[102] Rather than focusing on whether a person was taken into custody voluntarily or involuntarily, Judge Parker would consider a number of factors in determining whether a special relationship existed in a given case:

> 1) the authority and discretion state actors have to control the environment and the behavior of the individuals in their custody, 2) the responsibilities assumed by the State, 3) the extent to which an individual in state custody must rely on the State to provide for his or her basic needs, and 4) the degree of control actually exercised by the State in a given situation.[103]

---

98. *Id.*
99. *Id.*
100. *Id.* at 1306, 1308 (Parker, Robert M., J., with whom Politz, C.J., and Stewart, J., join, concurring specially).
101. *Id.* at 1309 & n.19 (Parker, Robert M., J., with whom Politz, C.J., and Stewart, J., join, concurring specially) (citing to and quoting from the original version of this article, KAREN M. BLUM, DeShaney*: Custody, Creation of Danger, and Culpability,* 27 LOY. L.A. L. REV. 435, 450 (1994)).
102. 44 F.3d at 1309 (Parker, Robert M., J., with whom Politz, C.J., and Stewart, J., join, concurring specially).
103. *Id.* at 1309-10 (Parker, Robert M., J., with whom Politz, C.J., and Stewart, J., join, concurring specially).

Applying these factors to Walton's situation, Judge Parker would have found the existence of a special relationship giving rise to an affirmative duty to provide for Walton's safety and well-being. He still would have reversed the denial of qualified immunity, however, because there was no evidence presented to demonstrate that Superintendent Alexander breached the constitutional duty owed by being deliberately indifferent to the safety needs of Christopher Walton.[104]

The requirement that a child be involuntarily in the total and full-time physical custody of the state before the relationship gives rise to an affirmative duty to protect, serves as an arbitrary, unsatisfactory, and unnecessary screening device for substantive due process claims in the school context. To acknowledge that school teachers and officials are unquestionably the primary caretakers of children during school hours and school activities and to impose upon such caretakers a constitutional duty of protecting schoolchildren from known and foreseeable harms is not to open the floodgates of constitutional litigation. As Chief Judge Sloviter noted, case law doctrines are in place that significantly limit the potential liability of state officials for substantive due process violations.[105]

The emphasis in the school cases, no less so than in the incarceration and institutionalization cases, should be on the factors of culpability and causation. As schoolchildren are in the custody and care of school officials while attending school—whether or not that attendance is compelled—those officials should have an affirmative duty under the Constitution to provide an environment that is, at least, not deliberately indifferent to the safety and health needs of those children.

---

104. *Id.* at 1307 (Parker, Robert M., J., with whom Politz, C.J., and Stewart, J., join, concurring specially).

105. In her dissent in *D.R.*, Chief Judge Sloviter noted:

> [A] state official's potential liability for violations of substantive due process has already been circumscribed by decisions imposing high standards of culpability, limitations on the type of conduct for which state entities can be held responsible, and qualified immunity for individual defendants. These decisions make it unlikely that a holding that schools have a duty to protect schoolchildren while they are in the functional custody of the school will markedly expand the liability of the school districts.

D.R., 972 F.2d at 1384 (Sloviter, C.J., dissenting) (citations omitted).

Public Housing and Employment Contexts

Courts have not been receptive to an affirmative duty under the Due Process Clause to protect persons living in public housing or those employed by a public employer. In *Dawson v. Milwaukee Housing Authority,*[106] the plaintiff, a resident of city public housing, was shot and seriously injured by another resident.[107] The plaintiff argued that his presence in publicly subsidized housing was the functional equivalent of being in custody, thereby creating a constitutional duty to protect him from harm at the hands of private actors.[108] In refusing to equate "subsidy with custody," Judge Easterbrook relied on pre-*DeShaney* precedent from the Seventh Circuit that held that the Due Process Clause does not guarantee safety in the public workplace.[109]

In *Collins v. City of Harker Heights,*[110] the Supreme Court unanimously affirmed that "the Due Process Clause does not impose an independent federal obligation upon municipalities to provide certain minimal levels of safety and security in the workplace."[111] *DeShaney* and *Collins* no doubt negate any argument that there is a general substantive due process right to

---

106. 930 F.2d 1283 (7th Cir. 1991).
107. *Id.* at 1283.
108. *Id.* at 1284.
109. *Id.* at 1285 (citing Walker v. Rowe, 791 F.2d 507, 510-11 (7th Cir.), *cert. denied*, 479 U.S. 994 (1986); *accord* Washington v. District of Columbia, 802 F.2d 1478, 1481-82 (D.C. Cir. 1986) (finding prison guard has no constitutional right to safe working environment); McClary v. O'Hare, 786 F.2d 83, 89 (2d Cir. 1986) (noting improper actions by employer are not tantamount to constitutional violations simply because employer is government official).
110. 112 S. Ct. 1061 (1992).
111. *Id.* at 1071. The plaintiff's husband was employed by the city in its sanitation and sewer department and was asphyxiated while clearing a sewer line. *Id.*; *see also* Skinner v. City of Miami, 62 F.3d 344, 348 n.2 (11th Cir. 1995) (in case involving hazing incident by firefighters, court determined that the "record does not support the dissent's implication that the City committed any deliberate acts to injure [plaintiff]. At most, the evidence suggests that certain fire department officials knew that hazing incidents had occurred at some points in the past. This, however, falls short of demonstrating that the City violated a substantive constitutional right."); Lewellen v. Metropolitan Government of Nashville, 34 F.3d 345 (6th Cir. 1994) (workman accidentally

safety in public workplaces or housing based on some notion of functional custody. However, support exists for imposing constitutional liability on government defendants in noncustodial contexts, where persons claim to have been harmed by exposure to risks created or increased by government employees or officials.

The Snake-Pit Cases

In concluding that the state had not deprived Joshua DeShaney of any constitutionally protected rights, the Supreme Court suggested that the result might have been different if the state had played a role in creating the dangers to which Joshua was exposed or had increased his vulnerability to these dangers.[112] This chapter now turns to an examination of cases in which plaintiffs have claimed that an affirmative duty of protection was owed, in situations admittedly noncustodial, based on a state-created-danger or enhancement-of-risk theory.[113]

---

injured on school construction project has no substantive due process claim), *cert. denied*, 115 S. Ct. 963 (1995); Figueroa v. United States, 7 F.3d 1405, 1413 (9th Cir. 1993) ("While we acknowledge that a broader understanding of deprivation of liberty may have emerged later . . . we hold that in 1987 there was no clearly established constitutional right not to be placed in a position of danger by a government employer absent some sort of governmental restriction on an individual's physical freedom to act to avert potential harm."); Walls v. City of Detroit, 993 F.2d 1548 (6th Cir. 1993) (finding plaintiff's attempt to distinguish *Collins* "unavailing, because it misunderstands one of the central tenets of the Supreme Court's holding in that case: the Constitution does not guarantee police officers and other municipal employees a workplace free of unreasonable risks of harm"); Searles v. Southeastern Pa. Transp. Auth., 990 F.2d 789, 792 (3d Cir. 1993) (rejecting plaintiff's argument "that the Constitution imposes a duty on a municipal transit authority to provide its passengers with minimal levels of safety and security during transportation").

112. *DeShaney*, 489 U.S. 189, 201 (1989).

113. No clear line separates the state-created-danger cases from the enhancement-of-risk cases, and most snake-pit situations may fairly be characterized as containing elements of both. This chapter treats these cases as categorically distinct only for purposes of organization and discussion.

State-Created-Danger Cases

DeShaney makes clear that the state's mere awareness of a risk of harm to an individual will not suffice to impose an affirmative duty to provide protection.[114] If the state creates the danger confronting the individual, however, it may then have a corresponding duty to protect. The state-created-danger theory for imposing an affirmative duty has been raised in a number of the school cases. As one federal district court has noted:

> The relationship between a state and its students does not constitute the special custodial relationship referred to in *DeShaney.* The absence of an affirmative constitutional duty to protect its students does not, however, mean that a state may create a dangerous situation and place students in harm's way without acquiring a corresponding duty to protect those students from resulting violations of their constitutional rights.[115]

In addition to their functional custody argument,[116] the plaintiffs in *D.R. v. Middle Bucks Area Vocational Technical School*[117] raised the state-created-danger theory. They alleged that the school officials created an environment in which the plaintiffs were subject to repeated sexual and physical abuse by other students.[118] The court first noted that "the state-created danger theory is predicated upon the state's affirmative acts which

---

114. *DeShaney*, 489 U.S. at 200 ("The affirmative duty to protect arises not from the State's knowledge of the individual's predicament or from its expressions of intent to help him. . . .").
115. Robbins v. Maine Sch. Admin. Dist. No. 56, 807 F. Supp. 11, 13 (D. Me. 1992).
116. *See supra* notes 52-73 and accompanying text.
117. 972 F.2d 1364 (3d Cir. 1992) (*en banc*), *cert. denied*, 113 S. Ct. 1045 (1993).
118. *Id.* at 1373. Specifically, the plaintiffs claimed that the defendants created or increased their risk of harm by (1) failing to report to the parents or other authorities the misconduct resulting in abuse to plaintiffs, (2) placing the class under the control of an inadequately trained and unsupervised student teacher, (3) failing to demand proper conduct of the student defendants, and (4) failing to investigate and put a stop to the physical and sexual misconduct.

work to plaintiffs' detriments in terms of exposure to danger."[119] The Third Circuit then distinguished the plaintiffs' principal cases for imposing liability by observing that in each of those cases, the state acted affirmatively to create the danger encountered.[120]

The court's conclusion that no duty to protect existed in *D.R.,* however, appeared to rest not on the lack of the defendants' affirmative acts, but rather on the perceived unrelatedness between the defendants' acts and the plaintiffs' harm. The court opined that although the defendants' conduct "may have created a recognizable risk that plaintiffs would receive little education in that class, and perhaps, physical injury due to the roughhousing[,] [p]laintiffs did not suffer harm . . . from that kind of foreseeable risk."[121] Thus, although the court underscored the action/inaction line as the constitutionally significant distinction between *D.R.* and the other state-created-danger cases, the opinion's language belies a greater concern with the element of causation.

The Court of Appeals for the Eighth Circuit expressed a similar concern in *Dorothy J. v. Little Rock School District.*[122] This case involved the

---

119. *Id.* at 1374.

120. *Id.* The plaintiffs relied heavily on three post-*DeShaney* cases recognizing the state-created-danger theory as a basis for § 1983 liability outside the custodial context. *See* Cornelius v. Town of Highland Lake, 880 F.2d 348, 359 (11th Cir. 1989) (concluding defendants owed plaintiff duty of protection where they had created risk of harm to plaintiff by exposing her to inmates who were inadequately supervised), *cert. denied,* 494 U.S. 1066 (1990); Wood v. Ostrander, 879 F.2d 583, 595-96 (9th Cir. 1989) (finding duty to provide protection where police officer put plaintiff in harm's way when he arrested driver of car in which plaintiff was passenger, impounded vehicle, and left plaintiff stranded in high-crime area), *cert. denied,* 498 U.S. 938 (1990); Swader v. Virginia, 743 F. Supp. 434, 435, 444 (E.D. Va. 1990) (finding affirmative duty where defendants created risk of harm by permitting inmate serving life sentence for rape to work unsupervised on prison property where prison employees and their families were required to live).

The continued validity of the rationale and holding of *Cornelius* has been questioned by a number of panels of the Eleventh Circuit. *See, e.g.,* Lovins v. Lee, 53 F.3d 1208, 1211 (11th Cir. 1995); Wooten v. Campbell, 49 F.3d 696, 700 n. 4 (11th Cir. 1995); Wright v. Lovin, 32 F.3d 538, 541 n.1 (11th Cir. 1994).

121. *D.R.*, 972 F.2d at 1374. The dissent in *D.R.* disagreed with the majority's conclusion "that harm from sexual assault was not a foreseeable risk." *Id.* at 1378 (Sloviter, C.J., dissenting).

122. 7 F.3d 729 (8th Cir. 1993).

sexual assault of a mentally handicapped student by a fellow student who was in legal custody of the state of Arkansas. After rejecting an argument that the state owed a duty to provide protection based on some notion of functional custody,[123] the court turned to the state-created-danger theory of liability. The plaintiff argued that the state defendants' act of placing a youth with known violent propensities in the same program with the plaintiff created the risk of harm to which the plaintiff was exposed.[124]

The court refused to hold that the defendants' acts put the plaintiff in harm's way and, thus, gave rise to a duty to protect, where the attack took place at least two years after the violent youth had been placed in the program.[125] The court observed that "[i]n most every circuit court decision imposing § 1983 liability because the State affirmatively created or enhanced a danger, 'the immediate threat of harm has a limited range and duration,' unlike the indefinite risk created by enrolling Louis C. in public school."[126] Concluding that the consequence was too remote from the challenged conduct, the court refused to translate what it viewed as a traditional tort claim into a due process deprivation.[127]

While the Third Circuit in *D.R.* and the Eighth Circuit in *Dorothy J.* focused on the causal connection between the defendants' acts and the plaintiffs' harm in analyzing the state-created-danger arguments raised in those cases, the Fifth Circuit has twice rejected plaintiffs' state-created-danger claims in the school context because of a failure to demonstrate the requi-

---

123. *Id.* at 732. The court concluded that "public schools are simply not analogous to prisons and mental institutions." *Id.*

124. *Id.* at 733. A similar argument was made in Hunter v. Carbondale Area School District, 829 F. Supp. 714 (M.D. Pa. 1993). Plaintiffs argued that defendant school officials created the danger to which decedent was exposed when they placed the decedent, a seventh-grade special education student, in detention with older students who harbored animosity toward the boy. *Id.* at 720. The older students chased and assaulted the decedent after the detention period, pursuing him to a stream where he drowned. *Id.* at 716-17. Noting that the state-created-danger theory "is viable in limited circumstances," the court found "nothing in the record . . . that suggest[ed] that either Defendant encouraged, facilitated or authorized students to engage in the conduct which took place." *Id.* at 720-21.

125. *Dorothy J.*, 7 F.3d at 733.

126. *Id.* at 733 n.4 (quoting Reed v. Gardner, 986 F.2d 1122, 1127 (7th Cir. 1993)).

127. *Id.* at 733.

site culpability on the part of the defendants. In *Leffall v. Dallas Independent School District*,[128] a sixteen-year-old high school student was fatally shot in the high school parking lot following a school-sponsored dance. In support of her constitutional claim against the school district and the school principal under § 1983, plaintiff argued that the school district and the principal had created a dangerous environment by sponsoring a school dance and providing only two unarmed security guards when it was common knowledge that gunfire occured frequently during and after school functions at Lincoln High School. The Fifth Circuit held that, even if there were a substantive due process right to protection from dangers arising out of the school-sponsored dance, the plaintiff's claim was subject to dismissal because "she did not allege facts that demonstrated deliberate indifference to those dangers on the part of the state actors."[129]

Likewise, in *Johnson v. Dallas Independent School District*,[130] the court found "no sufficiently culpable affirmative conduct"[131] on the part of the school defendants to sustain a state-created-danger substantive due process claim. The court identified three requirements that are key to establishing the requisite level of culpability under a state-created-danger claim: "[T]he environment created by the state actors must be dangerous; they must know it is dangerous; and, to be liable, they must have used their authority to create an opportunity that would not otherwise have existed for the third party's crime to occur."[132] The Fifth Circuit in *Johnson* concluded that while the defendants may have been negligent in their efforts to secure the school environment, their conduct did not rise to the level of deliberate or callous indifference.[133]

The Supreme Court's decision in *Collins* does not preclude the imposition of constitutional liability on state officials who deliberately place public employees in a dangerous situation without adequate protection. For example, in *L.W. v. Grubbs*,[134] the plaintiff, a registered nurse at a medium security prison for young male offenders, was kidnapped and raped

128. 28 F.3d 521 (5th Cir. 1994).

129. *Id.* at 532.

130. 38 F.3d 198 (5th Cir. 1994). The facts of *Johnson* are set out *supra* at notes 84, 85, and accompanying text.

131. *Id.* at 202.

132. *Id.* at 201.

133. *Id.*

134. 974 F.2d 119 (9th Cir.), *cert. denied*, 113 S. Ct. 2442 (1992).

by an inmate who had been assigned to work with her.[135] The plaintiff named as defendants her supervisors at the institution and alleged that, contrary to assurances that had been made, they selected a known violent sex offender to work alone with her in the clinic, thus "intentionally placing her in a position of known danger."[136] The district court granted the defendants' motion to dismiss for lack of a custodial context giving rise to a duty to protect and the plaintiff appealed.[137]

In reversing the dismissal, the Ninth Circuit stated that it was a mistake to read *DeShaney* as making "victim custody" a prerequisite to a due process claim for failure to protect.[138] The court noted two distinct exceptions to the general rule that the state has no affirmative duty to protect persons from violence inflicted by private actors: (1) the "special relationship" exception, stemming from a custodial relationship between the state and the victim, and (2) the "danger creation" exception, stemming from "affirmative conduct on the part of the state in placing the plaintiff in danger."[139]

The state-created-danger theory had been recognized by the Ninth Circuit in *Wood v. Ostrander,*[140] in which a third party had raped a woman after a police officer arrested the driver of the car in which she was a passenger, impounded the car, and left her alone in a high-crime area in the early hours of the morning.[141] Finding that the officer's actions had affirmatively placed her in danger, the court found her allegations sufficient to withstand scrutiny under *DeShaney.*[142] As in *Wood*, the court in *L.W.* concluded that the defendant's conduct "created the danger to which L.W. fell victim,"[143] a danger "that would not otherwise have existed."[144] The plaintiff's allegations that the defendants created the danger to which she was exposed, "and did so with a sufficiently culpable mental state," were sufficient to state a substantive due process claim under § 1983.[145]

---

135. *Id.* at 120.
136. *Id.*
137. *Id.*
138. *Id.* at 121.
139. *Id.*
140. 879 F.2d 583 (9th Cir. 1989), *cert. denied*, 498 U.S. 938 (1990).
141. *Id.* at 586.
142. *Id.* at 589-90.
143. *L.W.*, 974 F.2d at 121.
144. *Id.*
145. *Id.* at 123.

The defendants in *L.W.* argued that the Supreme Court's decision in *Collins* precluded a public employee from asserting a substantive due process claim against her supervisors for failure to protect.[146] The Ninth Circuit distinguished *Collins*, however, as a case in which the plaintiff asserted no affirmative culpable acts by the defendant city.[147] In holding that the city had no affirmative duty under the Due Process Clause to provide a safe work environment, the Supreme Court observed that the plaintiff in *Collins* had not claimed that "his supervisor instructed him to go into the sewer when the supervisor knew or should have known that there was a significant risk that he would be injured."[148] The *L.W.* plaintiff, unlike *Collins*, asserted that her supervisors knowingly put her in a position of danger and, thus, owed her a duty to provide protection.[149]

In *Gregory v. City of Rogers,*[150] the Court of Appeals for the Eighth Circuit, sitting en banc, was closely divided. The majority held that officers who arrested a designated driver owed no constitutional duty to protect the driver's intoxicated passengers from the dangerous situation created when the driver left the passengers in the vehicle, with the keys and unattended, outside the police station.[151] When one of the passengers attempted to drive home, the vehicle became involved in a single-car accident in which one passenger was killed and the other was injured.[152] The court concluded that even if the officers were aware of the intoxicated state of the passen-

---

146. *Id.* at 122.
147. *L.W.*, at 974 F.2d at 122.
148. Collins v. City of Harker Heights, 112 S. Ct. 1061, 1069 (1992).
149. *Id.* Other courts have recognized the viability of substantive due process claims asserted by public employees who have been subjected to known dangers by state officials. *See, e.g.*, Cornelius v. Town of Highland Lake, 880 F.2d 348, 359 (11th Cir. 1989) (recognizing substantive due process claim where plaintiff, town clerk, was abducted and held hostage by work squad inmates who were assigned to work in town hall without adequate supervision), *cert. denied*, 110 S. Ct. 1784 (1990); Swader v. Virginia, 743 F. Supp. 434, 444 (E.D. Va. 1990) (holding prison employee whose daughter was raped and killed by prisoner could state substantive due process claim against officials who allowed prisoner serving life sentence for rape to work unsupervised on prison property where plaintiff was required to live with her family).
150. 974 F. 2d 1006 (8th Cir. 1992) (*en banc*), *cert. denied*, 113 S. Ct. 1265 (1993).
151. *Id.* at 1011-12.
152. *Id.* at 1008.

gers, there was no affirmative act on the part of the defendants that placed the passengers in a position of danger.[153] Rather, it was the act of the designated driver in leaving them in an unattended car with keys that exposed the passengers to the danger encountered.[154]

The majority opinion disposed of the case on the grounds that the defendants owed no duty in a noncustodial situation in which they had not affirmatively created or enhanced the risk encountered by the victims.[155] The situation would have been different had the officers arrested the designated driver and left the passengers they knew to be intoxicated in the vehicle at the place of arrest.[156] This suggestion arguably makes the opinion turn more on elements of causation and culpability than on any distinction between acts of omission and commission.

In *Reed v. Gardner,*[157] the Court of Appeals for the Seventh Circuit applied the state-created-danger theory in reversing the dismissal of a case on the pleadings.[158] The complaint alleged that police officers violated the plaintiff's constitutional rights when they arrested the driver of a car and left the vehicle with an intoxicated passenger who shortly thereafter collided head-on with the plaintiff's vehicle, killing and injuring members of the plaintiff's family.[159] Assuming the truth of the well-pleaded factual allegations in the motion to dismiss, the court held that liability could be imposed on police officers who arrested a sober driver and left a passenger they knew or should have known was intoxicated to drive the vehicle, thereby creating the specific danger that the plaintiff and his family encountered.[160]

---

153. *Id.* at 1011. *See also* Foy v. City of Berea, 58 F.3d 227, 231-32 (6th Cir. 1995) (police owed no affirmative duty of protection to automobile passenger of intoxicated driver who was killed in automobile accident after officers ordered intoxicated individuals to leave college campus or submit to arrest).
154. *Id.* at 1012.
155. *See id.* at 1010-11.
156. *Id.* at 1011.
157. 986 F.2d 1122 (7th Cir. 1993).
158. *See id.* at 1125.
159. *Id.* at 1123.
160. *Id.* at 1125. On the face of the pleadings, there was no allegation that the driver was arrested by the defendants because she was intoxicated, although this fact was made known to the court by one of the defendants. *Id.* at 1124. It appears that had the district court judge converted the motion for a judgment on the pleadings into a summary judgment motion, this fact outside the

The court was quick to note that the defendants had a duty to protect only to the extent that their affirmative acts created or enhanced the danger faced by the victims.[161] Had the officers arrested one drunk driver and left the vehicle in the custody of another drunk driver, or had they observed and not interfered with the operation of a vehicle by a driver they knew to be intoxicated, no constitutional liability would have attached.[162] In either of these situations, the police would have done nothing to "place individuals in a position of danger that otherwise they would not have faced."[163]

The court's reasoning in *Reed* underscores the confusion engendered by any theory that turns "on the tenuous metaphysical construct which differentiates sins of omission and commission."[164] From a common-sense viewpoint, it is difficult to fathom why officers, who knowingly allow an intoxicated person to drive off in a vehicle, should be in constitutionally different positions depending upon whether they arrested a sober driver, leaving the drunk driver in control of the vehicle; arrested a drunk driver, leaving another drunk driver in control of the vehicle; or simply stood by and watched while someone they knew was intoxicated took control of the vehicle. Rather than focusing upon the affirmative nature of the conduct involved, the courts should ask whether the defendant's acts or omissions were the cause of the plaintiff's injuries and, if so, whether such acts or omissions reflect the requisite level of culpability to constitute a constitutional violation.

---

pleadings would have been legitimately considered and summary judgment for the defendants would have been affirmed on the theory that removing a drunk driver and failing to prevent her replacement with another intoxicated individual did not create or enhance the risk faced by the individuals involved. *Id.* at 1124, 1127.

Judge Posner would not have addressed "the difficult constitutional question" of whether a due process claim could be stated if the driver arrested by the defendants had been sober. *Id.* at 1128 (Posner, J., dissenting in part and concurring in part). He would have remanded to allow the district court to conduct a summary judgment proceeding, which in light of the facts introduced, would have put an end to the case without the need to resolve the constitutional issue. *Id.* at 1128-29 (Posner, J., dissenting in part and concurring in part).

161. *Id.* at 1126.

162. *Id.* at 1125.

163. *Id.*

164. White v. Rochford, 592 F. 2d 381, 384 (7th Cir. 1979).

Enhancement-of-Risk Cases

In *Sinthasomphone v. City of Milwaukee*,[165] three police officers responded to a call for help from two women who observed a young, naked, bleeding male wandering in the street.[166] The officers took control of the situation, declined assistance from others who were willing and able to provide it, and released the young man into the custody of a Mr. Jeffrey Dahmer, who shortly thereafter added the fourteen-year-old Laotian boy's name to the long list of his other unfortunate victims.[167] The plaintiffs and the estate and family of the victim brought a § 1983 action against the officers and the City of Milwaukee, asserting that the defendants' failure to protect him violated the victim's constitutional rights.[168]

The court noted both the legal difficulties posed by this case, as well as the "genius" of the complaint in trying to avoid those difficulties.[169] In denying the defendants' motion to dismiss, the court concluded that a key distinction between this case and *DeShaney* rested in the line between action and inaction. "[P]laintiffs have not merely alleged that the police officers failed to protect [the boy] . . . Rather, they allege[d] . . . that the officers actively prevented private citizens from helping [him] . . . [T]he allegations are not just of police inaction, but of police action. . . ."[170] Thus,

---

165. 785 F. Supp. 1343 (E.D. Wis. 1992).
166. *Id.* at 1346.
167. *Id.* at 1345-46. For a popular media account of this tragedy, *see,* for example, *Police May Have Left Boy with Slaying Suspect*, L.A. Times, July 27, 1991, at A2.
168. *Sinthasomphone*, 785 F. Supp. at 1346-46.
169. *Id.* at 1347.
170. *Id.* at 1349. *Sinthasomphone* is a good example of a case in which the plaintiffs relied on a number of different theories in an attempt to slip through the "cracks" in the surface of *DeShaney*. Although the action/inaction distinction would have been sufficient to sustain the complaint at the motion-to-dismiss stage, the court noted other allegations in the complaint that served to differentiate the case from *DeShaney. Id.* The allegations supported a claim that the boy was taken into "brief police custody," and released to an unrelated adult with no legal right to custody. *Id.* In addition, the court found that the complaint clearly stated a claim that the officers' conduct and the policy of the city operated to deny Sinthasomphone equal protection under the law. *Id.* at 1350. Plaintiffs alleged that it was the policy of the city to differentiate in the provision of protective services on the "basis of race, color, national origin, or sexual orientation." *Id.*

although the officers did not create the danger that befell Sinthasomphone, their interference with aid that would otherwise have been forthcoming significantly increased the risk of harm to which he was subjected.[171]

In *Losinski v. County of Trempealeau*,[172] Julie Losinski and her three children fled their trailer home after a particularly violent domestic dispute with her husband.[173] Ms. Losinski successfully obtained a "no contact" temporary restraining order and shortly thereafter commenced divorce proceedings.[174] She was granted permission to return to the trailer to retrieve some personal belongings.[175] Given her husband's violent nature and the presence of guns in the home, Ms. Losinski sought and was granted police protection for this purpose.[176] Ms. Losinski, accompanied by her mother, brother-in-law, and Deputy Hovell, proceeded to the trailer home where her husband confronted them and expressed his desire to speak with her alone.[177] She apparently consented to this wish and was allowed to enter the home with her husband.[178] When it became clear that an argument had

---

171. *See also* Ross v. United States, 910 F.2d 1422 , 1431 (7th Cir. 1990) (allowing claim stated under § 1983 where plaintiff alleged that her son's death was due to county's policy of preventing private assistance to drowning victims and failing to provide effective replacement protection), distinguished in Andrews v. Wilkins, 934 F.2d 1267 (D.C. Cir. 1991) (noting, whereas deputy in Ross used his authority as state actor to intrude into purely private rescue effort, police in *Andrews* enlisted private assistance as part of an ongoing police rescue effort).

    In a later opinion, the court held that the officers were entitled to qualified immunity on the substantive due process claim, concluding that "[e]ven assuming that the officers failed to do adequate police work, the situation was not sufficiently clear to allow the conclusion that they had to know the inevitable horror which would follow their actions." Sinthasomphone v. City of Milwaukee, 838 F. Supp. 1320, 1327 (E.D. Wis. 1993). *See also* Rogers v. City of Port Huron, 833 F. Supp. 1212, 1220 (E.D. Mich. 1993) (deciding "plaintiffs cannot establish that Officers . . . violated a clear constitutional right in preventing private citizens from rescuing Decedent in light of conflicting opinions within the circuits addressing this issue.").
172. 946 F.2d 544 (7th Cir. 1991).
173. *Id.* at 547.
174. *Id.*
175. *Id.*
176. *Id.*
177. *Id.*
178. *Id.*

erupted inside the trailer, the others entered the trailer.[179] There was no attempt on the part of Deputy Hovel to end the dispute or separate Ms. Losinski from her husband.[180] The argument continued in the bedroom and, as Deputy Hovell and the others stood in an adjacent hallway, the husband shot Ms. Losinski in the head and neck.[181] She died three days later.[182]

Ms. Losinski's three children and her estate brought an action against the county, the sheriff, Deputy Hovell, and their insurers, asserting both constitutional and state-law claims.[183] The complaint alleged that, by agreeing to provide protection to Ms. Losinski, the defendants created a special relationship that survived *DeShaney* analysis and that the failure to protect in this situation violated Ms. Losinski's rights under the Due Process Clause.[184]

In addressing the plaintiffs' due process claim, the court first rejected an argument that Ms. Losinski was owed an affirmative duty because she was in the "protective custody" of the state when harm befell her.[185] Adhering to a notion of custody characterized by restraint and involuntariness, the court quickly concluded that Ms. Losinski had been under no coercion to accept the state's protection.[186] With no coercion or restraint, the fact that the state had assumed some responsibility for her safety was insufficient to satisfy the "in custody" requirement of *DeShaney.*

The court found the plaintiffs' other argument more plausible: By offering protection to Ms. Losinski and assuming some responsibility for her welfare, the defendants created or increased the risk of harm to which she was exposed, and thus owed her an affirmative duty to render assistance.[187] Ultimately, however, the court rejected the constitutional claim as precluded by *DeShaney*, concluding that "[w]hile the issue [was] very close, . . . the essence . . . of *DeShaney* is state creation of dangers faced or involuntary subjection to known risks."[188] The court held neither element was satisfied

---

179. *Id.* at 547-48.
180. *Id.* at 548.
181. *Id.*
182. *Id.* at 547-48.
183. *Id.* at 548.
184. *Id.*
185. *Id.* at 550.
186. *Id.*
187. *Id.* at 550.
188. *Id.* at 550-51.

in *Losinski*.[189] The defendants had not created or enhanced the risk facing Ms. Losinski, nor did they subject her involuntarily to a known existing danger.[190] While recognizing that Ms. Losinski may not have gone to the trailer home had she not been accompanied by Deputy Hovel, the court explained that "[a]lthough the state walked with Julie as she approached the 'lion's den,' it did not force her to proceed."[191]

In *Pinder v. Commissioners of Cambridge*,[192] the plaintiff's former boyfriend, Pittman, had been taken into custody after physically attacking and threatening to kill the plaintiff and her children. The plaintiff informed the arresting officer, Johnson, that Pittman was on probation for a previous arson conviction relating to the plaintiff's home and expressed concern about returning to work and leaving her children at home. The plaintiff returned to work only when she was assured by Officer Johnson that Pittman would be kept in custody overnight because he could not be brought before a county commissioner until the next morning. In fact, Pittman was brought before a commissioner that same evening, charged with only misdemeanor offenses and released on his own recognizance. He went directly to plaintiff's home and set a fire that killed her three children who were home asleep.[193]

The plaintiff sued individually and on behalf of her minor children, claiming that Officer Johnson and the city of Cambridge had violated her and her children's constitutional right to due process by not providing protection in these tragic circumstances.[194] The district court denied Johnson's motion for summary judgment based on qualified immunity,[195] and a divided panel of the Fourth Circuit affirmed.[196] The issue for the en banc court was "simply whether the due process right Pinder claim[ed] was clearly established at the time of her dealings with Johnson."[197]

---

189. *Id.* at 550.
190. *Id.*
191. *Id.* at 550-51.
192. 54 F.3d 1169 (4th Cir. 1995) (*en banc*).
193. *Id.* at 1172.
194. *Id.*
195. Pinder v. Johnson, 821 F. Supp. 376 (D.Md. 1993).
196. Pinder v. Johnson, 33 F.3d 368 (4th Cir. 1994).
197. 54 F.3d at 1173. In addressing the qualified immunity issue, the court noted that it was concerned only with the state of settled law at the time of the challenged conduct, not with the current state of the law. *Id.*

Observing that *DeShaney* was decided just eighteen days before the events in *Pinder* took place and that the affirmative duty of protection that Pinder claimed was owed under the Due Process Clause was the very duty rejected in *DeShaney*, the majority of the en banc court concluded that Officer Johnson did not deprive Pinder and her children of an established right to protection from the violent acts of her boyfriend.[198]

While acknowledging the lack of a custodial relationship within the meaning of *DeShaney*, Pinder argued that the promise of Officer Johnson that Pittman would be incarcerated overnight, along with Johnson's charging Pittman with only misdemeanors, were affirmative acts that created the danger to which Pinder's children were exposed and a corresponding duty to protect. The court suggested that creation-of-danger cases represent no exception to *DeShaney*, but rather conform to the traditional § 1983 framework wherein a plaintiff asserts the violation of a constitutional right caused directly by someone acting under color of state law.[199] The majority of the en banc court, however, refused to view the case as one involving action rather than omission on the part of the state actor, rejected the notion that promises can create a special relationship and emphasized that *DeShaney* makes custody, not promises, the "crux of the special relationship rule."[200]

In deciding that the right to protection was not clearly established in *Pinder*, the court, in dicta, highlighted the "good reasons why the constitutional right to protection sought by Pinder was not clearly established by the courts."[201] Viewing the recognition of a broad affirmative right to protection as "the first step down the slippery slope of liability[,]" the court warned of any theory of liability that would make law enforcement officials guarantors of citizens' safety from private actors.[202] The Fourth Circuit

---

198. *Id.* at 1174.

199. *Id.* at 1176 n.*.

200. *Id.* at 1175. The dissent saw the case as one where Officer Johnson clearly placed Pinder and her children in a dangerous situation through false assurances that Pittman would be locked up overnight. To the extent that Johnson placed Pinder and her children in a dangerous position, he owed them a duty of protection. *Id.* at 1180-82 (Russell, J., joined by Ervin, C.J., Murnaghan, J., and Michael, J., dissenting).

201. *Id.* at 1178.

202. *Id.*

concluded that *DeShaney* should be taken as a "bright-line decision, in which the Court saw in the admittedly sympathetic case the first step on a long, litigious journey."[203]

The lower courts are obviously struggling to formulate a coherent theory for applying the "in custody" and "state-created danger" exceptions to *DeShaney's* no-affirmative-duty rule. A review of recent cases reveals the fine lines and distinctions courts are drawing. The comparison of *Gregory* and *Reed,* along with the examination of *Losinski* and *Pinder*, forces one to ask whether constitutional doctrine should be built on such parsing of facts. Characterizations about the custodial or noncustodial context of the case and, if noncustodial, whether defendants have committed sins of omission or commission, may determine not only whether a duty to protect exists at all, but also what level of culpability will be required in order to state a claim under the Due Process Clause.

The Culpability Factor

The Supreme Court has not definitively established the level of culpability that is required to make out a substantive due process claim based on a failure to protect, but has held that something more than "mere negligence" must be shown.[204] Indeed, in *Collins*, the Court implied that allegations of deliberate conduct that "shocks the conscience"[205] might be required to state a substantive due process claim outside of the custodial context.[206] Multiple standards, including gross negligence,[207] reckless-

---

203. *Id.*

204. Davidson v. Cannon, 474 U.S. 344, 347 (1986); Daniels v. Williams, 474 U.S. 327, 333 (1986).

205. Rochin v. California, 342 U.S. 165, 172 (1952) (pumping of criminal defendant's stomach to obtain evidence was determined to be "conduct that shocks the conscience").

206. *Collins*, 112 S. Ct. at 1071 (refusing to find city's alleged deliberate indifference to worker's safety was "arbitrary Government action that much 'shock the conscience' of federal judges"). In Searles v. Southeastern Pennsylvania Transportation Authority, 990 F.2d 789 (3d Cir. 1993), the court noted that the concepts of deliberate indifference and deliberate harm are quite distinct, the latter requiring an "intent to injure." *Id.* at 793.

207. *See, e.g.*, Simescu v. Emmet County Dep't of Social Servs., 942 F.2d 372, 375 (6th Cir. 1991) (holding gross negligence sufficient for substantive due

ness,[208] deliberate indifference,[209] intent,[210] and conscience-shocking conduct,[211] have been articulated by the lower federal courts.[212]

In *Fagan v. City of Vineland*,[213] the Court of Appeals for the Third Circuit, sitting *en banc*, addressed the issue of the level of culpability required to state a substantive due process claim in the context of a high-speed police pursuit that resulted in the deaths of three innocent bystanders. The

---

process claim, where gross negligence is described as defendant "'intentionally do[ing] something unreasonable with disregard to a known risk or a risk so obvious that he must be assumed to have been aware of it, and of a magnitude such that it is highly probable that harm will follow'" (quoting Nishiyama v. Dickson County, 814 F.2d 277, 282 (6th Cir. 1987) (*en banc*)). *But see* Lewellen v. Metropolitan Government of Nashville and Davidson County, 34 F.3d 345, 350 (6th Cir. 1994) ("*Nishiyama*'s test of a substantive due process violation, relying as it does on an explication of the standard for a particular type of 'gross negligence,' simply cannot be reconciled with what the Supreme Court said in Harker Heights."), *cert. denied*, 115 S. Ct. 963 (1995).

208. *See*, Germany v. Vance, 868 F.2d 9, 18 (1st Cir. 1989) (stating reckless or callous indifference is required for substantive due process violation).

209. *See, e.g.*, Salazar v. City of Chicago 940 F.2d 233, 238-39 (7th Cir. 1991) (holding deliberate indifference proper standard for substantive due process claim but also noting that it is synonymous with intentional or criminally reckless conduct).

210. *See, e.g.*, Lewellen v. Metropolitan Government of Nashville and Davidson County, 34 F.3d 345, 351 (6th Cir. 1994) ("What seems to be required is an intentional infliction of injury . . . or some other governmental action that is 'arbitrary in a constitutional sense.'"), *cert. denied*, 115 S. Ct. 963 (1995).

211. *See, e.g.*, Fagan v. City of Vineland, 22 F.3d 1296, 1303 (3d Cir. 1994) (*en banc*) ("Reexamination of our reckless indifference standard in light of *Collins* leads us to conclude that the substantive component of the Due Process Clause can only be violated by governmental employees when their conduct amounts to an abuse of official power that 'shocks the conscience.'").

212. *See* Barbara Kritchevsky, *Making Sense of State of Mind; Determining Responsibility in Section 1983 Municipal Liability Litigation,* 60 Geo. Wash. L. Rev. 417 (1992), where the author observes that "there appears to be no discernible difference between indifference, recklessness, wantonness, and willfulness." *Id.* at 470 n.279. *See also* Dorris v. County of Washoe, 885 F. Supp. 1383, 1388 n. 3 (D. Nev. 1995) (court engages in lengthy analysis of question of "what mental state is necessary in these 'due process third party harm' cases before the defendants can be held liable").

213. 22 F.3d 1296 (3d Cir. 1994) (*en banc*).

incident that initially gave rise to the chase was a passenger waving his arms through a car's open rooftop. When the driver of the vehicle failed to stop in response to an officer's activated overhead lights, a chase began and continued through residential neighborhoods. Other police vehicles became involved in the pursuit, which ended tragically when the pursued vehicle ran a red light and collided with a pickup truck, killing both occupants of the truck as well as one of the passengers in the fleeing vehicle.[214]

The accident survivors, along with the estates and relatives of those killed, brought actions under § 1983 against the officers and the city. They alleged that their substantive due process rights were violated by the officers' recklessness and by the city's failure to train the officers properly regarding high-speed pursuits. The district court granted summary judgment in favor of all defendants on the constitutional claims, holding that the alleged conduct of the officers could not be found to satisfy the applicable standard in this context. A jury could not find that the actions of the officers constituted "[b]ehavior that shocks the conscience, . . . outrageous behavior, or behavior that offends a sense of justice."[215]

A divided panel reversed the part of the district court's decision that held that a shocks-the-conscience standard was applicable to the due process claim, the majority holding that "reckless indifference to public safety" was the standard to be applied in police pursuit cases. A petition for rehearing *en banc* was granted, limited to the issue of "the appropriate standard to be applied in police pursuit cases alleging a violation of substantive due process."[216]

---

214. *Id.* at 1299, 1300.

215. Fagan v. City of Vineland, 804 F. Supp. 591, 603 (D.N.J. 1992) (footnote omitted), *aff'd in part, rev'd and remanded in part*, 22 F.3d 1283 (3d Cir. 1994) and 22 F.3d 1296 (3d Cir. 1994) (*en banc*).

216. *Fagan*, 22 F.3d at 1302 (*en banc*). Having found no underlying constitutional violation, the district court concluded there could be no liability on the part of the city for failure to train. 804 F. Supp at 606 (citing City of L.A. v. Heller, 475 U.S. 796, 799 (1986)). The Third Circuit panel was in agreement, however, that the city could be found independently liable for the violation of plaintiffs' constitutional rights, even if the individual officers were found not liable because they lacked the requisite mental state to be constitutionally accountable. *Fagan*, 22 F.3d at 1292. This aspect of the panel opinion was not considered in the *en banc* rehearing and has recently been criticized by another panel of the Third Circuit. In Mark v. Borough of Hatboro, 51 F.3d 1137 (3d Cir. 1995), the court made the following observation:

Significantly, the majority of the *en banc* court noted that the matter of whether there was a constitutional duty owed at all under the facts of *Fagan* was an issue not before the court, but that had it been argued, there may have been some question about the duty owed in a noncustodial context after *DeShaney*.[217] Operating on the assumption that there was a duty owed, however, the majority concluded that the duty could be breached in a police pursuit case only by conduct so abusive of official power that it "shocks the conscience."[218] The majority was of the opinion that the Supreme Court's decision in *Collins* dictated the shocks-the-conscience standard for substantive due process claims.

In *Collins*, the plaintiff's husband was a city employee who was asphyxiated while cleaning a sewer line. In her § 1983 suit against the city, plaintiff offered two theories of liability: 1) the city owed its employees an affirmative duty under the Due Process Clause to provide a safe workplace, and 2) the city was deliberately indifferent to the safety needs of its employees by failing to adequately train and warn with respect to safety issues.[219]

As already noted, the Court unanimously rejected the imposition of an affirmative constitutional duty to provide for minimal safety in the public workplace.[220] Furthermore, even assuming deliberate indifference on the part of the city in failing to train or warn with respect to known risks of harm, the Court refused to find a substantive due process violation where the omission could not "properly be characterized as arbitrary, or conscience-shocking, in a constitutional sense."[221]

The majority in *Fagan* interpreted *Collins* as dictating a shocks-the-conscience standard for substantive due process claims arising in a non-

---

> [T]he *Fagan* panel opinion appeared to hold that a plaintiff can establish a constitutional violation predicate to a claim of municipal liability simply by demonstrating that the policymakers, acting with deliberate indifference, enacted an inadequate policy that caused an injury. It appears that, by focusing almost exclusively on the 'deliberate indifference' prong of the Collins test, the panel opinion did not apply the first prong—establishing an underlying constitutional violation.

id. at 1153 n.13.

217. 22 F.3d at 1308 n.9 (*en banc*).

218. *Id.* at 1303.

219. 112 S. Ct. at 1069.

220. *See* notes 110-11, *supra*, and accompanying text.

221. 112 S. Ct. at 1070.

custodial context[222] and rejected the view that *Collins* was limited to cases where harm was alleged to result from governmental omissions rather than affirmative acts.[223]

The *en banc* dissent first attacked the majority's conclusion that the Supreme Court's decision in *Collins* was determinative of the issue in *Fagan*. Criticizing the *en banc* majority for "read[ing] too much into *Collins*[,]" the dissent understood *Collins* as simply rejecting the argument that public employers have an affirmative duty under the federal Constitution to provide for safety in the workplace.[224] In the absence of a duty, there was no need to address or decide the issue of what conduct would be required to constitute a breach. Furthermore, the dissent noted the Supreme Court's use of the term "arbitrary" as well as "conscience-shocking" in *Collins* in describing conduct that would be sufficient to state a claim under the Due Process Clause.[225] Finally, the dissent observed that it would be strange for the Supreme Court to resolve the question of what standard applies to substantive due process claims without reference to the many courts of appeals' decisions it would be undermining in announcing the shocks-the-conscience test.[226]

Assuming the majority's reliance on *Collins* was misplaced, the dissent found little in the way of independent analysis that would sustain the majority's adoption of a shocks-the-conscience test as a necessary standard for substantive due process claims and its rejection of reckless indifference as an insufficient standard for such claims.[227] The dissent looked to the Supreme Court's discussion of due process principles in *Daniels v. Williams*[228] and concluded that "the basic formulation is whether the challenged conduct is an intentional violation or an arbitrary exercise of governmental power in a particular case."[229] Furthermore, the dissent would

---

222. The court observed that "reckless disregard" was the appropriate standard in custody cases "because the government has restricted an individual's liberty and thereby increased his or her vulnerability to abusive governmental action or to private harm." 22 F.3d at 1306.
223. *Id.* at 1304-05 (citing numerous cases in support of position that the shocks-the-conscience standard has been applied to affirmative acts of government).
224. *Id.* at 1311 (Cowen, J., joined by Becker, Scirica, and Lewis, JJ., dissenting).
225. *Id.* at 1312.
226. *Id.* at 1312 n.1.
227. *Id.* at 1313-16.
228. 474 U.S. 327 (1986).
229. 22 F.3d at 1320-21.

hold that reckless indifference to public safety in the context of a high-speed pursuit is tantamount to intentional or arbitrary conduct and, thus, sufficient to make out a due process claim.[230] Faulting the majority for adopting a test that, by the majority's own admission, is "amorphous and imprecise,"[231] the dissent would have remanded the case for trial under the reckless indifference standard.

Under the *en banc* majority's approach in *Fagan*, what shocks the conscience will be a function of both the context in which the conduct occurs and the responsibilities of the officials charged with violating the Constitution. The shocks-the-conscience test would be satisfied by a government actor's recklessness or deliberate indifference to the basic needs of those who are in the state's custody.[232] Furthermore, where a governmental entity is shown to have failed to train its officers in exercising the power vested in them, and such failure is deliberately indifferent to the constitutional rights of persons with whom those officers come into contact, the failure to train may shock the conscience.[233] In noncustodial contexts involving individual state actors' liability, however, it would take more than reckless or deliberate indifference to shock the conscience, whether the conduct was characterized as an affirmative act or an omission.[234]

---

230. *Id.* at 1321. The dissent relied on a number of sources, including the *Restatement (Second) of Torts*, the *Model Penal Code, Black's Law Dictionary* and case law, to support its position that reckless conduct would qualify as intentional or, at least, arbitrary conduct for purposes of satisfying the due process standard. *See* 22 F.3d at 1323-25.
231. 22 F.3d at 1308 (majority opinion).
232. *Id.* at 1306 ("Although we have not articulated the issue in this way, it can fairly be said that the judicial conscience is shocked by a governmental employee's reckless disregard of the constitutional rights of an individual in custody.").
233. Thus, given the facts in *Fagan*, the *en banc* majority found the conduct of the individual officers not so egregious as to shock the conscience of the court, yet let stand the panel decision recognizing the possibility of a substantive due process claim against the city based on a failure to train in proper police pursuit procedures, where such failure was deliberately indifferent to the great likelihood that constitutional rights would be violated. *See Fagan*, 22 F.3d at 1292 (panel opinion).
234. *Compare* Uhlrig v. Harder, 64 F.3d 567, 572 at *4 (10th Cir. Aug. 30, 1995), where the court held that a substantive due process claim in a noncustodial context could be predicated on "reckless or intentionally injury-causing state

There is certainly precedent for applying different standards of culpability to the same constitutional provision. In the Eighth Amendment context, for example, prison conditions cases and medical needs cases are governed by a "deliberate indifference" standard,[235] while excessive force claims must satisfy a "malicious and sadistic" standard of culpability.[236] The ultimate question in both contexts is whether the alleged conduct or condition constitutes cruel and unusual punishment.[237]

---

action which 'shocks the conscience.'" The court explained, however, that to satisfy the 'shock the conscience' standard, a plaintiff must do more than show that the government actor intentionally or recklessly caused injury to the plaintiff by abusing or misusing government power. That is, the plaintiff must demonstrate a degree of outrageousness and a magnitude of potential or actual harm that is truly conscience shocking. The level of conduct required to satisfy this additional requirement cannot precisely be defined, but must necessarily evolve over time from judgments as to the constitutionality of specific government conduct. We do know, however, that the 'shock the conscience' standard requires a high level of outrageousness, because the Supreme Court has specifically admonished that a substantive due process violation requires more than an ordinary tort and that merely allowing unreasonable risks to persist in the workplace is not necessarily conscience shocking. *Id.* at *574.

235. *See, e.g.*, Farmer v. Brennan, 114 S. Ct. 1970, 1984 (1994) (holding that a prison official may be held liable under the Eighth Amendment for acting with deliberate indifference "only if he knows that inmates face a substantial risk of serious harm and disregards that risk by failing to take reasonable measures to abate it"); Helling v. McKinney, 113 S. Ct. 2475, 2481 (1993) (recognizing claim under Eighth Amendment based on prison officials' deliberate indifference to exposure of prisoner to levels of environmental tobacco smoke "that pose an unreasonable risk of serious damage to his future health"); Wilson v. Seiter, 111 S. Ct. 2321, 2326-27 (1991) (making deliberate indifference standard of Estelle v. Gamble, 429 U.S. 97 (1976), applicable to all complaints about conditions of confinement); Estelle v. Gamble, 429 U.S. 97, 103-04 (1976) (holding Eighth Amendment violated by deliberate indifference to prisoners' serious medical needs).

236. Hudson v. McMillian, 112 S. Ct. 995, 998-99 (1992) (adopting standard established in Whitley v. Albers, 475 U.S. 312 (1986), where force was used in context of prison riot, and making Whitley standard applicable "whenever prison officials stand accused of using excessive physical force in violation of the Cruel and Unusual Punishment Clause, [making] the core judicial inquiry . . . whether force was applied in a good-faith effort to maintain or restore discipline, or maliciously and sadistically to cause harm").

237. *Hudson*, 112 S. Ct. at 1000.

Likewise, in the substantive due process context, there is precedent for applying different standards of culpability depending upon the nature of the claim, the setting in which it arose, and the responsibilities of the state actors involved. In *Youngberg v. Romeo,*[238] a case involving the treatment of involuntarily committed, mentally retarded patients, the Supreme Court held that liability could be imposed "when the decision by the professional is such a substantial departure from accepted professional judgment, practice, or standards as to demonstrate that the person responsible actually did not base the decision on such a judgment."[239]

In *Shaw v. Strackhouse,*[240] a profoundly retarded resident of a state mental institution brought a § 1983 action against state employees, asserting a failure to protect him from abuse and sexual assault.[241] On appeal from a grant of summary judgment in favor of the defendants, the Third Circuit addressed the standard of care that state officials owe to those in their custody, and determined that the standard might vary depending upon the nature of the physical custody involved.[242]

The court concluded that while a deliberate indifference standard governed the liability of the nonprofessional employee-defendants, "the *Youngberg* professional judgment standard should have been applied to the primary care professionals, supervisors and administrators named as defendants."[243] In the court's opinion, professional judgment is a relatively deferential standard that, like recklessness and gross negligence, would fall "somewhere between simple negligence and intentional misconduct."[244] The plaintiff's burden is somewhat greater "when trying to establish deliberate indifference than when trying to establish a failure to exercise professional judgment."[245]

---

238. 457 U.S. 307 (1982).
239. *Id.* at 323. *See also* Estate of Porter by Nelson v. State of Illinois, 36 F.3d 684, 688 (7th Cir.1994) ("In determining whether an involuntarily committed patient's right to reasonable safety has been violated, courts may only 'make certain that professional judgment in fact was exercised.'").
240. 920 F.2d 1135 (3d Cir. 1990).
241. *Id.* at 1138-39.
242. *Id.* at 1144.
243. *Id.* at 1139.
244. *Id.* at 1146.
245. *Id.* at 1150.

A number of courts have applied the professional judgment standard to substantive due process claims raised by involuntarily placed foster children. In *Yvonne L. v. New Mexico Department of Human Services,*[246] the Court of Appeals for the Tenth Circuit expressed some doubt about any significant difference between the two standards in the context of foster care, yet adopted the professional judgment standard rather than deliberate indifference.[247] The court explained:

> The compelling appeal of the argument for the professional judgment standard is that foster children, like involuntarily committed patients, are 'entitled to more considerate treatment and conditions' than criminals. These are young children, taken by the state from their parents for reasons that generally are not the fault of the children themselves. 'The officials who place the children are acting in place of the parents.'[248]

The District Court for the District of Columbia has also held that it would be "inappropriate" to require children in foster care to demonstrate deliberate indifference on the part of their caretakers in order to make out a constitutional claim for relief under the Due Process Clause.[249] The court concluded that it would "judge the defendants' liability based on whether they have exercised competent professional judgment in the administration of the District's child welfare system."[250]

Conclusion

Given the variety and range of situations that may be covered by an affirmative duty theory under the Due Process Clause, it is not surprising

---

246. 959 F.2d 883 (10th Cir. 1992).
247. *Id.* at 894.
248. *Id.* (quoting Youngberg v. Romeo, 457 U.S. 307, 321-22 (1982)).
249. *See* La Shawn A. v. Dixon, 762 F. Supp. 959, 996 (D.D.C. 1991), *aff'd and remanded*, 990 F.2d 1319 (D.C. Cir. 1993).
250. *Id.* In a footnote, the court stated that it was persuaded to adopt the professional judgment standard since the plaintiffs were seeking only injunctive relief. *Id.* at 996 n.29. The suggestion was made that deliberate indifference may be a more appropriate standard in cases seeking damages, where there is greater concern about "the chilling effect that an unfavorable judgment may have on municipal policymakers." *Id.*

that the lower court opinions in this area reflect a sense of confusion and a need for guidelines and principles beyond the foundation poured in *DeShaney.* The two major questions are clear: (1) In what contexts beyond imprisonment and involuntary commitment is an affirmative duty of protection owed?, and (2) What level of culpability will the plaintiff be required to demonstrate to establish a breach of the duty in a given context?

This chapter suggests that the concept of custody set out in *DeShaney* should be interpreted expansively to include not only prisoners and involuntarily committed mental patients, but also

1. "voluntarily" committed mental patients,
2. foster children who are either voluntarily or involuntarily placed in the state's child welfare system, and
3. schoolchildren who are in an environment controlled by the state and who rely on state actors to provide for their basic needs, safety, and welfare while they are in that environment.

Within the context of custody, as in the noncustodial setting, different standards of culpability would apply depending upon the nature of the custody. Distinctions should not be based on the voluntary or involuntary aspect of the custodial arrangement, but rather on

1. the responsibilities assumed by the particular state actors involved,
2. the need for state actors to have more or less unfettered discretion in a particular area,
3. the degree of control actually exercised by the state in a given situation, and
4. the extent of reliance and the degree of vulnerability attributed to the person in the state's care.

Given these considerations, it would not be unreasonable to apply a professional judgment standard to those state actors who are trained and employed as professionals in state mental institutions, the state's child welfare system, and the public schools. The test should be:

1. whether the individual actor's behavior constituted a substantial departure from accepted professional judgment, practice, or standards;

2. whether such departure was virtually certain to be detrimental to the safety, health, or welfare of those persons within the professional's care; and
3. whether the constitutional injury complained of was in fact caused by the failure to adhere to accepted professional judgment. Conduct by professionals that represents a significant departure from accepted professional practice and that causes constitutional injury to those entrusted in their care should be actionable under § 1983.[251]

For nonprofessional state employees in these settings, liability should depend upon the plaintiff's ability to show that the constitutional injury was caused by the defendants' deliberate indifference to the safety, health, or well-being of those in their care. Deliberate indifference would be established in the Eighth Amendment context by satisfying the test set out in *Farmer v. Brennan*,[252] that is, by showing that a defendant had actual knowledge of the substantial risk faced by the inmate and failed to take reasonable steps to abate that risk. Outside the Eighth Amendment setting, however, the deliberate indifference standard should be satisfied if the plaintiff proves that a defendant consciously acted or chose not to act with actual or constructive knowledge of the obvious consequences of this conduct.[253]

---

251. The professional judgment standard, unlike the deliberate indifference standard, would entail a purely objective test, analogous to the "objective reasonableness" standard employed in Fourth Amendment excessive force cases. *See, e.g.*, Graham v. Connor, 490 U.S. 386 (1989). Thus, it would not be relevant to the test whether the professional actually knew that her conduct violated accepted professional practice or whether she intended a substantial deviation from accepted professional standards.
252. 114 S. Ct. 1970 (1994).
253. Being charged with knowledge of the obvious or very likely consequences of one's conduct does not mean that the individual defendant must have intended or actually been aware that such consequences would violate the victim's constitutional rights. This form of deliberate indifference is more akin to the concept of deliberate indifference established in City of Canton v. Harris, 489 U.S. 378, 388 (1989), permitting liability of a municipality for failure to train resulting in a constitutional violation to be premised on obviousness or constructive notice.

In noncustodial contexts, there are two different points at which the question of culpability plays a role. In assessing the threshold question of whether an affirmative duty to protect from harm inflicted by third persons should be recognized in noncustodial contexts, the test should be whether a state actor deliberately chose a course of conduct or failed to act, knowing that the act or omission was substantially certain to create an unreasonable risk of harm to the plaintiff or arbitrarily enhance the danger to which the plaintiff would be exposed. If the fact-finder answers this question affirmatively, then the second question should be whether the state actor who knowingly exposed the plaintiff to danger by the act or omission took any reasonable steps to ameliorate or to provide protection from the situation created.

The search for criteria to define the circumstances that should give rise to an affirmative duty to protect under the substantive Due Process Clause has been misguided by the view that *DeShaney* recognizes such a duty only in involuntary custodial situations, as well as the assumption that a uniform standard of culpability will apply to all such claims. If the constitutional backdrop for affirmative duty cases is a shocks-the-conscience standard, the degree of fault or level of culpability that will satisfy this test should vary depending on the nature of the custodial arrangement in the custody cases. In noncustodial creation-of-danger or enhancement-of-risk cases, liability of state actors should depend upon their knowingly putting the individual in a position of unreasonable risk of harm and then failing to take reasonable measures to protect that individual from the harm created.

Restricting the affirmative duty to contexts of imprisonment, involuntary institutionalization, and involuntary placement in a state's foster care system is an arbitrary, unfair, and unnecessary means of containing the expansion of substantive due process claims. The complexity and variety of situations in which the affirmative duty should be recognized dictate that careful attention be paid to the level of culpability required in order to establish a breach of the duty, and close scrutiny be given to the causal connection between the challenged behavior and the resulting harm.

Chapter Five
Municipal Liability Under § 1983

Michael S. Bogren

Section 1983 is the descendent of § 1 of the Civil Rights Act of 1871, 17 Stat. 13. The bill was introduced on March 28, 1871, as H.R. 320. Section 1 of the Bill, now § 1983, was debated on a limited basis and was passed without amendment.[1] The Act, also known as the Ku Klux Klan Act, grew out of a message sent to Congress by President Ulysses Grant on March 23, 1871.[2] The Bill was designed inter alia to provide a federal remedy where a state-created remedy was in existence, but was not available in practice.[3]

Monroe v. Pape

In 1961 the U.S. Supreme Court issued its decision in *Monroe v. Pape.*[4] *Monroe* greatly expanded the scope of official conduct actionable under § 1983 by holding that state officials acted "under color of law" even when they violated state or federal law.

The plaintiff, Monroe, alleged that thirteen Chicago police officers broke into his home, without a warrant, while he and his wife were in bed, made them stand naked in the living room, and ransacked every room in the house. The complaint further alleged that Mr. Monroe was taken to the police station and detained for ten hours while he was interrogated about a murder. He was subsequently released without criminal charges being filed against him. The complaint alleged that the police officers had no search warrant and no arrest warrant, but that they acted under color of law.[5]

The plaintiffs filed suit in federal court alleging a violation of their constitutional rights. The defendant police officers argued that the phrase

1. Monell v. Department of Social Services, 436 U.S. 658, 664-665 (1978).
2. Monroe v. Pape, 365 U.S. 167, 172 (1961).
3. Monroe v. Pape, 365 U.S. at 174.
4. 365 U.S. 167 (1961).
5. Monroe v. Pape, 365 U.S. at 169.

"under color of law" excluded acts of a state official who could point to no legal authority authorizing his actions. In addressing this argument, the Supreme Court first held that the federal remedy was supplementary to any state remedy, and that the state remedy need not be exhausted before the federal remedy could be utilized.[6]

In rejecting the defendants' construction of the phase "under color of law," the Court relied upon *United States v. Classic*[7] and *Screws v. United States,*[8] cases which analyzed 18 U.S.C § 242, the criminal counterpart to § 1983. The Court followed the holdings in *Classic* and *Screws*, and held that "misuse of power, possessed by virtue of state law and made possible only because the wrongdoer is clothed with the authority of state law, is action taken 'under color' of state law."[9]

The *Monroe* Court refused, however, to allow claims under § 1983 to be asserted against municipal corporations. The Court stated: " . . . we are of the opinion that Congress did not undertake to bring municipal corporations within the ambit of [Section 1983]."[10] The Supreme Court relied on the legislative history of the Ku Klux Klan Act, and specifically the rejection of the Sherman Amendment, to find municipal corporations excluded from § 1983. The Sherman Amendment, as originally proposed, included a provision which would have made the inhabitants of a municipality in which certain acts of violence occurred liable to pay full compensation to the person damaged.[11] The version of the Sherman Amendment which was finally adopted deleted all provisions for municipal liability.[12] The Supreme Court concluded its discussion of municipal liability in *Monroe* by stating:

> The response of the Congress to the proposal to make municipalities liable for certain actions being brought within federal purview by the Act of April 20, 1871, was so antagonistic that we cannot believe that the word 'person' was used in this particular Act to

---

6. Monroe v. Pape, 365 U.S. at 183.
7. 313 U.S. 299 (1941).
8. 325 U.S. 91 (1945).
9. Monroe v. Pape, 365 U.S. at 183.
10. Monroe v. Pape, 365 U.S. at 187.
11. Cong. Globe, 42d Cong., 1st Sess., p. 663.
12. Monroe v. Pape, 365 U.S. at 190.

> include [municipal corporations]. Accordingly, we hold that the motion to dismiss the complaint against the City of Chicago was properly granted.[13]

Municipal corporations were the purview of liability under § 1983 until 1978.

Monell v. Department of Social Services

In *Monell v. Department of Social Services,*[14] the Supreme Court revisited the holding of *Monroe v. Pape*, that municipal corporations could not be held liable under § 1983. Reexamining the debate in the 42nd Congress on the Civil Rights Act of 1871, and examining historical rulings which treated municipal corporations as natural persons for virtually all purposes of constitutional and statutory analysis,[15] the Supreme Court overruled *Monroe* and held that Congress *did* intend municipalities to be included among those "persons" to whom § 1983 applied.[16] That holding has spawned litigation which has resulted in conflicting circuit court decisions, fractured Supreme Court rulings, and few concrete rules to guide the practitioner.

Preliminary Matters

Prior to examining the bases of liability against municipalities under § 1983, it is necessary to understand various concepts which can come into play in litigating such claims. Practitioners seeking to prosecute or defend a municipality in an action under § 1983 must be familiar with these concepts.

Eleventh Amendment

The Eleventh Amendment states:

> The Judicial power of the United States shall not be construed to extend to any suit in law or equity, commenced or prosecuted against

---

13. Monroe v. Pape, 365 U.S. at 191-192 (footnote omitted).
14. 436 U.S. 658 (1978).
15. *Monell*, 436 U.S. at 665-689.
16. *Monell*, 436 U.S. at 690.

> one of the United States by Citizens of another State, or by Citizens or Subjects of any Foreign State.

To the uninitiated, the Eleventh Amendment appears to be of very limited terms. However, as the Supreme Court explained in *Hans v. Louisiana*,[17] the Amendment deprives a federal court of jurisdiction to entertain a suit brought by a citizen against his or her own state, as well as another state. The Supreme Court held that the history of Article III of the Constitution and the pre-existing common law did not contemplate federal jurisdiction over any suits against unconsenting states.[18] In spite of this jurisdictional bar, a state may waive Eleventh Amendment immunity and consent to suit against it in federal court.[19] In determining whether a state has waived its constitutional protection under the Eleventh Amendment, the courts will find waiver only where stated by express language or by such overwhelming implications from the text of a statute that there is no room for any other reasonable construction.[20]

Congress has the power to abrogate the Eleventh Amendment immunity consistent with the provisions of Section 5 of the Fourteenth Amendment.[21] However, just as statutes are strictly construed when determining whether a state has consented to suit, so too must the congressional intent to abrogate Eleventh Amendment immunity be unequivocal.[22]

The Supreme Court held in *Quern v. Jordan*[23] that § 1983 does not explicitly abrogate the immunity of the states, nor does it have a history which would lead to such a conclusion. Thus, the Court held that Eleventh Amendment immunity barred federal courts from obtaining jurisdiction over states in § 1983 actions.

It can become confusing to determine proper application of the Eleventh Amendment due to the fact that § 1983 creates liability on the part of every "person" who, under color of any statute, ordinance, regulation, custom or usage of any state, territory or the District of Columbia, causes a

---

17. 134 U.S. 1 (1890).
18. Hans v. Louisiana, 134 U.S. at 15.
19. Pennhurst State School and Hospital v. Halderman, 465 U.S. 89, 99 (1984).
20. Edelman v. Jordan, 415 U.S. 651, 673 (1974).
21. Fitzpatrick v. Bitker, 427 U.S. 445 (1976).
22. Pennhurst State School and Hospital v. Halderman, 465 U.S. at 99.
23. 440 U.S. 332, 345 (1979).

deprivation of any rights, privileges, or immunities secured by the Constitution or laws of the United States. This requirement is generally referred to as "state action," and defendants in § 1983 actions are typically referred to as "state actors."

Eleventh Amendment immunity from suit in federal courts extends to the states themselves and state agencies, but does not typically extend to counties and other political subdivisions, especially municipal corporations.[24] The issue to be determined in applying Eleventh Amendment immunity is whether the defendant is the state itself or, in the words of Monell, a "local government unit." This determination must be made by examining state law. The Supreme Court held in *Mount Healthy* that a Board of Education was not entitled to assert Eleventh Amendment immunity because under Ohio law the "state" did not include "political subdivisions," while "political subdivisions," in turn, *did* include local school districts.[25]

A determination must be made on a state-by-state basis as to whether a particular governmental entity is protected by Eleventh Amendment immunity. See *Fordyce v. City of Seattle*[26] (under Washington law a municipal corporation, such as the city of Seattle, is not a state agency); *Eaglesmith v. Ward*[27] (under California law County Office of Education [COE] is a state agency for Eleventh Amendment purposes as is a county school district); and *Roach v. West Virginia Regional Jail and Correctional Facility Authority*[28] (under West Virginia law a regional jail and correctional facility authority is a state agency for purposes of Eleventh Amendment immunity). This can lead to the rather anomalous result of a similar agency or office being both "state" and "local" in the same circuit, depending upon which state is involved.[29] It should be carefully noted that it is the federal court's assessment of certain factors that determines whether an agency or officer is "state" or "local," not state case law.[30]

---

24. Mount Healthy City School District Board of Education v. Doyle, 429 U.S. 274, 280 (1977); *Monell*, 436 U.S. at 690, n. 54.
25. *Mount Healthy*, 429 U.S. at 280.
26. 55 F.3d 436, 442 (9th Cir. 1995).
27. 73 F.3d 857, 860 (9th Cir. 1996).
28. 74 F.3d 46, 48 (4th Cir. 1996).
29. *Compare* Hufford v. Rodgers, 912 F.2d. 1338 (11th Cir. 1990), holding Florida sheriffs are local, with Parker v. Williams, 862 F.2d. 1471 (11th Cir. 1989), holding Alabama sheriffs to be state-level officers.
30. *See* Hufford v. Rodgers.

The Eleventh Amendment does not bar a claim where the action under § 1983 is brought in state court, since the Amendment, by its explicit terms, restrains only the "Judicial power of the United States."[31] Section 1983 actions may be brought in state court.[32] Thus, a plaintiff bringing suit against a state or state agency under § 1983 can avoid Eleventh Amendment immunity by filing suit in state court.[33] However, as will be discussed, the state is not a "person" for purposes of § 1983. So, the fact that Eleventh Amendment immunity does not bar a § 1983 claim brought in state court against the state does not give a plaintiff a claim that is free from defenses.

The Eleventh Amendment has also been held to apply to a suit seeking injunctive relief, as the language of the Eleventh Amendment speaks of suits "in law or equity."[34] There is an important exception to Eleventh Amendment immunity with respect to injunctive relief. A suit challenging the constitutionality of a state official's action is not deemed to be one against the state, and prospective injunctive relief may be issued by a federal court under such circumstances.[35] The Supreme Court has held, however, that while a federal court may award an injunction that governs the state official's future conduct, it still may not award monetary damages.[36] Thus, the federal courts may award *prospective* injunctive relief against a state official in a suit challenging the constitutionality of the official's action.[37]

The Supreme Court has also held that an award of attorney fees to a prevailing plaintiff under § 1988 is not barred by the Eleventh Amendment.[38] Therefore, a prevailing plaintiff who obtains prospective injunctive

---

31. Maine v. Thiboutot, 448 U.S. 1, 9 n. 7 (1980).
32. Martinez v. California, 444 U.S. 277 (1980).
33. Defendants have a right to remove actions arising under the Constitution and statutes of the United States to Federal Court. 28 U.S.C. § 1331; 28 U.S.C. § 1441. Once the case is removed, a state could seek to dismiss the federal claims on Eleventh Amendment grounds. The result, however, would be a classic Pyrrhic victory. The plaintiff could refile the claims in State Court where the action first started. A defendant should carefully consider Rule 11 before undertaking this course of action.
34. Cory v. White, 257 U.S. 85, 91 (1982).
35. Ex parte *Young*, 209 U.S. 123, 160 (1908).
36. Edelman v. Jordan, 415 U.S. 651, 666 (1974).
37. Pennhurst State School and Hospital v. Halderman, 465 U.S. at 103.
38. Hutto v. Finney, 437 U.S. 678, 697 (1978).

relief against a state official will be entitled to an award of attorney fees payable from the state treasury.

Official-Capacity Suits and Personal-Capacity Suits

It is imperative to understand the distinction between official capacity suits and personal capacity suits. In *Brandon v. Holt*,[39] the Supreme Court held that a suit brought against a public official "in his official capacity" imposed liability on the entity that person represented, rather than on the individual himself. As the Supreme Court explained in *Kentucky v. Graham:*[40]

> Personal-capacity suits seek to impose personal liability upon a government official for actions he takes under color of state law. Official-capacity suits, in contrast, 'generally represent only another way of pleading an action against an entity of which an officer is an agent.' As long as the government entity receives notice and an opportunity to respond, an official-capacity suit is, in all respects other than name, to be treated as a suit against the entity. It is not a suit against the official personally, for the real party in interest is the entity. Thus, while an award of damages against an official in his personal capacity can be executed only against the official's personal assets, a plaintiff seeking to recover on a damages judgment in an official-capacity suit must look to the government entity itself.

It is oftentimes difficult to ascertain whether a plaintiff seeks to sue an individual in his or her individual or official capacity. The Supreme Court has observed that "it is obviously preferable for the plaintiff to be specific in the first instance to avoid any ambiguity."[41] However, in the absence of an explicit statement in the complaint, the circuits are split as to how to determine whether a claim should be treated as an individual-capacity claim or an official-capacity claim.

The Second, Fourth, Fifth, Ninth, Tenth, and Eleventh Circuits have adopted the approach of looking to the substance of the plaintiff's claim, the relief sought, and the "course of proceedings" to determine the nature

---

39. 469 U.S. 464, 471-472 (1985).
40. 473 U.S. 159, 165-166 (1985).
41. Hafer v. Melo, 502 U.S. 21, 24, n.* (1991).

of a § 1983 suit when a plaintiff fails to allege capacity. Two circuits, the Eighth and Sixth, have adopted a bright-line rule that where the complaint is silent as to capacity, it is presumed that a defendant has been sued only in his or her official capacity. The First Circuit has not addressed the issue, but a district court in the First Circuit has adhered to the bright-line rule announced by the Sixth and Eighth Circuits.

The majority view in the circuits, which looks to the course of proceedings to determine the nature of the suit, is fairly consistent in its application. In *Rodriguez v. Phillips,*[42] the Second Circuit followed the "course of proceedings" test. (Relief sought in the complaint, defenses raised by the individual defendants, and the fact that the plaintiff continued the claim against the individual who was no longer employed rather than substituting the current office holder dictate a finding that the suit was a personal-capacity suit.) The other circuits applying the "course of proceedings" test have reached similar conclusions.[43]

In *Egerdahl v. Hibbing Community College,*[44] the Eighth Circuit continued to follow its previously announced rule that if a plaintiff's com-

---

42. 66 F.3d 470, 482 (2d Cir. 1995).
43. Melo v. Hafer, 912 F.2d 628, 636 (3d Cir. 1990), *aff'd* 502 U.S. 21 (1991) (claims asserted in the complaint together with defenses raised compel conclusion that defendant was sued in both her official and individual capacities); Biggs v. Meadows, 66 F.3d 56, 61 (4th Cir. 1995) (relief requested in the complaint together with defenses raised demonstrate that the plaintiff intended to sue the defendants in their individual capacity); Shoshone-Bannock Tribes v. Fish & Game Commission, Idaho, 42 F.3d 1278, 1284-1285 (9th Cir. 1994) (where state officials are named in a complaint seeking damages under § 1983, it is presumed that the officials are being sued in their individual capacity. However, since the plaintiff explicitly named one official in his individual capacity, the other officials were entitled to assume that they were being sued only in their official capacity); Houston v. Reich, 932 F.2d 883, 885 (10th Cir. 1991) (even though the caption of the pleadings did not indicate on what basis the defendants were being sued, the pleadings, pre-trial order and jury instructions made it clear that the suit was brought against the defendants in both their official and individual capacities); Hobbs v. Roberts, 999 F.2d 1526, 1531 (11th Cir. 1993) (allegation of "several" liability among defendants, dismissal of official who became successor in office after the date alleged in the complaint, and defenses raised demonstrated that individuals were sued in both their official and individual capacity).
44. 72 F.3d 615, 619-620 (8th Cir. 1995).

plaint is silent about the capacity in which an individual is being sued, the complaint is interpreted as including only official-capacity claims.

The Sixth Circuit announced the same bright-line test in *Wells v. Brown.*[45] However, the Sixth Circuit has not applied the bright-line rule with the same degree of certainty as has the Eighth Circuit. For example, in *Ritchie v. Wickstrom,*[46] the court held that although the complaint did not identify the capacity in which an individual defendant was being sued, "it becomes instantly clear that the suit against corrections officer Wickstrom is an 'individual capacity' suit not subject to Eleventh Amendment protections."

In *Sanderfer v. Nichols*,[47] the court seemed to apply a "course of proceedings" approach:

> The order substituting Jansen as a party defendant does not specify the capacity in which she is sued, and ordinarily, when the complaint in a § 1983 action does not specify that a defendant is sued in her individual capacity, we have held that such a defendant has been sued in her official capacity only. See *Wells v. Brown*, 891 F.2d 591 (6th Cir. 1989). However, because the district court ordered Jansen substituted as a party defendant but denied her summary judgment on qualified immunity grounds while granting summary judgment to the county, we will assume, for purposes of this action, that the district court's intent was to substitute Jansen in her individual capacity.

Finally, in *Charron v. Picano,*[48] a district court in the First Circuit held that the bright-line rule adopted by the Sixth and Eighth Circuits was preferable where the plaintiff neglected to identify the capacity in which a defendant was being sued.

As the Supreme Court noted in *Hafer v. Melo*, *supra*, the preferable approach is for a plaintiff to unequivocally state whether an individual is

---

45. 891 F.2d 591, 593 (6th Cir. 1989) ("It is not too much to ask that if a person or entity is to be subject to suit, the person or entity should be properly named and clearly notified of the potential for payment of damages individually.") *See also* Lovelace v. O'Hara, 985 F.2d 847, 850 (6th Cir. 1993).
46. 938 F.2d 689, 692 (6th Cir. 1991).
47. 62 F.3d 151, 152, n. 1 (6th Cir. 1995).
48. 811 F. Supp. 768, 772 (D.R.I. 1993).

being sued in his or her individual capacity, official capacity, or both. This places no greater burden on the plaintiff, clearly identifies the nature of the claim upon which a defendant is being called to defend, and avoids confusion. Most important from the practitioner's standpoint, this practice will avoid the potential loss of a viable cause of action if it is not properly pled.

Apart from Eleventh Amendment immunity issues, the capacity of an individual defendant is important for determining what claims may be brought against the defendant and what defenses can be raised. For example, while qualified immunity is available to an individual defendant sued in his or her individual capacity,[49] a municipality may not assert the qualified immunity of its officers or agents as a defense to liability for damages.[50] Thus, an individual sued in his or her official capacity could not raise the defense of qualified immunity, since the suit is, in fact, a claim against the governmental entity.

By the same token, while punitive damages can be assessed against a defendant sued in his or her individual capacity,[51] punitive damages cannot be assessed against a municipality.[52] Therefore, an official-capacity claim asserted against an individual would not allow the imposition of punitive damages, but an individual-capacity claim asserted against an individual state actor would.

Finally, and most important, to establish personal liability in a § 1983 action a plaintiff must show that the official, acting under color of state law, caused the deprivation of a federal right.[53] In an official-capacity action, however, the governmental entity's policy or custom must have caused the violation of federal law.[54] (The requirements for establishing liability against a governmental entity under *Monell* will be discussed in detail in Part III *infra.*)

When a plaintiff is determining the capacity in which an individual defendant is sued, it must be kept foremost in mind that a suit against an individual in his or her official capacity will require the same elements and

---

49. Anderson v. Creighton, 483 U.S. 635 (1987).
50. Owen v. City of Independence, 445 U.S. 622, 638, 657 (1980).
51. Smith v. Wade, 461 U.S. 30 (1983).
52. City of Newport v. Fact Concerts, Inc., 453 U.S. 247, 271 (1981).
53. Kentucky v. Graham, 473 U.S. 159, 166 (1985).
54. *Id.*

standard of proof as would be required to establish liability against the entity itself, as an official capacity suit *is* a suit against the entity.

The State Is Not a "Person" Under § 1983

In *Will v. Michigan Department of State Police,*[55] the Supreme Court addressed the issue of whether a state (or one its agencies) is a person under § 1983. The Supreme Court held that a state is not a "person" within the meaning of § 1983. Using its decision in *Quern v. Jordan, supra*, as a starting point, the Court relied on the legislative history of § 1983 and the long-established doctrine of sovereign immunity.[56] The Court concluded that neither a state nor its officials acting in their official capacities are "persons" under § 1983.[57]

The Supreme Court's ruling in *Will* created some confusion with respect to state officials. Defendants attempted to argue that when a plaintiff alleged that a state official was *acting* in "official capacity," as opposed to being *sued* in "official capacity," *Will* automatically barred the claim.

This confusion was resolved in *Hafer v. Melo*. The defendant in *Hafer* asserted that she could not be held personally liable for discharging employees of the state of Pennsylvania, because she *acted* in her official capacity as auditor general of Pennsylvania. In rejecting this contention, the Supreme Court stated:

> Of course, the claims considered in *Will* were official-capacity claims; the phrase 'acting in their official capacities' is best understood as a reference to the capacity in which the state actor is sued, not the capacity in which the officer inflicts the alleged injury. To the extent that *Will* allows the construction Hafer suggests, however, we now eliminate that ambiguity.
>
> * * *
>
> Hafer seeks to overcome the distinction between official- and personal-capacity suits by arguing that Section 1983 liability turns not on the capacity in which state officials are sued, but on the

55. 491 U.S. 58 (1989).
56. *Will*, 491 U.S. at 67-68.
57. *Will*, 491 U.S. at 71.

> capacity in which they acted when injuring the plaintiff. Under *Will*, she asserts, state officials may not be held liable in their personal capacity for actions they take in their official capacity.[58]
>
> The Court rejected Hafer's argument, stating:
>
> The requirement of action under color of state law means that Hafer may be liable for discharging respondents precisely because of her authority as auditor general. We cannot accept the novel proposition that this same official authority insulates Hafer from suit.[59]
>
> The Court concluded by holding:
>
> We hold that state officials, sued in their individual capacities, are 'persons' within the meaning of Section 1983. The Eleventh Amendment does not bar such suits, nor are state officers absolutely immune from personal liability under Section 1983 solely by virtue of the 'official' nature of their acts.[60]

One of the significant results of *Will* is that Eleventh Amendment immunity, which had no effect on a § 1983 claim brought against a state in state court, became relatively unimportant. Since a state was not a "person" under § 1983, it could not be sued for damages under § 1983 in either state or federal court. The practical effect of *Will* was explained by the Sixth Circuit:[61]

> Thus, in an effort to get a 'deep pocket,' the plaintiff in *Brandon* sued the Director in his official capacity. A public official is only a 'deep pocket,' however, if the governmental unit will pay the judgment. This may or may not occur. In order to provide the plaintiff in *Brandon* with the 'deep pocket' he would have had post-*Monell*, the Supreme Court simply declared that a suit against a public official in his 'official capacity' is a suit against the governmental unit.

---

58. Hafer v. Melo, 502 U.S. at 26-27.
59. Hafer v. Melo, 502 U.S. at 27-28.
60. Hafer v. Melo, 502 U.S. at 31.
61. Ritchie v. Wickstrom, *supra*, 938 F.2d at 691.

What goes around comes around, however, and the 'deep pocket' feeling of euphoria felt by plaintiffs post-*Brandon* was dampened somewhat when the Supreme Court issued its opinion in *Will v. Michigan Department of State Police*, 491 U.S. 58, 109 S.Ct. 2304, 105 L.Ed.2d 45 (1989).

In *Will*, the Supreme Court determined that states are not 'persons' within the meaning of Section 1983 and that 'a suit against a state official in his or her official capacity is not a suit against the official, but rather is a suit against . . . the state itself.'

Thus, at least for causes of action brought under § 1983, a plaintiff will fare no better in state court attempting to assert an official-capacity suit against a state official than he would in federal court. Practitioners representing states or state agencies and officials must bear in mind that Eleventh Amendment immunity is quasi-jurisdictional in that it can be waived. It is an affirmative defense which can be waived when the state appears and defends the action without raising the immunity as a defense.[62]

Prerequisites for a Claim Under § 1983

The deprivation of a federally protected right is the essence of a claim under § 1983. The claim may be a federal statutory right[63] or rights protected by the U.S. Constitution. Rights protected by the Constitution are the more prevalent claim asserted under § 1983.[64] It must be kept in mind that § 1983 creates no substantive rights. As the Supreme Court stated in *Chapman v. Houston Welfare Organization*:[65]

> . . . it remains true that one cannot go into court and claim a 'violation of § 1983'—for § 1983 by itself does not protect anyone against anything.

---

62. Atascadero State Hospital v. Scanlon, 475 U.S. 234 (1985).
63. Maine v. Thiboutot, 448 U.S. 1 (1980); Chapman v. Houston Welfare Rights Organization, 440 U.S. 600 (1979).
64. Wilson v. Garcia, 471 U.S. 261, 278 (1985).
65. 441 U.S. at 617.

In other words, § 1983 is not self-executing. It cannot be the federal statute which is claimed to have been violated. Section 1983 merely provides a remedy for the violation of an underlying federally protected right.

The existence of a constitutional violation (or the violation of certain federal statutes) is a fundamental prerequisite to hold a municipality liable under § 1983. In *City of Los Angeles v. Heller*,[66] the Supreme Court addressed the requirement of a constitutional violation. In a bifurcated trial the jury returned a verdict in favor of a defendant police officer and against the plaintiff, Heller, on an excessive force claim. The district court then dismissed the action against the city of Los Angeles, concluding that since the officer had been exonerated by the jury, there could be no basis for liability against the city. The Ninth Circuit reversed.[67]

The Supreme Court reversed the Ninth Circuit, stating: "[The city and its police commission] were sued only because they were thought legally responsible for [Officer] Bushey's actions; if the latter inflicted no constitutional injury on respondent, it is inconceivable that petitioners could be liable to respondent."[68] The Court concluded by stating:

> If a person has suffered no constitutional injury at the hands of the individual police officer, the fact that the departmental regulations might have authorized the use of constitutionally excessive force is quite beside the point.[69]

Circuit Court Decisions

All of the circuits, with the exception of the Third and the Tenth, have followed the Supreme Court's decision in *Heller*.[70]

---

66. 475 U.S. 796 (1986).
67. City of Los Angeles v. Heller, 475 U.S. at 798.
68. City of Los Angeles v. Heller, 475 U.S. at 799.
69. *Id.*
70. *See* DeFeliciano v. DeJesus, 873 F.2d 447 (1st Cir. 1989); Pitchell v. Callan, 13 F.3d 545, 549 (2d Cir. 1994); Gray v. Laws, 51 F.3d 426, 439 (4th Cir. 1995); Leatherman v. Tarrant County, 28 F.3d 1388, 1398, n.15 (5th Cir. 1994); Garner v. Memphis Police Department, 8 F.3d 358, 365 (6th Cir. 1993); Thompson v. Boggs, 33 F.3d 847, 859 (7th Cir. 1994); Robinson v. City of St. Charles, Missouri, 972 F.2d 974, 977 (8th Cir. 1992); Quintanilla v. City of Downey, 84 F.3d 353, 355 (9th Cir. 1996); Hardin v. Hayes, 52 F.3d 934, 939, n.8 (11th Cir. 1995).

In *Fagan v. City of Vineland*,[71] the Third Circuit stated that the language in *Heller* "should not be read so broadly as to automatically preclude municipal liability absent an individual police officer's liability."

While that statement may be true under some conceivable set of circumstances, the Third Circuit announced the rule in a setting where an individual officer had been found not to have inflicted constitutional injury on the plaintiff. In that circumstance, the court's ruling is difficult, if not impossible, to reconcile with *Heller*.

The Third Circuit attempted to distinguish *Heller* on the basis that the Supreme Court was faced with a Fourth Amendment issue, whereas the plaintiff in *Fagan* had raised a substantive due process claim arising out of a police pursuit. The perceived significance of that distinction was not explained.

The *Fagan* court also believed that the Supreme Court in *Heller* dismissed the claim against the city of Los Angeles because it sounded in *respondeat superior*, which is not a proper basis for imposing liability.[72] The Third Circuit went on to find that because an individual officer could be found liable under the circumstances of a pursuit only if his or her conduct "shocked the conscience," the city could still be held liable for failure to train upon a showing of "deliberate indifference."[73]

The problem with the *Fagan* analysis is that it misconstrues *Heller*, and violates the principle established by the Supreme Court in *City of Canton v. Harris*[74] for establishing municipal liability for failure to train.

Contrary to the Third Circuit's assertion, *Heller* did not analyze the claims against the city of Los Angeles as being claims of *respondeat superior*. The Supreme Court observed that the city of Los Angeles was sued "only because they were thought legally responsible for [Officer] Bushey's actions."[75] In the context of *Monell*, which the Supreme Court cited in *Heller*, it is not logical to believe that the Court was addressing a *respondeat superior* claim. Rather, the city was thought legally responsible for the officer's actions due to departmental regulations which "might have authorized the use of constitutionally excessive force."[76] Thus, the Third Circuit's attempt to distinguish *Heller* is not well-founded.

---

71. 22 F.3d 1283, 1291 (3d Cir. 1994).
72. *Fagan*, 22 F.3d at 1292.
73. *Fagan*, 22 F.3d at 1292.
74. 489 U.S. 390 (1989).
75. *Heller*, 475 U.S. at 1573.
76. *Heller*, 475 U.S. at 1573.

Additionally, the court in *Fagan* asserted that a different standard governed whether a police officer inflicted a constitutional injury and whether the city inflicted a constitutional injury for failure to train. This analysis ignores two significant points: there was a determination that the officer did not inflict a constitutional injury on the plaintiff in the first instance, and the Supreme Court's repeated statements in *City of Canton v. Harris, supra*, that a failure to train claim is dependent upon a constitutional injury inflicted by a municipal employee: "The claim in this case, however, is that if a concededly valid policy is *unconstitutionally applied by a municipal employee,* the City is liable if the employee has not been adequately trained and the constitutional wrong has been caused by that failure to train."[77] The Court noted that "respondent must still prove that the deficiency in training actually caused the *police officers' indifference to her medical needs.*"[78] The Supreme Court also stated in *City of Canton* that "In virtually every instance where a person has had his or her *constitutional rights violated by a city employee*, a § 1983 plaintiff will be able to point to something the city 'could have done' to prevent the unfortunate incident."[79]

The Tenth Circuit has joined the Third Circuit in departing from the clear holding in *Heller.* In *Williams v. City of Denver*,[80] the court stated in dicta that " . . . the City may be held liable for its own conduct even absent unconstitutional conduct by Officer Farr."[81]

On balance, *Fagan* and *Williams* are radical departures from the Supreme Court's decision in *Heller*. However, these decisions are the law in the Third and Tenth Circuits, and practitioners in those Circuits must be aware of the holdings.

The holding in *Heller* should not be misconstrued as a ruling that the dismissal of claims against individual defendants on the basis of qualified immunity will insulate a municipality from liability. *Heller* was based upon the fact that a determination was made that a police officer had not inflicted a constitutional injury upon the plaintiff. The Supreme Court was careful to point out that qualified immunity was not an issue in the case.[82]

---

77. City of Canton v. Harris, 489 U.S. at 387.
78. *Id.*, at 391. (Emphasis added)
79. *Id.*, at 392. (Emphasis added)
80. 99 F.3d. 1009 (10th Cir. 1996).
81. 99 F.3d. at 1013.
82. City of Los Angeles v. Heller, 475 U.S. at 798.

An individual defendant dismissed on the basis of qualified immunity stands in a different position than one who has been dismissed on a finding that no constitutional violation occurred. A detailed discussion of qualified immunity can be found in Chapter 11. For purposes of this discussion, however, it is enough to state that qualified immunity shields an individual defendant from liability and suit where there may have been a violation of the plaintiff's constitutional rights because the law was not "clearly established" that the defendant's actions were improper.[83]

While the Supreme Court has not explicitly addressed what impact qualified immunity of an individual defendant has on claims of municipal liability, it has held that qualified immunity does not apply to municipalities.[84] The Circuits which have addressed the issue are unanimous in holding that a municipality does not escape liability for a § 1983 violation based solely upon the qualified immunity of an officer who committed the violation.[85]

---

83. *See generally* Anderson v. Creighton, 483 U.S. 635 (1987).
84. Owen v. City of Independence, *supra*.
85. Walker v. Waltham Housing Authority, 44 F.3d 1042, 1047 (1st Cir. 1995) ("Perhaps a municipality might in rare cases be liable for a constitutional violation, even though the individual who acted for it was protected by qualified immunity."); Dodd v. City of Norwich, 827 F.2d 1, 6 (2d Cir. 1987) ("Where, as here, a police officer carries out municipal policy with the result that an arrestee is killed, there is a potential for municipal liability even though the police officer may be personally immune from liability . . . "); Babb v. Dorman, 33 F.3d 472, 476, n.7 (5th Cir. 1994) (affirming dismissal of conspiracy claim against municipality, but rejecting trial court's reasoning that a city could not conspire with a person who was qualifiedly immune, stating that municipal liability could be upheld notwithstanding the qualified immunity of the individual defendants); Garner v. Memphis Police Department, 8 F.3d 358, 365 (6th Cir. 1993) (" . . . a municipality may not escape liability for a § 1983 violation merely because the officer who committed the violation is entitled to qualified immunity."); Alexander v. City and County of San Francisco, 29 F.3d 1355, 1359 (9th Cir. 1994) (rejecting trial court's grant of summary judgment to municipality on the basis that because individual officers were entitled to qualified immunity, there could be no municipal liability); Hinton v. City of Elwood, Kansas, 997 F.2d 774, 782 (10th Cir. 1993) (" . . . a finding of qualified immunity does not shelter a municipality from liability.").

Municipal Liability After *Monell*

The Holding in Monell

As previously discussed, *Monell* overruled *Monroe v. Pape* to the extent that *Monroe* held that municipalities were not "persons" subject to suit under § 1983. *Monell's* explicit holding was:

> Our analysis of the legislative history of the Civil Rights Act of 1871 compels the conclusion that Congress *did* intend municipalities and other local government units to be included among those persons to whom § 1983 applies. Local governing bodies, therefore, can be sued directly under § 1983 for monetary, declaratory, or injunctive relief where, as here, the action that is alleged to be unconstitutional implements or executes a policy statement, ordinance, regulation, or decision officially adopted and promulgated by that body's officers. Moreover, although the touchstone of the § 1983 action against a government body is an allegation that official policy is responsible for a deprivation of rights protected by the Constitution, local governments, like every other § 1983 'person,' by the very nature of the statute, may be sued for constitutional deprivations visited pursuant to governmental 'custom' even though such a custom has not received formal approval through the body's official decisionmaking channels.[86]

However, after holding that a municipality was a "person" under § 1983 and could be sued for an officially adopted policy, or for a governmental custom which is the moving force behind a constitutional injury, the Court explicitly rejected liability on the basis of *respondeat superior*:

> On the other hand, the language of § 1983, read against the background of the same legislative history, compels the conclusion that Congress did not intend municipalities to be held liable unless action pursuant to official municipal policy of some nature caused a constitutional tort. In particular, we conclude that a municipality cannot be held liable *solely* because it employs a tortfeasor—or,

---

86. *Monell*, 436 U.S. at 690-691 (emphasis in original).

in other words, a municipality cannot be held liable under § 1983 on a *respondeat superior* theory.[87]

Tying the two holdings together, the Court concluded:

> We conclude, therefore, that a local government may not be sued under § 1983 for an injury inflicted solely by its employees or agents. Instead, it is when execution of a government's policy or custom, whether made by its lawmakers or those whose edicts or acts may fairly be said to represent official policy, inflicts the injury that the government as an entity is responsible under § 1983. Since this case unquestionably involves official policy as the moving force of the constitutional violation found by the District Court . . . we must reverse the judgment below. In so doing, we have no occasion to address, and do not address, what the full contours of municipal liability under § 1983 may be. We have attempted only to sketch so much of the § 1983 cause of action against the local government as is apparent from the history of the 1871 Act and our prior cases, and we expressly leave further development of this action to another day.[88]

The full contours of municipal liability under § 1983 remain unclear. The Supreme Court has, in some instances, attempted to define some of those contours. The Courts of Appeals have been left to address municipal liability where the Supreme Court has not. In both situations, the result has been inconsistent, leaving practitioners with few clear benchmarks.

The Search for "Policy" or "Custom"

In order to avoid imposition of liability under a theory of *respondeat superior*, the Supreme Court has consistently required a plaintiff to identify a municipal "policy" or "custom" that caused the constitutional injury. There are three ways that a plaintiff can establish a policy which could result in municipal liability:

---

87. *Monell*, 436 U.S. at 691 (emphasis in original).

88. *Monell*, 436 U.S. at 694-695.

1. A policymaker promulgates a generally applicable statement of policy, and the implementation of that policy results in a constitutional deprivation;
2. A course of action tailored to a particular situation, and not intended to have general application, when the action is taken by a policymaker or at the direction of a policymaker;
3. Where a policymaker has failed to act when the need to take action to control governmental agents is so obvious that the policymaker can be said to have been deliberately indifferent to the need.[89]

All three areas require, as an initial step, the identification of a policymaker.

Policymakers

Final Authority to Make Policy Under State Law

The policymaker is most easily identified in situations where the legislative body of the entity acts. There, unquestionably, the policymaker has established policy.[90] It is when the legislative body has not acted that difficult questions arise.

In *Pembaur v. City of Cincinnati*,[91] the Court held in a plurality opinion that officials other than the properly constituted legislative body of a municipality could create municipal policy. The Court stated:

> If the decision to adopt that particular course of action is properly made by that government's authorized decisionmakers, it surely represents an act of official government 'policy' as that term is commonly understood.[92]

---

89. Liability for a "custom" that has not been formally approved by a policymaker but which subjects a municipality to liability on the theory that the practice is so widespread as to have the force of law (Addickes v. S.H. Cress & Company, 398 U.S. 144, 167-168 [1970]) is typically analyzed under the third basis for finding a municipal policy.
90. *See* City of Newport v. Fact Concerts, 453 U.S. 247 (1981).
91. 475 U.S. 469 (1986).
92. *Pembaur*, 475 U.S. at 481 (footnote omitted).

Justice Brennan's plurality opinion went on to state:

> Having said this much, we hasten to emphasize that not every decision by municipal officers automatically subjects the municipality to § 1983 liability. Municipal liability attaches only where the decisionmaker possesses final authority to establish municipal policy with respect to the action ordered. The fact that a particular official—even a policymaking official—has discretion in the exercise of particular functions does not, without more, give rise to municipal liability based on an exercise of that discretion. The official must also be responsible for establishing final government policy respecting such activity before the municipality can be held liable. Authority to make municipal policy may be granted directly by a legislative enactment or may be delegated by an official who possesses such authority, and of course, whether an official had final policymaking authority is a question of state law.
>
> Thus, for example, the County Sheriff may have discretion to hire and fire employees without also being the county official responsible for establishing county employment policy. If this were the case, the Sheriff's decisions respecting employment would not give rise to municipal liability, although similar decisions with respect to law enforcement practices, over which the Sheriff is the official policymaker, would give rise to municipal liability. Instead, if county employment policy was set by the Board of County Commissioners, only that body's decisions would provide a basis for county liability. This would be true even if the Board left the Sheriff discretion to hire and fire employees and the Sheriff exercised that discretion in an unconstitutional manner; the decision to act unlawfully would not be a decision of the Board. However, if the Board delegated its power to establish final employment policy to the Sheriff, the Sheriff's decisions would represent county policy and could give rise to municipal liability.[93]

The Supreme Court attempted to clarify the issue of final authority to make municipal policy the following year in *City of St. Louis v. Praprotnik.*[94]

---

93. Pembaur, 475 U.S. at 481-482 (footnotes omitted).
94. 485 U.S. 112 (1988).

Unfortunately, a deeply divided Court again resulted in a plurality opinion. Relying heavily upon Justice Brennan's opinion in *Pembaur*, the Supreme Court reversed a finding of liability against the city of St. Louis for alleged retaliation in the disciplining and ultimate layoff of a city employee.[95]

The Court reiterated that identifying policymakers with final authority was not a question of federal law, but a question of state law. Moreover, the Court stated that the identification of policymakers was not a question of fact, but is a question for the Court to determine as a matter of law.[96] Acknowledging that there would be "a rich variety of ways in which the power of government is distributed," the Court was confident that "state law (which may include valid local ordinances and regulations) will always direct a court to some official or body that has the responsibility for making law or setting policy in any given area of a local government's business."[97]

The Court then touched upon the issue that has given rise to some of the most difficult determinations in this area: when a municipal policymaker has delegated policymaking authority to another official. The Court stated that the mere exercise of discretion by an employee will not give rise to a constitutional violation, as that result would be indistinguishable from *respondeat superior* liability.

The Court also acknowledged, however, that policymakers could not insulate a municipality from liability simply by delegating their policymaking authority to others.[98] The Court then outlined guiding principles in addressing the issue.

---

95. The employee, James Praprotnik, alleged that he had been first transferred and then laid off in retaliation for appealing an earlier suspension. The St. Louis legislative body was charged with enacting ordinances. It had created a civil service commission whose function was to hear appeals from city employees who believed that their rights had been violated by employment decisions. Praprotnik was disciplined by his supervisors, transferred to another unit, and ultimately laid off purportedly due to a lack of funding. All of the employment decisions were made by his immediate supervisors. Praprotnik had been able to obtain relief from some of the adverse decisions from the Civil Service Commission. His appeal to the Civil Service Commission for the layoff was postponed when Praprotnik filed suit in federal court challenging his layoff on the basis of a First Amendment violation.
96. *Praprotnik*, 485 U.S. at 124.
97. *Praprotnik*, 485 U.S. at 125 (footnote omitted).
98. *Praprotnik*, 485 U.S. at 126.

The Court, relying upon *Pembaur*, stated that the relevant authority to make municipal policy for *Monell* liability was necessarily the authority to make *final* municipal policy.

> When an official's discretionary decisions are constrained by policies not of that official's making, those policies, rather than the subordinate's departures from them, are the act of the municipality. Similarly, when a subordinate's decision is subject to review by the municipality's authorized policymakers, they have retained the authority to measure the official's conduct for conformance with *their* policies. If the authorized policymakers approve a subordinate's decision and the basis for it, their ratification would be chargeable to the municipality because their decision is final.[99]

Rejecting the Court of Appeals's conclusion that Praprotnik's supervisors were policymakers, the Court stated that simply going along with discretionary decisions made by subordinates was not a delegation to the subordinates to make policy. As the Court noted, "It is equally consistent with the presumption that the subordinates are faithfully attempting to comply with the policies that are supposed to guide them."[100]

The Court observed that it would be a different matter if a particular decision made by a subordinate was in the form of a policy statement and was then expressly approved by the policymaker. It would also be a different matter, the Court stated, if a series of decisions by a subordinate manifested a custom or usage of which the policymaker must have been aware, but failed to act. The Court then concluded by stating:

> But the mere failure to investigate the basis of a subordinate's discretionary decisions does not amount to a delegation of policymaking authority, especially where (as here) the wrongfulness of the subordinate's decision arises from a retaliatory motive or other unstated rationale. In such circumstances, the purposes of § 1983 would not be served by treating a subordinate employee's decision as if it were a reflection of municipal policy.[101]

---

99. *Praprotnik*, 485 U.S. at 127 (emphasis added).
100. *Praprotnik*, 485 U.S. at 130.
101. *Praprotnik*, 485 U.S. at 130.

The Supreme Court finally rendered a majority opinion on the issue of policymakers in *Jett v. Dallas Independent School District.*[102] The Court held that municipal policy could only be established by:

> . . . those officials or governmental bodies who speak with final policymaking authority for the local government actor concerning the action alleged to have caused the particular constitutional or statutory violation at issue.[103]

The courts of appeals have struggled with application of the "final policymaker" rule, but for the most part have attempted to adhere to the Supreme Court's guidelines. In *DeFeliciano v. DeJesus*,[104] the First Circuit reversed a jury verdict against Puerto Rico's Farm Credit Corporation. The jury had found in favor of the president of the governmental agency, but against the agency itself. In reversing the verdict as inconsistent, the First Circuit held that since the president was the only person with final authority to establish the agency's policy, a verdict in his favor precluded a finding of liability on the part of the agency.

In *Terminate Control Corp. v. Horowitz*,[105] the Second Circuit affirmed dismissal of a claim against the New York City Board of Education arising out of an alleged kickback scheme involving the board's Division of School Buildings (DSB) and various DSB officials. When the plaintiff refused to participate in the scheme, it was alleged that the DSB officials withheld contract payments.

In dismissing the claims against the Board of Education, the Second Circuit held that there was no evidence that the board was involved in the kickback scheme; that any board member played any role in the conduct in question; that any board member knew of the illegal activity aimed at the plaintiff; or that any board member had knowledge of or involvement in the extortion scheme. The court concluded that imposing liability on the Board of Education as a result of the actions of DSB supervisors would result in the sort of *respondeat superior* liability precluded by *Monell.*

---

102. 491 U.S. 701 (1989).
103. *Jett*, 491 U.S. at 737.
104. 873 F.2d 447, 450 (1st Cir. 1989).
105. 28 F.3d 1335, 1349 (2d Cir. 1994).

The Third Circuit took a slightly different approach in *San Filippo v. Bongiovanni*.[106] There the Third Circuit held that a question of fact existed on the issue of liability on the part of the Board of Governors of Rutgers University. The plaintiff alleged that the university president recommended his dismissal to the Board of Governors in retaliation for exercising First Amendment rights. While the plaintiff did not allege that the Board of Governors, which accepted the recommendation and discharged the plaintiff, acted in a retaliatory fashion itself, it was alleged that the board was deliberately indifferent to the president's retaliation.

The Third Circuit agreed that there was enough evidence for the board to suspect that the plaintiff's protected activities had been a substantial motivating factor in the decision to initiate dismissal proceedings. The court then held that a question of fact was created regarding whether the ultimate decisionmaker acted with deliberate indifference to the plaintiff's First Amendment rights by approving a recommendation potentially based upon improper motivation.[107]

---

106. 30 F.3d 424, 445-446 (3d Cir. 1994).
107. Other circuit decisions follow the Supreme Court's lead from *Pembaur, Praprotnik*, and *Jett*. Greensboro Professional Firefighters Ass'n v. City of Greensboro, 64 F.3d 962, 965-966 (4th Cir. 1995) (City not liable for actions of fire chief who had discretion to hire and fire, where the city manager and city counsel possessed the authority to fashion policy for employer-employee relations. "Appellants confused the authority to make final policy with the authority to make final implementing decisions."); Gonzalez v. Ysleta Independent School District, 996 F.2d 745, 754 (5th Cir. 1993) (Decision of school district's board of trustees to transfer a teacher to another classroom after allegation of sexual misconduct constituted a policy attributable to the school district, even though the transfer was contrary to school district's sexual abuse policy. "The board's decision to transfer . . . represents a final action by the entity charged with making and executing policy within the school district . . . "); Feliciano v. City of Cleveland, 988 F.2d 649, 655-656 (6th Cir. 1993) (City not liable for chief of police's order for police cadets to take drug tests. Chief of police subordinate to director of public safety, and there was no showing that the director did not retain the power to review policy statements issued by the chief of police regarding drug testing.); Auriemma v. Rice, 957 F.2d 397, 399-400 (7th Cir. 1992) (City not liable for chief of police's promotion and demotion decisions alleged to have been motivated by race. City ordinances unequivocally ban racial discrimination. "That a particular agent is the apex of the bureaucracy makes the decision 'final' but does not forge a

Conceptually this is one of the most difficult areas in § 1983 litigation. The practitioner must be aware of the distinction between policymaking authority and discretion in the execution of policy. The courts are reluctant to ascribe policymaking authority to a high-level official with discretion to act, in the absence of a clear statement under state or local law that the official is, in fact, a policymaker. Thus it is also an area that is sufficiently unsettled that practitioners can be creative in advancing both theories of liability and defenses.

Rules for Determining Policymakers

In *Jett*, the Supreme Court clarified two interrelated points from *Pembaur* and *Praprotnik* related to the issue of determining where policymaking authority lies. The Court held:

> Whether a particular official has 'final policymaking authority' is a question of state law; and
>
> The identification of a policymaker is a legal question to be resolved by the trial court before the case is submitted to the jury.[108]

As the Supreme Court readily admitted in *Praprotnik*, the "rich variety" of local government models can create some difficulty in identifying who a policymaker is in a given situation. Since the courts may look beyond state statutes to local ordinances and regulations, however, the Court was confident that the law will ultimately direct the trial court to some

---

link between 'finality' and 'policy.'" To hold the municipality liable . . . the agent's action must implement rather than frustrate the government's policy."); McGautha v. Jackson County, 36 F.3d 53, 56 (8th Cir. 1994) (Assistant director of collections department was not a final policymaker where his actions were reviewable by the county executive and were subject to written county policy.); Alexander v. San Francisco, 29 F.3d 1355, 1368 (9th Cir. 1994) (City not liable for police commander's direction to enter suspect's home without a warrant absent showing that San Francisco police commander is an authorized decisionmaker.); Welch v. Laney, 57 F.3d 1004, 1009 (11th Cir. 1995) (County liable for sheriff's employment decisions where sheriff was the "ultimate repository of county authority.").

108. *Jett*, 491 U.S. at 737.

official or body "that has the responsibility for making law or setting policy in any given area of a local government's business."[109]

Based upon this analysis, it is doubtful that prior decisions from a particular federal district court or circuit will be binding in terms of identifying a policymaker in subsequent cases. Unless the identical municipal entity is involved, a holding that the city manager of a given city is a policymaker is unlikely to be binding authority for determining that a city administrator is a policymaker in another lawsuit involving a different municipality.

It is also unclear from the Supreme Court the method by which the court determines who a policymaker is. The one thing that is clear is that this determination is to be made by the court, not the jury. The preferable way to make the determination would seem to be by way of a motion for summary judgment, either by the defendant challenging the identification of certain individuals as policymakers, or by the plaintiff seeking a determination that a given individual is a policymaker. In the absence of motions for summary judgment, however, the court must be provided with sufficient information by the parties to make the determination prior to submitting the case to the jury. It remains for the jury to determine whether the decisions of the policymaker have caused the deprivation of rights at issue.[110] Thus, the court must make the determination as to who a policymaker is before the case is submitted to the jury. Both plaintiffs and defendants should give early attention to either agreeing upon the identity of the policymaker or gathering the appropriate state and local laws, ordinances, and regulations which will allow the court to make that determination.

Single Decision of Policymaker Is Policy

In *City of Oklahoma City v. Tuttle*,[111] the Supreme Court held that proof of a single incident of unconstitutional activity is not sufficient to impose liability on a municipality unless the plaintiff could prove that the incident was caused by an existing unconstitutional policy which could in turn be attributed to a municipal policymaker.[112] The Court went on to hold that

---

109. *Praprotnik*, 485 U.S. at 125.
110. *Jett*, 491 U.S. at 737.
111. 471 U.S. 808 (1985).
112. *Tuttle*, 471 U.S. at 824.

where a policy is not itself unconstitutional, more proof than a single incident would be necessary to establish municipal liability.[113]

In *Pembaur*, the Supreme Court held that a single decision by a policymaker could result in municipal liability:

> If the decision to adopt that particular course of action is properly made by that government's authorized decisionmakers, it surely represents an act of official government 'policy' as that term is commonly understood. More importantly, where action is directed by those who establish government policy, the municipality is equally responsible whether that action is to be taken only once or to be taken repeatedly.[114]

Where a municipal policy is itself unconstitutional, a single application of that policy will result in municipal liability. By the same token, where a municipal policymaker makes a single decision, and that decision is applied, municipal liability will result. However, where there is no policy established by a policymaker, and the plaintiff attempts to impose liability on the basis of custom or practice, a single action by a municipal employee will not result in liability. As the Court explained in *Tuttle*, the word "policy" implies a course of action chosen from among various alternatives. A single action on the part of a non-policymaking employee is insufficient to create a policy attributable to the municipality.

Custom or Practice

In addition to imposing liability upon municipalities for the actions of policymakers which cause constitutional deprivations, a municipality can also be liable under § 1983 when its custom or practice causes constitutional deprivations. The Supreme Court in *Monell* explicitly recognized that municipalities could be liable for custom or practice:

> . . . Local governments, like every other § 1983 'person,' by the very terms of the statute, may be sued for constitutional depriva-

113. *Id.*
114. Pembaur, 475 U.S. at 481 (footnote omitted).

> tions visited pursuant to governmental 'custom' even though such a custom has not received formal approval through the body's official decisionmaking channels. . . . Congress included customs and usages in § 1983 because of the pursuant and widespread discriminatory practices of state officials . . . Although not authorized by written law, such practices of state officials could well be so permanent and well settled as to constitute a 'custom or usage' with the force of law.[115]

The courts have required substantial proof to support a claim of a municipal custom or policy. For example, in *Doe v. Claiborne County*,[116] the Sixth Circuit rejected a claim that a school board had a custom of failing to act to prevent the sexual abuse of students. The court stated that a custom must have "the force of law" and be a "legal institution" not memorialized by written law.[117]

While the cases rejecting attempts to impose liability upon custom or practice far outnumber those imposing liability, there are numerous cases in which custom or practice was the basis for municipal liability.[118]

There are no bright-line rules which will establish when a custom or practice exists. It is clear that there must be more than one event to give rise to a custom or practice. Additionally, the practice must be "longstanding" and "pervasive." Beyond that, the determination is subject to *ad hoc* review by the courts.

---

115. *Monell*, 436 U.S. at 690-691 (footnote omitted).
116. 103 F.3d 495 (6th Cir. 1996).
117. *Doe*, 103 F.3d at 507-508.
118. *See, e.g.*, Scott v. Moore, 85 F.3d 230, 334 (5th Cir. 1996) (Ten-year practice at jail to have unsupervised male jailer present with female detainees constituted custom or practice sufficient to impose liability.); Bordanarro v. McLeod, 871 F.2d 1151, 1155 (1st Cir. 1989) (Police department had longstanding practice, engaged in by virtually all officers, of breaking down doors without a warrant when arresting a felon.); Jones v. City of Chicago, 856 F.2d 985, 995 (7th Cir. 1988) (Police officers' keeping of "street files" was pervasive and of long standing, entitling jury to find that it had been approved by policymakers for the police department.); Leach v. Shelby County Sheriff, 891 F.2d 1241, 1247 (6th Cir. 1989) (Deliberate indifference to medical needs of physically incapacitated prisoners was so pervasive as to constitute custom and practice for the county sufficient to impose liability.).

Causation and Culpability

Even assuming that a plaintiff can establish the existence of a municipal policy or custom, that does not end the inquiry. Before liability upon a municipality can be imposed, a plaintiff must establish causation between the policy and the constitutional deprivation.

This link was established in *Monell,* in which the Court stated that "the touchstone of the § 1983 action against a government body is an allegation that official policy is *responsible* for the deprivation of rights"[119] under the Constitution. The Court also pointed out that "Congress did not intend municipalities to be held liable unless action pursuant to official municipal policy of some nature *caused* a constitutional tort."[120] The connection between policy and constitutional deprivation has been reiterated by the Supreme Court in every case since *Monell* when municipal liability has been addressed.

The Supreme Court's most recent pronouncement in the area of municipal liability focuses on the causation issue. In *Bryan County v. Brown,*[121] the plaintiff brought a claim for damages under § 1983, alleging that a county deputy used excessive force in arresting her and that the county was liable based on the sheriff's decision to hire the deputy, who had a misdemeanor assault conviction. The plaintiff obtained judgment at the district court level, and the judgment was affirmed by the Fifth Circuit.[122] The Supreme Court reversed, concluding that "Congress did not intend to impose liability on a municipality unless deliberate action attributable to the municipality itself is the 'moving force' behind the Plaintiff's deprivation of federal rights."[123]

The plaintiff's claims against Bryan County arose out of the sheriff's decision to hire a reserve officer without adequately checking his criminal background. The reserve officer had pleaded guilty to various driving-related offenses and other misdemeanors, including assault and battery, resisting arrest, and public drunkenness.

---

119. *Monell*, 436 U.S. at 690 (emphasis added).
120. *Monell*, 436 U.S. at 691 (emphasis added).
121. 117 S. Ct. 1382 (1997).
122. 67 F.3d 1174 (5th Cir. 1995).
123. *Bryan County*, 117 S. Ct. at 1386.

While Oklahoma law did not preclude the hiring of an individual as a police officer who had a misdemeanor conviction, the plaintiff asserted that the hiring policy of Bryan County, as instituted by its policymaker, Sheriff Moore, was so inadequate that it amounted to deliberate indifference to the plaintiff's constitutional rights.[124] The county stipulated that Sheriff Moore was the policymaker for the county regarding the sheriff's department.

However, the Court stated that it is not enough for a § 1983 plaintiff to merely identify conduct attributable to the municipality. Additionally, the plaintiff must demonstrate "a direct causal link between the municipal action and the deprivation of federal rights."[125]

Distinguishing situations where a municipality's legislative body has intentionally deprived a plaintiff of a federally protected right, the Court required "rigorous standards" of causation to be applied in Bryan County, where a plaintiff claimed that the municipality had not directly inflicted injury but had caused an employee to do so.[126] Since every injury at the hands of a municipal employee can be traced to a hiring decision in a "but-for" sense (but for the decision to hire the employee, the plaintiff would not have suffered an injury), the Supreme Court stated that "a court must carefully test the link between the policymaker's inadequate decision and the particular injury alleged."[127] The Court required that a plaintiff prove that a particular employee was "highly likely" to inflict the particular injury suffered by the plaintiff before municipal liability could attach. The Court explained that:

> . . . a finding of culpability simply cannot depend on the mere probability that any officer inadequately screened will inflict any constitutional injury. Rather, it must depend on a finding that this officer was highly likely to inflict the particular injury suffered by the plaintiff. The connection between the background of the particular applicant and the specific constitutional violation alleged must be strong.[128]

---

124. *Bryan County*, 117 S. Ct. at 1387.
125. *Bryan County,* 117 S. Ct. at 1388.
126. *Bryan County,* 117 S. Ct. at 1389.
127. *Bryan County*, 117 S. Ct. at 1391.
128. *Bryan County*, 117 S. Ct. at 1392.

After "carefully testing" the link between Sheriff Moore's hiring decision and the plaintiff's injury, the Court found the plaintiff's proofs to be inadequate. The Court concluded that the reserve deputy's criminal record was simply not of a nature that the sheriff would necessarily have determined that the use of excessive force would have been a plainly obvious consequence of the hiring decision.[129] Concluding, the Court held:

> Bryan County is not liable for Sheriff Moore's isolated decision to hire Burns without adequate screening, because respondent has not demonstrated that his decision reflected a conscious disregard for a high risk that Burns would use excessive force in violation of respondent's federally protected right.[130]

After *Bryan County*, the plaintiff who seeks to impose liability on a municipality for an injury inflicted by a non-policymaking employee bears a significant burden on the issue of causation.

The issue of causation is often tied to the issue of fault. As the Supreme Court explained in *Bryan County*, proof that a policymaker had intentionally deprived a plaintiff of a federally protected right necessarily establishes municipal liability. Similarly, where the action taken or directed by the policymaker violates federal law, the plaintiff will necessarily establish that the action was the moving force behind the injury. It is in the cases where some intervening act on the part of a lower-level employee inflicts the injury that the issue of causation arises.

The most common situation that falls within this category of cases is "failure to train." In *City of Canton v. Harris*,[131] the Supreme Court held that there are limited circumstances in which a "failure to train" can be the basis for liability under § 1983. In outlining those "limited circumstances," the Court again focused on the issue of causation. The Court held that a municipality could be liable under § 1983 only where its policy of failing to train was the "moving force" behind the constitutional violation.

In explaining the parameters for municipal liability, the Court held that a plaintiff would have to show much more than that the existing training program represented a policy for which the city is responsible. The Court

---

129. *Bryan County*, 117 S. Ct. at 1392-1393.
130. *Bryan County*, 117 S. Ct. at 1394.
131. 489 U.S. 378 (1989).

held that the municipality must choose an inadequate training program from among various alternatives. Giving as an example the need to train police officers in the constitutional limitations on the use of deadly force, the Court stated that in light of the duties assigned to police officers, the need for more or different training may become so obvious, and the inadequacy of the training so likely to result in constitutional violations, that the policymakers can reasonably be said to have been deliberately indifferent to the need for more or different training.[132]

The Court then emphasized that before liability can attach, an identified deficiency in a training program "must be closely related to the ultimate injury."[133] The plaintiff must prove that the deficiency actually caused the particular constitutional deprivation.[134] Implicitly, the fact that a deficiency in a training program could be said to lead to a higher likelihood of constitutional deprivations generally would be insufficient.

Similarly, if the evidence in a particular case demonstrates that the same result would have occurred regardless of the training program, municipal liability would not attach. It is only when an identifiable deficiency in the training program can be proven to have resulted in the specific constitutional violation that municipal liability can attach.

Circuit decisions on the issue of causation which pre-date *Bryan County* also required a strong showing of causation. For example, in *Walker v. City of New York*,[135] the Second Circuit rejected a claim of failure to train officers not to commit perjury on the basis of *causation*. While the court acknowledged that there had not been a training program with respect to the obligation not to commit perjury, the Second Circuit found the obligation not to commit perjury was so obvious to all without training that the failure to train was not "so likely" to produce a constitutional violation that the city could be held liable.[136]

In *Jones v. Wellham*,[137] the Fourth Circuit held that there was not the necessary affirmative link between a city policy and a violation where a police officer had been disciplined, but not discharged, for a sexual assault

132. *City of Canton*, 489 U.S. at 390.
133. *City of Canton*, 489 U.S. at 391.
134. *Id.*
135. 974 F.2d 293 (2d Cir. 1992).
136. *Walker*, 974 F.2d at 299-300.
137. 104 F.3d 620 (4th Cir. 1997).

ten years before committing a sexual assault on the plaintiff. The Fourth Circuit's standard for the connection between the policy and the injury was that the specific injury be "almost bound to happen, sooner or later, rather than merely likely to happen in the long run."[138]

In *Gazette v. City of Pontiac*,[139] the Sixth Circuit accepted the plaintiff's facts as true, but found no causal link between the municipal policy and the constitutional deprivation. The plaintiff alleged that when her mother was reported missing under circumstances which suggested foul play, the police assured her that they were taking appropriate action, but in fact did nothing. The mother was found murdered several days later and the plaintiff claimed that, had the police not lied to her, she could have investigated her mother's disappearance and found her before the murder.

In rejecting this argument, the Sixth Circuit Court stated that there was "no close causal connection between the police officers' lies and Bandy's death because many factors could have prevented the police officers, or Bandy's family and friends, from locating Bandy. The causal connection between the police officers' lies and Bandy's death simply is not sufficient to sustain a § 1983 claim. . . ."[140]

In *Ricketts v. City of Columbia*,[141] the Eighth Circuit found no causal link in a case where the plaintiff claimed that the casual treatment of domestic abuse cases by police resulted in her and her mother being attacked by her estranged husband. Specifically, the plaintiff alleged that had her estranged husband been arrested for previous domestic assaults, he would not have raped her and murdered her mother on the date in question. Rejecting this claim, the Eighth Circuit stated that such speculation could not "establish causation because it is equally plausible that an arrest for the prior harassment might as easily have spawned retaliatory violence from Sonny."[142]

The Supreme Court's decision in *Bryan County* establishes a significant hurdle for plaintiffs to overcome. In situations where the municipal policy is not directly tied to the constitutional injury (primarily in failure to train in negligent hiring cases), a plaintiff must now prove that the specific

---

138. *Jones*, 104 F.3d at 625.
139. 41 F.3d 1061 (6th Cir. 1994).
140. *Gazette*, 41 F.3d at 1066.
141. 36 F.3d 775 (8th Cir. 1994).
142. *Ricketts*, 36 F.3d at 780.

constitutional injury is directly related to the municipal policy, and that the former would be a "plainly obvious consequence" of the latter. It should be anticipated that the courts will not be lenient in assessing this nexus in light of *Bryan County*.

Deliberate Indifference: The Standard of Culpability

Closely related to the issue of causation is the issue of culpability. As with the issue of causation, where the municipal policy itself is unconstitutional, culpability is a given. For example, when a city's legislative body violates a First Amendment right through a legislative enactment (*Newport v. Fact Concerts, Inc.*[143]), liability is established when the decision itself is found to be unconstitutional. Similarly, where a municipal employee is discharged without procedural due process (*Owen v. Independence*[144]), the formal decision of the municipal legislative body discharging the employee without a hearing resulted in liability.

Claims not involving an allegation that the municipal action itself violated the Constitution present different issues of fault. In the examples of First Amendment violations and procedural due process violations, the "state of mind" requirement was all that was necessary to establish the underlying constitutional violation. That was true because the plaintiff was challenging the decision of the legislative body itself. However, where a plaintiff seeks to establish liability on the theory that a facially lawful municipal policy or action has led an employee to violate the plaintiff's constitutional rights, the plaintiff must demonstrate that the municipal action was taken with "deliberate indifference," quite apart from the underlying constitutional claim.

The simplest examples are found in *City of Canton* and *Bryan County*. In *City of Canton,* the plaintiff claimed that the individual police officer deprived her of due process by failing to obtain adequate medical care for her mental condition while she was in policy custody. In *Bryan County*, the plaintiff claimed that the individual police officer violated her Fourth Amendment rights. The claims against the municipal employer, however, were premised upon a policy of failing to train and a policy of improper hiring procedures. Thus, proving a due process violation in *City of Canton*

143. 453 U.S. 247 (1981).
144. 445 U.S. 622 (1980).

or a Fourth Amendment violation in *Bryan County* against the individual officer would not speak to the city's culpability.

In *City of Canton*, the Court held that liability could attach to a municipality where the failure to train amounted to deliberate indifference to the rights of persons with whom the police come into contact.[145] The deliberate indifference required a finding that the municipality made a deliberate choice to follow a course of action from among various alternatives.[146] The Court stated, "That a particular officer may be unsatisfactorily trained will not alone suffice to fasten liability on the city, for the officer's shortcomings may have resulted from factors other than a faulty training program."[147]

The Court also rejected the idea that liability could attach if the plaintiff proved that an injury could have been avoided if better or different training had been given. The Court observed that such a claim could be made about almost any encounter resulting in injury, yet would "not condemn the adequacy of the program to enable officers to respond properly to the usual and recurring situations with which they must deal."[148]

In *Bryan County*, the Supreme Court held that the sheriff's failure to thoroughly review a deputy's criminal record prior to hiring him was not enough to establish deliberate indifference. The Court stated:

> In layman's terms, inadequate screening of an applicant's record may reflect 'indifference' to the applicant's background. For purposes of a legal inquiry into municipal liability under § 1983, however, that is not the relevant 'indifference.' A plaintiff must demonstrate that a municipal decision reflects deliberate indifference to the risk that a violation of a particular constitutional or statutory right will follow the decision. Only where adequate scrutiny of an applicant's background would lead a reasonable policymaker to conclude that the plainly obvious consequence of the decision to hire the applicant would be deprivation of a third party's federally protected right can the official's failure to adequately scrutinize the applicant's background constitute 'deliberate indifference.'[149]

---

145. *City of Canton*, 489 U.S. at 388.
146. *City of Canton*, 489 U.S. at 389.
147. *City of Canton*, 489 U.S. at 390-391.
148. *City of Canton*, 489 U.S. at 391.
149. *Bryan County*, 117 S. Ct. at 1392.

In light of *Bryan County*, it is likely that the issue of culpability will receive greater scrutiny in the future. This has been an area in which the circuits have been inconsistent. Many times, after struggling with the difficult concepts of who is a policymaker and causation, the courts essentially assume culpability. The Supreme Court in *Bryan County*, however, makes clear that culpability is a separate issue, and a significant one to be addressed with careful scrutiny.

The decision in *Bryan County* reaffirms the circuit decisions which pre-dated it. *Bryan County* demonstrated that the "deliberate indifference" standard is the standard by which essentially all claims of municipal liability will be addressed. The circuits have traditionally required a showing of deliberate indifference before imposing municipal liability for a policy which is not facially invalid. However, prior to *Bryan County*, the circuits varied widely in what constituted "deliberate indifference."

For example, in *San Filippo v. Bongiovanni*,[150] the Third Circuit held that Rutgers University could be liable if it was deliberately indifferent to the plaintiff's First Amendment rights by approving a recommendation that the plaintiff be dismissed. The Third Circuit's discussion, however, did not appear to require a great deal of culpability on the part of the university before the deliberate indifference standard could be met. The court stated that the university could not be liable for a "mere failure to investigate" the rationale behind a recommendation to terminate.[151]

The court went on to state that the university "had reason to suspect" that the plaintiff's protected activities had been a motivating factor in the decision to initiate dismissal proceedings.[152] Finally, the court stated that the university was required to "tread with a certain amount of care to avoid the possibility of *inadvertently* punishing someone for exercising his First Amendment rights."[153] These facts led the Third Circuit to conclude that a factual issue existed as to whether the university had been deliberately indifferent.

In contrast, in *Jones v. Wellham*,[154] the Fourth Circuit held that there was no deliberate indifference as a matter of law for the actions of the chief

150. 30 F.3d 424 (3d Cir. 1994).
151. *San Filippo*, 30 F.3d at 446.
152. *Id.*
153. *San Filippo*, 30 F.3d at 446, n. 26.
154. 104 F.3d 620 (4th Cir. 1997).

of police. The chief had disciplined, but not discharged, a police officer in 1979 for a sexual assault. After six months, the chief returned the officer to street duty. In 1990, the same officer raped the plaintiff. In finding that the chief's actions did not constitute deliberate indifference, the Fourth Circuit stated that, with the benefit of hindsight, the chief's actions were "clearly unfortunate, might perhaps be thought to be imprudent, or even be found legally negligent, but that does not suffice; only decisions taken with deliberate indifference to the potential consequences of known risks suffices to impose municipal liability. . . ."[155]

In *Gonzalez v. Ysleta Independent School District*,[156] the Fifth Circuit rejected the plaintiff's claim that the school district had been deliberately indifferent by transferring a teacher to another school in the face of allegations of sexual abuse. In seeking to satisfy the the *City of Canton* test, the plaintiff argued that the school district made a deliberate choice from among various alternatives, such as suspending the teacher, ordering further investigation, scheduling a hearing, issuing a more severe reprimand, or providing for classroom monitoring. Instead, the school district chose to transfer the teacher to another school where he sexually abused the plaintiff's daughter.

The Fifth Circuit rejected this approach, stating that municipal liability "must be predicated upon a showing of 'fault,' not merely 'responsibility'."[157] The court went on to state that in order for municipal liability to attach, "plaintiffs must offer evidence of not simply a decision, but a 'decision by the city itself to violate the Constitution.'"[158] The Fifth Circuit then held as a matter of law that the actions of the board in reassigning the teacher did not amount to deliberate indifference because the board did not "ignore or turn a blind eye" to the complaint against the teacher, but undertook an investigation, and thus the school district could not be deliberately indifferent to the constitutional rights of the plaintiff. Even though the failure to impose a more a severe sanction was not only negligent, but also inconsistent with the school district's handling of other similar cases, the Fifth Circuit concluded that such facts simply did not give rise to deliberate indifference as a matter of law.[159]

---

155. *Jones*, 104 F.3d at 627.
156. 996 F.2d 745 (5th Cir. 1993).
157. *Gonzalez*, 996 F.2d at 757.
158. *Gonzalez*, 996 F.2d at 759.
159. *Gonzalez*, 996 F.2d at 762.

In a factually similar case, the Sixth Circuit reached the same result in *Doe v. Claiborne County.*[160] There, a high school student had been sexually assaulted by one of her teachers in 1992. In 1989, an allegation of sexual misconduct was made against the same teacher and in 1990, complaints were made that the teacher had sexually abused nine different girls at a middle school. An investigation was undertaken by a state agency at the school district's request and the teacher was initially not rehired by the board for the following school year. Shortly thereafter, however, a new superintendent was hired and the decision to rehire the teacher was approved by the school board. After being rehired, the teacher sexually abused the plaintiff.

In finding that the plaintiff had failed to demonstrate deliberate indifference as a matter of law, the court observed that the board members "might have been recklessly passive in the performance of their duties," and that it could be argued that "they were reckless in their failure, collectively, to inquire further into the allegations."[161] However, such conduct did not reach the level of deliberate indifference.

While the law will continue to develop as the circuits apply the *Bryan County* holding to specific cases, it appears that the Fifth Circuit's rationale in *Gonzalez* is most in keeping with the Supreme Court's decisions: In order for municipal liability to attach, a plaintiff must offer evidence of not simply a decision to choose among alternatives, but a "decision by the city itself to violate the Constitution."[162]

Supervisory Liability

The issue of supervisory liability is closely tied to the issue of municipal liability. The Supreme Court's only decision squarely addressing supervisory liability came in *Rizzo v. Goode*,[163] where the Court reversed an injunction entered by the district court against the mayor, city manager, and police commissioner of the city of Philadelphia which sought to control the manner in which citizen complaints about police officers were

---

160. 103 F.3d 495 (6th Cir. 1996).
161. *Doe*, 103 F.3d at 508.
162. *Gonzalez*, 996 F.2d at 759, quoting City of Canton, 489 U.S. at 494 (*O'Connor*, concurring).
163. 423 U.S. 362 (1976).

handled. In rejecting the district court's authority to enter such an injunction, the Court relied upon the fact that there was no showing that the supervisory defendants had in any way participated in any of the specific unconstitutional actions of individual police officers directed to specific citizens. The Court stated:

> Individual police officers not named as parties to the action were found to have violated the constitutional rights of particular individuals, only a few of whom were parties plaintiff. As the facts developed, there was no affirmative link between the occurrence of the various incidents of police misconduct and the adoption of any plan or policy by petitioners express or otherwise *showing their authorization or approval of such misconduct*; instead, the sole causal connection found by the District Court between petitioners and the individual respondents was that in the absence of a change in police disciplinary procedures, the incidents were likely to continue to occur, not with respect to them, but as to the member of the classes they represented.[164]

In rejecting the finding of liability against the supervisory officials, the Court distinguished cases where police supervisors presided over intentional, concerted and conspiratorial efforts to deprive discrete individuals of their constitutional rights.[165] The Court found that the distinguishing factor was that in the previous cases there was simply not a number of constitutional violations which occurred, but a pervasive pattern of intimidation flowing from a deliberate plan by the supervisory defendants to crush labor organizations.[166]

Concluding that the District Court exceeded its authority in issuing the injunction against the supervisory officials, the Court held:

> Here, the District Court found that none of the petitioners had deprived the respondent classes of any rights secured under the Constitution. Under the well-established rule that the federal 'judicial

164. *Rizzo,* 423 U.S. at 371.
165. The Court distinguished the facts in Rizzo from those in Hague v. CIO, 307 U.S. 496 (1939) and Allee v. Medrano, 416 U.S. 802 (1974).
166. *Rizzo*, 423 U.S. at 375.

> powers may be exercised only on the basis of a constitutional violation,' this case presented no occasion for the District Court to grant equitable relief against petitioners.[167]

The clear holding in *Rizzo* is that supervisory defendants cannot be found to have committed a constitutional violation absent direct participation in the specific constitutional deprivation alleged by a specific plaintiff. In the 20 years since the *Rizzo* decision, however, the Supreme Court's pronouncement has been less than faithfully applied by the circuits.

The circuits are unanimous in holding that supervisory liability cannot be predicated on a theory of *respondeat superior*, just as municipal liability may not be predicated on that basis. While there is a certain similarity in the various circuit approaches to supervisory liability, there is also a great deal of divergence.

The First Circuit has essentially adopted the same standard for supervisory liability as exists for municipal liability. A supervisor can be held liable "if (1) the behavior of his subordinates results in a constitutional violation, and (2) the supervisor's action or inaction was affirmatively linked to that behavior in that it could be characterized as supervisory encouragement, condonation or acquiescence, or gross negligence amounting to deliberate indifference."[168] Moreover, the affirmative link required between the action or inaction of a supervisor and the behavior of subordinates "contemplates proof that the supervisor's conduct led inexorably to the constitutional violation."[169]

The Second Circuit's test for supervisory liability is the most expansive and the least reconcilable with *Rizzo*. In a 1995 case the Second Circuit held that personal involvement of a supervisory defendant resulting in liability can be shown by evidence that:

> (1) The defendant participated directly in the alleged constitutional violation, (2) the defendant, after being informed of the violation through a report or appeal, failed to remedy the wrong, (3) the defendant created a policy or custom under which unconstitutional practices occurred, or allowed the continuance of such

---

167. *Rizzo*, 423 U.S. at 377.
168. Lipsett v. University of Puerto Rico, 864 F.2d 881, 902 (1st Cir. 1988).
169. Hugarty v. Somerset County, 53 F.3d 1367, 1380 (1st Cir. 1995).

> a policy or custom, (4) the defendant was grossly negligent in supervising subordinates who committed the wrongful acts, or (5) the defendant exhibited deliberate indifference to the rights of inmates by failing to act on information indicating that unconstitutional acts were occurring.[170]

The Third Circuit has a relatively simple test enunciated in a 1995 case. There the court held that in order to establish supervisory liability based upon the actions of a subordinate, plaintiffs must first prove the subordinate's conduct violated the plaintiff's constitutional rights, and then prove that the supervisor knew of the subordinate's conduct and approved it.[171]

The Fourth Circuit's test for supervisory liability is that liability can attach to supervisors only by proof of direct culpability in causing the injury, either by directly authorizing the action or by expressly or tacitly condoning a known pattern of comparable conduct by inaction. To establish culpability though tacitly condoning inaction, the plaintiff would have to offer evidence that the supervisors knew or reasonably should have known of a comparable pattern of conduct that was sufficiently widespread to pose a pervasive and unreasonable risk of constitutional injury to the plaintiff, and in the face of that knowledge the supervisors took no action to stop it, but remained deliberately indifferent to it.[172]

In the Sixth Circuit, the test for supervisory liability is that a supervisory employee cannot be held liable for the constitutional torts of those supervised unless it is shown that the supervisor "encouraged the specific incident of misconduct or in some other way directly participated in it."[173]

The Seventh Circuit's standard is similar to that of the Sixth Circuit. A supervisory defendant will not be liable for a constitutional violation for merely exercising supervisory authority over those who violated the plaintiff's rights. In order for a supervisory official to be held liable under

---

170. Conlon v. Coughlin, 58 F.3d 865, 873 (2d Cir. 1995).

171. Blanche Road Corp. v. Bensalem Township, 57 F.3d 253, 263 (1995).

172. McWilliams v. Fairfax County Board of Supervisors, 72 F.3d 1191, 1197 (4th Cir. 1996).

173. Lillard v. Shelby Board of Education, 76 F.3d 716, 727 (6th Cir. 1996) quoting Bellamy v. Bradley, 729 F.2d 416, 421 (6th Cir.), *cert. denied*, 469 U.S. 845 (1984).

§ 1983, a plaintiff must establish that the supervisor was personally involved or acquiesced in the alleged constitutional violation.[174]

Similar to the First Circuit, the Eighth Circuit's test for supervisory liability mirrors the test for municipal liability. In the Eighth Circuit, a supervisor may be held individually liable under § 1983 if he or she directly participated in a constitutional violation or if a failure to properly supervise and train the offending employee caused a deprivation of constitutional rights. The plaintiff must demonstrate that the supervisor was deliberately indifferent to, or tacitly authorized, the offending acts. This, in turn, requires a showing that the supervisor had notice that the training procedures and supervision were inadequate and were likely to result in the constitutional violation.[175]

In the Ninth Circuit, a supervisor can be liable under § 1983 as a result of personal involvement in either the constitutional deprivation or the creation or implementation of a policy so deficient that the policy itself is a repudiation of constitutional rights and the moving force of a constitutional violation.[176]

In the Tenth Circuit, a supervisor is not liable under § 1983 absent a showing that the supervisor personally participated in the incident or an affirmative link between the constitutional deprivation and the failure to supervise.[177]

In the Eleventh Circuit, supervisory liability occurs either when the supervisor personally participates in the alleged constitutional violation or when there is a causal connection between actions of the supervisor and the alleged constitutional deprivation. The causal connection required can be established by a showing of a history of widespread abuse that puts the supervisor on notice of the need to correct the conduct which results in the deprivation and the supervisor fails to do so.[178]

The divergence of the circuits on the issue of supervisory liability leads to the inescapable conclusion that the Supreme Court will have to revisit

---

174. Kelly v. Municipal Courts of Marion County, 97 F.3d 902, 909 (7th Cir. 1996).
175. Andrews v. Fowler, 98 F.3d 1069, 1078 (8th Cir. 1996).
176. Hansen v. Black, 885 F.2d 642, 646 (9th Cir. 1989); MacKinney v. Nielsen, 69 F.3d 1002, 1008 (9th Cir. 1995).
177. Grimsley v. McKay, 93 F.3d 676, 679 (10th Cir. 1996).
178. Dolihite v. Maughon, 74 F.3d 1027, 1052 (11th Cir. 1996).

this issue. In the meantime, however, the practitioner must make a careful study of the law as it relates to the particular circuits. Conduct which may give rise to supervisory liability in one circuit may not be actionable conduct in another. While there is a common thread among the circuit decisions on the issue of supervisory liability, there is no bright-line rule on which a practitioner can rely.

Conclusion

Municipal liability under § 1983 has undergone significant changes over the last 20 years. The Supreme Court's decisions in this area have been fractured and contiguous, leaving practitioners and the lower courts with a great deal of uncertainty. The complexity of the issue of municipal liability under § 1983 has caused some commentators, and not a few judges, to call for a repudiation of *Monell* and the imposition of *respondeat superior* liability. The makeup of the current Supreme Court does not make that occurrence likely in the near future.

Chapter Six

Dangerous Misperceptions: Protecting Police Officers, Society, and the Fourth Amendment Right to Personal Security*

Kathryn R. Urbonya

As detectives entered the home of O.J. Simpson and as police officers repeatedly struck Rodney King,[1] the nation questioned whether these actions violated the Fourth Amendment, which protects an individual's right to personal security.[2] In both cases, officers asserted that their actions were reasonably based on their objective assessment of danger: providing aid to possible victims in Mr. Simpson's home and protecting themselves from a disobedient suspect. Resolution of these Fourth Amendment issues centered on how to assess danger to police officers and community, with little consideration given to the right to personal security and privacy.

When police officers attempt to control suspects during arrests, they must exercise only reasonable force because the Fourth Amendment provides that individuals have a right "to be secure in their persons . . . against unreasonable . . . seizures."[3] Officers must also act reasonably when they render aid to victims[4] or frisk suspects.[5] In evaluating the use of force, the

---

* This chapter is adapted from "Dangerous Misperceptions: Protecting Police Officers, Society, and the Fourth Amendment Right to Personal Security," which originally appeared in 22 Hastings Constr. L. Q. 623 (1994).

1. Jerome H. Skolnick & James J. Fyfe, Above the Law: Police and the Excessive Use of Force 16 (1993) ("Mistrust and hostility predictably follow upon abuse and repression.").
2. The Fourth Amendment provides as follows:
   The right of the people to be secure in their persons, houses, papers and effects, against unreasonable searches and seizures shall not be violated, and no Warrants shall issue, but upon probable cause, supported by Oath or affirmation, and particularly describing the place to be searched, and the persons or things to be seized.
   U.S. Const. amend. IV.
3. U.S. Const. amend. IV.
4. *See infra* text accompanying notes 142-49, 358-72.
5. *See infra* text accompanying notes 72-137, 297-331.

U.S. Supreme Court has stated that reasonableness is an objective standard. In *Tennessee v. Garner*,[6] the Court addressed the issue of deadly force. It held that "if a suspect threatens an officer with a weapon or there is probable cause to believe that he has committed a crime involving the infliction or threatened infliction of serious physical harm, deadly force may be used if necessary to prevent escape, and if, where feasible, some warning has been given."[7] In applying this standard to the use of nondeadly force, the Court in *Graham v. Connor*[8] articulated three factors to consider in determining whether force was reasonable: "the severity of the crime," "whether the suspect poses an immediate threat to the safety of the officers or others," and "whether he is actively resisting arrest or attempting to evade arrest by flight."[9] Although these decisions provide some guidelines for determining reasonable force, many courts have drastically limited the Fourth Amendment right to personal security by determining that the presence of danger automatically justifies both aggressive and preventive actions.

As a result of this interpretation of the Reasonableness Clause, courts have misperceived how to assess reasonableness. Too often the presence of any danger results in the court's failure to perceive other significant issues for resolving whether the conduct was reasonable; whether police officers created the need to use force; whether police officers should have used lesser intrusive means to apprehend a suspect; whether the Fourth Amendment, under some circumstances, indicates that police officers should let suspects flee rather than use ever-increasing amounts of nonlethal force; whether juries are necessary to determine the reasonableness of a police practice; and whether police officers' actions before a seizure are relevant to the reasonableness inquiry. The courts should consider the presence of danger when they determine reasonableness; however, courts often erroneously assess the degree of danger by strongly deferring to the judgment of police officers. These serious misperceptions significantly diminish the Fourth Amendment right to personal security.

Because the Fourth Amendment reasonableness standard is an abstract standard, some guidelines are necessary to aid courts in discerning the

---

6. 471 U.S. 1 (1985). For a discussion of this case, *see infra* text accompanying notes 29-51.
7. *Garner,* 471 U.S. at 11-12.
8. 490 U.S. 386 (1989).
9. *Id.* at 396.

balancing process of the Fourth Amendment. Without guidelines, the reasonableness standard may become more rule-like,[10] with courts continuing to create legal fictions[11] and automatic presumptions of constitutionality.[12] These guidelines must take into account the history of the Fourth Amendment, particularly the fear of an unchecked constabulary. As Professor Tracey Maclin has stated, "The constitutional lodestar for understanding the Fourth Amendment is not an ad hoc reasonableness standard; rather, the central meaning of the Fourth Amendment is distrust of police power and discretion."[13]

When assessing the danger posed by suspects, courts, however, have strongly deferred to the judgment of police officers, rather than question

---

10. *See, e.g.*, KATHLEEN M. SULLIVAN, *Forward: The Justices of Rules and Standards*, 106 HARV. L. REV. 22, 56-69 (1992). Professor Kathleen Sullivan has stated that a rule "binds a decisionmaker to respond in a determinative way to the presence of delimited triggering facts. . . . A rule necessarily captures the background principle or policy incompletely and so produces errors of over- or under-inclusiveness." *Id.* at 58. A standard, however, "allow[s] the decisionmaker to take into account all relevant factors or the totality of circumstances." *Id.* at 59. It thus has fewer problems with over- or under-inclusiveness. *Id.* at 58. *See generally* T. ALEXANDER ALEINIKOFF, *Constitutional Law in the Age of Balancing*, 96 YALE L.J. 943, 946 (1987) (balancing includes both weighing competing interests and discerning the presence of "'compelling' or 'important' state interests").
11. *See infra* text accompanying notes 373-85.
12. *See infra* text accompanying notes 205-06, 224-26, 301-31.
13. TRACEY MACLIN, *The Central Meaning of the Fourth Amendment*, 35 WM. & MARY L. REV. 197, 201 (1993); *see also* Kopf v. Skyrm, 993 F.2d 374, 379 (4th Cir. 1993). In *Kopf*, the Fourth Circuit declared that history of the Fourth Amendment supports a robber's right not to be subject to unreasonable force during arrest:

    [The robber] was a criminal. He deserved to be arrested and punished; his story stirs little sympathy, much less outrage, in the crowd. The courts cannot be so impassive. We must always remember that unreasonable searches and seizures helped drive our forefathers to revolution. One who would defend the Fourth Amendment must share his foxhole with scoundrels of every sort, but to abandon the post because of the poor company is to sell freedom cheaply.

    Id. at 379-80. The Fourth Circuit added, "'[W]hile we are concerned with a shabby defrauder, we must deal with his case in the context of what are really the great themes of the Fourth Amendment.'" *Id.* at 380 (quoting United States v. Rabinowitz, 339 U.S. 56, 69 (1950) (Frankfurter, J., dissenting)).

the need for force.[14] Were courts to consider historical distrust of police power when reviewing reasonable force claims, one would expect less deference to police judgment and more concern for an individual's interest in personal security. When courts evaluate whether police used reasonable force, they should consider whether alternatives were available to police officers, instead of rubber-stamping their actions. By closely scrutinizing the judgment of police officers, courts would limit the types of conduct that establish a reasonable belief that suspects pose a danger to police officers and the community. A likely by-product of such an approach would be improved municipal training of police officers in using devices to restrain subjects.[15]

Rather than articulate an evolving standard of reasonableness, many courts erroneously use danger as proxy for reasonableness and have defined danger too broadly. The lack of any scrutiny is clear when courts permit police officers to frisk suspects for weapons.[16] Courts readily uphold frisks as preventive measures.[17] They should not, however, transfer their assessment of danger justifying a preventive measure to justify an aggressive measure, such as a shooting, because of the weighty interest in bodily integrity. Under the doctrine of furtive gestures, many courts, however, have used the same danger analysis to justify both a frisk and a shooting.[18] In short, many courts, without considering other important issues, have erroneously justified officers' shooting suspects simply because the suspect moved after an order to freeze.[19]

This chapter asserts that danger is not the only issue in resolving whether a police practice is unconstitutional. Other factors affect the balancing process of the Fourth Amendment. The goal of this chapter is to highlight the misperceptions of the Fourth Amendment. One common misperception is

---

14. *See generally* Maclin, *supra* note 13, at 200 ("If the Court can identify any plausible goal or reason that promotes law enforcement interests, the challenged police practice is considered reasonable and the constitutional inquiry is over.").
15. *See, e.g.*, City of Canton v. Harris, 489 U.S. 378, 390 n.10 (1989) (a municipality can be liable for its failure to train officers as to the constitutional limits on the use of deadly force).
16. *See infra* text accompanying notes 297-331.
17. *See infra* text accompanying notes 297-331.
18. *See infra* text accompanying notes 224-330, 314-17.
19. *See infra* text accompanying notes 186, 224-26.

that assessing danger is the same issue as assessing reasonableness. An analysis reveals that in both *Garner* and *Graham* danger was only a factor in determining the constitutionality of force during investigations and arrests. As will be shown, when the police officers act preventively rather than aggressively, the presence of danger more readily justifies the action. The chapter examines the common practice of frisking suspects, one allowing police officers to pat down the outer garments of suspects if they have reasonable suspicion to believe that the suspects may be "armed and dangerous."[20] Other common preventive practices include emergency searches and searches incident to arrests. Danger is a factor in determining the constitutionality of both practices.

This chapter also details the conflict in the lower courts as to how to measure reasonableness when officers act aggressively. The disagreement has centered on five important issues: what evidence is relevant; who decides whether conduct was reasonable; and the significance of the offense allegedly committed by the suspect, the suspect's actions, and the availability of less intrusive alternatives. How courts resolve these issues has depended upon the role they give to danger analysis. Those that find danger to be a weighty factor give little consideration to the other issues. Those that properly perceive the significance of danger analysis are more likely to evaluate other factors. In addition, the chapter will discuss the lower courts' misperception of the Fourth Amendment and the results of that misperception: officers may frisk suspects for weapons if they have mere suspicion; officers may use extremely intrusive means for conducting stops when drugs are involved; officers may view "emergencies" as opportunities for investigative searches; and officers may search an area incident to an arrest even if the suspects did not have access to that area at the time of the search.

In the final portion of the chapter, specific guidelines for assessing danger and the constitutionality of both aggressive and preventive actions are offered. These guidelines safeguard Fourth Amendment rights and check the unnecessary deference courts have given police officers by compelling courts to view their serious misperceptions of the right to personal security.

The debate between Justices Stevens and Kennedy in *Maryland v. Buie*[21] captures the essence of the courts' misperceptions of the Fourth Amendment. Justice Stevens thought a police officer was foolish for

---

20. Terry v. Ohio, 392 U.S. 1, 30 (1968).
21. 494 U.S. 325 (1990).

searching a basement of a home after another officer had arrested the resident for armed robbery and taken him outside the home;[22] Justice Kennedy thought that the action represented good police work because a second person or accomplice might have been hiding in the base ment.[23] Although walking downstairs into an unknown basement can create fear, the mere presence of danger, for Justice Stevens, did not justify the officers' continuing their search because they had already fulfilled the purpose of their entry—arresting the suspect pursuant to a warrant. For Justice Kennedy, further intrusion was permissible because some danger was present. Even though Justice Kennedy's perspective is harmonious with the trend in the lower courts, Justice Stevens's assessment of danger properly signifies the needed balancing of interests. Justice Stevens questioned whether the officers created the danger by going down the stairs. He also recognized that alternatives were available to minimize any potential danger. In this situation, the privacy interest in the home and the availability of alternatives reduced the weight Justice Stevens gave to the presence of danger. The Stevens perspective directs attention to the issues explored in this chapter. It highlights how one's view of danger in Fourth Amendment jurisprudence significantly affects the balance of interests.

Using Physical Force to Seize Suspects: Aggressive Actions

Although suspects for years have alleged that police officers used excessive force during their arrests, it was not until 1985 that the U.S. Supreme Court declared that these claims arise under the Fourth Amendment, which prohibits "unreasonable" seizures.[24] In two decisions, *Tennessee v. Garner*[25] and *Graham v. Connor,*[26] the Supreme Court created a standard of analysis for both deadly and nondeadly force claims under the Fourth Amendment. Central to its discussion were the text and history of the amendment.[27] In both decisions, assessing the danger a sus-

---

22. *Id.* at 337-38 (Stevens, J., concurring).
23. *Id.* at 329 (Kennedy, J., concurring).
24. Tennessee v. Garner, 471 U.S. 1, 8 (1985).
25. *Id.*
26. 490 U.S. 386, 394 (1989).
27. *Graham,* 490 U.S. at 394-97; *Garner,* 471 U.S. at 8-15.

pect presented to police officers and the community was a part of its analysis.[28]

In *Garner*, determining reasonableness required balancing interests: the right to personal security, which protects both the suspect and society from unreasonably intrusive police practices; society's interest in a fair adjudication of guilt; and society's interest in effective law enforcement.[29] Assessing danger required an evaluation of the offense allegedly committed by the suspect.[30] Measuring the degree of danger was important in determining whether it outweighed the suspect's "fundamental interest in his own life."[31] Only if the danger was significant could the police officer use deadly force. In applying the balancing standard under the Fourth Amendment, the Court strongly emphasized the nature of the offense the suspect allegedly committed.

The Court's assessment of danger in *Garner* drove its conclusion that the police officer used unreasonable force in shooting a fleeing suspect. The police officer had probable cause to believe that a person running from a house at night had just attempted to burglarize it.[32] The police officer, who did not believe that the suspect was armed, commanded him to halt.[33] When the suspect failed to follow the order, the officer shot the suspect in the back of the head.[34] A state statute authorized the use of deadly force to shoot any fleeing felon.[35] The Supreme Court held the statute unconstitutional as applied because it determined that not all fleeing felons are dangerous.[36]

To justify the use of deadly force, the offense must be one signifying great danger in order to outweigh a suspect's fundamental interest in life. In describing the seriousness of the offense, the Court appeared to state both a "standard" and a "rule":[37]

---

28. *Graham*, 490 U.S. at 396; *Garner*, 471 U.S. at 10-11.
29. *Garner*, 471 U.S. at 9-10.
30. *Id.* at 11.
31. *Id.* at 9.
32. *Id.* at 3-4.
33. *Id.* at 4.
34. *Id.*
35. *Id.* at 5.
36. *Id.* at 11.
37. *See supra* note 10.

> Where the officer has probable cause to believe that the suspect poses a threat of serious physical harm, either to the officer or to others, it is not constitutionally unreasonable to prevent escape by using deadly force. Thus, if the suspect threatens the officer with a weapon or there is probable cause to believe that the suspect has committed a crime involving the infliction or threatened infliction of serious physical harm, deadly force may be used if necessary to prevent escape, and if, where feasible, some warning has been given.[38]

The first sentence contains a standard: police officers may use deadly force on suspects when they seriously endanger the lives of officers or others. This standard considers all of the circumstances at the time of the shooting. The second sentence, however, suggests a rule for determining the requisite danger: when suspects commit a certain type of offense, they automatically signify danger to officers or the community.

Noticeably absent from the rule in the second sentence is a reference to *immediate* danger to officers or others. The literal language of the second part seems to suggest a presumption of danger for heinous offenses: until the person is caught, everyone is in danger. Thus, if a fleeing suspect has committed an offense involving the serious infliction of bodily harm, officers may shoot him or her even if they themselves or members of the public are not in immediate danger.[39]

Such an interpretation, however, is inconsistent with the standard in the first sentence, which logically distinguishes between both actual danger and possible danger. A standard may include a presumption, but not one that is mandatory because a standard allows consideration of all the surrounding circumstances. Immediacy would thus be a factor in calculating reasonableness.

Under this standard, police officers must explain how they or others were in danger at the time of the shooting. This interpretation is consistent with a statement in *Garner*: "Where the suspect poses no *immediate* threat

---

38. 471 U.S. at 11-12.
39. *See* John C. Hall, *Use of Deadly Force to Prevent Escape*, FBI L. Bull., Mar. 1994, at 31 (once suspect has committed an offense involving the infliction of serious bodily harm, police officers do not need "to calculate the 'probability' of future danger if the suspect were permitted to escape").

to the officer and no threat to others, the harm resulting from failing to apprehend him does not justify the use of deadly force to do so."[40] Read in context, then, some offenses may signify danger, but the surrounding circumstances determine the degree of danger.

In assessing danger, the Court looked at the history of the Fourth Amendment by considering the common law.[41] Although the common law rule allowed police officers to shoot fleeing felons, the Court rejected interpreting the Fourth Amendment to allow killing fleeing felons because modern felonies are significantly different from felonies at common law, which generally allowed capital punishment upon conviction.[42] The Court instead adapted the common law rule to modern times by requiring a relationship between the alleged offense and danger to the community. It also reflected this adaptation by creating a standard, not a rule, for evaluating force.

The Court also considered the history of the Fourth Amendment by noting the type of weapons available to police officers at common law.[43] It observed that officers then had "rudimentary" weapons, did not carry handguns "until the latter half of the last century," and engaged in "hand-to-hand" struggles.[44] To apply common law shooting rules to modern times, the Court stated, would be to ignore significant "technological" changes.[45]

To determine reasonableness of a shooting under the Fourth Amendment thus requires a consideration of a suspect's dangerousness. The Court wisely noted that assessing dangerousness is difficult, yet it justified linking reasonableness and danger by stating that "similarly difficult judgments must be made by the police in equally uncertain circumstances."[46]

In light of the difficulty in making a determination of dangerousness, it is not surprising that the Court was not unanimous in its determination that the fleeing nighttime burglary suspect was not a danger to the officer or the community. Justice O'Connor in her dissent thought that the offense signified the requisite danger.[47] She also interpreted the Fourth

40. *Garner,* 471 U.S. at 11 (emphasis added).

41. *Id.* at 12-15.

42. *Id.* at 13 n.11 (Although "[n]ot all felonies were always punishable by death, . . . the link was profound.").

43. *Id.* at 14-15.

44. *Id.*

45. *Id.* at 15.

46. *Id.* at 20.

47. *Id.* at 26-28 (O'Connor, J., dissenting).

Amendment reasonableness standard to force a suspect to comply with an officer's command. She stated, "[T]o avoid the use of deadly force and the consequent risk to his life, the suspect need merely obey the valid order to halt."[48] In short, she thought the way to preserve a suspect's right to personal security is to require compliance with an officer's order. She also criticized the majority for discussing when officers may use deadly force, rather than the narrower question of when officers may use handguns.[49] She wondered how officers are to know when either they or the suspects are using potentially lethal objects. She questioned the limits on the use of knives, baseball bats, and ropes.[50] In addition, she emphasized the importance of deferring to the judgment of police officers who have to make split-second decisions.[51]

Dangerousness is also a factor when evaluating the use of nondeadly force. In *Graham v. Connor*,[52] the Supreme Court explained that the Fourth Amendment reasonableness standard described in *Garner* was also applicable to the use of nondeadly force. After noting the balancing of interests required by the Reasonableness Clause, the Court attempted to provide some factors to consider in determining reasonableness: "the severity of the crime at issue, whether the suspect poses an immediate threat to the safety of officers or others, and whether he is actively resisting arrest or attempting to evade by flight."[53]

In articulating these factors, the Court did not state how to weigh the factors. In contrast to the *Garner* decision, which stated that the suspect has a fundamental interest in his life, the *Graham* Court did not state how to weigh a suspect's interest in personal security. Yet, in examining the three *Graham* factors, one can easily discern their derivation from *Garner* because they highlight the same considerations. In *Garner*, the Court considered the offense of burglary, the immediacy of danger to the police officer and the community, and the need to capture the fleeing felon, which are the specific factors articulated in *Graham*.

In attempting to provide some guidelines for using nondeadly force, the *Graham* Court emphasized that the force police officers may use in

48. *Id.* at 29 (O'Connor, J., dissenting).
49. *Id.* at 32 (O'Connor, J., dissenting).
50. *Id.* (O'Connor, J., dissenting).
51. *Id.* (O'Connor, J., dissenting).
52. 490 U.S. 386, 394-95 (1989).
53. *Id.* at 396.

apprehending suspects is governed by the word "reasonable,"[54] while the force prison officials may use is governed by the words "cruel" and "unusual punishments."[55] Even though prison officials are liable for the use of force only if they act maliciously, the *Graham* Court explained that police officers may violate the Fourth Amendment even if they act in subjective good faith.[56] A standard of reasonableness provides greater protection to suspects because it limits the amount of force police officers can use based on objective factors.

In articulating this protective standard, the Court, however, explained that this standard should be applied with consideration for the split-second decisions that police officers have to make.[57] Within that parameter, the Court emphasized that even split-second decisions must be reasonable and not merely made in subjective good faith. Specifically, it held that it will evaluate the decision to use force from the perspective of "a reasonable police officer on the scene."[58]

The *Garner* and *Graham* decisions thus provide only general guidelines as to how to measure reasonableness. An important factor in these guidelines is the danger posed by a suspect. Once officers reasonably perceive the requisite immediate danger, they may act aggressively in apprehending a suspect to protect police officers and society because the need to apprehend outweighs the suspect's right in bodily integrity. In recognizing the danger officers face in their work, the Court in both *Garner* and *Graham* noted that it had previously allowed officers to conduct a limited search of suspects during investigations in *Terry v. Ohio*.[59] Since the Court upheld this preventive police practice in *Terry* and its companion case of *Sibron v. New York*,[60] it has similarly considered the presence of danger in upholding numerous other preventive actions by police officers.[61]

---

54. *Id.* at 395-96.
55. *Id.* at 398 (citing Whitley v. Albers, 475 U.S. 312, 320-21 (1986)).
56. *Graham*, 490 U.S. at 398-99.
57. *Id.* at 397.
58. *Id.* at 396.
59. 392 U.S. 1, 24 (1968).
60. 392 U.S. 40, 64-65 (1968).
61. *See infra* text accompanying notes 142-54.

Frisking Suspects for Weapons: Preventive Actions

The need to limit danger to police officers and innocent bystanders is an issue in determining the constitutionality of numerous preventive police practices. These practices include searching a suspect,[62] conducting a protective sweep of an area,[63] ordering a suspect out of a vehicle,[64] taking a suspect to the police station,[65] inventorying the contents of a vehicle,[66] and even testing for illegal drugs.[67] When police officers decide to frisk a suspect, danger is the only question.[68] In the other areas, the presence of potential danger was at least one factor among many which the Supreme Court used to strengthen the government's justification for an intrusion.[69] The most important cases first establishing the significance of danger and its justification for intrusive police conduct were *Terry v. Ohio*[70] and *Sibron v. New York*.[71] Since these decisions, danger has been an important factor in upholding numerous police practices.

Danger as the Justification for a Terry *Frisk*

In *Terry* and *Sibron*, the Court approved of investigatory stops and limited searches under some circumstances. When police officers have reasonable suspicion that a suspect is armed and dangerous, they may conduct a "frisk."[72] This search allows officers to pat down a suspect's clothing, and, upon feeling an object that may be a weapon, to search

62. *See infra* text accompanying notes 72-119.
63. *See infra* text accompanying notes 120-37.
64. *See infra* text accompanying notes 346-47.
65. *See infra* text accompanying notes 151-54.
66. *See infra* text accompanying notes 146-49.
67. *See* National Treasury Employees Union v. Von Raab, 489 U.S. 656, 672 (1989) (suspicionless urine testing of customs agents who carry firearms is reasonable; employees must be able to properly exercise "judgment and dexterity").
68. *See infra* text accompanying notes 72-76.
69. *See supra* text accompanying notes 38-56 and *infra* text accompanying notes 139-54.
70. 392 U.S. 1, 24-25 (1968).
71. 392 U.S. 40, 64-65 (1968).
72. 392 U.S. at 20-27.

further.[73] This preventive action allows police officers to investigate crime without jeopardizing their safety or the community's safety. In discussing the role of danger for this preventive action, the *Terry* Court determined that the presence of danger in these circumstances outweighed an individual's interest in personal security under the Fourth Amendment.[74]

The Court interpreted the Fourth Amendment to allow police officers to seize and search suspects even if they did not have probable cause to arrest them.[75] Although the language of the amendment only referred to probable cause for warrants, the Court analyzed the word "reasonable" and determined that such conduct would be permissible if officers had reasonable suspicion to stop someone for a crime that was about to occur and to search him or her if they had reasonable suspicion that the suspect was "armed and dangerous."[76] The Court explicitly linked the ability to frisk to a reasonable perception of danger.

In both *Terry*[77] and *Sibron*[78] the Court considered the criminal nature of the suspect's activity as a factor in assessing the danger the suspect posed to the investigating officer. In *Terry*, an officer thought some men were about to burglarize a store because he saw them repeatedly walk near a certain store.[79] In *Sibron*, the officer thought that a suspect was buying drugs because he had spoken with drug addicts. In addition to the alleged offense, the Court in both cases also considered whether the suspect's actions during the confrontation with the officer reasonably heightened the sense of danger. In *Terry*, when the plainclothes officer approached the suspects, he identified himself as a policeman and asked them their names. When they "mumbled" a response, the officer grabbed one of the suspects and frisked him.[80] At this point the officer reasonably thought he was in

---

73. *Id.* at 29. The *Terry* Court clearly stated that the intrusion is to be incremental, with reasonable suspicion that the suspect may be armed and dangerous justifying each intrusion. *Id.* at 29-30. Frisks, which include touching the chest and groin areas, may be "annoying, frightening, and perhaps humiliating experience[s]." *Id.* at 25.
74. *Id.* at 27.
75. *Id.* at 24.
76. *Id.* at 30-31.
77. *Id.* at 30.
78. 392 U.S. at 62.
79. *Terry*, 392 U.S. at 6.
80. *Id.* at 7.

danger and a frisk was permissible.[81] In *Sibron*, however, the suspect's action in reaching into his pocket did not increase the sense of danger.[82]

The Court held that the frisk was unreasonable.[83] In contrast to the frisk in *Terry*, which was for "protection of [the officer] and others in the area,"[84] the frisk in *Sibron* was for gathering evidence. The Court noted that the officer did not specify any facts from which he could "reasonably infer [that] the individual was armed and dangerous."[85] By talking with drug addicts, the suspect did not lose his right to personal security.[86] The Court stated, "The suspect's mere act of talking with a number of known narcotics addicts over an eight-hour period no more gives rise to reasonable fear of life and limb on the part of the police officer than it justifies an arrest for committing a crime."[87]

Although the language of the Fourth Amendment does not refer to frisks or reasonable suspicion, the Court believed that the Reasonableness Clause of the Fourth Amendment allowed frisks in some circumstances. Its rationale was built on a type of exigent circumstance, with the frisk permissible based on reasonable suspicion, not probable cause.[88] It explained that police officers, who often may not have probable cause to arrest a

---

81. *Id.* at 7. The officer thought he felt a gun and later reached inside the suspect's pocket and removed it. *Id.*
82. *Sibron*, 392 U.S. at 64. When the officer approached the suspect and stated, "You know what I am after," the suspect "mumbled something and reached into his pocket." *Id.* at 45. The officer "simultaneously" put his hand in the pocket. *Id.*
83. *Id.* at 64-65.
84. *Terry*, 392 U.S. at 30.
85. *Sibron,* 392 U.S. at 64. Although the Court seemed to rely on the subjective belief of the officer that the suspect was not reaching for illegal drugs, the Court nevertheless reiterated the objective standard that it had established in *Terry. Id.*
86. *Id.* at 64. In the alternative, the Court noted that even if the officer would have had reasonable suspicion to believe that the suspect was armed, the officer violated *Terry* by failing to first pat down the outer clothing of the suspect. *Id.* at 65-66. By thrusting his hand directly into the suspect's pocket, the officer acted unreasonably. *Id.*
87. *Id.* The Supreme Court explicitly rejected finding danger based on being part of a group. *Id.* at 65.
88. *Terry,* 392 U.S. at 20-24.

suspect, have a duty to investigate crime that is about to occur.[89] The purpose of the stop is to dispel the officer's reasonable suspicion that crime is about to occur.[90] If such an investigation is necessary, then police officers must not put themselves in unnecessary danger. The Court declared that the presence of danger outweighed an individual's right to personal security.[91]

The balancing process for frisks resembles the balancing process in *Tennessee v. Garner*[92] and *Graham v. Connor,*[93] except that significantly greater protection attaches to the right to personal security when officers act aggressively. Although the suspects in both *Terry* and *Garner* were allegedly involved in burglarizing a place, the preventive action in *Terry* was reasonable in order to defuse potential danger from an impending burglary, while the aggressive action in *Garner* was unreasonable because the shooting was merely to stop the suspect's flight from the scene of the crime.

In upholding the need for preventive frisks, the *Terry* Court did not completely diminish the right to personal security. It stated that a frisk is a "serious intrusion upon the sanctity of the person."[94] In evaluating an individual's right to personal security, the Court also recognized that the practice of stopping and frisking suspects may severely undermine respect for the police when they use this practice to harass youths and minorities.[95]

Even in light of strong interests in the right to personal security and the freedom from harassment, the Court nevertheless approved of frisks when officers have reasonable suspicion to believe that a suspect is dangerous.[96] The *Terry* Court cited to the problem of violence in America:

---

89. *Terry*, 392 U.S. at 24.
90. *Id.* at 30.
91. *Id.* at 23.
92. *See supra* text accompanying notes 29-51.
93. *See supra* text accompanying notes 52-58.
94. *Terry*, 392 U.S. at 17. The Court noted that a frisk may include a touching of a person's "'arms and armpits, waistline and back, the groin and area about the testicles, and entire surface of the leg down to the feet.'" *Id.* at 17 (quoting PRIAR AND MARTIN, *Searching and Disarming Criminals*, 45 J. CRIM. L. C. & P.S. 481 (1954)).
95. *Id.* at 14 n.11.
96. *Id.* at 27.

> Certainly it would be unreasonable to require that police officers take unnecessary risks in the performance of their duties. American criminals have a long tradition of armed violence, and every year in this country many law enforcement officers are killed in the line of duty, and thousands more are wounded. Virtually all of these deaths and a substantial portion of the injuries are inflicted with guns and knives.[97]

In balancing the interests, the Court linked the reasonableness inquiry to assessing the danger posed by a suspect. The *Terry* Court found the necessary danger present because the officer had reasonable suspicion to believe that the suspects were about the burglarize a store.[98] The Court stated that such a search may be "designed to discover guns, knives, clubs, or other hidden instruments for the assault of the police officer."[99]

The suspect's alleged offense and his actions are thus factors in determining whether a frisk is reasonable. In upholding the frisk in *Terry* and finding it unlawful in *Sibron* the Court aptly noted that the reasonableness of any frisk depends upon the facts of a particular case.[100] Even though the *Terry* Court limited its holding to the facts of the case, it later analyzed the facts of other cases to determine whether the circumstances justified preventive frisks.

The Progeny of Terry

The progeny of *Terry* reveals that only a reasonable perception of danger justifies a frisk. Several decisions have discussed frisks associated with illegal drugs activity: *Minnesota v. Dickerson*[101] rejected extending *Terry* frisks to searches for drugs; *Ybarra v. Illinois*[102] prohibited police officers from frisking bar patrons when officers execute a search warrant for drugs; and *Adams v. Williams*[103] suggested that even if the alleged offense is pos-

---

97. *Id.* at 23-24.
98. *Id.* at 30.
99. *Id.* at 29.
100. *Id.* at 29 ("[t]hese limitations will have to be developed in the concrete factual circumstances of individual cases").
101. *See infra* text accompanying notes 104-06.
102. *See infra* text accompanying notes 107-112.
103. *See infra* notes accompanying text 113-19.

session of drugs, other circumstances may nevertheless support an officer's decision to frisk based on a reasonable perception of danger. These decisions reveal that the mere presence of drug activity does not justify searching individuals for weapons or drugs.

In *Dickerson*, the Supreme Court refused to extend the scope of a frisk to include a search for drugs.[104] The Court affirmed that a *Terry* frisk must be "strictly 'limited to that which is necessary for the discovery of weapons which might be used to harm the officers or others nearby.'"[105] Officers could, however, search suspects for drugs if, after doing a patdown, their sense of touch gave them probable cause to believe that the objects they felt were illegal drugs.[106] By limiting the *Terry* frisk to a search for weapons, the Court barred further encroachment into an individual's right to personal security.

The difficulty of assessing danger was pronounced in *Ybarra v. Illinois,*[107] a decision in which a majority of the Court refused to accept the dissent's bright line, which provided:[108] When officers are executing search warrants for drugs in a public place, frisks of the people present are permissible because guns are "'tools of the trade'"[109] of drug dealers and buyers.

The majority reiterated that individualized suspicion is the standard for *Terry* frisks. It refused to assume that just because individuals were present during the execution of a search warrant, they were necessarily armed or that the presence of a group automatically endangered the officers.[110] The dissent believed that a group danger theory was valid because the officers were looking at the search area and not the people present.[111] In

---

104. 113 S. Ct. 2130, 2136 (1993).
105. *Id.* at 2136 (quoting Terry v. Ohio, 392 U.S. 1, 26 (1968)).
106. *Id.* at 2137.
107. 444 U.S. 85, 94-96 (1979).
108. *Id.* at 98, 102 (Rehnquist, J., dissenting).
109. *Id.* at 106 (Rehnquist, J., dissenting) (quoting United States v. Oates, 560 F.2d 45, 62 (2d Cir. 1977)).
110. *Id.* at 92-93. The police officers had a warrant to search a bar and the bartender. It did not authorize them to search the bar's patrons. Even though the bar was associated with illegal drugs and twelve customers filled the small search area, the Court refused allow a general search for weapons. *Id.* at 90-92.
111. *Id.* at 106-07 (Burger, J., dissenting). The dissent contended that executing search warrants creates more danger than investigating crimes. *Id.* at 107.

finding the frisk of a bar patron unreasonable, the Court also noted that neither the customer's actions nor attire created a sense of danger.[112] Although in *Ybarra* the presence of drugs did not automatically signify danger, other offenses can. In *Adams v. Williams*,[113] the Court upheld a frisk of a suspect based on a tip that a person in a car had both a gun and some drugs.[114] The Court justified both the stop and the frisk by finding that the officer had reasonable suspicion to believe that the suspect did not have a permit for his gun.[115]

The Court's assessment of danger,[116] however, ignored one important fact—state law permitted its citizens to carry weapons as long as they were licensed.[117] In perceiving the requisite danger for a frisk, the Court seemed to rely on mere suspicion that the driver had a weapon in a high-crime area at night. The dissent did not believe that mere possession of a gun signified danger.[118] It suggested that if gun control is necessary, the Court should

---

112. *Id.* at 91. The patron wore a large jacket, which could conceal weapons. The Court did not interpret the presence of baggy clothing as creating a need for a frisk. *Id.*
113. 407 U.S. 143, 148-49 (1972).
114. *Id.* at 147-48.
115. *Id.* at 148.
116. *Id.* at 148. The facts of *Adams* reveal the complexities in assessing danger. *Id.* at 144-45. At 2:15 a.m. an informant walked up to a police officer in his cruiser and told him that a man in a nearby car was carrying a gun at his waist and had drugs. In this high-crime area, the officer walked over to the car and tapped on the window, asking the driver to step out. When the suspect rolled down the window instead of opening the door, the officer reached inside the car and relied on informant's tip that a gun was at the suspect's waist. He reached in and took it, even though it was not visible when he saw the suspect. Unlike the stop in *Terry*, the officer did not ask any questions to dispel his suspicion. Three factors were significant for the Court: the high-crime area, the suspect's failure to follow the officer's command, and the informant's tip that the suspect had a gun and some drugs. *Id.* at 147-49. The need for the frisk, according to the Court, did not arise simply because there was reasonable suspicion to believe that the suspect was involved in drugs. *Id.* at 148. The car's ability to block the officer's view of the suspect, according to the Court, created a "greater" threat to the officer's safety. *Id.* at 148.
117. *Id.* at 149-50 (Douglas, J., dissenting).
118. *Id.* at 149-50 (Douglas, J., dissenting). In another dissent, Justice Marshall perceived the majority as treating warrantless searches as the "rule rather than [as a] 'narrowly drawn' exception." *Id.* at 154 (Marshall, J., dissenting).

"water down the Second rather than the Fourth Amendment."[119] The majority's assessment of danger, however, prevailed, suggesting a strong concern for officer protection and less interest in the citizen's right to personal security.

The Court's heightened concern for protecting police officers compelled it to later expand the scope of a frisk to include a search of the area near a suspect. The constitutionality of this expanded search, however, also depended upon the same justification for the frisk of a person: reasonable suspicion that the officer was in danger. In *Michigan v. Long*,[120] the Court permitted officers to "frisk" the passenger compartment of a car,[121] and in *Maryland v. Buie*,[122] the Court allowed officers to conduct a protective "sweep" of an area while executing a warrant.

Although the *Long* Court recognized that danger is present during all traffic stops,[123] such danger does not justify searching the vehicle of all suspects. The Court stated that the circumstances facing the officer must create reasonable suspicion to believe that the suspect is dangerous.[124] In short, it found no automatic right to search cars when the driver is charged with a traffic offense.

For an officer to lawfully search the passenger compartment, the facts must signify danger. In *Long*, the danger existed, according to the majority, because the officer saw a knife on the floor of the car.[125] The presence of

---

119. *Id.* at 151 (Douglas, J., dissenting).
120. 463 U.S. 1032 (1983).
121. *Id.* at 1050. In *Long*, the search of the passenger compartment occurred when an officer saw a large knife on the floor during a traffic stop. The officer then frisked the suspect and searched the compartment. The search was not limited to objects in plain view. It included opening containers. The officer in *Long* lifted an armrest, saw an open pouch, and found marijuana. The Court upheld the search of the vehicle, finding that the officer had reasonable suspicion to perceive danger. *Id.*
122. 110 S. Ct. 1093 (1990).
123. *Id.* at 1047-48. The Court had previously recognized the danger inherent in traffic stops in Pennsylvania v. Mimms, 434 U.S. 106, 110 (1977). In *Mimms* the Court declared that police officers who lawfully stop drivers may order them out of the vehicle without any level of suspicion of danger. The Court held that the intrusion on the driver's liberty was de minimis and the officers' interest in safety was significant. *Id.*
124. *Id.* at 1049 n.14.
125. *Id.* at 1050.

this weapon gave the investigating officer the authority to search containers in the vehicle.[126] Although other facts also heightened the perception of danger,[127] the Court emphasized the danger associated with a large hunting knife.[128]

How to accurately measure this danger caused a division in the Court. The majority did not want to closely evaluate whether the officer could have used other means to protect himself;[129] the dissent, however, did.[130] The dissent thought the officer could have protected himself by keeping the driver outside the car. The officer could then safely enter the car.[131] It added that by finding danger in these circumstances[132] and by failing to scrutinize the means used, the majority did "violence to the requirements of the Fourth Amendment."[133]

---

126. *Id.*
127. *Id.* at 1035-37. The Court offered a lengthy description of the facts justifying the arrest: it was late at night in a rural area; the driver, who was under the influence of an "intoxicant," failed to respond coherently to the officer's requests for identification and registration; the officer saw a knife on the floor of the car; and the officer believed that the suspect, who was not arrested, might have access to other unknown weapons in the car when he returned to it. *Id.* at 1050.
128. *Id.* at 1052 n.16.
129. *Id.* at 1052. The Court declared, "[W]e have not required that officers adopt alternative means to ensure their safety in order to avoid the intrusion involved in a *Terry* encounter." *Id.* By limiting scrutiny of available alternatives, the Court diminished an individual's right to privacy by allowing officers to open containers in vehicles when they see a weapon.
130. *Id.* at 1065 (Brennan, J., dissenting).
131. *Id.* (Brennan, J., dissenting).
132. *Id.* at 1061 (Brennan, J., dissenting). The dissent wondered why the police officer should be able to search a closed container only because it "'could have contained a weapon.'" *Id.* (Brennan, J., dissenting) (quoting *id.* at 1050-51). In addition, it questioned what objects will justify an officer's search for "other" weapons. It noted that both a hammer and a baseball bat could be a deadly weapon. Having these objects in a car should not allow police officers to search containers looking for other "weapons." It also thought that the offense justifying the stop, driving under the influence of a drug, should not signify danger to a police officer. It contended that it "requires imagination to conclude that [the suspect] is presently dangerous." *Id.* at 1062.
133. *Id.* at 1064-65.

In contrast to the extremely heightened perception of danger in *Long*, the Court's view of danger in *Maryland v. Buie* was more realistic. It applied the *Terry* frisk doctrine to justify officers' conducting "protective sweeps" as they execute warrants. A sweep allows officers to inspect "those spaces where a person may be found"[134] if they have reasonable suspicion to believe that danger is present. Thus, as with *Terry* stops, police officers must have reasonable suspicion of danger.[135]

In examining the contours of reasonableness, the *Buie* Court built the doctrine of protective sweeps on the progeny of *Terry*. It relied on the safety concerns discussed in *Terry*, *Ybarra*, and *Long*.[136] These cases, it found, supported giving officers the authority to search the area imbued with the greatest expectation of privacy—the home. The Court noted that in contrast to an investigation on the street, an arrest in the home heightens the safety concerns of police officers because someone may "unexpectedly launch an attack."[137] The only restrictions specified were that officers have reasonable suspicion to believe that someone will harm them and that the search will last no longer than necessary to effectuate the arrest.

In establishing the protective sweep doctrine, the Court simply cited prior case law. It failed to explicitly describe the process of balancing interests. Once *Terry* and its progeny balanced danger against an individual's interest in personal security and privacy, the *Buie* Court discerned the central role of danger in analyzing the constitutionality of frisks.

---

134. *Id.* at 1099.

135. The task of ascertaining whether the facts create the requisite danger produced contrasting opinions in *Buie*. Although the majority remanded the case to the lower court for an application of its articulated standard for protective sweeps, *id.* at 1099-1100, Justices Stevens and Kennedy separately hinted how the lower court should decide the issue. Justice Stevens thought that a police officer's decision to go down basement stairs after arresting the person named in the warrant was foolhardy. *Id.* at 1100 (Stevens, J., concurring). Justice Kennedy, however, thought that the officer's decision was sound. Justice Kennedy stated, "[T]he officers would have been remiss if they had not taken these precautions." *Id.* at 1101 (Kennedy, J., dissenting). The contrasting views highlight the difficulty in assessing danger when it becomes the talisman for reasonableness.

136. *Id.* at 1098-99.

137. *Id.* at 1098.

Because the question of reasonableness should be an open-ended standard, the Court's fixation on danger has caused it to allow police officers to further limit the right to personal security. By balancing interests with a strong deference to safety concerns and avoiding consideration of alternatives available to police officers, the Court has sanctioned other police practices that implicate strong interests in both personal security and privacy.

Limiting Danger: Inherent Danger During Emergencies and Arrests

The presence of danger has also been a significant factor in determining what actions police officers may take during emergencies and during arrests. Although the Supreme Court has never stated that there is an "emergency" doctrine under the Fourth Amendment, it has discussed that officers may perform "community caretaking" functions and that they may act without a warrant if they have both probable cause and "exigent circumstances."[138]

In noting that exigencies often exist that require prompt action, the Court has under the caretaking doctrine justified police actions taken for the public good, even if these actions did not meet the standards for criminal investigations. In the criminal context, the Court has focused on protecting police when they arrest suspects. The justification for both actions is perceived danger, whether to the community or to the officer. An examination of these doctrines reveals how misperceptions of danger can significantly erode the protections afforded by the Fourth Amendment.

---

138. Although many of the exigent circumstances cases deal with the fear of losing evidence, *see, e.g.*, Welsh v. Wisconsin, 466 U.S. 740, 749-50 (1984) (warrantless entry of home held impermissible; even though evidence was intoxication may have dissipated by the time an officer would have gotten a warrant, the desired evidence related to a minor offense), danger analysis has at times allowed officers to enter a person's home without a warrant.

When the danger presented by a home is not a fire, but the presence of drugs and weapons, the entering of a home may also constitute a type of exigency. Although a federal statute, § 3109 (1985), limits a federal official's ability to enter without knocking, Justice White in Illinois v. Condon urged the Supreme Court to evaluate the need to knock when officers believe that the person to be arrested has both drugs and guns. Although he noted that some courts recognize exigent circumstances simply because drugs are inside, the decision did not address how to handle the entering when officers know that the suspect has just weapons.

Emergencies: Community Caretaking Functions

Police actions under the community caretaking doctrine are ones taken to protect society during emergencies.[139] The doctrinal justification is similar to the need for conducting *Terry* frisks except that the action is to protect the community, thereby making the reasonable suspicion standard inapplicable.[140] The standard articulated by the Court questions only whether the officers reasonably believed that an emergency existed.[141] Constitutionality thus depends on the assessment of an "emergency" or a public need for action.

Exigency based on the need for safety can arise when police officers enter a home without a warrant either to apprehend a killer or to provide aid to those injured inside the home. The Supreme Court recognized this type of exigency in *Mincey v. Arizona*.[142] In *Mincey*, the Court held that police officers could not conduct a detailed search of a home without a warrant even though the suspect had allegedly committed a murder.[143] Even though murder is a serious offense, the Court looked at all of the circumstances to determine if the requisite exigency existed. It found no exigency arising solely from the offense because once the officers removed the suspect from the house, the exigency disappeared. It did note, however, that an emergency would exist when police officers "reasonably believe that a person within is in need of immediate aid" or that a killer or other victims are inside.[144]

The Court has similarly allowed firefighters to enter burning buildings not only to extinguish a fire but to investigate its origins.[145] The need to protect the public is obvious. In these cases, the need to protect police officers and the public outweighs the suspect's interest in privacy.

---

139. *See infra* text accompanying notes 142-49.
140. *See infra* text accompanying notes 142-49.
141. *See infra* text accompanying notes 142-49.
142. 437 U.S. 385, 393-94 (1978).
143. *Id.*
144. *Id.* at 393. *See generally* Thompson v. Louisiana, 469 U.S. 17, 20 (1984) (officers went to home after receiving a call that a suicidal mother shot her husband; search after mother was removed from the home was impermissible).
145. *See* Michigan v. Clifford, 464 U.S. 287, 293 (1984) (plurality); Michigan v. Tyler, 436 U.S. 499, 506 (1978).

When a suspect is arrested, the Court has cited community safety as a justification for allowing police officers to inventory an arrested person's vehicle. The Court in *Cady v. Dombrowski*[146] recognized that when police officers remove guns from vehicles left by arrested drivers they perform a "community caretaking function."[147] These actions, according to the Court, are administrative.[148]

In interpreting the reasonableness of this preventive action, the Court also refused to carefully consider the availability of other alternatives.[149] Although the officer in this case had reason to believe that the car contained a gun, the Court's interpretation of the inventory doctrine does not require such a belief. The search was reasonable because the Court found it to be administrative, not investigative.

The central question under the community caretaking doctrine is whether the balance of interests justifies an officer's intrusive actions. Reasonableness becomes a question of weighing the right to privacy and personal security against the perceived danger. How one perceives danger, as with the other doctrines, can thus skew the balance.

Searches Incident to Arrests: Inherent Danger

Inherent danger is a part of the justification for searches incident to arrests. The automatic right to search an arrested person is built on three rationales: barring suspects from destroying evidence, lessening the likelihood of escape, and protecting police officers.[150] Although these reasons justify the search, the Court in *Chimel v. California*[151] stated that danger is present during all arrests.[152]

Because of this perception of inherent danger, the *Chimel* Court approved of searching an arrested person for weapons and the "area within

---

146. 413 U.S. 433 (1973).
147. 413 U.S. 433, 441 (1973).
148. *Id.* at 447.
149. *Id.* at 447. It stated, "The fact that the protection of the public might, in the abstract, have been accomplished by 'less intrusive' means does not, by itself, render the search unreasonable." *Id.*
150. *See, e.g.*, Chimel v. California, 395 U.S. 752, 763 (1968).
151. 395 U.S. 752 (1969).
152. *Id.* at 763.

his immediate control."[153] By examining the suspect and the area, the police officer could seize any weapon that would endanger the officer or help the suspect to escape.

The Court limited the search area to that near the suspect in order to safeguard the suspect's right to privacy as it furthered the officer's need for safety. It also required the search to be contemporaneous to the arrest because the need to search is based on need to protect the police officer, not to gather evidence. Because the officers in *Chimel* had searched the entire house without a warrant, the search was unconstitutional.

The authority to conduct this search, however, differs from the authority to conduct a *Terry* frisk. A frisk requires a police officer to have reasonable suspicion that a suspect is armed and dangerous; a search incident to an arrest requires that the prior arrest was lawful. The authority to search a suspect is automatic when the officer arrests a person because of the Court's perception of inherent danger. As a result, officers do not need to articulate the reasons for their searches for weapons under these circumstances.

Although the Court has used danger as a factor in evaluating both preventive and aggressive police actions, a misperception of danger associated with the latter is more troublesome. One is more willing to balance the scale in favor of officer safety when the intrusion does not implicate bodily integrity. Recently, when evaluating aggressive actions, the lower courts have too easily found danger present.[154] They have not properly weighed other Fourth Amendment interests: both the suspect's and society's interests in personal integrity and privacy. By not considering the availability of alternatives to police officers in these situations, the courts have erroneously deferred to the judgment of governmental officials. Such deference is misplaced because mistrust of governmental officials is implicit in the history of the Fourth Amendment.

Litigating Unreasonable Force Claims

Excessive force claims arise whenever police officers use force that is "unreasonable" within the meaning of the Fourth Amendment during investigations or arrests. In determining whether the force used was reason-

153. *Id.* at 763.

154. *See infra* text accompanying notes 186-203.

able, some courts have used the presence of danger as a litmus test.[155] Although most claims occur when police officers arrest suspects,[156] police officers also have to defend their use of force during *Terry* stops because of the intrusive means they often use to check potential danger.[157] An examination of these decisions reveals how courts, in trying to protect police officers and society, have undermined each citizen's right to personal security.

Danger to Police Officers and the Community During Arrests

In *Tennessee v. Garner*[158] and *Graham v. Connor*,[159] the Supreme Court made clear that the Fourth Amendment applies not only to when police officers may arrest suspects, but also to how they may arrest them. The Court declared that the Reasonableness Clause of the Fourth Amendment sets limits on the manner of effectuating seizures.

The *Graham* Court offered three factors to aid police officers in determining whether their conduct in arresting someone was reasonable: the offense committed, the immediate danger to police officers and others, and the suspect's resistance.[160] The Court, however, did not state that these were exclusive factors, nor did it explain the weight of each factor. The Court's lack of definiteness is not surprising because no guidelines can precisely describe the parameters of reasonableness.

Even with this open-ended standard, misperceptions are still possible. Numerous lower courts have misread *Garner* and *Graham* as requiring broad deference to police officers' statements that they feared for their lives.[161] In doing so, the reasonableness inquiry fails to be meaningful.

Assessing the danger confronting police officers and the community requires consideration of numerous issues: what circumstances are relevant to the issue of reasonableness; who decides what is reasonable; what offenses increase the likelihood of danger to police officers and others; what movements by suspects create the inference of serious danger; and what

---

155. *See infra* text accompanying notes 186-203, 224-26.
156. *See infra* text accompanying notes 168-273.
157. *See infra* text accompanying notes 342-51.
158. *See supra* text accompanying notes 29-51.
159. *See supra* text accompanying notes 52-58.
160. Graham v. Connor, 490 U.S. 386, 396 (1989).
161. *See infra* text accompanying notes 186-203.

level of scrutiny courts should use in considering the availability of less intrusive alternatives. An examination of these issues reveals the need to give police officers, juries, and courts greater guidance in determining the reasonableness of force. Without more guidelines, courts may continue to misperceive danger as the central issue in evaluating police practices.

Facts Relevant to the Reasonableness Inquiry

Although danger is a factor in determining the constitutionality of using deadly force, how courts perceive danger depends upon how they define relevancy. Courts disagree about the relevant time frame for evaluating an officer's actions: some courts freeze the time frame to include only those circumstances present at the moment the officer seized the suspect;[162] others include circumstances prior to the seizure.[163] How courts resolve this issue significantly affects the perception of danger.

Resolution of this issue has in part depended upon how courts interpret the *Graham* decision. In *Graham*, the Supreme Court stated that the reasonableness inquiry must be rooted in the reasonable perceptions of an officer:

> The 'reasonableness' of a particular use of force must be judged from the perspective of a reasonable officer on the scene, rather than the 20/20 vision of hindsight. . . . The calculus of reasonableness must embody allowance for the fact that police officers are often forced to make split-second judgments—in circumstances that are tense, uncertain, and rapidly evolving—about the amount of force that is necessary in a particular situation.[164]

The Court thus emphasized that built into the question of reasonableness is a consideration that police officers often need to make quick decisions, unlike courts and juries.

Yet, lower courts have interpreted this passage differently: some use it to narrowly construe the relevant facts,[165] some interpret it as requiring

---

162. *See infra* text and accompanying notes 168-72.
163. *See infra* text and accompanying notes 173-79.
164. 490 U.S. at 396-97.
165. *See infra* text accompanying notes 168-72.

broad deference to the judgment of police officers,[166] and others find the language as only underscoring the nature of police work.[167] An examination of these contrasting views reveals the need for guidelines in assessing relevancy.

One of the first cases to narrowly describe the relevant circumstances was *Greenidge v. Ruffin*.[168] In *Greenidge*, an undercover officer observed a woman enter a man's car. The officer thought that the woman was a prostitute soliciting an illegal act. Instead of having other officers back her up, the officer went to the vehicle, accidentally leaving behind her flashlight. With her police badge hanging from her neck, she went to the car, opened the door, identified herself as an officer, and ordered the two suspects "to place their hands in view."[169] When the occupants did not respond, the officer withdrew her weapon and repeated her order. She then saw the man "reach for a long cylindrical object from behind the seat."[170] She then fired at the man, causing him serious injury. The object turned out to be a wooden nightstick.

The Fourth Circuit in *Greenidge* held that two facts were not relevant to the reasonableness inquiry: the officer's failure to have a backup and her failure to use her flashlight. In determining whether the officer violated the Fourth Amendment, the court too narrowly defined what circumstances are relevant to the issue of reasonableness. The court declared that relevant

---

166. *See infra* text accompanying notes 173-80.

167. *See, e.g.*, Dickerson v. McClellan, 844 F. Supp. 391, 396 (M.D. Tenn. 1994). In Dickerson, the district court rejected the officer's argument for great deference:

> [I]n some cases these tough decisions must be second-guessed, for not every post hoc explanation, no matter how plausible or understandable, can justify every officer's behavior. The best a court can do is attempt to understand the situation as seen by the police and then apply standards of objective reasonableness within these confines. . . . [T]he court would point out that of course not all hindsight is barred in these cases; rather, only antiseptic hindsight. Judging the weight assigned to evidence is entirely appropriate, not to mention inevitable.

Id. The court sent to the jury the issue of whether police officers had used unreasonable force. *Id.* The jury, the court held, was to determine the facts and apply the standard of reasonableness to the ascertained facts. *Id.*

168. 927 F.2d 789 (4th Cir. 1991).

169. *Id.* at 790.

170. *Id.*

circumstances are the conditions confronting the officer the moment she pulled the trigger. In short, the court refused to consider the alternatives available to the officer in investigating a crime. For the Fourth Circuit, reasonableness did not include the officer's conduct prior to the shooting that could have created a need to use deadly force.

Since this decision, the Fourth Circuit has adhered to its narrow reading of relevance.[171] Other courts have also misread *Graham* to require a narrow time frame.[172]

---

171. *See* Drewitt v. Pratt, 999 F.2d 774, 780 (4th Cir. 1993). In *Drewitt*, a plainclothes police officer attempted to stop a person who was driving recklessly. *Id.* at 776. The officer, who did not display his badge, withdrew his weapon and shouted to the driver to stop. *Id.* When the vehicle stopped, the officer walked in front of it. *Id.* While he was in front of it, the vehicle sped forward, hitting the officer. *Id.* After landing on the hood of the vehicle, he shot the driver twice. *Id.* The Fourth Circuit held that the officer's failure to identify himself was not relevant to the determination of whether the shooting was reasonable. *Id.* at 780. After determining that there were no material facts in dispute, the court granted summary judgment for the officer. *Id. See generally* James v. City of Chester, No. 3:92-812-17, 1994 WL 198899, at *7 (D. S.C. May 18, 1994) (reasonableness requires examining the circumstances at the moment the officer used force; it was irrelevant that the officer did not "station a guard at the entrance to the . . . apartment, . . . [nor] the officer's failure to employ proper backup and use a flashlight").

172. *See, e.g.*, Carter v. Buscher, 973 F.2d 1328, 1333 (7th Cir. 1992). In narrowly defining the relevant time frame, the Seventh Circuit in *Carter* refused to consider the serious misjudgments of several police officers. Police officers believed that a suspect had hired someone to kill his wife. Because the suspect frequently bragged that he was always armed, police officers decided to create a ruse to arrest him on a highway in order to protect themselves and limit the likelihood of injury to bystanders. When the suspect agreed to help a stranger who was allegedly stranded on the road, police officers pretended to be the stranded motorist. When the suspect failed to get out of his car and examine the engine of the allegedly malfunctioning car, police officers became restless and approached him as he sat in his car. One officer shined a flashlight into his eyes and shouted "state police." The suspect began firing and hit an officer. After numerous rounds of fire, the suspect and an officer died.

For the Seventh Circuit, the relevant time frame began once the suspect started shooting the officer. *Id.* It refused to consider whether the officers had done anything to precipitate the gunfire. The officers' decision to arrest him on the road and to directly confront him as he was seated were not relevant to the issue of reasonableness. The Seventh Circuit rooted its decision in the

In contrast to these courts, others have more broadly defined the relevant facts for the reasonableness inquiry.[173] By expanding the time frame, the factfinder has greater opportunity for scrutinizing police practices. In doing so, the factfinder may perceive less danger.

A case revealing the importance of a broader time frame is the Seventh Circuit's decision in *Estate of Starks v. Enyart*,[174] a case markedly different from those narrowly defining relevancy. In *Estate of Starks*, the court found relevant all the actions of the police officers prior to a fatal shooting.[175] Police officers knew that the suspect had stolen a taxi without any violence.[176] The suspect later parked the taxi next to another car. An officer then parked his cruiser behind the suspect. Three officers then surrounded the vehicle: one at the driver's window, one at the rear, and another in front of the vehicle, standing behind a utility pole. When the suspect refused to comply with an officer's request to get out of the taxi, he put the car in reverse in order to give him more space to make a sharp turn around the utility pole. When the suspect drove forward, the officer behind the pole placed himself in danger "by moving out from behind the pole without leaving [him] time to stop the car."[177] All three officers then shot the suspect, killing him.

In this decision, the Seventh Circuit criticized the actions of the officers by determining that under the suspect's version of the facts, they created

---

language of *Garner* and its view that the reasonableness inquiry began only when the suspect was actually seized. *Id.* at 1332-33. The reasonableness question arose at the moment the officer shot the suspect. It stated, "The Fourth Amendment prohibits unreasonable *seizures,* not unreasonable, unjustified or outrageous conduct in general." *Id.* It explained that even if the plan to arrest him was poor, the reasonable inquiry began when the officers seized the suspect. It also quoted from the district court, which feared second-guessing the judgment of police officers: "'a contrary holding would create a cottage industry wherein federal courts would be called upon to second-guess police officers as to every discretionary decision regarding time and place of arrest.'" *Id.* at 1331.

173. *See, e.g.*, Estate of Starks v. Enyart, 5 F.3d 230, 233-35 (7th Cir. 1993); Gilmere v. City of Atlanta, 774 F.2d 1495, 1502 (11th Cir. 1985) (*en banc*), *cert. denied*, 476 U.S. 1115 (1986); Dickerson v. McClellan, 844 F. Supp. 391, 396-97 (M.D. Tenn. 1994).
174. 5 F.3d 230 (7th Cir. 1993).
175. *Id.* at 234.
176. *Id.* at 233.
177. *Id.* at 234.

the situation that caused them to use deadly force. It noted that the original offense was nonviolent and that deadly force was impermissible. It explained, "If a fleeing felon is converted to a 'threatening' fleeing felon *solely* based on the actions of a police officer, the police should not increase the level of intrusiveness."[178] To find the shooting reasonable under these circumstances, the court stated, would be to find reasonable a shooting of a driver who accidentally is about to kill a police officer.[179]

The Seventh Circuit thus did not define relevancy narrowly. In contrast to the *Greenidge* decision, which barred from consideration the facts that the officer failed to have a backup or use her flashlight, the Seventh Circuit found relevant actions prior to the shooting. In using a broader time frame, the court considered whether the officers created the need for force as an aspect of assessing danger. Other courts have similarly allowed broader time frames in assessing the degree of danger officers faced when they acted aggressively.[180]

---

178. *Id.*

179. *Id.* The court also added that the two officers who were not behind the telephone pole had to go to trial to resolve the Fourth Amendment claim against them. It refused to grant them immunity simply because a fellow officer's life was in danger based on his own misconduct. *Id.* at 235.

180. *See*, *e.g.*, Gilmere v. City of Atlanta, 774 F.2d 1495 (11th Cir. 1985) (*en banc*), *cert. denied*, 476 U.S. 1115 (1986); Dickerson v. McClellan, 844 F. Supp. 391, 396-97 (M.D. Tenn. 1994).

The Eleventh Circuit in *Gilmere* considered all of the circumstances that preceded an officer shooting the suspect. Two officers believed that a suspect, who had been drinking heavily, had threatened another driver with a gun from the trunk of his car. The officers went to the suspect's home and the suspect resisted going to the officers' cruiser. An officer then began beating him. The suspect reached for one of the officers' guns. It fell to the ground, and another officer shot the suspect as he "lunged toward" him. *Id.* at 1497 n.1. In assessing the danger posed to the officer who shot the suspect, the Eleventh Circuit held that the shooting was unreasonable. It stated, "[A]ny fear on the officer's part was the fear of retaliation against his own unjustified physical abuse. . . . [A] moment of legitimate fear should not preclude liability for harm which largely resulted from his own improper use of his official power." *Id.* at 1501. Danger was also lessened by the facts that the suspect was small, drunk, and lacked a weapon when the officers arrived. Danger arose because of the officers' provocation, not the suspect's conduct. The court upheld the jury's verdict that the officers acted unreasonably in killing the suspect. *Id.* at 1511.

Defining the relevant time frame thus affects the determination of reasonableness and the perception of danger. Those courts that narrowly define the relevant circumstances shield from scrutiny police practices preceding a shooting. Courts that more broadly define the relevant circumstances allow consideration of the facts preceding shootings. This latter approach does not freeze the time frame at the moment of the shooting. Although the Supreme Court in both *Garner* and *Graham* recognized that police officers often have to made quick decisions, the Court did not equate deference with no scrutiny. By more broadly defining the relevant circumstances, one acknowledges the importance of limiting governmental power that unduly infringes on the right to personal security. These contrasting viewpoints, however, are also apparent in how courts decide when a jury should determine whether the force used was unreasonable.

The Jury's Role: Civil Fourth Amendment Claims

When suspects sue police officers for injuries incurred during their arrests, they allege both that the officers seized them and that the officers used unreasonable force. The difficulty in establishing this type of claim centers on the second issue, reasonableness, because when police officers intentionally use physical force they have effectuated a Fourth Amendment seizure.[181]

By expanding the time frame to conduct prior to a challenged shooting, a federal district judge in Dickerson v. McClellan, 844 F. Supp. 391, 396 (M.D. Tenn. 1994), also sent the issue of reasonableness to the jury. The officers in Dickerson entered a house without a warrant, without knocking, or announcing their presence. All that they knew was that a shooting had occurred in the neighborhood. When the homeowner grabbed his gun to respond to unknown people entering his house, the officers shot him. In dispute was whether the homeowner pointed a gun at the officers. Instead of freezing the time frame at the moment of the shooting, the court held that the officers' misconduct prior to the shooting was relevant to issue of reasonableness. *Id.* It explained, "Acting on a hunch that someone could be in danger and then taking actions that could place themselves and anyone inside in greater danger are not objectively reasonable behaviors by an officer." *Id.* The court thus held that the issue of reasonableness required consideration of the officer's conduct prior to the shooting. *Id.*

181. *See, e.g.*, Kathryn R. Urbonya, *'Accidental' Shootings as Fourth Amendment Seizures*, 20 Hastings Const. L.Q. 337, 354-67 1993).

Although the issue of reasonableness sounds like a classic issue for a jury, courts have disagreed as to the jury's role in evaluating unreasonable force claims. At the center of this controversy is whether the objective reasonableness standard established in *Tennessee v. Garner* and *Graham v. Connor* tips the balance in favor of having courts decide reasonableness on summary judgment.

The typical unreasonable force case involves determining what actually happened at the scene. It is a rare case in which police officers and suspects agree on the facts. To resolve material, disputed facts, juries often have to make credibility determinations. In doing so, the jury fulfills its role as factfinder.[182] It also can determine how to apply the standard of reasonableness to the given facts.[183] Such a role falls within the classic function of a jury. Numerous courts have properly denied summary judgment in unreasonable force cases.[184]

In contrast, some courts have interpreted the Supreme Court's decisions in *Garner* and *Graham* as requiring them to defer to the judgment of police officers in evaluating reasonableness.[185] They emphasize the split-

---

182. *See, e.g.*, RONALD J. BACIGAL, *Putting the People Back into the Fourth Amendment*, 62 GEO. WASH. L. REV. 359, 363 (1994).

183. *See, e.g.*, BAGICAL, *supra* note 179, at 364 ("'[r]easonableness vel non was a classic question of fact for the jury'") (quoting AKHIL R. AMAR, *The Bill of Rights as a Constitution*, 100 YALE L.J. 1131, 1179 (1991)).

184. *See, e.g.*, Butler v. City of Norman, 992 F.2d 1053, 1055 (10th Cir. 1993) (jury must decide whether police officers beat handcuffed suspect with a flashlight and hit him in the groin); Kane v. Hargis, 987 F.2d 1005, 1008 (4th Cir. 1993) (jury must determine whether the officer who slammed the suspect's head into the pavement was in danger, in light of the fact that the suspect weighed 100 pounds and the officer weighed 200 pounds); Spann v. Rainey, 987 F.2d 1110, 1115 (5th Cir. 1993) (retrial granted because a jury could find unreasonable the striking of a diabetic in coma for failing to identify himself); Russo v. City of Cincinnati, 953 F. 2d 1036, 1044-45 (6th Cir. 1992) (jury might find unreasonable the officers' repeated use of their guns); Ansley v. Heinrich, 925 F.2d 1339, 1348 (11th Cir. 1991) (jury must decide whether the force was objectively reasonable); Walmsey v. City of Philadelphia, 872 F.2d 546, 547 (3d Cir. 1989), *cert. denied*, 493 U.S. 955 (1989) (jury must decide whether officer hit the suspect); Dickerson v. McClellan, 844 F. Supp. 391, 396 (M.D. Tenn. 1994) (jury must determine whether the suspect aimed at the officers).

185. *See infra* text accompanying notes 186-203.

second judgments that police officers must make, judgments requiring minimal scrutiny. Under this interpretation reasonableness becomes a proxy for respect for police officers. In several decisions courts have misinterpreted the jury's role.

The Eighth Circuit in *Krueger v. Fuhr*[186] nullified the power of the jury to determine reasonableness as it resolved on summary judgment a case involving an alleged furtive gesture by a suspect.[187] In *Krueger*, an officer alleged that he heard the suspect withdraw a knife as they both ran. By allegedly reaching toward his waist, the suspect heightened the officer's perception of danger. The court found this shooting reasonable as a matter of law, even though the knife was found forty-three feet from the suspect's body.

The Eighth Circuit was not bothered by the location of the knife because it stated, as other courts have,[188] that an officer need not see a weapon in order to believe that the suspect is armed and dangerous. A furtive gesture is sufficient. It reasoned that it was immaterial whether the suspect actually had a gun. The officer's decision to shoot the suspect in the back

---

186. 991 F.2d 435 (8th Cir. 1993).

187. *Id.* at 439. An officer in *Fuhr* heard that a suspect had just assaulted someone, that he had a knife, and that he was using drugs. When the officer saw a person lying on the ground and noted that he matched the description of the suspect, the officer withdrew his gun and ordered the suspect to freeze. The suspect got up and began running. When the officer was about three to four yards from the suspect, the officer believed that he could hear the suspect pull an object from his waist. Because he was afraid that he would run into the suspect, the officer slowed down and shot the suspect in the back and head.

188. *See, e.g.*, Sherrod v. Berry, 856 F.2d 802, 805 (7th Cir. 1988). In Sherrod, the Seventh Circuit held that whether a suspect is in fact armed is not relevant. *Id.* It stated, "[W]e categorically reject the district court's assertion that fairness requires that the jury be presented with facts unknown and unavailable to Officer Berry at the time of the shooting (that Sherrod was unarmed)." *Id.* It also expressed great deference to decisions by police officers: "The Sioux Indians have a prayer that asks for this wisdom: 'Grant that I may not judge another until I have walked a mile in his moccasins.'" *Id.* The dissent, however, thought whether the suspect actually had something in his pocket would aid the jury in determining the type of gesture the suspect in fact had made and resolving conflicts in testimony. *Id.* at 807 (Cummings, J., dissenting).

and head was also not troublesome for the Eighth Circuit because it boldly stated that "it is not remarkable that an escaping felony suspect would be shot in the back."[189] It specifically refused to question whether under the circumstances the officer should have let the suspect flee instead of kill him.[190] Even if one were to agree with the Eighth Circuit's factual interpretations, it is difficult to agree with the court's decision that it, rather than the jury, should decide the issue of reasonableness under these circumstances.

The Sixth Circuit also diminished the importance of the jury in *Smith v. Freland.*[191] Its scrutiny of the police officers' conduct was highly deferential, if not nonexistent. In *Smith*, a police officer signaled for a driver to pull over when he ran a stop sign. A high-speed pursuit then occurred, during which the driver allegedly twice used his car to swerve near a police car. When the suspect turned down a cul-de-sac, some officers set up a roadblock at the entrance of the road. Another officer parked his car in front of the suspect's car. On one side of the suspect was a fence and behind him was a swimming pool. The officer got out of his car. The suspect then rammed the car as he started driving away. The officer, who was not in any danger, then shot the driver as he headed for the roadblock.

In justifying this shooting, the Sixth Circuit hypothesized as to the need for the shooting: the suspect was heading toward the roadblock, thus endangering the lives of the officers at the roadblock, and the suspect, who seemed desperate to get away, "could have stopped his car and entered one of the neighboring houses, hoping to take hostages."[192] This latter "justification" is just plain fanciful. In determining that the conduct was reasonable as a matter of law, the Sixth Circuit refused to consider whether alternatives were available to the shooting officer:

> [U]nder *Graham*, we must avoid substituting our personal notions of proper police procedure for the instantaneous decision of the officer at the scene. We must never allow the theoretical, sanitized world of our imagination to replace the dangerous and complex world that policemen face every day. What constitutes

189. 991 F.2d at 439.
190. *Id.*
191. 954 F.2d 343 (6th Cir. 1992).
192. *Id.* at 343.

> 'reasonable' action may seem quite different to someone facing a possible assailant than to someone analyzing the question at leisure.[193]

Although danger is a factor in determining reasonableness, its mere presence does not justify a court's overwhelming deference to the judgment of officers. Nor does it justify usurping the jury's province in determining reasonableness.

The Ninth Circuit in *Scott v. Henrich*[194] also erroneously decided the reasonableness of a fatal shooting. The officers shot a suspect when he allegedly came to the door with a gun.[195]

In holding this conduct reasonable as a matter of law, the Ninth Circuit was not concerned that the gun allegedly possessed by the suspect did not have his fingerprints on it. It, like the Sixth Circuit, created reasons why the shooting was nevertheless reasonable as a matter of law. The court suggested that the fingerprints were missing perhaps because the suspect did not sweat enough, perhaps because the surface of the gun was "too rough to take prints,"[196] or perhaps because the smooth part of the gun was too small for a fingerprint.[197] In evaluating these facts, the court nevertheless found the shooting reasonable as a matter of law, despite its recognition that police officers should not benefit from killing the only opposing witness—the suspect.[198] As with other courts deciding factual issues, the court also warned that it was not its duty to consider whether the police officers had alternatives available to them.[199]

---

193. *Id.* at 346.
194. 994 F.2d 1338 (9th Cir. 1992).
195. *Id.* at 1340-41. In *Henrich*, two police officers were investigating a shooting from a two-story apartment. A young child stated that he had seen a man with a gun on the second story. One of the officers then saw a man in a window on that floor. The officers went to an apartment, knocked, and announced that they were police. According to the police officers, the suspect opened the door and had a gun in his hand. The officer nearest the door then fired a shot, missing the suspect. The second officer, believing that the suspect had fired, fired four shots at the suspect, killing him.
196. *Id.* at 1343.
197. *Id.*
198. *Id.* at 1341.
199. *Id.* at 1342 ("Officers . . . need not avail themselves of the least intrusive means of responding to an exigent situation; they need only act within that range of conduct we identify as reasonable.").

The Seventh Circuit also usurped the jury's role in *Ford v. Childers* by affirming the district court's grant of a directed verdict for an officer at the close of the plaintiff's case. In *Childers*, a police officer could see a masked man robbing a bank. He could not, however, see what was in the suspect's outstretched hand. When the suspect exited the bank, the officer allegedly ordered him to stop. A foot chase ensued. The officer allegedly again ordered him to stop. When he did not, the officer shot him in the back.

In determining that the conduct was reasonable, the Seventh Circuit relied on the nature of the offense committed by the suspect—armed robbery—to justify the shooting. It determined that this offense alone indicated that the suspect posed "a danger of serious harm to others if not immediately apprehended."[200] It rejected the expert's testimony that the officer should have considered other alternatives and the suspect's assertion that he did not hear the commands to stop.

The court relied on the language from *Garner* that stated that if an officer has "probable cause" to believe that the suspect has committed a violent offense, then deadly force may be used. It thought that there was no room for disagreement as to the serious nature of armed robbery. It created a per se rule justifying deadly force based on the category of the offense. It failed to discern that it was for the jury to assess the reasonableness of this shooting. In determining that the conduct was reasonable as a matter of law, this court also cited the split-second nature of the officer's decision. Even though it explicitly warned that such shootings should not be "an automatic response of a police officer attempting to capture a fleeing felon,"[201] it failed to set limits on such shootings and it failed to send the reasonableness of the shooting to the jury.

Finally, the Fourth Circuit in *Drewitt v. Pratt*[202] also determined as a matter of law that a shooting was reasonable. As with the prior cases, the court interpreted reasonableness as requiring significant deference to the judgment of police officers. In *Drewitt*, a plainclothes police officer had observed a reckless driver. Without showing his badge, the officer shouted to the driver to stop. When the driver did, the officer walked in front of the car and was hit. The officer rolled onto the hood and fired two shots, killing the driver.

200. *Id.* at 1275.
201. *Id.* at 1276.
202. 999 F.2d 774 (4th Cir. 1993).

The court held that it could decide the reasonableness inquiry. It found unimportant the officer's action in walking in front of a vehicle that had already crashed into another vehicle and had no lights on at night. It stated that any dispute in facts was "more imagined than real."[203] Because of its misperceptions, the court robbed the jury of its role in determining reasonable conduct.

Thus when courts show extreme deference to the judgments of police officers, they deprive juries of their role in determining whether the force used was reasonable within the meaning of the Fourth Amendment. Although a reasonableness standard does not lend itself to numerous bright-line rules, in the context of excessive force claims, juries are better able to examine the totality of circumstances. In doing so, they may help to clarify some important elements of the reasonableness standard as applied to the use of force. Two important issues for the juries are the nature of the original offense and the kinds of actions by suspects that justify a belief that the suspect is endangering a police officer or the community.

Offenses Signifying Danger to Officers and the Community

In *Garner*, the Supreme Court stated that officers may use deadly force if they have probable cause to believe that a suspect has "committed a crime involving the infliction or threatened infliction of serious physical harm."[204] This language seems to suggest that an officer may shoot a serial killer in the back, even if the officer himself is not in danger. The passage from *Garner*, however, needs to be read with the Court's immediacy requirement. To justify a shooting, a police officer must perceive immediate danger, whether to himself or the community. One important question is thus whether certain offenses automatically create the inference that the community is in danger unless police officers immediately seize the suspect.

The *Garner* Court did not specify which offenses justify a police officer shooting a suspect. It merely stated that a nighttime burglary suspect fleeing from a home did not signify the requisite danger to justify shooting him or her. When analyzing the *Garner* decision, some courts have weighed heavily the fact that the offense was violent. The Eighth Circuit in

---

203. *Id.* at 780.

204. Tennessee v. Garner, 471 U.S. 1, 11 (1985).

Krueger v. Fuhr[205] evaluated an armed assault, and the Seventh Circuit in *Ford v. Childers*[206] considered an armed robbery. In both cases, the officers, who had reason to believe that the suspects had weapons, shot them in the back when they failed to heed their commands to stop. These courts thus appeared to create a per se rule based on the offense the officer had probable cause to believe that the suspect had committed. This rule-making arises from these courts' decision that the shootings were reasonable as a matter of law.

Few courts, however, center their analysis on the alleged offense. They instead focus on other actions the suspect takes during the confrontation with the police. When the subsequent conduct involves a high-speed pursuit, some courts use the fact of the pursuit itself as an indication that the suspect is a danger to the community.[207] In this context, some courts view this latter offense as increasing danger, possibly justifying a shooting.[208]

Such analysis is possible because the Supreme Court decisions suggest that the police practice of pursuing individuals in cars is not governed by the Fourth Amendment because the officers do not "seize" drivers during pursuits.[209] Thus, some courts do not scrutinize the officer's decision to pursue under the Fourth Amendment, but nevertheless use the pursuit as a factor in assessing the danger presented by the pursued driver. As a result of this peculiar view of the Fourth Amendment, some courts have refused to evaluate the reasonableness of pursuing at high speeds suspects who failed to pay a highway toll,[210] who drove through a stop sign,[211] who spun tires

---

205. 991 F.2d 435 (8th Cir. 1993). For a discussion of this case, see *supra* text accompanying notes 186-90.
206. Ford v. Childers, 855 F.2d 1271 (7th Cir. 1988). For a discussion of this case, see *supra* text accompanying note 266.
207. *See, e.g.*, Smith v. Freland, 954 F.2d 343, 347 (6th Cir. 1992).
208. *See infra* text accompanying notes 191-93.
209. *See, e.g.*, RONALD J. BACIGAL, *The Right of the People to Be Secure*, 82 KY. L.J. 145, 162 (1994) ("The history of the chase cases suggests that the Court intends to achieve its agenda for enhancing police power by whatever means are necessary."); KATHRYN R. URBONYA, *The Constitutionality of High-Speed Pursuits Under the Fourth and Fourteenth Amendments*, 35 ST. LOUIS U. L.J. 205, 270-85 (1991).
210. *See, e.g.*, Cole v. Bone, 993 F.2d 1328, 1330 (8th Cir. 1993).
211. *See, e.g.*, Smith v. Freland, 954 F.2d 343, 344 (6th Cir. 1992), *cert. denied*, 113 S. Ct. 462 (1992).

leaving a gas station,[212] who were intoxicated while driving,[213] and who sped.[214] Some courts, however, have properly questioned whether the officers conducting the pursuit are the source of the danger to the community.[215]

Furtive Gestures: Inferring Danger to Police Officers

In analyzing the danger a suspect poses to police officers and the community, some courts have determined that a "furtive gesture" by the suspect justifies an officer to reasonably believe that the suspect was reaching for a weapon.[216] To justify a shooting under the "furtive gesture" doctrine, officers do not need to state that they saw a gun, a knife, or even a glint of steel because of the role of the action/reaction theory.[217]

---

212. *See, e.g.*, Temkin v. Frederick County Commissioners, 945 F.2d 716, 718 (4th Cir. 1991).
213. *See, e.g.*, Fraire v. City of Arlington, 957 F.2d 1268, 1270-71 (5th Cir. 1992). In Fraire, the Fifth Circuit stated that a suspect was dangerous within the meaning of Garner because he drank as he drove, drove erratically, and sped through "a residential subdivision, twice crashing the car." *Id.* at 1276 n.30.
214. *See, e.g.*, Horta v. Sullivan, 4 F.3d 2, 7 (1st Cir. 1993).
215. *See, e.g.*, Brower v. County of Inyo, 884 F.2d 1316, 1317 n. 1 (9th Cir. 1989) ("It might be argued that the substantial threat requirement was not met because any danger proceeded from the fact that the police gave chase. This is not to say that the police should never chase suspected car thieves, only that the danger created by the chase would not give them license to use deadly force when it is necessary to prevent escape."); Donovan v. City of Milwaukee, 17 F.3d 944, 951 (7th Cir. 1994) (jury could find that ramming of motorcyclist during pursuit was unreasonable; officer chased suspect because he failed to answer questions about a nearby explosion); *see generally* Fagan v. City of Vineland, 22 F.3d 1283, 1293 (3d Cir. 1994) (municipality may be liable under the Fourteenth Amendment for failing to train police officers not to conduct pursuits for minor traffic offense when circumstances indicate danger to the public).
216. *See, e.g.*, Krueger v. Fuhr, 991 F.2d 435, 438-39 (8th Cir. 1993). In Krueger, an armed assault suspect had allegedly made a furtive gesture by reaching for his waist. The officer, having other facts to support his belief that the suspect had a knife, shot him in the back. The Eighth Circuit found the requisite danger because of the prior armed assault and the furtive gesture. *Id.*
217. *See, e.g.*, Sherrod v. Berry, 856 F.2d 802, 806-07 (7th Cir. 1988). In Sherrod, the suspect had allegedly robbed a store and had previously committed other "assaultive crimes." *Id.* at 802. After police officers stopped the suspect, one

Furtive gestures appear to create the inference of danger because some experts believe that by the time a police officer sees a glint of steel, the suspect would be able to kill him or her.[218] A federal judge described this problem in *Mathews v. City of Atlanta*.[219] The court stated that police officers may draw their guns during arrests, even if they would not be justified under the *Garner* standard in using them.[220] It ruled that to find otherwise would be to constitutionally require police officers to put themselves in danger.[221]

---

officer behind the vehicle had his weapon pointed at the car as did the officer who approached the car. When the passenger failed to comply with an officer's repeated commands to raise his hand, the passenger then allegedly made a furtive gesture by quickly moving "'his hand into his coat . . . [as if] he was going to reach for a weapon.'" 856 F.2d at 803 (quoting the police officer's testimony). The officer then killed the passenger. The court stated that it was for the jury to determine whether this gesture justified the killing. *Id.* at 806-07. In determining that it was not relevant whether the suspect actually had a weapon, the court interpreted the Fourth Amendment to require consideration of the split-second nature of officers' decisions. *Id.* at 805. The Seventh Circuit stated, "[C]ourts and juries must determine the propriety of the officer's actions based upon a thorough review of the knowledge, facts and circumstances known to the officer at the time he exercised his split-second judgment as to whether the use of deadly force was warranted." *Id.* at 807 n.2.

218. *See, e.g.*, Kevin Parsons, *Decision to Use Force: The Confrontational Continuum*, in 8 Civil Rights Litigation and Attorney Fees Annual Handbook, 115, 119-20 (1992). Dr. Parsons, a frequent expert in trials involving the use of unreasonable force, described the problem of officers dealing with knives:

> Our own testing in conjunction with government contracts for the design of use of force training programs has shown that an individual can draw a knife from a concealed position and cover 21 feet to stab an individual in the face before the average police officer can unholster his weapon and fire one shot. Obviously, knowledge of such threats or lack of knowledge of such issues can have a significant impact upon the reasonableness of an officer's actions.

Id. at 120. Under this theory, if the officer waited to see a glint of steel, the suspect would have been able to assault him before he could have reached his gun. Dr. Parsons also noted that certain circumstances need to exist before a furtive gesture could create the inference of danger. In his example, the suspect must be within 21 feet of the officer. Thus, not all furtive gestures create the inference of danger.

219. 699 F. Supp. 1552, 1557 (N.D. Ga. 1988).

220. *Id.* at 1557.

221. *Id.*

To justify a shooting, police officers need to reasonably believe that the suspect had the ability to harm him, had the opportunity to do so, and that either his life or the lives of others were in jeopardy.[222] This latter element, jeopardy, captures *Garner*'s requirement that the suspect present an immediate danger to officers or the community.[223] Jeopardy is what courts

---

222. *See, e.g.*, Ellis v. Wynalda, 999 F.2d 243, 246-47 (7th Cir. 1993). In *Ellis,* the Seventh Circuit explicitly linked the furtive gesture doctrine with the Fourth Amendment's requirement of jeopardy. The suspect in *Ellis* had allegedly burglarized a pharmacy. He had broken into it by using a sledgehammer to create a hole in a back wall. After returning the hammer to his car, the suspect surreptiously took some drugs and money. When the investigating officer saw the hole, he withdrew his gun and later noticed a person outside. He commanded the suspect to stop. When the suspect stopped walking and turned around, he suddenly tossed the bag containing drugs at the police officer. This lightweight bag did not daze the officer or dislodge his gun. When the suspect began running, the officer shot him in the back. In analyzing all these facts, the court stated that a jury must decide the issue of whether the shooting was reasonable. *Id.* at 247.

    The court's discussion of furtive gestures focused on three facts: the suspect's clothing, the quick toss of the bag at the officer, the lack of harm to the officer. The suspect was wearing pants and a sleeveless shirt. *Id.* This attire, the Seventh Circuit stated, could not support a belief that the suspect had a hammer on him. It explained, "While it was possible that [the suspect] carried a concealed weapon, as much as it is possible that every felon might be carrying a weapon, [the officer] had no particular reason to believe that [the suspect] was armed. The court, in considering the clothing and the original offense, did not believe that it was reasonable at that moment to believe the suspect was armed." *Id.*

    The act of tossing a bag at an officer could be a furtive gesture because the suspect could have disarmed or dazed the officer, allowing him to reach for a weapon. In this case, however, the court noted that after tossing the bag, the suspect did not reach for a weapon. At that point, the court declared, a shooting would be unjustified because the officer could not reasonably believe that the suspect had a weapon. *Id.* The court wisely noted that jeopardy is a necessary condition for a gesture to be "furtive": "When an officer faces a situation in which he could justifiably shoot, he does not retain the right to shoot at any time thereafter with impunity." *Id.* Because the tossing of the bag did not result in the suspect reaching for a weapon, the officer could not later shoot the suspect in the back since he was no longer in jeopardy.

223. *See generally* Samples v. City of Atlanta, 916 F.2d 1548, 1551 (11th Cir. 1990) (expert testified that the three elements of ability, opportunity, and jeopardy represent the industry's standard for measuring force).

find when they determine that an action by the suspect was a "furtive gesture." The act of reaching for an unknown object at times may fulfill each of the three requirements: an officer believes that the suspect has the ability to harm, the opportunity to do so, and the intention to kill.

Under some circumstances a suspect's movement may reasonably create the belief that he or she is reaching for a gun,[224] knife,[225] or an unknown, but possibly threatening, object on the floor or backseat of a car.[226] The requirements may also be satisfied when a suspect throws an object at an officer.[227] In this category, the original offense may or may not assist the police officer in believing that the reaching movement was for a weapon. If the original offense involved a weapon, then the officer may more easily conclude that the suspect may have been reaching for a weapon.[228]

In many cases, however, courts do not consider the original offense and declare that the furtive gesture itself signified the requisite danger justifying a shooting.[229] Some courts also do not consider whether the officers could have prevented the furtive gesture by using other means to apprehend the suspect.[230]

---

224. *See, e.g.*, Sherrod v. Berry, 856 F.2d 802, 805 (7th Cir. 1988).

225. *See, e.g.*, Krueger v. Fuhr, 991 F.2d 435, 436 (8th Cir. 1993).

226. *See, e.g.*, Greenidge v. Ruffin, 927 F.2d 789, 790 (4th Cir. 1991) (reached toward backseat); Young v. City of Killeen, Texas, 775 F.2d 1349, 1351 (5th Cir. 1985) ("reached down to the seat or floorboard of his car").

227. *See, e.g.*, Ellis v. Wynalda, 999 F.2d 243, 247 (7th Cir. 1993).

228. *See, e.g.*, Krueger v. Fuhr, 991 F.2d 435, 436 (8th Cir. 1993) (suspect had allegedly assaulted someone and had a knife); Sherrod v. Berry, 856 F.2d 802, 803 (7th Cir. 1988) (armed robbery suspect).

229. *See, e.g.*, Ellis v. Wynalda, 999 F.2d 243, 247 (7th Cir. 1993) (tossing a heavy object at officer could constitute a furtive gesture); Young v. City of Killeen, Texas, 775 F.2d 1349, 1351 (5th Cir. 1985) (alleged sudden movement created danger).

230. *See, e.g.*, Reese v. Anderson, 926 F.2d 494, 500-01 (5th Cir. 1991); Young v. City of Killeen, Texas, 775 F.2d 1349, 1352-53 (5th Cir. 1985) (even if the officer negligently created the situation that made the shooting more likely, the suspect's furtive gesture justified the shooting).

In *Reese*, nine police officer had surrounded a robber in his vehicle. 926 F.2d at 196. Even though an officer's siren made it difficult for the car's occupants to hear the commands to put their hands above their heads, the court nevertheless upheld a shooting that followed an alleged furtive gesture. It stated that the officer's life would have been in danger if he would have had to shut off the siren because the act would have "divert[ed] his attention." *Id.*

For a gesture to justify a police officer's shooting, the suspect's act must signify danger to the police officer. In a society in which so many citizens are armed, courts and juries may be more willing today to assume that a furtive gesture justifies an officer's belief that the suspect was reaching for a weapon. If courts and juries automatically make this inference without considering the surrounding circumstances, including the alleged offense, then the right to personal security is more symbolic than real. In most situations, police officers would be wise to ascertain other facts to support the belief of immediate danger.

Lunging at Police Officers: The Need for Escalating Force

Other movements by suspects, though not actually furtive gestures, may also increase an officer's perception of danger. In contrast to the furtive gestures cases, in which police officers shoot suspects because they fear for their lives, police officers often escalate the amount of nonlethal force they use when suspects "lunge" at them. This aggressive act does signify danger. The issue in this area is the degree of danger a lunge represents and what type of force is a reasonable response to the suspect's aggressive action.

In evaluating the significance of a lunge, courts need to consider all of the circumstances to discern the danger presented by a suspect. In *Tom v. Voida*,[231] a suspect who had allegedly stolen a bicycle smashed a police officer's head into the pavement twice as the officer attempted to arrest him.[232] The Seventh Circuit determined the suspect's subsequent lunge significantly heightened the officer's perception of danger. In doing so, however, it did not let the jury decide whether the suspect's motion was one of

---

231. 963 F.2d 952 (7th Cir. 1992).

232. *Id.* at 958. The court noted that the officer did not try to use a chemical repellant because in doing so, the suspect would have had access to the officer's weapon. *Id.* at 962. It also noted that the officer did not have her nightstick with her. In considering these facts, the court found her conduct reasonable as a matter of law. The court stated that the medical evidence concerning the officer's injuries and numerous witnesses supported the officer's version of what happen. It reasoned that no alternatives were available to the officer other than killing the suspect. The court thus appeared to consider the offenses that the suspect committed prior to the shooting to support the officer's judgment that her life was in danger when the suspect allegedly lunged at her.

surrender or aggression. Similarly, in *Pride v. Does*,[233] the Eighth Circuit decided that a police officer could choke a suspect to prevent him from lunging at her.[234] The court held, as a matter of law, that the suspect was threatening because of his prior disorderly conduct, his profanity, "his intense expression on his face,"[235] and his intoxicated state.[236]

In contrast to these decisions, the Eleventh Circuit in *Gilmere v. City of Atlanta*[237] had the trial court find facts regarding the significance of a lunge by a person who had allegedly threatened another person with a weapon.[238] In a bench trial, the court determined that the officers had provoked the suspect into lunging. In creating the need to use deadly force, the police officers could not use the suspect's lunging as support for their asserted need to use deadly force.[239] In addition, the court noted that the police officers were not in fear for their lives because of the suspect's diminutive and inebriated condition at the time of the shooting.[240] The shooting was thus unreasonable.

When suspects lunge at officers, the reasonableness inquiry mandates consideration of all of the circumstances. A lunge alone may not justify a shooting based on danger. What type of police response is permissible depends upon not only how one assesses danger, but also how one views the reasonableness inquiry.

In examining unreasonable force claims, courts disagree as to their roles. Some courts consider whether other means were available to the

---

233. 997 F.2d 712 (10th Cir. 1993).
234. *Id.* at 714. The officer believed that her action was necessary "in order to restrain him from lunging toward her." *Id.*
235. *Id.*
236. *Id.* at 716. The handcuffed suspect, however, thought the force was merely retaliatory for his comments about her sexual orientation. Even though the suspect denied getting out of his chair, the court held that the choking under the circumstances was reasonable as a matter of law. *Id.* at 717. It relied on her affidavit, which stated that intoxicated people are often violent. Once again in assessing danger, the court broadly deferred to the officer's judgment as to the need for force. Once again a court erroneously deprived a jury of the opportunity to determine reasonableness.
237. 774 F.2d 1495 (11th Cir. 1985), *cert. denied*, 476 U.S. 1124 (1986).
238. *Id.* at 1502.
239. *Id.*
240. *Id.*

officer in seizing suspects. Other courts refuse to consider alternatives or fail to even discuss the role of alternatives. This disagreement can result in conflicting determinations of reasonableness.

Minimizing Danger: Available Alternative Analysis

One of the most disputed aspects of the reasonableness inquiry is whether it includes analysis of alternatives available to the seizing officers.[241] The Supreme Court indirectly discussed the role of alternatives in *Tennessee v. Garner*[242] as it examined the lawfulness of using deadly force to apprehend fleeing suspects. The *Garner* Court stated, "It is not better that all felony suspects die than that they escape."[243]

In balancing the interests of the suspect, society, and law enforcement, the Court recognized that in making this statement it was limiting the means police officers could use to apprehend some suspects. It noted, however, that in prohibiting some shootings, it was not necessarily barring police officers from apprehending fleeing suspects. It explained, "[I]t should be remembered that failure to apprehend at the scene does not necessarily mean that the suspect will never be caught."[244] In short, the Court recognized that means other than deadly force may nevertheless allow police officers to seize suspects.

This same issue, however, also surfaces when police officers use non-lethal means to apprehend suspects. The issue is whether the reasonableness inquiry also requires courts and juries to consider whether the seizing officers should have used less intrusive means.[245] Most courts that have

---

241. *See supra* text accompanying notes 168-80. In some respects this issue is similar to the issue of defining the relevant time frame for evaluating the officers' actions. The issues overlap to the extent that they both may discuss whether the officers' actions, which created the need for force, are relevant to resolving the issue of reasonableness. The issues are different in that if the officers did not create the need for force, the issue of alternatives focuses on only the means that the officer used to seize a suspect.
242. 471 U.S. 1 (1985).
243. 471 U.S. at 11.
244. *Id.* at 9 n.8.
245. *See, e.g.*, Soares v. Connecticut, 8 F.3d 917, 921 (2d Cir. 1993) (Graham did not create a per se rule allowing officers to use handcuffs during all arrests); Walton v. City of Southfield, 995 F.2d 1331, 1342 (6th Cir. 1993) (handcuffing may be unreasonable if officer knows that it would injure a suspect).

mentioned the availability of alternatives have not elaborated upon its significance.[246] The discussion tends to be linked with the issue of how much deference courts and juries should afford officers when deciding the issue of reasonableness.

Some decisions equate considering alternatives available to officers as signifying improper second-guessing of police officers. The Sixth Circuit[247] has strongly objected to second-guessing the judgment of police officers. It stated, "We must never allow the theoretical, sanitized world of our imagination to replace the dangerous and complex world that policemen face every day."[248] When the Sixth Circuit has looked at alternatives available to police officers, it has also afforded the judgment of officers great deference if they used nonlethal force to seize suspects.[249]

The Fifth Circuit has also limited its reasonableness inquiry by not exploring the significance of alternatives. In *Young v. City of Killeen, Texas,* the Fifth Circuit rejected using expert testimony about proper police procedure in analyzing the Fourth Amendment reasonableness issue, but considered it in upholding the trial court's state law negligence claim for the plaintiff. The expert testified as to six different actions the officer could have taken while trying to apprehend the suspect. The Fifth Circuit did not explain why the testimony was relevant to the negligence claim but not to the Fourth Amendment reasonableness claim, which is a claim that requires balancing of interests.

In another case, the Fifth Circuit also seemed to ignore a department investigative report that was critical of an officer.[250] The report criticized the officer's decision to chase a driver down a cul-de-sac and to stand in front of the pursued's vehicle, inviting "the truck to aim for him."[251] The court never mentioned that the officer could have used other means to seize the suspect.

In addition, the Seventh Circuit sent a mixed message as to the role of alternatives in *Tom v. Voida.*[252] Although it noted that the only means for self-defense available to the officer at the time of an impending attack was

---

246. *See infra* text accompanying notes 250-59.
247. *See, e.g.*, Smith v. Freland, 954 F.2d 343, 346 (6th Cir. 1992).
248. 954 F.2d at 343.
249. *See, e.g.*, Russo v. City of Cincinnati, 953 F.2d 1036, 1044-45 (6th Cir. 1992) (by using a Taser, the officer sought "to obviate the need for lethal force").
250. *See* Fraire v. City of Arlington, 957 F.2d 1268, 1276 (5th Cir. 1992).
251. *Id.* at 1276.
252. 963 F.2d 952, 958 (7th Cir. 1992).

her gun, the court never discussed the significance of her failure to have her nightstick with her. Although a baton can be both a lethal and a nonlethal weapon, the court did not hint that this omission was relevant to the issue of reasonableness.

A similar issue arises when courts have to consider violations of department procedure. Some courts find them relevant[253] and others do not.[254] Although courts soundly agree that such violations do not automatically signify a Fourth Amendment violation, some courts fail to explain why these violations are not relevant to the issue of reasonableness. Both the Ninth Circuit[255] and a federal district court[256] have failed to consider these violations as an aspect of reasonableness.

The Ninth Circuit declared that police guidelines dealing with barricaded suspects were designed for the protection of officers and the community, not suspects.[257] It then concluded that the violation was not relevant to the suspect's claim of unreasonable force.[258] Similarly a federal district held that even if the officers' plan to seize a mentally ill suspect signified recklessness, the plan had "no bearing on whether [the] officer reasonably believed plaintiff posed a serious threat of injury."[259]

Other courts, however, have recognized that the reasonableness inquiry requires considering all of the circumstances facing an officer. These courts often affirm that they are not using 20/20 hindsight to evaluate reasonableness. Instead, they have analyzed the officer's conduct in light of all of the circumstances, including the alternatives available to police officers when they acted.

Some Ninth Circuit decisions have highlighted the importance of this inquiry. In *Brower v. County of Inyo*,[260] it interpreted the *Garner* standard as requiring two inquiries: Did the suspect's conduct create a "significant threat" to the safety of officers? And if so, "did a reasonable nondeadly

253. *See, e.g.*, Soares v. Connecticut, 8 F.3d 917, 922 (2d Cir. 1993) (department handcuffing policy was relevant to, but not dispositive of, the issue of whether handcuffing constituted excessive force; reasonableness requires considering all of the circumstances of an arrest).
254. *See infra* text accompanying notes 255-59.
255. *See* Scott v. Henrich, 994 F.2d 1338, 1342 (9th Cir. 1992).
256. *See* O'Toole v. Kalmar, 1990 WL 19542, at *9 (N.D. Ill. Feb. 23, 1990).
257. *Scott,* 994 F.2d at 1342.
258. *Id.*
259. *O'Toole*, 1990 WL 19542, at *9.
260. 884 F.2d 1316 (9th Cir. 1989).

alternative exist for apprehending the suspect?"[261] It described the second inquiry as focusing on the "[n]ecessity" of using force, an inquiry that compels consideration of alternatives. The court in a later decision similarly stated that reasonableness requires consideration of "alternative courses of actions open" to officers.[262]

In discussing the role of alternatives, the Fourth Circuit has found expert testimony helpful in determining reasonableness. In *Kopf v. Skyrm*,[263] the Fourth Circuit recognized that experts clarify what is the "prevailing standard of conduct" for various weapons. For example, they may explain how to effectively use canines, slapjacks, handcuffs, mace, and guns. In describing these police tools, experts help the jury to know that while it should not use 20/20 hindsight to fault officers, neither should the jury use it "to absolve" them.[264] Other courts have similarly upheld the use of

---

261. *Id.* at 1318.

262. Hopkins v. Andaya, 958 F.2d 881, 887 (9th Cir. 1992). In *Hopkins*, an officer hit a suspect with his baton. When the suspect got the baton from the officer, he hit the officer. *Id.* at 883. The officer responded by shooting the suspect. *Id.* The officer then radioed for help, reloaded his gun, and hid behind a car. *Id.* When the suspect advanced again, the officer shot him. *Id.* In evaluating these facts, the Ninth Circuit stated the reasonableness of the second shooting required consideration of alternatives available to the officer:

> [The officer] was armed with several weapons and could hide behind a car. [He] had already called for help; he needed only delay [the suspect] for a short period of time. He could have evaded [him], or he could have attempted to subdue him with his fists, his feet, his baton, or the butt of his gun.

Id. The court held that these alternatives supported its denial of summary judgment for the officer. *Id.* at 888. A jury would have to consider the significance of these alternatives. *Id.*

263. 993 F.2d 374 (4th Cir. 1993).

264. *Id.* at 379. The court held that the trial court erred in excluding the expert testimony on the proper use of canines and slapjacks. *Id.* It explained that the role of experts depends upon the facts of each case:

> Where force is reduced to its most primitive form—the bare hands—expert testimony might not be helpful. Add handcuffs, a gun, a slapstick, mace, or some other tool, and the jury may start to ask itself: what is mace? what is an officer's training on using a gun? how much damage can a slapjack do? Answering these questions may often be assisted by expert testimony.

Id. The court added that even if the jury would not have difficulty understanding the police weapon, sometimes it must permit experts to testify as to the standard for using the weapon. *Id.*

expert testimony[265] and have distinguished between automatic deference to the judgment of officers and the reasonable scrutiny of the officers' actions on the scene.[266]

The Seventh Circuit in *Villanova v. Abrams*[267] has also stated that availability of alternatives is a part of the reasonableness inquiry under the Fourth Amendment. In evaluating a Fourth Amendment claim based on an unlawful seizure during a civil commitment, the court held that unreasonableness under the Fourth Amendment is the same issue as unreasonableness for negligence claims.[268] It stated that Justice Learned Hand's formula for negligence applied to the Fourth Amendment reasonableness issue: negligence occurs when the "burden of precautions" was less than the "weight of the loss" and "the probability of an accident."[269] This formula, it observed, considers the burden of alternatives, a burden evaluated in light of the likelihood of harm to individuals and the community.[270] It explicitly measured dangerousness based on the probability of harm if the suspect were free.[271] It also noted that under the reasonableness standard less intrusion is permitted if the person has committed "a trivial crime,"[272] a factor specifically articulated in *Graham v. Connor*.

---

265. *See, e.g.*, Samples v. City of Atlanta, 916 F.2d 1548, 1551-52 (11th Cir. 1990) (trial court properly allowed experts to testify as to "the prevailing standards in the field of law enforcement" on the use of force and as to whether the physical evidence supported the officers' testimony as to the suspect's acts and reactions to his use of force).
266. *See, e.g.*, Ford v. Childers, 855 F.2d 1271, 1276 (7th Cir. 1988) ("an officer oftentimes has only a split second to make the critical judgment of whether to use his weapon. But this fact alone will never immunize an otherwise unreasonable use of deadly force"); Dickerson v. McClellan, 844 F. Supp. 391, 396 (M.D. Tenn. 1994) (sometimes "tough decisions must be second-guessed, for not every post hoc explanation, no matter how plausible or understandable, can justify every officer's behavior").
267. 972 F.2d 792 (7th Cir. 1992).
268. *Id.* at 796. It stated, "The test of negligence at common law and of unlawful search or seizure challenged under the Fourth Amendment is the same: unreasonableness in the circumstances." *Id.*
269. *Id.*
270. *Id.* at 796-97.
271. *Id.*
272. *Id.* at 797.

The Seventh Circuit concluded that this algebraic formula is nevertheless a standard requiring judgment on the part of officials.[273]

The circuit courts of appeals thus disagree as to how to evaluate reasonableness. All courts focus on danger, whether to the officer or the community. The issue of available alternatives invites consideration of whether officers had less intrusive means to apprehend suspects. This issue, however, for some courts is intertwined with the difficult nature of police work, which often compels quick decisions. Alternative analysis can thus limit the scope of deference juries and courts afford police officers as they assess danger.

The difficulty of alternative analysis is perhaps most significant when courts consider how police officers should apprehend suspects who are experiencing serious psychological problems. In this situation, police officers must not only consider the danger facing the officers and the community, but also the danger the suspects present to themselves.

Danger to Officers, the Community, and Psychologically Disturbed Suspects

Interpreting danger is also the core issue when police officers seize individuals in order to protect them from harming themselves. In this context, police officers do not have either reasonable suspicion or probable cause to believe that a person has committed a crime. The justification for the seizure is protecting the seized individual from himself or herself. In evaluating these seizures, courts have again focused on danger when interpreting the reasonableness standard of the Fourth Amendment.

Courts have considered three types of claims: whether the officer had probable cause to believe that a person was a danger to himself or herself,[274] whether a "welfare" stop was reasonable within the meaning of the Fourth Amendment,[275] and whether the officers' use of force when they confronted a disturbed person was reasonable.[276]

A number of courts have noted that when police officers take psychologically disturbed individuals to a mental institution, they have seized

273. *Id.* at 796.
274. *See infra* text accompanying notes 278-82.
275. *See infra* text accompanying notes 352-72.
276. *See infra* text accompanying notes 283-92.

them within the Fourth Amendment.[277] The issue is whether the circumstances known to the officers gave them probable cause to believe that the suspect was a danger to himself or herself.[278] When officers seize individuals under these circumstances, they have to determine their psychological state. The Fourth Circuit in *Gooden v. Howard County, Maryland*[279] described the problem of such seizures. It explained that although officers cannot arbitrarily subject citizens to psychological evaluations, the standard for such seizures has not been defined by courts:

> Certainly the concept of 'dangerousness' which calls on lay police to make a psychological judgment is far more elusive than the question of whether there is probable cause to believe someone has in fact committed a crime. The lack of clarity in the law governing seizures for psychological evaluations is striking when compared to the standards detailed in other Fourth Amendment contexts, where probable cause to suspect criminal conduct has been painstakingly defined.[280]

After recognizing the problem of asking police officers to assess "psychological" dangerousness, the court further confused this difficult task by placing broad-ranging deference in the police officers' alleged facts. It found that case law had not defined "dangerousness with the requisite particularity"[281] to give officers guidance as to what conduct compels psychological evaluations. It strongly deferred to the judgment of police officers, criticizing the dissent for making every encounter with police officers into "credibility

---

277. *See, e.g.*, Maag v. Wessler, 960 F.2d 773, 775-76 (9th Cir. 1991); Harris v. Pirch, 677 F.2d 681, 686 (8th Cir. 1982).

278. *See, e.g.*, Glass v. Mayas, 984 F.2d 55, 58 (2d Cir. 1993) (officers acted pursuant to a state law that allowed an emergency psychiatric examination when they have "'reason to believe that the individual has mental disorder and that there is clear and imminent danger of the individual's doing bodily harm to the individual or another'") (quoting state law); Maag v. Wessler, 960 F.2d 773, 776 (9th Cir. 1991) (officer had probable cause to believe that suspect was a danger to himself).

279. 954 F.2d 960, 968 (4th Cir. 1992).

280. *Id.* at 968.

281. *Id.*

contest[s]."[282] In assessing danger, the majority thought that repeated screams from an apartment occupied by a single woman indicated that she was psychologically disturbed.

In addition to assessing psychological harm, officers also have to consider danger in the manner of their seizures. Sometimes officers have to use force to control a psychologically disturbed individual. When courts consider these claims, the officers generally assert that their forceful actions were in self-defense. What started out as an act to give aid turned into an act to protect oneself. Although this type of self-defense claim is similar to the assertions officers make in defending their use of force during arrest, the context is different because the officer is dealing with psychologically impaired citizens. A few cases have examined the use of force against such individuals.

When the suspect is psychologically impaired, many courts do not discuss whether the suspect's condition affects how to determine reasonableness. The Seventh Circuit in *Krueger v. City of Algoma*[283] did not discuss the officer's failure to know that a driver was suicidal, even though other officials knew.[284] It never questioned whether the officer should have used other means to seize the disturbed driver.

Similarly, the Sixth Circuit in *Russo v. City of Cincinnati*[285] never mentioned whether officers should closely examine the means they use to seize a person believed to be both suicidal and homicidal.[286] In analyzing the use of force, the court appeared to show great deference to the officers' deci-

---

282. *Id.* at 966 n.1.
283. 1 F.3d 537 (7th Cir. 1993).
284. *Id.* at 540-41. The court granted summary judgment for the officer, who stopped the driver. *Id.* at 540. Prior to committing a traffic violation, the driver had been taken into custody and threatened to kill himself if he got a ticket. *Id.* at 538. After the parents notified the police that their son had taken a gun, an officer stopped the son. *Id.* at 538-39. According to the officer, the individual got out of the car and pointed a gun at the officer, who hid behind his car. *Id.* at 539. The driver then killed himself. *Id.* In analyzing the stop, the court justified the stop because the driver had allegedly committed a traffic offense. *Id.* at 540. It appeared immaterial to the court that the police department knew that the driver was suicidal. The court never mentioned whether the officer should have seized the suspect in another manner.
285. 953 F.2d 1036 (6th Cir. 1992).
286. *Id.* at 1044.

sion to use nonlethal force to seize the individual and less deference to the decision to use lethal force.[287] Perhaps by sanctioning the initial use of a Taser on the subject, the court was recognizing the volatile task of seizing a disturbed individual.

The question of whether an officer shot a mentally unbalanced person in self-defense was an issue for the jury in *Samples v. City of Atlanta*.[288] An officer had observed a person in a telephone booth "screaming like a demented person."[289] The officer approached the person, who then threw a can at him. When the individual approached the officer with a knife, the officer shot him until he fell to the ground.[290] In determining that the lower court erred in granting summary judgment for the officer, the court did not mention whether the officer properly approached a person he thought was demented. The court only discussed the need for the jury to resolve disputed facts.[291]

When officers encounter psychologically disturbed individuals, the courts thus seem not to analyze the means officer use in apprehending them, nor do they seem to question whether the act of dealing with these individuals affects how to determine reasonableness. As with "welfare stops,"[292] the courts recognize the need for officers to seize unbalanced individuals who may represent a danger not only to themselves, but also to police officers and society. Many courts appear to state that danger was present, but do not set any limits on when action based on danger unnecessarily infringes on the right to privacy and personal security.

When officers act aggressively by intruding upon a person's right to personal security, such actions are constitutional if they are reasonable within the meaning of the Fourth Amendment. These actions often arise because of some perceived danger, whether to the officer or society. In some cases, the

---

287. *Id.* at 1044-45. It twice stated that the use of nonlethal force demonstrated "an effort to obviate the need for lethal force." *Id.*

288. 846 F.2d 1328 (11th Cir. 1988).

289. *Id.* at 1331.

290. *Id.* at 1331-32. Another court has held that once an officer lawfully shoots an individual, the officer may continue to shoot until the suspect ceases presenting any harm. *See* O'Neal v. DeKalb County, 667 F. Supp. 853, 858 (N.D. Ga. 1987) ("The Constitution does not require police officers to use a minimum of violence when attempting to stop a suspect from using deadly force against police officers or others.").

291. *Id.* at 1332-33.

292. *See infra* text and accompanying notes 358-72.

actions are to protect individuals from harming themselves. Determining the reasonableness of these actions requires consideration of numerous issues, with danger an important, but not controlling, factor. Danger analysis, however, has become the central issue when evaluating preventive actions taken by police officers. An examination of the lower courts' assessment of danger reveals their strong approval of preventive actions.

Litigating Preventive Actions: Asserting Authority and Self-Protective Searches

The Supreme Court has interpreted the Fourth Amendment to allow police officers in some circumstances to conduct protective searches as they investigate crimes and aid society. As with the use of force in apprehending suspects, the means officers use to conduct their investigations must be reasonable within the meaning of the Fourth Amendment.

When officers act to safeguard their well-being, courts have often found such preventive actions reasonable: they have allowed officers to conduct *Terry* frisks,[293] to search suspects incident to their arrests,[294] to search an area if it poses a danger to them,[295] and to enter a home without a warrant or knocking in order to safeguard their lives or the lives of others.[296] Often these actions are reasonable because they lessen the likelihood of harm to the officers or others.

Analyzing such preventive actions raises two difficult issues: what circumstances signify danger, justifying the use of preventive measures; and if danger is present, what preventive measures are constitutionally reasonable. An examination of some of the decisions discussing preventive actions reveals the complexity of these issues and the trend toward affording police officers great deference in their assessment of danger.

Danger During **Terry** *Stops: Protective Frisks and Protective Sweeps*

In order for police officers to lawfully frisk suspects, they must believe that danger is present. In *Terry v. Ohio*, the Court described the belief that the officer must have in two different ways: the officer must have reason-

---

293. *See infra* text accompanying notes 297-331.
294. *See infra* text accompanying notes 373-84.
295. *See infra* text accompanying notes 330-31.
296. *See infra* text accompanying notes 352-54.

able suspicion to believe that the suspect "is" armed and dangerous or that the suspect "may be" armed and dangerous. Since this decision in 1968, there is little doubt that courts only require reasonable suspicion that the suspect "may be" armed.[297] Similarly courts have allowed officers to use more intrusive actions to protect themselves than courts would have allowed in the past.[298] Today many courts and officers easily perceive danger when officers seize suspects.

When officers frisk suspects, they must be able to later articulate why they thought a particular suspect might be armed. In assessing this danger, only a few circumstances make this determination easy. When an officer sees a gun on a suspect before he or she lawfully stops the person,[299] the officer clearly has reason to believe that the suspect is armed. Such a belief also arises when the officer has reasonable suspicion to believe that the suspect has just committed an offense using a weapon, even though he or she did not see the weapon.

In most situations, however, courts and officers simply draw inferences from the circumstances at the time of the seizure. Thus, the central issue becomes what circumstances reasonably signify danger, justifying a frisk. In analyzing this issue, most courts consider all of the circumstances to determine whether a suspect may have been armed and dangerous.[300] Such discussions are understandable because the reasonableness inquiry mandates weighing all the circumstances. Courts nevertheless emphasize that certain facts strongly weigh in favor of finding danger.

An anonymous tip that someone at a certain location is armed is one fact that persuaded the Courts of Appeal for the District of Columbia[301] and the Second Circuit[302] to find a frisk reasonable. Although locating the described person was the only corroboration in these cases, the courts never-

---

297. *See, e.g.*, United States v. Clark, No. 92-3191, 1994 WL 240652, *5 (D.C. Cir. June 7, 1994) (in the past, the standard might have required a belief that the suspect was armed; today the standard is that the suspect may have been armed).
298. *Id.* (modern courts approve of preventive actions that "might have raised judicial eyebrows at the time the Terry decision was issued").
299. For an excellent discussion of lawful Terry stops, see Tracy Maclin, *The Decline of the Right to Locomotion: The Fourth Amendment on the Streets*, 75 Cornell L. Rev. 1258, 1264-83 (1990).
300. *See infra* text accompanying notes 306-17.
301. United States v. Clipper, 973 F.2d 944, 951 (D.C. Cir. 1992).
302. United States v. Bold, 19 F.3d 99, 104 (2d Cir. 1994).

theless found both the stop and the frisk reasonable. These courts held that a frisk was the only way the officer could safely investigate the alleged crime of possessing a gun.[303] The Second Circuit found it unappealing to make the officer "wait until the individual brandishes or uses the gun."[304] To support its conclusion, both courts relied on statistics not only to show the prevalence of guns, but also to document the danger from their misuse.[305]

---

303. *Bold,* 19 F.3d at 104; Clipper, 973 F.2d at 951.

304. 19 F.3d 99, 104 (2d Cir. 1994).

305. *Bold,* 19 F.3d at 104; Clipper, 973 F.2d at 951. The Second Circuit described in detail the dangers of guns throughout the nation and in New York, the place where the frisk occurred:

> The district court painted a frightening picture when it noted that (1) 200 million handguns and other lethal weapons are in circulation in the United States, (2) more than 4.2 million firearms are added to that total each year, and (3) these weapons caused some 37,000 gunshot deaths in the United States in 1990, and approximately 259,000 nonfatal injuries. . . . Moreover, New York City has a population of approximately 8 million, yet as the district court found, only 122,137 pistols are licensed in the city. Those circumstances might be supplemented by the facts that (1) the City of New York, where those officers served and protected, has a well-documented history of illegal hand-gun possession . . . and (2) New York State has approximately 18 million people according to the 1990 census, yet has only issued gun permits to approximately 18,000 people a year from 1982 to 1992. . . . In short, the overwhelming majority of the people in New York State and City are not licensed to carry handguns.

Bold, 19 F.3d at 104. In citing these statistics, the court was attempting to justify the officer's belief that both the stop and frisk were reasonable, despite the Second Amendment, which allows citizens to bear arms. *See generally* STEPHEN P. HALBROOK, A RIGHT TO BEAR ARMS: STATE AND FEDERAL BILLS OF RIGHTS AND CONSTITUTIONAL GUARANTEES x (1989) ("The complete history of the right to keep and bear arms remains hidden in many respects."); FRANKLIN E. ZIMRING & GORDON HAWKINS, THE CITIZEN'S GUIDE TO GUN CONTROL,146 (1987) ("There is a neat role reversal in the mostly liberal advocates of gun control urging reliance on settled precedent while many conservative anticontrol partisans plead for a radical judicial reinterpretation of this element of the Bill of Rights."); WILLIAM VAN ALSTYNE, *The Second Amendment and the Personal Right to Bear Arms*, 43 DUKE L.J. 1236, 1254 (1994) (the Second Amendment right to bear arms is limited; one may not have a right to own a howitzer or to carry a weapon into courtrooms or schools); THOMAS M. MONCURE, JR., *The Second Amendment Ain't About Hunting*, 34 HOW. L.J. 589, 597 (1991) (Second Amendment is about liberty).

Another fact strongly weighed by some courts in assessing danger is whether the suspect in the past had committed a crime using a weapon.[306] Although no courts have found this fact to be dispositive in upholding a *Terry* frisk, one court seemed to suggest that this fact goes a long way toward establishing the requisite danger.

In *State v. Valentine*,[307] the New Jersey Supreme Court upheld a frisk, stating that although this fact does not automatically create the inference of danger, other facts aided the officer's belief of reasonable suspicion. These other facts, frequently present during stops, related to the suspect's presence in a high-crime area late at night and his "weak alibi" when asked what he was doing.[308] The court emphasized the need for safety, noting that it "should not set the test of sufficient suspicion that the individual is 'armed and presently dangerous' too high when protection of the investigating officer is at stake."[309] Such deference to the officer's split-second judgment was appropriate, the court stated, because the decision could have "life-and-death consequences."[310] The court thus viewed the frisk as a minimal intrusion and the need for safety as great.

Another fact often held to justify a frisk is the particular crime that a suspect has allegedly committed. In contrast to an officer's reasonable suspicion that a suspect has just used a weapon in committing a crime, certain crimes automatically signify the presence of a weapon, for some courts. Numerous courts today believe that if an officer has reasonable suspicion to believe that a suspect possesses drugs, then the suspect must have a weapon.[311] When these courts draw this inference, they automatically uphold the officer's

---

306. *See, e.g.*, State v. Valentine, 134 N.J. 536, 636 A.2d 505 (1994).

307. 134 N.J. 536, 636 A.2d 505 (1994).

308. 134 N.J. at 550, 636 A.2d at 509-10.

309. 134 N.J. at 550, 636 A.2d at 509 (quoting United States v. Riggs, 474 F.2d 699, 705 (2d Cir.), *cert. denied*, 414 U.S. 820 (1973).

310. 134 N.J. at 550, 636 A.2d at 509.

311. *See, e.g.*, United States v. Cannon, 15 F.3d 896, 900 (9th Cir. 1994) (frisk permissible when officer reasonably believed that suspect was a cocaine dealer); United States v. Miller, 974 F.2d 953, 957 (8th Cir. 1992) ("Drug trafficking . . . created a wholly credible concern that at least some of the suspects might be armed."); United States v. Alexander, 907 F.2d 269, 273 (2d Cir. 1990) ("This court has repeatedly acknowledged the dangerous nature of the drug trade and genuine need of law enforcement agents to protect themselves from the deadly threat they may pose."); United States

frisk. Some courts, however, have limited the presumption by requiring a reasonable belief that the suspects were involved in "serious" drug offenses, such as heavy drug trafficking or selling cocaine.[312] Other offenses such as robbery[313] may also create this automatic presumption.

Other actions by suspects or passengers in a vehicle may also signify danger. As with unreasonable force claims, furtive gestures often allow officers to frisk an individual on the street[314] or in a car.[315] In most cases,

---

v. Oates, 560 F.2d 45, 62 (2d Cir. 1977) (guns are "'tools of the trade'" for narcotics dealers); State v. Evans, 67 Ohio St.3d 405, 412, 618 N.E.2d 162, 169 (1993) ("Right to frisk is virtually automatic when the subject is suspected of committing a crime, like drug trafficking, for which he is likely to be armed.").

312. *See, e.g.*, State v. Thomas, 110 N.J. 673, 677, 542 A.2d 912, 915 (1988); *but see* Wisconsin v. Guy, 172 Wis. 2d 86, 492 N.W.2d 311, 315 (1992), *cert. denied*, 113 S. Ct. 3020 (1993) ("To require police officers to distinguish between major and insignificant dealers or users before making a limited frisk for weapons would be impractical and could unreasonably put officers in danger." Yet the court refused to apply an automatic frisk rule, stating that "the constitutionality of each such frisk will continue to depend upon its facts.").

313. *See, e.g.*, United States v. Rundle, 461 F.2d 860, 864 (3d Cir. 1972); *but see* People v. Hampton, 606 N.Y.S.2d 628, 629 (1994) (even if officer had reasonable suspicion to believe that suspect was about to rob a taxi driver, frisk was unreasonable).

314. *See, e.g.*, United States v. Michelletti, 991 F.2d 183, 184-85 (5th Cir. 1993) (suspect, who had a "cocky attitude," exited bar with drink in one hand and his hand in his pocket; officer thought the hand should not have stayed in the pocket so long); Poole v. State, No. 92-2617, 1994 WL 248257, at *1-2 (Fla. Dist. Ct. App. June 10, 1994) (drug suspect, who reached for his waistband and put something in his pocket, refused to take his hand out of his pocket, creating a "bulge").

315. *See, e.g.*, United States v. Evans, 994 F.2d 317, 320-21 (7th Cir. 1993) (frisk of suspect and car were reasonable; the driver "leaned forward at a forty-five degree angle for several seconds); People v. Corpany, 859 P.2d 865, 867 (Colo. 1993) (officer properly frisked fanny pack after passengers in the back seat appeared to be putting something underneath the seat); State v. Smith, 134 N.J. 599, 606, 637, A.2d 158, 161 (1994) (person in back seat of car leaned forward, possibly passing an object; the passenger appeared nervous, cried after officer told her he was going to frisk her; her later statement, "It's not mine, they made me put it in there," justified the frisk).

unexplained hand movement constitutes a furtive action, creating the belief that the individual is reaching for a weapon. This inference, for many courts, is easily drawn when car occupants reach for an undisclosed object. Many courts believe that traffic stops are inherently dangerous.[316] In addition to hand movements, a step back after an officer told a suspect to stop, for the Fifth Circuit, signified that the person was giving "himself some space to draw a weapon."[317]

---

316. *See, e.g.*, United States v. Tellez, 11 F.3d 530, 533 (5th Cir. 1993) (stopping car with three passengers, one of whom may have violated parole, was "potentially dangerous"); Cousart v. United States, 618 A.2d 96, 101 (App. D.C. 1992) ("While the progress of the auto may have stopped at the time [the officer] arrived, there was nothing to suggest or show to the responding officers the danger was over."); *but see* State v. Pierce, No. A-19, 1994 WL 268056, at *15 (N.J. Sup. Ct. June 15, 1994). In Pierce, the New Jersey Supreme Court, after noting the danger arising from traffic stops, determined that some police practices designed to protect officers can be too intrusive:

> We are mindful that police officers are at risk whenever they make a vehicular stop, and that a significant percentage of assaults on police officers occur in the course of traffic stops. . . . Nevertheless, out of the substantial number of ordinary citizens who might on occasion commit commonplace traffic offenses, the vast majority are unarmed.

Id. at *13. It held that under its state constitution officers could not automatically search a vehicle when the driver is arrested for a traffic offense. *Id.*

317. United States v. Rideau, 969 F.2d 1572, 1575 (5th Cir. 1992). In Rideau, the dissent properly criticized the majority for allowing a frisk of an alleged inebriated person just because he stepped backward:

> [I]f [the suspect] had stepped forward, [the officer] most certainly would have viewed it as threatening. Had the defendant stepped to the right or left, it would have been interpreted as nervousness or an attempt to flee. If [the suspect] had remained stiffly frozen in place, it would have been viewed, presumably, as a show of guilt or of abnormal behavior caused by drugs or alcohol. . . . Perhaps if [the suspect] had graduated from charm school and had been taught how to look "cool and collected" in the face of approaching uniformed officers, he could have managed to avoid the patdown.

Id. at 1581. (Smith, J., dissenting). The dissent stated that by finding danger justifying the frisk, the majority nullified the Fourth Amendment right to personal security. *Id.* at 1584-85. It explained that although officers do often face danger, the Fourth Amendment does protect them from unnecessary danger: to frisk, they must have reasonable suspicion that a suspect is armed and dangerous. *Id.* at 1585.

In addition to unexplained movements, some courts more readily perceive danger when an officer conducts his or her investigation with many individuals nearby. Although no court would justify a frisk of an individual just because the person was part of a group, when one person in the group may be involved in crime, some courts more easily draw the inference of danger, allowing the officer to act preventively.

An extreme example of how readily some courts are willing to conclude that a person is armed is a federal district court's decision in *United States v. Jaramillo*.[318] In *Jaramillo*, officers believed that a person returning from a men's room in a small bar might be armed because two men had tossed a gun on the floor when they shouted for everyone to freeze.[319] The court held that an officer's frisk of the suspect was reasonable simply because the person was near the men who previously had a gun.[320] The presence of an actual gun aided the belief that another person in a bar may have one as well.

Other courts[321] have similarly invoked a "group danger" theory. The Fifth Circuit Court of Appeals[322] used the presence of many individuals in contrasting ways: an officer was justified in frisking a suspect in part because the presence of three men near them increased the officer's sense of danger, and the frisk was permissible in order to protect the three men and the officer from possible danger by the suspect.[323] In this context, officers

---

318. 822 F. Supp. 118, 120 (E.D.N.Y. 1993).
319. *Id.* at 120.
320. *Id.*
321. *See, e.g.*, United States v. Tellez, 11 F.3d 530, 533 (5th Cir. 1993) (officers "knew that they were entering a potentially dangerous situation by stopping a truck with three passengers, one whom they believed to be a parole violator"); United States v. Michelletti, 991 F.2d 183, 185 (5th Cir. 1993).
322. *Michelletti*, 991 F.2d at 185.
323. *Id.* The court upheld the frisk of a person who exited a bar with a drink in one hand and his hand in his pocket:

> The officer appreciated the risk involved if indeed there was some criminal intent on the part of the four men. The officer also surmised, in the alternative, that the three men and the police might be in danger if the [suspect] had ill intent and was actually armed. The fact that he kept his hand in his pocket at all times, given the surrounding circumstances, was reason enough to suspect [him] of possibly being armed and warranted the patdown frisk for the officers' and, possibly, the bystanders' safety.

Id. The court thus found that a frisk was permissible in part because of

also sometimes assert that the sense of danger was heightened because of the suspect's attitude.[324] One court approved of frisking young kids who were disorderly and wearing baggy clothing because it wondered whether the youths were "emboldened by having a weapon."[325]

Another important fact related both to the question of group danger and to the type of offense is the presence of individuals at a place to be searched for illegal drugs.[326] The issue is whether this situation inherently signifies that a person present is armed and dangerous. The Supreme Court refused to address this issue in *Guy v. Wisconsin;*[327] only Justices White and Thomas, in their dissent from the Court's denial of certiorari, thought assessing danger in this context was necessary to resolve the sharp conflict in the lower courts.

Some courts had upheld the frisks by automatically drawing two inferences: people present had some involvement with drugs and people involved with drugs often possess weapons.[328] Other courts, however, held that mere presence at the searched place was a tenuous connection to drug activity.[329] The center of this disagreement is the assessment of danger.

---

the danger presented by four individuals and in part because of the need to protect three of those same individuals.

324. United States v. Villanueva, 15 F.3d 197, 199 (1st Cir. 1994) (disorderly conduct by suspect increases sense of danger); *Michelletti*, 991 F.2d at 185 (suspect had "a bit of a cocky attitude").

325. *Villanueva*, 15 F.3d at 199 (1st Cir. 1994) ("With the plethora of gun carrying, particularly by the young, we must have sympathy, to an extent, with police officers' apprehensions."). In *Villanueva*, the First Circuit noted that baggy clothing can increase an officer's sense of danger: "While defendant's clothing was in current style, and so could not affirmatively be held against him, . . . its capacity for concealment was not irrelevant." *Id.* The type of clothing that the suspects were wearing thus became one fact increasing the officer's sense of danger.

326. *See generally* United States v. Reid, 997 F.2d 1576, 1577 (D.C. Cir. 1993) (upholding frisk of person who had just left an apartment that the officers were just about to search; court determined that an officer reasonably believed that he was in danger by having the person "behind" him as he executed the search warrant for drugs).

327. 113 S. Ct. 3020, 3021 (1993).

328. *Id.* (collecting cases).

329. *Id.* (collecting cases).

The presence of other individuals also becomes an issue when officers conduct protective sweeps as they attempt to execute an arrest warrant. In this context, officers search an area rather than a person; yet, as with frisks, they must have reasonable suspicion that a person present may pose danger to them. Some courts rely on the presence of drugs to justify such searches,[330] while other courts find the connection between drugs and danger too remote to justify a search.[331]

The issue of what facts create reasonable suspicion to believe that officers must either search an area or a person in order to protect themselves is one resolved by considering all of the facts known to an officer. Although many courts have refrained from finding a single fact dispositive, they nevertheless use common situations, such as a high-crime area or the lateness of the hour, as facts that increase the inference of danger.

When officers frisk individuals or search areas, courts seem to easily conclude that the requisite danger was present. Such conclusions are often rooted in the need for officers to take preventive actions to minimize the harm to themselves and sometimes to others. This deference is also apparent when courts evaluate the means officers use during *Terry* stops.

---

330. *See, e.g.*, United States v. Horne, 4 F.3d 579, 586 (8th Cir. 1993) (protective sweep was permissible because officers, while executing a search warrant for a fugitive at a home where drugs had been previously seized, "had no way of knowing how many people were there"); United States v. Coleman, 969 F.2d 126, 131 (5th Cir. 1992) (valid search of pouch in a car because "[w]eapons and violence are frequently associated with drug transactions.").

331. *See, e.g.*, United States v. McQuagge, 787 F. Supp. 637, 654-55 (E.D. Tex. 1991) (search of van was not a protective sweep). A federal district court in *McQuagge* explicitly rejected the link between drugs and weapons:

> The Court has . . . repeatedly repudiated the notion that peace officers can assume danger merely from the nature of a crime, the area in which the confrontation occurred, or the likelihood of danger in a situation. These pronouncements similarly mandate that this court reject the idea that the peace officers can assume danger merely because many, or even most, drug dealers are armed and dangerous.

Id. The court thus did not infer that because a suspect was involved with drugs he had a gun in his van.

Preventive Actions During Terry *Stops*

The perception of danger is also central to the issue of whether officers violated the Fourth Amendment by using unreasonable means to effectuate a *Terry* stop. As with the use of force to arrest a suspect, reasonableness is the standard, and courts view this standard with the same focus—danger to the officers. When evaluating the issue of whether the force used by the officer was unreasonable, most courts have applied the factors it uses to distinguish *Terry* stops from arrests. The Seventh Circuit,[332] however, has also considered the three factors detailed in *Graham v. Connor*: the crime, the threat to officers and others, and resistance and flight.[333] A brief examination of some of the means officers use to stop individuals reveals that the courts' and officers' perception of danger has permitted officers to use psychologically and physically intrusive force during *Terry* stops.

With reasonableness the issue, most courts apply a totality of the circumstances standard when evaluating the actions of police officers during *Terry* stops.[334] The Eighth Circuit[335] has listed some factors, also applied by other courts,[336] for evaluating the use of force:

---

332. *See, e.g.*, United States v. Weaver, 8 F.3d 1240, 1244 (7th Cir. 1993) (handcuffing during stop was reasonable); Tom v. Voida, 963 F.2d 952, 958 (7th Cir. 1992) (tackling suspect during stop was reasonable).

333. Professor Richard Williamson has also properly noted that the means officers use during *Terry* stops should be evaluated in light of the Fourth Amendment standard articulated in Tennessee v. Garner. RICHARD WILLIAMSON, *The Virtues (and Limits) of Shared Values: The Fourth Amendment and Miranda's Concept of Custody*, 1993 U. ILL. L. REV. 379, 403 (1993) ("Just as killing a fleeing felon suspect under certain conditions may constitute an unreasonable means of seizing a person, so too would the use of excessive force or other debilitating tactics—such as handcuffing—during the period of nonarrest detention".).

334. *See, e.g.*, United States v. Perea, 986 F.2d 633, 644-45 (2d Cir. 1993); United States v. Harrington, 923 F.2d 1371, 1373 (9th Cir.), *cert. denied*, 112 S. Ct. 164 (1991); United States v. Saffeels, 759 F.2d 633, 638 (8th Cir.), *cert. denied*, 474 U.S. 837 (1985).

335. United States v. Saffeels, 759 F.2d 633, 638 (8th Cir.), *cert. denied*, 474 U.S. 837 (1985).

336. *See, e.g.*, United States v. Perea, 986 F.2d 633, 644-45 (2d Cir. 1993). The Second Circuit in Perea listed the following factors to aid courts in distinguishing arrests from stops:

> the number of officers and police cars involved, the nature of the crime and whether there is reason to believe the suspect might be armed, the strength of the officers' articulable suspicions, the erratic behavior of or suspicious movements by the person under observation, and the need for immediate action by the officers and lack of opportunity for them to have made the stop in less threatening circumstances.[337]

This standard raises many of the same factual issues analyzed when officers act aggressively and use force to arrest a suspect: the alleged crime committed, the need to act quickly for protection, and the suspect's resistance and furtive gestures. When interpreting this standard, courts also similarly express broad-ranging deference to a police officer's decision to act. Although during *Terry* stops police officers are to use means that will quickly "confirm or deny their suspicions,"[338] some courts have interpreted the U.S. Supreme Court's decision in *United States v. Sharpe*[339] as requiring minimal scrutiny. In *Sharpe*, the Court stated that courts "should not indulge in unrealistic second-guessing":[340]

> The fact that the protection of the public might, in the abstract, have been accomplished by 'less intrusive' means does not, by itself, render the search unreasonable. The question is not simply whether some other alternative was available, but whether the police acted unreasonably in failing to recognize it or to pursue it.[341]

> the amount of force used by police, the need for such force, and the extent to which the individual's freedom of movement was restrained, . . . and in particular such factors as the number of agents involved . . . ; whether the target of the stop was suspected of being armed . . . ; the duration of the stop, . . . ; the physical treatment of the suspect . . . , including whether or not handcuffs were used.

Id. The court stated that if the force used was too intrusive for a stop, then the suspect was de facto arrested. *Id. Accord* United States v. Hastamoir, 881 F.2d 1551, 1556 (11th Cir. 1989).

337. *Perea*, 986 F.2d at 639-40.
338. United States v. Sharpe, 470 U.S. 675, 693 (1985).
339. 470 U.S. 675 (1985).
340. United States v. Sanders, 994 F.2d 200, 204 (5th Cir. 1993) (quoting United States v. Sharpe, 470 U.S. 675, 687 (1985)).
341. *Sharpe*, 470 U.S. at 687.

As with the force used during arrests, reasonableness becomes the touchstone for evaluating the use of force during *Terry* stops.

As a result of this perceived deference and danger, courts usually uphold *Terry* stops, even though the officers used intrusive means generally associated only with arrests.[342] Officers during *Terry* stops have pointed guns at suspects,[343] handcuffed them,[344] tackled them,[345] com-

---

342. *See, e.g.*, United States v. Tilmon, 19 F.3d 1221, 1224 (7th Cir. 1994) ("For better or for worse, the trend has led to the permitting of the use of handcuffs, the placing of suspects in police cruisers, the drawing of weapons and other measures more traditionally associated with arrest than with investigatory detention."); United States v. Harrington, 923 F.2d 1371, 1373 (9th Cir.), *cert. denied*, 112 S. Ct. 164 (1991) ("Use of force during a *Terry* stop does not convert the stop into an arrest if the force is justified by concern for the safety of the officer or others.").

343. *See, e.g.*, *Tilmon*, 19 F.3d at 1227 ("'It is not nice to have a gun pointed at you by a policeman but it is worse to have a gun pointed at you by a criminal, so there is a complex tradeoff involved in any proposal to reduce (or increase) the permissible scope of investigatory stops.'") (quoting United States v. Serna-Barreto, 842 F.2d 965, 968 (7th Cir. 1988)); United States v. Garza, 10 F.3d 1241, 1246 (6th Cir. 1993) ("Courts have *generally* upheld . . . stop 'with weapons drawn.'") (quoting United States v. Hardnett, 804 F.2d 353, 357 (6th Cir. 1986), *cert. denied*, 479 U.S 1097 (1987); United States v. Perdue, 8 F.3d 1455, 1462 (10th Cir. 1993) ("Although effectuating a *Terry* stop by pointing guns at a suspect may elevate a seizure to an 'arrest' in most scenarios, it was not unreasonable under these circumstances."); United States v. Sanders, 994 F.2d 200, 205 (5th Cir. 1993) ("Other circuits have held uniformly that, in and of itself, the mere act of drawing or pointing a weapon during an investigatory detention does not cause it to exceed the permissible bounds of a *Terry* stop or to become a de facto arrest.") (collecting cases); *but see generally* People v. Hampton, 606 N.Y.S. 628, 630 (N.Y. App. Div. 1994) (both stop and frisk were invalid; officer, who thought a cab driver was being robbed in a high-crime area, impermissibly pointed his gun at a suspect).

344. *See, e.g.*, *Tilmon*, 19 F.3d at 1228 ("Handcuffing—once highly problematic—is becoming quite acceptable in the context of a Terry analysis."); United States v. Wilson, 2 F.3d 226, 232 (7th Cir. 1993). The Seventh Circuit in Wilson upheld the officer's decision to handcuff a suspect during a *Terry* stop because of its assessment of danger:

[T]he encounter occurred in the dead of night in a residential community. We have no information about how well illuminated the area was, but it is safe to assume that the hour considerably increased the potential danger level. Furthermore, when he finally accosted [the suspect], [the officer] was not

pelled them to lie on the ground,[346] and put them in police cruisers.[347] Although the courts have not created per se rules stating that officers

---

> accompanied by other officers. The suspect was hiding under a porch and the officer ordered him to crawl out. At this point, we believe that the officer was justified in handcuffing [the suspect] in the interest of his own safety and the safety of anyone else who might have been in the area.

Id. The court upheld the use of handcuffs, even though it did not know the officer's ability to see the suspect, nor what crime the person had allegedly committed. Other courts have similarly upheld the use of handcuffs during Terry stops as sound preventive measures. See United States v. Sanders, 994 F.2d 200, 205 (5th Cir. 1993), *cert. denied*, 114 S. Ct. 608 (1993) (handcuffing in some circumstances is permissible even though "it substantially aggravates the intrusiveness and is not typically part of a *Terry* stop"); United States v. Miller, 974 F.2d 953, 957 (8th Cir. 1992) (handcuffing permissible because the "suspects in the vicinity outnumbered the officers by six to three" and because the officers had reason to believe that the suspects were involved in drug trafficking); United States v. Crittendon, 883 F.2d 326, 329 (4th Cir. 1989).

345. Tom v. Voida, 963 F.2d 952, 958 (7th Cir. 1992).

346. *See, e.g., Tilmon,* 19 F.3d at 1228 ("When a suspect is considered dangerous, requiring him to lie face down on the ground is the safest way for police officers to approach him, handcuff him and finally determine whether he carries any weapons."); United States v. Perdue, 8 F.3d 1455, 1463 (10th Cir. 1993) ("Directing suspect to lie on the ground provided the officers with a better view of the suspect and prevented him from obtaining weapons which might have been in the car or on his person."); Courson v. McMillian, 939 F.2d 1479, 1496 (11th Cir. 1991) (officer reasonably ordered passenger in car to lie on ground because her companions were difficult to handle). The Fifth Circuit in *Sanders* found reasonable an officer's decision to force a suspect to lie on the ground while pointing a gun at him:

> Admittedly, being held at gunpoint by police would be a powerful incentive for most persons neither to flee nor resist an impending investigation. Such a situation is not, however, equally inspirational for everyone. For example, some individuals will be sufficiently familiar with police procedures to believe that the officer will not actually use deadly force against them—particularly in close proximity to innocent bystanders—or will be so hesitant to use force that the suspect can "get the jump" on the officers. Others, such as persons who have been consuming drugs or alcoholic beverages, might misjudge the gravity of the situation and might be confused as to which responses on their part are or are not appropriate. A

may always use these means,[348] they often perceive sufficient danger to justify these actions.

For example, the Seventh Circuit[349] has stated that even if the force used was too intrusive for a *Terry* stop, the force may nevertheless be reasonable depending on the "degree of suspicion" and the "duration of the restraint."[350] The court implied that a continuum of force exists for *Terry* stops as well as arrests: if officers lack probable cause for an arrest but use more force than permitted for a *Terry* stop, the force may nevertheless be reasonable depending upon the officers' suspicion and the degree of intrusion.[351]

In considering the preventive actions taken by police officers during *Terry* stops, most courts uphold the use of intrusive means. Although the means officers use during these stops can be psychologically jarring, the implicit message of many courts is that these means are designed to prevent further harm to the officer, suspect, and perhaps the community. They very easily perceive danger when officers act preventively.

With reasonableness as the standard for analyzing force claims under the Fourth Amendment, courts have interpreted this standard by focusing on danger. In addition to analyzing danger associated with *Terry* stops and arrests, courts have also considered danger the key issue in determining whether officers may enter a home without a warrant to aid someone during emergencies. How courts assess danger in this context is important because the home, unlike other places, signifies a profound expectation of privacy, an expectation worthy of consideration in balancing interests under the Fourth Amendment.

---

third ground will be so desperate to avoid apprehension that they will knowingly take any risk to evade the police.

Sanders, 994 F.2d at 207. Although the court refused to create a rule automatically justifying the such use of force, it may offer similar conjectures in other cases. *Id.* at 206.

347. *See, e.g.*, United States v. Cannon, 15 F.3d 896, 900 (9th Cir. 1994) (having suspect sit in cruiser was a "reasonable precautionary measure" as the officer did a computer check);

348. *See, e.g.*, *Sanders*, 994 F.2d at 206.

349. Tilmon, 19 F.3d at 1226 (court adopted a "sliding scale" to evaluate how intrusive police means may be under certain circumstances).

350. *Id.*

351. *Id.*

Rescuing Actions: Emergencies as Inherent Danger

The need to assess danger is pronounced when police officers justify their actions by asserting that their actions were necessary because of an emergency or a need to protect the community from harm. This type of danger assessment occurs when officers perform "community caretaking" functions, as first discussed by the Supreme Court in *Cady v. Dombrowski*.

The *Cady* Court held that officers, who are not suspicious of any criminal activity, may act to protect the public if their actions are reasonable within the meaning of the Fourth Amendment. When interpreting reasonableness in this context, courts have disagreed as to the degree of danger that must be present in order to justify suspicionless seizures. In reaching different conclusions, the courts have not uniformly weighed the interests of the seized individual, society, and the need for caretaking.

Assessing danger was the key to resolving the motion to suppress evidence at O.J. Simpson's preliminary hearing. The court's ruling from the bench in that case centered on whether the detectives who entered Mr. Simpson's home reasonably believed that an emergency existed. To support its determination that an emergency did exist, the court detailed its findings of fact. In doing so, the court stated that what constitutes an emergency is "a gray area of the law."

In the *Simpson* case, detectives, who had previously observed the bloody crime scene involved in the murder of Nicole Simpson and Ronald Goldman, went to Mr. Simpson's house. The court determined that the detectives initially went to the house for two reasons: to inform Mr. Simpson of the deaths and to have him assume responsibility of his two children, who had been taken to the police station. After ringing the doorbell for fifteen minutes and after noticing that lights were on and vehicles were in the driveway, they called the security company for Mr. Simpson's home. When the security company arrived and provided the detectives with Mr. Simpson's number, a detective called and got the answering machine. Soon one detective noticed blood on a vehicle rented by Mr. Simpson. Based on these facts, the court determined that it was reasonable to believe that an emergency existed, which justified a detective climbing a wall that surrounded three residences.

The court also found that the emergency justified other actions by the detectives. A detective went into the guest quarters and spoke with a man who stated that he had heard a loud noise earlier that had worried him. The detective then examined tennis shoes in the room. The court found that this action was reasonable because an emergency still existed; according to the court, the detective could examine them because he had earlier seen bloody footprints leading away from the crime scene. Yet in the rest of the findings, the court linked each action to the detectives' goal in locating people in the houses, people who could also have been harmed by the killer at the other residence. The court thus perceived that the officers' actions did not violate the Fourth Amendment because they reasonably believed that other people could have been in danger.

Other courts in assessing danger have also allowed police officers to enter homes in order to provide aid to a person,[352] to search for unknown victims,[353] and to seize a weapon because it signifies potential danger to residents.[354] Some courts, however, have more closely scrutinized the actions of entering a home.[355]

---

352. *See, e.g.*, Wayne v. United States, 318 F.2d 205, 210 (D.C. App. 1962) (need to give aid to unconscious person); State v. Plant, 236 Neb. 317, 326, 461 N.W.2d 253, 262 (1990) (officer reasonably believed that entering house was necessary "for the protection of three small unaccounted-for children"); Duquette v. Godbout, 471 A.2d 1359, 1362 (R.I. 1984) ("Distraught mother . . . believed [her] child to be in peril within the apartment."). When officers reasonably believe that an emergency exists, some courts also uphold warrantless entries on the ground that if they had not acted they would "have been derelict in their duty in light of all the knowledge that they possessed." *Id.*

    In Wayne, the District of Columbia Appellate Court stated that courts should defer to the judgment of police officers in assessing the danger:

    People could well die in emergencies if police tried to act with the calm deliberation associated with the judicial process. Even the apparently dead are saved by swift police response. A myriad of circumstances . . . [exist]: smoke coming out of a window or under a door, the sound of gunfire in a house, threats from inside to shoot through the door at police, reasonable grounds to believe that an injured or seriously ill person is being held within.

    Wayne, 318 F.2d at 211. In these situations, the court determined that deference is reasonable. *Id.*

353. *See, e.g.*, People v. Davis, 441 Mich. 1, 13, 497 N.W.2d 910, 915 (1993) (emergency entries "need not be subject to traditional probable cause analysis, but . . . their legality should be evaluated on the basis of whether the police 'reasonably believed' a person needed aid").

354. *See, e.g.*, United States v. Doe, 764 F.2d 695, 698 (9th Cir. 1985) (after son killed his father on the porch, officer could reasonably enter house to retrieve the gun put in the house by a bystander); State v. Nebraska, 237 Neb. 598,

Courts have also recognized that police officers may perform community caretaking functions in other contexts.[356] One court has strongly checked an officer's ability to perform "welfare stops"[357] by its interpretation of the Fourth Amendment.

The Utah Court of Appeals in *Provo City v. Warden*[358] stated that in some circumstances officers may perform suspicionless seizures in order to aid citizens. In balancing the interests under the Fourth Amendment, the court stated that such seizures are permissible only when "the circumstances demonstrate an imminent danger to life or limb."[359] It found that the facts of the cases signified such danger because an officer was acting on information from two individuals that a driver was planning to commit suicide. It derived this limitation by the heavy weight it gave to a citizen's right to privacy and personal security.[360] This strong weight, it reasoned, was also necessary in order to prohibit "pretexual police activities."[361] Some other courts, though not specifically limiting stops related to imminent danger, have stated that serious safety concerns would justify an officer's suspicionless intrusion.[362]

---

467 N.W.2d 375, 381 (1991) (person in house shot person on porch; officer reasonably seized gun in the house to "protect the lives" of those near and "to determine if there were any other victims").

355. *See, e.g.*, People v. Davis, 441 Mich. 1, 23, 497 N.W.2d 910, 920 (1993) (officers who entered a motel room after a reported shooting should have asked desk clerk in which room the shooting had occurred; level of intrusiveness is a factor in determining the reasonableness of emergency assistance).
356. *See, e.g.*, In re Forfeiture of $176,598 v. $176,598 U.S. Currency, 443 Mich. 261, 272, 505 N.W.2d 201, 206 (1993) (the following are emergencies: "remov[ing] a former girlfriend following a domestic dispute, . . . removing an intoxicated person from the street, . . . entering an abandoned boat to ascertain ownership and the safety of mariners, . . . [and] searching an unconscious person for identification").
357. *See, e.g.*, Provo City v. Warden, 844 P.2d 360, 361 (Utah App. 1992), *aff'd*, No. 930059, 1994 WL 257117 (Utah June 10, 1994).
358. 844 P.2d 360 (Utah App. 1992).
359. *Id.* at 364.
360. *Id.*
361. *Id.*
362. *See, e.g.*, United States v. King, 990 F.2d 1552, 1560-64 (10th Cir. 1992) (police officer, who was about to ask driver at jammed intersection to quit honking, could ask him to leave his car upon seeing a loaded weapon in the

Other courts, however, have appeared to trust police officers to perform such acts out of concern for citizens rather than as a subterfuge seizure or search.[363] They have not interpreted reasonableness as to require danger to a person's life or bodily integrity. These courts consider all of the circumstances to determine whether the aid was reasonable.

For example, some courts have found it reasonable to stop a driver because he had mist on his rear window,[364] because he was driving on the shoulder of a road late at night with a flashing turn signal,[365] and because he slowed down in a turn lane and rolled down his window when he was near an officer.[366] One court remanded for the trial court to determine whether an officer acted reasonably in stopping a driver in order to prevent a hat from blowing out of the driver's truck.[367] In resolving the issue of reasonableness, one court[368] stated that it must consider whether alternatives were available to the officer to provide the aid.[369]

---

car; officer erred in drawing her weapon, in a state where citizens may carry guns, and threatening to kill him if he failed to follow her order); United States v. Dunbar, 470 F. Supp. 704, 707 (D. Conn. 1979), *aff'd*, 610 F.2d 807 (2d Cir. 1979). The district court stated that the purpose of the Fourth Amendment was "to minimize governmental confrontations with the individual." 470 F. Supp. at 708. It nevertheless held that suspicionless stops were permissible when the officers would be providing significant aid to an individual:

> The most rigorous view of the Fourth Amendment would not bar police officers from stopping a motorist to inform him that a bridge beyond a bend in the road had just been washed away. Some might contend that, as soon as time permitted, even this situation could be handled less intrusively by placing barricades to close the road, but a stopping of cars to warn and suggest alternative routes scarcely seems unreasonable.

Id. at 707. The court thus recognized that in emergencies police officers may seize individuals without reasonable suspicion.

363. *See infra* text accompanying notes 364-69.
364. Russell v. Municipality of Anchorage, 706 P.2d 687, 688 (Alaska 1985).
365. State v. Goetaski, 209 N.J. Super. 362, 366, 507 A.2d 751, 752 (1986).
366. Crauthers v. Alaska, 727 P.2d 9, 10 (Alaska 1986).
367. State v. Chisholm, 39 Wash. App. 864, 867, 696 P.2d 41, 42 (1985).
368. 149 Wis. 2d 663, 439 N.W.2d 840, 848 (1987), *rev'd on other grounds*, 155 Wis. 2d 77, 454 N.W.2d 763 (1990).
369. 149 Wis. 2d at 682, 439 N.W.2d at 848 (court is to consider "the availability, feasibility and effectiveness of alternatives to the type of intrusion actually accomplished").

Even those courts that use a general reasonableness standard occasionally strike down alleged "caretaking" actions. Some courts have found it unreasonable to stop a driver in order to discuss possible past parking violations,[370] to finish a previously consensual conversation,[371] or to give directions to someone who appears lost.[372] These courts find the action by the police officers unreasonable because of the slight weight they give to the interest in helping individuals under these circumstances and the great weight accorded to a citizen's interest in personal security and privacy.

Determining what constitutes an emergency thus requires consideration of the presence of danger. Some courts require significant danger while other courts look at the circumstances to determine whether the aid was reasonable. In deriving these different standards, the courts are implicitly disagreeing as to whether the Fourth Amendment presumptively ascribes to officers a level of trust in their search and seizure decisions. Other preventive actions similarly focus on the need to protect officers and society.

Protective Searches Incident to Arrests: Bright-line Fictions

Officers have three justifications for a search incident to a suspect's arrest: protecting the officer who takes a suspect into custody, limiting escapes, and prohibiting the destruction of evidence.[373] When courts uphold these searches, rarely do they specify how the searches furthered these justifications. The only issues generally mentioned under this doctrine are whether the areas searched were within the suspect's control and whether the search was contemporaneous with the arrest. Two of these doctrinal elements, however, have become meaningless for many courts. Instead of analyzing the facts of a particular case, courts have relied on fictions to justify their interpretation that a search was permissible. Under this doctrine, fictions, rather than danger analyses, are dispositive.

The fiction that an area was within a suspect's immediate control is one of the most discernible in Fourth Amendment jurisprudence. Courts

---

370. State v. Anderson, 149 Wis.2d 663, 439 N.W.2d 840, 847 (1989), *rev'd on other grounds*, 155 Wis.2d 77, 454 N.W.2d 763 (1990).
371. McDougal v. State, 580 So.2d 324, 324 (Fla. App. 1991).
372. United States v. Dunbar, 470 F. Supp. 704, 707 (D. Conn. 1979), *aff'd* 610 F.2d 807 (2d Cir. 1979).
373. *See supra* notes 151-53 and accompanying text.

have upheld searches under the following circumstances: searches of a suspect's vehicle, even though at the time of the search he was in a police cruiser;[374] searches of a car, even though the suspect was shot, handcuffed, and surrounded by police officers;[375] searches behind a dresser, even though it was unlikely that the suspect could have reached there;[376] searches of a closet, even though the suspect was handcuffed and surrounded by police officers;[377] searches of handbags and suitcases held by the suspect at time of his arrest, even though the officer took them upon arrest.[378] These bizarre interpretations of the search incident to an arrest doctrine indicate absolute deference to the officer's decision to search an area. Only a few courts have realistically placed boundaries on this discretion.[379]

Several courts have explicitly stated the officers need not closely examine the facts of a particular case and determine whether the suspect had actual access.[380] A search may be reasonable even if access was "slight."[381]

---

374. *See, e.g.*, United States v. Lugo, 978 F.2d 631, 634-35 (10th Cir. 1992); United States v. Karlin, 852 F.2d 968, 971 (7th Cir. 1988), *cert. denied*, 489 U.S. 1021 (1989); Davis v. Robbs, 794 F.2d 1129, 1131 (6th Cir. 1986), *cert. denied*, 479 U.S. 992 (1986).
375. *See, e.g.*, State v. Calovine, 23 Conn. App. 123, 126, 579, A.2d 126, 128 (1990).
376. United States v. Palumbo, 735 F.2d 1095, 1097 (8th Cir. 1984), *cert. denied*, 469 U.S. 934 (1989).
377. United States v. Queen, 847 F.2d 346, 353-55 (7th Cir. 1988).
378. United States v. Nohara, 3 F.3d 1239, 1243 (9th Cir. 1993); United States v. Morales, 923 F.2d 621, 627 (8th Cir. 1991).
379. *See, e.g.*, United States v. Lugo, 978 F.2d 631, 634-35 (10th Cir. 1992) (invalid search because "once [the suspect] had been taken from the scene, there was obviously no threat that he might reach in his vehicle and grab a weapon or destroy evidence"); United States v. Fafowora, 865 F.2d 360, 362 (D.C. Cir.), *cert. denied*, 493 U.S 829 (1989) (police officers who approach individuals outside their vehicle may not search the car); United States v. Cotton, 751 F.2d 1146, 1148 (10th Cir. 1985) (search may be broader when officers search vehicles as opposed to other areas because of the diminished expectation of privacy); United States v. Lyons, 706 F.2d 321, 330 (D.C. Cir. 1983) (once police have control of an object and "there is no longer any danger that the arrestee might gain access to the property to seize a weapon or destroy evidence, a search of that property is not incident to the arrest").
380. *See, e.g.*, United States v. Arango, 879 F.2d 1501, 1506-07 (7th Cir. 1989), *cert. denied*, 493 U.S. 1069 (1990). In Arango, the Seventh Circuit described this common deference:

Although one court stated that an officer should not consider a suspect to be either "an acrobat" or "Houdini,"[382] searches are routinely upheld that require such rare physical skills. Similarly, some courts have also failed to give meaning to the doctrinal requirement that searches must be contemporaneous with arrests.[383]

Prior to the embedding of these fictions in Fourth Amendment jurisprudence, some circuits had examined the totality of the circumstances to assess actual access.[384] The standard for this assessment was similar to the standard for analyzing the means officers use during *Terry* stops. For example, the Ninth Circuit[385] considered the number of suspects and officers, the suspects'

> [The law] does not require the arresting officer to undergo a detailed analysis, at the time of arrest, of whether the arrestee, handcuffed or not, could reach into the car to seize some item within, either as a weapon or to destroy evidence, or for some altogether different reason. The facts surrounding each arrest are unique, and it is not by any means inconceivable under those various possibilities that an arrestee could gain control of some item within the automobile. The law simply does not require the arresting officer to mentally sift through all these possibilities during an arrest, before deciding whether he may lawfully search within the vehicle.

Id. See also United States v. Queen, 847 F.2d 346, 353 (7th Cir. 1988) (courts should not second-guess police officers because they "cannot be expected to make punctilious judgments regarding what is within and what is just beyond the arrestee's immediate control").

381. *Queen*, 847 F.2d at 353.
382. United States v. Lyons, 706 F.2d 321, 330 (D.C. 1983) (quoting United States v. Mapp, 476 F.2d 67, 80 (2d Cir. 1973)).
383. *See, e.g.*, United States v. Karlin, 852 F.2d 968, 971 (7th Cir. 1988), *cert. denied*, 489 U.S. 1021 (1989) (issue is whether suspect had access to area at time of arrest, not at time of search); United States v. Palumbo, 735 F.2d 1095, 1097 (8th Cir. 1984), *cert. denied*, 469 U.S. 934 (1989) (upheld search even though it was unlikely that suspect had access to area at time of arrest).
384. *See, e.g.*, United States v. McConney, 728 F.2d 1195, 1207 (9th Cir.), *cert. denied*, 469 U.S. 824 (1984).
385. United States v. McConney, 728 F.2d 1195, 1207 (9th Cir.), *cert. denied*, 469 U.S. 824 (1984). Later the Ninth Circuit replaced the actual access standard with a fiction. See United States v. Turner, 926 F.2d 883, 887-88 (9th Cir.), *cert. denied*, 112 S. Ct. 103 (1991). In *Turner*, the Ninth Circuit held that officers may search an area if the suspect had access to it at the time he was arrested, even if later he was removed in handcuffs. *Id.*

location, and the use of guns. This totality of circumstances standard, however, later gave way to the fiction, which did not require actual access.

In determining the constitutionality of searches incident to arrests, some courts have not applied a totality of circumstances standard. The fiction adopted by some courts is not linked to any of the justifications supporting the search. Instead, the primary goal seems to be affording officers broad discretion in deciding whether to search an area.

Although the standard of reasonableness cannot provide police officers with many bright lines to guide their actions, analyzing circumstances based upon doctrinal justifications seems to be at least a floor for judicial scrutiny. In assessing the circumstances surrounding preventive actions by police officers, such as *Terry* frisks and emergencies, courts have often fused the issue of reasonableness with the issue of danger. In the context of searches incident to arrest, danger has not only disappeared from the analysis, but analysis at times is nonexistent.

The common thread to these doctrines is the Fourth Amendment reasonableness standard. An important issue in Fourth Amendment jurisprudence is how courts discern danger and how they weigh it in determining the constitutionality of both aggressive and preventive actions.

Dangerous Misperceptions of the Fourth Amendment: The Substitution of Judicial Perspective for Executive Judgments

When police officers strike suspects or when they act preventively by performing frisks, searches incident to arrests, or community caretaking functions, the constitutionality of their actions depends upon whether they were reasonable within the meaning of the Fourth Amendment. Although in each of these areas the Supreme Court has articulated doctrinal elements for this reasonableness inquiry, many courts in evaluating the conduct of police officers have focused almost exclusively on the danger presented by the situation.

This focus has at times resulted in courts finding the assessment of danger to be synonymous with the reasonableness inquiry. Although the reasonableness inquiry under the Fourth Amendment is not formulaic, it does include more than an assessment of danger. In addition to society's interest in law enforcement, the reasonableness inquiry encompasses both society's and the individual's interest in personal security.

By centering the inquiry on the danger presented by circumstances, some courts err by interpreting the Fourth Amendment to require almost absolute deference to an officer's perception of danger. In doing so, they have often failed to scrutinize other important aspects of the confrontation: the gravity of the offense committed by a suspect, the availability of other means to apprehend the suspect, the role officers played in creating the need for force, the jury's role in determining what actually happened, and the intrusive nature of many preventive actions. This misapplied deference is pronounced when the circumstances involve a psychologically disturbed individual, a frisk, a community caretaking function, or a search incident to an arrest. An examination of each of these misperceptions reveals how courts should interpret the reasonableness inquiry.

Danger Is Only a Factor in Determining Reasonableness

The right to be free from "unreasonable searches and seizures" is a right that courts should interpret in light of the history and purpose of the Fourth Amendment. These two inquiries contour the reasonableness standard by revealing that assessing danger is not synonymous with determining reasonableness. The constitutionality of a police practice requires consideration of numerous issues, with danger assessment as only a single factor. Although scholars disagree as to the role the warrant clause plays in the Fourth Amendment analysis, they nevertheless recognize that reasonableness compels consideration of numerous interests.[386] Describing these interests and weighing them are the key issues in litigation arising from the use of physical force against a suspect and litigation involving preventive actions.

The history of the Fourth Amendment indicates a need to protect individuals and society from oppressive governmental actions. Because governmental practices during the colonial era were intrusive and arbitrary, the framers of the Fourth Amendment erected a shield to protect citizens from unreasonable practices. After examining this history, Professor Tracey Maclin soundly concluded that the Reasonableness Clause represents a mistrust of police power.

---

386. *See, e.g.*, Akhil R. Amar, *Fourth Amendment First Principles*, 107 Harv. L. Rev. 757, 759-61 (1994); Carol S. Steiker, *Second Thoughts About First Principles*, 107 Harv. L. Rev. 820, 824 (1994).

Evaluating how police officers use this police power, however, is not limited to examining only those practices present at common law because the framers could not have intended to freeze from scrutiny newer methods arising from technological developments. As Professor Carol Steiker has noted, "[U]se of the term 'reasonable' . . . positively invites constructions that change with circumstances."[387] The history and purpose of the amendment thus indicate a need to evaluate police practices to make sure that they do not unreasonably infringe upon the "right of the people to be secure."

Determining the scope of this right is thus the same question as determining what is an unreasonable search or seizure. Reasonableness emerges as the standard for measuring police practices. This inquiry, however, requires a balancing of interests, not a quick glance to determine if the practices are rational. Although reasonableness as a standard can hardly be described precisely, the history and purpose of the amendment nevertheless should guide how to identify the interests and how to weigh them.

Balancing interests under the Fourth Amendment, as with balancing interests under other amendments, is a process linked to perceived values represented in the amendment. In the context of aggressive actions against suspects, the U.S. Supreme Court in *Tennessee v. Garner* and *Graham v. Connor*[388] emphasized the importance of personal security both to the individual seized and to society.

In *Garner*, the Court highly valued an individual's right to life and society's interest in a fair adjudication of guilt. It held that in some situations these interests outweigh society's interest in effective law enforcement. It thus held that officers act unreasonably when they shoot some fleeing felons.

Similarly, in *Graham*, the Court detailed three factors that help to measure the degree of intrusiveness of police practices: the crime committed, the immediacy of harm to officers or the community, and the suspect's resistance. In listing these factors, the Court offered guidelines in evaluating police practices.

The Court in *Terry v. Ohio* also described the importance of the right to personal security as it upheld an officer's limited ability to frisk suspects.

---

387. *McConney,* 728 F.2d at 824.

388. 490 U.S. 386, 395 ("'Reasonableness' of a particular seizure depends not only on when it is made, but also on how it is carried out.").

It stated, "[A] frisk is a serious intrusion upon the sanctity of the person, which may inflict great indignity and arouse strong resentment, and it is not to be undertaken lightly."[389]

It held that this preventive action, one not designed to inflict bodily injury, is one that must be carefully limited to the need to protect officers from armed and dangerous suspects. Only under these circumstances would the Fourth Amendment permit officers to pat down a suspect because the right to personal security "belongs as much to the citizen on the streets of our cities as to the homeowner closeted in his study to dispose of his secret affairs."[390] This right thus broadly protects both bodily integrity and privacy.

When interpreting these decisions, however, some lower courts have misunderstood the reasonableness inquiry. They have interpreted the Court's discussion of danger in *Garner*, *Graham*, and *Terry* as the standard for measuring reasonableness. In doing so, they have shifted the balance to the goal of promoting law enforcement.

Woefully absent from this perspective is a recognition of the history of the amendment. If mistrust of police power was the impetus for passage of the Fourth Amendment, then interpreting the amendment to strongly further law enforcement interests makes no sense. Balancing thus requires evaluating conflicting interests, not just discerning the presence of danger. When courts focus their attention solely on the issue of danger, they fail to consider other interests furthered by the Fourth Amendment.

The Gravity of the Offense Is a Factor in Determining Reasonableness

One important factor in the calculus of reasonableness is the offense the suspect allegedly committed, which compelled an investigation, an attempt to apprehend, or any protective measures. The Supreme Court explicitly mentioned this factor in both *Garner* and *Graham* as it described how to evaluate the use of force by police officers. It also stated in *Wisconsin v. Welsh* that the gravity of the offense is an important factor in determining the presence of exigent circumstances. In *Terry*, the Court also used the nature of the suspected offense, armed robbery, as a factor in determining whether the investigating officer could have believed that the suspect was armed and dangerous.

389. Unites States v. Terry, 392 U.S. 1, 17 (1968).
390. *Id.* at 9.

In assessing the use of force against suspects, many courts have failed to consider the nature of the alleged offense. They have instead focused on two issues: the threat posed by the suspect and the suspect's resistance. They have interpreted these factors as creating a "dangerousness" standard. Such an interpretation, however, is misguided. The second *Graham* factor questions not only if there was a threat, but also if the threat was present at the time the officer acted. This immediacy requirement limits the use of force by focusing on the actual need. Similarly, the third factor simply questions whether the suspect resisted. It does not necessarily imply that all resistance must be checked by ever-increasing uses of force.

These erroneous interpretations do not adequately consider the first factor: the crime the person allegedly committed that required police officers to seize him. If an eleven-year-old boy stole a pair of sunglasses from a discount store and resisted the officers' commands to stop, should they tackle him and use pain compliance techniques to control him if they know the boy, where he lives, and that their actions may incite nearby youths observing the confrontation? Because the Reasonableness Clause requires a balancing of interests, such an action is unreasonable in light of the offense committed and the surrounding circumstances.

The significance of the crime allegedly committed depends upon the circumstances of the confrontation between the officer and suspect. For example, if a childless suspect has just killed his wife, he has just committed a crime involving the "serious infliction of bodily injury." A literal reading of this language from *Garner* might seem to suggest that officers could automatically shoot him when they see him. Yet, under the circumstances he may not pose an immediate danger to anyone else.

In short, even though he committed a heinous act, he is not an immediate threat to anyone else. He has already killed the only person who was logically at risk. Although he may pose a threat to himself, it would be unreasonable to kill him unless the surrounding circumstances somehow shift to signify an immediate danger to police officers and the community. By barring officers from shooting him, the suspect's right to personal security is preserved as is society's interest in a fair adjudication of his guilt.

The focus on danger analysis perhaps has risen from reliance on the continuum of force model for apprehending suspects. Many officers are trained to escalate the degree of force if the suspect resists their commands. The continuum itself does not signify that there ever is any need to let the suspect go. Only at the end of the continuum, which authorizes the use of deadly force, is there a check, one established by the Supreme Court in *Tennessee v. Garner*. In the nondeadly force context, officers sometimes may be constitutionally required to let suspects go rather than to use escalating force.

The balance of interests, represented by the reasonableness standard, at times should limit the use of nondeadly force in apprehending suspects, even when they flee. An interest that sometimes tilts the balance toward allowing flight is the individual's right to bodily integrity. Although the dissent in *Garner* argued that all suspects can maintain this interest by stopping, the majority properly interpreted the balancing process to protect a suspect's *fundamental* interest in his life. The suspect did not have to stop in *Garner* for the Constitution to protect this interest.

Although one's interest in life is significantly stronger than one's interest in bodily integrity, the balancing process should question whether at times this interest, as in *Garner*, outweighs the interest in law enforcement. By considering the nature of the alleged offense, courts and officers can better distinguish the scope of reasonable conduct. Determining when police officers should cease using nonlethal force and let a suspect flee is a question also linked to the question of the availability of alternative means to seize suspects. This issue, like the alleged offense, is also one frequently ignored by courts.

Judicial Scrutiny Does Not Constitute Impermissible Second-Guessing of Police Officers' Split-Second Judgments

Courts often fail to consider the availability of alternative means of action because of an implicit belief that such scrutiny constitutes impermissible second-guessing of officers' split-second judgments. Such broad-ranging deference, however, is inappropriate and contrary to our well established doctrine of judicial review. Analyzing the availability of alternative means is an important factor in determining reasonableness.

Understanding the role of available alternatives is difficult because the Supreme Court has not spoken clearly on this issue. When considering some preventive actions, the Court has not carefully evaluated available alternatives. In the seminal decisions of *Garner* and *Terry*, however, the Court clearly limited the means officers could employ when investigating and apprehending suspects. Scrutiny of means, however, does not necessarily require identifying the least intrusive practice. It entails consideration of whether the police practice was reasonable in light of available alternatives.

One of the Court's most deferential opinions addressing preventive actions is *Michigan v. Sitz*,[391] in which the Court held that police officers may stop drivers at roadblocks for the purpose of determining whether they are intoxicated. The Court upheld the practice as a safety measure, one allowing officers to seize individuals even though they have no reason for believing that they are intoxicated. In balancing the interests of the parties, the Court determined that this practice compelled a driver to stop for only a few seconds, that the police officers' actions were not arbitrary, that drunk driving was a serious problem, and that roadblocks were an "effective" means of stopping drunk drivers.

Even though the Court did explicitly evaluate the means used by the officers, it was reluctant to give the means heightened review. It stated, "[F]or the purposes of Fourth Amendment analysis, the choice among such reasonable alternatives remains with the governmental officials who have a unique understanding of, and a responsibility for, limited public resources, including a finite number of police officers."[392] It nevertheless determined that the practice was reasonable. It merely refused to decide which plan for stopping drunk driving was "ideal."[393]

The Court in some other preventive decisions has also expressed a reluctance to closely scrutinize means. In *Cady v. Dombrowski* and *Pennsylvania v. Mimms*, the Court held reasonable a police officer's decision to search a towed car for a gun and to order a suspect out of a car during a traffic stop. In *Cady*, the issue was the community's safety, and in *Mimms*, it was the officer's safety. In both decisions, the Court did not identify the least intrusive means available.[394]

When the practice involves serious infringements of bodily integrity and privacy, the Court is more willing to closely evaluate the means. For

---

391. 496 U.S 444, 448-49 (1989).

392. 496 U.S. at 443.

393. *Id.* at 453.

394. *See, e.g.*, Nadine Strossen, *The Fourth Amendment in the Balance: Accurately Setting the Scales Through the Least Alternative Analysis*, 63 N.Y.U. L. Rev. 1173, 1176 (1988) ("The Court's Fourth Amendment balancing analyses have neither systematically evaluated the marginal law enforcement benefits of challenged searches and seizures nor regularly incorporated the 'least intrusive alternative' requirement.").

example, *Garner* limited the use of deadly force, *Graham* limited the use of nondeadly force, *Terry* limited the nature of a frisk, and *Winston v. Lee* limited the government's ability to obtain evidence by performing surgery on a suspect. The heightened scrutiny of means in these situations is proper because the Reasonableness Clause requires a balancing of interests. When a police practice significantly intrudes upon bodily security and privacy, then it is reasonable for the Court to examine the fit between the need for the practice and the means used.

When the balance is so heavily weighted against the police practice, the lack of alternatives is an important issue. In this situation, the lack of another alternative is relevant, but not dispositive of the reasonableness question. For example, in *Garner* the Court barred killing the fleeing burglary suspect, even though it assumed that the officers would not apprehend him later. Similarly, in *Winston*, the Court barred surgery to remove a bullet from the suspect, even though it was the only way to retrieve this evidence. The availability of alternatives thus becomes one issue in the reasonableness inquiry. Its significance depends upon the circumstances of each case.

Some Conduct Prior to a Seizure Is Relevant to Determining Reasonableness

Examining alternatives also requires consideration of when to begin scrutinizing the means used by officials. This question arises when officers precipitate the need for greater force during a seizure. Some courts limit their scrutiny of means to the point at which the officers seized a suspect. Such bright-line temporal limitations, however, seriously undermine the right to personal security by failing to consider the officers' prior conduct. The confusion as to when to evaluate the means used by the officers results from the Supreme Court's language about the nature of policing and its incredibly narrowing "seizure" definitions.

The disagreement as to temporal limitations stems from the Supreme Court's discussion of policing in *Graham*. The *Graham* Court stated that when courts and juries determine reasonableness, they should remember that "police officers are often forced to make split-second judgments—in circumstances that are tense, uncertain, and rapidly evolving."[395] In examining this language, some courts confuse the nature of policing with defer-

395. Graham v. Connor, 490 U.S. 386, 397 (1989).

ence to police officers' decisions. Although the Court stated that the nature of policing is a factor in determining reasonableness, it did not state that because policing is difficult strong deference is necessary. Such an interpretation fails to take into consideration how police officers are trained. When police officers practice shooting their weapons, they often do so in conditions designed to simulate situations requiring quick judgment. An ability to make quick decisions simply describes a skill required of police officers. It does not prohibit examining whether their actions prior to the seizure created the need for force.

Determining how far back in time courts and juries should look when determining whether officers created the need for force is the most difficult issue associated with temporal limitations. Although the moment an officer seizes a suspect seems like a logical starting point, conduct prior to seizure at times may be significantly linked to the seizure. Like the classic question of proximate cause, how far to go back in time is a policy question implicit in the standard of reasonableness.

The temporal question probably would not exist except for the Court's ever-narrowing seizure definitions. Prior to the Court's seizure definition in *California v. Hodari D.*, courts more readily determined that officers had seized suspects by their actions. The *Hodari D.* Court drastically limited the circumstances constituting a seizure as it held that a "show of authority" by police officers does not automatically constitute a seizure within the meaning of the Fourth Amendment. By adding to its definition that the suspect must comply with the assertion of authority, the Court moved the point of seizure further ahead in time.

By considering actions prior to a seizure, courts are not expanding the scope of the Fourth Amendment because only those actions causally linked with the seizure should be relevant to the reasonableness inquiry. Thus, if the suspect never complied with the show of authority, then no seizure occurred and the prior conduct is not governed by the Fourth Amendment. If, however, the officers shot the suspect because he failed to comply with the show of authority, then the officers' prior actions may be causally linked to the seizure. Considering actions prior to the seizure may in some circumstances further the constitutional right to personal security because reasonableness is the standard and the Federal Rules broadly define relevance.

Reasonableness Is a Constitutional Standard, Not One Governed by State Law or National Police Practices

Although the Fourth Amendment prohibits "unreasonable searches and seizures," it does not specify how to determine reasonableness. Such an open-ended standard invites consideration of possible sources for ascertaining its meaning. When courts and juries have to determine whether officers violated the Fourth Amendment, they are necessarily distinguishing a constitutional violation from a state law violation, such as battery or trespass. This distinction is important when considering the role of experts in determining the reasonableness of a police practice. Although their testimony may be relevant to resolving reasonableness, their opinion does not resolve the Fourth Amendment question.

If policing experts were to resolve the issue of reasonableness, then in one sense the judiciary would be stripped of its power to interpret the Constitution. The Supreme Court in *Garner* recognized its role when it rejected the well-established police practice of killing fleeing felons. Although this practice was established at common law and a majority of police departments still adhered to the common law rule, the Court nevertheless interpreted the balancing process implicit in the Reasonableness Clause as prohibiting it. Similarly, in *Graham*, the Court affirmed that any arbitrary use of physical force does not necessarily violate the Fourth Amendment. Arbitrary force must rise to the level of a constitutional violation to be actionable.

Distinguishing constitutional torts from state torts, however, has been difficult for courts. Some courts have erroneously interpreted the Fourth Amendment as creating a negligence standard. Such an interpretation, however, strips from the amendment its rich history, one that informs courts and juries as to how to protect the interests of citizens and society.

Even though both the Fourth Amendment and negligence claims consider the availability of alternatives, they are different. Although no treatise could clearly delineate how to make this distinction, courts and juries properly interpret the Fourth Amendment when they consider the interests it protects. Simple reliance on the common law or national police standards undervalues the right to personal security.

In Civil Cases Juries Must Often Determine What Constitutes Objective Reasonableness

Who determines what constitutes objectively reasonable conduct is an important issue when the Fourth Amendment issue arises in a civil action under § 1983. Although a court in criminal cases finds facts during suppression hearings on Fourth Amendment issues, when civil cases raise Fourth Amendment issues, courts sometimes misunderstand the objective reasonableness standard. Some courts deprive the jury of its role both in determining what happened and in applying the standard of reasonableness.

Although the jury system is still not free from the significant problem of racial bias, it nevertheless plays an important role in evaluating police practices. Many courts, however, have erroneously interpreted the decisions in *Garner* and *Graham* as urging them to resolve the issue of reasonableness. This error arises from perceiving the decisions as requiring broad-ranging deference to police officers' decisions.

One of the most important functions of the jury is determining credibility. The need for such determinations is obvious when officers kill a suspect and no witnesses are present, and when the officers assert that their actions were justified because the suspect made a furtive gesture. Determining whether an action was "furtive" is an extremely important jury issue because when courts automatically defer to the officers' written assertions, they may unknowingly give them a license to murder at will. In this situation, assessing credibility is essential.

One scholar has further advocated the use of a jury in criminal cases to resolve Fourth Amendment suppression motions.[396] This practice would allow juries to reject some legal fictions easily accepted by some courts, such as the broad searches permitted by the courts' interpretation of the search incident to arrest doctrine. Few jurors would believe that many suspects possess unusual skills to reach guns and contraband. Yet, even if juries were to review some of these claims, such review would not overly deter police practices because many jurors believe that criminal defendants are only "second-class citizens."[397]

---

396. *See generally* BAGICUL, *supra* note 212.

397. MACLIN, *supra* note 17, at 238. Juries also often fail to check the misuse of police power because of racial prejudices. *See, e.g.*, JODY D. ARMOUR, *Race Ipsa Loquitur: Of Reasonable Racists, Intelligent Bayesians, and Involun-*

Although some cases involving police practices can be resolved on summary judgment when material facts are not in dispute, courts should be careful not to infringe upon the jury's role as factfinder when credibility is a key issue, as it is in many police misconduct cases.

Justifying Preventive Actions Based on Danger Is Different From Justifying Aggressive Actions Based on Danger

Although factfinders assess danger when examining both aggressive and preventive actions by police officers, danger that justifies preventive actions is different from danger that justifies aggressive actions. Although danger in one context should constitute the same perception of danger in the other context, the lower courts' interpretations of preventive actions signify a presumption that many preventive actions based on danger are reasonable. Such a presumption carried over to aggressive actions would represent serious undermining of the right to personal security.

The need for a dual standard of danger is apparent when considering a factfinder's assessment that a suspect was "armed and dangerous," justifying a protective frisk, and the finding that the suspect was armed, justifying the use of deadly force. When many courts determine the constitutionality of a particular frisk, they easily perceive that the officers were in danger. For example, many courts seem to presume that if an officer is investigating a suspect for drug possession, the officer may frisk the suspect because he is "armed and dangerous." Similarly, courts have allowed officers to use incredibly intrusive measures during *Terry* stops as preventive measures. Although pointing guns at suspects should convert most stops into arrests, many courts have allowed this intensive show of authority as a preventive measure. In addition, courts have allowed officers to frisk suspects merely because they failed to comply with the officer's command to freeze. The war on drugs has resulted in police officers having greater preventive power to control suspects.

These same facts, however, applied in the context of aggressive actions should not justify the use of significant force. Although many courts have failed to recognize that frisks constitute "serious intrusion[s]," they should

---

tary Negrophobes, 46 STAN. L. REV. 781, 784 (1994) ("Exploitation of racial fears [was] evident in the trial of the four white Los Angeles police officers who beat Rodney King.").

assess differently the need to strike or shoot suspects based on similar facts. When officers act aggressively, they significantly infringe the constitutional right to personal security. In this context, because of the heightened interest associated with bodily integrity, the availability of alternative methods of apprehending becomes more important than in the context of preventive actions. A suspicious movement by a suspect more readily supports a frisk than a strike by a police officer.

Although such a distinction in danger analysis may seem obvious, the broad language that some courts use in discussing danger does not suggest such a limitation. Determining reasonableness, however, requires consideration of all of the circumstances. An important circumstance in determining reasonableness is the magnitude of the infringement caused by the officer. The perception of danger is thus not an automatic justification for an aggressive action by police officers.

The Community Caretaking Function Doctrine Requires Reasonable Conduct

Danger analysis has also been a significant aspect of the community caretaking function doctrine. The doctrine by its very nature emphasizes that in some situations officers may avoid complying with the usual procedures of the Fourth Amendment in order to aid society. Interpreted broadly, however, this doctrine can seriously undermine the Fourth Amendment right to personal security. The need for a narrow scope of this doctrine is apparent when considering the magistrate's ruling on the motion to suppress evidence at O.J. Simpson's preliminary hearing.

The court held that detectives lawfully entered Mr. Simpson's house in order to render aid to possible victims inside. Under this doctrine, officers did not have to have probable cause to believe that someone was in danger. They merely had to have a reasonable belief that someone may be hurt. What is reasonable in this context, however, should also depend upon the degree of infringement on the right to personal security. If the justification for entering a home is to save a person known to be hurt, the balance tips in favor of entry.

On the other hand, when speculation is the basis of entry, perhaps entry is still permissible if officers may not invoke the plain view doctrine to justify seizing items they would not have had access to but for the entry. In that situation, the officers do truly perform an act of public service; they leave at the doorstep any desire to investigate criminal conduct.

Although the community caretaking function and its relationship to the exclusionary rule is a topic mandating extensive scrutiny, it is an important piece of the courts' assessment of danger under the Fourth Amendment. As with other doctrines, the exigencies of the day may too often tip the balance to the side of law enforcement. The right to personal security and privacy must also weigh heavily in assessing the need to act as the community's caretaker.

Reasonableness Requires an Actual Access Standard for Searches Incident to Arrests

Determining what constitutes reasonable police practices is difficult. Yet when the police practice is a search incident to an arrest, many courts have abandoned the reasonableness inquiry for a bright-line fiction: the area in a suspect's control is that area he or she had access to prior to being arrested. In doing so, they have not required that the suspect have actual access to the areas at the time of the search. This fiction thus cuts the doctrine loose from its underlying justifications of protecting officers, preventing escapes, and preserving evidence. The development of this fiction underscores the need for a reasonableness standard that seriously considers the right to personal security.

When the Court in *Chimel v. California* detailed the scope of searches incident to arrests, it scrutinized the means used by the officers. It rejected allowing officers to search an entire house simply because the homeowner had allegedly committed a crime. In analyzing this decision, Professor Nadine Strossen commended the Court for its emphasis on narrowly tailored means.[398] She interpreted the decision as requiring police officers to use the least intrusive police practice to further their reasonable concerns about safety and destruction of evidence. The decision thus signified that the Fourth Amendment required scrutiny of an intrusive police practice.

Through the years many courts abandoned such scrutiny, interpreting the progeny of *Chimel* as documenting the need for a bright line. That

398. *See* STROSSEN, *supra* note 503.

bright line became the area not in the defendant's actual control, but the area where he or she had been prior to the search. Although the need for such bright lines is understandable, the lines must have some relationship with the doctrinal justifications.

By losing reasonableness as the standard for evaluating such searches, some courts failed to give any weight to the right of privacy protected by the Fourth Amendment. Such a decline in analysis can occur when courts give broad deference to police officers' decisions and little weight to the right to personal security. Such deference has crept into the consideration of other preventive actions. When deference becomes routine, courts are more likely to create legal fictions—fictions not rooted in the facts of the case nor in the history of the amendment. Perhaps the development of the search incident to arrest doctrine signifies the scope of the reasonableness analysis for other Fourth Amendment doctrines if the courts fail to discard their misperceptions. Abandoning the legal fiction associated with searches incident to arrest is a beginning toward restoring reasonableness to its place in Fourth Amendment jurisprudence.

Conclusion

Dangerous misperceptions of the Fourth Amendment have seriously eroded the constitutional right to personal security, a right that protects both suspects and society from unreasonable police practices. These misperceptions have occurred because courts have erroneously interpreted the Fourth Amendment's prohibition of "unreasonable searches and seizures" as raising a single question: Does the challenged police practice rationally further the government's interest in protecting police officers and society from danger? By fusing the reasonableness standard with the assessment of danger, many courts have failed to understand the history of the Fourth Amendment and the balancing of interests mandated by the Reasonableness Clause.

The history of the Fourth Amendment reveals a mistrust of unchecked police power. The strong deference courts show to the judgments of police officers conflicts with this history of mistrust. By failing to recognize this important historical perspective, courts have skewed the balance of interests in favor of upholding intrusive police practices rather than beginning the balancing process with level scales.

This pronounced deference has affected the balancing process in numerous ways. In focusing solely on the danger a suspect represents to police officers and society, courts have often failed to discern society's interest in personal security. The devaluing of this right is particularly apparent when courts refuse to consider whether officers could have used less intrusive means to apprehend suspects.

Courts also undermine the right to personal security by not considering the nature of the offense that first prompted investigation. The type of offense is important because officers should recognize that sometimes they are constitutionally required to let suspects go rather than use ever-increasing amounts of force. This highly deferential standard of review has also resulted in courts refusing to consider whether the officers created the need for force and in their deciding fact-bound cases on summary judgment.

In determining reasonableness, courts should consider that danger is only a factor, one that the right to personal security and privacy may at times outweigh. Inherent in this balancing process is a recognition that aggressive police actions, such as the use of force during arrests, are markedly different from preventive actions, such as *Terry* frisks, searches incident to arrests, and community caretaking functions.

Even though preventive actions also intrude upon the right to personal security, the perception of possible danger more easily justifies upholding a preventive action than an aggressive action. The goal of a preventive action is to protect suspects, officers and others from possible bodily harm; the goal of an aggressive action, however, is to directly attack suspects' interest in bodily integrity in order to protect officers and others from possible harm.

Courts should thus balance differently the need to frisk suspects for weapons and the need to strike or shoot them. The broad language many courts use in describing the danger officers face during investigations masks this important difference. The right to personal security deserves protection from the courts' dangerous misperceptions of the Fourth Amendment.

Chapter Seven
The Constitutional Rights of Public Employees
Mary Massaron Ross

Justice Holmes once wrote an opinion holding that the Massachusetts Constitution did not protect the constitutional right of a public employee to speak freely since his job was conditioned on his agreement to suspend his free speech rights.[1] The justice assumed that there is a difference for constitutional purposes between the government as a lawmaking body and the government as a proprietor or employer.[2]

Whatever the merits of that approach, the federal courts long ago took a different path.[3] Decisionmaking with respect to public employees differs fundamentally from employment decisionmaking in the private sector. Public employees are protected by the Constitution. Public employers act as an arm of the state in their capacity as an employer as in other areas. As a result, public employers' ability to interact with their employees is limited by the Constitution.[4]

The Due Process Clause and the Equal Protection Clause of the Fourteenth Amendment protect public employees. They are shielded by the Fourth Amendment from an invasion of their privacy interests. Public employees may sue their employers for illegal searches. They need not implicate themselves in criminal conduct as a condition of employment. Growing litigation

---

1. McAuliffe v. New Bedford, 155 Mass 216, 29 NE 517 (1892).
2. *See* discussion in G. Edward White, Justice Oliver Wendell Holmes: Law and Inner Self at 285-86 (1993).
3. "[T]he theory that public employment which may be denied altogether may be subjected to any conditions, regardless of how unreasonable, has been uniformly rejected. . . . It is too late in the day to doubt that the liberties of religion and expression may be infringed by the denial of or placing of conditions upon a benefit or privilege." Keyishian v. Board of Regents, 385 U.S. 589, 605-06 (1967).
4. Public employment is also frequently governed by civil service requirements and collective bargaining agreements under various labor laws including special public employment labor laws. For an excellent discussion of the interplay between these aspects of public employment, *see Developments in the Law—Public Employment,* 97 Harv. L. Rev. 1611 (1984).

arises out of constitutional protections for First Amendment free speech and association interests of public employees.[5] The complex analysis employed to resolve public employment disputes that center around constitutional rights provides a fertile ground for Section 1983 litigation.

Who Is a Public Employer?

Before discussing the constitutional rights of public employees, it is worthwhile to consider whether the employer is acting under color of state law so that constitutional protections come into play.[6] 42 U.S.C. § 1983[7] requires that the complained-of conduct result from state action, and state

---

5. Public employers are also limited by numerous federal and state laws which impose additional limits on the governmental employer's ability to deal with public employees. *See, e.g.*, the Whistleblower Protection Act, 5 U.S.C. § 1201; Title VII, Civil Rights Act of 1964, as amended, 43 U.S.C. 2000e -2, -3 (a); the Americans with Disabilities Act, 42 U.S.C. § 12112 (a). The requirements of these and other statutes are beyond the scope of this article. This article is limited to a discussion of civil rights available in the public sector in an action pursuant to Section 1983.
6. The question of when conduct sufficiently implicates a governmental entity or is carried out by a policymaker so that the entity may be held liable is addressed elsewhere in this book. *See generally* Owens v. City of Independence, 445 U.S. 622, 628-29 (1980) (employment decision made by city council amounted to official policy); Jett v. Dallas Indep. School District, 491 U.S. 701, 737 (1989) (decisionmaker with final policymaking authority may amount to official policy of governmental entity). It will be discussed only in passing in this article.
7. Section 1983 provides in pertinent part:

   Every person who, under color of law of any statute, ordinance, regulation, custom, or usage, of any State or Territory or the District of Columbia, subjects or causes to be subjected, any citizen of the United States or other person residing within the jurisdiction thereof to the deprivation of any rights, privileges, or immunities secured by the Constitution and laws, shall be liable to the party injured in an action at law, sued in equity, or other proper proceeding for redress.

   Section 1983 does not apply to private conduct or to actions by federal agencies or federal officials. Wheeldin v. Wheeler, 373 U.S. 647, 650 n.2 (1963). Employees bringing an action against federal agencies or officials may sue directly those allegedly responsible. Bivens v. Six Unknown Named Agents of Federal Bureau of Narcotics, 403 U.S. 388 (1971).

action can readily be found when the state is the employer.[8] The issue becomes more difficult when the employer is a private entity that works closely with the government or performs traditionally public functions.[9]

Courts analyze whether the employer performs a public function and whether the government controls the employer's employment policies on a case-by-case basis.[10] If the employer's conduct amounts to state action, it triggers constitutional protections.[11]

Although some federal courts had held that an independent contractor is not protected by the same constitutional strictures as public employees,[12] the Tenth Circuit rejected this distinction in *Umbehr v. McClure*,[13] and the Supreme Court recently affirmed its ruling.[14] First Amendment retaliation claims are now available to independent contractors.[15] The extent to which independent contractors will be protected by other constitutional rights remains for future litigation.

---

8. Local governmental entities are "persons" for 1983 purposes. Monell v. Department of Social Services, 436 U.S. 658, 663 (1978). Individuals working for such entities may be sued if they acted under color of law while engaging in the complained-of conduct. Lugar v. Edmondson Oil Co., Inc., 457 U.S. 922 (1982).
9. *See, e.g.*, Janusaitis v. Middleburg Volunteer Fire Department, 607 F.2d 17 (2d Cir. 1979) (dismissal of fireman by volunteer fire department was state action because traditionally sovereign function).
10. *See generally* Henry H. Perritt, Jr., 2 Employee Dismissal Law & Practice § 6.2, at 2-6 (3d ed. 1992).
11. For an analysis of the symbiotic relationship, government involvement, and nexus tests for state action, *see* Sheldon H. Nahmad, 1 Civil Rights & Civil Liberties: The Law of Section 1983, § 2.05, at 65-70 (3d ed. 1991). *See also* Martin A. Schwartz and John E. Kirklin, 1A Section 1983 Litigation: Claims & Defenses, at 510-88 (3d ed. 1997).
12. Triad Assoc., Inc. v. Chicago Hous. Auth., 892 F.2d 583, 588 (7th Cir. 1989), *cert. denied,* 498 U.S. 845 (1990); Horn v. Kean, 796 F.2d 668, 675-77 (3d Cir. 1986) (*en banc*).
13. 44 F.3d 876 (10th Cir. 1995).
14. Board of County Commissioners, Waubansee County v. Umbehr, 116 S. Ct. 2342 (1996).
15. O'Hare Truck Service, Inc. v. City of Northlake, 116 S. Ct. 2353 (1996). For a discussion of the cases and tips on how governments can avoid exposure, *see* T. S. Welch & B.L. Goldstein, 44 The Fed. Lawyer 38 (1997).

Due Process Rights of Public Employees

Violations of the Fourteenth Amendment can be based on the denial of procedural due process, the denial of substantive due process, or the violation of any provisions of the Bill of Rights that have been incorporated into the Fourteenth and made applicable to the states. Courts have recognized broad rights flowing from this provision.

To establish a due process claim, a plaintiff must first show that he or she was deprived of a constitutionally cognizable property or liberty interest. This issue often provides the basis for an early motion for summary judgment. Defendants try to force a litigant to define and limit the claim at an early stage of the litigation. If the case proceeds to trial, a narrow precisely defined claim is more easily understood by the jury and may provide a basis for limiting the admission of unfavorable testimony. It can assist in focusing the legal and factual issues in the case and prevent a free-floating inquiry into the wisdom of the governmental decisionmaking that gave rise to the lawsuit. Plaintiffs, on the other hand, frequently leave their claim as broad as possible so that they are not limited in the proofs at trial and can shift theories as the case proceeds without the need to seek leave to file an amended complaint.

Property Interests

Property interests are not created by the Due Process Clause of the U.S. Constitution. They arise from state law.[16]

In *Board of Regents of State Colleges v. Roth*,[17] the Supreme Court explained:

> Property interests, of course, are not created by the Constitution. Rather, they are created and their dimensions are defined by existing rules or understandings that stem from an independent source such as state law. To have a property interest and a benefit, a person clearly must have more than an abstract need or desire for it. He must have more than a unilateral expectation of it. He must, instead, have a legitimate claim of entitlement to it.[18]

---

16. Jones v. University of Central Oklahoma, 13 F.3d 361, 365 (10th Cir. 1993).
17. 408 U.S. 564 (1972).
18. 408 U.S. at 577.

The independent source of a property right may be a statute, policy, practice, regulation, or guideline.[19] State law defines the expectation or entitlement, but federal law determines whether the practice "rises to the level of a 'legitimate claim of entitlement' protected by the Due Process Clause."[20] The rules or understanding need not be formal or explicit; "agreements implied from words and conduct in the light of surrounding circumstances" may be sufficient to invoke constitutional protections.[21]

The hallmark of a protected property interest is the right to continued employment.[22] To establish a protected interest in a government job, the employee must point to a statutory or contractual right which supports a legitimate claim to continued employment.[23] Lesser rights, such as an interest in terms and conditions of employment, may not rise to the level of a constitutionally cognizable property interest.

The Third Circuit's opinion in *Portman v. County of Santa Clara*[24] illustrates the distinction between the deprivation of a benefit, which does not automatically give rise to protected property interest, and a protected form of tenure, which does. A state employee argued that he had a protected property interest in accrued sick pay and medical benefits. Despite the existence of a genuine issue of material fact as to the former employee's right to the benefits under state law, the *Portman* court concluded that the deprivation of benefits did not amount to the deprivation of constitutionally protected property interest.[25] An accumulation of sick leave and medical insurance is not a protected property interest.[26]

---

19. Bishop v. Wood, 426 U.S. 341, 347 (1976); Rivera-Muriente v. Agosta-Alice, 959 F.2d 349 (1st Cir. 1992).
20. Memphis Light, Gas & Water Div. v. Craft, 436 U.S. 1, 9 (1978).
21. Perry v. Sindermann, 408 U.S. 593, 602 (1972).
22. Shawgo v. Spradlin, 701 F.2d 470, *cert. denied,* 464 U.S. 965 (1983).
23. Bailey v. Floyd County Bd. of Education, 106 F.3d 135 (6th Cir. 1997).
24. 995 F.2d 898 (9th Cir. 1993).
25. *Portman*, 995 F.2d at 906. The *Portman* court reviewed cases from other jurisdictions. In dicta, the court suggested that while most benefits are not constitutionally protected, the entitlement to retirement or disability benefits probably is protected. *Id.*
26. Ramsey v. Board of Educ., 844 F.2d 1268 (6th Cir. 1988). *See* Henry H. Perritt, 2 Employee Dismissal Law and Practice, § 6.10, at 19-25 (3d ed. 1992). *See also* Charles v. Baesler, 910 F.2d 1349, 1353-55 (6th Cir. 1990). The Sixth Circuit's analysis is that state-created property interests are all protected by procedural due process, but substantive due process protections

Provisions that merely establish disciplinary procedures are also distinguishable from those that create a right to continued employment.[27] They do not ordinarily create a constitutionally protected property right. A deprivation of due process rights typically occurs when an employee is fired.

Courts have been hostile to claims based on other lesser employment decisions.[28] The reassignment or transfer of an employee does not ordinarily implicate a protected property interest.[29] Employees typically have no right to a particular assignment even if a transfer involves a loss of rank, status, or salary.[30] Although a constructive discharge may amount to the deprivation of a protected property interest,[31] harassing an employee may not be enough.[32] A demotion or transfer may constitute a constructive discharge, but generally an employee is not entitled to retain a specific subjectively preferred job.[33]

---

are afforded to only a more limited subset of those interests, a subset defined by federal constitutional principles. *Charles*, 910 F.2d at 1353. *See also* McKinney v. Pate, 20 F.3d 1550, 1555-58 (11th Cir. 1994), *cert. denied,* 513 U.S. 1110 (1995) (holding substantive due process rights are created by the Constitution while rights created by state law need only be protected by observing the elements of procedural due process).

27. Campbell v. City of Champion, 940 F.2d 1111 (7th Cir. 1991). The employment handbook relied upon by a public employee contained no promissory language but set forth progressive discipline procedures. Relying upon Lim v. Central DuPage Hosp., 871 F.2d 644, 648 (1989), the court held that a contract that "merely creates a right to procedure does not create a property interest within the meaning of the due process clause." *Id. See also* Campbell v. Mercer, 926 F.2d 990 (10th Cir. 1991) (only substantive restrictions on the employer's discretion are relevant to the existence of a constitutionally cognizable interest).
28. Ferraro v. City of Long Branch, 23 F.3d 803, 805-06 (3d Cir. 1994); Maples v. Martin, 858 F.2d 1546, 1550 (11th Cir. 1988); Volk v. Coler, 845 F.2d 1422, 1430 (7th Cir. 1988); Kelleher v. Flawn, 761 F.2d 1079, 1087 (5th Cir. 1985).
29. Anglemyer v. Hamilton County Hosp., 58 F.3d 533, 538-39 (10th Cir. 1995).
30. Anglemyer, 58 F.3d at 539-40. *See also* HON. HARVEY BROWN AND SARAH V. KERRIGAN, *42 U.S.C. 1983: The Vehicle for Protecting Public Employees' Constitutional Rights,* 47 BAYLOR L. REV. 619, 632-35 (1995).
31. *See, e.g.*, Bishop, 426 U.S. at 350; Rathjen v. Litchfield, 878 F.2d 836, 838 (5th Cir. 1989).
32. Lyznicki v. Board of Educ., 707 F.2d 949, 951 (7th Cir. 1983).
33. Jett v. Dallas Indep. Sch. Dist., 798 F.2d 748, 755 (5th Cir. 1986), *aff'd in part*, 491 U.S. 701 (1989).

Due process rights are not required where the public employer can demonstrate that its employee voluntarily resigned. In *Lenz v. Dewey*,[34] the Tenth Circuit held that a bank president (operating a bank under the control of state regulators) relinquished any property interest he may have had in stock ownership and a directorship of the bank's holding company by voluntarily resigning from a holding company's board. Offered the choice between resignation from the holding company board with payment of his stock or termination without stock payment, the bank president resigned. The economic compulsion inherent in the choice did not amount to a constructive discharge; the decision was voluntary and deprived the plaintiff of any actionable claim. The protected property interest may be taken away as long as the employer gives the process that is due. In contrast, substantive due process claims based on fundamental rights cannot be denied or impinged upon regardless of the procedures used.[35]

Formal Creation of a Property Interest

The strongest basis for a property interest is a right created by a statute, ordinance, or contract. Courts scrutinize the terms of these measures to see if they provide the employee with a right to continued employment. Where state law prohibits firing a public employee except for cause, courts have recognized a protected property interest, which cannot be taken away without procedural due process.[36] A unilateral expectancy of continued employment does not give rise to a constitutionally protected interest.[37]

The analysis basically tracks the approach used by many state courts in resolving wrongful termination claims. Those who work at the will of their employer may be fired without notice under traditional contract law. Those who can only be fired for a "just cause" have an enforceable contract under state law.

Federal courts conclude that at-will employees lack a right to continued employment that amounts to a protected property interest. But if they have a right to their job under state law, then the government must provide due process before they are fired.

---

34. 64 F.3d 547 (10th Cir. 1995).
35. Copeland v. Philadelphia Police Dep't, 840 F.2d 1139, 1144-48 (3d Cir. 1988), *cert. denied*, 490 U.S. 1004 (1989).
36. Cleveland Bd. of Educ. v. Loudermill, 470 U.S. 532 (1985).
37. *Bishop*, 426 U.S. at 345-47.

Frazier v. Garrison I.S.D.[38] exemplifies this protection for those with a state law right to continued employment. Teachers, discharged for failing a Texas teacher competency examination, sued claiming that the test was discriminatory and that their procedural due process rights had been violated. They argued that they had a constitutionally protected property interest in continued employment based upon contract rights under a state statute. Texas law provides a public school teacher with a "constitutionally protected property interest in continued employment if he can demonstrate a reasonable expectation of continued employment."[39] The teachers' employment contract, as defined by the Texas Education Code, provided for fixed term and continuing term contracts. The Fifth Circuit ruled that teachers employed under a fixed term contract had a protected property interest in continued employment that gave rise to due process rights.[40]

Employees frequently ground their right to continued employment on a state statute, a formal employment contract, or an informal contract created orally or by a handbook.[41] In *Bailey v. Floyd County Board of Education*, a local Head Start director raised all three of these grounds for recognizing a right to continued employment. But the court ruled that she worked at the will of the school board and thus failed to establish a protected property interest.[42]

Carter v. City of Philadelphia[43] illustrates the formal creation of a property interest by a state statute. The plaintiff, a police officer with the city of Philadelphia for over twenty years, passed a promotional examination but

---

38. 980 F.2d 1514 (5th Cir. 1993).
39. Frazier, 980 F.2d at 1529 (citations omitted).
40. The court affirmed the lower court's grant of defendant's motion for summary judgment because the teachers failed to establish that the procedures available to them to challenge their test scores and termination were constitutionally inadequate. *See also* Goodreau v. School Districts No. 37 of Oklahoma City, 923 F.2d 1429 (10th Cir. 1987) (school aide had property interest in employment since statute provided for termination only for cause); Brown v. Trench, 787 F.2d 167 (3d Cir. 1986) (county ordinance that provided for just cause termination created property interests); Perry v. Haytch, 724 F.2d 362 (3d Cir. 1983) (tenure in court job created by court personnel regulations amounted to property interest).
41. Bailey v. Floyd County Bd. of Education, 106 F.3d 135 (6th Cir. 1997).
42. 106 F.3d at 135.
43. 989 F.2d 117 (3d Cir. 1993).

was never promoted. Eight lower-ranked individuals were. The plaintiff sued claiming that he had a property interest in promotion arising out of the Pennsylvania Veterans Preference Act. The district court granted the defendants' motion to dismiss.

The Third Circuit disagreed. It held that the statute took precedence over any local laws and entitled the plaintiff to a preference when his promotion was under consideration. Because the statutory language was clear and unequivocal, the court afforded the employee constitutional protection. This conclusion runs contrary to those cases that suggest that a protected property interest may only arise with respect to continued employment. The Third Circuit did not explain this apparent expansion of procedural due process protections; it may not have been raised. But the case provides a basis for arguing that hearing rights must be afforded in cases that do not involve the right to continued employment.

Property interests may also be created by formal contracts. Two types of contracts have been found to create property interests protected by the Fourteenth Amendment.[44] The first is a contract that confers a protected status, such as a tenure contract providing for permanent employment. The second is a contract explicitly providing that the employee may be terminated only for cause.

In *Sanguigni v. Otisburg Board of Public Education*,[45] the plaintiff, a public high school teacher asserting a property interest in her coaching positions, argued that when she was removed from coaching, she was deprived of procedural due process. She claimed that the collective bargaining agreement gave her a protected property interest, but the court found that it was not a tenure contract or one for just cause employment. The court suggested that she might have fared better if she had alleged that she worked under an informal agreement providing her with tenure as coach.

A contract for a definite term, which limits termination during the term to good cause, creates a protected property interest.[46] In *Archer v. Sanchez*,[47] a university fired an employee without notice after only six months of a one-year term contract. Although the personnel manual provided that the

---

44. Sanguigni v. Otisburg Bd. of Public Educ., 968 F.2d 393 (3d Cir. 1992).
45. 968 F.2d 393 (3d Cir. 1992).
46. Archer v. Sanchez, 933 F.2d 1526 (10th Cir. 1991).
47. 933 F.2d 1526 (10th Cir. 1991).

employee served at the university president's pleasure, the plaintiff argued that the university had to provide notice and a hearing before firing him during his term. The Tenth Circuit agreed with the plaintiff because "his employment contract for a specific term is recognized under New Mexico law as a property right which cannot be taken away without some procedural protection reflecting fundamental fairness."[48]

Informal Creation of a Property Interest

A *de facto* tenure system, such as where there are "mutually explicit understandings" which include a promise of continued employment, may amount to a protected property interest.[49] These understandings have been found in policies, handbooks, or oral promises.

Difficult problems of proof may arise where the claim is based upon unwritten policies or customs. Claims based on such informal agreements require a careful analysis of state law. In the decade of the 1980s, the traditional rule permitting termination at will was whittled down extensively and riddled with exceptions.[50] In the 1990s, the balance has tipped the other way.[51] Because state law provides the basis for determining whether a protected right exists, at the outset of any procedural due process litigation, it is critical to evaluate the scope of protection afforded an employee in that state.

Despite difficulties in proving claims based on informal policies or understandings, litigation continues in this area. The Seventh Circuit, for example, considered whether a school board policy conferred a property interest in continued employment on a former high school secretary in *Hohmeier v. Leyden Community High School District 212*.[52] The secretary disputed the district court's reliance on state contract law as the only way to establish a property interest. She contended that since the government employer's policy

---

48. *Archer*, 933 F.2d at 1530.
49. *Perry*, 408 U.S. 593.
50. For a discussion of the employment at will rule, its erosion, and the current status of state law, *see* PERRITT, *supra,* note 10 at §§ 1.1 - 1.76.
51. *See, e.g.*, Rowe v. Montgomery Ward, 437 Mich. 627, 473 N.W.2d 268 (1991) *overruling* Toussaint v. Blue Cross and Blue Shield of Michigan, 408 Mich. 579 N.W.2d 880 (1980) (because the theory it had recognized was a transparent invitation to the factfinder to decide *not* what the 'contract' was, but what 'fairness' requires").
52. 954 F.2d 461 (7th Cir. 1992).

was promulgated pursuant to the school board's statutory rulemaking authority, it gave rise to constitutionally cognizable property entitlements.

The court agreed that rulemaking could give rise to an interest in continued employment. But it concluded that the rule at issue was not binding, since it did not contain explicit language making it mandatory.

An employment manual may give rise to a protected property interest if state contract law gives employees enforceable rights based upon its existence and terms. In *Cummings v. South Portland Housing Authority*,[53] for example, the First Circuit applied state law to conclude that the handbook at issue contained clear and express language to restrict the public employer's ability to discharge employees. When hired as a department head in charge of maintenance, the plaintiff was told that he had to serve a probationary period after which he would be a permanent employee and the personnel policy would govern his employment. During his probationary period, the plaintiff provided an undated letter of resignation, to be used if he failed to fulfill his responsibilities. Long after the probationary period had elapsed, his employer presented the resignation letter to the plaintiff and refused to provide a requested termination hearing.

The First Circuit held that an employee generally has a constitutionally protected property interest in continued employment "when he reasonably expects that his employment will continue."[54] At-will employment contracts do not ordinarily create a reasonable expectation of continued employment. But the employment manual contained two sections that included language creating a constitutionally protected interest. The language clearly restricted the employer's ability to terminate employees and specifically stated that all actions affecting employees would be based on merit and ability. This language in the manual entitled the plaintiff to due process procedural protections.

A litigant may claim that a custom or policy of providing a warning and a hearing before an employee is fired gives rise to a protected interest. But custom or policy will not override the terms of a statute or ordinance. *Heck v. City of Freeport*[55] represents one such case.

The plaintiff, a general inspector of the city, was appointed by the mayor with approval by the city council. He was replaced when a new

53. 985 F.2d 1 (1st Cir. 1993).
54. *Id.* at 2.
55. 985 F.2d 305 (7th Cir. 1993).

mayor took office. The Seventh Circuit rejected his claim of a property interest in continuing employment insofar as it was based on a provision regarding removal of officials under the city's municipal code because the provision pertained to removal during the term of an office and not to reappointments by a succeeding mayor. The plaintiff also argued that the city never fired anyone without a warning and a hearing. But the statutory scheme at issue in *Heck* negated a protected interest arising out of an informal custom or practice because the claimed practice was inconsistent with official law.[56]

Although the municipality in *Heck* was protected from trial by the language in its code, the case highlights the difficulties that can arise where a litigant relies on informal customs or policies. Municipalities are well-advised to check the language of their ordinances and policies to ensure that they use at-will terminology if their goal is to avoid the creation of a property interest.

Federal courts are reluctant to deviate from explicit language in a duly-enacted local ordinance or contract based upon less formal policies or agreements of a government employer. In *Campbell v. City of Champion,*[57] the plaintiff argued that a handbook's language overrode at-will language in an ordinance. Courts will generally recognize the primacy of the text of a statute or ordinance as the Seventh Circuit did in *Campbell* and *Heck.*

A promise to create a tenured position for a public employee did not create a protected property interest in *Gallegos v. City and County of Denver.*[58] The deputy manager of public works for finance administration claimed that the mayor had promised to eventually make her position a career services position with all the attendant benefits, including the job security not afforded by her non-tenured appointed position. She argued that the mayor's promise amounted to the informal creation of a property interest. Strict guidelines govern the creation of career services positions, and the record revealed no evidence that the mayor had authority to circumvent these procedures.

As a result, the Tenth Circuit held that the plaintiff lacked a legitimate claim of entitlement to the nonexistent career services position. The mayor's

---

56. *Id.* at 310-311.
57. Campbell v. City of Champion, 940 F.2d 1111 (7th Cir. 1991).
58. 984 F.2d 358 (10th Cir. 1993), *cert. denied*, 508 U.S. 972 (1993).

promise was nothing more than a future expectation or goal of the department, the breach of which was not actionable.

In *Perry v. Sindermann*,[59] the Supreme Court ruled that a *de facto* tenure system gave rise to a constitutional claim. On the same day, the Court rejected a potential claim based on the nonrenewal of a one-year term contract.[60] These rulings teach that a due process claim must be predicated on the deprivation of an expectation of continued employment, rather than a hope or expectancy. The Supreme Court's affirmance of *Vail v. Board of Education*[61] illustrates the tension between the protection of property interests in employment and the notion advocated by Judge Posner in dissent, that every breach of contract claim should not give rise to a federally litigated constitutional claim.[62]

The Seventh Circuit considered whether post-deprivation state remedies would suffice to provide whatever process was due. The *Vail* court concluded that the Supreme Court's ruling in *Parratt v. Taylor*[63] governed only where the loss of property was due to a "random and unauthorized act by a state employee."[64] The court rejected Judge Posner's suggestion that the plaintiffs' right was "just a right to a particular remedy-damages. . . ."[65] Since a state court breach of contract action was available, Judge Posner took the position that no due process deprivation had occurred.[66]

Judge Posner's view was rejected in *Vail* and later decisions by the Seventh Circuit. In *Cushing v. City of Chicago*,[67] the Seventh Circuit held that the availability of a state court contract action based on an employee's claim

---

59. 408 U.S. 564 (1982).
60. *Roth*, 408 U.S. 564.
61. 706 F.2d 1435 (7th Cir. 1983), *aff'd by an equally divided court*, 466 U.S. 377 (1984).
62. *Vail*, 706 F.2d at 1449-56.
63. 451 U.S. 527 (1981). In *Parratt*, the Supreme Court ruled that procedural due process claims arising from the random and unauthorized deprivation of a property interest may be satisfied by an adequate post-deprivation judicial remedy. The Supreme Court refined its analysis in Daniels v. Williams, 474 U.S. 327 (1986), holding that negligence was not sufficient to amount to a due process deprivation.
64. Logan v. Zimmerman, 455 U.S. 422 (1982).
65. *Vail,* 706 F.2d at 1453.
66. *Id.* at 1453-54.
67. 3 F.3d 1156 (7th Cir. 1993).

that he was entitled to medical benefits did not bar a procedural due process claim. Because the employer could readily provide a predeprivation hearing, its failure to do so gave rise to a claim. The court distinguished *Zimmerman v. Burch*,[68] because the city's refusal to pay the plaintiff's medical benefits was not random and unauthorized but allegedly resulted from a city policy.

But the availability of a state breach of contract action and its impact on due process claims remains unclear. In *McKinney v. Pate*,[69] the Eleventh Circuit reinstated a jury verdict. Two members of the panel concurred pointing out that the court's prior decisions were inconsistent with Supreme Court due process jurisprudence. These judges embraced the view that Judge Posner advocated in *Vail*, that the termination of a public employee implicated procedural not substantive due process. In their view, the termination was random and unauthorized. The court dismissed the claim because adequate state remedies were available.[70] Thereafter, in an en banc opinion, the Eleventh Circuit adopted the views of the concurrence.[71]

Practitioners should check the law in their circuit on this point. Defense counsel should consider raising the argument that adequate state post-termination remedies mandate dismissal of the due process claim.[72]

What Is Due Process re: Property Interest?

Established principles of due process require, as a prerequisite to an intentional deprivation of a protected property interest, that the government provide notice and an opportunity for a hearing. In *Cleveland Board of Education v. Loudermill*,[73] the court summarized essential "notice" and "opportunity to respond" requirement as follows:

> The opportunity to present reasons, either in person or in writing, why proposed action should not be taken is a fundamental due process requirement. The tenured public employee is entitled to

---

68. 489 U.S. 113 (1990).
69. 985 F.2d 1502 (11th Cir. 1993), *cert. denied*, 513 1110 (1995).
70. McKinney, 985 F.2d at 1507-11.
71. McKinney v. Pate, 994 F.2d 772 (11th Cir. 1993) (*en banc*). *See also* Charles v. Baesler, 910 F.2d 1349, 1353-54 (6th Cir. 1990).
72. For an in-depth discussion of the Parratt v. Taylor doctrine, *see* SCHWARTZ & KIRKLIN, *supra*, n. 11 at 361-89.
73. 470 U.S. 532 (1985).

> oral or written notice of the charges against him, an explanation of the employer's evidence, and an opportunity to present his side of the story.[74]

Emphasizing the importance of the employee's interest in retaining his or her job, the *Loudermill* court pointed out that the opportunity for the employee to present his or her side of the case was "of obvious value in reaching an accurate decision."[75]

The pretermination hearing did not need to be "elaborate."[76] The court determines its adequacy by examining the government's interest in imposing the deprivation immediately, the private interest of those affected by the government's conduct, the risk of erroneous deprivations as a result of the challenged procedures, and the probable value of additional or different procedural safeguards.[77] A public employee who is given post-termination administrative procedures must only be given oral or written notice of the charges against him or her, an explanation of the employer's evidence, and an opportunity to present his or her side of the story.[78]

When post-termination administrative procedures are available, pretermination procedures function only as an initial check against mistaken decisions to determine whether there are reasonable grounds to believe the charges against the employee are true and support the proposed action. The pretermination process need not resolve the propriety of the discharge.[79] By recognizing that less than a full-blown pretermination hearing was adequate for due process purposes, the Supreme Court struck a balance between an employee's interest in retaining employment and presenting her side of the story, and the public employer's interest in quickly removing an unsatisfactory employee.[80]

This minimal pretermination process differs from the more complete procedural safeguards required in a judicial proceeding.[81] The right to call

---

74. *Loudermill*, 470 U.S. at 546.
75. *Id.* at 543.
76. *Id.* at 546. *See* Mathews v. Eldridge, 424 U.S. 319 (1976).
77. Mathews, 424 U.S. at 335.
78. *Loudermill*, 470 U.S. at 546.
79. *See* Linton v. Fredrick County Bd. of County Comm'rs, 964 F.2d 1436 (4th Cir. 1992).
80. *Loudermill*, 470 U.S. at 546.
81. Fred S. Friendly, *Some Kind of Hearing*, 123 V. Pa. L. Rev. 1267 (1975).

witnesses and present evidence, the right to counsel, an unbiased tribunal, a record of the evidence, the right to cross-examine adverse witnesses, and other procedural protections for decisionmaking may ultimately be required at a post-termination hearing.[82]

Numerous federal courts have considered whether the process provided to an employee meets the *Loudermill* standard. A sample of these opinions confirms that the requirements for a pretermination hearing are minimal.[83] That being the case, public employers should consider treating all public sector discharges as ones requiring due process.

In *Duchesne v. Williams*,[84] the Sixth Circuit explained that the right of reply hearing is intended to invoke the discretion of the decisionmaker. The hearing may satisfy the requirements of due process although the decisionmaker participated in the investigation or the decision to fire the employee.[85]

In *Vukadinovich v. Board of School Trustees of the Michigan City Area Schools*,[86] a teacher sued the school board claiming that the circumstances surrounding his termination violated his constitutional right to procedural due process. After being notified that the board would consider canceling his employment contract, the teacher formally requested a hearing. The school board's private attorney presided over the hearing without objection and made rulings concerning the admissibility of evidence, but did not act as a prosecutor for the school administration or participate in the school board's deliberations. During the hearing, both the school administration and the teacher presented evidence, questioned witnesses, and argued their respective positions.

The Tenth Circuit rejected the teacher's complaint that the hearing was conducted by the school board's attorney and held that the plaintiff failed to overcome the presumption of honesty and integrity attributed to those who serve as adjudicators. The court followed the Supreme Court's holding in

---

82. Schaper v. City of Huntville, 813 F.2d 709, 716 (5th Cir. 1987); Wells v. Dallas Indep. Sch. Dist., 793 F.2d 679, 683 (5th Cir. 1986).
83. *See, e.g.*, Delahoussaye v. City of New Iberia, 937 F.2d 144, 151 (5th Cir. 1991).
84. 849 F.2d 1004 (6th Cir. 1988) (*en banc*).
85. Myrick v. City of Dallas, 810 F.2d 1382, 1387 (5th Cir. 1987); Brasslett v. Cota, 761 F.2d 827, 837 (1st Cir. 1985); Vanelli v. Reynolds Sch. Dist. No. 7, 667 F.2d 773, 780 n. 10 (9th Cir. 1982).
86. 978 F.2d 403 (7th Cir. 1992), *cert. denied*, 114 S. Ct. 133 (1993).

Withrow v. Larkin,[87] a case in which the court held that performing dual roles in an adjudicative setting does not, without more, violate due process. [88]

Because the pretermination hearing is not an "adjudication," the decisionmaker need not be impartial.[89] Post-termination adversary-trial type hearings are available to ferret out bias, pretext, deception, or corruption that may have caused the complained-of decision. Post-termination hearings can be state judicial proceedings, collective bargaining grievance procedures, or arbitration hearings.[90] But a biased post-termination proceeding is not constitutionally adequate.[91] Nor does subsequent review of post-termination proceedings cure the defect.[92]

Although it is safer to provide a hearing in person, courts have approved notice and a hearing by memo. In *Williams v. Texas Tech Univ. Health Sciences Center*,[93] the court found that a former public employee received the minimal process required when he was informed in writing of the complaints against him, had the opportunity and did respond. In this case, a tenured professor in charge of research in the department of surgery was compensated by salary and fringe benefits, a portion of which came from an income plan for faculty members. The department's chair decided that the professor had not generated enough grant money and notified him that funds from the income plan would no longer be available to him.

The Fifth Circuit ruled that the professor had received the requisite procedural protection. The record revealed that the department chair had sent the plaintiff a memo warning that he would not receive funds from the income plan and the plaintiff had responded. The minimal process required by *Mathews v. Eldridge*[94] had been satisfied.[95]

---

87. 421 U.S. 35 (1975).
88. *Id. See also Myrick*, 810 F.2d at 1387.
89. Walker v. City of Berkeley, 951 F.2d 182, 183 (9th Cir. 1991). *See also* Hicks v. City of Watonga, 942 F.2d 737, 746 (10th Cir. 1991).
90. *See, e.g.*, Maples v. Martin, 858 F.2d 1546, 1551 (11th Cir. 1988); Lewis v. Hillsborough Transit Auth., 726 F.2d 668 (11th Cir. 1984), *cert. denied*, 469 U.S. 822 (1984); Archuleta v. Colorado Dept. of Institutions, Div. of Youth Services, 936 F.2d 483 (10th Cir. 1991).
91. Clements v. Airport Authority of Washoe County, 69 F.3d 321, 333 (9th Cir. 1995).
92. 69 F.3d 321.
93. 6 F.3d 290 (5th Cir. 1993), *cert. denied*, 510 U.S. 1194 (1994).
94. 424 U.S. 319 (1976).
95. *Williams,* 6 F.3d at 293.

The Eighth Circuit also approved a notification by letter that was coupled with the opportunity for a response. In *Simons v. City of Grand Forks*,[96] the plaintiff sued after he was dismissed from his position as city assessor. Before his termination, the plaintiff received a letter from the mayor stating that he was considering recommendations made by the civil service commission as a result of grievances filed against the plaintiff. The plaintiff responded to this letter as requested by the mayor. He then received a termination letter which listed eight reasons for the termination and advised the plaintiff of his right to post-termination review.[97]

The sole issue on appeal was whether the pretermination procedure satisfied due process. The court concluded that it did.[98] The mayor's letter provided clear written notice to the plaintiff of the allegations and afforded him complete access to all evidence used in making the decision. The court found that the plaintiff had ample time to present his side and eventually responded in writing to the allegations. As a result, dismissal of the procedural due process claims was appropriate.

A thirty-minute meeting with a supervisor may be enough to satisfy the requirements of due process. In *Browning v. City of Odessa, Texas*,[99] a firefighter with an exemplary record until he experienced personal problems with a co-worker was fired. After the assistant fire chief recommended that the plaintiff be terminated, the fire chief told the firefighter of the circumstances that led to the dismissal recommendation and allowed him to respond. After this hearing, the firefighter was demoted and placed on probation. He was then discharged because he protested and refused to return to work.

The Sixth Circuit pointed out that the fire chief had notified the plaintiff of the proposed termination, discussed the reasons, and allowed plaintiff to present any arguments in his favor. Even though the meeting between the fire chief and the firefighter lasted for only thirty minutes, nothing more was required since the plaintiff had the option of a full evidentiary post-termination hearing. He failed to exercise this option, a choice that the court took into account when it ruled.

---

96. 985 F.2d 981 (8th Cir. 1993).
97. *Williams*, 985 F.2d at 982.
98. *Id.* at 983.
99. 990 F.2d 842 (6th Cir. 1993).

Although a minimal pretermination hearing is generally required, courts have occasionally approved discharges with no pretermination hearing. If an important governmental interest is at stake, a substantial assurance exists that the deprivation is not baseless or unwarranted, and a need for prompt action justifies postponing the hearing, a post-termination hearing may suffice. *Ambus v. Granite Board of Education*[100] illustrates this situation. A tenured teacher at a high school was terminated with no notice or hearing after the school board became aware that the teacher had been arrested for distributing marijuana. The teacher claimed he was deprived of his right to procedural due process and argued that a post-termination procedure was insufficient.

Relying upon *FDIC v. Mellen,*[101] the Tenth Circuit approved the school board's procedure. The school board presented substantial evidence that, before suspending the teacher, the assistant superintendent had verified that the teacher had indeed been arrested on drug charges. Because an arrest and the filing of charges by the government requires probable cause, the school had a sufficient basis for a temporary deprivation of a property interest without a prior hearing. The court held that the substantiated knowledge that the teacher had been arrested for drug sales raised a substantial government interest justifying immediate suspension without pay. The plaintiff had been notified before the suspension and was informally provided with an opportunity to correct any erroneous information on which the suspension and subsequent termination was based.

While the lack of a pretermination hearing was approved in *Ambus*, this represents the exception and not the rule. *Loudermill* itself suggests some hearing is required before the employee is fired.[102] But in rare circumstances, the Supreme Court has now held that an employee is not entitled under the Due Process Clause to notice and a hearing before a suspension without pay when the government has an interest in immediate suspension and there are reasonable grounds to support it.[103] In *Gilbert v. Homar,*[104] the Court considered a state university employee's claim. The employee had been arrested and charged with possession of marijuana, possession with intent to deliver,

100. 975 F.2d 1555 (10th Cir. 1992).
101. 486 U.S. 230, 240 (1988).
102. *Loudermill,* 470 U.S. at 544-45.
103. Gilbert v. Homar, 117 S. Ct. 1807 (1997).
104. *Id.*

and criminal conspiracy to violate the controlled substances law. When the state police notified the employee's supervisor, he was suspended without pay. Although the criminal charges were later dismissed, the state university continued with its own investigation, met with the employee to hear his version of the story, and ultimately demoted him.

The Court specifically declined to decide whether a discipline short of termination gave rise to a protected property interest since the point was not contested.[105] The Court applied the *Loudermill* test to balance the government's interest in immediate action in response to the serious charges against the lesser risk from a suspension rather than a termination. The Court found that when an independent third party has determined there is probable cause to believe that the employee committed a serious crime, the need for a hearing lessens. *Gilbert* confirms the *Ambus* court's reasoning and recognizes an exception to the pretermination hearing requirement if the employee has been indicted or arrested and formally charged with a crime. Government employers should continue to be cautious in firing someone without a hearing, though. Even if the deprivation is ultimately approved, the lack of constitutionally adequate procedures supports an award of nominal damages.[106]

Liberty Interests

The U.S. Supreme Court first recognized a liberty interest in employment in the case of *Meyer v. Nebraska*,[107] where it established "the rights of an individual . . . to engage in any of the common occupations of life."[108] The Supreme Court expanded this notion to give rise to a protected liberty interest. In *Easton v. Sundram*,[109] the Second Circuit explained:

> In *Paul v. Davis*, 424 U.S. 693, 701, 96 S. Ct. 1155, 1170, 47 L. Ed. 2d 405 (1976), the Supreme Court held that "reputation alone, apart from some more tangible interests such as employment, is [n]either 'liberty' [n]or 'property' by itself sufficient to invoke the procedural protection of the Due Process Clause."

---

105. *Id.* at 1811.
106. Knudson v. City of Ellensburg, 832 F.2d 1142, 1149 (9th Cir. 1987).
107. 262 U.S. 390 (1923).
108. *Id.* at 399.
109. 947 F.2d 1011 (2d Cir. 1991), *cert. denied*, 504 U.S. 911 (1992).

* * *

> Our cases have interpreted *Paul* to mean that some 'stigma plus' is required to establish a constitutional deprivation.[110]

To qualify as a liberty interest, and thus invoke the procedural guarantees contained in the Due Process Clause, "a right or status previously recognized by state law [must be] distinctly altered or extinguished" by state action.[111] To establish a deprivation of a liberty interest without due process of law, a public employee must show: 1) a false statement 2) of a stigmatizing nature 3) attending his or her discharge 4) made public 5) by the governmental employer 6) without a meaningful opportunity for an employee name clearing hearing.[112]

The concept of liberty protected by the Due Process Clause has long included occupational liberty, which has been defined as "the liberty to follow a trade, profession or other calling."[113] The courts have not recognized a substantive right not to be stigmatized, but a liberty interest preventing stigmatization without procedural protections.[114] Injury to reputation alone is not protected.[115]

The courts have consistently drawn a distinction between occupational liberty and the right to a specific job. The Supreme Court has noted that "[I]t stretches the concept too far to suggest that a person is deprived of 'liberty' when he simply is not rehired in one job but remains as free as before to seek another."[116] It is the liberty to pursue a calling or occupation, and not the right to a specific job, that is secured by the Fourteenth Amendment.[117]

Defamation that is incident to the government's refusal to re-employ an individual can implicate a liberty interest. A liberty interest is involved if "(1) the individual's good name, reputation, honor or integrity are at stake by such charges as immorality, dishonesty, alcoholism, disloyalty, communism or subversive acts or (2) the State imposes a stigma or other

---

110. *Easton*, 947 at 1016.
111. *Paul*, 424 U.S. at 711.
112. Warren v. Crawford, 927 F.2d 559, 565 (11th Cir. 1991).
113. Wroblewski v. City of Washburn, 965 F.2d 452, 455 (7th Cir. 1992).
114. Wells v. Doland, 711 F.2d 670, 676 (5th Cir. 1983).
115. *Paul*, 424 U.S. 693.
116. *Roth,* 408 U.S. at 5775.
117. Lawson v. Sheriff of Tippecanoe County, 725 F.2d 1136, 1138 (7th Cir. 1984).

disability on the individual which forecloses other opportunities."[118] Liberty is not infringed when the individual is only somewhat less attractive to some other employers, as through a label of incompetence or poor management skills.[119] To be actionable, there must be permanent exclusion from or protracted interruption of employment.[120]

Stigmatizing information must be equivalent to charges of "dishonesty or immorality" that might seriously damage an employee's reputation.[121] Charges that carry the stigma of moral turpitude may implicate a liberty interest, but charges of incompetence or inability to get along with others do not.[122]

In *Hyland v. Wonder*,[123] the court held that the employer's statement to the press regarding a volunteer's ability to work as a peace officer was not egregious enough to give rise to due process protection. The court emphasized that these were not charges of immorality or dishonesty that could "cripple an individual's ability to earn a living."[124] Other cases have made it clear that statements that the terminated employee was overpaid do not rise to the level of those that implicate a liberty interest,[125] and statements that the employee had poor work habits, was incompetent, or inefficient are insufficient to amount to stigma.[126]

Public disclosure of the allegedly stigmatizing information is usually required. The Seventh Circuit opinion in *Johnson v. Martin*[127] is illustrative of this rule. A probationary police officer was required to provide a urine sample for drug testing. The results of the officer's test showed

---

118. *Wroblewski*, *supra*, at 456 quoting Perry v. FBI, 781 F.2d 1294, 1300 (7th Cir. 1986).
119. *Id.* quoting Munson v. Friske, 754 F.2d 683, 693 (7th Cir. 1985).
120. *Id.*
121. Russillo v. Scarborough, 935 F.2d 1167 (10th Cir. 1991).
122. Wheaton v. Webb-Petette, 931 F.2d 613 (9th Cir. 1991).
123. 972 F.2d 1129 (9th Cir. 1992), *cert. denied*, 508 U.S. 908 (1993).
124. *Hyland*, 972 F.2d at 1142.
125. Erickson v. Pierce County, 960 F.2d 801 (9th Cir. 1992), *cert. denied*, 506 U.S. 1035 (1992).
126. *See*, *e.g.*, Russillo v. Scarborough, 935 F.2d 1167, 1172 (10th Cir. 1991); Munson v. Friske, 754 F.2d 683, 693 (7th Cir. 1985); Erickson, 960 F.2d 801; Mitchell v. Glover, 996 F.2d 164, 167 (7th Cir. 1993); Stritzl v. United States Postal Serv., 602 F.2d 249, 252 (10th Cir. 1979).
127. 943 F.2d 15 (7th Cir. 1991).

positive for the presence of drugs. Following disciplinary proceedings in which the plaintiff denied using drugs, he was fired. The police officer sued claiming that the police department's actions discharging him and placing the information in his personnel file damaged his reputation in the community. He claimed his constitutionally protected liberty interest in his reputation was violated.

The Seventh Circuit held that the police officer could not prove public disclosure of the allegedly stigmatizing information. The officer conceded that the drug test results had not been disseminated to any potential future employer. He argued, however, that the stigmatizing information contained in his personnel file "will as a matter of logic and common sense have an adverse effect on . . . [his] ability to obtain future employment in the field of law enforcement as well as other areas."[128] The police officer relied on a Second Circuit case, *Brandt v. Board of Coop. Education Serv.*,[129] in which the court held that the public disclosure requirement of constitutional defamation is satisfied if a litigant shows that stigmatizing information is placed in his or her personnel file.

In rejecting this conclusion, the Seventh Circuit relied upon the Supreme Court's decision in *Bishop v. Wood*.[130] The Supreme Court explained that if the reasons for the discharge have not been made public, the communication "cannot properly form the basis for a claim that petitioner's interest in his 'good name, reputation, honor, or integrity' was thereby impaired."[131]

The mere reporting of defamatory accusations of a third party does not make a governmental agency or official liable for the deprivation of a protected liberty interest. In *Melton v. City of Oklahoma,*[132] a police officer, discharged after being accused of perjury in a departmental criminal investigation, argued that the publication of two stories in which the city quoted others had violated his liberty interest. The stories revealed accusations of perjury made against the officer by the FBI. The mere reporting of defama-

---

128. *Johnson*, 943 F.2d at 16.
129. 820 F.2d 41 (2d Cir. 1987).
130. 426 U.S. 341 (1976). *See also* Simpkins v. Sandwich Community Hosp., 854 F.2d 215 (7th Cir. 1988) (employee accused of improper recordkeeping regarding drugs; charges not made public so no liberty interest implicated). *But see* Burris v. Willis Indep. Sch. Dist., Inc., 713 F.2d 1087, 1092 (5th Cir. 1983).
131. *Bishop*, 426 U.S. at 348.
132. 928 F.2d 920 (10th Cir. 1991), *cert. denied*, 502 U.S. 906 (1991).

tory accusations of others is not enough to make the government employer liable. If the governmental entity overtly or impliedly adopts the defamatory accusation as the basis for its actions, the result might differ. In *Melton*, the statements attributed to the supervisor and published in the press did not stigmatize the officer because nothing that the supervisor reported was false. The supervisor neither accepted the FBI accusation of perjury as truth nor did he himself accuse the plaintiff of perjury. He accurately recounted a third party's statements.

A temporal relation between the remark and the termination is required. Thus, the Seventh Circuit concluded that a remark made long after the former employee's discharge did not violate any liberty interest.[133] Likewise, the First Circuit held that a defamatory remark made well after the discharge failed to implicate a liberty interest in employment.[134]

The Second Circuit agreed with this approach in *Salpaugh v. Monroe Community Hospital*.[135] The court held that the trial court had improperly dismissed the plaintiff's claim that her liberty interest had been violated by comments made to a prospective employer. The Second Circuit criticized the district court for failing to determine whether the statements were made during the termination process, which would amount to a protected liberty interest, or after the plaintiff was terminated, in which case there would not be a protected liberty interest.

What Is Due Process re: Liberty Interest?

If a court finds that the statements were sufficiently stigmatizing to give rise to a protected liberty interest, then the public employee is entitled to due process. In *Board of Regents v. Roth*,[136] the U.S. Supreme Court held that the hearing necessary to protect an employee's liberty interest is one that provides the person with "an opportunity to clear his name."[137] The hearing to provide the plaintiff with an opportunity to clear his name need not be separate from the hearing provided before depriving the plaintiff of a property interest.

---

133. Sudeikis v. Chicago Transit Authority, 774 F.2d 766 (7th Cir. 1985).
134. Laureano-Agosto v. Garcia Caraballo, 731 F.2d 101 (1st Cir. 1984).
135. 4 F.3d 134 (2d Cir. 1993), *cert. denied*, 510 U.S. 1164 (1994).
136. 408 U.S. 564 (1972).
137. *Roth*, 408 U.S. at 573, n.12.

In *Schleck v. Ramsey County*,[138] the court held that the pretermination hearing under *Loudermill*[139] was sufficient to protect both interests. In *Schleck*, the plaintiffs were offered an extensive post-termination hearing, but it was never conducted because they declined to avail themselves of the opportunity. Based upon the plaintiffs' failure to accept the offer of a hearing, the court concluded that there was no violation of due process rights.

There is no need for hearing if the statements or charges have been admitted by the plaintiff.[140] But otherwise the employee is entitled to a public hearing at which to clear his name.[141] If provided upon the request of the public employee, a name clearing hearing can cure the violation.[142] If the employee retains his position, "the only claim of stigma he has derives from the injury to his reputation. . . . "[143] By itself, this is not enough to state a claim.[144] But the loss of employment coupled with stigmatizing statements, absent an opportunity to clear the employee's name, amounts to the deprivation of a liberty interest.[145] If the employee insists on a public hearing at which the charges are disseminated, then the employer is not responsible for the public dissemination of the information.[146]

Substantive Due Process

The scope and parameters of a substantive due process claim in the public employment context are unclear. Federal courts have been reluctant to recognize substantive due process claims if a specifically delineated constitutional right exists.[147] In a plurality opinion, the Supreme Court em-

---

138. 939 F.2d 638 (8th Cir. 1991).
139. *Loudermill*, 470 U.S. 532.
140. *See* Codd v. Velger, 429 U.S. 624 (1977).
141. Rosenstein v. City of Dallas, 876 F.2d 392, 396 n. 8 (5th Cir. 1989); Chilingirian v. Boris, 882 F.2d 200, 205-06 (6th Cir. 1989).
142. Arrington v. County of Dallas, 970 F.2d 1441, 1447 (5th Cir. 1992).
143. Paul v. Davis, 424 U.S. 693 (1976).
144. Schultea v. Wood, 27 F.3d 1112, 1117 (5th Cir. 1994).
145. *Id.*
146. Campos v. Giullot, 743 F.2d 1123 (5th Cir. 1984).
147. *See* Albright v. Oliver, 510 U.S. 266, 270-75 (1994). Albright arose in the context of a malicious prosecution claim but the analysis applies equally to the employment setting.

phasized the open-ended nature of substantive due process and concluded that the more specific constitutional provision should be employed to provide the rule of decision.[148] Yet substantive due process claims have been raised on the basis of arbitrary conduct or where government policies interfere with fundamental rights.

It is important to carefully analyze the basis for the claim. Conduct challenged as arbitrary is subject to a rational basis test, an approach that should make it easy for the government to prevail. Conduct challenged because it interferes with a fundamental right is subject to strict scrutiny, an approach that is much more helpful to the plaintiff.

Government employees may have a constitutional interest in personal appearance.[149] *Pence v. Rosenquist*[150] illustrates this principle. The *Pence* court held that school officials lacked any rational basis for refusing to let a person with a mustache, no matter how neatly trimmed, drive a school bus.[151] The record failed to show that the "plaintiff's mustache negatively affected his driving skills, or relationship with his passengers, nor that it tended to generate any kind of problem which endangered their health or safety."[152] The policy was, therefore, so irrational that it was arbitrary in a constitutional sense.[153] The *Pence* court rejected the notion that a government employee's liberty interest in his or her choice of personal appearance was so insignificant as to preclude a claim.[154]

But if the government can show some reason for its regulations, they will be upheld. In *Lowman v. Davis*, the Eighth Circuit upheld a hair length regulation against a challenge that it lacked a rational basis. The state park management grounded the hair-length requirement in its need to make members of the park management team more identifiable to the public, make it more likely that park officials would be obeyed, and promote an esprit de

148. *Id.*
149. Lowman v. Davies, 704 F.2d 1044 (8th Cir. 1983).
150. 573 F.2d 395 (7th Cir. 1978).
151. *Pence*, 573 F.2d at 398.
152. *Id.*
153. *Id.* at 399.
154. The *Pence* court withdrew the holding of a prior case rejecting such claims, Miller v. School District Number 167, Cook County, Ill., 495 F.2d 658 (7th Cir. 1974), in favor of a rule providing for case by case evaluation of the rational relationship between the government policy and claimed public purpose. *Pence*, 573 F.2d at 399-401.

corps among team members.[155] The *Lowman* court accepted the proffered reasons over a strong dissent which pointed to the absence of logical or factual support for a connection between the regulation and the stated goals.[156]

Likewise, in *Tardif v. Quinn*[157] the school's termination of a nontenured high school teacher for wearing too-short skirts survived a challenge on constitutional grounds. The court affirmed the lower court's ruling emphasizing its narrow scope of review.[158]

These cases stand as a warning to attorneys representing government defendants to provide support for challenged regulations. The government needs to point to a legitimate interest and demonstrate that the regulation furthers the interest.

A claimed fundamental right to privacy has sometimes been the basis for a constitutional challenge. *Sullivan v. Meade Independent School District No. 101*[159] involved an unmarried teacher's challenge of the school board for firing her because she lived with a person of the opposite sex. The Eighth Circuit ducked the constitutional issue but found that the school board had acted in good faith. Since a mistake in judgment fails to demonstrate a substantive due process violation, the court refused to award any damages.[160] The teacher did not seek reinstatement so there was no need to resolve the constitutional issue.

Substantive due process claims have more typically been predicated on fundamental rights, such as the right to marry.[161] Despite the potential to affect the right to marry, several federal circuits have approved municipal anti-nepotism policies. *Waters v. Gaston County, N.C.*,[162] illustrates this line of cases. In *Waters*, county employees who sought to marry in violation of an anti-nepotism policy challenged the county by contending that

---

155. *Lowman*, 704 F.2d at 1046.
156. *Id.* at 1047-48.
157. 545 F.2d 761 (1976).
158. *Tardif,* 545 F.2d at 763-64.
159. 530 F.2d 799 (8th Cir. 1976).
160. *Sullivan*, 530 F.2d at 808-09.
161. *See, e.g.*, Littlejohn v. Rose, 768 F.2d 765, 769-72 (6th Cir. 1985), *cert. denied,* 475 U.S. 1045 (1986) (denial of public employment because of involvement in constitutionally protected behavior such as decision to seek a divorce states a claim).
162. 57 F.3d 422 (4th Cir. 1995).

the policy intruded on their constitutional right to marry.[163] The policy prohibited employees from marrying each other if they were employed in the same division or unit or if one had supervisory authority over the other.[164]

The *Waters* court acknowledged that the policy affected the marriage; the Seventh Circuit nevertheless reasoned that it did not forbid marriage altogether or require permission of the government to marry.[165] Fundamental rights were not therefore involved. The policy passed constitutional muster under a rational basis test since it fostered workplace goals such as avoiding conflicts between work and family obligations, reducing favoritism, limiting interoffice dating, and decreasing the likelihood of sexual harassment in the workplace.[166]

Occasionally, courts have considered substantive due process claims arising in other circumstances. In *McWilliams v. Fairfax County Board of Supervisors*,[167] the Fourth Circuit analyzed an employee's claim that he suffered physical assaults during his co-workers' sexual harassment of him. The court acknowledged that the complained-of conduct "sufficed to support a finding that he suffered constitutional injury" under the substantive due process clause's "protection against unreasonable bodily intrusions by state actors."[168]

The claim fell, however, when the record failed to support a finding that the unwelcome conduct was authorized or tacitly allowed by the municipal employer or its supervisors.[169] The court also rejected a failure to train theory since the record included no proof of a pattern of such conduct or evidence to show specific deficiencies in the training that caused the misconduct.[170]

While it remains difficult to prevail on substantive due process claims, particularly in the public employment context, the theory should not be

---

163. *Waters,* 57 F.3d at 424.
164. *Id.*
165. *Id.* at 426.
166. *Id.* at 426-27. *See also* Parks v. City of Warner Robins, Ga., 43 F.3d 609, 613-15 (11th Cir. 1995); Shawgo v. Spradlin, 701 F.2d 470, 482-83, *cert. denied*, 464 U.S. 965 (5th Cir. 1983); Wright v. Metrohealth Medical Center, 58 F.3d 1130, 1134-38 (6th Cir. 1995), *cert. denied*, 116 S. Ct. 1041 (1996); Parsons v. County of Del Norte, 728 F.2d 1234 (9th Cir.), *cert. denied*, 469 U.S. 846 (1984).
167. 72 F.3d 1191 (4th Cir.), *cert. denied*, 117 S. Ct. 72 (1996).
168. *McWilliams*, 72 F.3d at 1197.
169. *Id.*
170. *Id.* at 1197-98.

overlooked. Adding a substantive due process claim may allow for broader discovery and, if not dismissed before trial, allows the plaintiff to argue that the government defendant was arbitrary and unreasonable in its conduct. Since juries tend to be more concerned with the fairness of the government employer's action than with technical legal requirements, this can be very helpful to the plaintiff.

First Amendment Claims

In the employment setting, the First Amendment right to the expression of individual opinion has created both practical problems and doctrinal difficulties. Courts have struggled to balance the government employer's need for efficiency, workplace discipline, harmony, and productivity with the traditional tolerance of "verbal tumult, discord, and even offensive utterance," as "necessary side effects of . . . the process of open debate" that is protected by the Constitution.[171] The Supreme Court has recognized that "when an employee counsels her co-workers to do their job in a way with which the public employer disagrees, her managers may tell her to stop, rather than relying on counter-speech."[172] Yet, the Court recognizes the value of protecting government employees who seek to participate in public debate.

The tension between these overarching themes has led to shifts in approach, balancing tests, and a reluctance to make rulings that intrude too far into the workplace. The rules tend to be narrow and fact-based. Judge Easterbrook acknowledged the difficult choices foisted upon government employers for whom "taking *any* action" may be risky.[173] The scope of First Amendment protections for public employees represents an area of increasing litigation. Courts continue to elaborate upon the constitutional protections to be afforded to public sector workers under the First Amendment and to expand the actionable theories.

The protection of government employees' free speech rights can be traced to *Keyishian v. Board of Regents*,[174] where the Court held that even if a public employee could be fired without cause, the right to free expression

171. Cohen v. California, 403 U.S. 15, 24-25 (1971).
172. Waters v. Churchill, 511 U.S. 661 (1994).
173. Walsh v. Ward, 991 F.2d 1344 (7th Cir. 1993).
174. 385 U.S. 589 (1967).

could not be infringed by the denial of or placing of conditions on a benefit or privilege.[175] *Keyishian* represented the culmination of a line of cases decided during the Cold War and involving government efforts to require loyalty oaths from all public employees.[176] The Supreme Court stepped in to prevent government employers from proceeding with efforts to search out suspected communists by delving into their political activities and ordering public workers to pay political obeisance to the government.

A public employer may not discharge an employee on a basis that infringes constitutionally protected speech or associations. In bringing a case based on the violation of a public employee's First Amendment rights, the terminated employee must establish that the conduct at issue was entitled to constitutional protection.[177] The employee must then prove that the constitutionally protected conduct was substantial or a motivating factor behind the termination.[178] The employer may then show by a preponderance of the evidence that it would have made the decision to terminate even if the employee had not engaged in the protected conduct.[179] The premise underlying the causation rule is that the "constitutional principle at stake is sufficiently vindicated if . . . [the] employee is placed in no worse a position than if he had not engaged in the conduct."[180]

Often, litigation over the employee's First Amendment rights arises in the context of whether a defendant is entitled to qualified immunity.[181] Un-

---

175. *Keyishian*, 385 U.S. at 606.

176. *See, e.g.*, Garner v. Board of Public Works of Los Angeles, 341 U.S. 716 (1951) (upholding ordinance requiring employees to take a loyalty oath and sign an affidavit disclosing whether they had ever been a member of the Communist Party); Adler v. Board of Education, 342 U.S. 485 (1952) (upholding statute making membership in a subversive group a basis for denying employment to public school teachers); Wieman v. Updegraff, 344 U.S. 183 (1952) (holding state employees could not be required to take an oath that they have not innocently associated with subversive groups); Shelton v. Tucker, 364 U.S. 479 (1960) (striking down ordinance that required teachers to disclose every organization to which they had belonged during preceding five years).

177. Mount Healthy City School Dist. Board of Education v. Doyle, 429 U.S. 274, 287 (1977); Erickson v. Pierce County, 960 F.2d 801 (9th Cir. 1992); Garrett v. Barnes, 961 F.2d 629 (7th Cir. 1992).

178. Mount Healthy, 429 U.S. at 287.

179. *Id.*

180. *Id.* at 286.

181. *See, e.g.*, Stough v. Gallagher, 967 F.2d 1523 (11th Cir. 1992); Click v. Cope-

der this analysis, the court must determine whether the government official's conduct violated "clearly established statutory or constitutional rights of which a reasonable person would have known."[182] These cases may be helpful in interpreting the scope of First Amendment rights.

Freedom of Speech

A state or other governmental entity cannot condition public employment on a basis that infringes on the employee's constitutionally protected interest in freedom of expression.[183] The employee's right to freedom of speech is not absolute. To determine whether a public employer has infringed upon an employee's protected right of free speech, the court applies a multi-level analysis. The court must decide, as a matter of law, whether the speech at issue touches on a matter of public concern.[184] To determine this, the court looks to the time, place, and manner of the speech in question.[185]

If the speech addresses a matter of public concern, the court applies the *Pickering* balancing test, to weigh the interest of the employee "as a citizen, commenting upon matters of public concern," against the "interest of the state, as an employer, in promoting the efficiency of the public services it performs through its employees."[186] If the employee's interest in making the statement outweighs the state's interest, then the employee bears the burden of proving that speech was a motivating factor in the employment decision.[187]

If the employee satisfies this burden, then the employer must prove by a preponderance of the evidence that it would have reached the same deci-

---

land. 970 F.2d 106 (5th Cir. 1992); Pounds v. Griepenstroh, 970 F.2d 338 (7th Cir. 1992), *cert. denied,* 507 U.S. 910 (1993); DiMarco v. Rome Hosp. and Murphy Memorial Hosp., 952 F.2d 661 (2d Cir. 1992); Meyers v. City of Cincinnati, 979 F.2d 1154 (6th Cir. 1992); Burns v. County of Cambria, 971 F.2d 1015 (3d Cir. 1992) *cert. denied* 506 U.S. 1081 (1993).

182. Stough v. Gallagher, 967 F.2d 1523, 1525 (11th Cir. 1992) (quoting Harlow v. Fitzgerald, 457 U.S. 800, 818 (1982)).
183. Pickering v. Board of Education, 391 U.S. 563 (1968); Perry v. Sindermann, 408 U.S. 593 (1972); Rankin v. McPherson, 483 U.S. 378 (1987).
184. *Rankin*, 483 U.S. at 384; Connick v. Meyers, 461 U.S. 138 (1983).
185. 483 U.S. at 384-85.
186. *Pickering*, 391 U.S. at 568.
187. *Mount Healthy,* 429 U.S. 274.

sion in the absence of the protected conduct.[188] In conducting this analysis, the focus should be on what the employer thought was said and not on what the trier of fact ultimately determines to have been said.[189]

Matter of Public Concern

It is well settled that persons do not relinquish their First Amendment rights to comment on matters of public interest by becoming government employees.[190] Generally, speech is not protected if it is merely the airing of a personal grievance. The court will analyze the content, form, and context of the given statement to determine whether it could "be fairly considered as relating to any matter of political, social or other concern to the community."[191] If, however, the speech is of general interest, on topics such as disclosure of public officials' wrongdoing or waste and inefficiency of the particular governmental entity, it will likely be considered a matter of public concern. In applying the "content, form, and context" analysis, the Supreme Court has directed courts to consider whether the speech at issue was made in the employee's role as citizen or as employee.

> [W]hen a public employee speaks, not as a citizen upon matters of public concern, but instead as an employee upon matters only of personal interest, absent the most unusual circumstances, a federal court is not the appropriate forum in which to review the wisdom of a personnel decision taken by a public agency allegedly in reaction to the employee's behavior.
>
> * * *
>
> Whether an employee's speech addresses a matter of public concern must be determined by the content, form, and context of a given statement, as revealed by the whole record.[192]

Courts pay particular interest to the context in which the speech was presented to prevent plaintiffs from adding the public concern issue to their

---

188. *Id.* at 287.
189. Waters v. Churchill, 114 S. Ct. 1878 (1994).
190. *Rankin,* 483 U.S. at 383-84.
191. *Connick,* 461 U.S. at 146-48.
192. *Id.* at 147.

claim after the fact. "[R]etrospective embellishment cannot transform personal grievances into matters of public concern."[193] Judge Posner explained that while chitchat is not protected, speech need not be earth-shattering to fall under the First Amendment:

> [T]he Supreme Court . . . did not mean matters of transcendent importance, such as the origins of the universe or the merits of constitutional monarchy; they meant matters in which the public might be interested, as distinct from wholly personal grievances —which . . . are too remote from central concerns [of the First Amendment] to justify judicial interference with the employment relation . . . and casual chitchat, which is not protected by the First Amendment at all.[194]

Content is the most important factor. But the subject may be a matter of public concern and statements about the subject not be protected. For example, an employee who complains about secondhand smoke is not engaging in protected speech when his complaints are purely on his own behalf and in his own interest.[195] A further illustration of this distinction can be seen in the courts' conflicting approach to speech about sexual harassment. Courts have focused on the speaker's motivational role and concluded that sexual harassment complaints are not protected since they have a "private and informal flavor."[196] When the specific statements related solely to a personal problem, these courts have held that the speech does not merit First Amendment protection.[197]

The Third Circuit recently criticized these opinions in *Azzaro v. County of Allegheny*.[198] The *Azzaro* court disagreed with earlier opinions that gave controlling significance to the speaker's primary purpose or motive in mak-

---

193. Dodds v. Childers, 933 F.2d 271, 274 (5th Cir. 1991). *See also* Hyland v. Wonder, 972 F.2d 1129 (9th Cir. 1992), *cert. denied*, 508 U.S. 908 (1993).

194. Dishnow v. School Dist. of Rib Lake, 77 F.3d 194, 197 (7th Cir. 1996).

195. Brown v. Disciplinary Committee of Edgerton Volunteer Fire Dept., 97 F.3d 969, 974 (7th Cir. 1996). *See also* Smith v. Fruin, 28 F.3d 646, 653 (7th Cir. 1994), *cert. denied*, 513 U.S. 1083 (1995).

196. Saulpaugh v. Monroe Community Hosp., 4 F.3d 134 (2d Cir. 1993), *cert. denied*, 510 U.S. 1164 (1994); Woodward v. City of Worland, 977 F.2d 1392 (10th Cir. 1992), *cert. denied*, 509 U.S. 923 (1993).

197. *Id.*

198. 110 F.3d 968 (3d Cir. 1997).

ing the challenged statement.[199] The *Azzaro* court found several lessons to the contrary in *Connick*. First, the community has an interest in the "free exchange of information and ideas relating to matters of public concern. . . . "[200] That interest is implicated by private speech as well as public.[201] Second, *Connick* suggests that some information is likely to be of public concern. For example, speech about racial discrimination in the assignment of school personnel, the district attorney's failure to discharge its responsibilities in investigating and prosecuting crimes, and actual or potential wrongdoing are matters of public concern.[202] Third, *Connick* teaches that the speaker's motive is not dispositive of whether speech relates to a matter of public concern.[203] In the Third Circuit's view, if a "complainant reports sexual harassment by a public official, her speech touches on a matter of public concern, even if motivated by purely personal considerations because it exposes the potential malfeasance of a public official."[204]

While sexual harassment has most often been treated as an unprotected personal grievance, an employee's statements to a news reporter about racial or sexual harassment will be protected. This injection of the speech into a public forum may transform it from a personal grievance to a matter of public concern. [205] But if an employee contacts the media, the press release or public comment does not always make the speech a matter of public concern.[206]

Nor must speech be made publicly in order to be protected.[207] In *Givhan v. Western Line Consol. School,*[208] the Court held that even private speech could be protected in some cases.[209] The line between pro-

---

199. *Azzaro,* 110 F.3d at 979.
200. *Id.* at 977.
201. *Id.*
202. *Id.* at 978.
203. *Id.*
204. *Id.*
205. Matulin v. Village of Lodi, 862 F.2d 609, 613-14 (6th Cir. 1988); *see also* Rode v. Dellarciprete, 845 F.2d 1195, 1202 (3d Cir. 1988).
206. Rahn v. Drake Center, 31 F.3d 407 (6th Cir. 1994), *cert. denied*, 115 S. Ct. 2578 (1995).
207. Givhan v. Western Line Consol. School, 439 U.S. 410, 414 (1979).
208. *Id.*
209. *Mount Healthy*, 429 U.S. at 283-84.

tected and unprotected speech in this area is a thin one and practitioners should scrutinize the facts with care.

Although speech about harassment has caused difficulty in classification, courts have recognized certain subject matters as "inherently of public concern."[210] Speech regarding illegal campaign activity, criminal misuse of public funds, wastefulness, and inefficiency in managing governmental entities are inherently matters of public concern.[211] Even when such speech is uttered in private to the employee's supervisor, it retains its public character. But the argument that any activity that occurs within a government office is a matter of public concern has been routinely rejected.[212]

In *Dorsett v. Board of Trustees for State Colleges & Universities*,[213] the court specifically analyzed this issue regarding educational institutions.

> In public schools and universities across this nation, interfaculty disputes arise daily over teaching assignments, room assignments, administrative duties, classroom equipment, teacher recognition, and a host of other relatively trivial matters. A federal court is simply not the appropriate forum in which to seek redress for such harm.[214]

Federal courts have upheld speech rights when a professor criticized the public school curriculum (and its supporters) for reflecting bias against minorities. Likewise, a school guidance counselor's articles in a local newspaper and comments to the media were protected speech because the counselor was "participating in a public debate on matters of interest to the public."[215]

First Amendment rights may be afforded in cases where an employee refuses to speak.[216] In *Langford v. Lane*, an employee was fired after she refused to tell her employer what grievances she planned to air at a public meeting the next day. The court held that the worker's refusal to speak

---

210. Roth v. Veteran's Admin., 856 F.2d 1401, 1405 (9th Cir. 1988).
211. Chateaubriand v. Gaspard, 97 F.3d 1218, 1222 (9th Cir. 1995).
212. Caine v. Hardy, 943 F.2d 1406, 1416 (5th Cir. 1991), *cert. denied*, 503 U.S. 936 (1992). *See also* Thomson v. Scheid, 977 F.2d 1017 (6th Cir. 1992), *cert. denied*, 508 U.S. 910 (1993); Wallace v. Texas Tech University, 80 F.3d 1042 (5th Cir. 1996).
213. 940 F.2d 121 (5th Cir. 1991).
214. *Dorsett*, 940 F.2d at 123.
215. *Dishnow*, 77 F.3d at 196-197.
216. *See* Langford v. Lane, 921 F.2d 677 (6th Cir. 1991).

was afforded First Amendment protection under the *Connick* framework, stating "[T]he protection of the First Amendment extends equally to the right to speak freely and the right to refrain from speaking at all."[217] Insults and profanity do not generally amount to speech on a matter of public concern. Calling the dean of a university a Hitler or engaging in rude or insulting speech is not protected.[218]

Expressive conduct may amount to protected speech. For example, a police officer "wearing a blackened face, dressed in bib overalls and a black curly wig, and carrying a watermelon," might be engaged in protected speech if the costume was intended to express a message.[219] The officer's claim was ultimately rejected since he testified that he did not intend to comment on any issue of interest to the public; he wanted to entertain the other guests at the party.[220]

On the other hand, an off-duty police officer who wore a blackened face and a wig during a public musical show was engaged in protected speech since the performances were a "form of artistic expression" of interest to the public.[221] Wearing a flag patch to protest discrimination or a peace pin to support peace were protected.[222]

False statements may be protected speech.[223] At a minimum, "absent proof of false statements knowingly or recklessly made by him, a teacher's exercise of his right to speak on issues of public importance may not furnish a basis for his dismissal from public employment."[224]

Courts have disagreed about how to apply this analysis.[225] The Seventh Circuit held and the Tenth suggested in dicta that false statements are pro-

---

217. *Id.* at 680 (quoting Wooley v. Maynard, 430 U.S. 705, 714 (1977)).
218. McBride v. City of Roanoke, 871 F. Supp. 885 (W.D. Va. 1994); Landrum v. Eastern Ky. Univ., 578 F. Supp. 241 (E.D. Ky 1984).
219. Tindle v. Caudell, 56 F.3d 966 (8th Cir. 1995).
220. 56 F.3d at 970.
221. Bergler v. Battaglia, 779 F.2d 992 (4th Cir. 1985), *cert. denied*, 476 U.S. 1159 (1986).
222. Leonard v. City of Columbus, 705 F.2d 1299 (11th Cir. 1983), *cert. denied*, 468 U.S. 1204 (1984); Smith v. U.S., 502 F.2d 512 (5th Cir. 1974).
223. *Pickering*, *supra*, 391 U.S. at 566-74.
224. *Id.* at 1738.
225. *Compare* Brenner v. Brown, 36 F.3d 18, 20 (7th Cir. 1994) *with* Wulf v. City of Wichita, 883 F.2d 842, 859 n. 24 (10th Cir. 1989) *and* Brasslett v. Cota, 761 F.2d 827, 840-41 (1st Cir. 1985) *and* Moore v. City of Kilgore, 877 F.2d 364, 376 (5th Cir.), *cert. denied*, 493 U.S. 1003 (1989).

tected absent proof that the inaccuracies were knowing or reckless.[226] The First, Fifth, and Ninth Circuits have rejected a per se rule in favor of a rule that considers recklessness as to the truth as part of the *Pickering* balancing test, which is examined more closely below.[227]

Pickering Balancing Test

In *Pickering*, the Supreme Court ruled that once a public employee demonstrates that the speech addressed is a matter of public concern, the employee's interest in speaking on matters of public concern must be balanced against "the interest of the state, as an employer, in promoting the efficiency of the public services it performs through its employees."[228]

The courts consider a number of factors in completing this balancing of interests:

1. The need for harmony in the office or workplace;
2. Whether the government's responsibilities require a close working relationship to exist between the plaintiff and co-workers when the speech in question has caused or could cause a relationship to deteriorate;
3. The time, manner, and place of the speech;
4. The context in which the dispute arose;
5. The degree of public interest in the speech; and
6. Whether the speech impeded the employee's ability to perform his or her duties.[229]

Other relevant considerations include "whether the statement impairs discipline by superiors or harmony among co-workers, has a detrimental

---

226. *See Brenner*, 39 F.3d at 20; *Wulf*, 883 F.2d at 859 n.24.

227. Johnson v. Multnomah County, Oregon, 48 F.3d 420, 423-24 (9th Cir.), *cert. denied*, 115 S. Ct. 2616 (1995); *Brasslett*, 761 F.2d at 840-41; American Postal Workers Union v. U.S. Postal Service, 830 F.2d 294, 305-06 (D.C. Cir. 1987); *Moore*, 877 F.2d at 376.

228. Pickering v. Board of Education, 391 U.S. 563, 568 (1968).

229. Stever v. Independent School Dist. No 625, 943 F.2d 845, 850 (8th Cir. 1991) (citing Bowman v. Pulaski County Special School Dist., 723 F.2d 640, 644 (8th Cir. 1983)). *See also* Martinez v. City of Opa-Locka, 971 F.2d 708 (11th Cir. 1992)

impact on close working relationships for which personal loyalty and confidence are necessary, impedes the performance of the speaker's duties or interferes with the regular operation of the enterprise."[230] The "inappropriate or controversial character of the statement is irrelevant to the question whether it deals with a matter of public concern."[231]

The content of public expression must be assessed to determine if the statements impede the employee's job performance or interfere with the operations of the government employer.[232] Sometimes the public nature of the speech is enough to tip the balance. In *McMullen v. Carson*,[233] an employee of the sheriff's office said in a televised news broadcast that he was a Ku Klux Klan recruiter. Public outrage made his "discharge . . . necessary to prevent a deleterious effect on the Sheriff's ability to enforce the law in the community."[234] Private expression may invoke additional factors such as whether the speech threatens the "employing agency's institutional efficiency . . . not only by the content of the employee's message but also by the manner, time, and place in which it is delivered."[235]

Pickering balancing involves a case-by-case analysis of the government interests and the protected speech.[236] The Eleventh Circuit evaluated a police officer's right to conduct a letter-writing campaign that was critical of the police department without giving the department the opportunity to investigate her complaints internally before going public.[237] Although the officer had an interest in expressing her opinion on the alleged malfeasance of her superiors, it was outweighed by the police department's need to maintain a close working relationship within the department.

The court gave substantial weight to the fact that the department was a quasi-military organization with a need to protect confidentiality, the esprit de corps, and the discipline required in such groups.[238] The department regulation did not bar the officer from voicing her complaints; it merely delayed her right to go public until an internal investigation was

---

230. *Rankin*, 483 U.S. at 388.
231. *Id.* at 386-88.
232. Givhan v. Western Line Consol. School, 439 U.S. 410 n 4.
233. 754 F.2d 936 (11th Cir. 1985).
234. *McMullen*, 754 F.2d at 937.
235. *Id.*
236. Busby v. City of Orlando, 931 F.2d 764, 774 (11th Cir. 1991).
237. 931 F.2d at 669-770.
238. *Id.* at 773-75.

complete.[239] Presumably, a complete bar to such speech would not have passed muster.

In *Moore v. City of Wynnewood*,[240] the Tenth Circuit applied *Pickering* to hold that the government interests outweighed those of the speaker. A former deputy chief of police, demoted for criticism of the department's race relations, sued. His insider's perspective on the department's racial problems was important to the public debate, but the city had "a strong interest in controlling the speech of its employees when they purport to speak for the city or one of its departments."[241] The officer wore his uniform and was on duty at the city council meeting when he spoke. He left his post to attend the meeting "despite being the only officer on duty" at the time.[242] These factors coupled with the need for close working relationships in the department tipped the balance in favor of the city.[243]

The *Moore* court refused to make the city prove that the speech actually disrupted the department. Although the government cannot rely on "purely speculative allegations" that speech will disrupt operations, it need not "wait for speech to actually disrupt core operations before taking action."[244] The department's small size and the officer's leadership position increased the likelihood that the speech would interfere with the officer's ability to function.[245]

But the Second Circuit reversed a district court for failing to require a factual basis for its conclusion that a police officer's speech threatened effective police operations.[246] The Second Circuit later backed away from this requirement on the basis of *Waters v. Churchill*.[247] The record showed no harm to the officer's professional relationships and minimal impact on public perception of the department. Courts have typically required the

---

239. *Id.* at 774.
240. 57 F.3d 924 (10th Cir. 1995).
241. *Moore*, 57 F.3d at 933-34.
242. *Id.* at 934.
243. *Id.* at 934-35.
244. *Id.* at 934. *See also* Jeffries v. Harleston, 52 F.3d 9 (2d Cir.), *cert. denied*, 116 S. Ct. 173 (1995).
245. *Moore*, 57 F.3d at 934-35.
246. Bieluch v. Sullivan, 999 F.2d 666 (2d Cir. 1993), *cert. denied*, 510 U.S. 1094 (1994).
247. 114 S. Ct. at 1887, 1890 (1994).

government to prove its interests and the harm that allegedly flows from the speech.[248]

The Third Circuit required proof of actual disruption in *Zamboni v. Stamler*.[249] In its view, a finding of potential disruption is not enough. The record must contain proofs that the speech impeded the speaker's proper job performance or interfered with the regular operations of the school.[250] Disruption of the workplace must not have been serious where the government employer reproduced and disseminated the article in the workplace.[251]

Practitioners should check the law of their circuit on this point. Since the extent of proofs showing disruption is unclear, the government employer should present as strong a case as possible.

The weight given to the disruptive effect of speech depends, in part, on the responsibilities of the employee.[252] Thus, if an employee "serves in a sensitive capacity that requires extensive public contact, the employee's private speech may pose a substantial danger to the agency's successful functioning."[253] A police officer whose job involved building community support for the department and fostering credibility with all constituent groups of a multi-ethnic city could be fired for making statements critical of immigrants and deploring the need to speak Spanish.[254] The officer made his comments while preaching a sermon, but the remarks were published in the press. His speech fell outside the scope of the First Amendment because it posed a substantial danger to the police department's successful accomplishment of its mission.[255]

A probation officer's public criticism of the police department and local court system during a call-in radio show did not outweigh the government's interest in promoting the efficiency of its judicial system.[256] Since loyalty and confidence are critical to the probation officer's position

---

248. Anderson v. McCotter, 100 F.3d 723 (10th Cir. 1996); Considine v. Board of County Commissioners of the County of Adams, 910 F.2d 695 (10th Cir. 1990).
249. 847 F.2d 73, 78-79 (3d Cir. 1988), *cert. denied*, 488 U.S. 899 (1988).
250. *Zamboni*, 847 F.2d 79.
251. Rode v. Dellarciprete, 845 F.2d 1195, 1202 (3d Cir. 1988).
252. *Rankin*, 483 U.S. at 388.
253. Sims v. Metropolitan Dade County, 972 F.2d 1230 (11th Cir. 1992).
254. 972 F.2d at 1234-38.
255. *Id.* at 1238. *See also* Jeffries v. Harleston, 52 F.3d 9 (2d Cir.), *cert. denied*, 116 S. Ct. 173 (1995).
256. Jefferson v. Ambroz, 90 F.3d 1291 (7th Cir. 1996).

and his statements potentially injured the probation officer's relationship with other law enforcement agencies, the government could reasonably conclude that he could no longer perform his duties effectively.[257]

The government employer's conduct must be judged in light of the speech as the employer interpreted it. In *Waters v. Churchill*,[258] the Court held that substantial weight must be afforded to the right of the "government's interest in achieving its goals as effectively and efficiently as possible. . . ."[259] The *Waters* court, evaluating a government employer's discharge of an employee based on mistaken facts, approved the use of personnel procedures that differ from evidentiary rules and required courts to "look to the facts as the employer reasonably found them to be."[260] The *Waters* court ruled that "[i]f an employment action is based on what an employee supposedly said, and a reasonable supervisor would recognize that there is a substantial likelihood that what was said was protected, the manager must tread with a certain amount of care."[261]

The Court's approach is intended to protect employers from situations in which "reasonable employers would disagree about who is to be believed, or how much investigation needs to be done, or how much evidence is needed to come to a particular conclusion."[262] Liability will not result from mistaken though reasonable conduct. Government employers may "rely on hearsay, on past similar conduct, on their personal knowledge of people's credibility, and on other factors that the judicial system ignores."[263] *Waters* carves out a broader sphere of action for government employers. They may, for example, prohibit employees from being rude, a standard that would be too vague if applied to the public at large.[264] The *Waters* court gives "substantial weight to government employers' reasonable predictions of disruption. . . ."[265]

---

257. 90 F.3d at 1297.
258. 114 S. Ct. 1878 (1994).
259. *Waters*, 114 S. Ct. at 1887-88.
260. *Id.* at 1889.
261. *Id.*
262. *Id.*
263. *Id.* at 1888.
264. *Id.* at 1886.
265. For a critical discussion of the Waters opinion *see* E. J. VELAZQUEZ, *Waters v. Churchill: Government-Employer Efficiency, Judicial Deference, and the Abandonment of Public-Employee Free Speech by the Supreme Court*, 61 BROOKLYN L. REV. 1055 (1995).

Some courts, unsympathetic to the trouble resulting from a critical employee's gripes, have found a strong interest in ensuring government discretion and control over the management of its employees. In *Williams v. Alabama State University*,[266] the court recognized the employer's "prerogative to remove employees whose conduct hinders efficient operation. . . . "[267] The *Williams* court resolved the case on immunity grounds, an easy out where the issue is close. But the language suggests a far-reaching right to terminate troublesome employees. It would be unwise for a government employer to count on such a favorable application of the balancing test.

Because *Pickering* is a fact-specific test, the government employer is entitled to immunity unless the balance "would lead to the inevitable conclusion that the discharge of the employee was unlawful."[268] Because the rule "turns upon a fact-intensive balancing test, it can rarely be considered 'clearly established' for purposes of the *Harlow* qualified immunity standard."[269] Judge Easterbrook acknowledged the difficulties inherent in administering a balancing approach, noting that litigation is both expensive and error-prone in *Walsh v. Ward*.[270]

The question of whether speech is on a matter of public concern and the balancing of the speaker's First Amendment interest against the government's interests are both legal determinations for the court.[271] It is reversible error to instruct a jury to perform the *Pickering* balancing test.[272] The court should instruct the jury which speech is protected, ask it to determine whether the protected speech was a substantial factor in the detrimental employment decision and, if so, whether the employer would have reached the same decision in the absence of that speech.[273] The failure to object to instructions submitting the question of what speech is protected to the jury waives the issue.[274] Government defendants must ask the court

---

266. 102 F.3d 1179 (11th Cir. 1997).
267. *Williams,* 102 F.2d at 1184.
268. Dartland v. Metropolitan Dade County, 866 F.2d 1321, 1323-24 (11th Cir. 1989).
269. Bartlett v. Fisher, 972 F.2d 911, 916 (8th Cir. 1992) (citing cases showing that at least five circuits agree); Burnham v. Ianni, 98 F.3d 1007 (8th Cir. 1996).
270. 991 F.2d 1344 (7th Cir. 1993).
271. Gardetto v. Mason, 100 F.3d 803 (10th Cir. 1996).
272. 100 F.3d at 817.
273. *Id.* at 816-18.
274. Feldman v. Philadelphia Housing Authority, 43 F.3d 823, 831 (3d Cir. 1994).

on the record to make a finding that speech is not on a matter of public concern and to balance the interests of the parties.[275] Otherwise they will not be in a position to appeal from the failure to do so.

Causation

Once an employee establishes speech on a matter of public concern and persuades the court that *Pickering* balancing prohibits taking an adverse employment action based on the speech, the employee must then show that protected speech was a substantial or motivating factor in the adverse action.[276] The rule of causation adopted by the Supreme Court in *Mount Healthy City School District Board of Education v. Doyle* requires the plaintiff to show that the government employer would not have reached the same decision in the absence of the protected conduct. The plaintiff must allege facts showing that protected speech motivated the adverse employment action. The government agency may then show that it would have reached the same decision even absent the protected conduct.[277]

At a minimum, these showings require the plaintiff to demonstrate that the employer knew about and disagreed with the protected speech.[278] An extended period of time between the protected speech and the adverse employment action undercuts the existence of any causal link.[279] But showing that the adverse employment decision followed protected speech, by itself, is insufficient.[280]

In the absence of evidence that the government employer knew about the protected speech, summary judgment is in order.[281] When opposing a motion for summary judgment, the employee must point to specific nonconclusory facts reasonably linking protected speech to employer discipline.[282] The employee may not "rely on the mere fact that an adverse employment action followed speech that the employer would have

---

275. Dishnow v. School District of Rib Lake, 77 F.3d 194, 197-98 (7th Cir. 1996).
276. *Mount Healthy*, 429 U.S. 274.
277. *Id.*
278. O'Connor v. Chicago Transit Authority, 985 F.2d 1362 (7th Cir. 1993).
279. *Id.* at 1368.
280. Barnard v. Jackson County, 43 F.3d 1218, 1226 (8th Cir.), *cert. denied*, 116 S. Ct. 53 (1995).
281. Cabrol v. Town of Youngsville, 106 F.3d 101, 108 (5th Cir. 1997).
282. Bailey v. Floyd County Bd. of Educ., 106 F.3d 135, 144-145 (6th Cir. 1997).

liked to prevent."[283] The employee must link the speech to the adverse employment action.[284]

Courts have struggled with the requirements for a prima facie case.[285] Temporal proximity must be coupled with other evidence that is sufficient to support an inference of retaliation.[286] This determination is ordinarily a question of fact.[287]

Because the ultimate fact of retaliation turns on the defendants' state of mind, it is particularly difficult to establish by direct evidence.[288] A plaintiff will typically prove the case with circumstantial evidence.[289] Often, this is accomplished by persuading the jury that the employer's explanation for the adverse action is pretextual.[290] This can be done by showing that a discriminatory motive more likely motivated the employer, or that the employer's explanation is unworthy of credence.[291]

The Supreme Court has recognized that a government employer may have mixed motives.[292] To prevail, the government employer must show that it would have made the same decision based on legitimate reasons.[293] If the employer's dual motivations arose at different times, the employer must establish that it would have taken the same action at the same time.[294] If an employee is discharged because of protected speech, a First Amendment violation has occurred even if some other circumstance occurs or comes to the employer's attention that would have resulted in a decision

---

283. *Bailey*, 106 F.3d at 145 citing Collyer v. Darling, 98 F.3d 211, 229 (6th Cir. 1996); Wright v. Illinois Dept. of Children & Family Services, 40 F.3d 1492, 1500 (7th Cir. 1994).
284. *Bailey*, 106 F.3d at 145.
285. *See* Bartlik v. U.S. Department of Labor, 73 F.3d 100 (6th Cir. 1996).
286. *See, e.g.*, Durant v. Independent School Dist. No. 16 of LeFlore County, Okla., 990 F.2d 560, 564 (10th Cir. 1993).
287. Matulin v. Village of Lodi, 862 F.2d 609, 613 (6th Cir. 1988).
288. Ramirez v. Oklahoma Dept. of Mental Health, 41 F.3d 584, 595-96 (10th Cir. 1994).
289. Harrington v. Harris, 108 F.3d 598, 606 (5th Cir. 1997).
290. 108 at F.3d 598.
291. Amburgey v. Corhart Refractories Corp., Inc., 936 F.2d 805, 813 (5th Cir. 1991).
292. Price Waterhouse v. Hopkins, 490 U.S. 228, 109 S. Ct. 1775, 104 L. Ed. 2d 268 (1989) (dual-motivation defense in employment discrimination context).
293. *Price Waterhouse,* 490 U.S. at 251; *Mount Healthy*, 429 U.S. at 287.
294. Sagendorf-Teal v. County of Rensselaer, 100 F.3d 270, 275 (2d Cir. 1996).

to fire the employee. But the later circumstance cuts off liability for damages and avoids the remedy of reinstatement.[295]

Although many defendants do not want to instruct the jury on a mixed-motive defense, the Seventh Circuit says that if the plaintiff offers one motive for the action and the defendant says it was based on something else, "the jury should be told what to do if it concludes that the employer had both motives."[296] Courts have distinguished mixed-motive cases from pretext cases.[297] Some courts take the position that in a pretext case, the burden of proof never shifts.[298] But if there is credible evidence of both permissible and impermissible factors influencing the challenged decision, once the plaintiff proves an impermissible factor motivated the employer, the burden shifts to the employer to prove as an affirmative defense that it would have made the same decision anyway.[299]

Defense counsel should carefully evaluate the evidence to decide whether to pursue a pretext or mixed-motive defense. The theory chosen may affect the jury instructions and the burden of proof. Practitioners should carefully review the abundant case law governing jury instructions and burden of proof in the context of employment discrimination. Although some courts have borrowed from Title VII, ADEA, and other bodies of law to resolve instructional issues in the context of First Amendment analysis,[300] the Seventh Circuit rejected that approach in *Gooden v. Neal.*[301]

Freedom of Association

Except under limited circumstances, a public employer may not terminate an employee because of political beliefs or associations. The U.S.

---

295. McKennon v. Hashville Banner Publishing Co., 513 U.S. 352 (1995) (after-acquired evidence does not bar all relief but can limit damages and render reinstatement and front pay inappropriate).
296. Gooden v. Neal, 17 F.3d 925, 928-29 (7th Cir. 1994), *cert. denied*, 573 U.S. 816 (1994).
297. *See Price Waterhouse*, 490 U.S. at 260.
298. Luciano v. Olsten Corp., 110 F.3d 210, 215 (2d Cir. 1997).
299. *Id.*
300. Hawkins v. Hennepin Technical Center, 900 F.2d 153 (8th Cir. 1990); Sagendorf-Teal v. County of Rensselaer, 100 F.3d 270, 275 (2d Cir. 1996). *See* SCHWARTZ & KIRKLIN, *supra* n. 11 at 206-27.
301. 17 F.3d 925, 928 (7th Cir.), *cert. denied*, 513 U.S. 816 (1994). *But see* McMillian v. Svetanoff, 878 F.2d 186, 190 n. 3 (7th Cir. 1989).

Supreme Court has addressed this issue on three occasions and determined that a violation of the First Amendment occurs when governmental employees are discharged on the basis of their political beliefs or associations.

This represents a break with the tradition of patronage in American political history, a history typified by Governor William Marcy's statement that "to the victor belong the spoils of the enemy."[302] Traditionally, when a new president, governor, sheriff, or other public official took office, he or she cleaned house by firing the employees of his or her predecessor and replacing them with cronies.[303] Gradually, civil service reform efforts replaced some patronage jobs with a bureaucratic merit-based system.[304] But these efforts left some of the patronage system in place.

Then, in 1976, the Supreme Court expanded First Amendment protection to bar discharge or threats of discharge of employees solely because of their partisan political affiliation or nonaffiliation.[305] In *Elrod v. Burns*, the Supreme Court criticized patronage as a restraint on freedom of belief and association.[306] In *Elrod*,[307] several non-civil service employees of a sheriff's office sued when they were dismissed or threatened with dismissal because they were not affiliated with the current political party. The Supreme Court examined the interest of government efficiency and effectiveness and reasoned that such dismissals were not the least restrictive means to those ends. In the Court's view, the "need to ensure that policies which the electorate has sanctioned are effectively implemented" could be met by limiting patronage dismissals to policymaking employees only.[308]

The *Elrod* Court did not enunciate a clear line for determining when an employee occupies a policymaking position. The most important factor is

---

302. Brian L. Porto, *The Constitution & Political Patronage: Supreme Court Jurisprudence and the Balancing of First Amendment Freedoms*, 13 Pace L. Rev. 87 (1993) (citing Martin Tolchin & Susan J. Tolchin, To the Victor 323 (1971)).
303. In fact, the concept of judicial review was first announced in connection with deciding the propriety of just such an attempt in Marbury v. Madison, 1 Cranch 137, 2 L. Ed. 60 (1803).
304. Porto, *supra,* note 294 at 89-91.
305. Elrod v. Burns, 427 U.S. 347 (1976).
306. 427 U.S. at 354-58.
307. *Id.*
308. *Id.* at 357.

the nature of the employee's responsibilities. Employees who are nonpolicy-making usually have limited responsibility. Nonpolicymaking employees are those who cannot easily undermine the goals of the party. In contrast, an employee in a policymaking position most likely has responsibilities that are broadly defined and allow for the exercise of substantial discretion:

> In determining whether an employee occupies a policymaking position, consideration should also be given to whether the employee acts as an advisor or formulates plans for the implementation of broad goals.[309]

Under *Elrod*, patronage dismissals must be limited to policymaking positions. All other such dismissals are unconstitutional under the First and Fourteenth Amendments.

The Court rejected the argument that patronage dismissals contribute to the democratic process by helping partisan politics. In the Court's view, "any contribution of patronage dismissals to the democratic process does not suffice to override [the] severe encroachment of First Amendment freedoms."[310] This conclusion has elicited sharp criticism from political scientists and legal scholars who fear it will weaken political parties and democratic accountability to the voters.[311]

Four years after *Elrod*, the Supreme Court refined its analysis of patronage dismissals involving a policymaking or confidential employee.[312] The Court replaced the inquiry into whether the employee was a policymaker or confidential employee with a functional test that looks for a connection between the employee's political views and the ability to perform the specific responsibilities of the job.[313]

In *Branti v. Finkel*, two assistant public defenders sued when they were terminated by a newly appointed public defender because they were Re-

---

309. *Id.* at 368.
310. *Id.* at 372-73.
311. *See* J. Moeller, *The Supreme Court's Quest for Fair Politics*, 1 Constitutional Commentary 203-23 (1984); K. J. Meier, *Ode to Patronage: A Critical Analysis of Two Recent Supreme Court Decisions*, 41 Pub. Admin. Rev. 558-63 (1981); M. A. Fitts, *The Vices of Virtue: A Political Party Perspective on Civic Virtue Reforms of the Legislative Process*, 136 U. Pa. L. Rev. 1567-45 (1988).
312. Branti v. Finkel, 445 U.S. 507 (1980).
313. 445 U.S. at 517.

publicans. The *Branti* Court's analysis is instructive. Assistant public defenders can effectively perform their office without political allegiance to the public defender's party. Since the assistant public defender represents clients, his allegiance must be to them and not to partisan and political concerns. Further, the assistant public defender's access to confidential information arises more out of the attorney-client relationship than partisan political activity.

The *Branti* Court altered the test formulated in *Elrod* and concluded that the assistant public defenders should not be discharged based on their political affiliations.[314] The court noted that "under some circumstances, a position may be considered political even though it is neither confidential nor policymaking in character."[315] For example, speech writers and other assistants to a political office holder may not be policymakers or confidential employees. But party affiliation is an appropriate requirement for the effective performance of their job.[316]

An employee who performs primarily ministerial functions and has little autonomy or discretion in performing his job is not subject to patronage dismissal.[317] *Billingsley v. St. Louis County*[318] illustrates the application of the *Branti* test to a county council administrative assistant who was fired for refusing to participate in her boss's election campaign. A clerk involved in mailing procedures and ordering office supplies could not be fired for her political associations because her "duties did not encompass areas that would be influenced by the . . . [her] political views."[319] On the other hand, a staff legal assistant who advised the city clerk on legal and personnel matters and represented him in judicial and administrative hearings could be replaced on political grounds.[320] The administrative assistant at issue in *Billingsley* fell between the two extremes.

---

314. *Id.*
315. *Id.* at 518.
316. *Id.*
317. Matlock v. Barnes, 932 F.2d 658, 664 (7th Cir. 1991), *cert. denied*, 502 U.S. 909 (1991); Soderbeck v. Burnett County, 752 F.2d 285, 288 (7th Cir. 1985), *cert. denied*, 417 U.S. 1117 (1985).
318. 70 F.3d 61 (8th Cir. 1995).
319. Billingsley, 70 F.3d at 63 (citing Bornes v. Bosley, 745 F.2d 501, 505 (8th Cir. 1984), *cert. denied*, 471 U.S. 1017 (1985)).
320. *Id.* at 63-64 (citing Bauer v. Bosley, 802 F.2d 1058 (8th Cir. 1986), *cert. denied*, 481 U.S. 1038 (1987)).

Since the county council administrative assistant was the sole intermediary between the elected official and his clients, received telephone calls from constituents and communicated the elected official's response, and dealt with sensitive legislative issues, a reasonable official could have assumed she could be replaced.[321]

Labels or job titles are not controlling. The question is whether the hiring authority can demonstrate that party affiliation is an appropriate requirement for the effective performance of the public office involved.[322] Thus, generalizations cannot be made on the basis of one court's conclusion that a particular position is confidential.[323] Even if a bailiff or deputy sheriff or correctional officer is subject to patronage dismissal, it does little to advance the argument to point to earlier opinions dealing with bailiffs, sheriffs, or correctional officers without discussing the job responsibilities.[324]

This point is significant both as a guide to the proofs necessary in a patronage case and for consideration of any qualified immunity defense. Since it is the particular duties of the jobholder rather than his or her job title that controls, immunity is likely to be available in close cases.[325] But the Sixth Circuit recently warned that there need not be a separate patronage decision on the particular position before qualified immunity can be denied.[326] Thus, government employers should tread with care if the question is a close one.

The Sixth Circuit has outlined four categories of public occupations that are validly subject to patronage considerations.[327] The categories are:

1. Positions specifically named in relevant federal, state, county, or municipal law to which discretionary authority with respect to the

---

321. *Id.* at 64.
322. Flenner v. Sheahan, 107 F.3d 459 (7th Cir. 1997).
323. Meeks v. Grimes, 779 F.2d 417, 420 n. 2 (7th Cir. 1988).
324. *Flenner*, 107 F.3d at 463.
325. *See, e.g.*, Beauregard v. Olsen, 85 F.3d 1402, 1405 (11th Cir. 1996); Parrish v. Nikolits, 86 F.3d 1088 (11th Cir. 1996), *cert. denied*, 1997 WL 256087; Pounds v. Griepenstroh, 970 F.2d 338, 341 (7th Cir. 1992), *cert. denied*, 507 U.S. 910 (1993); Rakovich v. Wade, 850 F.2d 1180, 1209 (7th Cir.), *cert. denied*, 488 U.S. 968 (1988).
326. McCloud v. Testa, 97 F.3d 1536, 1556 (6th Cir. 1996).
327. 97 F.3d at 1556, 1557.

enforcement of that law or the carrying out of some other policy of political concern is granted;

2. Positions to which a significant portion of the total discretionary authority available to category one position-holders has been delegated; or positions not named in law, possessing by virtue of the jurisdiction's pattern or practice the same quantum or type of discretionary authority commonly held by category one positions in other jurisdictions;
3. Confidential advisors who spend a significant portion of their time on the job advising category one or category two position-holders on how to exercise their statutory or delegated policymaking authority, or other confidential employees who control the lines of communications to category one positions, category two positions, or confidential advisors; [and]
4. Positions that are part of a group of positions filled by balancing out political party representation, or that are filled by balancing out selections made by different government agents or bodies.[328]

The categories provide a road map for litigating a patronage dismissal. The government employer should look for relevant statutes or policies giving the employee discretionary authority to enforce the law or carry out some policy of political concern to the public. If the government can demonstrate that the employee is a confidential advisor or communicator for the policymaker, patronage considerations are probably permissible. Finally, if the government can show that the position is filled by a representative of a political party or agency, patronage will be allowed.

More recently, in *Rutan v. Republican Party of Illinois*,[329] the U.S. Supreme Court extended First Amendment protection to employment practices other than dismissals that were based on political patronage. The Court held that the rule of *Elrod* and *Branti* extends to promotion, transfer, recall, and hiring decisions based on party affiliation and support.[330]

In *Rutan*, petitioners sued alleging that the governor used a hiring freeze procedure to establish a political patronage system that limited state employment and beneficial employment decisions to those supported by the

---

328. *Id. See also* Mumford v. Basinski, 105 F.3d 264, 272 (6th Cir. 1997).
329. 110 S. Ct. 2729 (1990).
330. 110 S. Ct. at 2739.

Republican Party. Of the three petitioners, one had been denied promotions for several years; another was denied a promotion and later a transfer because he did not have the support of the local party officials; and the third was repeatedly denied state employment, again because he was without the support of party officials.

The Supreme Court reviewed the *Elrod* and *Branti* decisions and underscored its earlier conclusion that there are various ways a governmental employer can meet its agenda:

> A government's interest in securing effective employees can be met by discharging, demoting or transferring staff members whose work is deficient. A government's interest in securing employees who will loyally implement its policies can be adequately served by choosing or dismissing certain high-level employees on the basis of their political views.[331]

In the *Rutan* Court's view, the democratic process is no more furthered by other patronage-related employment decisions than by patronage dismissals. The Court noted that political parties have survived the decline in patronage-related employment. The Court also found that patronage-related employment decisions "impair the elective process by discouraging free political expression by public employees."[332] These conclusions are not free from doubt. Justice Powell, in his *Branti* dissent, pointed out that successful "implementation of policy often depends upon the cooperation of public employees who do not hold policymaking posts."[333] But the Court nevertheless expanded *Elrod-Branti* by holding that the First Amendment prohibits patronage hiring the same as transfer, demotion, or discharge.[334]

The *Elrod-Branti* analysis has been consistently applied when the court determines that the motivation for terminating an employee was solely for political affiliation.[335] But the circuits have not agreed on the proper analysis for cases involving both speech and political association.[336] If the employee was discharged because of his political affiliation *and* po-

---

331. *Id.* at 2737.
332. *Id.*
333. *Branti*, 445 U.S. at 529-30. (Power, Jr., dissenting).
334. *Rutan*, 110 S. Ct. at 2739.
335. *See, e.g.*, Stough v. Gallagher, 967 F.2d 1523 (11th Cir. 1992).
336. Rodriguez v. Munoz, 808 F.2d 138, 143-44 (1st Cir. 1986) (hybrid speech and affiliation case poses difficulty).

litical activity (speech and association mixed), the analysis differs depending upon the jurisdiction.

The Fourth, Fifth, and Eighth Circuits have adopted versions of the "unified spectrum" approach, which regards *Elrod* as an application of *Pickering*. In the Fourth and Eighth Circuits, if an employee is terminated for "overt activity involving arguably protected speech (either solely or in addition to party affiliation)," the *Pickering* balancing test must be applied.[337] The Fifth Circuit has also adopted the *Pickering* balancing test for these cases, although it views "dismissals based on political activity as falling in the center of a spectrum anchored by pure patronage cases at one end and pure speech cases at the other."[338]

Kinsey v. Salado[339] involved both speech and political association. It fell squarely under the Fifth Circuit's earlier decision in *McBee v. Jim Hogg County*.[340] The Fifth Circuit evaluates each case on a spectrum. Cases involving only discharge for political party affiliation, such as *Elrod* and *Branti*, were "at the extreme of the employee's side, where little, if any, weighing is called for. . . . They did not campaign, they did not even speak: they merely thought."[341] At the employer's end of the spectrum, *Ferguson v. Thomas*[342] and *Duke v. North Texas State University*[343] exemplified the balance where the employer/government's interests must be given serious consideration.

Under this approach, the scope of patronage cases is very narrow. If the case has a speech component, then the government interests must be weighed and balanced. If the case involves solely political affiliation, then *Elrod* governs and the employee's interests take priority. The *Kinsey* court applied this spectrum approach to evaluate the position of the plaintiff, who occupied a high-level policymaking job. For purposes of balancing, his position fell "much closer to the employer's end of the spectrum, where the government's interests more easily outweigh the employee's (as a private citizen)."[344]

---

337. Jones v. Dodson, 727 F.2d 1329, 1337 (4th Cir. 1984); Horton v. Taylor, 767 F.2d 471, 481 (8th Cir. 1985).
338. *Rodriguez*, 808 F.2d at 144 n.6.
339. 950 F.2d 988 (5th Cir.), *cert. denied*, 504 U.S. 941 (1992).
340. 730 F.2d 1009 (5th Cir. 1984).
341. *McBee*, 730 F.2d 1009.
342. 430 F.2d 852 (5th Cir. 1970)
343. 469 F.2d 829 (5th Cir. 1972), *cert. denied*, 412 U.S. 932 (1973).
344. *Kinsey*, 950 F.2d at 993.

The First Circuit found both of these approaches were not entirely satisfactory.[345] *Rodriguez v. Munoz* involved both political patronage and free speech. In remanding the case, the First Circuit ordered the district court to determine whether the plaintiff's position was the type where political affiliation was an appropriate requirement. If the answer to this question was yes, then the district court was to enter judgment for the defendant.[346] If, however, the district court decided that plaintiff's position did not require political affiliation, then the district court was to balance the plaintiff's First Amendment rights against the employer's interests.[347]

In *Horton v. Taylor*,[348] the Eighth Circuit criticized the view that *Elrod* and *Branti* are at one end of the spectrum where little or no weighing is required; this fails to differentiate between *Pickering/Connick* and *Elrod/ Branti*. According to the *Horton* court, *Elrod* and *Branti* do not require balancing because they did not involve conduct that would threaten the efficient conduct of public office. On the other hand, *Pickering* and *Connick* involved expression that could "'threaten the integrity of employer-employee relations, and therefore each case required the interests to be balanced anew.'"[349]

In *Sanguigni v. Pittsburgh Board of Public Education,*[350] the First Circuit discussed this disagreement among the circuits and followed a case-by-case approach. A faculty member claimed that her right to freedom of association was violated because the school administration retaliated against her for statements trying to organize faculty opposition to the administration. The *Sanguigni* court did not decide whether the *Connick* analysis "generally applies to claims involving freedom of association."[351] It merely found that *Connick* governed the plaintiff's freedom of association claim in the case before it "because that claim is based on speech that does not implicate associational rights to any significantly greater degree than the employee speech at issue in *Connick*."[352]

---

345. *Rodriguez*, 808 F.2d at 144.
346. *Id.* at 144.
347. *Id.* at 145-46.
348. 767 F.2d 471, 480 (8th Cir. 1985).
349. *Id.* (citing *McBee*, 730 F.2d 1009 (Rubin, J., dissenting)).
350. 968 F.2d 393 (3d Cir. 1991).
351. *Sanguigni,* 968 F.2d at 400.
352. *Id. See also* Billingsley v. St. Louis County, 70 F.3d 61, 63 (8th Cir. 1995) (tests devised to implement *Branti* have led to inconsistent results).

The Seventh Circuit has held that *Connick v. Myers*[353] applies to freedom of association claims even when speech on a matter of public concern is not involved.[354] The Sixth Circuit likewise applies the *Connick* "public concern" test to association as well as speech claims.[355] Those courts that apply the same test do so on the basis that there is no hierarchy of interests protected by the First Amendment. Therefore, the related speech, association, and petition rights should be evaluated in the same way.

Those urging a sharp break between the protections for speech and association rights suggest that limiting the protection of association rights under *Connick* is inconsistent with the Supreme Court's prior rulings.[356] Narrowing the reach of *Elrod-Branti* weakens protections for public employees because it replaces a bright-line rule prohibiting patronage dismissals with a balancing test that may afford substantial weight to the government's interests.

The Sixth Circuit recently distinguished political candidacy from political affiliation and held that the former could be a basis for firing an employee in *Carver v. Dennis*.[357] Retention of a government job cannot be based on political beliefs or affiliations. But discharging an employee for announcing her candidacy against her boss was permissible.

While this holding seems startling in light of the broad protection given employees in other cases, the result is as much to do with the record as anything else. The Sixth Circuit found no evidence that the basis for the plaintiff's termination was her exercise of her right to speak out on matters of public concern.[358] There was no evidence that the employee "either held or voiced any opinions or anything."[359] Nor were there allegations that by

---

353. 461 U.S. 138, 144-45 (1983).
354. Griffin v. Thomas, 929 F.2d 1210, 1211 (7th Cir. 1991) (recognizing split in circuits and adopting view that *Pickering* balancing is required in associational rights cases).
355. Boals v. Gray, 775 F.2d 686, 691-92 (6th Cir. 1985) (holding employee who is disciplined solely in retaliation for membership in and support of a union states a valid First Amendment claim.)
356. *See* Hatcher v. Board of Public Education and Orphanage, 809 F.2d 1546, 1558-59 (11th Cir. 1987).
357. 104 F.3d 847, 853 (6th Cir. 1997). *See also* Brazil-Breashears v. Bilandic, 53 F.3d 789, 791 (7th Cir.), *cert. denied*, 116 S. Ct. 188 (1995) (right to run for office is not fundamental but is subject to balancing tests).
358. *Carver*, 104 F.2d at 852.
359. *Id.*

running for office she was advancing the political ideas of a particular set of voters. Since running for office is not, itself, a fundamental right, the plaintiff's First Amendment rights were not implicated.[360] A neutral rule prohibiting or limiting government employees from running for political office while on the public payroll is likely to be enforced. Courts distinguish restrictions on candidacy from those due to an employee's political views.

There is a split regarding whether political differences must be partisan to be protected by the First Amendment. The Ninth Circuit has held that *Elrod-Branti* does not protect an employee who personally opposes the incumbent in a nonpartisan election.[361] But the Sixth Circuit found it clearly established that *Elrod-Branti* protects nonideological factions of the same party from patronage retaliation.[362] Firing someone out of personal pique is unlikely to be protected; firing someone for their political leanings even if they are nonpartisan is more likely to give rise to a claim.

The Supreme Court has recognized that the First Amendment protects the right of association in two lines of cases.[363] The clearest and broadest protection has been afforded to political or social associations. The First Amendment protects the freedom to engage in association for the advancement of beliefs, which applies to political, economic, religious, or cultural matters.[364]

While patronage cases involving political or social affiliations have resulted in the most frequent litigation, the right of association has been applied to protect intimate human-relations implication in lifestyle choices, nepotism policies, and other interests.[365] The right to associate may extend to the right to meet with others on a personal or social basis.[366] The protec-

---

360. *Id.* at 52-53. *See also* Bart v. Telford, 677 F.2d 622, 624 (7th Cir. 1982) (incumbent mayor could require city employee to take a leave of absence to run for mayor).
361. Thomas v. Carpenter, 881 F.2d 828, 831 (9th Cir. 1989), *cert. denied*, 494 U.S. 1028 (1990).
362. *McCloud*, 97 F.3d at 1537; Monks v. Marlinga, 923 F.2d 423 (6th Cir. 1991). *But see* Correa v. Fischer, 982 F.2d 931 (5th Cir. 1993) (no First Amendment violation when new county attorney fired member of former county attorney's staff because he disliked his predecessor).
363. City of Dallas v. Stanglin, 490 U.S. 19, 22-24 (1989).
364. Roberts v. U.S. Jaycees, 468 U.S. 609 (1984).
365. *See, e.g., Roberts*, 468 U.S. 609 (1984); Wallace v. Texas Tech University, 80 F.3d 1042, 1051 (5th Cir. 1996).
366. Wilson v. Taylor, 733 F.2d 1539, 1544 (11th Cir. 1984).

tion afforded to social or personal relationships can be seen in *Wilson v. Taylor*.[367] A police officer, fired for dating the adopted daughter of a convicted felon who was reputedly a member of organized crime, sued. The court held that the relationship was protected under the First Amendment. The city did not argue that even if dating were protected, a law enforcement officer's rights could be curtailed due to the nature of police work. So the court did not answer this question.

The Eleventh Circuit recently considered the issue of the scope of protection for intimate associations in *Shahar v. Bowers*.[368] The plaintiff, a homosexual female whose employment offer with the state law department was withdrawn after she made known her plans to participate in a marriage ceremony with her female companion, sued.

Noting a choice of three tests for the conduct, the *Pickering* balancing test, the *Elrod-Branti* test, and strict scrutiny, the court decided that strict scrutiny was the most appropriate since it evaluated the right to marry as an intimate association and, in this case, one inextricably intertwined with the plaintiff's religious beliefs. As a homosexual engaged in a religious marriage ceremony, she was protected from adverse employment action unless it was narrowly tailored to serve a compelling state interest.[369] After a poll of the judges, the opinion was vacated and the case was reheard *en banc*. The Eleventh Circuit ended up with an opinion that gives leeway here as it has been given in nepotism policies.[370]

Assuming but not deciding the existence of a right of intimate association and a right of expressive association, the Eleventh Circuit declined to apply strict scrutiny to the government employer's decision.[371] Emphasizing that the "government's role as employer is different from its role as sovereign," the court applied the *Pickering* balancing test to evaluate the constitutionality of the decision to terminate the employee on the basis of

---

367. 733 F.2d 1539 (11th Cir. 1984).

368. 70 F.3d 1218 (11th Cir. 1995), *vacated,* 78 F.3d 499 (1996).

369. *Shahar*, 70 F.3d at 1226.

370. Shahar v. Bowers, 114 F.3d 1097 (11th Cir. 1997) (*en banc*). *See, e.g., Waters, supra*. In *Waters*, the court avoided strict scrutiny by concluding that a policy that does not forbid marriage altogether or require government permission does not implicate fundamental rights. *See also* Montgomery v. Carr, 101 F.3d 1117 (6th Cir. 1996) (rational basis scrutiny for right of association claims arising from anti-nepotism policies).

371. 114 F.3d 1097, 1102-03.

her "purported 'marriage' to another woman"[372] The court underscored the government interest "in staffing its offices with persons the employer fully trusts . . . when the pertinent employee helps make policy, handles confidential information, or must speak or act—for others to see—on the employer's behalf."[373] The court applied a common-sense balancing approach and concluded that the public perception that the Attorney General (who was litigating against homosexual sodomy) had changed his views outweighed the employee's rights. The *Shahar* court emphasized the breadth of the "powers of the government as an employer" and its willingness to dispense with hard proofs of public perception in favor of deferring to the Attorney General's judgment about them.[374]

In *Swank v. Smart*,[375] the Seventh Circuit held that the First Amendment did not protect a police officer discharged, at least in part, because of conversations with a 17-year-old college student while he was off-duty. Judge Posner's opinion provides an excellent discussion of the parameters of lifestyle claims. Because the speech between the officer and the teen-age student was not on a matter of public concern, no free speech claim existed. Because the officer took pains to emphasize that no intimate association of the kind to which a right of privacy attaches had taken place, no fundamental right was involved. As a result, the test for the government conduct was whether it was arbitrary. The court held that it was not. At least some family relationships fall within the ambit of the First Amendment right of association. But not all such relationships do.[376] The precise boundaries of the right of intimate association remain to be developed.

In other opinions addressing off-duty conduct, courts have held that the First Amendment does not provide a right to continued government employment in a capacity that is undermined by the employee's off-duty expressive conduct. In *Sims v. Metropolitan Dade County*,[377] the court considered whether supervisors of the county department of community af-

---

372. 114 F.3d at 1098, 1103.

373. 114 F.3d at 1103.

374. 114 F.3d at 1108-11.

375. 898 F.2d 1247 (7th Cir.), *cert. denied*, 498 U.S. 853 (1990).

376. *See, e.g.*, Rode v. Dellarciprete, 845 F.2d 1195, 1204-205 (3d Cir. 1988) (brother-in-law relationship not an intimate association that is protected). *See also* Walters v. Village of Oak Lawn, 548 F. Supp 417, 419 (N.D. Ill. 1982) (loss of consortium not constitutionally protected).

377. 972 F.2d 1230 (11th Cir. 1992).

fairs were protected by immunity for their action in suspending an employee for his off-duty remarks expressing frustration at being required to speak Spanish at restaurants and urging blacks to boycott certain establishments. The court held that the nature of the employee's job, the public employer's purpose of avoiding racial and cultural resentment, and belief that the off-duty statements would undermine the employer's ability to accomplish its purpose, all meant that the employer's discharge of the employee was appropriate.

Freedom to Petition

The First Amendment petition clause protects an employee's right to petition the government for a redress of grievances.[378] This basis for protection has often been ignored, perhaps because free speech analysis is often available and reaches the same result.[379] The Supreme Court has not "discussed the scope of the constitutional right to petition in the context of an allegedly retaliatory discharge of a public employee. . . ."[380] But the Court's teachings suggest that an employer cannot retaliate against an employee for filing a lawsuit or a grievance.[381]

Courts have generally applied the *Connick* requirement that speech be on a matter of public concern to claims involving retaliation for the filing of grievances or lawsuits.[382] The right to petition is subject to the same analysis as the right to free speech.[383] Courts subsume the right to petition the government into that of free speech.[384] They have been un-

---

378. Genas v. State of New York Dept. of Correctional Services, 75 F.3d 825 (2d Cir. 1996); Boyle v. Burke, 925 F.2d 497, 505 (1st Cir. 1991).
379. *See* discussion in Margo Pave, *Public Employees and the First Amendment Petition Clause: Protecting the Rights of Citizen-Employees Who File Legitimate Grievances and Lawsuits Against Their Government Employers*, 90 NW. U. L. Rev. 304 (1995).
380. San Filippo v. Bongiovanni, 30 F.3d 424, 435 (3d Cir. 1994), *cert. denied*, 513 U.S. 1082 (1995).
381. Renfroe v. Kirkpatrick, 722 F.2d 714, 715 (11th Cir.), *cert. denied*, 469 U.S. 823 (1984); Yatvin v. Madison Metro School Dist., 840 F.2d 412, 419-20 (7th Cir. 1988).
382. *See, e.g.*, Rathjen v. Litchfield, 878 F.2d 836 (5th Cir. 1989).
383. Valot v. Southeast Local School Dist. Board of Education, 107 F.3d 1220 (6th Cir. 1997).
384. Belk v. Town of Minocqua, 858 F.2d 1258 (7th Cir. 1988).

sympathetic to the argument that the petition clause provides broader protection.[385]

But occasionally, courts have rejected the *Connick* requirement.[386] *Stellmaker v. De Petrillo*[387] illustrates this broader reading of the petition clause. A teacher complained that she had been demoted for filing a grievance against the director and superintendent of the school district. The government raised *Connick* and argued that the grievance did not touch on a matter of public concern. But since the retaliation was not due to speech, the court bypassed *Connick's* requirement and looked to other petition clause cases for guidance. Because these cases extended First Amendment protection to petitions raising "employment conditions and even personal injury claims," the *Stellmaker* court ruled for the plaintiff.[388] The parameters and requirements for a petition clause case have not yet been clearly enunciated. But practitioners should not overlook the theory in appropriate cases.

Fourth Amendment

Workplace searches are subject to the Fourth Amendment protection. Under the Fourth Amendment, a public employer engages in a search whenever it invades a space in which an employee has a reasonable expectation of privacy. The Supreme Court has provided a framework for analyzing whether searches and seizures pertaining to office space and personal effects are unreasonable in *O'Connor v. Ortega*.[389] While a psychiatrist at a state hospital on administrative leave pending review of charges against him was absent, his office was searched and officials seized various personal items from his desk and file cabinets. The Supreme Court pointed out that a public employee's expectation of privacy in his or her office or personal space might be "reduced by virtue of actual office practices and procedures, or by legitimate regulation."[390] But the Fourth Amendment does apply.

---

385. Day v. South Park Independent School Dist., 768 F.2d 696, 697-701 (5th Cir. 1985), *cert. denied*, 474 U.S. 1101 (1986).
386. *San Filippo*, 30 F.3d 424.
387. 710 F. Supp. 891 (D. Conn. 1989).
388. Stellmaker, 710 F. Supp. at 892. *See also* Fuchilla v. Prockop, 682 F. Supp. 247 (D. N.J. 1987); McCoy v. Goldin, 598 F. Supp. 310, 315 (S.D. N.Y. 1985).
389. 480 U.S. 709 (1987).
390. *O'Connor*, 480 U.S. at 717.

Where a school guidance counselor's desk was searched by a school board member after hours to try to find out the identity of the person who had drawn a cartoon ridiculing the policies of the school board, a Fourth Amendment right to privacy was implicated.[391] The school board member gained access to the office after hours with the help of a janitor with a passkey. The court found that the counselor had a reasonable expectation of privacy in his office; it was not open to the public and the superintendent of schools agreed that the desk was considered private.

If no specific regulation or practice alerts a public worker to the possibility of a search, the employee probably has a reasonable expectation of privacy in a desk or locker.[392] A police officer, whose locker was secured with a private lock, had a reasonable expectation of privacy when the department failed to show that it routinely opened such lockers without permission.

If an employee's desk is frequently invaded by others, the employee lacks exclusive control of the area, or legitimate regulations authorize others to be within the area, then the employee lacks any reasonable expectation of privacy and the Fourth Amendment does not come into play.[393] *Schowengerdt v. United States* illustrates these principles. The Ninth Circuit held that a government employee lacked a reasonable expectation of privacy in his office, desk, or credenza, because his employer had extensive security procedures in place. The office environment was characterized by frequent office searches and surveillance for compliance with security precautions. And the employer used trained security investigators to monitor the workplace. As a result, the employee lacked any Fourth Amendment privacy right.

An employer may reduce expectations of privacy by announcing a policy of searching lockers, work areas, and other internal spaces.[394] The Sixth Circuit held that a search of employees' lockers did not violate the Fourth Amendment where the employer's regulations permitted lockers to be searched at any time and the employees signed a waiver stating that their lockers were subject to inspection at any time.[395]

---

391. Gillard v. Schmidt, 579 F.2d 825 (3d Cir. 1978).
392. U.S. v. Speights, 557 F.2d 362 (3d Cir. 1977).
393. *See* Schowengerdt v. United States, 944 F.2d 483 (9th Cir. 1991), *cert. denied*, 112 S. Ct. 1514 (1992).
394. American Postal Workers Union v. U.S. Postal Service, 871 F.2d 556 (6th Cir. 1989).
395. 871 F.2d at 560.

Likewise, the Ninth Circuit Court of Appeals held that no Fourth Amendment privacy interest was implicated where postal regulations permitted searches by supervisors and inspectors. Any Fourth Amendment expectation of privacy that might otherwise have arisen was eliminated by the postal regulations.[396]

But a sign or warning will not always eliminate a Fourth Amendment expectation of privacy.[397] Employees of a commuter railroad facility retained a reasonable expectation of privacy in their cars despite signs posted authorizing such searches. Although the employees saw the signs and could have parked elsewhere, the signs did not inform them "of the grounds for the search, the extent of the search or the frequency or regularity of the searches."[398] The Seventh Circuit held that the employees would "have modestly but not drastically, diminished expectations of privacy."[399] Since no searches had previously taken place, the court found "only a vague possibility that they might be searched. . . ."[400] This suggests that regular searches may be necessary in order to eliminate the expectation of privacy that would otherwise exist.

While the Seventh Circuit warns against crying "wolf" with warnings about searches, the Sixth Circuit has held that once a policy permits searches, they need not be carried out to negate an expectation of privacy. In *American Postal Workers Union v. U.S. Postal Service*,[401] a collective bargaining agreement permitted random and unannounced locker inspections. The past failure to implement this provision did not mean it could not be carried out. This result, while grounded on the lack of an expectation of privacy, may also have been based on implied consent since the collective bargaining agreement provided for searches. If a union consents to drug testing of public employees as part of a collective bargaining agreement, the employee will not be able to raise a Fourth Amendment claim.[402]

---

396. United States v. Bunkers, 521 F.2d 1217 (9th Cir.), *cert. denied*, 423 U.S. 989 (1975).
397. *See* McGann v. Northeast Illinois Regional Commuter RR, 8 F.3d 1174 (7th Cir. 1993).
398. 8 F.3d at 1180.
399. *Id.* at 1182.
400. *Id.*
401. 871 F.2d 556, 560-61 (6th Cir. 1989).
402. Bolden v. Southeastern Pennsylvania Transit Authority, 953 F.2d 807 (3d Cir. 1991), *cert. denied*, 112 S. Ct. 2281 (1992). *See* ANDREW M. SAUDER,

Drug testing of public employees is sometimes permissible.[403] The Supreme Court has made clear that the collection and testing of urine is a search under the Fourth Amendment.[404] Whether the urine test is a permissible depends on the reasonableness of the search and the reasonableness of the manner of the search. *Skinner v. Railway Labor Executives Ass'n* held that neither a warrant nor probable cause are necessary "when 'special needs, beyond the normal need for law enforcement, make the warrant and probable-cause requirement impracticable.'"[405] The court must evaluate whether the government interest "justifies the privacy intrusions absent a warrant or individualized suspicion."[406]

In *Skinner*, the Court held that workers engaged in safety-sensitive tasks could be subjected to drug testing without a warrant or probable cause. Likewise, in *Von Raab* the Court upheld such testing for suspicionless drug testing of customs officers who were directly involved in drug interdiction or required to carry a firearm. The court must balance the government's interest against the employee's expectation of privacy. Factors considered include the government's interest in safety, the employee's knowledge of the drug testing program, whether the policy and test results are used for criminal prosecution or kept confidential, and the government's need to maintain public confidence in public employees.

Reasonableness is tested under two prongs. First, is the search justified in its inception? Second, is it related in scope? A drug test or workplace search is justified at its inception if there are reasonable grounds for expecting misconduct.[407] Proof of an existing drug problem is unnecessary.[408] The search must be related in scope to the circumstances for which it was justified.[409] When a drug testing policy requires reasonable suspicion before testing, it satisfies the second prong of the reasonable-

---

Bargaining Away Fourth Amendment Rights in Labor Dispute Resolution: Bolder v. SEPTA, 38 VILL. L. REV. 1133 (1993).

403. Skinner v. Railway Labor Executives Ass'n, 489 U.S. 602, 633 (1989); National Treasury Employees Union v. Von Raab, 489 U.S. 656, 677 (1989).

404. *Von Raab,* 489 U.S. at 665.

405. *Id.* at 619.

406. *Id.* at 621.

407. *O'Connor,* 480 U.S. at 726.

408. Harmon v. Thornburgh, 878 F.2d 484, 487-88 (D.C. Cir. 1989), *cert. denied, sub nom.* Bell v. Thornburgh, 493 U.S. 1056 (1990).

409. New Jersey v. T.L.O., 469 U.S. 325, 340-42 (1985).

ness standard because the intrusion is not excessive in light of the nature of the suspected drug use.[410]

The justification for a workplace search need not amount to the probable cause required to obtain a search warrant. In *Ortega*, the Supreme Court explained that an employer may search the workplace with "reasonable grounds for suspecting that the search will turn up evidence that the employee is guilty of work-related misconduct, or that the search is necessary for a non-investigatory work-related purpose."[411]

Reasonable suspicion may be based on objective facts, such as observed behavior suggesting drug use or inferences based on facts.[412] It depends on both the content of the information provided and its degree of reliability.[413] Direct observation or physical evidence that an employee's ability to perform his job was impaired because of drug use is not necessary.[414] Information that would lead a reasonable person to suspect the employee of on-the-job drug use or impairment is enough.[415] The source of the information may be a person with a close personal relationship[416] or an informant's report.[417]

The government's interest in testing may be compelling enough to justify testing without individualized suspicion.[418] If the employee is engaged in a safety-sensitive task, drug testing may be permitted without a warrant or probable cause. Courts will scrutinize the testing policy or regulation to ensure that it curtails discretion in the administration of the tests.[419]

Random drug testing has been upheld for police officers because the police industry is a highly regulated quasi-military organization whose members are armed.[420] The administrative search exception to the Fourth

---

410. 469 U.S. at 342.
411. *O'Connor,* 480 U.S. at 726.
412. *See, e.g.*, Copeland v. Philadelphia Police Dept., 840 F.2d 1139, 1144 (3d Cir. 1988), *cert. denied*, 490 U.S. 1004 (1989).
413. Benavidez v. City of Albuquerque, 101 F.3d 620, 624 (10th Cir. 1996).
414. 101 F.3d at 624.
415. *Id.*
416. Garrison v. Dept. of Justice, 72 F.3d 1566, 1569-70 (Fed. Cir. 1995).
417. 72 F.2d at 1570.
418. Von Raab, 489 U.S. at 668; Skinner, 489 U.S. at 634.
419. *See, e.g.*, McDonnell v. Hunter, 809 F.2d 1302, 1309 (8th Cir. 1987).
420. Policeman's Benevolent Ass'n of N.J. v. Twp. of Washington, 850 F.2d 133 (3d Cir. 1988), *cert. denied*, 490 U.S. 1004 (1989); McDonnell v. Hunter, 809 F.2d 1302 (8th Cir. 1987).

Amendment permits random urinalysis testing to ensure confidence in the police department.[421] Random drug testing is also permitted for public employees in safety-sensitive positions. Workers involved in the nuclear power industry, railroad industry, or other transportation areas, such as bus drivers, may be subject to such tests.[422] But it is the government employer's burden to show that drug use by its employees poses a danger to the public.[423]

Courts have also upheld drug testing as part of the job application process. In *Middlebrooks v. Wayne County*,[424] the Michigan Supreme Court found that urinalysis testing was permissible in connection with a job application. The position sought entailed riding a lawn mower on highway medians and embankments, driving front-end loaders, and operating other heavy equipment. Despite the fact that county general service workers are less regulated than railroad employees or commercial drivers, the job duties posed a greater threat to the public than the operation of normal cars, vans, and trucks.[425] Since the record showed applicants were provided notice of the testing, were not arbitrarily selected for testing, and the information was used only for determining suitability for the job, the testing was upheld.

The Fourth Amendment limits the scope of the search. The search is permissible when the measures adopted for it are reasonably related to the objectives of the search and not excessively intrusive in light of the purpose for the search. Courts look at whether urine samples are only tested for specified drugs, whether samples must be provided under the direct observation of a monitor, whether the tests are provided in a hospital environment by a medical professional, and whether the information is kept confidential.[426]

Sometimes Fourth Amendment claims are coupled with generalized right to privacy allegations that may also be analyzed under the First Amend-

---

421. *Policeman's Benevolent Ass'n,* 850 F.2d at 134, 141-42.
422. Bolden v. Southeastern Pennsylvania Transp. Authority, 953 F.2d 807 (3d Cir. 1991), *cert. denied*, 504 U.S. 943 (1992).
423. Taylor v. O'Grady, 888 F.2d 1189 (7th Cir. 1989) (remanding drug-testing challenge in prison context to determine whether employees subjected to testing had regular access to inmate population, had a reasonable opportunity to smuggle drugs in, or had access to firearms).
424. 446 Mich 151, 521 N.W.2d 774 (1994).
425. 521 N.W.2d at 778-81.
426. *See Von Raab*, 489 U.S. at 662-71; *Skinner,* 489 U.S. at 622-26.

ment. In *O'Brien v. DiGrazia*,[427] the court considered claims brought by police officers who had been suspended for failing to fill out a questionnaire seeking financial information. The court held that even if the Fourth Amendment was applicable to the request to fill out the questionnaire, the order requiring a list of sources of income, assets, and copies of income tax returns was not so lacking in justification as to be unreasonable.

Some courts have found a privacy interest that bars unnecessary or overbroad investigations into an employee's sexual practices or private life.[428] Government lawyers should review employment questionnaires with care to determine whether they comply with case law in this area.

Fifth Amendment

The Fifth Amendment's protection against self-incrimination has potential application to a public employer's internal investigations. The U.S. Supreme Court has ruled that public employers may discipline employees who refuse to answer questions that directly relate to job performance, but may not require employees to waive their constitutional protection with respect to the use of answers in a criminal prosecution of the employee.[429]

The Supreme Court has also held that interrogations of public employees must comply with the Fifth Amendment guarantee against compelled self-incrimination.[430] Thus, public employers may not require their employees to provide a questionnaire asking about the private use of illegal drugs if the information may be disclosed to law enforcement agencies.[431] Nor may city officials require their employees to waive the constitutional privilege against compelled self-incrimination as a condition of employment.[432] The Third Circuit distinguished a questionnaire during the ap-

---

427. 544 F.2d 543 (1st Cir. 1976), *cert. denied*, 431 U.S. 914 (1977).
428. Thorne v. El Segundo (Thorne I), 726 F.2d 459 (9th Cir. 1983), *cert. denied*, 469 U.S. 979 (1984); Thorne v. El Segundo (Thorne II), 802 F.2d 1131 (9th Cir. 1986); Schowengerdt v. General Dynamics Corp., 823 F.2d 1328 (9th Cir. 1987).
429. Gardner v. Broderick, 392 U.S. 273 (1968).
430. United Sanitation Men's Ass'n v. Commission of Sanitation, 392 U.S. 280 (1968).
431. American Federation of Gov't Employees v. United States R.R. Bd., 742 F. Supp. 450 (N.D. Ill. 1990).
432. Hester v. City of Milledgeville, 598 F. Supp. 1456 (M.D. Ga. 1984).

plication process on the basis that it was not compulsory.[433] An employee has no right to lie or make a false statement to his employer, but denying charges and their underlying facts may not be used as a basis for a falsification charge.[434]

433. Fraternal Order of Police v. City of Philadelphia, 859 F.2d 276 (3d Cir. 1988).
434. King v. Erickson, 89 F.3d 1575, 1584 (Fed. Cir. 1996).

Chapter Eight
The Section 1983 Land Use Case
Richard G. Carlisle

This year marks the 75th anniversary of the Supreme Court's decision in *Pennsylvania Coal v. Mahon.*[1] The legal profession's particular fascination with *Pennsylvania Coal* is demonstrated by the case having been cited in the state and federal courts over 100,000 times since it was decided in 1922.

One reason for such long-standing interest has been that, while the Fifth Amendment's[2] injunction against taking private property without just compensation is self-enforcing, the primary vehicle for enforcing other constitutional rights, § 1983, could not—until 1978—be used to sue local government. In that year, the Supreme Court decided *Monell v. Department of Social Services,*[3] holding that municipalities were "persons" directly liable under § 1983 when their official policies caused a deprivation of a federal right—whether under the Fifth Amendment or otherwise.

Notwithstanding *Monell*, however, the Fifth Amendment remains the primary vehicle for challenging land use cases. Accordingly, this chapter will trace taking jurisprudence from its origins in *Pennsylvania Coal* to the Supreme Court's dramatic, even surprising, opinion in *Dolan v. City of Tigard.*[4]

---

1. Pennsylvania Coal v. Mahon, 260 U.S. 393 (1922).
2. The Fifth Amendment to the United States Constitution provides that: "no person shall . . . be deprived of . . . property, without due process of law; nor shall private property be taken for public use, without just compensation." U.S. Const. amend V.
3. 436 U.S. 658 (1978).
4. 114 S. Ct. 2309 (1994). In Williamson County Regional Planning Comm'n v. Hamilton Bank, 473 U.S. 172, 199 n.17 (1985), Justice Blackmun observed that "the attempt to determine when regulation goes so far that it becomes, literally or figuratively, a 'taking' has been called the 'lawyers equivalent to the physicist's hunt for the quark.'" Monell, 436 U.S. 658, provided the current Supreme Court with an opportunity to de-emphasize the Fifth Amendment in favor of due process and equal protection challenges under the Fourteenth Amendment. Nonetheless, the (largely unsuccessful) hunt for the "taking quark" continues.

Taking Without Just Compensation

Pennsylvania Coal, Euclid, *and* Nectow

Given its continuing importance in taking jurisprudence, a complete understanding of the *Pennsylvania Coal* case is necessary. In *Pennsylvania Coal*, the Mahons sought an injunction to prevent the Pennsylvania Coal Company from mining under their property in such a way as to remove support and cause subsidence. The Coal Company had executed a deed conveying the surface to the Mahons, but in express terms reserved certain specific property rights to mine the subsurface. The Coal Company alleged that these specific property rights arising from the Mahon contract had been taken away by the Kohler Act, where that act prohibited the mining of anthracite coal in such a way as to cause the subsidence of any structure used for human habitation.

Under these facts, Justice Holmes observed:

> As applied to this case, the statute is admitted to destroy previously existing rights of property and contract. The question is whether the police power can be stretched so far.
>
> Government hardly could go on if to some extent values incident to property could not be diminished without paying for every such change in the general law. As long recognized, some values are enjoyed under an implied limitation and must yield to the police power. But obviously the implied limitation must have its limits, or the contract and due process clauses are gone. One fact for consideration in determining such limits is the extent of the diminution. When it reaches a certain magnitude, in most if not all cases there must be an exercise of eminent domain and compensation to sustain the act. So the question depends upon the particular facts.[5]

In the next paragraph, Holmes turned to analysis of the application of the Kohler Act to the Mahons's "single private house."[6] Upon the "particular facts" of the case, Justice Holmes balanced the judgment of the legislature against the extent of the diminution in value of the Coal Company's

---

5. Pennsylvania Coal v. Mahon, 260 U.S. 393 at 433.
6. *Id.*

property, finding the public interest in the statute to be limited and the destruction of the subsurface rights, preserved by the Coal Company in the Mahon deed, to be extensive.[7] Accordingly, Justice Holmes reversed the decree for the Mahons granted by the Supreme Court of the State of Pennsylvania, which had enjoined the Coal Company from mining under the Mahons's property.[8]

Having resolved the only Article III case or controversy before the Court, Holmes, nonetheless, noted that the attorney general of the state, the city of Scranton, and the representatives of other "extensive interests" were allowed to take part in the argument (not, of course, as parties), stating:

> It seems, therefore, to be our duty to go farther in the statement of our opinion, in order that it may be known at once, and that *further* suits should not be brought in vain.
>
> It is our opinion that the act cannot be sustained as an exercise of the police power, so far as it affects the mining of coal under streets or cities in places where the right to mine such coal has been reserved.[9]

This because:

> The rights of the public in a street purchased or laid out by eminent domain are those that it has paid for. If in any case its representatives have been so shortsighted as to acquire only surface rights without the right of support, we see no more authority for supplying the latter without compensation than there was for taking the right of way in the first place and refusing to pay for it because the public wanted it very much.[10]

---

7. *Id.* at 413-14.
8. *Id.* at 416. It is interesting to note that "equitable relief is not available to enjoin an alleged taking. . . . " Ruckelshaus v. Monsanto Co., 467 U.S. 986, 1016 (1984). Therefore, today, the Coal Company could not invoke the Fifth Amendment as a defense to a taking for public use; instead, it could only bring a suit for invalidation (no public use) or for compensation. *Cf.* Connolly v. Pension Benefit Guar. Corp., 475 U.S. 211 (1986) (no invalidation remedy for facial challenges).
9. *Pennsylvania Coal,* 260 U.S. at 414 (emphasis added).
10. *Id.* at 415.

Thus, having dealt with the particular case or controversy between the Mahons and the Coal Company, Justice Holmes hypothesized a "further" case between a city, such as the City of Scranton, and a mine operator who had reserved the right to mine coal under streets. Under the situation hypothesized, Holmes did not find the "average reciprocity of advantage that has been recognized as a justification" for other laws, such as the law upheld in *Plymouth Coal Company v. Pennsylvania*, 232 U.S. 531 (1914).[11]

Then, still in the context of "going farther in the statement of his opinion" than an examination of the case or controversy between the Mahons and the Coal Company warranted, Holmes announced his famous aphorism: "The *general rule* at least is, that while property may be regulated to a certain extent, if regulation goes too far it will be recognized as a taking."[12]

In the next two sentences, Holmes, twice, again characterized the above statement as a "general" rule and, additionally, stated: "As we already have said, this is a question of degree—and therefore *cannot* be disposed of by general propositions."[13]

The point is this: Justice Holmes's decision in *Pennsylvania Coal* must be split into two parts. Part I was the Mahons's bill in equity (just compensation was *not* sought by the Coal Company) seeking to prevent the Coal Company from mining under their property; and, Part II, the hypothetical case, concerning not a single private house, but the rights of the public in a street purchased or laid out by eminent domain, where a city had acquired only surface rights without the right of support.

As to Part I, Justice Holmes thought "it clear that the statute does not disclose a public interest sufficient to warrant so extensive a destruction of

---

11. *Id.* (citing Plymouth Coal Co. v. Pennsylvania, 232 U.S. 531 (1914)) (statute requiring a pillar of coal to be left along the line of adjoining property).
12. *Id.* (emphasis added). A similar statement had appeared as early as 1900 in 1 Lewis, Eminent Domain, t.14 (2d ed. 1900) ("but the moment the legislature passes beyond mere regulation and attempts to deprive the individual of his property, then the act becomes one of eminent domain."). *See* Hudson County Water Co. v. McCarter, 209 U.S. 349, 355 (1908) ("[I]f [regulation] should attempt to limit [development rights] so far as to make an ordinary building lot wholly useless, the rights of property would prevail over the other public interests, and the police power would fail."); *see also* Block v. Hirsh, 256 U.S. 135, 155 (1921); Martin v. District of Columbia, 205 U.S. 135, 139 (1907).
13. *Pennsylvania Coal*, 260 U.S. at 416 (emphasis added).

the defendants' constitutionally protected rights."[14] He held that the public interest shown by the statute was limited in that it sought to protect the private rights of the Mahons, who did not also own the subsurface. The statute was therefore not justified as a protection of personal safety; and, by deed, the Mahons had assumed the risk and waived all claims for damages that could arise from mining coal underneath their property. What had been taken from the Coal Company was not viewed by Holmes to have served the *public* interest, but instead, as the Kohler Act was applied in the Mahon/Coal Company controversy (the state was not a party), to have protected only the Mahons against risks assumed in their deed, while admittedly destroying previously existing rights of property and contract abiding in the Coal Company. As applied to the Mahon property, what was taken from the Coal Company was *not* taken for public use.[15] Accordingly, Justice Holmes found that the Mahons's bill in equity, relying as it did upon the Kohler Act, could not be sustained.

While volunteering his advisory opinion on hypothetical cases involving hypothetical parties in Part II of his opinion, Justice Holmes did not, nor could he, endorse resolution of cases not yet subject to the jurisdiction of the federal courts under Article III of the Constitution. As to his hypothetical case, and the general rule that if a regulation goes too far it will be recognized as a taking, Holmes specifically denounced resolution of this "question of degree" through general rules because, as a question of degree, it "cannot be disposed of by general propositions."[16]

---

14. *Id.* at 414.
15. The Fifth Amendment's injunction—"[N]or shall private property be taken for public use, without just compensation"—states, not only that private property may not be taken without just compensation, but also that the taking of private property (with or without just compensation) must be for a *public use*. The exercise of governmental power, whether the power of eminent domain or the police power, must always be for a public purpose under the Due Process Clause. *Cf.* Hawaii Housing Auth. v. Midkiff, 467 U.S. 229 (1984). If private property is *not* taken for public use, the Just Compensation Clause does not come into play at all and the Due Process Clause provides the proper vehicle for judicial review, if only because it subsumes the public use requirement of the Fifth Amendment. Injunctive relief (including invalidation), restitution, declaratory judgment or damages would be available to the court in fashioning appropriate relief, but "just compensation" would not.
16. *Pennsylvania Coal*, 260 U.S. at 416.

The general rule of *Pennsylvania Coal*, "if regulation goes too far it will be recognized as a taking," was not some sort of pronouncement that can be "violated" in the sense of violation of a legislative rule. As oracular prophesies so often are, it was a brief and enigmatic statement that would not prove itself to be particularly helpful in resolving future cases.[17] It was, instead, only what it was labeled to be: a general prediction that in some future case, the application of the Kohler Act to a specific property (*e.g.*, property below a street in the City of Scranton) *might* result in a taking for a *public* use for which just compensation must be paid.

Justice Holmes accepted the invitation of the Attorney General of the state of Pennsylvania, the City of Scranton, and the representatives of other "extensive interests" and discussed, without deciding, whether the Kohler Act might be sustained so far as it affected the mining of coal under streets or cities in places where a specific interest in the right to mine such coal has been reserved. Justice Holmes expressed his views, but did not, and could not, resolve all future cases challenging either the Kohler Act or any other legislation by the "general propositions" expressed. He did not resolve all future cases or controversies by his "general rule"; instead he qualified his views by emphasizing that the existence of a regulatory taking "is a question of degree" that can only be resolved on the basis of concrete factual situations.

Thus, by dividing the discussion in *Pennsylvania Coal* into two parts, Justice Holmes's opinion reveals itself to be primarily, if not solely, a resolution of the dispute between the Mahons and the Pennsylvania Coal Company. As to that dispute, Holmes found that the taking from the coal company was not for a public use, because the Kohler Act did not disclose a public interest sufficient to warrant destruction of the subsurface estate acquired by the coal company from the Mahons. Secondarily, he went further to volunteer his advice on another hypothetical set of facts, the taking for a public use of rights reserved to the coal company under-

---

17. In Keystone Bituminous Coal Ass'n v. DeBenedictus, 480 U.S. 470 (1987), Freilich, Leitner & Carlisle filed an amicus brief arguing that a facial attack by an association of coal companies to legislation "strikingly similar" to the Kohler Act should fail because *Pennsylvania Coal* was merely an advisory opinion, and that a taking for a public use provides no basis for a facial attack. Justice Stevens held that the "uphill battle" of making a facial attack on legislation is "especially steep." *Id.* at 495.

neath streets. Numerous attempts over the years have been launched to analyze what Justice Holmes meant by the *obiter dictum* in the second part of his opinion. Was his analysis taking analysis? Was it due process analysis?[18]

The answer to the inquiry of what, specifically, Justice Holmes meant is that, although he was clearly directing his remarks to the Fifth Amendment, he meant to speak only in general terms. Specifically, he meant nothing, because of the advisory and aphoristic nature of his comments. Justice Holmes looked to subsequent developments in the law to specify the nature of analysis under the Due Process and Just Compensation Clauses.

One such development came four years later in the landmark case *Euclid v. Ambler Realty Company.*[19] Ambler Realty Company, the owner of a tract of land containing sixty-eight acres in the Village of Euclid, Ohio, challenged an ordinance adopted by the village council establishing a comprehensive zoning plan. The land owned by Ambler was restricted by the plan in a manner that excluded certain uses previously permitted and placed certain bulk limitations on the property, such as a limit on the height of structures.[20]

Ambler sought a declaration that the ordinance was unconstitutional and an injunction restraining its enforcement as to the company's property. In support of its prayer, Ambler alleged:

> [T]hat the ordinance attempts to restrict and control the lawful uses of appellee's land so as to confiscate and destroy a great part of its value; that it is being enforced in accordance with its terms; that prospective buyers of land for industrial, commercial and residential uses in the metropolitan district of Cleveland are deterred from buying any part of this land because of the existence of the ordinance and the necessity thereby entailed of conducting burdensome and expensive litigation in order to vindicate the right to use the land for lawful and legitimate purposes; that the ordinance constitutes a cloud upon the land, reduces and destroys its value, and has the effect of diverting the normal industrial, commercial and residential development thereof to other and less favorable locations.[21]

---

18. *Cf.* Williamson County v. Hamilton Bank Regional Planning Comm'n, 473 U.S. 172, 198 (1985) (discussing the meaning of Holmes's words).
19. Euclid v. Ambler Realty Co., 272 U.S. 365 (1926).
20. *Id.* at 379-80.
21. *Id.* at 384-85.

The village directed a motion to dismiss to these allegations on the ground that Ambler "had made no effort to obtain a building permit or apply to the zoning board of appeals for relief," and consequently, that the suit was premature.[22]

Justice Sutherland held that this motion was properly overruled[23] for reason that:

> The effect of the allegations of the bill is that the ordinance of its own force operates greatly to reduce the value of appellee's lands and destroy their marketability for industrial, commercial and residential uses; and the attack is directed, and not against any specific provision or provisions, but against the ordinance as an entirety. Assuming the premises, the existence and maintenance of the ordinance, in effect, constitutes a present invasion of appellee's property rights and a threat to continue it. Under these circumstances, the equitable jurisdiction is clear.[24]

Justice Sutherland then posed the question that must always be resolved when the *general unconstitutionality* of a regulation is challenged on its face: "Is the ordinance invalid in that it violates the constitutional protection 'to the right of property in the appellee by attempted regulations under the guise of the police power, which are unreasonable and confiscatory?'"[25]

The answer to this question comes only through due process, not taking, analysis. Justice Sutherland delineated the scope of the due process inquiry in a case where the general constitutionality of the legislative scheme is challenged.

First, in an often-quoted section of the opinion, he acknowledged the breadth of the police power: "Regulations, the wisdom, necessity and validity of which, as applied to existing conditions, are so apparent that they

---

22. *Id.* at 386.
23. Justice Sutherland's holding in this regard provides an interesting contrast to the recent holdings of the Supreme Court in Williamson County Regional Planning Comm'n v. Hamilton Bank, 473 U.S. 172 (1985); and MacDonald, Sommer & Frates v. Yolo County, 477 U.S. 370 (1986).
24. *Euclid*, 272 U.S. 365, 386 (1926).
25. *Id.*

are not uniformly sustained, a century ago, or even half a century ago, probably would have been rejected as arbitrary and oppressive."[26]

Second, the opinion cautioned that, even in a case challenging the general constitutionality of a regulatory scheme on its face, the question of whether the police power exists so as to justify such a regulation "is to be determined, not by an abstract consideration . . . , but by considering [the regulation] in connection with the circumstances and the locality."[27]

Third, after discussing reasons for the wisdom of zoning regulations, Justice Sutherland described the nature of an inquiry into the general constitutionality of a statutory scheme:

> [T]he reasons are sufficiently cogent to preclude us from saying, as it must be said before the ordinance can be declared unconstitutional, that such provisions are clearly arbitrary and unreasonable, having no substantial relation to the public health, safety, morals, or general welfare.
>
> It is true that when, if ever, the provisions set forth in the ordinance in tedious and minute detail, come to be concretely applied to a particular premises, including those of the appellee, or to particular conditions, or to be considered in connection with specific complaints, some of them, or even many of them, may be found to be clearly arbitrary and unreasonable. But where the equitable remedy of injunction is sought, as it is here, not upon the ground of a present infringement or denial of a specific right, or of a particular injury in process of actual execution, but upon the broad ground that the mere existence and threatened enforcement of the ordinance, by materially and adversely affecting values and curtailing the opportunities of the market, constitute a present and irreparable injury, the court will not scrutinize its provisions, sentence by sentence, to ascertain by a process of piecemeal dissection whether there may be, here and there, provisions of a minor character, or relating to matters of administration, or not shown to contribute to the injury complained of, which, if attacked separately, might not withstand the test of constitutionality.[28]

---

26. *Id.* at 387.
27. *Id.* at 388.
28. *Id.* at 395 (citations omitted).

Finally, Justice Sutherland refused to speculate upon the value or marketability of the lands held by Ambler Realty Company because the application of the ordinance to those lands was not before the Court.[29] Accordingly, because only policy itself was before it, the Court held:

> Under these circumstances, therefore, it is enough for us to determine, as we do, that the ordinance in its general scope and dominant features, so far as its provisions are here involved, is a valid exercise of authority, leaving other provisions to be dealt with as cases arise directly involving them.
>
> And this is in accordance with the traditional policy of this Court. In the realm of constitutional law, especially, this Court has perceived the embarrassment which is likely to result from an attempt to formulate rules or decide questions beyond the necessities of the immediate issue. It has preferred to follow the method of a gradual approach to the general by a systematically guarded application and extension of constitutional principles to particular cases as they arise, rather than by out of hand attempts to establish general rules to which future cases must be fitted. This process applies with peculiar force to the solution of questions arising under the due process clause of the Constitution as applied to the exercise of the flexible powers of police, with which we are here concerned.[30]

It is difficult to ascertain how an approach other than that chosen by Justice Sutherland in *Euclid* is possible when there is a facial attack upon a regulatory scheme, an attack on the police power itself.[31] The *Euclid*

---

29. *Euclid*, 272 U.S. at 397. Accordingly, the impact of a regulation cannot be assessed in a facial challenge.
30. *Id.* (footnote omitted). *Cf.* Pennsylvania Coal v. Mahon, 260 U.S. 393 (1922), where, uncharacteristically, Justice Holmes did "attempt to formulate" such rules.
31. Conceivably, it might be argued that a regulation, on its face, necessarily results in such a complete deprivation or diminution of value among all the subjects of regulation, that the regulation on its face can be deemed, *generally*, a Fifth Amendment taking, and thus invalid unless just compensation is paid. However, such compensation, even then, could be awarded only on a case-by-case basis. And, given a sufficient public use and the constitutionally man-

approach is one of a due process inquiry as to the general constitutionality of a regulation under the Fourteenth Amendment, leaving questions of specific unconstitutionality and economic injury for later inquiry as facts develop and evidence is proffered with respect to the application of the regulation to a particular parcel.

Nectow v. City of Cambridge[32] was Justice Sutherland's counterpoint to *Euclid*, addressing the issue of the specific unconstitutionality of land use regulations. In *Nectow*, a zoning ordinance of the City of Cambridge had, in point of fact, been applied to a specific parcel of ground owned by Nectow. Nectow sought a mandatory injunction directing the city to pass upon her application, as submitted. The case was referred to a master who viewed the property and made extensive findings of fact with respect to the application of the ordinance to the particular premises.

After reviewing the master's findings, Justice Sutherland stated the test for a challenge to the specific constitutionality of a regulation as *applied* to a particular piece of property:

> [A] court should not set aside the determination of public officers in such a matter unless it is clear that their action 'has no foundation in reason and is a mere arbitrary or irrational exercise of power having no substantial relation to the public health, the public morals, the public safety or the public welfare in its proper sense.'[33]

This, of course, is similar to the test applied in *Euclid*. However, given the specific application of an ordinance to a particular piece of property, the Court was not faced with the prospect of invalidating a regulation in its entirety as to all properties, but only with deciding the validity of *applying* a regulation under a particular set of facts to one parcel. Consequently, Justice Sutherland concluded:

> That the invasion of the property of Plaintiff in error was serious and highly injurious is clearly established; and, since a necessary

---

dated availability of just compensation in individual cases, the separation of powers doctrine precludes invalidation, a remedy Justice Holmes also sought to avoid in cases such as Lochner v. New York, 198 U.S. 45 (1905).

32. Necton v. City of Cambridge, 277 U.S. 183 (1928).
33. *Id.* at 187-88 (quoting *Euclid*, 272 U.S. at 395).

> basis for the support of that invasion is wanting, the action of the zoning authorities comes within the ban of the Fourteenth Amendment and cannot be sustained.[34]

The impact of the regulation of Nectow's property was fully developed; therefore, that impact could be balanced against the public's need for inclusion of her property in a residential district.[35] *Nectow*, as with *Euclid*, applied the Fourteenth, not the Fifth Amendment.

To this day, *Pennsylvania Coal, Euclid*, and *Nectow*, all cases decided during the 1920s, form the bedrock foundation for challenges to land use regulations. For fifty years, the Supreme Court essentially ignored *Pennsylvania Coal* and it has been the least reliable of these three precedent-setting cases.

Taking Reawakening

Beginning in 1978 (the same year *Monell*[36] was decided), the Supreme Court awakened from over fifty years of stony sleep, in newfound fascination with the Fifth Amendment.[37] This reawakening began with the *Penn Central Transportation Company v. New York City*[38] decision con-

---

34. *Id.* at 188-89. Again, neither the amount of scrutiny nor the burden of proof shifts in an "as applied" case. Instead, additional facts are admissible which allow the additional test of "impact" to be assessed. *See* discussion *supra* at footnote 30.
35. *Id.* at 188.
36. *See supra* note 3 and accompanying text.
37. In these years, very few zoning cases were decided. One notable exception was Goldblatt v. Town of Hempstead, 369 U.S. 590 (1962). In Goldblatt, the town enacted an ordinance regulating dredging and pit excavating below the water table and imposed an affirmative duty to refill excavations below that level. An important, sometimes forgotten, aspect of the case was that the Supreme Court refused to hear Goldblatt's taking claim because the record did not suggest that the prohibition of mining reduced the value of a lot in question. The Court also held that there was "a dearth of relevant evidence" necessary to evaluate the reasonableness of the ordinance. Because Goldblatt had the burden of proof in the face of the town's presumption of reasonableness, his constitutional defenses failed and the town was allowed to enjoin further mining by Goldblatt.
38. Penn Central Transp. Co. v. New York City, 438 U.S. 104 (1978).

cerning whether the "application" of New York City's Landmarks Preservation Law to the parcel of land occupied by Grand Central Terminal had "taken" its owners' property in violation of the Fifth and Fourteenth amendments.[39] Before considering Penn Central's specific contentions, Justice Brennan[40] carefully reviewed the factors that shaped taking jurisprudence:

1. that the fifth amendment is 'designed to bar government from forcing some people alone to bear public burdens which, in all fairness and justice, should be borne by the public as a whole . . . ;'[41]
2. that no 'set formula' exists for determining when 'justice and fairness' require just compensation from economic harm caused by public action;[42] and
3. the following factors will be accorded particular significance: economic impact of regulation on the claimant, e.g., diminution in value of the property; character of the governmental action, e.g., physical invasion; and the degree of the regulations' interference with investment-backed expectations.

The Court, however, also held that the question of whether a taking has occurred required an "ad hoc factual inquiry"[43] and "depends largely 'upon the particular circumstances' [in that] case."[44]

As mandated by the language of the Fifth Amendment itself, that inquiry must be in the context of a record fully developed as to the economic impact of the regulation on a particular claimant.[45] Because government may execute the same law or program to affect recognized economic values in varying degrees and different ways, it is only when execution of

---

39. *Id.* at 107, 119.
40. *Id.* at 123-28.
41. Armstrong v. United States, 363 U.S. 40 (1960).
42. *See* Goldblatt v. Town of Hempstead, 369 U.S. 590 (1962).
43. Penn Cent. Transp. Co. v. New York City, 438 U.S. 104, 124 (1978).
44. *Id.* at 124. The three *Penn Central* factors discussed in the present text represent the Supreme Court's highest watermark in establishing standards for the field, capable of evolving into a reliable precedent. Unfortunately, these factors have not been fully developed and decisions continue to be guided by the factual circumstances of each case.
45. *Id.*

laws causing economic harm "interfere(s) with interests that were sufficiently bound up with the reasonable expectations of the claimant to constitute 'property' for Fifth Amendment purposes" that the taking inquiry even can begin.[46]

The general constitutionality of a law can still be examined under the *due process* calculus of *Euclid*, but the Fifth Amendment does not mandate compensation for abstract, facial challenges to regulations or policy itself. Conduct implementing or executing policy is necessary.[47] Moreover, inquiry into the extent of actual injury to investment-backed expectations sits at the threshold of just compensation analysis: "That inquiry may be narrowed to the question of the severity of the impact of the law on appellants' parcel, and its resolution in turn requires a careful assessment of the impact of the regulation on the Terminal site."[48]

Finding that the Landmarks Preservation Law as applied to the Terminal site did not interfere in any way with the present uses of the Terminal, the Court concluded "that the application of New York City's Landmarks Law has not effected a 'taking' of appellant's property."[49] Dissenting, Justices Rehnquist and Stevens were of the view that the Landmarks Law's application to the Terminal site had not been sufficiently developed in the record to resolve this threshold question: "Because the record on appeal is relatively slim, I would remand to the Court of Appeals for determination of whether TDR's constitute a 'full and perfect equivalent for the property taken.'"[50]

---

46. *Id.* at 125.
47. *See* Monell v. Dept. of Social Servs., 436 U.S. 658 (1978) and its progeny as to when official policy can be said to have caused a deprivation of constitutional rights. The brief for the United States as *amicus curiae* supporting petitioners in Williamson County Regional Planning Comm'n v. Hamilton Bank, 473 U.S. 172 (1985) suggested that the Court require not just some application of challenged provisions, but a final decision as to how those provisions would be applied in a particular case before a claim for compensation ripened. Amicus Brief, at 15 (the time of "taking" *generally* is never to be determined from the date of publication of a plan or enactment of a regulation) (citing ROBERT H. FREILICH, *Solving the "Taking" Equation: Making the Whole Equal the Sum of Its Parts*, 15 URB. LAW. 447, 473 (1983)).
48. Penn Cent. Transp. Co. v. New York City, 438 U.S. 104, 136 (1978).
49. *Id.* at 138.
50. *Id.* at 152.

Penn Central had opened the floodgates.[51] In quick succession, a number of inverse condemnation cases resulted in the formation of three general types of taking cases: physical takings, title takings, and economic entitlement takings.

Physical Takings—Loretto

A physical invasion, or regulatory activity that produces a physical intrusion sufficient to support an action for inverse condemnation, has been found in a variety of circumstances. The general rule regarding takings is that if the government physically invades land, the regulation will generally be held to be a *per se* taking unless such acquisition secured a private benefit to the landowner or was a "temporary deprivation," in which case the *Penn Central* balancing test is applied.[52]

The general rule for physical taking is clearly established in *Loretto v. Teleprompter Manhattan CATV Corp.*,[53] which applied the "rule of reason" balancing test to temporary regulation. The Supreme Court, in the *Loretto* decision, announced a per se rule requiring that an enactment that authorizes a "permanent physical occupation" of a landowner's prop-

---

51. While *Penn Central* best represented the dramatic shift in the role of the Supreme Court in land use cases, it should be noted that in 1974, the Court also decided Village of Belle Terre v. Boraas, 416 U.S. 1 (1974) (upholding single family zoning restrictions against equal protection challenges).
52. *See* Hodel v. Irving, 481 U.S. 704 (1987); Andrus v. Allard, 444 U.S. 51 (1979); Griggs v. Allegheny, 369 U.S. 84 (1962). The dissent in Loretto v. Teleprompter Manhattan CATV Corp., 458 U.S. 419, 442-56 (1982) (Blackmun, J., dissenting), characterized Justice Marshall's majority opinion as having established a *per se* takings rule. The dissent viewed the majority's opinion as the sole example of abandonment of the balancing approach previously followed by the Court. *Id.* at 451. Although the majority opinion does, in passing, discuss the dissent's characterization of its holding as a per se rule, *id.* at 435 n.12, the majority still alluded to the Penn Central case in arriving at a decision and held that one fact—permanent physical occupation of an owner's property—was dispositive of its taking analysis. Whether or not, as the dissent suggested, this constitutes a per se takings rule can be answered definitively only by the Supreme Court. In any event, if such a rule has been announced, it is clearly limited to circumstances where a permanent physical occupation has in fact been established.
53. Loretto v. Teleprompter Manhattan CATV Corp., 458 U.S. 419 (1982).

erty constitutes a taking regardless of the nature of the governmental interest involved.

In *Loretto*, an apartment owner claimed a taking occurred because a New York statute authorized a cable TV company to install cable lines and boxes containing roof cables on the roof of his apartment building. The Supreme Court held that a *permanent physical occupation authorized by government* is a taking even though the physical interference with the landowner's property is minimal. The Court found that the taking in *Loretto* destroyed the apartment owner's right to exclude and therefore established that a taking had occurred. Additionally, the Court held that the *per se* taking rule does not apply to temporary physical invasions or cases when "a regulation merely restricts the use of property." In all taking claims where a permanent physical invasion has not taken place, the Supreme Court reaffirmed in *Loretto* that it will engage in an *ad hoc* "multi-factor" inquiry into the "economic impact of the regulation, the extent to which it interferes with investment-backed expectations and the character of the government action."[54]

Title Takings—Nollan

A taking of title will be established when it is shown that the government has taken possession of property, which is owned by an individual or private group, even though there has been no physical trespass upon the property. This proposition is displayed in *Nollan v. California Coastal Comm'n*.[55] In *Nollan*, the Supreme Court put municipalities on notice that drafting and implementing regulatory conditions in the development approval process that effectuate acquisition of title or the interference with possession can result in a finding that private property has been taken for public use requiring the payment of just compensation.

The Nollans were beachfront landowners who wanted to replace their dilapidated small bungalow with a larger house. They were granted a permit from the California Coastal Commission with the condition that the Nollans grant an easement, by deed, for the public to pass across their beach. The easement required was a lateral one that would pass across a portion of their property bounded by the mean high tide line on one side and their seawall on the other.

---

54. *See id.* at 432.
55. Nollan v. California Coastal Comm'n., 483 U.S. 825 (1987).

The Commission's stated rationale was that the new structure would obscure the view of the ocean, thus discouraging access, and burdening the public's right to traverse along the shore front. It would prevent the public "psychologically . . . from realizing a stretch of coastline exists nearby that they have every right to visit." The Nollans challenged the condition on the grounds that it constituted a taking under the Fifth Amendment. The Superior Court agreed, but the Court of Appeals reversed, finding the condition did not deprive the Nollans of all reasonable use of their property.

The U.S. Supreme Court reversed again and required that an "essential nexus" exist between the state's underlying public purpose and any condition attached to the permit effectuating a transfer of title. This "essential nexus" analysis involved an inquiry into whether a reasonable causal connection exists between the prevention of the perceived adverse impacts of the development and the conditions the government has imposed on the permit. The permit condition was invalidated because it "fail[ed] to further the end advanced" where there was no relationship between the stated objectives of ensuring visual access to the beach and preventing psychological access barriers, as well as the "requirement that people already on the beaches be able to walk across the Nollans' property."

Because the condition involved a *"permanent physical occupation of property"* (and arguably because the condition was not a legislative act), the Court employed a heightened scrutiny in determining the "fit" between the condition imposed and the underlying objectives. As Justice Scalia noted, "in that context there is heightened risk that the purpose is avoidance of the compensation requirement." However, the Court also made it clear that regulations that involve acquisition of title are not *per se* unconstitutional. It was within the Commission's power to either condition the building permit on the dedication of an easement, or to deny the permit outright.

Economic Entitlement Takings

Economic entitlement takings comprise the majority of inverse condemnation cases. Although no physical invasion or taking of title of the property is involved, the deprivation of the use and enjoyment of the property causing permanent diminution in the value of such property can sometimes result in a taking. To determine economic impact, the property interest must be viewed in its totality and the person claiming a taking must have ownership or entitlement to the property taken.[56] Faced with such a requirement, courts that must determine when property value has been injured or destroyed have developed a two-tier inquiry to determine if the Fifth Amendment has been violated: (1) the purpose of the regulation must serve a legitimate state interest and the means chosen must substantially advance the intended purpose;[57] or (2) the court will determine if there is a reasonable beneficial use remaining for the property when viewed as a whole.[58]

1st Tier Inquiry—"Public Use" Review: The role of the courts in reviewing exercises of police power is "an extremely narrow one."[59] In *Hawaii Housing Auth. v. Midkiff,*[60] the Supreme Court held that the police power may extend to any conceivable public purpose, coterminous with the power of eminent domain. "[T]he Court has made it clear that it will not substitute its judgment for a legislature's judgment as to what constitutes a public use 'unless the use be palpably without reasonable foundation.'"[61]

More recently, in the context of an equal protection challenge, the Court has restated this position in *Federal Communications Commission v. Beach Communications, Inc.,* holding that:

> In areas of social and economic policy, a statutory classification that neither proceeds along suspect lines nor infringes fundamental constitutional rights must be upheld against equal protection

---

56. *See* Concrete Pipe & Products, Inc. v. Construction Laborers Pension Trust, 113 S. Ct. 2264 (1993); Andrus v. Allard, 444 U.S. 51 (1979); Penn Cent. Transp. Co. v. New York City, 438 U.S. 104 (1978); *see also* Robert H. Freilich *et al.*, *Supreme Court Review: The New Conservative Paradigm Impacts State and Local Government*, 23 Urb. Law. 499, 608 (1991). *But see* Lucas v. South Carolina Coastal Council, 112 S. Ct. 2886 (1992); Florida Rock Indus., Inc. v. United States, 18 F.3d 1560 (1994); Loveladies Harbor, Inc. v. United States, 1994 WL 259489 (Fed. Cir.).
57. *See supra* note 16 and accompanying text (re: "public use" challenges).
58. As will be seen, such economic impact assessment can either result in a per se taking or a balancing test will be applied. The concept of economic "entitlement" is discussed more fully *infra* at Part II.B.3.b.
59. Berman v. Parker, 348 U.S. 26 (1954).
60. Hawaii Housing Auth. v. Midkiff, 467 U.S. 229 (1984).
61. *Id.* (citing United States v. Gettysburg Elec. R. Co., 160 U.S. 668, 680 (1896)).

> challenge if there is any reasonably conceivable state of facts that could provide a rational basis for the classification. . . . This standard of review is a paradigm of judicial restraint. 'The Constitution presumes that, absent some reason to infer antipathy, even improvident decisions will eventually be rectified by the democratic process and that judicial intervention is generally unwarranted no matter how unwisely we may think a political branch has acted.'[62]

2nd Tier Inquiry—Economic Entitlement: This level of inquiry will only be reached if the regulation passes muster under the legitimacy review. If a regulation fails legitimacy review, then any attempt to take should be enjoined because it is not for a "public use" or invalidated for violation of the due process requirements of the Fourteenth Amendment.

Under economic entitlement review, the court examines whether there is reasonable beneficial use remaining for the property, when viewed as a whole. This level of review is possible only if the property owner has ripened the controversy by obtaining "a final and authoritative determination of the type and intensity of development legally permitted on the subject property."[63]

Denial of All Economically Beneficial Use of Property—Lucas: In rare cases, economic entitlement review standing alone will be dispositive. As in the case of the *Loretto*[64] decision, the Supreme Court announced a second *per se* taking rule in *Lucas v. South Carolina Coastal Council*.[65] If a regulation denies *all use* of property to which a person is entitled, the finding of taking must be automatic and the court will normally bypass further inquiry.

In this 1992 case, David Lucas, owner of two beachfront lots in South Carolina, claimed that he was denied "all economically viable use" of his property by the South Carolina Beachfront Management Act. He did not challenge the validity of the Act. According to the South Carolina Supreme

62. Federal Communications Commission v. Beach Communications, Inc., 113 S. Ct. 2096, 2101 (1993) (citations omitted).
63. MacDonald, Sommer & Frates v. Yolo County, 477 U.S. 340 (1986). *See* discussion *infra* at Part IV.
64. *See* discussion *supra* at Part II.B.1.
65. 112 S. Ct. 2886 (1992) (amicus brief, Freilich, Stone, Leitner & Carlisle).

Court, "Lucas maintain[ed] that if a regulation operates to deprive a landowner of 'all economically viable use' of his property, it has worked a taking for which compensation is due, regardless of any other considerations."

The South Carolina court disagreed, finding that there is not a "set formula" to determine when a taking occurs, only a number of factors to consider. In fact, according to the court, the single factor test as advanced by Lucas was expressly rejected by the *Keystone Bituminous Coal*[66] majority. Lucas's failure to attack the legislation in any way caused the court to find that he had conceded that the regulation fell into the "nuisance-like exception" line of cases[67] and was not an illegitimate use of police power, and, therefore, no compensation was due.

The U.S. Supreme Court disagreed. In a majority opinion written by Justice Scalia, the Court essentially held that the scope of the nuisance exception, described above, was too broad and lacked sufficient basis in the law. Scalia began his opinion with a reaffirmation:

> We think, in short, that there are good reasons for our frequently expressed belief that when the owner of real property has been called upon to sacrifice all economically beneficial uses in the name of a common good, that is, to leave his property economically idle, he has suffered a taking.[68]

The opinion continued with a historical review of the "harmful or noxious uses" exception[69] to the taking/compensation rule.

In its opinion the Court noted that over time, the "harmful or noxious use" language upon which governmental entities had based regulation that proscribed certain uses without compensation transformed into the current legislative basis of "harm preventing regulation." The effect of the govern-

---

66. Keystone Bituminous Coal v. DeBenedictis, 480 U.S. 470 (1987).
67. Goldblatt v. Hempstead, 369 U.S. 590 (1962); Miller v. Schoene, 276 U.S. 272 (1928); Hadachek v. Sebastian, 239 U.S. 394 (1915); Mugler v. Kansas, 123 U.S. 623 (1887).
68. *See Lucas,* 112 S. Ct. 2886.
69. Prior to *Lucas,* it was generally recognized that where the character of government action was to prevent harm, the regulation could virtually prohibit all uses of the property without constituting a taking. Keystone Bituminous Coal, 480 U.S. 470; Hadachek, 239 U.S. 394; Euclid v. Ambler Realty Co., 272 U.S. 365 (1926).

mental action remained the same but the boundaries of application widened.

The Court found the broader range of regulation without compensation available to governmental entities to be unsustainable. Justice Scalia opined that "[a] fortiori the legislature's recitation of a noxious use justification cannot be the basis for departing from our categorical rule that total regulatory taking must be compensated. If it were, departure would virtually always be allowed."[70] Consequently, the Court held that for an act of governmental regulation to be upheld, which deprived a landowner of all use of the property, the regulation may only "proscribe use interests [which] were not part of his title to begin with."[71] This means, in the explanation of the Court, that the regulation must be tied to a common-law property or nuisance principle which prohibited the use even without the regulation—an inquiry that involves three factors:

1. The degree of harm to public land and resources, or adjacent private property, posed by the claimant's proposed activities;
2. The social value of the claimant's activities and its suitability to the location in question; and
3. The relative ease with which the alleged harm can be avoided through measures taken by the claimant and the government.[72]

The Court added:

> The fact that a particular use has long been engaged in by similarly suited owners ordinarily imports a lack of any common-law prohibition (though changed circumstances or new knowledge may make what was previously permissible no longer so). So also does the fact that other landowners, similarly situated, are permitted to continue the use denied to the claimant.[73]

It is interesting to note that the Court instructed lower courts to turn to the Restatement (Second) of Torts to determine what prohibitions were placed on use of the property. The Restatement, however, looks to statutory enactments.

---

70. *Lucas,* 112 S. Ct. at 2899.
71. *Id.*
72. *Id.* at 2901.
73. *Id.*

> In respect to certain types of intentional invasion, there has been a crystallization of legal opinions as to gravity and utility, with the result that the invasions are held to be reasonable or unreasonable as a matter of law. This crystallization may appear in the form of a legislative enactment. . . .[74]

This comment in the Restatement accords with the belief that once a statute has been passed, it passes into the common law.[75] What restrictions, then, are applicable to what property owner? The post-*Lucas* decisions are mixed, but generally have not shown any substantial changes in existing taking jurisprudence.

In *Stevens v. City of Cannon Beach,*[76] an Oregon appellate court applied *Lucas* to hold that the denial of an owner's application for permits to build a seawall as part of a future hotel development of vacant lots in the dry sand area of the city was not a taking because the owner's property interests before the permit denial never included development rights to build a seawall that could interfere with the public's use of the dry sand area.

Likewise, in *Wilson v. Commonwealth,*[77] the Massachusetts Supreme Court found *Lucas* to be of no assistance in deciding that no taking occurred in the destruction of oceanfront properties by natural forces while administrative procedures were underway by the Department of Environmental Quality Protection to determine if the property owners could build a revetment which would have protected their properties.

Citing *Lucas*, the court in *Bernardsville Quarry v. Borough of Bernardsville*[78] held that a municipal ordinance limiting quarry operations was not a taking because (although the quarry was not an actual nuisance) the quarry had a harmful impact on the public welfare sufficient to justify a protective governmental response to limit the quarrying activities. The court found that the property retained its value and that the quarry owner could have reasonably foreseen the municipal regulation.

---

74. Restatement (Second) of Torts § 826 cmt. a (1979).
75. Guido Calabresi, A Common Law for the Age of Statutes, 83-85 (1982).
76. Stevens v. City of Cannon Beach, 835 P.2d 940 (Or. Ct. App. 1992).
77. Wilson v. Commonwealth, 597 N.E.2d 43 (Mass. 1992).
78. Bernardsville Quarry v. Borough of Bernardsville, 608 A.2d 1377 (N.J. 1992).

Finally, in *Berrios v. City of Lancaster,*[79] the district court cited *Lucas* to hold that (to determine if compensation is required when the government takes property in the exercise of its police power) the court must look at the economic impact of the regulation and the extent to which the regulation interfered with distinct investment-backed expectations. Although the court found the entire property interest of the plaintiffs to be taken and extinguished by the city's regulation which condemned the plaintiffs' rented housing as unfit for human habitation, the court distinguished the case from *Lucas* because the regulation was not newly legislated and could have been anticipated since sixty days' notice to vacate was provided. Also, there was no reasonable investment-backed expectation to retain possession of the housing beyond the sixty-day notice because their investment was paid in thirty-day periods.[80]

In any event, *Lucas*'s categorical taking rule clearly addressed only claims where property is rendered valueless in perpetuity.[81] In his opening paragraph, Justice Scalia emphasized that the petition for certiorari squarely raised the question of whether regulatory prohibitions rendered Lucas's parcels permanently valueless. Repeatedly, throughout his opinion, Justice Scalia emphasized the draconian prohibitions of the Beachfront Management Act and its "complete extinguishment of property value" and "permanent ban on construction insofar as Lucas's lots were concerned." The Act permanently deprived of "any reasonable economic use of the lots . . .

---

79. Berrios v. City of Lancaster, 798 F. Supp. 1153 (E.D. Pa. 1992).
80. A suggested approach to the design and application of land use regulations in order to avoid *Lucas*'s claims includes keeping the following in mind when drafting:
   a. Focus on intensity of uses rather than blanket statements of uses permitted, thereby allowing potential uses;
   b. Consider the use of performance standards where applicable, incorporate a site plan review process;
   c. Designate critical areas based on "hard" criteria keeping in mind existing property and nuisance regulations and the basis of the regulation in the preservation of public health or welfare;
   d. Allow relief in all regulations—consider variances, special permits, or conditional uses;
   e. If a moratorium must be imposed, keep it short.

   See Terry D. Morgan, *Taking Law: Strategies for Dealing with Lucas*, 45 Land Use L. & Zoning Dig. 3 (Jan. 1993).
81. Lucas v. South Carolina Coastal Council, 112 S. Ct. 2886, 2891 (1992).

and eliminated the unrestricted right of use, and render[ed] them valueless."[82] Justice Scalia stressed the Act's "obliteration of the value of petitioner's lots." Justice Scalia found that a categorical taking occurred because the Act's prohibitions were "unconditional and permanent" and a "total deprivation of beneficial use."[83]

Justice Scalia made perfectly clear, when he referred to "*all* economically beneficial uses," that "all" means "all." Property must be rendered "valueless" by reason of the application of a regulatory scheme.[84] Justice Scalia refused to entertain any argument (as addressed in the dissents) that "valueless" did not mean "valueless."[85]

Seemingly, therefore, Lucas's holdings as to a per se, categorical, taking should be confined to inverse condemnation of fee simple title—a conclusion buttressed by other Supreme Court cases. In *Penn Central*, the Court explained that:

> 'Taking' jurisprudence does not divide a single parcel into discrete segments and attempt to determine whether rights in a particular segment have been entirely abrogated. In deciding whether a particular governmental action has effected a taking, this Court focuses rather both on the character of the action and on the nature and extent of the interference with rights in the parcel as a whole. . . . [86]

Similarly in *Andrus v. Allard*,[87] the Court stated that "where an owner possesses a full 'bundle' of property rights, the destruction of one 'strand' of the bundle is not a taking, because the aggregate must be viewed in its entirety."[88] In the same vein, Justice Stevens in his dissent in *First English Lutheran Church of Glendale v. City of Los Angeles* stated: "Regulations are three dimensional: they have depth, width, and length. . . . It is obvious

82. *Id.* at 2890.
83. *Id.* at 2894.
84. *Id.* at 2895.
85. *Id.* at 2896 n.9. Two of the dissenting Justices found the lower court's finding the property was valueless to be erroneous. *See id.* at 2908 (Blackmun, J., dissenting), 2925 (Souter, J., statement).
86. Penn Cent. Transp. Co. v. City of New York, 438 U.S. 104 (1978).
87. 444 U.S. 51 (1979).
88. *Id.* at 65-66.

that no one of these elements can be analyzed alone to evaluate the impact of a regulation, and hence to determine whether a taking has occurred."[89]

Notwithstanding the holdings in these cases, however, Justice Scalia further stated that the "rhetorical force" of the "no economically viable use" rule is "greater than its precision, since the rule does not make clear the 'property interest' against which the loss of value is to be measured."[90] Nonetheless, for the time being, it appears that Justice Scalia's "deprivation fraction" will be defined according to the factual circumstances of the *Lucas* case, namely, that a land use regulation must effectively take fee simple title in perpetuity before a categorical taking will be found.[91] See discussion re: *Penn Central, supra,* and also *Fulling v. Palumbo*.[92]

Post-*Lucas* decisions have declined to pursue Justice Scalia's invitation to find a taking in other circumstances:

> [F]or example, (where) a regulation requires a developer to leave 90 percent of a rural tract in its natural state, it is unclear whether we would analyze the situation as one in which the owner has been deprived of all economically beneficial use of the *burdened por-*

89. First English Lutheran Church of Glendale v. City of Los Angeles, 482 U.S. 304 (1987), *on remand*, 210 Cal. App. 3d 1353 (1989). *See also* Keystone Bituminous Coal Assn v. DeBenedictus, 480 U.S. 470 (1987).
90. Lucas v. South Carolina Coastal Council, 112 S. Ct. 2886 (1992).
91. *See also id.* at 2894 n.7; Loretto v. Teleprompter Manhattan CATV Corp., 458 U.S. 419 (1982) (discussed *supra*, at Part II.B.1.). In dictum, however, Justice Scalia also indicates that a noncategorical taking may be found in certain circumstances where all economically viable use of the property is not deprived. Lucas, 112 S. Ct. at 2895 n.8. In this footnote, Justice Scalia observes that an owner whose property has been diminished in value 95 percent may not benefit from the categorical rule created in Lucas, but as the Court has acknowledged "[t]he economic impact of the regulations on the claimant and . . . the extent to which regulation has interfered with distinct investment-backed expectations are keenly relevant to taking analysis *generally*." *Id. Cf.* Agins v. City of Tiburon, 447 U.S. 255 (1980); Andrus v. Allard, 444 U.S. 51 (1979); Penn Cent. Transp. Co. v. New York City, 438 U.S. 104 (1978). If the regulation has taken all use of the property, the *Lucas* Court held that the landowner must be compensated unless the regulation is based on common-law property or nuisance principles. *Lucas*, 112 S. Ct. at 2900. If, however, the landowner is left with some use of the property, it appears that the inquiry will return to the balancing of interests.
92. *See* Fulling v. Palumbo, 233 N.E.2d 272 (N.Y. 1967).

> *tion of the tract*, or as one in which the owner has suffered a mere diminution in value of the tract as a whole.[93]

In *Powers v. Skagit County*,[94] a Washington appellate court construed *Lucas* to require compensation for a taking whenever land use restrictions deny a landowner *all* economically viable use of his property. If the restriction denies the landowner some but not all economically viable use, the court must examine whether there is a reasonable beneficial use remaining for the property when viewed as a whole or if the restriction is unduly oppressive which requires a balancing of interests.

Additionally, in *Reahard v. Lee County*,[95] the Eleventh Circuit, after waiting for the release of the *Lucas* opinion, noted that *Lucas* left open how the categorical taking rule set forth in the Court's opinion applied to situations in which a part of a landowner's property was rendered unusable by a regulation. Therefore, the court relied on *Nollan* to hold that the balancing tests to be used in a taking analysis were whether the regulation substantially advanced a legitimate state interest and whether the regulation denied an owner all or substantially all economically viable use of his property.

The Supreme Court also appears to have resolved any remaining dilemma in *Concrete Pipe & Products of California, Inc. v. Construction Laborers Pension Trust*, [96] where Justice Souter, writing for the Court, stated that "[t]o the extent that any portion of the property is taken, that portion is always taken in its entirety; the relevant question, however, is whether the property taken is all, or only a portion of the parcel in question."[97]

---

93. *Lucas*, 112 S. Ct. at 2890 n.7.
94. Powers v. Skagit County, 835 P.2d 230 (Wash. Ct. App. 1992).
95. Reahard v. Lee County, 968 F.2d 1131 (11th Cir. 1992).
96. 113 S. Ct. 2264, 2290 (1993).
97. *Id. See also* Presbytery of Seattle v. King County, 787 P.2d 907 (Wash. 1990) (expressly overruling Allingham v. Seattle, 749 P.2d 160 (Wash. 1988), which had allowed partial taking challenges; taking must be determined by viewing statute's effect on entire parcel). *But see* McAndrews v. Bank of New England, 796 F. Supp. 613 (D. Mass. 1992); Bernardsville Quarry v. Borough of Bernardsville, 608 A.2d 1377 (N.J. 1992); Sintra, Inc. v. Seattle, 829 P.2d 765, 771 (Wash. 1992) ("court also asks if the regulation destroys one or more of fundamental attributes of property ownership—right to possess, to exclude others and to dispose of property"); Robinson v. Seattle, 830 P.2d

Economic Value—Claim of Entitlement Versus Entitlement: Thus, for those cases where only a portion of the value of the parcel in question is taken, the decision of whether an economic entitlement taking has been effectuated by government returns to analysis of the *Penn Central* balancing test.[98] A pervasive *Penn Central* question which must be answered when considering a taking of property is that of value.

For example, the Ninth Circuit ruled in *Moore v. City of Costa Mesa*[99] that a land use regulation is not a taking unless it "destroys a major portion of the property's value." In *Ellison v. County of Ventura,*[100] a California court found that no taking occurs unless the landowner can demonstrate that something of value was taken. In *Ellison,* the property *increased* in value between time of purchase and time of trial. As pointed out by a Nevada court in *Stephans v. Tahoe Regional Planning Agency,*[101] the relevant inquiry is not the amount of value that has been destroyed but rather the amount that remains, or the extent of permitted use.[102]

The Fifth Amendment does not guarantee the most profitable use of property.[103] In fact, a general land use regulation may sometimes deprive an owner

---

318 (Wash. 1992), *cert. granted* (both cases), No. 92-487 (amicus curiae National League of Cities, The U.S. Conference of Mayors and the National Association of Counties, brief written by Freilich, Leitner & Carlisle). The Supreme Court recently refused a case that posed this exact question. Tull v. Virginia, 23 Envr. Rptr. 1111 (1991), *cert. denied*, 113 S. Ct. 191 (1992).

98. *See supra* note 45 and accompanying text.
99. Moore v. City of Costa Mesa, 886 F.2d 260, 263 (9th Cir. 1989).
100. Ellison v. County of Ventura, 217 Cal. App. 3d 455 (1990).
101. Stephans v. Tahoe Regional Planning Agency, 697 F. Supp. 1149 (D. Nev. 1988).
102. *See also* Barancik v. County of Marin, 872 F.2d 834 (9th Cir. 1988) (applying the arbitrary and capricious standard, the court upheld a 60-acre parcel, zoning regulation that was coupled with a development rights transfer provision designed to protect agricultural areas); William C. Haas Co. v. City of San Francisco, 605 F. 2d 1117 (9th Cir. 1979), *cert. denied*, 445 U.S. 928 (1980) (95 percent diminution); Long Beach Equities v. County of Ventura, 231 Cal. App. 3d 1016 (1991) (Freilich, Stone, Leitner & Carlisle) (loss of substantially all economic use of the land) (citing Lake Naciemento Ranch Co. v. San Luis Obispo City, 841 F.2d 872 (9th Cir. 1987)); Agins v. City of Tiburon, 447 U.S. 255 (1980).
103. Goldblatt v. Town of Hempstead, 369 U.S. 590 (1962); Jackson Court Condominiums v. City of New Orleans, 874 F.2d 1070, 1080 (5th Cir. 1989); Estate of Scott, 778 S.W. 2d 585, 584-592 (Tex. Ct. App. 1989).

of the best use or uses of his property without just compensation.[104] Similarly, mere diminution in value does not establish a taking.[105]

Notwithstanding these cases, many litigants tend to see the Fifth Amendment as a sort of insurance system guaranteeing a return, even on a bad investment. A common factual pattern is seen where a developer purchases agriculturally zoned property on the suburban fringe and then files suit claiming a taking after an upzoning request is denied. Certainly, such a developer is entitled to the procedural protections of the Fourteenth Amendment because he has a legitimate *claim* of entitlement in the zoning proceedings.[106] However, the Fifth Amendment should not protect such *claims*. Instead, the Fifth Amendment protects a possessory interest in property—entitlement itself.[107]

The only argument available to such a developer is that he enjoyed a reasonable investment-backed expectation to future profits. However, in

---

104. *Goldblatt,* 369 U.S. at 59. *See also* MacLeod v. Santa Clara County, 749 F.2d 541, 548-549 (9th Cir. 1984); Murmur Corp. v. Board of Adjustment, 718 S.W.2d 790, 798 (Tex. Ct. App. 1986). "For this reason 'the taking issue . . . is resolved by focusing on the uses the regulations permit' and the residual value of the property." Pace Resources v. Shrewsbury Tp., 808 F.2d 1023, (2d Cir. 1987) (citing Penn Cent. Transp. Co. v. New York City, 438 U.S. 104 (1978)).

105. *See* Penn Cent. Transp. Co. v. New York City, 438 U.S. 104, 131 (1978). *See also* Hadachek v. Sebastian, 239 U.S. 394 (1915) (although there was shown to be an 87 to 93 percent diminution in property value, there was no taking); Deltona Corp. v. United States, 657 F.2d 1184, (Cl. Ct. 1981), *cert. denied*, 455 U.S. 1017 (1982) ("[t]he decisions of the Supreme Court 'uniformly reject the proposition that diminution in property value, standing alone, can establish a 'taking.' Instead the 'takings' issue in these contexts [of 75 to 99 percent reduction in value] is resolved by focusing on uses that the regulations permit"); Jentgen v. United States, 657 F.2d 1210, 1213 (1981), *cert. denied*, 455 U.S. 1017 (1982) (even drastic diminution in property value does not result in a taking of property); *Haas*, 605 F.2d at 1120 (value reduced from $2,000,000 to $100,000 did not constitute a taking); Woodson Lumber Co. v. City of College Station, 752 S.W. 2d, 744 (Tex. Ct. App. 1988) (mere decrease in value does not constitute a taking).

106. *See* Board of Regents v. Roth, 408 U.S. 564 (1972); Perry v. Sindermann, 408 U.S. 593 (1972).

107. *See generally* John J. Costonis, *Presumptive and Per Se Takings: A Decisional Model for the Taking Issue*, 58 N.Y.U. L. Rev. 465 (1983); James L. Oakes, *"Property Rights" in Constitutional Analysis Today*, 56 Wash. L. Rev. 583 (1981); *cf.* Charles Reich, *The New Property*, Yale L.J. 733 (1964).

Andrus v. Allard, the Supreme Court explained: "[L]oss of future profits—unaccompanied by any *physical* property restriction—provides a slender reed upon which to rest a taking claim. Prediction of profitability is essentially a matter of reasoned speculation that courts are not especially competent to perform."[108]

The difficulty in recovering loss of future profits for refusal to upzone is buttressed by those cases finding the lack of a taking even where a *downzoning* occurs. Investment-backed expectations are reasonable only if they take into account the power of the state to regulate for the public welfare.[109] All property is held subject to the valid exercise of the police power, and the general rule still remains that compensation is not required for all losses resulting from that exercise.

Zoning classifications thus must not be viewed as grants of entitlement, but, instead, as limitations on entitlements. One would not view, for example, a regulation setting speed limits on local roads as an entitlement. Zoning classifications do not give rise to reasonable investment-backed expectations that the property may be used for the designated purposes, since zoning classifications (like speed limits) are subject to future exercises of police power.[110] Any right to be within the protection of the Fifth Amendment must be more than a mere expectancy based upon the continuance of an existing law. Surely, then, Fifth Amendment rights cannot be based upon the mere expectancy of future laws being passed.[111]

---

108. Andrus v. Allard, 444 U.S. 51, 66 (1979) (emphasis added). *See also* Jackson Court Condominiums v. City of New Orleans, 874 F.2d 1070 (5th Cir. 1989) (diminution in value caused by market forces, as opposed to the city, not a taking); Park Ave. Tower Assocs. v. City of New York, 746 F.2d 135 (2d Cir. 1984), *cert. denied*, 470 U.S. 1087 (1985) (entering summary judgment against plaintiffs who claimed that a zoning change reducing maximum floor area ratio from 18 to 13 deprived them of reasonable return on their investments amounting to a taking); Pompa Constr. Corp. v. City of Saratoga Springs, 706 F.2d 418 (2d Cir. 1983) ("The burden was not on the City to prove the economic viability of each permitted use by dollar and cents data").
109. Pace Resources v. Shrewsbury Tp., 808 F.2d 1023, 1033 (2d Cir. 1987).
110. City of Univ. Park v. Benners, 485 S.W.2d 773, 778 (Tex. 1972), *app. dism.*, 411 U.S. 901 (1973).
111. It should also be noted that even interference with an investment-backed expectation (or vested right) triggers only application of the Penn Central balancing test. *See* United States v. Lock, 471 U.S. 84 (1985); Pace Resources, 808 F.2d at 1033.

Time as a Factor: The finding of a taking as a result of governmental regulation is also incomplete without analysis of the crucial factor of time. The word "all" has three meanings. First, it is spatial in the sense that a regulation may have impact on merely a portion of the acreage owned. Second, a regulation may interfere with less than all of the ownership interests represented by the "bundle of sticks" comprising title. And, finally, a regulation may, spatially, render all ownership interests valueless—but for a limited period of time.

First English Evangelical Lutheran Church of Glendale v. County of Los Angeles [112] has been cited, erroneously, for the proposition that denial of all economically viable use even on a temporary basis is a *per se* taking.[113] However, if the regulation is temporary and reasonable in length, all reasonable use has not been denied because there is future use remaining. Thus, for temporary regulations, the test is whether the regulation left a reasonable use over a reasonable period of time.[114]

For example, in *Woodbury Place Partners v. City of Woodbury,*[115] Woodbury Place Partners challenged as a taking a two-year interim moratorium on subdivision approval which prevented the partnership from developing property it owned in the city. The partners successfully showed that the moratorium deprived them of all economically viable use of the property during the two-year period and alleged that action constituted a *per se* taking requiring just compensation.

---

112. 482 U.S. 304 (1987), *on remand*, 210 Cal. App. 3d 1353 (1989).

113. *See* Gus Bauman, *The Supreme Court Becomes Serious About Takings Law*, 10 Zoning & Plan. L. Rep. 145 (Sept. 1987); Nathaniel S. Lawrence, *Regulatory Takings: Beyond the Balancing Test*, 20 Urb. Law. 389 (1988); Craig A. Peterson, *Land Use Regulatory Takings Revisited: The New Supreme Court Approaches*, 39 Hastings L.J. 335, 371-76 (1988).

114. *See* Lawton v. Steele, 152 U.S. 133 (1894); Guinnane v. City & County of San Francisco, 197 Cal. App. 3d 862 (1987); Golden v. Planning Bd. of Ramapo, 285 N.E.2d 291 (N.Y. Ct. App. 1972), *appeal dismissed*, 409 U.S. 1003 (1973); Arverne Bay Constr. Co. v. Thatcher, 15 N.E.2d 587 (N.Y. 1938); Linda Bozung & Deborah Alessi, *Recent Developments in Environmental Preservation and the Rights of Property Owners*, 20 Urb. Law. 969 (1988); Thomas E. Roberts, *Moratoriums Are Alive and Well*, 48 Urb. Land 34, 36 (Sept. 1989).

115. Woodbury Place Partners v. City of Woodbury, 492 N.W.2d 258 (Minn. Ct. App. 1992).

The Minnesota Court of Appeals declined to find a taking. The court found that the "property's economic viability was delayed rather than destroyed."[116] While acknowledging that no other cases had specifically addressed "the dimension of length of time as it applied to the totality of a taking," the court found that the Supreme Court's "inclination to measure the economic burden against the value of the property as a whole, rather than against discrete segments," compelled a rejection of the taking argument.[117] Accordingly, the taking analysis of *Lucas* was found to be inapplicable: "[w]e interpret the phrase 'all economically viable use for two years' as significantly different from 'all economical use' as applied in *Lucas*."[118]

A New **Lochner** *Era?*

As stated by Justice Stevens, regulations are clearly "three-dimensional: they have depth, width, and length . . . " and these elements will be analyzed alone or in combination to evaluate the impact of a regulation to determine whether a taking has occurred. However, these issues pale in importance when compared to the issue of what presumptions and burdens will be applied in the process of making that decision.

In our society, presumptions and burdens flow from what Laurence Tribe has described as vertical and horizontal separation of powers doctrine.[119] The tension between the legislative, judicial, and executive branches of government has been discussed previously in this chapter.[120] In general terms, where the legislature has exercised its police power, the judiciary, generally, has refrained from announcing any specific criteria or tests limiting the exercise of that power.

For example, in *Lawton v. Steele,* [121] the Court stated:

---

116. *Id.* at 261.
117. *Id.* at 262.
118. *Id.* at 261.
119. LAURENCE H. TRIBE, AMERICAN CONSTITUTIONAL LAW, at 18-560 (2d ed. 1988). No department, branch, or level of government is empowered to achieve dominance on its own. And, of course, vertical separation exists by reason of principles of dual sovereignty, full faith and credit, federalism, and comity that exists to separate federal and state exercises of police power.
120. *See supra* Part II.A. regarding *Euclid* and *Nectow.*
121. Lawton v. Steele, 152 U.S. 133, 137 (1894).

> To justify the State in . . . interposing its authority in behalf of the public, it must appear, first, that the interests of the public . . . require such interference; and, second, that the means [are] reasonably necessary for the accomplishment of the purpose, and are not unduly oppressive upon individuals.

In applying this test, debatable questions as to the reasonableness of legislative acts are not for the courts, but for the legislature.[122] If the existence of any rational basis for legislative acts is fairly debatable, the judiciary will uphold those acts because of their presumption of validity—along with the application of those acts on a case-by-case basis.[123] And, most important, cases have left no doubt that persons claiming injury by reason of the application of legislation have the burden on reasonableness.[124]

However, in *Nollan*,[125] the Supreme Court first raised the potential that the presumptions and burdens applied for evaluating a taking claim may differ from those applied to due process challenges. *Nollan* held that the latter merely require that a public body "could rationally have decided" that a land use regulation adopted could achieve its objective—thus triggering minimal scrutiny.[126] To survive a takings claim (or at least one involving the taking of title as was the case in *Nollan*), the Supreme Court appeared to apply a different test—namely that the regulation must "substantially advance" a legitimate state interest.[127] In *Nollan*, Justice Scalia justified a more demanding standard with a particularly emotional exercise of judicial will—arguing that "the right to build on one's own property—even though its exercise can be subjected to legitimate permitting requirements—cannot remotely be described as a 'governmental benefit' justifiable in exchange for a taking of title."[128]

Scalia's observations were not central to his decision because the easement condition imposed in *Nollan* was easily found to employ means not

122. Sproles v. Binford, 286 U.S. 374, 388 (1932).
123. *See supra* note 33 and accompanying text.
124. *See, e.g.*, Bibb v. Navaho Freight Lines, 359 U.S. 520, 529 (1959); United States v. Carolen Prods. Co., 304 U.S. 144, 154 (1938).
125. *See supra* note 56 and accompanying text.
126. Nollan v. California Coastal Comm'n, 483 U.S. 825, 834 n.3 (1987).
127. *Id.* This holding was criticized by Justice Brennan in his dissent. *Id.* at 848 (Brennan, J., dissenting).
128. *Id.* at 833-34 n.2.

reasonably necessary for the accomplishment of the public purpose of maintaining views of the ocean. However, in Justice Rhenquist's decision in *Dolan v. City of Tigard,* [129] the Court expressly abandoned the *Euclid/ Nectow* [130] "rational basis" test—precisely because that test allowed only a "minimal level of scrutiny" by the judiciary. Instead, the majority adopted its evolving "rough proportionality"[131] test—abandoning the separation of powers doctrine that had, after all, led to the "rational basis" test in the first place. And, to put an end to "out-and-out plans of extortion" by rascally politicians telling people what they can build on their own property, the Supreme Court took the dramatic, even surprising, step of shifting the burden of proof to the city to require it to "make some sort of individualized determination" that the dedication required by the city "is related both in nature and extent to the impact of the development."[132]

The Dolans had sought a building permit to demolish a 9,700-square-foot building and to construct a replacement 17,600-square-foot building for an electric and plumbing supply business on 1.67 acres of land in Tigard's downtown central business district. The property was within an "action area" overlay zone, which allowed the city to attach conditions to the Dolans's development at the building permit stage in order to accommodate projected transportation and public facility needs.

Pursuant to the requirements of Oregon's comprehensive land use management program, the City of Tigard codified its comprehensive plan in a Community Development Code (CDC). The CDC required the Dolans and all others located in the central business district to comply with a 15

---

129. 114 S. Ct. 2309 (1994).

130. *See supra* note 33 and accompanying text.

131. One approach in developing a definition for "rough proportionality" is to consider a developer's pro rata share of contribution based on the impact of the development. This theory is discussed in Christopher Lake Dev. Co. v. St. Louis County, 36 F.3d 1269 (8th Cir. 1994).

132. In his dissent, Justice Stephens stated that the majority, in so doing, "made a serious error by abandoning the traditional presumption of constitutionality and imposing a novel burden of proof on a city implementing an admittedly valid comprehensive land use plan." *Dolan*, 114 S. Ct. at 2326. *See* discussion in the dissent at footnote 6 concerning the Court's return to the era of Lochner v. New York, 198 U.S. 45 (1905). *Cf.* Chief Justice Rehnquist's rejection of *Lochner* in his dissent in Community Communications Co. v. City of Boulder, 455 U.S. 40, 67 (1982) (Rehnquist, C.J., dissenting).

percent open space requirement. Tigard granted the Dolans's application, but required them to transfer title to the city of a fifteen-foot easement strip that was within the 100-year flood plain for a storm drainage system. The city also required dedication of an eight-foot easement strip for construction of a pedestrian and bicycle pathway as a condition of the permit. The exactions required dedication of approximately 10 percent of the Dolans's total property, which dedications were applied to the 15 percent open space requirement.

The Tigard Planning Commission's final order for the permit based the two easement conditions on the Comprehensive Master Drainage Plan and the Pedestrian/Bicycle Pathway Plan, which purportedly established a "reasonable relationship" between the Dolans's developmental impacts and the need for increased drainage and alternative means of transportation, respectively. The Oregon Supreme Court upheld the district court's finding that Tigard's exaction did not create a taking of the Dolans's property.

The Supreme Court reversed the Oregon Supreme Court and held that, to justify its exactions: (1) there must be an "essential nexus" present that satisfies *Nollan*; (2) the city (as opposed to the property owner) must demonstrate "rough proportionality" between the harm caused by the new land use and the benefit obtained by the condition; and (3) the city must establish the constitutionality of its condition by making an "individualized determination" that the condition satisfies the proportionality requirement.

On the critical issues of presumptions and burdens addressed in *Dolan*, there are really only two ways to even remotely justify the *Dolan* decision in light of historical precedent. The first is to limit its application to cases where dedications are imposed solely in an *ad hoc* adjudicative manner. The second is to limit its scope to cases requiring a landowner to transfer title to the city.[133]

There are a number of cases that limit *Dolan* to adjudicative decisions. One such case is *Harris v. City of Wichita,*[134] where landowners challenged regulations imposed by the city placing use restrictions on land located at either end of the runway at McConnell Air Force Base. The plaintiffs owned

---

133. A third view would be to limit the application of *Dolan* only in instances where there exists both an ad hoc, nonlegislative condition and the transfer of title.

134. Harris v. City of Wichita, 862 F. Supp. 287 (D. Kan. 1994).

land that was located in the Airport Overlay District (AOD), which was affected by the regulations, and argued that the regulations created a *per se* taking of their property. Upon initial disposal of the case, the district court found that the taking claims were not ripe for adjudication as to the plaintiffs' "as applied" taking challenge, and that the facial challenge to the regulations did not stand as the AOD schemes were reasonable, and not arbitrary and capricious.

After this decision, the plaintiffs filed a motion for reconsideration of the court's ruling on the facial challenge, arguing that the U.S. Supreme Court announced a new standard in *Dolan v. City of Tigard* which should be applied to the case. The district court denied the motion for reconsideration, stating that *Dolan* did not apply to the case. *Dolan* was specifically distinguished from prior land use cases, the court noted, on two grounds: (1) *Dolan* was based on an adjudicative decision to condition a building permit relating to an individual parcel, and (2) the requirement was that the Dolans *deed* portions of their property to the city.

> Furthermore, the City's and County's decisions were legislative rather than adjudicative in nature. The City and County classified entire areas of land surrounding McConnell Air Force Base, not merely the individual parcels owned by plaintiffs. Therefore, *Dolan*'s rough proportionality test does not apply to this case. The court properly assessed this case under the standards applicable to zoning regulations.[135]

Recently, a California court decided *San Mateo County Coastal Landowners' Ass'n v. California Coastal Comm'n,*[136] where it was held that the *Dolan* "rough proportionality" test did not apply to a legislative determination of mandatory agricultural and open space easement requirements for the entire county. "*Dolan* makes it clear that it does not reach the type of legislative determination classifying entire areas of a county . . . [r]ather, its reach is limited to adjudicative decisions conditioning permit applications on particular parcels."[137]

---

135. *Id.* at 294.

136. San Mateo County Coastal Landowners' Ass'n. v. California Coastal Comm'n., 45 Cal. Rptr. 2d 117 (Cal. Ct. App. 1995).

137. *Id.* at 131.

In *Southeast Cass Water Resource Dist. v. Burlington Northern R.R. Co.,*[138] the North Dakota Supreme Court held that an express and generally legislated duty imposed upon a railroad company to provide for improvements, as opposed to an "adjudicative decision to condition," did not require analysis under *Dolan*. This case focused on a water resource district imposing costs on a railroad in order to alter bridges and culverts because of increased water flow.

However, in *Schultz v. City of Grants Pass,*[139] the Oregon Court of Appeals struck down two novel efforts to circumvent *Dolan*. Petitioners owned a 3.85 acre parcel of property located within an urban growth boundary. When petitioners applied for a development permit to partition their property, the city approved the application, subject to conditions, including a ten-foot "dedication for county right of way" along a length of both parcels that abutted a street. In response to the landowners' taking challenge, the city argued that, because the dedication condition was based on city ordinances, it was the "functional equivalent" of a legislative decision and, therefore, not subject to the requirements of *Dolan*. The court stated that the city was mischaracterizing its actions, and misunderstanding *Dolan*.

Since the city ordinances *required* the imposition of a dedication, the city argued, the decision to impose the dedication was actually legislative in nature and therefore not subject to *Dolan*'s heightened scrutiny. The court thought otherwise, stating that "what triggers the heightened scrutiny of exactions is the fact that they are 'not simply a limitation on the use' to which an owner may put upon his or her property, but rather a requirement that the owner deed portions of the property to the local government."

Similarly, in *Parking Ass'n. of Georgia v. City of Atlanta,*[140] an association of companies that managed and owned parking lots challenged the city's ordinance requiring curbs, landscaping, and trees for these parking lots. The Georgia Supreme Court held that the ordinance was not a taking of property; however, the legislative/adjudicative debate was fur-

---

138. Southeast Cass Water Resource Dist. v. Burlington Northern R.R. Co., 527 N.W.2d 884, 896 (N.D. 1995).
139. Schultz v. City of Grants Pass, 884 P.2d 569 (Or. Ct. App. 1994).
140. Parking Ass'n. of Georgia v. City of Atlanta, 450 S.E.2d 200 (Ga. 1994), *cert. denied*, 115 S. Ct. 2268 (1995).

ther sparked by Justice Thomas's dissent from the denial of certiorari (joined by Justice O'Connor) in *Parking Association of Georgia*, where he stated:

> It is hardly surprising that some courts have applied *Dolan's* rough proportionality test even when considering a legislative enactment. It is not clear why the existence of a taking should turn on the type of governmental entity responsible for the taking. A city council can take property just as well as a planning commission can. Moreover, the general applicability of the ordinance should not be relevant in a taking analysis. . . . The distinction between sweeping legislative taking and particularized administrative taking appears to be a distinction without a constitutional difference.

The following collection of cases shows how some courts will only apply the findings of *Dolan* to cases that involve land dedications. For example, in *McCarthy v. City of Leawood,*[141] the Kansas Supreme Court declined to apply the *Dolan* rough proportionality requirement to impact fees. In this case, landowners challenged a city ordinance that conditioned issuance of building permits and plat approval on the payment of impact fees by the landowner. The court stated "[t]he landowners cite no authority for the critical leap which must be made from a fee to a taking of property."[142] Similarly it was found in *Country Joe, Inc. v. City of Eagan*[143] that the rough proportionality of *Dolan* does not apply to the payment of a one-time fee, a building permit, for general street improvements.

Applied directly to development exactions, the court in *Clajon Production Corp. v. Petera*[144] stated:

> [b]efore conducting the governmental interest inquiry, we must first determine whether the 'essential nexus' and 'rough proportionality' tests apply at all to regulatory taking claims. Based on a close reading of *Nollan* and *Dolan*, we conclude that those cases

141. McCarthy v. City of Leawood, 894 P.2d 836, 845 (Kan. 1995).

142. *Id.*

143. Country Joe, Inc. v. City of Eagan, 548 N.W.2d 281 (Minn. Ct. App. 1996).

144. Clajon Production Corp. v. Petera, 70 F.3d 1566 (10th Cir. 1995).

> (and the tests outlined therein) are limited to the context of development exactions where there is a physical taking or its equivalent.[145]

However, the Oregon Court of Appeals, from which the *Dolan* case originated, held in *Clark v. City of Albany*[146] that the rough proportionality test applies specifically to a situation where the landowner is responsible for constructing traffic improvements rather than dedicating parcels of property to the city to construct such improvements. In *Clark*, a developer submitted a site plan to the City of Albany for a fast-food drive-in restaurant, and the city approved the site plan pursuant to the satisfaction of certain conditions by the developer. Of five conditions, number four required that, "prior to issuance of building permits, design for street improvements" must be provided by the developer. Condition five similarly required the developer to "provide financial assurances for or construct improvements" for an adjacent roadway.[147]

The court said of these conditions:

> [T]he fact that *Dolan* itself involved conditions that required a dedication of property interests does not mean that it applies *only* to conditions of that kind. This case is not the appropriate one for line-drawing because, in our view, there is no relevant and meaningful distinction between conditions that require conveyances and conditions like the fourth and fifth ones here. For purposes of taking analysis, we see little difference between a requirement that a developer convey title to the part of the property that is to serve a public purpose, and a requirement that a developer himself make improvements on the affected and nearby property and make it available for the same purposes. The fact that the developer retains title in, or never acquires title to, the property that he is required to improve and make available to the public, does not make the requirement any the less a burden on his use and interest than corresponding requirements that happen also to entail memorialization in the deed records.[148]

---

145. *Id.* at 1578.
146. Clark v. City of Albany, 904 P.2d 185 (Or. Ct. App. 1995).
147. *Id.* at 187.
148. *Id.* at 189. *See also* J.C. Reeves Corp. v. Clackamas County, 887 P.2d 360 (Or. Ct. App. 1994) (rough proportionality applies to development conditions not involving transfer of title).

Dolan has even been applied in analyzing the "taking" of a retiree health benefit fund. In *Templeton Coal Co. v. Shalala,*[149] a federal district court considered the constitutionality of the Coal Industry Retiree Health Benefit Act of 1992 because of a challenged violation of the taking clause. The Act required former coal mining companies to be liable for a new retiree health benefit fund. A challenge to the law was brought by four companies previously involved in the coal mining industry. In addition to a brief mention of *Dolan,* the court analyzed *Concrete Pipe* in order to render its decision. The court held that the Coal Act was not a taking.

However, in *Unity Real Estate Co. v. Hudson,*[150] another district court decided that the same Act was a "taking." In reaching its conclusion, the court relied on a special report and recommendation that is included in the opinion. In this report, the relationship between the past employment and the burden of the Coal Act was considered. The author of the report felt that the Act lacked the rough proportionality required by *Dolan.*[151]

All of these cases are important and instructive. However, in one of the most watched cases of the post-1978 takings era, the California Supreme Court, in *Ehrlich v. City of Culver City,*[152] held that the heightened scrutiny/shifted burden approach dictated in *Dolan* does not apply to legislative acts.

In *Ehrlich,* between 1973 and 1975, plaintiffs acquired 2.4 acres of vacant land and obtained approval to develop the property as a tennis club and recreational facility. The city amended its zoning and general plan ordinances from R-1 (single family residential) and C-2 (retail commercial) to C-3 (commercial). The property was operated by various owners as a recreational facility until 1988, when plaintiff closed the facility due to financial loss. The plaintiff applied for a zoning change and plan amendment to allow construction of a thirty-unit condominium complex valued at $10 million.[153]

---

149. Templeton Coal Co. v. Shalala, 882 F. Supp. 799 (S.D.Ind. 1995).
150. Unity Real Estate Co. v. Hudson, 889 F. Supp. 818 (W.D.Pa. 1995).
151. *Id.* at 847. Several other courts have applied the rough proportionality test to impact fee calculations. These cases include Clajon Production Corp. v. Petera, 70 F.3d 1566 (10th Cir. 1995) and Northern Ill. Home Builders Assn. v. County of DuPage, 649 N.E.2d 384 (Ill. 1995).
152. Ehrlich v. City of Culver City, 911 P.2d 429 (Cal. 1996). Freilich, Kaufman, Fox & Sohagi briefed and argued the case for Culver City.
153. As previously noted, Justice Scalia in Dolan v. City of Tigard stated that "the right to build on one's own property—even though its exercise can be sub-

The city expressed an interest in acquiring the property as public recreational facilities, but in April 1989 decided not to purchase the property due to financial and other constraints.[154] The application for a condominium development was also turned down over concerns of loss of recreational land uses in the city. In subsequent discussions, the development was approved. In lieu of placing four tennis courts on the property, the plaintiff was required to pay $280,000 to be used by the city for additional recreational facilities at another location (recreation fee). The plaintiff was also required to pay an exaction based on the city's "Art in Public Places" program, which totaled $33,200, *or* to place an equivalent amount of art on its own property.

The plaintiff challenged both the art requirement and the recreation fee under the California Mitigation Fee Act and also alleged an unconstitutional taking. Plaintiff paid the recreation fee under protest, received building and other permits to proceed with the development, and preserved the right to challenge the fee through the lawsuit. Residential units were then sold to the public.

---

jected to legitimate permitting requirements—cannot remotely be described as a 'governmental benefit' justifiable in exchange for a taking of title." 483 U.S. 825, 833-34 n.2 (1987). Whether or not, invoking the doctrine of unconstitutional conditions, Justice Scalia would apply heightened scrutiny (or even find a taking) for refusal to upzone is difficult to ascertain. There is, however, the potential that the same wide-ranging, essentially standardless inquiry into the reasonableness of local regulation applied to permitting requirements may also be applied by a majority of the Court to all matters of claimed entitlements as well. *See supra* at Part II.B.3. Justice Stephens in his dissent in *Dolan* equates Scalia's approach to a substantive due process inquiry. Analytically, a condition attached to obtaining an entitlement not presently enjoyed could be examined under the *Euclid/Nectow* approach exploring a "rational basis" for that condition. However, if a prospective property interest is subjected to an unconstitutional condition, it is difficult to understand how a taking could occur.

154. The public's intent to acquire property, if it can be shown, is always a key factor in a judicial finding of a taking. Though not discussed in the opinion, the city's prior interest in acquisition of title may differentiate this case from other cases where an impact fee is charged in the absence of such intent. *Compare* this with the discussion in *Nollan* re: "Out-and-out plans of extortion." Nollan v. California Coastal Comm'n, 483 U.S. 825, 837 (1987).

The case came to the California Supreme Court through a long procedural history. The trial court originally ruled that the recreation fee was invalid, but that the art fee was not unconstitutional. The court of appeals affirmed the trial court judgment in its entirety, but then reversed that portion of the judgment invalidating the recreation fee. Upon certiorari, the U.S. Supreme Court vacated that decision and directed the court of appeals to review its decision in light of *Dolan*. Upon remand from the Supreme Court, a divided court of appeals reached the same result.

Before the California Supreme Court, four separate opinions were filed by the seven-justice panel. A plurality of four justices (Arabian, Lucas, George & Werdegar) agreed that the heightened scrutiny of *Dolan* may apply to permit condition in which the city attempts to use its police power as "leverage" to force the property owner to surrender a benefit (potentially including situations where fees are required).

The Supreme Court in *Dolan* stated that the heightened scrutiny applies to dedications of land that implicate the property owner's right to exclude people from the land. The California Supreme Court applied a broader standard, and stated that heightened scrutiny is triggered when there is a "risk that the local permitting authority will seek to avoid the obligation to pay just compensation" and not merely when the right to exclude is at issue.

The case was remanded to determine the proper amount of the recreation fee that the city could impose. While a plurality decided that the rough proportionality test should be used to test the recreation fee, it also determined that it could not conclude—based on the facts before the court—whether the amount of $280,000 was fair and was based on "individualized findings" required by the increased costs the city would face due to the loss of the plaintiff's recreation land.[155] The Art in Public Places

---

155. The plurality did give strong indications of how the city could prove that the fee was roughly proportional. The recreation fee could be based on:
   (a) Additional administrative expenses incurred in redesignating other property within Culver City for recreational use, or
   (b) Public costs in approving the condominium project, in the form of diminished ability to attract private recreation development, and greater costs in attracting a developer of suitable recreational facilities because the subject property is no longer available for public use.
   (c) As an alternative to imposing the fee, the court suggested that the city could require the plaintiff to transfer the restricted land use (recreation facilities) to

requirement was found to be constitutional and was not tested under the *Nollan/Dolan* framework.

In summary, what can be seined from the pages of *Ehrlich* are two victories for local government. Notwithstanding the fact that the *Ehrlich* court applied *Dolan* to fees (in addition to dedications of land), importantly, it did so only when "such exactions are imposed—as in this case—neither generally nor ministerially, but on an individual and discretionary basis. . . ."[156] In other words, they were only imposed in "a context in which the constraints imposed by legislative and political processes are absent or substantially reduced. . . ."[157] The *Dolan* test, according to the *Ehrlich* court, applies only when a city is acting in the absence of legislative authority providing standards creating a "logical connection between the condition and the purported justification for an outright ban on development."[158] No such legislation existed in Culver City; therefore the case was remanded for further consideration under the *Dolan* standard.

The second victory for local government was more subtle. In upholding the Art in Public Places Ordinance, the *Ehrlich* court came up with a *third* reason[159] to escape the *Dolan* test: by arguing that a "fee is not a development exaction of the kind subject to the *Nollan/Dolan* takings analysis."[160] Culver City's Art in Public Places Ordinance required that a fee be paid in the amount of 1 percent of the total building valuation *or* that the plaintiff contribute an approved work of art of an equivalent value either on-site (in which case it remains the property of the applicant) or donated for placement elsewhere in the city.

The *Ehrlich* court concluded that such a requirement was "akin to traditional land use regulations imposing minimal building setbacks, parking and lighting conditions, landscaping requirements, and other *design* conditions such as color schemes, building materials and architectural ameni-

---

a comparable site owned by the plaintiff, which would return the city to the status quo as it existed prior to approval of the condominium project. The city could then impose a fee in lieu of this unique "recreational use transfer," thus justifying a fee that would serve the same purpose as reserving plaintiff's land for recreational facilities at an alternative site.

156. *Ehrlich*, 911 P.2d at 44.

157. *Id.*

158. *Id.* at 445.

159. The first two are where title transfers or nonlegislative decisions are made.

160. *Ehrlich*, 911 P.2d at 450.

ties."[161] Such aesthetic conditions were held (without further explanation) to be a valid exercise of the city's traditional police power and, as such, not to amount to a taking "merely because they might incidentally restrict a use, diminish the value, or impose a cost in connection with the property."[162]

Nollan/Dolan/Ehrlich aside, it is clear that we are living at a time in which the "Madisonian Clockwork" of the separation of powers doctrine needs a horologer. Judicial power to declare legislative policies void, whether on their face or as applied, must be exercised with restraint. Legislative, and even executive policies,[163] must be identified precisely (to avoid decision on abstract, hypothetical, or moot constitutional questions). Questions of constitutional invalidity must be raised in the plaintiff's first pleadings. A plaintiff must have a direct and personal interest in the question. The presumption of validity requires construction where possible in favor of constitutionality. Attacks on policy that merely argue the wisdom, fairness, justice, or expediency of the policy in abstract terms must always fail. Simply stated, courts are not supposed to substitute their judgment for that of another level or coordinate branch of government.

In consequence of the general presumption in favor of validity of policies (again, both on their face and as applied), and the duty of the courts to resolve all doubts in favor of their validity, the rule is fixed such that the party who alleges the unconstitutionality of a policy has a heavy burden in sustaining that claim. As this author stated (as an editor of the 1983 edition of *Sword & Shield*):

> . . . the burden in policy cases should require a plaintiff to show that no rational basis, which might support the policy exists. Presumptions of validity require proof showing unconstitutionality beyond a reasonable doubt. Certainly, the availability and scope of judicial review will vary depending upon the facts and circumstances of each case. The principle remains the same, and, as pertains to non-statutory review under principles embodied in

---

161. *Id.*

162. One must, of course, ask whether the court's decision would have remained the same had the fee not been imposed pursuant to ordinance but, instead, pursuant to "leveraging" criticized by the court with respect to the recreation fee.

163. The presumption of validity has historically attended judicial, legislative, and executive policies. *Cf.* Pacific States Box & Basket Co. v. White, 296 U.S. 176, 185 (1935); United States v. Chemical Found., 272 U.S. 1, 14-15 (1926).

> the constitution (as opposed to procedures mandated by statutes for review of agency decisions), this presumption of validity attends judicial, legislative, and executive policies.[164]

Nothing has changed. Or has it? If *Dolan*'s reach is not restricted, we have entered a new *Lochner* era.

Ripeness

Nollan/Dolan presage that something may have changed. But (in addition to restricting *Dolan*'s reach to title transfers effectuated by nonlegislative acts) one final, all-important doctrine should prevent the pendulum from swinging further in the direction of judicial activism: ripeness.

Since 1978, decision after decision has enforced the requirement of a final decision by government before the Fifth Amendment's Just Compensation Clause provides a remedy—a requirement that implicitly recognizes that an individual must show definitively that it is the government's *institutional* intent to acquire dominion or control over a specific parcel of property before relief will be granted. Thus, in a leading case, *Williamson County Regional Planning Comm'n v. Hamilton Bank,*[165] the Court required resort to state inverse condemnation proceedings and full utilization of all variance procedures because the Court could not objectively ascertain whether the institution itself, Williamson County, intended to allow Hamilton Bank to develop its property until the institution's procedures were utilized.[166]

---

164. Richard G. Carlisle, *Owen v. City of Independence: Toward Constructing a Model for Municipal Liability After Monell*, in Section 1983 Sword & Shield: Civil Rights Violations: The Liability of Urban, State and Local Government 95 (1983).
165. Williamson County Regional Planning Comm'n v. Hamilton Bank, 473 U.S. 172 (1985).
166. *Cf.* Portsmouth Harbor Land v. United States, 260 U.S. 327, 329-30 (1922) (more than single trespass required to show taking). Hamilton Bank and cases such as Portsmouth Harbor show the difference between temporary regulatory interference, which is not protected by the Fifth Amendment, and a temporary taking, which is protected. Just compensation is a remedy mandated by the Fifth Amendment (the sole instance of a constitutional remedy) for any taking, even a temporary regulatory taking; however, temporary regulatory interference will rarely constitute a taking. *See supra* notes 53-55 and accompanying text.

Earlier, in *Pruneyard Shopping Center v. Robins,*[167] Justice Rehnquist had emphasized the need for an adequate record to decide whether or not application of a regulation has sufficient impact upon the entire "group of rights inherent in the citizen's [ownership]" as to warrant inquiry under the taking clause.[168] Because Pruneyard had the burden of making such a record, a state law concerning the right to solicit signatures on shopping center property was upheld: "There is nothing to suggest that preventing appellants from prohibiting this sort of activity will unreasonably impair the value or use of their property as a shopping center."[169]

In *Agins v. City of Tiburon,*[170] Agins's property had been downzoned by the city of Tiburon, but the full application of downzoning ordinances to Agins's property had not been ascertained because Agins never sought approval for development under those ordinances.[171] Agins filed a complaint against the city in state court seeking, in Count 1, $2 million in damages for inverse condemnation and, in Count 2, a declaration that the zoning ordinances were facially unconstitutional.

The court noted that, "The gravamen of both claims was that the city had taken Agins's property without just compensation in violation of the Fifth and Fourteenth Amendments."[172] In his opinion, Justice Powell confirmed the holding of the state court that the zoning ordinances "on their face" did not take Agins's property without just compensation,[173] treating that challenge as a due process challenge by relying upon the "seminal" decision in *Euclid v. Ambler Realty Co.* for guidance on how to weigh private and public interests when a regulation is challenged on its face.[174] Because the regulations passed by the city of Tiburon substantially advanced legitimate governmental goals, those regulations were upheld.[175] Because the impact of the city's regulations was yet to be ascertained and because Agins had not pursued his reasonable investment-backed expectations by submitting a development plan to local officials, the specific con-

167. Pruneyard Shopping Center v. Robins, 447 U.S. 74 (1980).
168. *Id.* at 82-83 n.6.
169. *Id.* at 83.
170. Agins v. City of Tiburon, 447 U.S. 255 (1980).
171. *Id.* at 257.
172. *Id.* at 258.
173. *Id.* at 255.
174. *Id.* at 261.
175. *Agins*, 447 U.S. at 261. *Cf.* Berman v. Parker, 348 U.S. 26 (1954).

stitutionality under the Taking Clause of the city's regulations, as applied, was not deemed ripe for consideration by the Court.[176]

Hodel v. Virginia Surface Mining & Reclamation Ass'n [177] was a facial challenge to the Surface Mining and Reclamation Act of 1977. Relying upon *Agins*, the Court, in an opinion by Justice Marshall, held that challenges to the application of that Act were premature and not ripe for judicial resolution.[178] In so doing, Justice Marshall held that the taking inquiry "suffers from a fatal deficiency" when a particular piece of property owned by a person claiming just compensation has not been identified as taken by application of a regulation. Absent such an identification, a court must necessarily inquire into the constitutionality of statutes without the benefit of "an actual factual setting that makes such a decision necessary."[179]

"*[A]d hoc*, factual inquires" must be conducted, said Justice Marshall, with respect to "specific property," and the "particular estimates of economic impact and ultimate valuation relevant to the unique circumstances."[180]

---

176. In a case better known for its dissent than its majority opinion, the majority in San Diego Gas & Elec. Co. v. City of San Diego, 450 U.S. 621 (1981) found that the existence of disputed fact issues as to the amount of development that would be permitted by the city precluded Supreme Court review under 28 U.S.C. § 1257 of a California Court of Appeal decision. Discussing Agins v. City of Tiburon, 447 U.S. 255 (1980), the Court held that this decision was not reviewable as a final judgment or decree because the state court had not decided whether any taking had in fact occurred.
177. Hodel v. Virginia Surface Mining & Reclamation Ass'n, 452 U.S. 264 (1981).
178. *Id.* at 296-97 nn.37-40.
179. *Id.* at 294-95.
180. *Id.* at 295. When a party, such as the association in *Hodel*, challenges the facial validity of a regulation without challenging whether or not that regulation advances legitimate government goals, the challenge should be doomed to failure. The general constitutionality of a regulation can be determined only through analysis of whether or not a regulation advances such goals—patently a due process, not a just compensation, inquiry. *Cf.* Keystone Bituminous Coal Ass'n v. DeBenedictus, 480 U.S. 470 (1987) (*supra* note 18.); Hawaii Housing Auth. v. Midkiff, 467 U.S. 229, 244 n.7 (1984) (*supra* note 16 and Part II.B.3.a); Village of Belle Terre v. Boraas, 416 U.S. 1 (1974); Berman v. Parker, 348 U.S. 26 (1954); Euclid v. Ambler Realty Co., 272 U.S. 365 (1926) (*supra*, note 24). Accordingly, such facial challenges are not subject to the strict finality requirements applicable to as applied challenges. Yee v. Escondido, 274 Cal.Reptr. 551 (Cal. Ct. App. 1990), *cert. granted in part*, 502 U.S. 905 (1991), and *judgment affirmed by*, 503 U.S. 519 (1992).

In *Ruckelshaus v. Monsanto Co.*,[181] Justice Blackmun found that interference with reasonable investment-backed expectations was a factor "so overwhelming" that it disposed of the taking question regarding the property involved in that case.[182] However, absent careful proof of interference with such expectations, the *Ruckelshaus* Court found that no taking had occurred. If interference had been shown by Monsanto, the Court might have proceeded with a taking inquiry. However, certain portions of the regulations involved in that case had not been applied, preventing any claim of loss of market value. Consequently, the Court held that "any finding that there has been an actual taking would be premature."[183]

Furthermore, Justice Blackmun went on to hold in *Ruckelshaus* that, "Equitable relief is not available to enjoin an alleged taking of private property for a public use, duly authorized by law, when a suit for compensation can be brought against the sovereign subsequent to the taking."[184] Because a suit to obtain compensation for a taking can *always* be brought against the sovereign in federal court or in state court, this holding is an absolute bar to invalidation suits seeking injunctive relief for violation of the Just Compensation Clause. Invalidation is only available where the taking is not for a public use, in other words, where a regulation does not advance legitimate governmental goals.[185]

---

181. Ruckelshaus v. Monsanto Co., 467 U.S. 986 (1984).
182. *Id.* at 1005.
183. *Id.* at 1013.
184. *Id.* at 1016.
185. *Cf. Hodel, supra* notes 180-83 and accompanying text, and *Nectow, supra* note 33. A proceeding for just compensation, again, should always be available where a public body has taken property for public use. Such is the mandate of the Fifth Amendment, and a distinguishing characteristic from the protections afforded by the Fourteenth Amendment. Where a deprivation of Fourteenth Amendment rights under color of law occurs, the federal courts are always "alert to adjust their remedies so as to grant necessary relief" and compensation is not mandated. Marbury v. Madison, 5 U.S. (1 Cranch) 137 (1903); Bell v. Hood, 327 U.S. 678 (1946). Section 1983, of course, provides an action at law, suit in equity, or other proper proceeding for redress to ensure that a full range of remedies is available for such a deprivation. In appropriate cases, equitable relief is available for a Fourteenth Amendment deprivation. City of Los Angeles v. Lyons, 461 U.S. 95, 112 (1983). Damages are also available under Williamson County Regional Planning Comm'n v. Hamilton Bank, 473 U.S. 170, 197 (1985).

In *United States v. Riverside Bayview Homes, Inc.*, the Corps of Engineers brought an action to enjoin Bayview Homes from filling wetlands in violation of certain federal regulations. In considering the court of appeals's position that the Corps's regulatory authority must be narrowly construed to avoid a taking without just compensation in violation of the Fifth Amendment, Justice White stated in no uncertain terms: "[W]e have made it quite clear that the mere assertion of regulatory jurisdiction by a governmental body does not constitute a regulatory taking."[186]

Relying on the holding in *Ruckelshaus* ("equitable relief is not available to enjoin an alleged taking"), the Court rejected the court of appeals's logic that the challenged regulatory program *might* someday be applied to "in some instances result in the taking of individual pieces of property."[187] Such a possibility was viewed as no justification for the use of narrowing constructions to limit regulatory programs "if compensation will in any event be available in those cases where a taking has occurred."[188]

In *MacDonald, Sommer & Frates v. County of Yolo*,[189] as with the cases previously discussed, the Court embraced the task of developing the meaning of the Just Compensation Clause of the Fifth Amendment.[190] The critical issues of whether the application of regulation to a particular parcel gives rise to a taking and when, in point of time, that taking occurs were squarely addressed in *Yolo County*:

> It follows from the nature of a regulatory takings claim that an essential prerequisite to its assertion is a final and authoritative

---

186. United States v. Riverside Bayview Homes, Inc., 106 S. Ct. 455 at 459.
187. *Id. Cf.* Justice Holmes's opposite approach in *Pennsylvania Coal*, discussed *supra* at Part II.B.
188. Riverside Bayview Homes, 106 S.Ct. at 459. *Cf.* Connolly v. Pension Benefit Guaranty Corp., 475 U.S. 211 (1986) (upholding the Employee Retirement Income Security Act regulation from a facial challenge, notwithstanding the prospect that the Act as applied might give rise to an action for compensation).
189. 477 U.S. 340 (1986).
190. The majority opinion in *Yolo County* was not merely a procedural dance around the question of whether federal, state, and local governments must pay money to a landowner whose property has been "taken" temporarily (or permanently) by the application of governmental regulations. In due time, that question will answer itself, if it has not already been answered. *See* Riverside Bayview Homes, 474 U.S. at 126 ("governmental land-use regulations may under extreme circumstances amount to a 'taking' of . . . affected property").

> determination of the type and intensity of development legally permitted on the subject property. A court cannot determine whether a regulation has gone 'too far' unless it knows how far the regulation goes. As Justice Holmes emphasized throughout his opinion for the Court in *Pennsylvania Coal Company v. Mahon*, 'this is a question of degree—and therefore cannot be disposed of by general propositions.'[191]

In *Yolo County*, the Court wanted to know, not only the nature and extent of development permitted before the taking (the "before value"), but also the nature and extent of development permitted after the "taking" (the "after value"), before making government pay for development rights unconstitutionally taken by the application of regulations limiting development. In *Yolo County*, the Supreme Court, with almost mathematical precision, required identification of "before" and "after" values so that the property acquired could be ascertained unequivocally.[192]

Citing *Hamilton Bank*, the *Yolo County* Court emphasized that the effect of the application of regulations cannot be measured until a final decision is made as to how regulations will be applied showing the extent of actual injury to the value of property and investment-backed profit

---

191. *Yolo County*, 477 U.S. at 348 (citations omitted).
192. Thus, if Blackacre's 100 acres were zoned for 100 single-family lots, and downzoned to open space and the enforcement of that zoning decision permanently took all 100 units of density, then government might be seen as having intended to acquire a conservation easement to that 100 acres so that just compensation would have to be paid. Just compensation analysis would focus on the fair market value of what the owner had lost (before value minus after value). Taking analysis would focus on the character of the government action and on what the government had acquired—what was taken by government that an individual once owned, that the public now enjoys. *Cf.* Kaiser Aetna v. United States, 444 U.S. 164 (1979). Taking analysis focuses upon the interest in property government acquired. Just compensation analysis focuses upon the value of property an individual lost. Once property is taken, courts will require payment of full fair market value for any diminution, however slight. Paradoxically, however, slight diminution is almost never a taking.

expectations.[193] Such an inquiry, again, is the "essential prerequisite" to takings analysis. The language of the Taking Clause, along with Article III, proscribes any other approach. The final and definitive application of a regulation may or may not in extreme circumstances amount to a taking; however, the regulation itself, pure policy, can never take private property.[194] And, at the other end of the spectrum, notwithstanding *Dolan*, the ripeness doctrine should require an *ad hoc* to be affirmed through the institution's applicable variance and appeal mechanisms before a taking can be found. The underlying form of a Fifth Amendment claim is proof that it was government's institutional intent to acquire dominion and control over a specific parcel of property.

---

193. *Id. Cf.* Justice Holmes's opposite approach in Pennsylvania Coal, discussed *supra* at Part II.B.

194. The Supreme Court's holding in Yolo County in this regard, as with similar holdings in Hamilton Bank, pertain to allegations of a taking without just compensation under the Fifth Amendment, not to allegations of a deprivation of property without due process of law under the Fourteenth Amendment. This distinction should be emphasized because, in a proper case, an inchoate proceeding or a final decision denying an application could result in a due process violation, even though it did not give rise to a taking without just compensation. The Court in Yolo County stated:

> A property owner is of course not required to resort to piecemeal litigation or otherwise unfair procedures in order to obtain this determination (of what use, if any, may be made of the affected property). *See* Williamson Planning Comm'n v. Hamilton Bank, 473 U.S. at 179, 105 S. Ct. at 3112-113 (Stephens, J. concurring in judgment); United States v. Dickinson, 331 U.S. 745, 749 (1947).

Thus, if an applicant seeks a final decision of the type and intensity of development legally permitted, but is unreasonably frustrated in that search, a due process violation arises by reason of the "unfair procedures" themselves, quite aside from any taking. It would be paradoxical to hold that an applicant must obtain a determination of permitted development on the one hand, while allowing government to refuse to make such a determination on the other. The Just Compensation Clause requires a final determination of permitted development; the Due Process Clause does not.

Chapter Nine
Prison and Jail Litigation Under § 1983

David J. LaBrec
Katie Anderson

Prison litigation affects every segment of our society—law enforcement, taxpayers, inmates, and virtually every entity or individual concerned with the human condition and crime in our society. As a society, Americans almost unanimously agree that convicted criminals should be punished, set apart from others, but they should not be subjected to cruel and unusual punishment. The U.S. Constitution codifies this belief.

The Eighth Amendment, made applicable to state governments by the Fourteenth Amendment, reads as follows:

> Excessive bail shall not be required, nor excessive fines imposed, nor *cruel and unusual punishments* inflicted.

The U.S. Supreme Court has interpreted these words "in a flexible and dynamic manner"[1] and further clarified what this means by stating, "Conditions must not involve the wanton and unnecessary infliction of pain, nor may they be grossly disproportionate to the severity of the crime warranting punishment."[2]

But the Court also has made it clear that the Eighth Amendment's ban on cruel and unusual punishment does not guarantee the comfort of those incarcerated. Most notably, the Court stated that "the Constitution does not mandate comfortable prisons."[3] Similarly, at least one circuit has held that "[w]hile the temperature in extended lockdown may be uncomfortable, that alone cannot support a finding that the plaintiff was subjected to cruel and unusual punishment in violation of the Eighth Amendment."[4]

---

1. Rhodes v. Chapman, 452 U.S. 337, 345 (1981) citing Gregg v. Georgia, 428 U.S. 153 (1976).
2. *Id.* at 347.
3. *Id.* at 349.
4. Woods v. Edwards, 51 F.3d 577, 581 (5th Cir. 1995).

Interestingly, the circuit courts are split on how to review prisoners' complaints. In his concurring opinion in *Rhodes v. Chapman*, Justice Brennan suggested that "a court considering an Eighth Amendment challenge to conditions of confinement must examine the totality of the circumstances."[5] Several circuits have addressed this totality standard.

For example, the Fifth Circuit follows this rule:

> In determining whether conditions of confinement are unconstitutional under the Eighth Amendment or the Fourteenth Amendment, we do not assay separately each of the institutional practices but look to the totality of conditions. Our task is limited to enforcing constitutional standards rather than assuming superintendence of jail administration.[6]

Meanwhile, the Eighth Circuit believes that even though an individual prisoner's complaint does not itself involve an Eighth Amendment violation, such a violation could still exist when that complaint is considered in light of the totality of circumstances.[7] Note, however, that the Supreme Court has stated that "nothing so amorphous as 'overall conditions' can rise to the level of cruel and unusual punishment when no specific deprivation of a single human need exists."[8]

Additionally, and perhaps most importantly, to be liable under § 1983, prison officials must exhibit "deliberate indifference" to at least one prisoner's health or safety.[9] Such deliberate indifference requires more than mere negligence or inattentiveness.

This chapter addresses several issues arising from jail and prison confinement that are currently evolving, including overcrowding, security, classification, health and medical care, diet and nutrition, exercise, visitation, suicides, right to counsel, discipline, and other similar topics that are facing our prison system today. Some of the decisions of various courts seem to go far to preserve and protect prisoners' rights, while other rulings ap-

---

5. *Rhodes*, 452 U.S. at 362-63.
6. Jones v. Diamond, 636 F.2d 1364, 1368 (5th Cir. 1981); *see also* McCord v. Maggio, 910 F.2d 1248 (5th Cir. 1990).
7. Tyler v. Black, 811 F.2d 424, 433 (8th Cir. 1987), *modified*, 865 F.2d 181 (8th Cir. 1989).
8. Wilson v. Seiter, 501 U.S. 294, 305 (1991).
9. Farmer v. Brennan, 114 S.Ct. 1970, 1977 (1994).

pear to be insufficient to truly protect such rights. Regardless of where one's sympathies lie, it is clear that prisoners and those who house them must keep current with this evolving area of the law.[10]

Is Public Perception Reality?

Prisoners are not stripped of their constitutional rights by the mere fact that they are incarcerated. However, the governmental entities overseeing the prison system have significant expenses that are incurred when they remedy prisoners' grievances. To what extent must prison officials respond to prisoner complaints? In recent years, prison inmate lawsuits have proliferated and their numbers continue to increase. Prison inmates have rising voices, complaining of everything from minor discomforts to serious grievances.

Recently, moviegoers have been mesmerized by horrific prison tales on the big screen. Kevin Bacon portrayed an abused prisoner at Alcatraz who literally spent years "in the hole" or "dungeon." Based on a true story, *Murder in the First* contained graphic scenes of a prisoner in isolation for an inordinate amount of time and both the mental and physical abuse he suffered. *The Shawshank Redemption*, another box office hit, described the hopeless life of prisoners in America's past, including abusive treatment by prison officials.

While the American public is enticed by plots and themes of awful prison life in yesteryear, it is also interested in the current state of the prison system. "Forty-Eight Hours" recently aired a piece on prisoners titled "Hard Time." This program addressed America cracking down on crime and enforcing longer prison sentences because citizens are tired of living in fear. At the conclusion, Dan Rather asked: Are we going too far?

The first segment of "Forty-Eight Hours," "Chain Reaction," covered chain gangs being reintroduced in Alabama, a state where the prison population has quadrupled in the past decade. A later segment, "Crime Pays," explained the problem many jailers face in controlling their prison population because prisoners often occupy 90 percent of a jail while prison

---

10. The "privatization" of prisons is an evolving area also. The U.S. Supreme Court recently held that two prison guards who were employed by a private firm, not the state, were not entitled to qualified immunity for allegedly using restraints on a prisoner in a manner that violated the Constitution. Richardson v. McKnight, 117 S. Ct. 2100 (1997).

officials only control 10 percent of a facility. The program also discussed Jail Expo, an annual conference sponsored by the American Jail Association, which offers innovative electronics for sale to jail administrators who cannot afford a large staff. After all, as one jailer said, the prison system requires citizens to spend a great deal of money on a segment of society that is not giving anything back.

In another segment, journalist Tom Wicker remembered the worst prison uprising in America's history at New York's Attica State Prison on September 9, 1971. Thirty-nine people died by police fire. Apparently, the prisoners were subjected to unlivable conditions, such as total restriction from all activities including education and recreation. Because of their inhumane treatment, the prisoners fought for what they believed to be their basic human rights.

Media programs such as these are instrumental in demonstrating the competing interests of affording all people their basic liberties versus not spending undue time and resources on a portion of society that has committed wrongs against society.

As with all in life and law, a balance must be reached. Taxpayers are not anxious to chip in more of their hard-earned wages in order that those who have violated the law can have all the modern comforts. Nevertheless, the U.S. Constitution provides guarantees to all. To strike a constitutional balance and, thus, for harmony to prevail, the government must at least meet the minimum requirements found in the Constitution. While many provisions of the Constitution are applicable, such as the Due Process Clause, the First Amendment, etc., the majority of prisoners' § 1983 claims are brought pursuant to the Eighth Amendment.

How Many Prisoners Can Be Incarcerated and How Should They Be Separated?

Overcrowding necessarily involves the limitation of general movement as well as potential for physical and mental injury. Additionally, vandalization of cells and an atmosphere of violence can often be attributed to overcrowding of inmates.[11] The experience of Harris County, Texas, is illustrative.

The overcrowding in Harris County jails caused by overflow prisoners from the Texas Department of Corrections stressed all systems of the jail, including food service, programming, elevators, recreation, classification,

11. *See* Hutto v. Finney, 437 U.S. 678, 688 (1978).

maintenance, visiting, supplies of clothing and bedding, security, medical care, and mental health services.[12]

Hoping to alleviate some of the overcrowding, the district court ordered the county to deliver at least 290 transfer-ready felons per week to the Texas Department of Corrections. However, the state refused to accept the transfer, and the county could not comply with the court's order. The district court eventually found that these conditions resulted in extreme overcrowding where 2,800-2,900 prisoners slept on the floor each night, forming a "human carpet" and compromising fire safety.[13] The court later ordered the state to pay a per diem amount for each state inmate being housed by the county that exceeded the population cap, and the Fifth Circuit has recently upheld the decision.[14]

The Supreme Court has held that "double-bunking" is not unconstitutional as a matter of law where cells were seventy-five square feet and inmates were not confined to the cells during all hours of the day.[15] The Eighth Circuit, however, disapproves of the practice of double-bunking inmates who have exhibited assaultive and predatory behavior toward staff or other inmates.[16]

Inmate Classification/Segregation

Prisons have an affirmative duty to protect inmates from violence.[17] But the courts recognize that prison officials cannot be expected to prevent all attacks.[18] In *Hadley v. Peters*,[19] the plaintiff was attacked by his cellmate for calling him a bum. The court acknowledged that "[v]iolence is unfortunately endemic in American prisons," and then held that the prison officials could not be liable for problems caused by the plaintiff's own contentious nature. The plaintiff was attacked by his cellmate for calling

12. Alberti v. Sheriff of Harris County, 937 F.2d 984, 988 (5th Cir. 1991).
13. *Id.* at 990.
14. Alberti v. Klevenhagen, 46 F.2d 1347 (5th Cir. 1995).
15. Bell v. Wolfish, 441 U.S. 520 (1979).
16. Tyler v. Black, 811 F.2d 424, 434-35 (8th Cir. 1987).
17. Farmer v. Brennan, 114 S.Ct. 1970 (1994).
18. Hadley v. Peters, 841 F. Supp. 850 (C.D. Ill. 1994), *aff'd* 70 F.3d 117 (7th Cir. 1995).
19. *Id.*
20. 841 F. Supp. at 858.

him a bum.[20] Therefore, classification and segregation must at least take into account the potential violence of each inmate, given his or her criminal history.

An inmate has no right to a particular classification, so long as the classification is not unreasonable or arbitrary. In *McCord v. Maggio*,[21] the Fifth Circuit Court noted that "It is well settled that '[p]rison officials must have broad discretion, free from judicial intervention, in classifying prisoners in terms of their custodial status.'"[22] Inmates are classified based on many other considerations, in addition to their propensity for violence.

Pretrial Detainees—Pretrial detainees, those in custody awaiting trial who have not been adjudged guilty, have a right to be free from punishment until they are so adjudged. They may be subjected to only those restrictions and privations which are inherent to confinement itself or are justified by compelling necessities of jail administration, such as effective management, security, order, and discipline.[23]

Because of their unique status, pretrial detainees must be classified and separated from convicted persons to the extent reasonably possible, except where detention in the same cell is required for institutional security.[24] Even though such confinement may have a punitive effect, it will be tolerated when it furthers a legitimate governmental objective, such as addressing a specific institutional violation, if it is not excessive in light of that violation.[25]

Race—Should race be considered in classification of prisoners? Though justice is supposed to be color-blind, the law has begun to acknowledge that people are not. Prospective jurors cannot be peremptorily stricken on the basis of race. So too, decisions with respect to prisoner housing should also be "race-neutral." Fear of racial violence is not a sufficient justification for a broad policy of racial segregation where the fear is generalized or vague.[26]

Nonetheless, prison officials in Ohio were granted a modification of a consent decree that originally prohibited racial discrimination in the as-

---

21. McCord v. Maggio, 910 F.2d 1248 (5th Cir. 1990).
22. *Id.* at 1251 (citing Wilkerson v. Maggio, 703 F.2d 909 (5th Cir. 1983)).
23. Bell v. Wolfish, 441 U.S. 520 (1979).
24. Jones v. Diamond, 636 F.2d 1364, 1376 (5th Cir. 1981).
25. Collazo-Leon v. U.S. Bureau of Prisons, 51 F.3d 315, 318 (1st Cir. 1995).
26. Sockwell v. Phelps, 20 F.3d 187 (5th Cir. 1994).

signment of inmate housing. After implementation of the decree, which called for random cell assignments, a riot ensued and resulted in the murder of nine inmates and one corrections officer.

The court agreed that the new random celling policy, if it were enforced, would pose security problems and would ignore pragmatic penological concerns. The court noted, however, that to allow an indefinite continuation of the status quo in segregating inmates by race would run afoul of the Constitution.[27]

Health/HIV—Prison officials must consider potential health problems in classifying inmates. By housing an inmate who poses a health risk with others, prison officials may violate the general inmate population's right to be free from cruel and unusual punishment. However, medical testing of inmates for HIV implicates constitutional questions concerning privacy. Several courts have addressed this question in the context of inmates who are HIV positive.

One circuit court has boldly stated that the identity and segregation of HIV-positive prisoners obviously serves a legitimate penological interest.[28] By contrast, however, another court held that placing an HIV-positive inmate in an area where mentally disturbed inmates were kept was not reasonably related to legitimate penological concerns.[29]

Sex—One clear basis for segregation of inmates is by sex, yet this test is not always easy to apply. In *Farmer v. Brennan*,[30] a transsexual male was placed in the male population and was allegedly raped. The U.S. Supreme Court remanded the case for application of its articulated test of "deliberate indifference."

Though the case law does not articulate clear-cut standards for all classification decisions, it is clear that prison officials may consider such factors as (1) the status of the prisoner as a pretrial detainee or a convict, (2) race, (3) health, and (4) sex.

---

27. White v. Morris, 832 F. Supp. 1129 (S.D. Ohio 1993).
28. Moore v. Mabus, 976 F.2d 268 (5th Cir. 1992) (failing to explain what legitimate interest is served). *See also* Harris v. Thigpen, 941 F.2d 1495, 1515-21 (11th Cir. 1991) (finding that a blanket HIV testing and segregation policy in the Alabama prison system did not violate any constitutionally protected privacy rights of inmates).
29. Nolley v. County of Erie, 776 F.2d 715 (W.D.N.Y. 1991).
30. 114 S.Ct. 1970 (1994).

Prisoners' Health and Fitness

Medical Care[31]

It is elementary that in order to state an Eighth Amendment claim with respect to medical care, a prisoner must show he or she was treated with deliberate indifference.[32] Deliberate indifference has been defined as official and actual knowledge and disregard of an excessive risk of inmate health or safety. It is equated with the standard for criminal recklessness.[33]

In *Farmer*, the Court held that while prisoners need not prove actual advance notice to prison officials of potential injury, they must show their subjective awareness of the risk of harm. In fact, some courts have said that the deliberate indifference must also result in "substantial harm" before a plaintiff has a constitutional claim.[34] The deliberate indifference standard has been applied in various prison medical care contexts.

In one context, pain and suffering endured by a prisoner that was not incorporated in his sentencing does not violate the Constitution unless a prison official intended the prisoner to suffer.[35]

State caretakers may not intentionally delay medical care or knowingly interfere with treatment.[36] However, the courts will generally defer to the discretion of prison officials in administering medication and treatment to prisoners.

For example, in *Burrell v. Griffith*,[37] an inmate was hurt playing basketball. He was taken to the hospital, where he was X-rayed and given an injection for pain. The doctor at the jail later referred the inmate to a bone and joint clinic, where he was given painkillers, physical therapy, and other

---

31. Much of the information contained in this section on medical care is taken, with permission, from *The Duty to Provide Medical Care* by Robert S. Lafferrendre and Haven Tobias, of counsel to Pierce, Couch, Hendrickson, Baysinger & Green, presented at the Defense Research Institute on Civil Rights and Governmental Tort Liability Seminar, January 19-20, 1995.
32. Farmer v. Brennan, 114 S.Ct. 1970, 1979 (1994).
33. *Id.*
34. *See* Mendoza v. Lynaugh, 989 F.2d 191 (5th Cir. 1993).
35. Wilson v. Seiter, 501 U.S. 294 (1991).
36. Young v. City of Augusta, Georgia, 59 F.3d 1160, 1169 n.17 (11th Cir. 1995) citing Estelle v. Gamble, 429 U.S. 97 (1976).
37. 158 F.R.D. 104 (E.D. Tex. 1994).

treatment. Much of the prescribed treatment was later disallowed by jail officials. For instance, the jail doctor changed the inmate's prescribed narcotic medication to another non-narcotic prescription in the interest of keeping illegal drugs away from inmates.

The inmate filed suit, alleging negligence and lack of due medical care. The court held that where there were differing medical opinions, plaintiff's allegations failed to state a claim. The court reasoned that:

> Plaintiff objects to second opinion solicited by the jail officials and the corresponding treatment alterations, including the change in medication. This is nothing more than what the average citizen could expect when encountering two different doctors. Defendants do not guarantee that prisoners receive absolutely correct medical treatment, as there is no such thing, and everyone takes a risk as to diagnosis and treatment.[38]

The Constitution does not guarantee absolutely correct medical treatment. Rather, for prison and jail inmates, it requires only that prison officials not be deliberately indifferent to *serious* medical needs.[39]

A "serious medical need" is one that has been diagnosed by a physician as requiring treatment or a medical need that is so obvious that even a lay person could easily recognize the necessity for a doctor's attention.[40] In this context, medical needs include both physical and mental health needs.[41]

Medical records which indicate sick calls, examinations, diagnoses, and medications provided to the inmate may be used to rebut a claim of deliberate indifference to serious medical needs.[42]

Transsexualism has been recognized as a serious medical need that should be treated the same as any other psychiatric disorder. It has been described as a condition where a physiologically normal person experiences discomfort or discontent about nature's choice of his or her sex.[43]

---

38. *Id.* at 106 citing McCraken, 562 F.2d at 24.
39. Estelle v. Gamble, 429 U.S. 97, 104 (1976); Farmer, 114 S.Ct. at 1980 (1994).
40. Sheldon v. Pezley, 49 F.3d 1312, 1316 (8th Cir. 1995) (denying recovery to an inmate who refused to be re-handcuffed and transmitted to the shower, where the nurse could have better visibility).
41. Madrid v. Gomez, 889 F. Supp. 1146, 1255 (D. Cal. 1995).
42. *See* Banuelos v. McFarland, 41 F.3d 232, 235 (5th Cir. 1995).
43. Long v. Nix, 877 F. Supp. 1358, 1364 (D. Iowa 1995), *aff'd*, 86 F.3d 761 (8th Cir. 1996).

An inmate who had been cured of lung cancer believed his health was jeopardized by his exposure to his cellmate's secondhand smoke. He unsuccessfully sued the state officials because he failed to show that the smoke exacerbated a serious medical condition. The sole testifying physician opined that because the inmate was cured of his lung cancer, the smoke of which he complained affected him no more than any other prisoner, and was therefore not a greater danger to him.[44]

A jail employee who failed to give an inmate his medication for a heart condition, allegedly causing the inmate to have high fever, severe lower back pains and bronchitis, was found not to be deliberately indifferent. The inmate did not allege that the defendants were aware of his condition or that they intentionally withheld his medication.[45] Even where an inmate alleged that his medical condition (asthma) was included in his medical records, prison officials were not found to be deliberately indifferent because the inmate did not inform the officials of his need for an inhaler.[46]

Along with classification of inmates, pretrial detainee medical claims are scrutinized under the due process clauses of the Fifth and Fourteenth Amendments instead of the Eighth Amendment. However, some courts have held that with respect to providing pretrial detainees with such basic necessities as medical care, the minimum standard is the same as that allowed by the Eighth Amendment.[47] At a minimum then, a detainee must show that he has been deprived of at least a single human need in order to successfully claim a due process violation.[48] The Seventh Circuit originally held that a detainee was entitled to receive "prompt and reasonable medical attention," but later adopted the Eighth Amendment approach used by a majority of the circuits.[49] The Fifth Circuit has held that pretrial detainees are entitled to reasonable medical care unless the failure to supply that care is reasonably related to a legitimate government objective.[50]

---

43. Long v. Nix, 877 F. Supp. 1358, 1364 (D. Iowa 1995), *aff'd*, 86 F.3d 761 (8th Cir. 1996).
44. Goffman v. Gross, 59 F.3d 668, 671 (7th Cir. 1995).
45. Summers v. Sheahan, 883 F. Supp. 1163, 1168 (D. Ill. 1995).
46. Ware v. Fairman, 884 F. Supp. 1201, 1206 (D. Ill. 1995).
47. *See, e.g.*, Hamm v. DeKalb County, 774 F.2d 1567, 1574 (11th Cir. 1985).
48. *Wilson,* 501 U.S. at 305.
49. Salazar v. City of Chicago, 940 F.2d 233 (7th Cir. 1991).
50. *See* Cupit v. Jones, 835 F.2d 82 (5th Cir. 1987).

Recently, some prisons and jails have begun charging inmates for the expense of medical care. In *Johnson v. Department of Public Safety & Correctional Services*,[51] the court did not hesitate to conclude that a prison policy requiring inmates to co-pay for medical treatment was not "intolerable" such as to "shock the conscience." In *Johnson*, the terms of the policy would only subject inmates who abused the prison medical services to the co-pay requirement.[52] On the other hand, a policy that contains no exceptions to a co-payment requirement unconstitutionally deprives inmates of meaningful access to health care.[53] Withholding medical care for want of payment from an inmate who cannot afford to pay violates his constitutional rights.[54]

Finally, in the medical care context one court has recognized a different standard for potential liability of supervisory personnel. In determining a supervisor's liability for deliberate indifference in providing medical care, the Eleventh Circuit recognizes a three-prong test:

1. whether the supervisor's failure to adequately train and supervise subordinates constituted deliberate indifference to an inmate's medical needs;
2. whether a reasonable person in the supervisor's position would understand that the failure to train and supervise constituted deliberate indifference; and
3. whether the supervisor's conduct was causally related to the subordinate's constitutional violation.[55]

Diet, Exercise, and Recreation

Prisons must provide "nutritionally adequate food that is prepared and served under conditions which do not present an immediate danger to the

---

51. 885 F. Supp. 817, 820 (D. Md. 1995).
52. *Id; see also* Shapely v. Nevada Bd. of State Prison Comm'rs, 766 F.2d 404, 408 (9th Cir. 1985) (upholding dismissal of inmate's claim that the three-dollar charge for a medical visit violated his constitutional rights where he failed to allege that he was denied medical treatment because he could not pay the three dollars).
53. *See* Collins v. Romer, 962 F.2d 1508, 1514 (10th Cir. 1992).
54. Martin v. Debruyn, 880 F. Supp. 610, 615 (D. Ind. 1995).
55. Adams v. Poag, __F.3d__, 1995 WL 475796 at *1 (11th Cir. 1995).

health and well-being of the inmates who consume it."[56] Serving plain but nutritious food to inmates does not offend the Constitution.[57] Although "likely dull," a jail diet consisting mainly of starches and carbohydrates with few vegetables or fruits meets the requirement that prisoners be furnished reasonably adequate food.[58]

Even when a prisoner complains of vermin-infested food, he cannot recover for a constitutional violation unless he can prove that the jailers knew of the foreign object. An inmate must show both that the defendants were deliberately indifferent to the fact that food which contained vermin was routinely served and that the inmate complained about this to the defendants, who then did nothing about it.[59] Food that contains foreign objects, while unpleasant, does not amount to a constitutional deprivation.[60] In the words of the Seventh Circuit, "inmates cannot expect the conveniences and services of a good hotel."[61]

Although the Supreme Court has not ruled on whether or to what extent prison officials may deliberately withhold all food from an inmate, it has found that a restricted diet for a limited period of time is constitutional.[62] One district court has attempted on two occasions to establish the parameters for withholding of food as a disciplinary measure. In *Moss v. Ward*,[63] the court held that withholding food from an inmate for four days was an unconstitutionally disproportionate measure of punishment for the inmate's refusal to return a plastic cup. More recently, in *Williams v. Coughlin*,[64] the same court held that the deprivation of five meals within two days for an inmate's refusal to relinquish a food tray and cup was sufficiently serious to be of constitutional dimensions.

---

56. Ramos v. Lamm, 639 F.2d 559, 570-71 (10th Cir. 1980), *cert. denied*, 450 U.S. 1041 (1981); *see also* French v. Owens, 777 F.2d 1250, 1255 (7th Cir. 1985), *cert. denied*, 479 U.S. 817 (1986).
57. Zingmond v. Harger, 602 F. Supp. 256, 262-63 (N.D. Ind. 1985).
58. Jones v. Diamond, 636 F.2d 1364, 1378 (5th Cir. 1981).
59. Summers v. Sheahan, 883 F. Supp. 1163, 1170 (N.D. Ill. 1995).
60. Hamm v. DeKalb County, 774 F.2d 1567, 1575 (11th Cir. 1985), *cert. denied*, 475 U.S. 1096 (1986).
61. *Summers*, 883 F. Supp. at 1170 citing Harris v. Fleming, 839 F.2d 1232, 1235 (7th Cir. 1988).
62. *See* Hutto v. Finney, 437 U.S. 678, 686-87 (1978).
63. 450 F. Supp. 591 (W.D.N.Y. 1978).
64. 875 F. Supp. 1004, 1012 (W.D.N.Y. 1995).

No other expressed parameters for food or diet have been clearly set. As long as the meals meet the recognized daily requirements, both nutritionally and calorically, two meals instead of three per day may suffice.[65]

Finally, prisons need not provide inmates with special diets based on religion when it would place an undue burden on the prison system both financially and administratively, or when it could give rise to a proliferation of false claims by other individuals.[66]

With respect to exercise, many courts agree that regular exercise of some type is crucial for the psychological and physical fitness of inmates.[67] Nevertheless, "what constitutes adequate exercise will depend on the circumstances of each case, including the physical characteristics of the cell and jail and the average length of stay of the inmates."[68] The Ninth Circuit has held that prisoners with lengthy terms of confinement must be given an opportunity for outdoor exercise.[69] In contrast, the Fifth Circuit ruled the same year that there is no constitutional requirement for outdoor exercise.[70]

Though the amount of recreation constitutionally required depends on the facts of each case, it is clear that inmates must not be denied free movement such that their muscles suffer atrophy or that their individual health is threatened.[71]

Where a prisoner has a reasonable opportunity for exercise and does not allege any significant physical deterioration, no constitutional claim is presented.[72] The lack of formal recreation will not support a constitutional claim when an inmate still has the right to exercise. Relevant factors include access to a day room and the measurements of the areas to which the inmate is confined.[73]

---

65. *See* Green v. Ferrell, 801 F.2d 765, 770 (5th Cir. 1986).
66. Udey v. Kastner, 805 F.2d 1218, 1219 (5th Cir. 1986).
67. *See* Bailey v. Shillinger, 828 F.2d 651, 653 (10th Cir. 1987).
68. Housley v. Dodson, 41 F.3d 597, 599 (10th Cir. 1994).
69. *See* Spain v. Procunier, 600 F.2d 189, 199 (9th Cir. 1979).
70. *See* Dailey v. Byrnes, 605 F.2d 858, 860 (5th Cir. 1979); *see also* Carver v. Knox County, Tenn., 753 F. Supp. 1370, 1390 (E.D. Tenn. 1989) (suggesting opportunity for outdoor exercise is not constitutionally required unless inmates are required to spend more than a year in jail), *aff'd in part, rev'd in part on other grounds*, 887 F.2d 1987 (6th Cir. 1989).
71. *See* French v. Owens, 777 F.2d 1250, 1255 (7th Cir. 1985), *cert. denied*, 479 U.S. 817 (1986).
72. Buffington v. O'Leary, 748 F. Supp. 633, 634 (N.D. Ill. 1990).
73. *See* Pippins v. Adams County Jail, 851 F. Supp. 1228, 1232 (C.D. Ill. 1994).

Inmate Visitation

Visitation has been recognized to have rehabilitative benefits, including better community adjustment upon release.[74] But while allowing broad visitation may be a good idea, the Constitution creates no liberty interest in prison visitation.[75] Courts are particularly deferential to the decisions of prison administrators with respect to visitation.[76]

Visiting restrictions will generally be upheld unless a prisoner can show that prison officials exaggerated their response to a perceived problem, that the response was irrational, or that there was no real threat to the security and order of the institution.[77] Denying visitation to a particular visitor is also well within the terms of confinement ordinarily contemplated by a prison sentence.[78] In *Percy v. Jabe*,[79] the court held that it was proper to place a visitor on the permanent restriction list when it was believed that the visitor had smuggled contraband to the inmate.

In *Caraballo-Sandoval v. Honsted*,[80] a female visitor suspected of passing contraband to an inmate was removed from the visitation list. The officials were concerned about her background as a clerk in the prison and her knowledge of prison security measures. They also questioned whether her relationship with the inmate was established prior to his incarceration as required by the prison's visitation rules.

After changing her last name to that of the inmate, she was able to visit until she was recognized. At some point, the inmate and his persistent visitor were married. The couple filed suit, claiming that the wardens unfairly prevented the visitation.

The court held that no liberty interest was created by a regulation giving the warden discretion to restrict visitation for reasons such as security. The court also concluded that the officials had discretion to terminate visitation and that inmates have no absolute right to visitation as long as visitation policies meet legitimate penological interests. Additionally, the court

---

74. Kozlowski v. Coughlin, 871 F.2d 241, 242 (2d Cir. 1989).
75. Evans v. Johnson, 808 F.2d 1427, 1428 (11th Cir. 1987).
76. Doe v. Sparks, 733 F. Supp. 227, 230 (W.D. Pa. 1990).
77. *Bell*, 441 U.S. at 555.
78. Hewitt v. Helms, 459 U.S. 460, 468 (1983).
79. 823 F. Supp. 445, 448 (E.D. Mich. 1993).
80. 35 F.3d 521 (11th Cir. 1994).

found that the language of the visitation policy did not create a liberty interest in visitation.

In deciding visitation issues courts will also consider whether state law creates a substantive right to visitation or whether it merely establishes procedures for prison officials to follow.[81] Such a right is created if officials' discretion with respect to visitation is substantially limited.[82] The courts look to see if the provision regarding visitation uses mandatory language, such as "shall," which limits such discretion.[83]

The U.S. Supreme Court has conclusively stated in *Block v. Rutherford*[84] that prisons may restrict contact visits for legitimate security reasons.[85] However, inmates have a fundamental right to counsel and a prisoner's right of access to the courts includes visits with a lawyer.[86] To deny such visits between inmate and attorney, prison officials must show a legitimate penological interest.[87]

At least one circuit court has recognized that the size of the facility may be considered. Visitation measures that are achievable in larger institutions may not be reasonable in the smallest of local jails.[88]

Jail Suicides

In a 1994 case, inmate Donald Parsons alleged that the Marshall County deputy sheriff repeatedly and intentionally told him that his fiancee was having sexual intercourse with three different men. As a result, Parsons attempted to commit suicide by slashing his wrists multiple times. The district court found that the deputy's statements, while no doubt ill-advised, did not rise to the level of deliberate indifference to support an Eighth Amendment claim.[89]

---

81. *See, e.g.*, Villanova v. Abrams, 972 F.2d 792, 798 (7th Cir. 1992).
82. Kentucky Dep't of Corrections v. Thompson, 490 U.S. 454 (1989).
83. Long v. Norris, 929 F.2d 1111, 1117 (6th Cir. 1991), *cert. denied*, 502 U.S. 863 (1991).
84. 468 U.S. 576 (1984).
85. *Block*, 468 U.S. at 586-87.
86. *See* Ching v. Lewis, 895 F.2d 608, 610 (9th Cir. 1990).
87. Barnett v. Centoni, 31 F.3d 813, 816 (9th Cir. 1994).
88. Penland v. Warren County Jail, 797 F.2d 332, 335 (6th Cir. 1986).
89. Parsons v. Board of County Comm'rs, 873 F. Supp. 542 (D. Kan. 1994).

As in other types of prison litigation, a plaintiff must show that the prison officials acted with deliberate indifference. The courts have recognized that prison suicide cases may be considered under the Eighth Amendment standards established in medical care cases.[90]

In the context of jail suicide, deliberate indifference includes a question of whether a defendant was deliberately indifferent to both an individual's mental condition as well as the likely consequences of that condition.[91] A finding of deliberate indifference requires that officials have notice of the suicidal tendency of the inmate before being held liable for his suicide.[92] Deliberate indifference can only be established where a plaintiff demonstrates a strong likelihood, rather than a mere possibility, that suicide will result from a defendant's actions or inaction.[93]

In *Edwards v. Gilbert*, a juvenile who had been tried as an adult and convicted of sexual assault hanged himself with a bed sheet. The circuit court reversed the denial of summary judgment for the defendants because defendants did not know that the inmate was a suicide risk; the inmate had never threatened or attempted to commit suicide.

The risk of suicide must be particular to the individual. The fact that other suicides have occurred in a jail does not mean that the authorities should conclude that all prisoners are likely to commit suicide. The test is whether a defendant was "deliberately indifferent to an individual's mental condition and the likely consequences of that condition."[94]

In *Mullins v. Stratton*,[95] the plaintiff failed to establish that the jail policy with respect to monitoring suicidal inmates caused him harm. The jail's policy and procedure manual provided that if an inmate was a suicide risk, he should be observed every twenty minutes, otherwise a sixty-minute staggered schedule should be maintained. The plaintiff alleged a pattern of obvious indifference in the lack of observation for signs of scars, marks,

---

90. Plasko v. City of Pottsville, 852 F. Supp. 1258, 1262 (E.D. Penn. 1994) (requiring a plaintiff to establish (1) detainee had a particular vulnerability to suicide, (2) the custodial officer knew or should have known of that vulnerability, and (3) those officers acted with a reckless indifference to the detainee's particular vulnerability).
91. Wright v. Wagner, 641 F.2d 239, 242 (5th Cir. 1981).
92. Popham v. City of Talladega, 908 F.2d 1561, 1564 (11th Cir. 1990).
93. Edwards v. Gilbert, 867 F.2d 1271 (11th Cir. 1989).
94. Tittle v. Jefferson County Comm'n, 10 F.3d 1535, 1541 (11th Cir. 1994).
95. 878 F. Supp. 1016 (E.D. Ky. 1995).

behavior, and other indications of suicidal tendencies. The court concluded that there was not a custom at the jail which was so permanent and well-settled as to constitute a custom or usage with the force of law and concluded that the monitoring policy was not clearly unconstitutional.

In *Anderson v. County of Kern*,[96] inmates brought a § 1983 claim complaining of the placement of mentally disturbed and suicidal persons in safety cells. The safety cells were padded and used to temporarily confine violent or suicidal prisoners. The court opined that the test under the Eighth Amendment is (1) whether the placement of mentally disturbed or suicidal inmates in safety cells constituted an infliction of pain or a deprivation of the basic human needs (such as adequate food, clothing, shelter, sanitation, and medical care) and (2) if so, whether prison officials acted with the requisite culpable intent such that the infliction of pain was unnecessary and wanton.

Access to the Courts

Rejecting arguments that many prisoners would be ill-equipped to use the tools of the legal profession, the U.S. Supreme Court has ordered that prisons must provide "prisoners with adequate law libraries or adequate assistance from persons trained in the law."[97] The Court was careful to leave open a broad range of possibilities to satisfy this requirement:

> It should be noted that while adequate law libraries are one constitutionally acceptable method to assure meaningful access to the courts, our decision here . . . does not foreclose alternative means to achieve that goal. . . . Among the alternatives are the training of inmates as paralegal assistants to work under lawyers' supervision, the use of paraprofessionals and law students, either as volunteers or in formal clinic programs, the organization of volunteer attorneys through bar associations or other groups, the hiring of lawyers on a part-time consultant basis, and the use of full-time staff attorneys working either in new prison legal assistance organizations or as part of public defender or legal services offices.[98]

---

96. 45 F.3d 1310 (9th Cir. 1995), *petition for cert. filed,* 64 U.S.L.W. 3144 (U.S. Aug. 16, 1995).
97. *Id.* at 1314.
98. Bounds v. Smith, 430 U.S. 817, 828 (1977).

The only standard articulated by the Court was that the right of access must enable a prisoner to set forth a nonfrivolous claim that meets all procedural prerequisites.

Since this 1977 ruling, the Supreme Court has not comprehensively addressed the extent of legal assistance that must be afforded. Various circuit courts have tried to define those parameters.[99] In *Knop v. Johnson*,[100] the Sixth Circuit concluded that if a law-abiding citizen does not have a constitutional right of access to the public purse for legal assistance to pursue or defend all types of legal claims, certainly it should not be the case that such a constitutional right arises as a result of incarceration.

The Tenth Circuit Court of Appeals recently held that a state has no affirmative duty to assist inmates in civil matters other than habeas corpus proceedings or civil rights actions regarding their condition of current confinement.[101] The court stated that the constitutional right of access does not require a state to supply legal assistance beyond preparation of initial pleadings in civil rights actions regarding the conditions of confinement and habeas corpus pleadings. The court did proscribe, however, that a state may not erect barriers that impede the rights of access of incarcerated persons to file other legal actions.[102]

In *Abdul-Akbar v. Watson*,[103] the court stated that the standard is whether the legal resources available to a prisoner will enable him to identify the legal issues he desires to present to the relevant authorities, and to make his communications with and presentations to those authorities understood. In *Geder v. Godinez*,[104] the court held that a prisoner failed to state a violation of the constitutional right to meaningful access to the courts when he failed to allege or present any evidence of delay or

---

99. Schrier v. Halford, 60 F.3d 1309 (8th Cir. 1995) (upholding the district court's ruling that as a matter of law the Constitution does not require the states to provide a law library or its legal equivalent to inmates pursuing general civil claims arising only under state law).
100. 977 F.2d 996, 1002-09 (6th Cir. 1992), *cert. denied*, 113 S.Ct. 1415 (1993).
101. Carper v. Deland, 54 F.3d 613 (10th Cir. 1995) (discussing constitutionality of plan where two private attorneys assisted inmates in preparing state and federal petitions for writs of habeas corpus and initial pleadings in civil rights actions regarding conditions of confinement).
102. *Id.* at 615-16.
103. 4 F.3d 195, 203 (3d Cir. 1993).
104. 875 F. Supp. 1334, 1341 (N.D. Ill. 1995).

interruption in pending or contemplated litigation resulting from this deprivation. Whatever the standard, inmates are not constitutionally entitled to unfettered direct access to law libraries.

In addition to the ambiguity with respect to what is considered meaningful or adequate access, the extent of injury that a prisoner must show to claim deprivation of this right of access is also unclear. The *Geder* court seemed to require the inmate to show evidence of actual delay or interruption in litigation, effectively requiring an inmate to show actual harm.[105]

Conversely, the Third Circuit has found that a prisoner need not show that a deprivation of access to a law library caused him an independent injury where the deprivation was so significant as to constitute an injury in and of itself.[106] The Eighth Circuit believes that unless an inmate is completely denied access to the law library, he must assert actual injury or prejudice.[107] "A court's inquiry does not end with a finding that an inmate suffered the loss of some legal materials, or was denied access to the prison law library or assistance from those trained in the law."[108]

Recently, the U.S. Supreme Court has clarified the need for an inmate to show an actual injury from any deprivation of legal materials and has emphasized the important roles of the separate and distinct branches of government. In *Lewis v. Casey*,[109] the Supreme Court reviewed the district court's finding that the State of Arizona Department of Corrections had a variety of shortcomings regarding the prison's library facilities. Specifically, the district court concluded that two groups of inmates were particularly affected by the system's inadequacies: lockdown prisoners and illiterate or non-English-speaking inmates.

The district court granted a permanent injunction, specifying in minute detail the times that libraries were to be kept open, the number of hours of library use to which each inmate was entitled, the minimal educational requirements for prison librarians, and the content of a videotaped legal-research course for inmates.

---

105. *Id.* at 1339. *See* Smith v. Shawnee Library Sys., 60 F.3d 317, 323 (7th Cir. 1995).
106. Kershner v. Mazurkiewicz, 670 F.2d 440 (3d Cir. 1982). *See also* Sowell v. Vose, 941 F.2d 32, 34-35 (1st Cir. 1991).
107. Hamm v. Groose, 15 F.3d 110 (8th Cir. 1994).
108. *Id.* at 112.
109. 116 S. Ct. 2174 (1996).

The Supreme Court reiterated the standards set out in *Bounds v. Smith*,[110] stating that an inmate must show that the alleged inadequacies of a prison's library facilities or legal assistance program caused him "actual injury." Should a court fail to identify anything more than isolated instances of actual injury, a finding of a systemic violation is invalid. This requirement of actual injury derives ultimately from the doctrine of standing, "a constitutional principle that prevents courts of law from undertaking tasks assigned to the political branches."[111]

The Court further opined that no abstract, freestanding right to a law library or legal assistance exists; therefore, an inmate cannot establish relevant actual injury simply by establishing that the prison's law library or legal assistance program is sub-par in some theoretical sense. The inmate must demonstrate that the alleged shortcomings in the library or legal assistance program hindered efforts to pursue a legal claim.

"In other words, *Bounds* does not guarantee inmates the wherewithal to transform themselves into litigating engines capable of filing everything from shareholder derivative actions to slip-and-fall claims," the Court noted. "The tools it requires to be provided are those that the inmates need in order to attack their sentences, directly or collaterally, and in order to challenge the conditions of their confinement."[112]

The Court concluded that the injunction issued by the trial court failed to accord adequate deference to the judgment of the prison authorities in determining how best to ensure that inmates have a reasonably adequate opportunity to file nonfrivolous legal claims challenging their convictions or conditions of confinement.

Prisoners must be furnished basic supplies to render their access to the courts meaningful.[113] Indigent inmates must be provided, free of charge, with paper and pen to draft legal documents, with notarial services to authenticate them, and with stamps to mail them. Access to the courts, however, does not also include "a federally protected right to use a typewriter or to have one's pleadings typed."[114] Peripheral resources such as pads, pens, pencils, and photocopy machines are not required by the Constitution.

---

110. 430 U.S. 817 (1977).
111. *Lewis*, 116 S. Ct. 2179.
112. 116 S. Ct. at 2181.
113. *Bounds*, 430 U.S. 817 (1977).
114. Stubblefield v. Henderson, 475. F.2d 26 (5th Cir. 1973).

Juveniles' constitutional rights do not necessitate the same procedures and methods of adults' rights. For instance, the Supreme Court has never extended the same criteria for access to the courts to juvenile delinquents.[115] In contrast, one district court has extended such rights where the stipulated record disclosed that most of the juveniles had been committed to the institution without having been represented by counsel.[116]

Correspondence/Reading Materials

In *Thornburgh v. Abbott*,[117] the U.S. Supreme Court overruled its 1974 decision in *Procunier v. Martinez*,[118] holding that prison mail censorship had to be "generally necessary" to protect a governmental interest. Since *Thornburgh*, prison regulations affecting the sending of publications to prisoners must be analyzed under a reasonableness standard and are valid if they are reasonably related to legitimate penological interests.[119] Legitimate penological interests include preserving prison security and maintaining order and discipline.[120] If prison officials want to reject a publication, they may do so based on the publication's potential implications for prison security. "In the volatile prison environment," the Second Circuit noted, "it is essential that prison officials be given broad discretion to prevent such disorder."[121]

Unjustified censorship of incoming mail violates inmates' constitutional rights of access to the courts and freedom of speech and association. The Supreme Court has ruled that prison officials may censor mail, but not simply to eliminate "unflattering or unwelcome opinions or factually inaccurate statements."[122]

The Fifth Circuit Court of Appeals, in *Brewer v. Wilkinson*,[123] has unequivocally stated that requiring that the prisoner be present when his mail is opened shields protected expression, and violating the regulation may

---

115 . Twyman v. Crisp, 584 F.2d 352, 358 (10th Cir. 1978).

116. Alexander v. Boyd, 876 F. Supp. 773, 789 (D. S.C. 1995) citing Morgan v. Sproat, 432 F. Supp. 1130, 1158 (S.D. Miss. 1977).

117. 490 U.S. 401 (1989).

118. 416 U.S. 396 (1974).

119. 490 at 413.

120. *Id.* at 415-16.

121. Security & Law Enforcement Employees v. Carey, 737 F.2d 187, 203 (2d Cir. 1984).

122. 416 U.S. at 413.

123. 3 F.3d 816, 825 (5th Cir. 1993), *cert. denied*, 114 S.Ct. 1081 (1994).

inhibit the inmate's ability to speak, protest and complain openly, directly and without reservation with the court. The Fifth Circuit also concluded that there was sufficient evidence in the record for a reasonable person to infer that there existed a pattern and practice of opening inmates' incoming court mail outside their presence, thus impinging upon their constitutional rights.[124] Likewise, the Third Circuit held that such a violation rises to the level of a constitutional violation where the prison opens mail sent to an inmate from a court outside his presence.[125]

Outgoing mail should be unrestricted unless it falls into categories that present a threat to the order or security of the prison, such as "escape plans, plans relating to ongoing criminal activity, and threats of blackmail or extortion."[126] In addition, when an inmate misuses the mail system by including defamatory remarks intended for the warden, he or she may properly be disciplined.[127]

For a claim to rise to the level of a constitutional violation, a litigant must show prejudice. It is not enough to show that mail was opened and read outside an inmate's presence.[128]

In addition to considerations regarding mail, prison officials can only limit other reading materials if they do so on a content-neutral basis or only for legitimate penological interests. A regulation is content-neutral if it prohibits behavior based on a reason other than the particular content or viewpoint contained in the otherwise free speech. The "government may not regulate use based on hostility—or favoritism—towards the underlying message expressed."[129] If, for instance, the prison were to banish all written materials during meal times because they afford inmates an increased chance to harbor contraband, then such a regulation would be permissible and would not impede freedom of speech.

One area of particular concern to prison officials is pornography. Can prison officials ban pornography? Not absolutely. Under proper circumstances prison officials may disallow sexually explicit materials. It does

---

124. *Id.* at 825.
125. Bieregu v. Reno, 59 F.3d 1445, 1452 (3d Cir. 1995).
126. Thornburgh v. Abbott, 490 U.S. 401, 412 (1989).
127. Leonard v. Nix, 55 F.3d 370, 375 (8th Cir. 1995).
128. Walker v. Navarro County Jail, 4 F.3d 410, 413 (5th Cir. 1993); *see also* Black v. Callahan, 876 F. Supp. 131 (N.D. Tex. 1995).
129. R.A.V. v. City of St. Paul, Minnesota, 505 U.S. 377, 386 (1992).

not infringe First Amendment rights to disallow "obscene" materials; however, "what may be sexually explicit is not necessarily obscene. . . . Public officials have no legitimate governmental interest in imposing their own standards of sexual morality on the inmates."[130]

To be obscene, material must meet the three-prong test articulated in *Miller v. California*:

1. the work, taken as a whole, must appeal to the prurient interest in sex;
2. the work must portray sexual conduct in a patently offensive way; and
3. the work, taken as a whole, must not have any serious literary, artistic, political or scientific value.[131]

In order to be constitutionally acceptable, a regulation may permit suppression of sexually oriented material only if the material comports with a standard of obscenity defined by the courts and the legislature rather than one articulated by prison authorities.[132] In other words, prison officials would need to use the community standards to determine what is "obscene" as opposed to using their own definitions. Thus, the question becomes: Is it being sold down the street at the local convenience store? If so, it may not be obscene.

Even if the sexually explicit material does not rise to the level of "obscenity," prison officials can still limit access to it. However, they must follow two important steps. First, prison officials can reject any publication for good reason pursuant to specific criteria, but they must review each issue separately.[133] In other words, a general ban on all issues of a certain magazine would not be acceptable. Each issue must be separately considered.

Second, the regulations disallowing the material must be reasonably related to legitimate penological interests.[134] Without dispute, a prison has an interest in security, discipline, order, public safety, and rehabilitation.

---

130. 416 U.S. 15, 24 (1973).
131. 413 U.S. 15, 24 (1973).
132. Pepperling v. Crist, 678 F.2d 787, 790 (9th Cir. 1982).
133. Jackson v. Ward, 458 F. Supp. 546, 561 (W.D.N.Y. 1978).
134. Thornburgh v. Abbott, 490 U.S. 401, 412 (1989).
135. *See* Thompson v. Patteson, 985 F.2d 202, 206 (5th Cir. 1993) (finding that pornographic materials could exacerbate problems of nonconsensual homosexual acts within the prison).

Sexually explicit publications have been found to negatively impact these valid penological interests.[135]

Prisoner Discipline

"[T]he problems that arise in the day-to-day operation of a corrections facility are not susceptible of easy solutions," the Court stated in *Bell v. Wolfish.*[136] "Prison administrators should be accorded wide-ranging deference in the adoption and execution of policies and practices that in their judgment are needed to preserve internal order and discipline and to maintain institutional security."[137]

Despite the Supreme Court's articulated belief that prison officials should be granted broad discretion, [138] there are limits. There must be mutual accommodation between the institutional purposes and due process.

As the Supreme Court recognized in *Wolff v. McDonnell,*[139] prison disciplinary proceedings "take place in a closed, tightly controlled environment peopled by those who have chosen to violate the criminal law and who have been lawfully incarcerated for doing so." Due to the needs and exigencies of the institutional environment, imprisonment makes unavailable many of the rights and privileges afforded an ordinary citizen. Additionally, the *Wolff* court discussed prison disciplinary proceedings, which are not part of a criminal prosecution and therefore do not necessitate the full panoply of rights due a defendant in such proceedings.

As long as the conditions or degree of confinement to which a prisoner is subjected as a form of "discipline" is within the sentence imposed and is not otherwise violative of the Constitution, the Due Process Clause does not in itself subject an inmate's treatment by prison authorities to judicial oversight.[140] In fact, to make a claim under the Due Process Clause, the prisoner must first demonstrate that a protected liberty or property interest was infringed by the defendant's action.[141]

---

136. 441 U.S. 520 (1979).
137. 441 U.S. at 547.
138. 441 U.S. at 554.
139. 418 U.S. 539, 561 (1974).
140. Montanye v. Haymes, 427 U.S. 236, 242 (1976).
141. Blizzard v. Hastings, 886 F. Supp. 405, 408 (D. Del. 1995).
142. *Wolff*, 418 U.S. at 563-67.
143. 115 S.Ct. 2293 (1995).

In *Wolff*, the Supreme Court set out minimum requirements of procedural due process that must be afforded prisoners:

- written notice of the claimed violation at least twenty-four hours in advance of the inmate's appearance at a disciplinary hearing;
- a written statement of the factfinders as to the evidence relied upon and the reason for disciplinary action taken, unless the exclusion of certain items of evidence is necessary for personal or institutional safety reasons;
- an opportunity to call witnesses and present documentary evidence in defense when permitting the inmate to do so would not be unduly hazardous to institutional safety or correctional goals. However, the Court stated that prison officials must have the discretion, without being subject to unduly crippling constitutional impediments, to determine when calling witnesses would potentially cause safety concerns to other inmates and the staff.[142]

In *Sandin v. Conner*,[143] the Court reaffirmed the principles stated in *Wolff*. States may, under certain circumstances, create liberty interests which are protected by the Due Process Clause. However, the Court expressly limited such interests to freedom from restraint which, while not exceeding the sentence in such an unexpected manner as to give rise to protection by the Due Process Clause of its own force, "nonetheless imposes atypical and significant hardship on the inmate in relation to the ordinary incidents of prison life."[144]

In so holding, the Court abandoned the methodology applied in *Hewitt v. Helms*,[145] which produced two undesirable effects. It created disincentives for states to codify prison management procedures in the interest of uniform treatment and "led to the involvement of federal courts in the day-to-day management of prisons, often squandering judicial resources with little offsetting benefit to anyone."[146]

Inmates charged with an offense that would deprive them of good-time credit are entitled to those minimum procedures appropriate under the cir-

---

144. *Id.* at 2300.
145. 459 U.S. 460 (1983).
146. *Sandin,* 115 S.Ct. at 2299.
147. Spaulding v. Collins, 867 F. Supp. 499, 507 (S.D. Texas 1993) citing Wolff, 418 U.S. at 557.
148. Baxter v. Palmigiano, 425 U.S. 308, 315 (1976).

cumstances and required by the Due Process Clause to ensure that their rights are not arbitrarily abrogated.[147] Inmates do not have a right to either retain or appoint counsel in disciplinary hearings.[148] Despite all the due process in the world, inmates cannot be punished for acts that they could not have known were prohibited. Prior notice or fair warning of the prohibited conduct is required.[149]

Several factors may be considered by prison officials when administering inmate discipline. In *Ferreira v. Duval*,[150] Manuel Ferreira acted as one of the leaders in a group demonstration by inmates. At his disciplinary hearing, he was found guilty of three offenses: (1) disobeying an order by lying to or showing insolence toward a staff member, (2) disrupting or interfering with the security or orderly running of the institution, and (3) participating in or encouraging an unauthorized group demonstration. Officials considered numerous factors in administering Ferreira's discipline: he was a leader of the demonstration; he had a great number of prior, similar disciplinary infractions; and he did not accept responsibility for the incident. Though the court did not specifically so hold, such factors are proper considerations when administering discipline to an inmate.

Perhaps a more difficult question for jail personnel is the amount of discipline that can be fairly used. Reasonable punishment may be imposed to enforce reasonable prison disciplinary requirements even with respect to pretrial detainees.[151] However, it is not always clear what is reasonable. Jailers may use what amounts to excessive force in administering discipline in certain circumstances. Inmates who file suit for excessive force in violation of the Cruel and Unusual Punishments Clause will succeed only if they can prove that the force was applied maliciously and sadistically to

---

149. Reeves v. Pettcox, 19 F.3d 1060 (5th Cir. 1994) (reversing lower court's approval of sanction given to an inmate for placing his food tray outside his cell when he had no knowledge of the act being prohibited). *See also* Montana v. Commissioners Court, 659 F.2d 19, 23 (5th Cir. 1981), *cert. denied*, 455 U.S. 1026 (1982) (stating that punishment for an entire cell block for contraband found in one cell was likely unconstitutional and should not have been dismissed by the trial court).
150. 887 F. Supp. 374 (D. Mass. 1995).
151. Collazo-Leon v. U.S. Bureau of Prisons, 51 F.3d 315, 318 (1st Cir. 1995).
152. Hudson v. McMillian, 503 U.S. 1, 6-7 (1992).
153. Graham v. Connor, 490 U.S. 386, 395 n.10 (1989) quoting Whitley v. Albers, 475 U.S. 312, 327 (1979) (citations omitted).

cause harm. If it was applied in a good faith effort to maintain or restore discipline, they cannot prevail.[152]

Post-conviction excessive force claims are to be raised under the Eighth Amendment rather than the Fourteenth Amendment:

> [T]he Due Process Clause protects a pretrial detainee from the use of excessive force that amounts to punishment. . . . After conviction, the Eighth Amendment 'serves as the primary source of substantive protection . . . in cases . . . where the deliberate use of force is challenged as excessive and unjustified.' . . . Any protection that 'substantive due process' affords convicted prisoners against excessive force is, we have held, at best redundant of that provided by the Eighth Amendment.[153]

In *Sheldon v. Pezley*,[154] the Eighth Circuit upheld the district court's dismissal of an inmate's complaint that a "pain compliance hold" was used on him. The use of this device involves bending a person's wrist with no pressure applied. If the person refuses to comply with an order, then the wrist is bent to cause only sufficient pain to cause the person to comply with the order being given. In *Sheldon*, the officers testified that no force was actually ever applied to the inmate.

To state a claim for excessive force, an inmate must allege more than that the defendant had malicious and sadistic intentions. An inmate must allege some injury in order to sustain an excessive force claim.[155]

Conclusion

As the ongoing struggle between society and those inmates it imprisons inevitably continues, this area of the law will continue to evolve. Inmates' counsel will continue to assist them in bringing legitimate and often illegitimate claims at the courthouse and attorneys representing those who imprison and retain them will continue to defend those cases.

What is needed is an active attempt on both sides of these cases which is designed to inform and educate prison officials about what is constitu-

---

154. 49 F.3d 1312 (8th Cir. 1995).
155. Warren v. Humphrey, 875 F. Supp. 378, 382 (E.D. Texas 1995).

tionally permissible, thereby reducing the significant cost and congestion in the court system that results from prison litigation.

Taxpayers continue to resist increased taxes for enhanced institutions of confinement. However, prisoners' suits are costly on the citizens as well. For the best resolution of prison litigation, parties and counsel should work together to find effective, cost-efficient solutions to problematic areas such as overcrowding and poor treatment.

Chapter Ten

A Student's Constitutional Rights in the Public School Setting

Margaret-Ann F. Howie

Once upon a time in America, a public school teacher or an administrator could administer corporal punishment, and then depend upon a parent to double the penalty at home: everyone in the community accepted responsibility for a young person's conduct and development.[1] Those halcyon days of community corporal punishment are long behind us, and teachers who attempt to do the same today would find themselves in violation of the laws of several states.[2] Even as the global village shrinks, we live as and among strangers in our own neighborhoods.

This intimate distance has become increasingly evident in our public schools. Today's public schools are charged with both the moral[3] and academic[4] development of our young people. As our society struggles to determine the precise scope of public schools' role, this distance has both increased and decreased. Indeed, in recent years, public educators have moved from standing *in loco parentis*[5] to becoming arms of the state.[6]

---

1. As the recently popularized African proverb states: "It takes a whole village to raise a child."
2. Although the U.S. Supreme Court has ruled that the Eighth Amendment protection does not extend to students receiving corporal punishment, Ingraham v. Wright, 430 U.S. 651 (1977), many states have flatly prohibited corporal punishment. (*See, e.g*, Md. Ed. Code Ann., § 7-305.).
3. The recent demand for "values-based" education is a good example.
4. Federal law makes this a requirement for children with disabilities. Education for All Handicapped Children Act (EAHCA) (20 U.S.C. § 1401 *et seq*.), reenacted as Individuals with Disabilities Education Act (IDEA), requires local school systems to provide to all children with disabilities a "free appropriate public education" and "related services" in the "least restrictive environment."
5. "A person stands *in loco parentis* when he puts himself in the situation of a lawful parent by assuming the obligations incident to the parental relation without going through the formalities necessary to a legal adoption." 9 Am. Jur.2d

However, the modern classroom is far from a breeding ground for civil rights violations. Rather, most courts balance the rights of students against the rights of public schools to maintain order and discipline. In many cases the schools' rights may outweigh the students'.

This chapter presents an overview of the seminal court decisions concerning the First and Fourth Amendment rights of public school students. Additionally, it briefly addresses recent developments in students' rights under the Thirteenth Amendment. In analyzing these cases, this chapter attempts to present a basic framework of the constitutional rights of students in our nation's public schools, recognizing that this particular target moves with agility.

Student Expression: The Articulable Distance

Its subsequent equivocation notwithstanding, the U.S. Supreme Court has unequivocally declared that students do not "shed their constitutional rights to freedom of speech or expression at the schoolhouse gate."[7]

Parent and Child, § 75 (1987). According to Blackstone, a parent is said to delegate part of the parental authority to a school master who then stands "*in loco parentis*, and has such portion of the power of the parent . . . as may be necessary to answer the purposes for which he is employed." 1 BLACKSTONE, COMMENTARIES, at 453.

6. This conclusion has been reached by the U.S. Supreme Court. "[A] few courts have concluded that school officials are exempt from the dictates of the [Constitution] by virtue of the special nature of their authority over schoolchildren. Teachers and school administrators, it is said, act *in loco parentis* in their dealings with students: their authority is that of the parent, not the State, and is therefore not subject to the limits of the [Constitution]. Such reasoning is in tension with contemporary reality and the teachings of this Court. . . . In carrying out . . . disciplinary functions pursuant to [school policies] school officials act as representatives of the State, not merely as surrogates for the parents, and they cannot claim the parents' immunity from the strictures of the [Constitution]." New Jersey v. T.L.O., 469 U.S. 325, 336-337 (1985). The courts do not attempt to reconcile the expansion of young people's rights. However, at least one scholar has argued that post-World War II society, in part, created the modern view of adolescence, and its altered view of the rights of young people. FRANKLIN E. ZIMRING. THE CHANGING LEGAL WORLD OF ADOLESCENCE. (New York: The Free Press, 1982).
7. Tinker v. Des Moines Independent Community School District, 393 U.S. 503, 506, 89 S.Ct. 733, 21 L.Ed. 2d 731, 736 (1969).

The U.S. Supreme Court first articulated this principle in *Tinker v. Des Moines Independent Community School District*,[8] when high school students sought an injunction under § 1983 to prevent school officials from disciplining them for violating the school district's dress code. The challenged dress code prohibited students from wearing black arm bands to protest the Vietnam War.

Several facts are noteworthy: In a school system of more than 18,000 students, only five were suspended for violating the dress code. No evidence of "threats or acts of violence on school premises" was found, nor was there any "evidence whatsoever of petitioners' interference, actual or nascent, with the schools' work or of the collision with the rights of other students to be secure and to be let alone."[9] Additionally, the school system did not prohibit wearing "all symbols of political or controversial significance."[10] Therefore, the regulation's sole purpose was to suppress the students' speech about Vietnam. "A particular symbol—black arm bands worn to exhibit opposition to this nation's involvement in Vietnam—was singled out for prohibition."[11] In fact, an internal school memorandum noted that "the schools are no place for demonstrations," and, if the students were dissatisfied with the political process, then "it should be handled with the ballot box and not in the halls of our public schools."[12]

The Court found this singular prohibition to be particularly reprehensible. As a result, it clearly articulated the distance that existed between the rights of the public school student and the reach of the public school administration:

> In our system, state-operated schools may not be enclaves of totalitarianism. School officials do not possess absolute authority over their students. Students in school as well as out of school are 'persons' under our Constitution. They are possessed of fundamental rights which the State must respect, just as they themselves must respect their obligations to the State. In our system, students may not be regarded as closed-circuit recipients of only that which

---

8. 393 U.S. 503, 89 S.Ct. 733, 21 L.Ed.2d 731 (1969).
9. 393 U.S. at 508.
10. 393 U.S. at 510.
11. 393 U.S. at 510-511.
12. 393 U.S. at 508, n.3.

> the State chooses to communicate. They may not be confined to the expression of those sentiments that are officially approved. In the absence of a specific showing of constitutionally valid reasons to regulate their speech, students are entitled to freedom of expression of their views.[13]

Two competing sets of rights were involved. These included the students' First Amendment rights, which the Court stated are available to students "applied in light of the special characteristics of the school environment."[14] The case also examined the authorities' need to maintain control, noting that "the Court has repeatedly emphasized the need for affirming the comprehensive authority of the States and of school officials, consistent with fundamental constitutional safeguards, to prescribe and control conduct in the schools."[15] Therefore, the "problem lies in the area where students in the exercise of First Amendment rights collide with the rules of the school authorities."[16]

Schools, the Court concluded, cannot suppress speech "because of an undifferentiated fear or apprehension of disturbance."[17] Rather, in order to suppress the students' speech, the Court ruled that a public school must prove that a student's First Amendment exercise would "materially and substantially" disrupt the school program.

Indeed, the *Tinker* court noted that the public school setting was the ideal venue for self-expression, especially on controversial subjects, as long as the student does not "materially and substantially interfere with the requirements of appropriate discipline in the operation of the school."[18] The Court waxed eloquent in its defense of students' rights:

> Under our Constitution, free speech is not a right that is given only to be so circumscribed that it exists in principle but not in fact. Freedom of expression would not truly exist if the right could be exercised only in an area that a benevolent government has

---

13. 393 U.S. at 511.
14. 393 U.S. at 506.
15. 393 U.S. at 507.
16. 393 U.S. at 507.
17. 393 U.S. at 508.
18. 393 U.S. at 513.

> provided as a safe haven for crackpots. The Constitution says that Congress (and the States) may not abridge the right to free speech. This provision means what it says. We properly read it to permit reasonable regulation of speech-connected activities in carefully restricted circumstances. But we do not confine the permissible exercise of First Amendment rights to . . . a supervised and ordained discussion in a school classroom.[19]

Subsequent cases have demonstrated, however, that the distance between the students' rights and the schools' reach has never been greater. Instead, the Supreme Court has strived to substantially shorten it.

For instance, in *Bethel School Dist. No. 403 v. Fraser*,[20] the Supreme Court clarified the "material and substantial disruption" standard. In *Fraser*, a high school student, in spite of warnings from teachers concerning its appropriateness, delivered a speech before the entire student body. The speech was full of graphic and sexually explicit metaphors.[21] Fraser received a three-day suspension for violating a *Tinker*-fashioned school rule prohibiting the use of obscene language, specifically "conduct which materially and substantially interferes with the educational process."[22]

The Court found there to be a "marked distinction" between the student's speech in *Fraser* and the students' arm bands in *Tinker*. The Court noted that:

> [I]n upholding the students' right to engage in nondisruptive, passive expression of a political viewpoint in *Tinker* this Court was

19. 393 U.S. at 513.
20. 478 U.S. 675, 106 S.Ct. 3159, 92 L.Ed.2d 549 (1986).
21. Mr. Fraser's speech, part of which was reproduced in Justice Blackmun's dissent, read: "I know a man who is firm—he's firm in his pants, he's firm in his shirt, his character is firm—but most of all, his belief in you, the students of Bethel, is firm. Jeff Kuhlman is a man who takes his point and pounds it in. If necessary, he'll take an issue and nail it to the wall. He doesn't attack things in spurts—he drives hard, pushing and pushing until finally—he succeeds. Jeff is a man who will go to the very end—even the climax, for each and every one of you. So vote for Jeff for A.S.B. vice-president—he'll never come between you and the best our high school can be." As quoted at 106 S.Ct. at 3167 (Blackmun, J. dissenting). A later Court characterized the speech as "not legally obscene." *Hazelwood, infra*, at 567.
22. 106 S.Ct. at 3162.

> careful to note that the case did not concern speech or action that intrudes upon the work of the schools or rights of other students [citations omitted].[23]

According to the Court, because *Fraser*'s speech did not merit First Amendment protection, school administrators had the authority to suppress it. The First Amendment rights of school children, the Court reasoned, are not co-extensive to those of adults. Therefore, "it does not follow that simply because the use of an offensive form of expression may not be prohibited to adults making . . . a political point, the same latitude must be permitted to children in public school. The First Amendment gives a high school student the classroom right to wear *Tinker*'s armband, but not *Cohen*'s jacket. [citations omitted]"[24] However, the exercise of a student's First Amendment rights need not "materially disrupt" the school program in order for a disciplinary code to suppress that right. On the contrary, as the Court noted subsequently:

> [T]he decision in *Fraser* rested on the 'vulgar,' 'lewd,' and plainly offensive character of a speech delivered at an official school assembly rather than on any propensity of the speech to 'materially disrup[t] classwork or involv[e] substantial disorder or invasion of the rights of others.'[25]

In *Hazelwood School District v. Kuhlmeier*,[26] the Supreme Court closed the distance created in *Tinker* through what the dissent characterized as "brutal censorship."[27] The students in that case were three high school newspaper staff members. They asserted that school officials (in particular, their principal, Robert Reynolds, and their journalism teacher,

---

23. 106 S.Ct. at 3163.
24. *Fraser, supra*, 106 S.Ct. at 3164. Cohen, an adult, had been arrested for wearing in a courthouse a jacket that read: "Fuck the draft." Cohen v. California, 403 U.S. 15, 91 S.Ct. 1780, 29 L.Ed.2d 284 (1971). The Court upheld Cohen's right to express his political viewpoint in a public place, regardless of the offense it caused.
25. Hazelwood School District v. Kuhlmeier, 484 U.S. 260, at 271, fn. 4, 108 S.Ct. 562, 98 L.Ed.2d 592 (1988).
26. 484 U.S. 261, 208 S.Ct. 562, 98 L.Ed.2d 592 (1988).
27. 108 S.Ct. at 159.

Howard Emerson) had violated their First Amendment rights when they deleted two full pages of the school newspaper written by members of the Journalism II class.

Page proofs of each issue were normally submitted to the principal for prepublication review. The principal objected to two stories: one detailing three students' experiences with pregnancy, the other describing the impact of divorce on students. Although pseudonyms were used in the pregnancy story, Principal Reynolds believed that the identity of the students could be discovered from the story's content. Additionally, he was concerned about the discussion of sexual activity and birth control and its impact upon younger students at the school. Lastly, Reynolds believed that the divorce story, which identified students by name, required parental consent prior to publication. Reynolds directed the journalism teacher to exclude two pages of the newspaper even though the pages contained articles to which Reynolds did not object.

The Court, while paying necessary tribute to its holding in *Tinker*, found the principal's actions to be constitutional. It noted a marked distinction between *promotion* of student speech and *toleration* of student speech. The Court also found persuasive the level of involvement in the newspaper's production: students received grades and academic credit; public funds were expended from the school board's budget; and the publication was to be developed within the school's educational mission. Ultimately, therefore, the school retained control over the content of the publication. "Accordingly, school officials were entitled to regulate the contents of [the school newspaper] in any reasonable manner," the Court concluded. "It is this standard, rather than our decision in *Tinker*, that governs this case."[28]

The Court went on to acknowledge that the First Amendment does not require that "a school affirmatively . . . promote particular student speech.[29] Therefore, public schools may exercise authority over school-sponsored publications, theatrical productions, and other expressive activities that students, parents, and members of the public might reasonably perceive bear the imprimatur of the school."[30]

Because a school may exercise greater control over student expression that is part of the curriculum, a public school may rightly "disassociate

28. 108 S.Ct. at 569.
29. 108 S.Ct. at 569.
30. 108 S.Ct. at 569.

itself" from speech that is ungrammatical, poorly written, or unsuitable for immature audiences.[31] Therefore, the *Tinker* standard would not apply to the school's determination to lend its name and resources to the dissemination of student expression:

> [W]e hold that educators do not offend the First Amendment by exercising editorial control over the style and content of student speech in school-sponsored expressive activities so long as their actions are reasonably related to legitimate pedagogical concerns.[32]

The Court refused to concede that specific written regulations would be required to define educators' prepublication control.[33] Rather, the majority found all of Principal Reynolds' actions to be reasonable, including the deletion of two full pages of the newspaper. However, Justice Brennan (joined by Justices Marshall and Blackmun) disagreed:

> The Court opens its analysis in this case by purporting to reaffirm *Tinker*'s time-tested proposition that public school students 'do not shed their constitutional rights to freedom of speech or expression at the schoolhouse gate.' That is an ironic introduction to an opinion that denudes high school students of much of the First Amendment protection that *Tinker* itself prescribed. Instead of 'teach[ing] children to respect the diversity of ideas that is fundamental to the American system,' and 'that our Constitution is a living reality, not parchment preserved under glass,' the Court today "teach[es] youth to discount important principles of our government as mere platitudes.'[34]

In effect, Principal Reynolds' scissors severed the *Tinker*-established distance between the students' rights and the school's control.

Subsequent federal cases have continued to articulate the limits and the extent of a school's power over speech and expression.[35] Courts have

---

31. 108 S.Ct. at 570.
32. 108 S.Ct. at 571.
33. 108 S.Ct. at 571, fn. 6.
34. 108 S.Ct. at 580.
35. A notable example is found in Pyle by Pyle v. South Hadley School Comm., 861 F. Supp. 157 (D.Mass. 1994), where the federal district court struck down a school dress code that prohibited students from wearing clothing

become increasingly sensitive to administrative concerns about school violence. For example, in *Lovell v. Poway Unified School District*,[36] a high school student asserted violations of her free speech and due process rights resulting from a three-day suspension for allegedly threatening to shoot a counselor because of a proposed schedule change.[37] Lovell argued that the discipline also violated § 1983.

The Ninth Circuit concluded, however, that threats are not protected by the First Amendment. Moreover, the court noted that "given the level of violence pervasive in schools today, it is no wonder that [the guidance counselor] felt threatened. . . . We recognize that violence is prevalent in public schools today, and that teachers and administrators must take threats by students very seriously."[38]

The power of *Tinker* and its progeny rests in its simple affirmation of students' rights: As our society has become increasingly aware of the violence that pervades the public schools, the simple has become complex, eliminating distance in order to ensure safety. Not unlike the biblical Samson, that which once gave strength has been excised. A similar emasculation appears with respect to students' Fourth Amendment rights.

---

that "harasses, threatens, intimidates or demeans" any individual or group because of "sex, color, race, religion, handicap, national origin or sexual orientation." The court noted that the "harassment provision of the dress code [was] aimed directly at the content of the speech, not at its potential for disruption or vulgarity." The question was certified to state court by the First Circuit Court of Appeals. 55 F.3d 20 (1st Cir. 1995); 667 N.E.2d 869 (Mass. 1996). However, not all dress codes violate the First Amendment: The federal district court in Albuquerque ruled that freedom of expression does not extend to a student's wearing of baggy pants, even though the student claimed that the attire expressed his identification with black culture. Bivens v. Albuquerque Public Schools, 899 F. Supp. 556 (D.N.M. 1995). *See also* Jeglin v. San Jacinto Unified School District, 827 F. Supp. 1459 (C.D. Cal.1993) (anti-gang dress code prohibiting clothing with sports team insignia); Oleson v. Board of Education School District No. 228, 676 F. Supp. 820 (N.D. Ill. 1987) (anti-gang dress code prohibited males from wearing earrings).

36. 90 F.3d 367 (9th Cir. 1996).
37. The trial court could not conclusively determine what was said. According to the student, she merely uttered a "figure of speech." According to the guidance counselor, however, the student said: "If you don't give me this schedule change, I'm going to shoot you." 847 F. Supp. 780, 783 (S.D. Cal. 1994).
38. 90 F.3d at 373-4.

From Reasonable Distance to Reasonable Intimacy

The Supreme Court's seminal case on students' Fourth Amendment rights is *New Jersey v. T.L.O.*[39] The case, which held that the exclusionary rule does not apply to the public school setting, set the standard for analyzing the legality of student searches in public schools.

Two high school girls were caught smoking in the lavatory, in violation of school rules. Both violators were questioned by Assistant Vice Principal Choplick. While T.L.O.'s co-violator admitted to smoking, T.L.O. denied that she had been smoking and asserted firmly that she did not smoke at all.

Mr. Choplick demanded to inspect T.L.O.'s purse; he immediately observed a pack of cigarettes. Upon reaching into her purse for the cigarettes, he then noticed cigarette rolling papers. A thorough search ensued and uncovered a small amount of marijuana, a pipe, empty plastic bags, a roll of money in one dollar bills, and a list of students purportedly who owed T.L.O. money. When T.L.O.'s case was referred to juvenile court for disposition of charges of possession and sale of marijuana, T.L.O. argued that Choplick's search of her purse had violated her Fourth Amendment rights.

Although the Court declined to hold that the search was illegal, it concluded that the Fourth Amendment's prohibition on illegal searches and seizures did indeed apply to searches by public school officials. In so doing, the Court majority sought guidance from *Tinker*:

> We have held school officials subject to the commands of the First Amendment . . . if school authorities are state actors for the purposes of the constitutional guarantees of freedom of expression . . . it is difficult to understand why they should be deemed to be exercising parental rather than public authority when conducting searches of their students. . . . Today's public school officials do not merely exercise authority voluntarily conferred on them by individual parents; rather, they act in furtherance of publicly mandated educational disciplinary policies.[40]

---

39. 469 U.S. 325, 105 S.Ct. 733, 83 L.Ed.2d 720 (1984).
40. 469 U.S. at 336.

The Court went on to balance the school officials' need to search against the "invasion which the search entails."[41] It determined that a student would possess a legitimate expectation of privacy in personal articles carried to school. At the same time, the Court noted that teachers and administrators possessed a "substantial interest . . . in maintaining discipline in the classroom and on school grounds."[42]

Unlike in criminal cases, however, searches in the public schools bear no warrant requirement or probable cause standard. "Rather," the Court stated, "the legality of a search of a student should depend simply on the reasonableness, under all the circumstances, of the search."[43] The standard of reasonableness will govern the objectives of the search, and will be guided, moreover, by the nature of the infraction and the age and sex of the student. In applying the reasonableness to the facts presented, the Court concluded that Mr. Choplick's search of T.L.O.'s purse complied with the Fourth Amendment.

The Court increased the school's reach, however, in a subsequent case.

Reasonable Intimacy

In *Vernonia School District 47J v. Acton*,[44] the Supreme Court held that random urinalysis drug tests of student athletes was constitutional. The case is a marked departure from the individualized suspicion that the Court found vital in *T.L.O.*

The petitioner school district observed a sharp increase in drug use; the district court noted that the disciplinary problems had reached "epidemic" proportions. Indeed, the school district found that athletes led the drug culture. Athletes who used drugs presented a particular concern to the school district, because of the increased risk of sports-related injury.

After proposing a student athlete drug policy to parents and receiving their unanimous approval, the school board adopted the policy. Its stated purpose was to prevent drug use by student athletes, protect athletes' health and safety, and provide assistance programs to drug users.

---

41. 469 U.S. at 337.
42. 469 U.S. at 339.
43. 469 U.S. at 341.
44. 454 U.S. 263, 115 S.Ct. 2386, 132 L.Ed.2d 564 (1995).

The policy applied to all students participating in interscholastic athletics. Athletes were tested at the beginning of each season. During the season, 10 percent of the athletes were randomly tested each week. When tested, students were monitored by adults of the same sex; the samples, in turn, were forwarded to an independent laboratory and tested for the presence of amphetamines, cocaine, and marijuana. Only the superintendent, principals, assistant principals, and athletic directors had access to the results.

The Court acknowledged that *T.L.O.* was based upon individualized suspicion. First and foremost, it noted that the reasonableness of every search must be balanced between the individual's Fourth Amendment interests and the promotion of legitimate governmental interests. The Court easily disposed of the privacy interests of student athletes but reasoned that "central . . . to the present case, is the fact that the subjects of the Policy are (1) children who (2) have been committed to the temporary custody of the State as school master."[45]

In interpreting its prior holding in *T.L.O.*, the court noted that "*T.L.O.* did not deny, but indeed emphasized that the nature of that power is custodial and tutelary, permitting a degree of supervision and control that could not be exercised over free adults."[46] Thus, "while children assuredly do not shed their constitutional rights . . . at the schoolhouse gate, the nature of those rights is what is appropriate for children at school."[47]

The Court applied a yet more relaxed reasonableness standard to the privacy interests of student athletes, and noted that there "is an element of communal undress inherent in athletic participation."[48] As such, "somewhat like adults who choose to participate in a 'closely regulated industry,' students who voluntarily participate in school athletics have reason to expect intrusions upon normal rights and privileges, including privacy."[49] Lastly, the Court concluded that the character of the complained intrusion was "negligible"[50] because the results were disclosed to a limited class of persons. Also, the test was only conducted to determine the presence of illegal drugs, and the drugs for which the urine was screened did not vary based upon the identity of the student.

---

45. 115 S.Ct. at 2391.
46. 115 S.Ct. at 2392.
47. 115 S.Ct. at 2392.
48. 115 S.Ct. at 2393.
49. 115 S.Ct. at 2393.
50. 115 S.Ct. at 2393.

Most important, however, the Court considered whether the governmental interest was "important enough"[51] to justify these types of searches. Although, it failed to definitively state "whether that relatively high degree of governmental concern"[52] is necessary, the Court found that the government's concern was both "compelling"[53] and immediate. It refused to find less intrusive measures (e.g., suspicion-based testing) to be required: "In many respects . . . testing based on suspicion of drug use would not be better, but worse."[54]

Nonetheless, the Court refused to hold that all suspicionless drug testing in public schools would be constitutional. Rather,

> [T]he most significant element in this case was the first we discussed: that the policy was undertaken in furtherance of the government's responsibilities, under a public school system, as guardian and tutor of children entrusted to its care. . . . [W]hen a government acts as a guardian and tutor the relevant question is whether the search is one that a reasonable guardian and tutor might undertake.[55]

Apparently, in the view of the Court, it would not be unreasonable for parents or guardians to subject their children to random drug testing.[56]

Mandatory Community Service

The purposes of public education as they relate to students' rights are perhaps best illustrated in recent challenges to mandatory community ser-

---

51. 115 S.Ct. at 2394.
52. 115 S.Ct. at 2395.
53. 115 S.Ct. at 2395.
54. 115 S.Ct. at 2396.
55. 115 S.Ct. at 2397.
56. Lower federal courts have addressed a number of other issues related to student searches: Cornfield v. Consolidated High School District No. 230, 991 F.2d 1316 (7th Cir. 1993) (nude strip search); Williams v. Ellington, 936 F.2d 881 (6th Cir. 1991) (strip search); Horton v. Goose Creek Independent School District, 690 F.2d 470 (5th Cir. 1982) and Doe v. Renfrow, 475 F. Supp. 1012 (N.D. Ind. 1979), *rev'd on another issue*, 631 F.2d 91 (7th Cir.) (per curiam) *cert. den.*, 451 U.S. 1022, 101 S.Ct. 3015, 69 L.Ed.2d 395 (1982) (canine sniffing of students and lockers).

vice programs.[57] Courts acknowledge that the role of the public school extends beyond the academic realm. This recognition was evident in *Immediato v. Rye Neck School District,*[58] where the Second Circuit Court of Appeals refused to hold that a school district's mandatory community service requirement for high school graduation violated the Thirteenth Amendment's prohibition on involuntary servitude.[59]

The school district's program required the completion of forty hours of community service during one's high school career. There were no exceptions to this requirement.[60] The school district permitted students to choose from a number of different organizations on its approved list, including charities, public agencies, political, or not-for-profit groups. Although the school district retained ultimate approval authority, students also had the option of suggesting their own organizations. Students could complete their forty-hour requirement at any time during their four-year high school career, even during the summer. Students determined their own work schedule and were responsible for their own transportation.

The plaintiffs argued that the program, in spite of its laudable goals, amounted to involuntary servitude. The court, however, believed that a "contextual approach" to the labor's ultimate purpose was necessary in order to analyze it properly. It noted that "involuntary servitude" was intended to "cover those forms of compulsory labor akin to African slavery which in practical operation would tend to produce undesirable results."[61] The proper

---

57. In Maryland, for example, community service is a requirement of graduation. *See* Code of Maryland Regulations, Md. Regs. Code Tit. 13A § 03.02.03 (D) (1994) "Student Service." Challenges have been mounted (and defeated) in both the Fourth and the Third Circuits. Steirer v. Bethlehem Area School District, 987 F.2d 989 (3d Cir. 1993) and Herndon v. Chapel Hill-Carrboro City Board of Education, 89 F.3d 174 (4th Cir. 1996).
58. 73 F.3d 454 (2d Cir. 1996).
59. The student plaintiff also asserted that his privacy and substantive due process rights had been violated. His parents, in turn, argued that the program unconstitutionally impinged upon their liberty interest in raising their child without governmental interference.
60. The program, which had been incorporated into the school district's curriculum, also required a corresponding classroom discussion. At this time, under the auspices of a mandatory course titled "Managing Your Future," students discussed their experiences and how their service could assist them with making career choices.
61. 73 F.3d at 459.

inquiry must look beyond the compulsory nature of the labor to the "whole set of conditions existing in the imposition of a mandatory community service program in a public high school."[62]

Unlike African slavery, the conditions of the program were not onerous; the program was not exploitative; and the work was not severe.[63] Additionally, the court found that the governmental interest in public education was amply supported by mandatory community service:

> The state's interest in education extends to teaching students the values and habits of good citizenship, and introducing them to their social responsibilities as citizens. The District reasonably concluded that the mandatory community service program would expose students to the needs of their communities and to the various ways in which a democratic system of volunteerism can respond to those needs. In so doing, the mandatory community service program helps students recognize their place in their communities, and, ideally, inspires them to introspection regarding their larger role in our political system. . . .[64]

Conclusion

Our public schools are, depending upon the peculiarities of the reviewing court, both parent and public entity—both intimately involved with us and distantly removed from us. As the court determines which of these roles fits the public schools, the analysis of the students' rights changes. As is evident from the case law presented in this chapter, the most obvious interpretation often changes.

---

62. *Id.* at 460.
63. Nonetheless, the court refused to extend blanket approval to "any and every service program that a public school system may devise. . . . If, for instance, the students were required to spend their Saturdays at the homes of their teachers, washing their cars, painting their houses, and weeding their gardens, the extent, nature, and conditions of 'service' and more obviously exploitative purpose of the program might indeed warrant a finding of involuntary servitude." *Id.* at 490.
64. 73 F.3d at 462.

However, this mercurial nature of legal decisionmaking is not disturbing.[65] Rather, we know how far we must go to reach Utopia. As W.E.B. DuBois noted, "To make . . . in . . . education that ever-necessary combination of the permanent and the contingent—of the ideal and of the practical in workable equilibrium—has been . . . as it ever must be in every age and place, a matter of infinite and frequent mistakes."[66]

---

65. On the contrary: it is quite comforting. We have moved from Plessy v. Ferguson, 163 U.S. 537 (1896) (separate but equal), to Brown v. Board of Education of Topeka, 347 U.S. 497 (1954) (separate is unconstitutional).
66. William Edward Burghardt DuBois, The Souls of Black Folk, New York: New American Library, 1982, at 124.

Chapter Eleven

Individual Immunity Defenses Under § 1983

Robert F. Brown

While the text of § 1983 ostensibly creates a cause of action against "every person" who, while acting under color of state law, deprives another of a federal or constitutional right, "every person" does not include all persons. The U.S. Supreme Court has created special immunity defenses for certain classes of individual defendants who are sued in their individual capacities. These persons may be entitled to an absolute immunity from suit and damages or to assert a qualified immunity from suit and damages, depending on the particular functions exercised by the individuals.

Recognition and Evolution of Immunity Defenses

Section 1983 was enacted to deter public officials from abusing their authority in a manner that deprives persons of their federally protected rights and to provide a remedy to victims of unconstitutional acts.[1] Section 1983, however, contains no language addressing either absolute or qualified immunity for public officials alleged to have violated § 1983. Rather, individual immunity defenses from § 1983 liability are judicially created doctrines that stem from the common law as it existed when Congress enacted the Civil Rights Act of 1871, Section 1 of which is now codified as § 1983. These historically recognized common law immunities were public policy driven and designed to protect public officials from litigation that might tend to chill the officials' proper exercise of discretion and divert the attention of public officials from their duties by unnecessary and time-consuming litigation.[2] As stated by the U.S. Supreme Court in *Owen v. City of Independence*, "[w]here the immunity claimed by the defendant was

1. *See* Carey v. Piphus, 435 U.S. 247, 253-54 (1978).
2. *See*, *e.g.*, Wood v. Strickland, 420 U.S. 308, 319-20 (1975); Pierson v. Ray, 386 U.S. 547, 554-55 (1967).

well established at common law at the time § 1983 was enacted, and where its rationale was compatible with the purposes of the Civil Rights Act, we have construed the statute to incorporate that immunity."[3]

Source of Federal Immunities

The Supreme Court has consistently recognized individual immunity defenses that were well-established in 1871 when Congress enacted the Civil Rights Act of 1871. Regardless of strong policy considerations, the Court has not, however, provided immunities from § 1983 actions where such immunities did not exist in 1871.[4]

In developing the federal immunities applicable in § 1983 litigation, the Supreme Court has chosen not to be influenced by the various state law doctrines of immunity for governmental entities and government officials. Rather, the Supreme Court has held that federal law controls the immunity analysis under § 1983 even if the matter in question is pending in state court.[5] Pursuant to the Supremacy Clause of the U.S. Constitution, federal laws are enforceable in state courts, and state courts are charged with the parallel responsibility of enforcing those laws according to their regular modes of procedure.[6]

> No one disputes the general and unassailable proposition relied upon by the [state] Supreme Court below that States may establish the rules of procedure governing litigation in their own courts. By the same token, however, where state courts entertain a federally created cause of action, the 'federal right cannot be defeated by the forms of local practice.'[7]

---

3. 445 U.S. 622, 638 (1980).
4. *See, e.g.*, Tower v. Glover, 467 U.S. 914, 922 (1984) (where no immunity was available in 1871 providing public defenders an absolute immunity from liability for intentional misconduct that deprives clients of their federal rights, even strong public policy reasons do not support providing public defenders such immunity under § 1983).
5. *See* Howlett v. Rose, 496 U.S. 356, 369 (1990) ("A state court may not deny a federal right, when the parties and controversy are properly before it, in the absence of a 'valid excuse.'").
6. *Id.* at 367.
7. Felder v. Casey, 487 U.S. 130, 138 (1988) (quoting Brown v. Western R. Co. of Alabama, 338 U.S. 294, 296 (1949)).

Since immunity under the Civil Rights Act is a question of federal law, state courts are obligated to recognize and apply federal law regarding immunities to suits brought under § 1983.[8]

Distinction Between Immunity from Damages and Immunity from Injunctive Relief

There is a distinction from immunity from damages and immunity from injunctive relief. For example, in *Supreme Court of Virginia v. Consumers Union of the United States*,[9] the U.S. Supreme Court held that the Virginia Supreme Court and its Chief Justice could be sued under § 1983 for injunctive relief in their capacities as enforcers of the Virginia Supreme Court's disciplinary rules for lawyer advertising, which rules had been challenged on First Amendment grounds.[10] The Court held that the Virginia Supreme Court could not, however, be sued for injunctive relief in its legislative capacity in promulgating the challenged rules or in its judicial capacity in adjudicating the constitutionality of the rules.[11]

Similarly, in *Pulliam v. Allen*,[12] the Supreme Court held that judges are not absolutely immune from injunctive relief under § 1983.[13] The Court, noting that actions in prohibition and mandamus had historically been used at common law to enjoin judicial actions, held that the lack of absolute immunity from injunctive relief for judicial actions, as compared to immunity from damage suits, would not have a chilling effect on judicial independence.[14]

Individual- Versus Official-Capacity Suits

In *Kentucky v. Graham*,[15] the Supreme Court attempted "to unravel once again the distinction between personal- and official-capacity suits."[16]

---

8. *See* Martinez v. State of California, 444 U.S. 277, 284 n.8 (1980).
9. 446 U.S. 719 (1980).
10. *Id.* at 736.
11. *Id.* at 731-34.
12. 466 U.S. 522 (1984).
13. *Id.* at 541-42.
14. *Id.* at 536-40.
15. 473 U.S. 159 (1985).
16. *Id.* at 163.

> Personal-capacity suits seek to impose personal liability upon a government official for actions he takes under color of state law. Official-capacity suits, in contrast, 'generally represent only another way of pleading an action against an entity of which an officer is an agent.' As long as a government entity receives notice and an opportunity to respond, an official-capacity suit is, in all respects other than name, to be treated as a suit against the entity. It is *not* a suit against the official personally, for the real party in interest is the entity. Thus, while an award of damages against an official in his personal capacity can be executed only against the official's personal assets, a plaintiff seeking to recover on a damage judgment in an official-capacity suit must look to the government entity itself.[17]

Consequently, individuals sued in their official capacities only are not entitled to assert individual immunity defenses.

Functional Approach to Immunity Analysis

The Supreme Court utilizes a functional approach in determining whether a particular class of individual defendants is entitled to absolute immunity or qualified immunity.

> Running through our cases, with fair consistency, is a 'functional' approach to immunity questions other than those that have been decided by express constitutional or statutory enactment. Under that approach, we examine the nature of the functions with which a particular official or class of officials has been lawfully entrusted, and we seek to evaluate the effect that exposure to particular forms of liability would likely have on the appropriate exercise of those functions. Officials who seek exemption for personal liability have the burden of showing that such an exemption is justified by overriding considerations of public policy, and the Court has recognized a category of 'qualified' immunity that avoids unnecessarily extending the scope of the traditional concept of absolute immunity.[18]

---

17. *Id.* at 165-66 (citations omitted) (emphasis in original).
18. Forrester v. White, 484 U.S. 219, 224 (1988).

Utilizing a functional analysis, the Supreme Court has determined that state and regional legislators (when acting in a legislative capacity), judges (when acting within their jurisdiction), and prosecutors (when acting as advocates in the criminal process) are all absolutely immune from liability for damages under § 1983.[19] Under a functional approach, determining what type of immunity applies to a particular official in a given case turns on the nature of the act being performed, rather than on the position or title held by the official.

For example, state and regional legislators, when acting administratively rather than legislatively, are protected only by the affirmative defense of qualified immunity.[20] Moreover, prosecutors, when acting in an investigative capacity rather than as advocates in a criminal process, are not entitled to absolute immunity, but are entitled only to assert the defense of qualified immunity.[21]

A critical distinction between absolute immunity and qualified immunity is that absolute immunity does not look to the reasonableness of the defendant's actions; rather, an absolute immunity analysis is complete once it is determined that the defendant's function entitles that defendant to an absolute immunity, regardless of the defendant's subjective or objective good faith. As is explained below, the functional approach to immunity analysis has extended absolute immunity beyond even legislators, judges, and prosecutors to other individual defendants who are engaged in legislative, judicial, or prosecutorial acts.

Absolute Immunity

Under a functional approach, absolute immunity protects certain government officials for their official acts regardless of the legality or constitutionality of the acts. Courts have consistently recognized two policy rationales justifying the recognition of absolute immunity: (1) the fear of damages may chill an official's exercise of discretion, and (2) the process

---

19. *See* Tenney v. Brandhove, 341 U.S. 367, 379 (1951) (state legislators); Lake Country Estates, Inc. v. Tahoe Regional Planning Agency, 440 U.S. 391, 405-06 (1979) (regional legislators); Stump v. Sparkman, 435 U.S. 349, 356-57 (1978) (judges); Imbler v. Pachtman, 424 U.S. 409, 427 (1976) (prosecutors).
20. *See* Lake Country Estates, 440 U.S. at 402-06.
21. Burns v. Reed, 500 U.S. 478, 492-96 (1991).

of defending civil rights claims may divert the official's attention from his or her duties.

Legislators

Federal law is well-settled that legislators are entitled to an absolute immunity from suit under 1983 for conduct in furtherance of their legislative duties.[22] Utilizing a functional approach, however, the Court has limited the application of absolute legislative immunity to acts within the sphere of legitimate legislative activities.[23]

The landmark case of *Tenney v. Brandhove*[24] discusses the historical antecedents of legislative immunity. Justice Frankfurter wrote that legislators

> are immune from deterrents to the uninhibited discharge of their legislative duty, not for their private indulgence but for the public good. One must not expect uncommon courage even in legislators. The privilege would be of little value if they could be subjected to the cost and inconvenience and distractions of a trial upon a conclusion of a pleader, or to the hazard of the judgment against them based upon a jury's speculation as to motives.[25]

This language was repeated favorably in *Lake Country Estates, Inc. v. Tahoe Regional Planning Agency*.[26] Justice Frankfurter in *Tenney* quoted language from *Coffin v. Coffin*,[27] in describing the parameters of absolute legislative immunity:

> I will not confine it to delivering an opinion, uttering a speech, or haranguing in debate; but will extend it to the giving of a vote, to

22. *See Owen* 445 U.S. at 663 n.6; *Lake Country Estates*, 440 U.S. at 402-06; *Tenney,* 341 U.S. at 379.
23. *See Lake Country Estates,* 440 U.S. at 402-06 (court used functional approach to determine that a bi-state regional planning agency created by California and Nevada was entitled to absolute legislative immunity for its adoption and enforcement of a regional land use plan); *Tenney*, 341 U.S. at 379 (state legislators absolutely immune from liability for damages when they act "in a field where legislators traditionally have power to act").
24. 341 U.S. 367 (1951).
25. *Id.* at 377.
26. 440 U.S. 391, 405 (1979).
27. 4 Mass. 1, 27 (1808).

> the making of a written report, and to every other act resulting from the nature, and in the execution, of the office; and . . . securing to every member exemption from prosecution, for everything said or done by him, as a representative, in the exercise of the functions of that office, without inquiring whether the exercise was regular according to the rules of the house, or irregular and against their rules.[28]

Public policy considerations also favor "the recognition of absolute immunity for elected local officials performing legislative functions. Local officials are directly accountable for their words and votes. In fact, the electoral process is a far stronger protection for the public where the legislator is local rather than state or federal."[29] Many local legislators serve for little or no salary.

> Adding the risk [to the local legislator] of a lawsuit at every vote hardly makes the task more attractive. Local government should not be reserved for only those who can afford to hire lawyers and defend against potential personal liability. Furthermore, absolute legislative immunity protects the legislative process from encroachment by or subordination to the judiciary or individual plaintiffs. For the good of the public, local legislators must be able to speak their minds and vote their consciences without fear of personal liability under 42 U.S.C. §1983. Finally, no potential plaintiff will be disadvantaged by this immunity. If liability is found, all taxpayers will pay the damages that the local officials, in discharge of legislative duties in behalf of the public, may be found to have caused. Of course, local legislators must face the political consequences of this liability.[30]

Although the Supreme Court has not yet spoken on this issue, at least eight federal appellate courts have extended absolute legislative immunity to local legislators performing legislative functions.[31]

---

28. *Tenney*, 341 U.S. at 374.
29. Heiar v. Crawford County, Wisconsin, 558 F.Supp. 1175, 1180 (W.D. Wis. 1983), aff'd in part, vacated in part, 746 F.2d 1190 (7th Cir. 1984), *cert. denied*, 472 U.S. 1027 (1985). *Cf. Tenney*, 341 U.S. at 378.
30. *Heiar*, 558 F.Supp. at 1180-81.
31. *See* Haskell v. Washington Township, 864 F.2d 1266, 1277 (6th Cir. 1988); Aitchison v. Raffiani, 708 F.2d 96, 98-100 (3d Cir. 1983); Reed v. Village of

The Functional Approach: Legislative Versus Administrative Acts

Under the functional approach, only those persons whose actions are legislative in nature are entitled to the protection of absolute legislative immunity.[32]

Legislators are absolutely immune while passing laws, holding committee meetings, or when acting "in a field where legislators traditionally have power to act."[33] Legislative immunity has been found for budgeting decisions,[34] ordinance enactment,[35] zoning decisions,[36] and other matters held to be legislative in nature.[37]

Shorewood, 704 F.2d 943, 952-53 (7th Cir. 1983); Espanola Way Corp. v. Meyerson, 690 F.2d 827, 829 (11th Cir. 1982), *cert. denied*, 460 U.S. 1039 (1983); Kuzinich v. County of Santa Clara, 689 F.2d 1345, 1349-50 (9th Cir. 1982); Hernandez v. City of LaFayette, 643 F.2d 1188, 1193-94 (5th Cir. 1981); Bruce v. Riddle, 631 F.2d 272, 279 (4th Cir. 1980); Gorman Towers, Inc. v. Bogoslavsky, 626 F.2d 607, 611-14 (8th Cir. 1980).

32. *See, e.g.*, *Lake Country Estates*, 440 U.S. at 402-06 (regional legislators); *Consumers Union*, 446 U.S. at 731-34 (state supreme court justices in promulgating attorney conduct rules); Gravel v. United States, 408 U.S. 606, 616-21 (1972) (legislative aides when performing acts for which a legislator would be immune).
33. *Tenney*, 341 U.S. at 379.
34. Baker v. Mayor and City Council of Baltimore, 894 F.2d 679, 681 (4th Cir. 1990) (mayor and council were acting in a legislative capacity when they eliminated city employee positions under a budget ordinance and, thus, were entitled to immunity); *Aitchison*, 708 F.2d at 98-100 (mayor and city council were absolutely immune for eliminating position of assistant building inspector).
35. Shoultes v. Laidlaw, 886 F.2d 114, 117 (6th Cir. 1989) (mayor and city council who voted for unconstitutional zoning ordinance held absolutely immune); Mears v. Town of Oxford, 762 F.2d 368, 371 (4th Cir. 1985) (town commissioners who passed ordinance limiting marina expansion were acting in a legislative capacity and were absolutely immune).
36. *Bruce*, 631 F.2d at 279 (members of county council were absolutely immune in passing rezoning ordinance); *Gorman Towers*, 626 F.2d at 611-14 (city board of directors were absolutely immune for passing zoning amendment).
37. Schultz v. Sundberg, 759 F.2d 714, 717 (9th Cir. 1985) (senate president was absolutely immune in compelling legislator to attend session through use of senate sergeant-at-arms and state troopers); Agromayor v. Goldberg, 738 F.2d 55, 58-60 (1st Cir. 1984) (Puerto Rico speaker of the house was absolutely immune in refusing to hire individual of rival political party as a legislative press officer); Kuzinich v. City of Santa Clara, 689 F.2d 1345, 1349 (9th Cir.

When local legislators are acting with respect to a specific situation that does not amount to policymaking, they may not have legislative immunity. For example, in the land use area, a vote to change zoning laws or to establish general rules for the use of property may be a legislative act, but an individual decision on a single parcel of land may not be a legislative act. The mere fact that the complained-of action occurred by way of a vote does not automatically mean the action is legislative. A number of federal appellate courts have recognized that "[a]lthough a local legislator may vote on an issue, [the act of voting] alone does not necessarily determine that he or she was acting in a legislative capacity."[38]

The U.S. Supreme Court has not outlined any definitive test for determining when a particular action taken by a local official is considered legislative and when it is not. Nevertheless, the Fifth and First Circuits have adopted two tests to aid in this determination.[39]

The first test focuses on the nature of the facts used to reach a given decision. Under that test, if the underlying facts on which a decision is based are "legislative facts," such as generalizations concerning a policy or state of affairs, then the decision is legislative. If, on the other hand, the facts used in the decisionmaking are more specific, such as those that relate to particular individuals or situations, then the decision is administrative.[40]

The second test focuses on the "particularity of the impact of the state action." Under this test, if the action involves establishment of a general policy, it is legislative. If it singles out specific individuals and affects them differently from others, it is administrative.[41] Other federal appellate courts

---

1982) (members of local legislative bodies had complete immunity from suits based on their legislative acts); Green v. DeCamp, 612 F.2d 368, 372 (8th Cir. 1980) (state senators who released committee report to media were entitled to legislative immunity).

38. Brown v. Griesenauer, 970 F.2d 431, 437 (8th Cir. 1992); Crymes v. DeKalb County, Ga., 923 F.2d 1482, 1485 (11th Cir. 1991). *See also* Roberson v. Mullins, 29 F.2d 132, 134 n. 3 (4th Cir. 1994) (recognizing that member of local governmental body does not necessarily act in legislative capacity when participation takes form of a vote).

39. *See* Hughes v. Tarrant County, 948 F.2d 918, 921 (5th Cir. 1991); Cutting v. Muzzey, 724 F.2d 259, 261 (1st Cir. 1984).

40. *Hughes,* 948 F.2d at 921; *Cutting*, 724 F.2d at 261.

41. *Hughes,* 948 F.2d at 921; *Cutting*, 724 F.2d at 261.

have adopted the same or similar tests for determining the scope of absolute legislative immunity.[42]

Judges

Absolute judicial immunity was recognized as part of the common law well before the adoption of the Civil Rights Act of 1871.[43] In *Pierson v. Ray*, the Supreme Court recognized absolute judicial immunity for damages under § 1983, stating, "The immunity of judges for acts within the judicial role is . . . well established, and we presume that Congress would have specifically so provided had it wished to abolish the doctrine [when it enacted § 1983]."[44]

It was not until the Supreme Court's 1978 decision in *Stump v. Sparkman*,[45] however, that the Court articulated two limits on judicial immunity. The Court held that (1) acts in the clear absence of a court's jurisdiction are not entitled to immunity, although immunity does extend to acts in mere excess of jurisdiction, and (2) only judicial acts are protected.[46]

The Supreme Court has articulated at least three policy bases justifying absolute judicial immunity from § 1983 suits: (1) the recognition of the common law history of immunity for judges, (2) the desire not to chill judicial discretion, undermine the finality of judicial proceedings, or unfairly punish judges from exercising discretion, and (3) the availability of alternative methods of addressing judicial abuse by way of appeal, judicial conduct proceedings, criminal prosecution, and the will of the electorate for elected judges.[47]

---

42. *See, e.g.*, *Roberson*, 29 F.3d at 135; *Brown*, 970 F.2d at 437; Acevedo-Cordero v. Cordero-Santiago, 958 F.2d 20, 23 (1st Cir. 1992); *Crymes*, 923 F.2d at 1485; Ryan v. Burlington County, N.J., 889 F.2d 1286, 1290-91 (3d. Cir. 1989); Cinevision Corp. v. City of Burbank, 745 F.2d 560, 580 (9th Cir. 1984), *cert. denied*, 471 U.S. 1054 (1985).
43. *See* Bradley v. Fisher, 13 Wall. 335 (1871).
44. 386 U.S. 547, 554-55 (1967).
45. 435 U.S. 349 (1978).
46. *Id.* at 356-62. *See also* Mireles v. Waco, 112 S.Ct. 286, 288 (1991).
47. *See Pierson*, 386 U.S. at 554-55; *Stump*, 435 U.S. at 355-57.

The Functional Approach: Judicial Versus Nonjudicial Conduct

The functional approach to absolute judicial immunity protects judges at all levels as well as those who act like judges.[48] Only judicial acts, however, are protected by absolute immunity.[49] In determining whether conduct constitutes a judicial act, the Supreme Court has stated that

> the factors determining whether an act by a judge is a 'judicial' one relate to the nature of the act itself, i.e., whether it is a function normally performed by a judge, and to the expectations of the parties, i.e., whether they dealt with the judge in his judicial capacity.[50]

The Supreme Court has upheld judicial immunity even in extreme circumstances.[51] Lower courts have also upheld such immunity in a variety of circumstances.[52] Even judges acting outside of, or in excess of, their juris-

---

48. *See, e.g.*, Butz v. Economou, 438 U.S. 478, 512-13 (1978) (absolute immunity extended to hearing examiners).
49. *See, e.g.*, Cleavinger v. Saxner, 474 U.S. 193, 203-06 (1985) (hearing officers in a prison disciplinary proceeding functioned as adjudicators in an administrative matter and were only entitled to qualified immunity).
50. *Stump*, 435 U.S. at 362.
51. *See, e.g., Mireles,* 112 S.Ct. at 288-89 (judge was acting within his judicial function when he ordered deputies to physically bring lawyer who was late into his courtroom and excessive force was allegedly applied; judge had absolute judicial immunity since ordering lawyer who was physically present in the courthouse to come to his courtroom was a judicial function); *Stump*, 435 U.S. at 357-60 (judge of court of general jurisdiction who ordered sterilization of fifteen-year-old girl was absolutely immune even if Indiana law did not authorize his acts).
52. *See, e.g.*, Myers v. Vogal, 960 F.2d 750 (8th Cir. 1992) (judge who sentenced juvenile as adult was still acting within his jurisdiction and was entitled to absolute judicial immunity); John v. Barron, 897 F.2d 1387, 1391-92 (7th Cir. 1990) (judge was absolutely immune in removing trustee of charitable trust); Mills v. Criminal Dist. Court No. 3, 837 F.2d 677 (5th Cir. 1988) (trial judge was absolutely immune against allegations of denial of a fundamentally fair trial); Glick v. Koenig, 766 F.2d 265, 269 (7th Cir. 1985) (judge who allegedly conspired with prosecutor in speeding ticket case was entitled to absolute immunity); Halloway v. Walker, 765 F.2d 517, 522-23 (5th Cir. 1985) (judge was absolutely immune for placing company in receivership and running company improperly); Adams v. McIlhany, 764 F.2d 294, 297-99 (5th Cir. 1985) (judge who sentenced woman to thirty days in jail for contempt because she had

diction are entitled to absolute judicial immunity unless the judge is acting in *clear excess* of territorial jurisdiction.[53]

Judges are not typically entitled to immunity when acting outside of their judicial offices. For example, in *Zarcone v. Perry*,[54] a judge ordered a sandwich vendor brought before him in handcuffs because he sold "putrid" coffee. In the resulting civil rights suit, the judge was held not to have been performing a judicial act and the jury's verdict of $80,000 in compensatory damages and $60,000 in punitive damages was subsequently upheld.[55]

---

accused the judge of accepting bribes was absolutely immune); Emory v. Peeler, 756 F.2d 1547, 1551 (11th Cir. 1985) (judge who singled out and chastised juror for not voting for death penalty was absolutely immune); Green v. Maraio, 722 F.2d 1013, 1017-18 (2d Cir. 1983) (judge who allegedly told court reporter to alter trial transcript after criminal defendant was sentenced was absolutely immune, as was the court reporter who acted pursuant to the judge's explicit instructions); Scott v. Hayes, 719 F.2d 1562, 1566-67 (11th Cir. 1983) (judge who ordered party in divorce proceeding to have vasectomy as a condition of obtaining a favorable property settlement was absolutely immune).

53. *See, e.g.*, Rosenthal v. Justices of the Supreme Court of California, 910 F.2d 561, 565-66 (9th Cir. 1990) (even if judge acts outside of jurisdiction, he still has absolute judicial immunity so long as acts themselves are judicial); King v. Love, 766 F.2d 962, 965-66 (6th Cir. 1985) (municipal court judge who acted in excess of his jurisdiction by jailing driver was still absolute immune since court had subject matter jurisdiction over the underlying offense); Billingsley v. Kyser, 691 F.2d 388, 389 (8th Cir. 1982) (judge who amended plaintiff's criminal sentence while plaintiff's appeal was pending was immune even though the judge had lost jurisdiction over the matter); Turner v. Raynes, 611 F.2d 92, 93-94 (5th Cir. 1980) (Texas justice of the peace with limited criminal jurisdiction was absolutely immune even if he convicted plaintiff of nonexistent crime). Contra Maestri v. Jatkofsky, 860 F.2d 50, 53 (2d Cir. 1988) (town judge, who could only hear criminal cases in his own town and in towns immediately adjacent, was not entitled to absolute immunity when he heard a case beyond those limits and issued arrest warrants for acts that took place in a town not within his jurisdiction); Dykes v. Hosemann, 743 F.2d 1488, 1496-97 (11th Cir. 1984) (judge acting in clear and complete absence of personal jurisdiction loses judicial immunity).
54. 572 F.2d 52 (2d Cir. 1978).
55. *Id.* at 54-55. *See also* Harris v. Harvey, 605 F.2d 330, 336 (7th Cir. 1979) (where judge initiated criminal proceedings against black police officer based upon racially improper motives and made racial remarks to press, he was not entitled to absolute immunity and jury's award of $60,000 in compensatory damages and $200,000 in punitive damages was accordingly upheld).

Judges are not absolutely immune when they act in an administrative capacity,[56] or when they act as supervising employers.[57] A judge acting in other capacities is not entitled to judicial immunity. For example, a judge who acts as a prosecutor, preparing complaint forms and then acting on them as a judge, is immune for the judicial acts, but not for the prosecutorial acts.[58] A judge acting as a legislator, issuing court rules, is absolutely immune in the legislative capacity, but not in enforcing the rules, which is an administrative capacity.[59] Even judges who are absolutely immune for damages may be subject to suit for declaratory and injunctive relief.[60]

Others Who May Perform Judge-Like Functions

Executive officials performing judge-like functions are also immune,[61] as are parole officers acting in a judicial capacity.[62] Persons acting pursu-

---

56. *See, e.g.*, Atcherson v. Siebenmann, 605 F.2d 1058, 1063-64 (8th Cir. 1979) (judge who allegedly unlawfully terminated employee was entitled only to assert qualified immunity defense); *King*, 766 F.2d at 968-69 (judge who deliberately mislead an officer about the identity of the person named in a warrant, which lead to that person's arrest, committed a nonjudicial act for which no judicial immunity was available).
57. *See, e.g.*, Forrester v. White, 484 U.S. 219, 229-30 (1988) (state court judge was acting in an administrative capacity when he demoted and dismissed probation officer and, thus, was not absolutely immune from § 1983 damages suit brought by disgruntled ex-employee); Goodwin v. Circuit Court of St. Louis County, 729 F.2d 541, 545 (8th Cir. 1984) (judge who allegedly transfered female hearing officer on the basis of her sex was not entitled to absolute immunity).
58. *See* Lopez v. Vanderwater, 620 F.2d 1229, 1234-35 (7th Cir. 1980).
59. *Consumers Union*, 446 U.S. at 731-34.
60. *See id.* at 736. *But see* Alia v. Michigan Supreme Court, 906 F.2d 1100, 1101-02 (6th Cir. 1990) (state supreme court justices were acting in their legislative capacity in enacting mediation rule and, thus, were entitled to legislative immunity from civil rights action regardless of whether relief sought was money damages or injunctive relief).
61. *See, e.g.*, *Butz*, 438 U.S. at 513-14 (administrative law judge and hearing examiner in agriculture department were acting in a judicial capacity when they attempted to revoke plaintiff's registration with the department and, thus, were absolutely immune); Scott v. Schmidt, 773 F.2d 160, 164-65 (7th Cir. 1985) (members of Illinois Racing Board were acting in a judicial capacity in suspending and denying horse owner's racing license where owner allegedly took a bribe to fix a horse race and, thus, were absolutely immune);

ant to court order or in conjunction with judicial activities are typically entitled to absolute immunity.

Mills v. Killebrew, 765 F.2d 69, 72 (6th Cir. 1985) (lawyers who served on mediation panel were entitled to absolute immunity); Vakas v. Rodriquez, 728 F.2d 1293, 1296-97 (10th Cir. 1984) (members of Kansas Board of Healing Arts hearing disciplinary charges against doctors were absolutely immune); Sprecher v. Graber, 716 F.2d 968, 972-73 (2d Cir. 1983) (SEC officials enjoyed absolute immunity insofar as alleged misconduct in connection with SEC investigation fell within scope of judicial or prosecutorial functions); Simons v. Bellinger, 643 F.2d 774, 777-78 (D.C. Cir. 1980) (unauthorized practice of law committee of bar association had absolute immunity in determining compliance with laws and rules governing practice of law); Ashbrook v. Hoffman, 617 F.2d 474, 476-77 (7th Cir. 1980) (commissioners appointed by the court to conduct a partition sale of the divorced plaintiffs' property were sufficiently related to the judicial process to entitle them to quasi-judicial absolute immunity from federal suit for damages arising from their conduct in handling sale and in distributing proceeds of sale).

62. *See, e.g.*, Farrish v. Mississippi State Parole Bd., 836 F.2d 969, 973-76 (5th Cir. 1988) (parole board members were absolutely immune in deciding whether to grant or deny parole); Johnson v. Rhode Island Parole Board Members, 815 F.2d 5, 8 (1st Cir. 1987) (parole board members were entitled to absolute immunity from liability for damages in § 1983 suit for actions taken within the proper scope of their official duties); Nelson v. Balazic, 802 F.2d 1077, 1078 (8th Cir. 1986) (parole board members who paroled individual who subsequently kidnapped, raped and sodomized plaintiffs were absolutely immune for their decision to parole the perpetrator); Evans v. Dillahunty, 711 F.2d 828, 830-31 (8th Cir. 1983) (regional parole commissioner, who rejected parole panel's recommendation, resulting in prisoner spending four extra months in prison, acted within scope of his official duties in reviewing the recommendation and, therefore, was entitled to absolute immunity); Sellars v. Procunier, 641 F.2d 1295, 1302-03 (9th Cir. 1981) (state parole board officials are entitled to absolute immunity from suits by prisoners for actions taken when processing parole applications since, under "functional comparability" test, parole board officials perform functionally comparable tasks to judges when they decide to grant, deny or revoke parole, and parole board officials face same risk of constant unfounded suits by those disappointed by parole board's decisions). *But see* Jones v. Moore, 986 F.2d 251, 253 (8th Cir. 1993) (parole officer was absolutely immune in revoking parole, but not in issuing false violation report); Harper v. Jeffries, 808 F.2d 281, 284 (3d Cir. 1986) (parole board members were absolutely immune when carrying out adjudicatory functions, but not when performing executive or administrative functions); Ray v. Pickett, 734 F.2d 370, 373-74 (8th Cir. 1984) (probation officer, in filing report with

For example, state officials charged with the duty of executing a facially valid court order enjoy absolute judicial immunity.[63] Court clerks acting in a ministerial role, however, are entitled only to qualified immunity with respect to certain functions.[64]

---

the U.S. Parole Commission to secure a parole violator's warrant, was not functioning in an adjudicatory or prosecutorial capacity and, thus, was not entitled to absolute immunity in suit claiming intentional falsification of report); Anderson v. Boyd, 714 F.2d 906, 908 (9th Cir. 1983) (absolute immunity does not extend to the knowing dissemination of false information concerning a parolee to persons outside the parole system).

63. *See* Valdez v. City and County of Denver, 878 F.2d 1285, 1287-88 (10th Cir. 1989). *See also* Carroll v. Gross, 984 F.2d 392, 393 (11th Cir. 1993) (members of the Florida State Bar were acting as agents of the Florida Supreme Court in connection with disciplinary proceeding and were entitled to absolute immunity); Turney v. O'Toole, 898 F.2d 1470, 1473-74 (10th Cir. 1990) (superintendent and psychologist at public mental health facility were entitled to absolute quasi-judicial immunity from juvenile's civil rights action insofar as action was based upon fact of juvenile's confinement pursuant to court order, even assuming order was infirm as matter of state law, but such immunity did not extend to any liability arising from placement of juvenile in maximum security ward; superintendent and psychologist were only qualifiedly immune for any liability arising from placement).

64. *See* Antoine v. Byers & Anderson, 113 S.Ct. 2167, 2171-72 (1993) (court reporter was not absolutely immune from damages liability for failing to produce transcript of federal criminal trial; tasks performed by court reporter were not discretionary and were not functionally comparable to that of judge); Henriksen v. Bentley, 644 F.2d 852, 856 (10th Cir. 1981) (clerks entitled only to qualified immunity when exercising ministerial and nondiscretionary duty to file court papers). *But see* Boyer v. County of Washington, 971 F.2d 100, 102 (8th Cir. 1992) (court clerk who signed and issued arrest warrant was entitled to absolute immunity); Kincaid v. Vale, 969 F.2d 594, 601 (7th Cir. 1992) (court clerks were entitled to absolute immunity against § 1983 action brought by two inmates who alleged that clerks had deprived them of their constitutional right to access to courts by refusing to file inmates' civil suit in Indiana Superior Court; clerks' acts were done at judicial direction and were nonmechanical functions integral to judicial process); Rogers v. Bruntrager, 841 F.2d 853, 856 (8th Cir. 1988) (court clerks held to have absolute immunity from actions for damages arising from acts they are specifically required to do under court order or at a judge's direction); McCaw v. Winter, 745 F.2d 533, 534 (8th Cir. 1984) (court clerk who followed judge's order in selecting jury was absolutely immune); Scott v. Dixon, 720 F.2d 1542, 1546-47 (11th Cir. 1983) (court clerk who issued

Those who are an integral part of the judicial system are also absolutely immune.[65] For example, grand jurors exercising discretionary judgment on the basis of evidence presented to them in grand jury proceedings are entitled to absolute immunity.[66]

Prosecutors

Prosecutors generally enjoy absolute immunity when performing prosecutorial acts.[67] As discussed below, however, prosecutors are not absolutely immune for all actions taken. Following a functional approach, the courts have held that while prosecutors are entitled to immunity for traditional litigation activities, they are not absolutely immune for activities such as office administration, criminal investigations, or news releases.

Imbler articulated a number of justifications for immunizing prosecutors for their prosecutorial acts. Those justifications, which are substantially similar to those advanced to justify absolute judicial immunity, include: (1) the recognition of the common law history of immunity for

---

arrest warrant under authority granted by state law was immune from suit even if he conspired with another by issuing criminal arrest warrant to collect debt).

65. *See, e.g.*, Millspaugh v. County Dept. of Public Welfare, 937 F.2d 1172, 1176 (7th Cir. 1991) (social service worker initiating child abuse proceeding was absolutely immune); Property Management & Investments, Inc. v. Lewis, 752 F.2d 599, 602 (11th Cir. 1985) (court appointed receiver was entitled to absolute immunity in performing acts within the scope of his authority and in carrying out judge's orders); Kurzawa v. Mueller, 732 F.2d 1456, 1458 (6th Cir. 1984) (state employees who were responsible for prosecution of child neglect and delinquency petitions in state courts, and psychologist and psychiatrists whose findings following examination of child were used by department of social services and state courts to determine what environment best suited interests of child, all of whom were integral parts of judicial process, were entitled to absolute immunity in action brought by parents individually and as next friends of their son alleging violation of their civil rights).
66. *See* DeCamp v. Douglas County Franklin Grand Jury, 978 F.2d 1047, 1050-51 (8th Cir. 1992) (members of grand jury had absolute immunity against § 1983 claims against them arising from grand jurors' "co-authoring" of report issued following investigation of child abuse and other charges; grand jurors' comments in report involved exercise of discretionary, quasi-judicial function).
67. *See* Imbler, 424 U.S. at 430-31; Burns, 500 U.S. at 490-91.

prosecutors, (2) policy considerations designed to protect prosecutors from unfounded litigation that would divert attention from their duties and effect independent decisionmaking, and (3) the availability of alternative checks on prosecutor's activities by various post-trial and appellate procedures, and professional disciplinary review mechanisms.[68]

The Functional Approach: Advocacy Versus Investigative Acts

Prosecutors are absolutely immune when performing prosecutorial acts such as initiating the prosecution, presenting the case in court and taking appeals.[69] Similarly, prosecutors are immune for their decisions to prosecute or not prosecute.[70] Activities associated with prosecutorial decisions are also

---

68. *See* Imbler, 424 U.S. at 424-27.
69. *See, e.g.*, Imbler, 424 U.S. at 430-31; Hansen v. Black, 885 F.2d 642, 646 (9th Cir. 1989) (city prosecutor entitled to absolute immunity for charging arrestee with violation of city ordinance); Ryan v. Bilby, 764 F.2d 1325, 1328 (9th Cir. 1985) (prosecutor involved in taxpayer's prosecution for failure to file tax returns was absolutely immune for damages under § 1983); Siano v. Justices of Mass., 698 F.2d 52, 57-58 (1st Cir. 1983); (county district attorney entitled to prosecutorial immunity from allegations that he initiated prosecution in bad faith and used tactics during trial that violated the criminal defendant's rights to due process and a fair trial); Lee v. Willins, 617 F.2d 320, 322 (2d Cir. 1980) (prosecuting attorneys entitled to prosecutorial immunity from § 1983 action based upon alleged falsification of evidence and coercion of perjured testimony); Henzel v. Gerstein, 608 F.2d 654, 657 (5th Cir. 1979) (alleged unlawful acts of prosecutors, including filing information without investigation, filing charges without jurisdiction, filing a baseless detainer, offering perjured testimony, suppressing exculpatory evidence, refusing to investigate complaints about prison system and threatening defendant with further criminal prosecutions, were all acts protected by prosecutorial immunity).
70. *See, e.g.*, Pinaud v. County of Suffolk, 52 F.3d 1139, 1149-52 (2d Cir. 1995) (prosecutor who presented case to grand jury and accepted plea agreement was entitled to absolute immunity for those acts, but not for delaying for three weeks the transfer of the prisoner back to federal custody after all state charges had been dismissed); Brummett v. Camble, 946 F.2d 1178, 1181 (5th Cir. 1991) (prosecutor was entitled to absolute immunity even if he had interest in bank which initiated complaint and even if he knew the charges were baseless); Newcomb v. Ingle, 944 F.2d 1534, 1536 (10th Cir. 1991) (decision not to prosecute entitled to absolute immunity); Fields v. Soloff, 920 F.2d 1114, 1119 (2d Cir. 1990) (prosecutors were absolutely immune in presenting

protected,[71] including immunity for plea bargaining activities,[72] and immunity in preparing for trial and in presenting the case in court.[73]

Acts of prosecutors not directly related to the decision to prosecute or the presentation of cases are typically not entitled to absolute immunity.

---

case to grand jury and in deciding whom to prosecute); Celia v. O'Malley, 918 F.2d 1017, 1019-20 (1st Cir. 1990) (prosecutors were absolutely immune in prosecuting case without seeking indictment from grand jury); Webster v. Gibson, 913 F.2d 510, 513-14 (8th Cir. 1990) (prosecutor was absolutely immune in failing to file information, even if ordered to do so by the court).

71. *See, e.g.*, Grant v. Hollenbach, 870 F.2d 1135, 1138-39 (6th Cir. 1989) (prosecutor bringing child abuse charges who allegedly conspired with complainant was entitled to absolute immunity); Baez v. Hennessey, 853 F.2d 73, 74-75 (2d Cir. 1988) (signing by assistant district attorney of erroneous indictment that grand jury did not return was prosecutorial act for which he was absolutely immune); Umphlet v. Connick, 815 F.2d 1061, 1062-63 (5th Cir. 1987) (district attorney was entitled to prosecutorial immunity from liability in § 1983 action for enforcement of state statute); Morrison v. City of Baton Rouge, 761 F.2d 242, 246-48 (5th Cir. 1985) (prosecutor who maliciously presented evidence to a grand jury in a manner calculated to clear a suspect of wrongdoing was absolutely immune); Powers v. Coe, 728 F.2d 97, 103-04 (2d Cir. 1984) (prosecutor who presented matter to the grand jury in breach of an agreement not to prosecute was absolutely immune); Lerwill v. Joslin, 712 F.2d 435, 441 (10th Cir. 1983) (city attorney who only had power to file criminal charges based on a violation of city ordinances was absolutely immune for wrongfully filing state felony charge); Gray v. Bell, 712 F.2d 490, 502-03 (D.C. Cir. 1983) (prosecutor was immune in presenting evidence to grand jury); Dellums v. Powell, 660 F.2d 802, 805-07 (D.C. Cir. 1981) (U.S. Attorney General was absolutely immune in ordering prosecution of Vietnam War demonstrators).

72. *See, e.g.*, Krohn v. United States, 742 F.2d 24, 29-30 (1st Cir. 1984) (federal prosecutor had absolute immunity from allegations that he conspired to convert plaintiff's property by striking deal with defense counsel to learn the location of plaintiff's safe-deposit box); McGruder v. Necaise, 733 F.2d 1146, 1148 (5th Cir. 1984) (prosecutor who offered to drop criminal charges against arrestee if he would dismiss a civil suit against the county jail was absolutely immune); Taylor v. Kavanagh, 640 F.2d 450, 453-54 (2d Cir. 1981) (prosecutor was absolutely immune in plea bargaining role).

73. *See, e.g.*, *Burns,* 500 U.S. at 490-91 (prosecutor was absolutely immune in presenting application for search warrant, but not in advising police on investigation); Geter v. Fortenberry, 849 F.2d 1550, 1554 (5th Cir. 1988) (act of setting a trial date was a prosecutorial act requiring absolute immunity).

For example, a prosecutor acting in other ways, such as conducting investigations, making representations to the court, or issuing news releases, may be entitled to a qualified immunity, but not absolute immunity.

Prosecutors who are involved in investigative functions are not usually entitled to absolute immunity.[74] Similarly, prosecutors are not entitled to absolute immunity for exercising law enforcement functions,[75] for giving legal advice,[76] or in making public statements.[77]

---

74. *See, e.g.*, Buckley v. Fitzsimmons, 113 S. Ct. 2606, 2616-17 (1993) (prosecutor's alleged misconduct, when endeavoring to determine whether a boot print at a crime scene had been left by a suspect was an investigatory, administrative function, rather than a prosecutorial function, for which the prosecutor was entitled to only qualified immunity in suspect's subsequent § 1983 suit); Houston v. Partee, 978 F.2d 362, 365-66 (7th Cir. 1992) (prosecutors who discovered exculpatory evidence after person was convicted and did not disclose it to the defense had no absolute immunity since they were acting in an investigative capacity); McSurely v. McClellan, 697 F.2d 309, 319-20 (D.C. Cir. 1982) (alleged conduct of prosecutor in participating in a public meeting for the purpose, known to him to be unconstitutional, of preventing plaintiffs from disseminating ideas, preparing flagrantly unconstitutional arrest and search warrants, participating in raid on plaintiff's home which went far beyond warrant, and conspiring with representatives of Senate subcommittee to transfer to them documents that had been illegally seized and were irrelevant to the subcommittee's business, and which were required by court order to be returned to plaintiffs or retained in safekeeping, did not implicate state prosecutor's protected advocate function and, thus, was not protected by absolute immunity from suit); Marrero v. City of Hialeah, 625 F.2d 499, 505-06 (5th Cir. 1980) (prosecutor participating in illegal search and seizure was not entitled to absolute immunity); Hampton v. Hanrahan, 600 F.2d 600, 633-34 (7th Cir. 1979) (prosecutors who arranged for police raid on Black Panther headquarters were not entitled to absolute immunity); Jacobson v. Rose, 592 F.2d 515, 524 (9th Cir. 1978) (where district attorney ordered and joined with sheriff's office in implementing illegal wiretap, he was not entitled to absolute immunity).
75. *See, e.g.*, Latimore v. Widseth, 986 F.2d 292, 294-95 (8th Cir. 1993) (prosecutor was not absolutely immune in disclosing to media that prisoner would be a witness in a case when that prisoner was subsequently attacked by other inmates); Buckley v. Fitzsimmons, 919 F.2d 1230, 1244 (7th Cir. 1990) (no absolute immunity for coercive interrogation of defendants by prosecutor); Day v. Morganthau, 909 F.2d 75, 77-78 (2d Cir. 1990) (prosecutor who ordered person arrested for trespassing was not entitled to ab-

A prosecutor's out-of-court treatment of seized evidence or property is not protected by absolute immunity.[78] Additionally, when prosecutors order the destruction of exonerating material, they are not entitled to absolute immunity.[79]

Others Who Perform Prosecutorial-like Functions

Other people performing prosecutorial-like functions are entitled to immunity.[80] Social workers initiating or "prosecuting" child neglect or child abuse proceedings have generally been held to have absolute immunity.[81]

---

solute immunity); Price v. Moody, 677 F.2d 676, 678 (8th Cir. 1982) (no immunity if prosecutor orders mistreatment of prisoner).

76. *See, e.g.*, *Burns*, 500 U.S. at 491-92 (prosecutor giving legal advice to policeman on how to conduct investigation was not entitled to absolute immunity); Benavidez v. Gunnell, 722 F.2d 615, 617 (10th Cir. 1983) (no absolute immunity when prosecutor gave legal advice to police).
77. *See, e.g.*, *Buckley*, 113 S.Ct. at 2617-18 (press statements by prosecutors not subject to absolute immunity); Stepanian v. Addis, 699 F.2d 1046, 1048 (11th Cir. 1983) (federal prosecutor's statements made at a press conference announcing criminal indictment were not subject to absolute immunity).
78. *See* Coleman v. Turpen, 697 F.2d 1341, 1346 (10th Cir. 1982) (participation in illegal sale of seized property was not protected by absolute immunity).
79. *See* Henderson v. Fisher, 631 F.2d 1115, 1120 (3d Cir. 1980) (prosecutor who allegedly failed to preserve exculpatory evidence was not entitled to absolute immunity).
80. *See, e.g.*, Wang v. New Hampshire Bd. of Registration in Medicine, 55 F.3d 698, 701-02 (1st Cir. 1995) (administrative board members initiating professional misconduct charges against a doctor were entitled to absolute prosecutorial immunity).
81. *See, e.g.*, Millspaugh v. County Dept. of Public Welfare, 937 F.2d 1172, 1175-76 (7th Cir. 1991) (social service worker initiating child abuse proceeding was absolutely immune); Vosburg v. Department of Social Services, 884 F.2d 133, 135-38 (4th Cir. 1989) (in filing a petition for removal of a child from her home, as opposed to conduct in investigating the possibility that removal petition should be filed, Virginia state social workers were acting in a prosecutorial rather than an investigative or "policing" capacity, and, thus, were absolutely immune from any liability arising from the decision to file a removal petition); Salyer v. Patrick, 874 F.2d 374, 378 (6th Cir. 1989) (social worker investigating child abuse case was absolutely immune); Meyers v. Contra Costa County Dept. of Social Serv., 812 F.2d 1154, 1157-58 (9th Cir. 1987)

The cases, however, are not entirely consistent.[82] Activities that have attributes of prosecutorial-like conduct may also be protected.[83]

(absolute immunity provided for social welfare workers who were investigating child abuse); Coverdell v. Department of Social and Health Services, 834 F.2d 758, 762-63 (9th Cir. 1987) (social workers prosecuting child abuse cases are absolutely immune); Kurzawa v. Mueller, 732 F.2d 1456, 1458 (6th Cir. 1984) (social service department employee enjoys absolute immunity in removing child from home and placing it in foster home).

82. *See, e.g.*, Snell v. Tunnell, 920 F.2d 673, 690-92 (10th Cir. 1990) (social workers who sought pre-petition conditional protective custody order as part of their investigation into neglect at private home being operated as emergency shelter were entitled to only qualified immunity from § 1983 civil rights liability); Hodorowski v. Ray, 844 F.2d 1210, 1213-15 (5th Cir. 1988) (conduct of child protective service workers in temporarily removing children from parents' home without first obtaining court order was more akin to function of police than prosecutor, so that workers were not protected by absolute prosecutorial immunity from civil rights liability arising from removal, but rather were entitled only to qualified immunity); Austin v. Borel, 830 F.2d 1356, 1360-63 (5th Cir. 1988) (child protection workers who allegedly filed false charges against parents were not entitled to absolute immunity).

83. *See, e.g.*, Spear v. Town of West Hartford, 954 F.2d 63, 66 (2d Cir. 1992) (city manager's decision to initiate a lawsuit in pursuit of city's governmental interests was similar to the filing of an administrative complaint and, thus, was entitled to absolute immunity); Hamill v. Wright, 870 F.2d 1032, 1037 (5th Cir. 1989) (director of county's domestic relations office was entitled to full prosecutorial immunity from civil rights claim based upon his decision to bring contempt proceedings against parent for failure to pay child support); Werle v. Rhode Island Bar Association, 755 F.2d 195, 198-99 (1st Cir. 1985) (members of state bar unauthorized practice of law committee were acting as public prosecutors and were entitled to absolute immunity); Walden v. Wishengrad, 745 F.2d 149, 152-53 (2d Cir. 1984) (attorney employed by county social services department who prosecuted child protective orders in family court was acting as a prosecutor and was absolutely immune); Demery v. Kupperman, 735 F.2d 1139, 1142-45 (9th Cir. 1984) (deputy attorney general prosecuting an administrative complaint against a doctor to revoke his medical license was absolutely immune in allegedly inducing witnesses to testify falsely); Malachowski v. City of Keene, 787 F.2d 704, 712 (1st Cir. 1981) (policeman who initiated juvenile delinquency proceeding in his capacity as juvenile officer was acting like a prosecutor and was entitled to absolute immunity).

Witnesses

Witnesses testifying at trial are entitled to absolute immunity.[84] As described below, however, the circuits are split as to whether witness immunity should be extended to those testifying at proceedings other than trial, such as probable cause and grand jury hearings.

The Supreme Court in *Briscoe* articulated two bases for justifying absolute immunity for witnesses testifying at trial: (1) the common law had historically recognized immunity for witnesses, and (2) public policy dictated that witnesses should not fear testifying truthfully for fear of a subsequent lawsuit based upon their testimony.[85]

Some circuits hold that witnesses are entitled to immunity for their testimony at proceedings other than trial.[86]

Some circuits, however, have refused to extend absolute witness immunity to proceedings other than testifying at trial.[87] One apparent rationale between the divergent cases denying absolute immunity and those granting absolute immunity is the distinction between being a fact witness and being a complaining witness, i.e., fact witnesses could lie and defame at common law with immunity in order to protect the integrity of the judi-

---

84. *See* Briscoe v. LaHue, 460 U.S. 325, 334 (1983).
85. *Id.* at 333-34.
86. *See* Williams v. Hepting, 844 F.2d 138, 141-43 (3d Cir. 1988) (witness entitled to absolute immunity for alleged perjured testimony given in preliminary criminal hearing); Alioto v. City of Shively, 835 F.2d 1173, 1174 (6th Cir. 1987) (police officers were absolutely immune from civil rights liability for their alleged conspiracy to give false and incomplete testimony in grand jury proceedings); Holt v. Castaneda, 832 F.2d 123, 127 (9th Cir. 1987) (extending absolute witness immunity to adversarial pretrial proceedings). Kincaid v. Eberle, 712 F.2d 1023, 1024 (7th Cir. 1985) (granting absolute immunity to grand jury witnesses).
87. *See, e.g.*, White v. Frank, 855 F.2d 956, 961 (2d Cir. 1988) (police officers who act as complaining witnesses do not have absolute immunity); Anthony v. Baker, 767 F.2d 657, 660 (10th Cir. 1985) (refusing to extend absolute witness immunity to grand jury witnesses); San Filippo v. United States Trust Co., 737 F.2d 246, 255 (2d Cir. 1984) (no absolute immunity for alleged conspiracy between prosecutor and witnesses to secure false testimony before grand jury); Wheeler v. Cosden Oil & Chemical Co., 734 F.2d 254, 261 (5th Cir. 1984) (denying absolute immunity to witness who testified at probable cause hearing).

cial process, but complaining witnesses were never afforded such immunity for malicious prosecution. While this may be a distinction without a difference with respect to law enforcement officials, it is a distinction that appears to have been drawn by some circuits.

Qualified Immunity

The U.S. Supreme Court has held that government officials performing discretionary functions are entitled to qualified immunity from suit and damages where "their conduct does not violate clearly established statutory or constitutional rights of which a reasonable person would have known."[88] The critical issue is not whether a defendant actually infringed upon a plaintiff's rights: "Even defendants who violate constitutional rights enjoy a qualified immunity that protects them from liability for damages unless it is further demonstrated that their conduct was unreasonable under the applicable standard."[89]

To aid in that determination, the Court has reaffirmed that "whether an official protected by qualified immunity may be held personally liable for an allegedly unlawful action turns on the 'objective legal reasonableness' of the action . . . assessed in light of the legal rules that were 'clearly established' at the time it was taken."[90] For the relevant legal standards to be "clearly established," the "contours" of the right alleged to have been violated "must be sufficiently clear that a reasonable official would understand that what he is doing violates that right."[91]

The Evolution of Qualified Immunity

The doctrine of qualified immunity, like the absolute immunities discussed earlier in this chapter, is a judicially created doctrine that recognizes the common law immunity of public officials for their "good faith" actions. The public policy behind such qualified immunity includes attracting competent individuals to public sector jobs, encouraging individuals to

---

88. Harlow v. Fitzgerald, 457 U.S. 800, 818 (1982); Mitchell v. Forsyth, 472 U.S. 511, 526 (1985).
89. Davis v. Scherer, 468 U.S. 183, 190 (1984).
90. Anderson v. Creighton, 483 U.S. 635, 639 (1987) (citations omitted).
91. *Id.* at 640.

serve in elected offices, allowing public officials to exercise unfettered discretion in serving the public good, and avoiding exposing public officials to unnecessary litigation that would distract them from their civic responsibilities. This concept of "good faith" qualified immunity has evolved from a two-pronged, objective and subjective test, to a one-pronged, objective test.

Wood v. Strickland *and the Subjective Test*

In *Wood v. Strickland*,[92] the U.S. Supreme Court defined qualified immunity in § 1983 actions as including both an objective and subjective element. The Court, in a case involving the liability of school board members for disciplinary actions against students, articulated the standard as follows:

> [A] school board member is not immune from liability for damages under § 1983 if he knew or reasonably should have known that the action he took within his sphere of official responsibility would violate the constitutional rights of the student affected, or if he took the action with the malicious intention to cause a deprivation of constitutional rights or other injury to the student.[93]

Under the two-pronged *Wood* test, public officials could be held liable under § 1983 for violations of federal law when their conduct was either objectively unreasonable or in subjective bad faith.

The use of a subjective "good faith" standard in the application of qualified immunity, however, proved problematic because it triggered an examination of the public official's subjective state of mind at the time of the alleged unconstitutional act. Such a factual determination obviously frustrated the intent of qualified immunity to quickly resolve insubstantial lawsuits by way of a motion to dismiss or a motion for summary judgment.

Harlow v. Fitzgerald *and the Objective Test*

In *Harlow v. Fitzgerald*,[94] the Supreme Court recognized this problem and significantly redefined the standard for qualified immunity by abandoning the subjective prong of the qualified immunity test and holding that

---

92. 420 U.S. 308 (1975).
93. *Id.* at 322.
94. 457 U.S. 800 (1982).

§ 1983 defendants would only be liable for damages when their conduct violated clearly established federal law.[95] The Court discussed the parameters of its newly defined objective qualified immunity test as follows:

> [W]e conclude today that bare allegations of malice should not suffice to subject government officials either to the costs of trial or to the burdens of broad-reaching discovery. *We therefore hold that government officials performing discretionary functions generally are shielded from liability for civil damages insofar as their conduct does not violate clearly established statutory or constitutional rights of which a reasonable person would have known.*
>
> Reliance on the objective reasonableness of an official's conduct, as measured by reference to clearly established law, should avoid excessive disruption of government and permit the resolution of many insubstantial claims on summary judgment: *On summary judgment, the judge appropriately may determine, not only the currently applicable law, but whether that law was clearly established at the time an action occurred. If the law at that time was not clearly established, an official could not reasonably be expected to anticipate subsequent legal developments, nor could he fairly be said to 'know' that the law forbade conduct not previously identified as unlawful.* Until this threshold immunity question is resolved, discovery should not be allowed. If the law was clearly established, the immunity defense ordinarily should fail, since a reasonably competent public official should know the law governing his conduct. Nevertheless, if the official pleading the defense claims extraordinary circumstances and can prove that he neither knew nor should have known of the relevant legal standard, the defense should be sustained. But again, the defense would turn primarily on objective factors.
>
> By defining the limits of qualified immunity essentially in objective terms, we provide no license to lawless conduct. The public interest in deterrence of unlawful conduct and in compensation of victims remains protected by a test that focuses on the objective legal reasonableness of an official's acts. Where an official could be expected to know that certain conduct would violate

---

95. *Id.* at 818-19.

> statutory or constitutional rights, he should be made to hesitate; and a person who suffers injury caused by such conduct may have a cause of action. But where an official's duties legitimately require action in which clearly established rights are not implicated, the public interest may be better served by action taken 'with independence and without fear of consequences.'[96]

Breaking Down the Harlow *Standard*

The U.S. Supreme Court has stated that "government officials performing *discretionary functions* generally are shielded from liability for civil damages insofar as their conduct does not violate clearly established statutory or constitutional rights of which a reasonable person would have known."[97] The discretionary versus ministerial function dichotomy in decisionmaking, however, has rarely been used as a disqualifier for undertaking a qualified immunity analysis.

For example, in *Horta v. Sullivan*,[98] the court downplayed the importance of discretionary versus ministerial functions in a qualified immunity analysis.

> [In] spite of the reference to discretionary functions [in *Harlow*], it has never since been clear exactly what role, if any, this concept is supposed to play in applying qualified immunity. Judge Cummings, writing for the Seventh Circuit, warned that 'it would be unwise to engage in a case by case determination of Section 1983 immunity based upon the ministerial versus the discretionary nature of the particular official act challenged.'[99]

Other circuits also have recognized the danger in rejecting qualified immunity claims merely on the basis of a determination that the functions involved are ministerial, rather than discretionary.

> The distinction between ministerial and discretionary duties of public officials has a long history. However, the plaintiffs have cited, and we can find, no recent case other than that before us in which

---

96. *Id.* (emphasis added, citations and footnotes omitted).
97. *Id.* at 818 (emphasis added).
98. 4 F.3d 2 (1st Cir. 1993).
99. *Id.* at 11 (quoting Coleman v. Frantz, 754 F.2d 719, 727 (7th Cir. 1985)).

> a court has rejected qualified immunity simply because the official in question was performing a ministerial duty.[100]

In *Davis v. Scherer*,[101] the Supreme Court dramatically circumscribed the viability of the ministerial duty exception to qualified immunity. In *Davis*, the plaintiff, a discharged employee of the Florida Highway Patrol, sued certain public officials of the Florida Department of Highway Safety and Motor Vehicles under § 1983 alleging that his due process rights had been violated.[102] The trial and appellate courts had denied the public officials qualified immunity because they had not followed certain administrative regulations in discharging the plaintiff and, therefore, were held not to have acted in a discretionary capacity.[103] In rejecting this contention, the Supreme Court stated as follows:

> Appellee's contention mistakes the scope of the 'ministerial duty' exception to qualified immunity in two respects. First, as we have discussed, breach of a legal duty created by the personnel regulation would forfeit official immunity only if that breach itself gave rise to the appellee's cause of action for damages. This principle equally applies whether the regulation created discretionary or ministerial duties. Even if the personnel regulation did create a ministerial duty, appellee makes no claim that he is entitled to damages simply because the regulation was violated. . . .
>
> [T]he District Court's findings that appellants ignored a clear legal command does not bear on the 'ministerial' nature of appellants' duties. *A law that fails to specify the precise action that the official must take in each instance creates only discretionary au-*

100. McIntosh v. Weinberger, 810 F.2d 1411, 1432 (8th Cir. 1987), partially vacated and remanded on other grounds sub. nom. Turner v. McIntosh, 487 U.S. 1212 (1988) (citation omitted). *See also* Ricci v. Key Bancshares of Maine, Inc., 768 F.2d 456, 464 (1st Cir. 1985) ("[B]reaking down discretionary acts . . . into discretionary and ministerial components would seem to vitiate much of the protection of discretionary action which absolute immunity was designed to provide."); *Horta,* 4 F.3d at 15 ("[I]t would be the rare case indeed where an officer is denied qualified immunity because the officer is found to have engaged in 'ministerial' rather than 'discretionary' conduct.").
101. 468 U.S. 183 (1984).
102. *Id.* at 185-87.
103. *Id.* at 188-89.

> *thority; and that authority remains discretionary however egregiously it is abused.*[104]

The Court also held that "[o]fficials sued for constitutional violations do not lose their qualified immunity merely because their conduct violates some statutory or administrative provision."[105] The Court reasoned that the officials could lose their immunity only if the breach of the state regulation, rather than a constitutional duty, gave rise to the plaintiff's damages claim.[106]

The narrow application of the ministerial duty exception to qualified immunity also has been recognized by the Fifth Circuit in *Gagne v. City of Galveston*.[107]

> Although the Supreme Court's qualified immunity opinions have given special attention to the need to avoid inhibiting the ardor of public officials whose positions entail the exercise of discretionary authority, the Court has never implied that the immunity defense is lost when an official is engaged in routine tasks. Indeed, any such suggestion was firmly rejected in footnote 14 of *Davis v. Scherer*, where the Court emphasized that the so-called 'ministerial duty' exception to qualified immunity is extremely narrow in scope. . . . Thus, if an official is required to exercise his judgment, even if rarely or to a small degree, the Court would apparently not find an official's duty to be ministerial in nature.[108]

Conduct That Does Not Violate Clearly Established Statutory or Constitutional Rights of Which a Reasonable Person Would Have Known

The doctrine of qualified immunity shields an official performing discretionary functions from liability for damages under § 1983 so long as the

---

104. *Id.* at 196 n.14 (emphasis added).
105. *Id.* at 194.
106. *Davis*, 468 U.S. at 194 n.12 ("For the reasons that we discuss, officials sued for violations of rights conferred by a statute or regulation, like officials sued for violation of constitutional rights, do not forfeit their immunity by violating some other statute or regulation. Rather, these officials become liable for damages only to the extent that there is a clear violation of the statutory rights that give rise to the cause of action for damages.").
107. 805 F.2d 558, 559-60 (5th Cir. 1986), *cert. denied*, 483 U.S. 1021 (1987).
108. *Id.* at 559-60.

official's conduct does not violate clearly established constitutional or statutory rights of which a reasonable person would have been aware. Whether an official can be held personally liable for taking an allegedly unlawful action turns on the "objective legal reasonableness" of the action, assessed in light of the legal rules that were "clearly established" at the time the action was taken.[109] To be clearly established, the "contours" of the right allegedly violated must be sufficiently clear that a reasonable official would understand what he or she is doing violates that right.[110]

The appropriate inquiry is whether a reasonable official could have thought that he or she acted in accordance with the Constitution in taking the action of which is complained.[111] As noted by the U.S. Supreme Court in *Hunter*, "the court should ask whether the [government official] acted reasonably under settled law in the circumstances, not whether another reasonable, or more reasonable, interpretation of the events can be constructed . . . years after the fact."[112]

This deferential standard is also applicable in a summary judgment context: "If, upon viewing the evidence in the light most favorable to the nonmovant, reasonable public officials could differ on the lawfulness of the defendant's actions, the defendant is entitled to qualified immunity."[113] The qualified immunity standard "gives ample room for mistaken judgments."[114]

To properly apply the test for qualified immunity, a court must determine whether the law, as applied to a specific factual situation, was clearly established in such a way that the officials involved should have known that their decision or actions violated constitutional rights or federal law. Simple negligence on the part of a public official is not enough.[115]

---

109. *See Harlow*, 457 U.S. at 818-19.
110. *See Anderson*, 483 U.S. at 640.
111. *See* McCleary v. Navarro, 112 S.Ct. 2324 (1992); Hunter v. Bryant, 502 U.S. 224, 228 (1991).
112. *Hunter,* 502 U.S. at 228.
113. Harper v. Harris County, 21 F.3d 597, 600 (5th Cir. 1994).
114. Malley v. Briggs, 475 U.S. 335, 343 (1986). *See also Hunter,* 502 U.S. at 229 ("[A]ccommodation for reasonable error exists because 'officials should not err always on the side of caution' because they fear being sued.") (citing Davis v. Scherer, 468 U.S. 183, 196 (1984)).
115. *See* Daniel v. Williams, 474 U.S. 327, 238 (1986); Davidson v. Cannon, 474 U.S. 344, 346-47 (1986).

> That qualified immunity protects government actors is the usual rule; only in exceptional cases will government actors have no shield against claims made against them in their individual capacities. Unless a government agent's act is so obviously wrong, in the light of pre-existing law, that only a plainly incompetent officer or one who was knowingly violating the law would have done such a thing, the government actor has immunity from suit.[116]

What Is a Clearly Established Right and How Is It Determined?

In *Anderson v. Creighton*,[117] the Supreme Court required increased fact specificity from plaintiffs alleging that a public official had violated clearly established law. The Court clarified the qualified immunity standard by rejecting the notion that public officials were expected to be able to give concrete application to lofty, abstract principles of constitutional law:

> The operation of [the *Harlow*] standard . . . depends substantially upon the level of generality at which the relevant 'legal rule' is to be identified. For example, the right to due process of law is quite clearly established by the Due Process Clause, and thus there is a sense in which any action that violates that cause (no matter how unclear it may be that the particular action is a violation) violates a clearly established right. Much the same could be said of any other constitutional or statutory violation. But if the test of 'clearly established law' were to be applied at this level of generality, it would bear no relationship to the 'objective legal reasonableness' that is the touchstone of *Harlow*. Plaintiffs would be able to convert the rule of qualified immunity that our cases plainly establish into a rule of virtually unqualified liability simply by alleging violation of extremely abstract rights. *Harlow* would be transformed from a guarantee of immunity into a rule of pleading.[118]

The Court has held that qualified immunity must be analyzed at an "objective, albeit fact-specific" level of abstraction:

---

116. Lassiter v. Alabama A&M Bd. of Trustees, 28 F.3d 1146, 1149 (11th Cir. 1994).
117. 483 U.S. 635 (1987).
118. *Id.* at 639.

> [O]ur cases establish that the right the official is alleged to have violated must have been 'clearly established' in a more particularized, and hence more relevant, sense: The contours of the right must be sufficiently clear that a reasonable official would understand that what he is doing violates that right.[119]

The objective reasonableness of the action in question is to be assessed in light of the constitutional norms that were "clearly established" at the time the action was taken.[120]

How Is the Law Clearly Established?

It is unquestioned that U.S. Supreme Court precedent directly on point establishes clearly settled law of which a reasonable public official either knows or should know. What constitutes "clearly established law" outside of U.S. Supreme Court precedent, however, is simply not clearly established. The question of which, and how many, courts must speak on an issue has not been addressed by the Supreme Court. For example, the Sixth Circuit has interpreted "clearly established law," other than black letter statutory provisions, to mean law that has been established by decisions of (1) the U.S. Supreme Court, (2) the U.S. Court of Appeals in which the incident occurred, (3) other U.S. courts of appeals, or (4) the highest state court in the state where the action arose.[121]

Some cases suggest that Supreme Court precedent or case law from the defendant's own jurisdiction is necessary to clearly establish a constitutional right, while others rely on case law from other jurisdictions.[122]

---

119. *Id.* at 640.
120. *Id.* at 639-40.
121. *See* Robinson v. Bibb, 840 F.2d 349, 351 (6th Cir. 1988).
122. *Compare* Azeez v. Fairman, 795 F.2d 1296, 1301-02 (7th Cir. 1986) (noting that "the State of Illinois is not bound to comply with every constitutional ruling by every district judge in the United States" and referring to "[t]he test in this circuit for a prison regulation challenged on religious grounds") (emphasis added) with LeClair v. Hart, 800 F.2d 692, 695 (7th Cir. 1986) (denying immunity even though "the Supreme Court has never passed upon the precise type of recording which is involved in this case" because "the lower courts have encountered no difficulty in . . . cases involving analogous circumstances" and Ward v. County of San Diego, 791 F.2d 1329, 1332 (9th Cir. 1986) (in the absence of binding precedent, courts should look to all available cases, including those from other circuits).

Some courts of appeals have granted immunity despite case law favoring the plaintiff simply because the number of such cases was insufficient.[123]

If the relevant precedents conflict either within the defendant's own jurisdiction or among various jurisdictions, almost all courts conclude that the right asserted by the plaintiff is not clearly established.[124]

Lower courts conflict as to whether dictum and opinions issued over dissents are relevant in determining whether a right is clearly established.[125]

When Is the Law Clearly Established?

In determining whether the law is "clearly established," courts must look to specific, concrete examples that shed an illuminating light on the factual scenario under review.

> For the law to be clearly established to the point that qualified immunity does not apply, the law must have earlier been developed in such a concrete and factually defined context to make it obvious to all reasonable government actors, in the defendant's place, that 'what he is doing' violates federal law. Qualified immunity is a doctrine that focuses on the actual, on the specific, on the details of concrete cases.[126]

---

123. *See, e.g.*, Walnut Properties, Inc. v. City of Whittier, 861 F.2d 1102, 1113 (9th Cir. 1988), *cert. denied*, 490 U.S. 1006 (1989) (referring to three federal court of appeals decisions and three federal district court decisions as only a "few cases"); Coleman v. Frantz, 754 F.2d 719, 730 n.15 (7th Cir. 1985) (requiring "caselaw which clearly and consistently recognized the constitutional right").
124. *See, e.g., Walnut Properties,* 861 F.2d at 1113 (granting immunity despite admitting that six federal decisions supported plaintiff, with none to the contrary); Benson v. Allphin, 786 F.2d 268, 275 n.16 (7th Cir.), *cert. denied*, 479 U.S. 848 (1986) (suggesting that rights can never be clearly established if the circuits conflict until the Supreme Court resolves the issue).
125. *Compare* Hall v. Medical College of Ohio at Toledo, 742 F.2d 299, 309 (6th Cir. 1984), *cert. denied*, 469 U.S. 1113 (1985) (dismissing earlier cases as dictum, and noting that relevant Supreme Court opinion was issued by divided Court) with LeClair v. Hart, 800 F.2d 692, 694 n.3 (7th Cir. 1986) (holding that split decisions are equally authoritative as unanimous ones).
126. *Lassiter,* 28 F.3d at 1149-50 (citation omitted).

Established case law must provide a bright line that the officials have clearly transgressed.[127]

In fact, preexisting law must dictate that the official's decision or actions violated well-established constitutional rights.

> For qualified immunity to be surrendered, pre-existing law must dictate, that is, truly compel (not just suggest or allow or raise a question about), the conclusion for every like-situated, reasonable government agent that what defendant is doing violates federal law *in the circumstances*.[128]

Who Is the Reasonable Person to Whom **Harlow** *Refers, and to What Extent Does Actual Knowledge of a Violation of Rights Play in an Objective Analysis?*

While *Harlow* protects discretionary conduct that does not violate clearly established statutory or constitutional rights of which "a reasonable person would have known,"[129] neither *Harlow* nor any subsequent Supreme Court precedent has discussed who is the reasonable person to whom *Harlow* refers. Is the reasonable person a reasonable public official in the abstract, or a reasonable person in the defendant's position?

---

127. *See, e.g.*, Hodge v. Jones, 31 F.3d 157, 167 (4th Cir. 1994) (Under the doctrine of qualified immunity, "officials are not liable for bad guesses in gray areas; they are liable for transgressing bright lines."); Post v. City of Fort Lauderdale, 7 F.3d 1552, 1557 (11th Cir. 1993) ("If case law, in factual terms, has not staked out a bright line, qualified immunity almost always protects the defendant."); Barts v. Joyner, 865 F.2d 1187, 1190, 1194 (11th Cir. 1989) ("The *Harlow* decision sets up a bright-line test that is a powerful constraint on causes of action under § 1983," and "the line is not to be found in abstractions—to act reasonably, to act with probable cause, and so forth—but in studying how these abstractions have been applied in concrete circumstances.").
128. *See Lassiter,* 28 F.3d at 1150 (emphasis in original). *See also* Alexander v. University of North Florida, 39 F.3d 290, 291 (11th Cir. 1994), *cert. denied*, U.S. 115 S.Ct. 1699 (1995) (to avoid qualified immunity, a plaintiff must point to preexisting law that "dictates" and "compels" the conclusion that the defendants violated the constitution").
129. *Harlow,* 457 U.S. at 818.

Some lower courts refer to what is reasonable for a defendant in that defendant's position.[130] These cases seem to imply that the court should consider the defendant's position in determining whether that defendant acted reasonably. The author is aware of no case, however, that directly discusses this issue.

Another issue not answered in *Harlow* or its progeny is whether there is a subjective prong involved when a defendant has actual knowledge of a violation of rights, even if the rights are not clearly established. In determining whether a government official acted reasonably, case law strongly supports ignoring the subjective intent of the official and looking only to a test of objective legal reasonableness.[131]

It can certainly be argued that while a defendant's subjective state of mind is not relevant to determine whether there is a violation of clearly

---

130. *See, e.g.*, Auriemma v. Wise, 910 F.2d 1449, 1455 (7th Cir. 1990) ("reasonable police chief of a large metropolitan police force"); Abel v. Miller, 824 F.2d 1522, 1531 (7th Cir. 1987) ("a reasonably competent prison official"); Schlegel v. Bebout, 841 F.2d 937, 945 (9th Cir. 1988) ("a reasonable PUC official").

131. *See Anderson*, 483 U.S. at 641 (despite that courts may inquire into "information possessed" by the defendant, the defendant's "subjective beliefs . . . are irrelevant"); Mitchell v. Forsyth, 472 U.S. 511, 517 (1985) (in *Harlow*, "this Court purged qualified immunity doctrine of its subjective components"); *Lassiter*, 28 F.3d at 1150 ("The subjective intent of government actor defendants plays no part in qualified immunity analyses."); *Post*, 7 F.3d 1552 at n.6 ("Qualified immunity invokes an objective standard; that is, if a reasonable person in the defendant's place could have acted the same way, the defendant's subjective intent is irrelevant."); American Civil Liberties Union of Maryland, Inc. v. Wicomico County, Maryland, 999 F.2d 780, 784 (4th Cir. 1993) ("The existence of qualified immunity 'generally turns on the objective legal reasonableness of the actions; without regard to the knowledge or subjective intent of the particular official.") (citations omitted); Cartier v. Lussier, 955 F.2d 841, 843 (2d Cir. 1992) ("A subjective inquiry into an official's personal belief is rejected in favor of an objective analysis of what a reasonable officer in defendant's position would believe."); Courson v. McMillian, 939 F.2d 1479, 1487 (11th Cir. 1991) ("The Supreme Court has developed an objective-reasonableness test for evaluating actions of a government official claiming qualified immunity. . . . The use of this test precludes the determination by district courts of subjective good faith in government officials' conduct in section 1983 actions.").

established law, the defendant's actual subjective knowledge may be important for determining whether that defendant is liable for violating clearly established law if that public official knew that he or she was violating clearly established law, even where an objective, reasonable defendant would not have known that he or she was violating clearly established law. The author is aware of no case that directly addresses this issue and those that mention it do so only in passing.[132]

The Extraordinary Circumstances Exception

In *Harlow*, the Supreme Court, without discussion, indicated that there could be "extraordinary circumstances" where defendants who violated clearly established law proved that they should not have known of the relevant legal standard.

> If the law was clearly established, the immunity defense ordinarily should fail, since a reasonably competent public official should know the law governing its conduct. Nevertheless, if the official pleading the defense claims *extraordinary circumstances* and can prove that he neither knew nor should have known the relevant legal standard, the defense should be sustained. But again, the defense would turn primarily on objective factors.[133]

---

132. *Compare* Perry v. Larson, 794 F.2d 279, 284 n.1 (7th Cir. 1986) ("it would be illogical to extend good faith immunity to a government official who has intentionally violated an individual's constitutional rights") and Fujiwara v. Clark, 703 F.2d 357, 359 n.3 (9th Cir. 1983) (noting that the Harlow standard "has elements of subjectivity" because qualified immunity is available only if the defendant "neither knew nor should have known of the relevant legal standard") with Kompare v. Stein, 801 F.2d 883, 887 (7th Cir. 1986) ("[i]t is irrelevant whether a particular defendant knew at the time she acted . . . that her actions violated someone's constitutional rights") and Bothke v. Flour Engineers & Constructors, Inc., 834 F.2d 804, 811 (9th Cir. 1987) (the defendant's "'subjective beliefs' about the lawfulness of her conduct are 'irrelevant'").
133. *Harlow*, 457 U.S. at 819 (emphasis added).

The most common assertion of the extraordinary circumstances exception is when public officials rely on the advice of legal counsel as authority for their actions.[134]

Other cases strongly suggest that mere reliance on an attorney's advice cannot be used as a shield from liability from actions that violate the constitution and clearly established law.[135]

---

134. *See* Pritchett v. Alford, 973 F.2d 307, 316 (4th Cir. 1992) ("mistaken official advice by legal counsel" given as an example of extraordinary circumstances that might insulate defendant from liability even if the defendant violated clearly established law.); V-I Oil Co. v. State of Wyoming, Dept. of Environmental Quality, 902 F.2d 1482, 1489-90 (10th Cir. 1990) (even though the defendant violated clearly settled Fourth Amendment law when he searched the plaintiff's business premises, the defendant was entitled to qualified immunity given the extraordinary circumstances presented by high-ranking government attorneys advising the defendant that the search was lawful).
135. *See* Melton v. City of Oklahoma City, 879 F.2d 706, 730-31 (10th Cir. 1989) (court rejected police chief's defense of good faith reliance on advice of city attorney where law was clearly established, stating that "[a]dopting the proffered position would immunize officials from liability via the simple expedient of consulting counsel"); Watertown Equip. Co. v. Norwest Bank Watertown, 830 F.2d 1487, 1495 (8th Cir. 1987) (reliance on their attorney's advice did not make the bank and its vice-president qualifiedly immune un der § 1983 from liability to lender where the law was clearly established that the actions complained of were unlawful); Kompare v. Stein, 801 F.2d 883, 887 (7th Cir. 1986) ("It is irrelevant whether a particular defendant knew at the time she acted (or failed to act) that her actions violated someone's constitutional rights. The question is whether the state of the law was such that a reasonable person would have known her actions were unconstitutional.") (citation omitted); Wentz v. Klecker, 721 F.2d 244, 248 (8th Cir. 1983) (rejecting advice of counsel as defense to § 1983 liability since "state employees may not rely on their ignorance of even the most esoteric aspects of the law to deny individuals their due process rights"); Bier v. Fleming, 717 F.2d 308, 312 (6th Cir. 1983) (reversed trial court's rejection of qualified immunity defense, premised upon defendant's failure to follow the advice of counsel, because the law in question was not clearly established).

Chapter Twelve

Admissibility of Investigatory Reports in § 1983 Civil Rights Actions—A User's Manual*

Martin A. Schwartz

In many parts of the nation, strained relations between the police and private citizens have placed law enforcement operations under intense public scrutiny. From coast to coast, commissions and internal affairs units are being employed to investigate allegations of law enforcement misconduct and corruption. These investigations typically culminate in the issuance of an investigatory report. In some instances these reports have been highly critical of law enforcement agencies and, not surprisingly, well-publicized by the media.

In New York, the Mollen Commission found the New York City Police Department rampant with corruption throughout its ranks, a complete collapse of command responsibility, and a powerful "code of silence."[1] Five years earlier, in that same state, the New York Temporary Commission of Investigation found that the Suffolk County District Attorney's Office and Police Department tolerated and ratified serious incidents of police misconduct.[2] In California, the Christopher Commission, created in response to the Rodney King beating, found the Los Angeles Police Department guilty of widespread use of excessive force, racism, and inadequate supervision, and discovered a seriously flawed civilian complaint review system resulting primarily from the officers' code of silence.[3]

---

* This chapter is adapted from "Admissibility of Investigatory Reports in § 1983 Civil Rights Actions—A User's Manual," which originally appeared in 79 MARQ. L. REV. 453 (1996).

1. City of New York, COMMISSION TO INVESTIGATE ALLEGATIONS OF POLICE CORRUPTION AND THE ANTI-CORRUPTION PROCEDURES OF THE POLICE DEPARTMENT (July 7, 1994). *See* C. KRAUSS, *2-Year Corruption Inquiry Finds a 'Willful Blindness' In New York's Police Department,* N.Y. TIMES, July 7, 1994, at 1.
2. Temporary Commission of Investigation of the State of New York, AN INVESTIGATION OF THE SUFFOLK COUNTY DISTRICT ATTORNEY'S OFFICE AND POLICE DEPARTMENT (1989). *See* Gentile v. County of Suffolk, 129 F.R.D. 435 (E.D.N.Y. 1990), *aff'd*, 926 F.2d 142 (2d Cir. 1991).
3. REPORT OF THE INDEPENDENT COMMISSION ON THE LOS ANGELES POLICE DEPARTMENT (July 7, 1991). *See* Montiel v. City of Los Angeles, 2 F.3d 335 (9th Cir. 1993).

Not all law enforcement investigatory reports are of such a grand scale. Investigatory reports of law enforcement activities may concern particular incidents,[4] systemic problems,[5] or both. A particularly well-publicized incident, such as that involving Rodney King, may be symptomatic of what is thought to be a systemic problem and, thus, trigger a broad-based investigation.

Are these investigatory reports of law enforcement activities admissible in federal civil rights actions brought under § 1983, challenging the constitutionality of the conduct of law enforcement officers?[6] Various courts have held that reports of a particular incident are relevant to the issue of the individual liability of the particular officer or officers charged with constitutional wrongdoing,[7] and reports on systemic issues may be highly probative on the issue of municipal liability.[8] Whether based on an individual incident, a systemic problem, or both, courts have ruled that

---

4. For decisions involving investigatory reports of particular incidents, *see, e.g.*, Kinan v. City of Brockton, 876 F.2d 1029 (1st Cir. 1989); McQuaig v. McCoy, 806 F.2d 1298 (5th Cir. 1987); Perrin v. Anderson, 784 F.2d 1040 (10th Cir. 1986); Wilson v. Beebe, 743 F.2d 342 (6th Cir. 1984), *vacated on other grounds*, 770 F.2d 578 (6th Cir. 1985) (*en banc*); Swietlowich v. County of Bucks, 610 F.2d 1157 (3d Cir. 1979).
5. For decisions involving investigatory reports of systemic problems, *see, e.g.*, Falk v. County of Suffolk, 781 F. Supp. 146 (E.D.N.Y. 1991); Gentile v. County of Suffolk, 926 F.2d 142 (2d Cir. 1991), *aff'd* 129 F.R.D. 435 (E.D.N.Y. 1990); Anderson v. City of N.Y., 657 F. Supp. 1571 (S.D.N.Y. 1987).
6. For an overview of the law pertinent to § 1983 actions contesting law enforcement activities, *see infra* notes and accompanying text.
   § 1983 provides:
   Every person who, under color of any statute, ordinance, regulation, custom, or usage, of any State or Territory or the District of Columbia, subjects, or causes to be subjected, any citizen of the United States or other person within the jurisdiction thereof to the deprivation of any rights, privileges, or immunities secured by the Constitution and laws, shall be liable to the party injured in an action at law, suit in equity, or other proper proceeding for redress. For the purposes of this section, any Act of Congress applicable exclusively to the District of Columbia shall be considered to be a statute of the District of Columbia.
   42 U.S.C. § 1983 (1988).
7. *See infra* notes and accompanying text.
8. *See, e.g.*, *Gentile*, 129 F.R.D. at 459-60. *See infra* notes and accompanying text.

because these reports carry the imprimatur of government, they may be given great weight by the trier of fact.[9] However, the reliability of investigatory reports can and does vary greatly from case to case, and this weight may or may not be deserved.[10]

The admissibility of governmental investigatory reports typically raises difficult and contentious issues. As a starting point, the report itself, when offered for its truth, is hearsay.[11] Moreover, investigatory reports frequently contain findings and conclusions that are not based upon the investigating officer's personal knowledge.

An investigation may involve not only an analysis of the scene of the incident, but also the investigator's interviews and discussions with individuals who themselves may or may not have personal knowledge. A hearing may or may not be held. If a hearing is held, the reliability of the testimony given can vary greatly from case to case, and indeed, from witness to witness. Investigations may also rely upon written documents, including studies and reports, which are themselves hearsay.

Other variables may significantly impact upon the report's reliability. The time when the investigation was carried out in relation to the pertinent events, the procedures used in conducting the investigation, the thoroughness of the investigation, and the skills, experience, motivations, and biases of the investigating officers can and do differ greatly from case to case.[12] It is therefore not difficult to see how the reliability of investigatory reports can vary greatly from case to case.

Nevertheless, Congress found overall that governmental investigatory reports are sufficiently reliable to justify the creation of a specific hearsay exception for them. Rule 803(8)(C) of the Federal Rules of Evidence creates a hearsay exception "in civil actions and proceedings and against the Government in criminal cases" for public records containing "factual findings resulting from an investigation made pursuant to authority granted by law, unless the sources of information or other circumstances indicate lack

---

9. *See infra* notes 229 and accompanying text.
10. *See infra* notes and accompanying text.
11. Rule 801(c) of the Federal Rules of Evidence defines hearsay as "a statement, other than one made by the declarant while testifying at the trial or hearing, offered in evidence to prove the truth of the matter asserted." A "statement" is defined in part as "an oral or written assertion . . . intended by the person as an assertion." FED. R. EVID. 801(a).
12. *See infra* notes 146-63 and accompanying text.

of trustworthiness."[13] Under this rule, investigatory reports may be admitted into evidence even though the investigators, the preparers of the report, and the suppliers of information are not subject to cross-examination at trial.[14]

The Rule 803(8)(C) hearsay exception goes far beyond the common law exception for public records,[15] is controversial and complex, raises numerous difficult evidentiary issues, and has generated a great deal of scholarly commentary.[16] As one federal district court observed:

---

13. Federal Rule of Evidence 803(8)(C) provides a hearsay exception for: "in civil actions and proceedings and against the Government in criminal cases, factual findings resulting from an investigation made pursuant to authority granted by law, unless the sources of information or other circumstances indicate lack of trustworthiness."
14. Rule 803 does not require the opportunity for such cross-examination. *See* Steven P. Grossman & Stephen J. Shapiro, *The Admission of Government Fact Findings Under Federal Rule of Evidence 803(8)(C): Limiting the Dangers of Unreliable Hearsay*, 38 Kan. L. Rev. 767, 773 (1990).
15. At common law there was "disagreement among the decisions" over the admissibility of investigatory reports. Fed. R. Evid. 803(8)(c) advisory committee's note. The disagreement was "due in part, no doubt, to the variety of situations encountered, as well as to differences in principle." *Id.* The prevailing view was that investigatory reports were admissible only insofar as they reflected the officer's firsthand knowledge and not for their evaluative conclusions. Charles T. McCormick, *Can the Courts Make Wider Use of Reports of Official Investigations?,* 42 Iowa L. Rev. 363 (1957). Professor McCormick's article advocated broader admissibility of investigatory reports, including those containing opinions. *Id.* at 365. The Supreme Court has referred to Professor McCormick's "influential article relied upon by the [Advisory] Committee. . . . " Beech Aircraft v. Rainey, 488 U.S. 153, 166 n.10 (1988).
16. *See* Grossman & Shapiro, *supra* note, at 767; Jonathon E. Grant, *The Trustworthiness Standard for the Public Records and Reports Hearsay Exception*, 12 W. St. L. Rev. 53 (1984); Kevin F. Bruen, Comment, *Evidence Opinions and Conclusions Admissible Under Federal Rule of Evidence 803(8)(C).* Beech Aircraft Corp. v. Rainey, 109 S. Ct. 439 (1988), 23 Suffolk U. L. Rev. 929 (1989); James M. Garner, Comment, *The Public Documents Hearsay Exception for Evaluative Reports: Fact or Fiction?* 63 Tul. L. Rev. 121 (1988); Kimberly K. Greene, Comment, *The Admissibility of Evaluative Reports Under Federal Rule of Evidence 803(8)*, 68 Ky. L.J. 197 (1979-80); Ross P. Masler, Comment, *The Towering Inferno: Trustworthiness of the Tower Report Under Federal Rule of Evidence 803(8)(C)*, 55 Brook. L. Rev. 625 (1989); Comment, *The Admissibility of Police Reports Under the Federal Rules of Evidence*, 71 Nw. U. L. Rev. 691 (1976); Cheryl Musselman-Brown, Note,

> Section (C) . . . is quite complex, and represents a major change from common law principles. For, quite contrary to what was generally permitted at common law, under the aegis of 803(8)(C), materials representing the distillation of a process that may have involved years of investigation and the taking of thousands of pages of testimony may be presented to the trier of fact in one fell swoop.[17]

Because it is "such a potent litigation tool, the parties are prone to skirmish mightily over the trustworthiness *vel non* of public records and reports."[18]

The admissibility of investigatory reports raises an unusually broad range of potentially significant evidentiary issues. To begin with, a number of important issues are raised by Rule 803(8)(C) itself, including: (1) what is encompassed within the rule's reference to "factual findings resulting from an investigation?"[19] (2) how should an investigatory report's "trustworthiness" be evaluated?[20] and (3) does the Rule 803(8)(C) hearsay exception encompass the accompanying data and information upon which the findings are based?[21] Of these Rule 803(8)(C) issues, trustworthiness is by far the most frequently and sharply contested issue.

But that is not all. In addition to the issues raised by Rule 803(8)(C), other significant evidentiary issues may be contested; namely, relevance and Rule 403 balancing,[22] the Rule 407 exclusionary rule for subsequent remedial measures,[23] and the invocation of a governmental privilege.[24]

Admitting Opinions and Conclusions in Evaluative Reports: The Trustworthiness Inquiry—Beech Aircraft v. Rainey, 64 Wash. L. Rev. 975 (1989); Penelope E. Nicholson, Note, *The Scope of Federal Rule of Evidence 803(8)(C)*, 59 Tex. L. Rev. 155 (1980); Note, *The Trustworthiness of Government Evaluative Reports Under Federal Rule of Evidence 803(8)(C)*, 96 Harv. L. Rev. 492 (1982).

17. Zenith Radio Corp. v. Matsushita Elec. Indus. Co., 505 F. Supp. 1125, 1143 (E.D. Pa. 1980), *rev'd in part on other grounds*, 723 F.2d 238 (3d Cir. 1983), *rev'd on other grounds*, 475 U.S. 574 (1986).
18. Zenith, 505 F. Supp. at 1146.
19. *See infra* notes 78-119 and accompanying text.
20. *See infra* notes 144-63 and accompanying text.
21. *See infra* notes 120-43 and accompanying text.
22. *See infra* notes 211-37 and accompanying text.
23. *See infra* notes 238-57 and accompanying text.
24. *See infra* notes 258-311 and accompanying text. Authentication is not a serious problem because "[o]fficial records frequently are admissible without a

At this point in time, twenty years after the adoption of the Federal Rules of Evidence, a somewhat specialized and extensive body of decisional law has developed governing the admissibility of investigatory reports in federal § 1983 actions. Decisions concerning the admissibility of investigatory reports in non-§ 1983 cases can, of course, be quite pertinent in § 1983 actions. Nevertheless, it stands to reason that the evidentiary decisions in § 1983 actions are likely to be the most relevant, persuasive precedents when the admissibility issue arises in a § 1983 action. Experienced attorneys who prosecute and defend § 1983 actions generally agree that an investigatory report is typically very powerful evidence in these cases.[25] Before analyzing the various evidentiary issues, however, an overview of the law governing § 1983 claims arising out of encounters with law enforcement officers will place admissibility of these reports in its proper context. We then look at the Rule 803(6) business records rule, the Rule 803(8) public records rule, and the relationship between these two rules.

The chapter next turns to the heart of the matter, analyzing the various facets of the Rule 803(8)(C) hearsay exception for investigatory reports and giving special attention to the critical issues of "trustworthiness." The chapter then discusses aspects of relevance, including Rule 403 balancing and the Rule 407 exclusionary rule for subsequent remedial measures. Finally, the chapter analyzes the potentially pertinent governmental privileges.

---

foundation witness because the self-authentication provisions of Rule 902 obviate the need for live foundation testimony." GLEN WEISSENBERGER, FEDERAL RULES OF EVIDENCE § 803.41, at 427 (1987). *See* FED. R. EVID. 902(1) (public documents under seal); (2) (public documents not under seal); (3) (certified copies of public documents); (5) (official publications); (8) (acknowledged documents). *See also* CHRISTOPHER B. MUELLER & LAIRD C. KIRKPATRICK, EVIDENCE, § 8.47, at 997 (1995).

25. Telephone interview with Lawrence J. Brennan, Chief, Bureau of Tort and Civil Rights Litigation, Nassau County Attorney, Sept. 14, 1994 (reports may be given "very strong weight"); personal interview with Frederick K. Brewington (experienced plaintiffs' lawyer), Oct. 27, 1994 (reports are "very important"); telephone interview with William Gibney, Managing Attorney, Prisoners' Legal Services, Sept. 22, 1994 (weight may depend upon sophistication of the jury); telephone interview with John Williams (experienced plaintiffs' lawyer), Sept. 22, 1994 (report can be "very powerful").

Overview

Section 1983 provides a cause of action against those who, under color of state or local law, violated the plaintiff's federally protected rights.[26] It does not itself establish or create federally protected rights, but only "gives a remedy" when the claimant demonstrates a violation of rights protected by the federal Constitution or, in some instances, by a federal statute other than § 1983.[27]

Large numbers of § 1983 actions arise out of encounters with law enforcement officers. These claims may challenge, inter alia, the constitutionality of an investigatory stop, arrest, detention, search, or prosecution. A large proportion of the claims assert the use of excessive force by the police in the course of making an arrest.[28] Excessive force-arrest claims are litigated under a Fourth Amendment objective reasonableness standard.[29] Under this standard, the constitutionality of the officer's use of force must be evaluated in light of the particular circumstances known to the officer "from the perspective of a reasonable officer on the scene, rather than with the 20/20 vision of hindsight," and "must embody allowance for the fact that police officers are often forced to make split-second judgments—in circumstances that are tense, uncertain, and rapidly evolving—about the amount of force that is necessary in a particular situation."[30]

---

26. *See, e.g.*, West v. Atkins, 487 U.S. 42, 48 (1988); Gomez v. Toledo, 446 U.S. 635, 640 (1980); Flagg Bros. v. Brooks, 436 U.S. 149, 155 (1978).
27. Chapman v. Houston Welfare Rights Org., 441 U.S. 600, 617 (1979). *Accord* Albright v. Oliver, 114 S. Ct. 807 (1994); Graham v. Connor, 490 U.S. 386 (1989); Wilson v. Garcia, 471 U.S. 261, 278 (1985); Oklahoma City v. Tuttle, 471 U.S. 808, 816, *reh'g denied*, 473 U.S. 925 (1985); Baker v. McCollan, 443 U.S. 137, 140 n.3 (1979).

    The federal statutes that are enforceable under § 1983 raise an issue of some complexity. *See* 1 Martin A. Schwartz & John E. Kirklin, Section 1983 Litigation: Claims, Defenses, and Fees ch. 4 (2d ed. 1991 & 1996 Cum. Supp. No.1). Section 1983 claims arising out of encounters with law enforcement officers are typically premised upon alleged federal constitutional, not federal statutory, violations.
28. *See* Schwartz & Kirklin § 3.6, at 137 & n.238.
29. Graham v. Connor, 490 U.S. 386 (1989). *See also* Tennessee v. Garner, 471 U.S. 1 (1985) (deadly force).
30. Graham, 490 U.S. at 396-97. *See also* Sherrod v. Berry, 856 F.2d 802 (7th Cir. 1988) (*en banc*).

The § 1983 claim may be asserted against the officer involved in the encounter in the officer's personal capacity, against the municipal entity, or, as is common, against both the officer and the entity.[31] Law enforcement officers sued in their personal capacities may assert the qualified immunity defense, which raises the issue of whether the officer violated clearly established federal law.[32] Because there is no *respondeat superior* liability under § 1983, a municipal entity may be found liable only if it is shown that the enforcement of a municipal policy or practice, or the final decision of a policymaker, caused the violation of the plaintiff's federally protected rights.[33] The Supreme Court has ruled that a municipality's deliberately indifferent training that caused the deprivation of the claimant's federally protected rights may give rise to § 1983 municipal liability.[34] By

---

31. Suing an official in an official capacity is tantamount to suing the entity. Kentucky PBA Bureau of State Police v. Graham, 473 U.S. 159 (1985); Brandon v. Holt, 469 U.S. 464, 471-72 (1985); Monell v. Department of Social Servs. of the City of N. Y., 436 U.S. 658, 690 n.55 (1978). On the distinctions between individual- and official-capacity claims, *see Graham,* 473 U.S. at 165-66. *See also* Hafer v. Melo, 112 S. Ct. 358 (1991). On the relationship between individual and municipal liability, *see* SCHWARTZ & KIRKLIN, *supra* note.

    The text refers to "municipal" entities, as opposed to state entities, because the great percentage of claims arising out of encounters with law enforcement officers involve municipal, not state, officials. States, state agencies, and state officials in their official capacities are not "persons" who may be sued under § 1983 for monetary relief. Will v. Michigan State Police, 491 U.S. 58 (1989).
32. *See, e.g.*, Hunter v. Bryant, 112 S. Ct. 534 (1991) (Bivens action; warrantless arrest); Anderson v. Creighton, 483 U.S. 635 (1987) (Bivens action; warrantless search); Malley v. Briggs, 475 U.S. 335 (1986) (arrest warrant application). *See generally* Harlow v. Fitzgerald, 457 U.S. 800 (1982) (establishing objectively reasonable qualified immunity standard). The lower courts are in conflict over whether qualified immunity may be asserted as a defense to a Fourth Amendment excessive force claim or whether, in this context, the qualified immunity defense is superfluous. *See* SCHWARTZ & KIRKLIN, *supra* note, § 9.21 & 1996 Cum. Supp. No. 1 (collecting decisions under subheading "Excessive Force").
33. Monell v. Department of Social Servs. of the City of N.Y., 436 U.S. 658 (1978). *See also* City of St. Louis v. Praprotnik, 485 U.S. 112 (1988); Pembaur v. City of Cincinnati, 475 U.S. 469 (1986).
34. City of Canton v. Harris, 489 U.S. 378 (1989).

logical extension, the lower federal courts have applied this ruling to claims arising out of failures to supervise, discipline, and take remedial action.[35] Investigatory reports may contain especially important information and evidence when the municipal liability claim is premised upon an alleged custom or practice of official wrongdoing or upon inadequate training, supervision, discipline, and remedial actions.

Business and Public Records Exceptions Under the Rules of Evidence

Business Records

Federal Rule of Evidence 803(6) establishes the familiar hearsay exception for regularly kept "business" records.[36] Although commonly referred to as the "business records rule," it is actually broader in scope. Rule

---

35. SCHWARTZ & KIRKLIN, *supra* note, § 7.10 & 1996 Cum. Supp. No. 1.
36. The advisory committee's note to Rule 803(6) explains that regularly kept business records are thought to be unusually reliable because of the regularity with which they are prepared and maintained, their systematic checking by auditors and others, the business duty to make accurate records, and the reliance on these records by the business in making decisions. An analysis of Rule 803(6) and its interpretive decisional law reveals that the following requirements must be established in order to satisfy the business record rule:
1. The record must be "kept in the course of a regularly conducted business activity." FED. R. EVID. 803(6).
2. It must be "the regular practice of that business activity to make the . . . record." *See, e.g.*, Wheeler v. Sims, 951 F.2d 796 (7th Cir.), *cert. denied*, 113 S. Ct. 320 (1992) (§ 1983 action).
3. The record must be made by an employee with personal knowledge, or from information transmitted by a person who has personal knowledge and a business duty to transmit the information. All other intermediaries must *also* be under a business duty to transmit. The advisory committee's note to Rule 803(6), citing what it describes as the "leading case" of Johnson v. Lutz, 170 N.E. 517 (N.Y. 1930), explains that when the supplier of the information, such as a bystander, or any other participant in the record-making process does not act in the regular course of business, an "essential link" of reliability is broken. FED. R. EVID. 803(6) advisory committee's note.
4. If the person supplying the information does not have a business duty to transmit the information, this requirement alternatively can be satisfied by showing that the transmittal of the information meets some other hearsay exemption or exception, such as an admission, excited utterance, or declaration

803(6) broadly defines *business* to "include business, institution, association, profession, occupation, and calling of every kind, whether or not con-

---

against interest. 2 JOHN W. STRONG, ET AL., MCCORMICK ON EVIDENCE § 290, at 275 (4th ed. 1992); 4 JACK B. WEINSTEIN & MARGARET A. BERGER, WEINSTEIN'S EVIDENCE § 803(6)[04] (1987).

5. The record must be "made at or near the time" of the transaction. FED. R. EVID. 803(6).

These "foundation" requirements must be substantiated by the "testimony of the custodian [of the records] or other qualified witness. . . ." FED. R. EVID. 803(6). This foundation testimony can be given by anyone who has personal knowledge of the organization's recordkeeping procedures. "[T]here is no requirement that this witness must have firsthand knowledge of the matter reported or actually have prepared the report or observed its preparation." WEINSTEIN & BERGER, *supra* § 803(6)[04].

Even if all of the requisites of the business record hearsay exception are met, Rule 803(6) authorizes exclusion of the record if "the source of information or the method or circumstances of preparation indicate lack of trustworthiness." FED. R. EVID. 803(6). This encompasses the so-called motivational problems that arise when reports are prepared for purposes of litigation—that is, the Palmer v. Hoffman, 318 U.S. 109 (1943) problem. *See, e.g.*, Wheeler v. Sims, 951 F.2d 796 (7th Cir.), *cert. denied*, 488 U.S. 1008 (1992) (§ 1983 action); Dorsey v. City of Detroit, 858 F.2d 338 (6th Cir. 1988) (§ 1983 action); Stone v. Morris, 546 F.2d 730 (7th Cir. 1976) (§ 1983 action).

When a record meets the requirements of the business record rule, Federal Rule of Evidence 803(7) provides that the failure of the record to include a transaction that one would ordinarily expect to be in a record of a regularly conducted business activity is admissible to prove the nonoccurrence of the event. The same 803(6) proviso appears in Rule 803(7): "unless the sources of information or other circumstances indicate lack of trustworthiness." A hypothetical example in the § 1983 setting would be a prison hospital record's failure to show the admission of a particular prisoner on a particular occasion that is introduced into evidence to show that the prisoner did not receive medical care on that date. There are few reported decisions under Rule 803(7). *See* STEPHEN A. SALTZBURG ET AL., FEDERAL RULES OF EVIDENCE MANUAL 1504-05 (6th ed. 1994) (annotating four cases). Rule 803(7) is a potentially very useful tool for accomplishing the frequently difficult task of proving a negative. Although the absence of an entry in a business record is probably not even hearsay because there is simply no out-of-court statement being introduced, there were some pre-rule decisions to the contrary, and Rule 803(7) sought "to set the question at rest in favor of admissibility." FED. R. EVID. 803(7) advisory committee's note.

ducted for profit."[37] Thus, it is broad enough to include the records of governmental entities.[38]

A business record may consist of "[a] memorandum, report, record, or data compilation, in any form. . . . "[39] The reference to "data compilation" is intended to cover computer-generated records.[40] The record may include opinions and diagnoses, such as those contained in medical records[41] and police reports.[42] The fact that the business record rule encompasses governmental records raises the issue, discussed below, concerning the relationship between the business and public records hearsay exceptions.[43] Before pursuing that issue, however, let's turn first to the Federal Rule of Evidence 803(8) exception for public records.

Public Records

Like hearsay exceptions generally, the public records exception is based upon the general trustworthiness of public records. Public records are generally believed to be sufficiently trustworthy because it is assumed that

---

37. FED. R. EVID. 803(6).
38. *See* Malek v. Federal Ins. Co., 994 F.2d 49 (2d Cir. 1993) (department of social services worker's notes within business records rule); Wheeler v. Sims, 951 F.2d 796 (7th Cir.) (prisoner's file), *cert. denied*, 488 U.S. 1008 (1989); Dorsey v. City of Detroit, 858 F.2d 338 (6th Cir. 1988) (police report); Ward v. Arkansas State Police, 714 F.2d 62 (8th Cir. 1983) (police department investigatory report); Stone v. Morris, 546 F.2d 730 (7th Cir. 1976) (a prison is a "business" under the business record rule). *But see* Garcia v. Gloor, 618 F.2d 264, 272 (5th Cir. 1980) ("The admissibility of such official documents under the Federal Rules of Evidence is not determined by business records rules standards, but by Rule 803(8), which provides for the admissibility of the reports of public agencies."), *cert. denied*, 449 U.S. 1113 (1981); United States v. American Cyanamid Co., 427 F. Supp. 859 (S.D.N.Y. 1977).
39. FED. R. EVID. 803(6).
40. FED. R. EVID. 803(6) advisory committee's note. On the admissibility of computer-generated records, *see* 2 STRONG, *supra* note, § 294; MICHAEL H. GRAHAM, HANDBOOK OF FEDERAL EVIDENCE § 803.6 (3d ed. 1991).
41. 2 STRONG, *supra* note, § 293.
42. *See, e.g.*, Dorsey v. City of Detroit, 858 F.2d 338 (6th Cir. 1988) (§ 1983 action: police report containing officer's opinion of nature and severity of plaintiff's injuries was within the business records rule; report should have been excluded, however, because of defendants' failure to produce it during discovery).
43. *See infra* notes 59-77 and accompanying text.

public officials will prepare accurate reports.[44] The public records exception is also justified by the public interest in avoiding having public officials testify in court about the subject matter of governmental reports.[45] Further, there is great likelihood that the record will be more reliable than the official's present testimony reflecting memory of events that may have occurred many years ago.[46]

Public records may be utilized at trial for several purposes: to refresh a witness's recollection, to memorialize an event under the doctrine of past recollection recorded, to impeach with a prior inconsistent statement, and to rehabilitate by showing a prior consistent statement.[47] Rule 803(8), however, creates an independent hearsay exception for public records, allowing them to be introduced for their truth. Of course, like the other hearsay exceptions, Rule 803(8) only removes the bar of the exclusionary rule against hearsay. Public records and reports that satisfy Rule 803(8) must still clear other hurdles of admissibility, such as relevance, Rule 403, specific exclusionary rules such as that for remedial measures under Rule 407, authentication, and the various privileges.

The Rule 803(8) hearsay exception is limited to records prepared by governmental entities. In *Lamphere v. Brown University*,[48] a Title VII gender discrimination suit, the First Circuit ruled that the opinions of a hearing panel comprising university faculty members did not come within Rule 803(8) because "the panels are not public agencies, and its members are not public officials."[49]

---

44. Fed. R. Evid. 803(8) advisory committee's note.
45. Strong, *supra* note, § 296.
46. *Id.*; Fed. R. Evid. 803(8) advisory committee's note.
47. Graham, *supra* note 40, § 803.8, at 892 n.3.
48. 685 F.2d 743, 749 (1st Cir. 1982).
49. *Id. See also* Marsee v. United States Tobacco Co., 866 F.2d 319 (10th Cir. 1989) (Rule 803(8)(C) inapplicable because report not prepared by public officials); *In re* Japanese Elecs. Prods. Antitrust Litig., 723 F.2d 238, 272 (3d Cir. 1983) (documents "authored by Matsushita rather than by a 'public office or agency' [not within] Rule 803(8)(C)"), *rev'd on other grounds,* 475 U.S. 574 (1986); John McShain, Inc. v. Cessna Aircraft Co., 563 F.2d 632 (3d Cir. 1977) (Rule 803(8) exempts from hearsay rule only reports by public officials).

    Although the investigation must be carried out by governmental officials, the information may be obtained from individuals having no involvement "whatsoever" with government. Grossman & Shapiro, *supra* note, at 768 & n.3 (citing numerous cases).

Rule 803(8) establishes three categories of public records and reports. It "has extraordinary breadth."[50] Subdivision (A) provides an exception for public records of "the activities of the office or agency." This covers records of the agency's internal affairs; that is, of its functions and activities, such as employment, inventory, and disbursement records.[51] There is no requirement that the record be based upon personal knowledge or even upon a governmental duty to transmit the information. If the record is not sufficiently trustworthy, however, it can be excluded under Rule 403.

Subdivision (B) provides a hearsay exception for public records setting forth "matters observed pursuant to duty imposed by law as to which matters there was a duty to report. . . ."[52] Thus, for example, in civil cases, a police officer's report of an accident or other law enforcement matter based upon the officer's personal knowledge comes within subdivision (B).[53]

The public records and reports covered by subdivisions (A) and (B) are fairly straightforward and noncontroversial. The same cannot be said of the subdivision (C) hearsay exception for investigatory reports. Rule 803(8)(C) provides a hearsay exception in civil cases for public records setting forth "factual findings resulting from an investigation made pursuant to authority granted by law, unless the sources of information or other circumstances indicate lack of trustworthiness."[54] This "represents

---

50. Mueller & Kirkpatrick, *supra* note, § 847, at 975.
51. *See* 2 Strong, *supra* note, § 296; Fed. R. Evid. 803(8)(A) advisory committee's note.
52. The subdivision (B) hearsay exception does not encompass "in criminal cases matters observed by police officers and other law enforcement personnel." Fed. R. Evid. 803(8)(B) (emphasis omitted). This clause has been interpreted as barring the prosecution, but not the defense, from introducing these reports in criminal cases. *See* 2 Strong, *supra* note, § 296, at 508.
53. *See, e.g.*, Baker v. Elcona Homes Corp., 588 F.2d 551 (6th Cir. 1978), *cert. denied*, 441 U.S. 933 (1979).
54. Fed. R. Evid. 803(8)(C). In addition to civil cases, Rule 803(8)(C) authorizes the admission of investigatory reports "*against* the Government in criminal cases." *Id.* (emphasis added). This language makes clear that investigatory reports may not be introduced under this subdivision by the government against a criminal defendant. This limitation was included in Rule 803(8)(C) because of Confrontation Clause concerns. *See* United States v. Oates, 560 F.2d 45 (2d Cir. 1977).

a tremendous expansion of the typical public records exception,"[55] is controversial, and raises multifaceted and often highly contentious evidentiary issues. It is the only public records hearsay exception "that reaches material based on outside information," potentially embracing "multiple layers of hearsay as information is passed among public officials"[56] before being finally recorded in what is offered at trial. Nevertheless, it is justified on the ground that "public officials have factfinding and evaluative expertise. . . . "[57]

Rule 803(8)(C) as written requires that (1) the report contain "factual findings," (2) "resulting from an investigation made pursuant to authority granted by law," and (3) is sufficiently trustworthy to justify its admission into evidence.[58] Before analyzing these issues, however, we pause to discuss the relationship between the Rule 803(6) business record rule and the Rule 803(8) public record rule.

Relationship Between Business and Public Records Rules

A great deal of uncertainty surrounds the relationship between the Rule 803(6) business records and the Rule 803(8) public records hearsay excep-

---

55. ABA Section on Litigation, Emerging Problems Under the Federal Rules of Evidence 237 (2d ed. 1991) (hereinafter Emerging Problems).
56. Mueller & Kirkpatrick, *supra* note, § 8.47, at 976. *But see* Miller v. Field, 35 F.3d 1088 (6th Cir. 1994) (§ 1983 action: limiting Rule 803(8)(C) to cases in which the report is based upon the preparer's personal knowledge). For an analysis of Miller v. Field, *see infra* notes 126-43 and accompanying text.
57. Mueller & Kirkpatrick, *supra* note, § 8.48, at 980. *See also id.* § 8.48, at 979-80 (Rule 803(8)(C) parallels the treatment the Federal Rules of Evidence affords expert witnesses). There is no requirement, however, that the investigators and authors of the report be qualified as experts. Clark v. Clabaugh, 20 F.3d 1290 (3d Cir. 1994).
58. Fed. R. Evid. 803(8)(C). Rule 803(10) is the public records counterpart to Rule 803(7). *See supra* note 36. It provides that the nonoccurrence of an event may be shown by its absence in a "regularly made and preserved" public record. Rule 803(10) *also* allows the absence of a public report to be shown by "certification in accordance with Rule 902," or testimony "that diligent search failed to disclose the record. . . . " The advisory committee's note to Rule 803(10) states that it covers "situations in which absence of a record may itself be the ultimate focal point of inquiry . . . as well as cases where the absence of a record is offered as proof of the nonoccurrence of an event ordinarily recorded."

tions. This issue has had its most significant, frequent, and difficult applications in criminal cases. This is because of the restrictions in Rules 803(8)(B) and (C) against introducing law enforcement and investigatory reports against criminal defendants, and because of Confrontation Clause concerns.[59] These are not pertinent factors in civil rights actions filed under § 1983.

In civil cases, two major questions are presented: (1) when a public record is sought to be introduced, which provision should the court look to in the first instance, 803(6) or 803(8), or is either permissible? and (2) are public records that do not meet the requirements of the public records rule potentially admissible under the business records rule?

It would seem natural that the specific Rule 803(8) hearsay exception for public records would be the first rule to which a federal court would turn when a hearsay issue is raised regarding public records. In fact, "there is some tendency to rely upon Rule 803(8) instead of Rule 803(6) for governmental entities since the more particular rule usually controls."[60] A number of courts have taken this approach in § 1983 cases involving investigatory reports.[61]

On the other hand, there are a surprising number of federal circuit court decisions in § 1983 cases that evaluate the admissibility of public records solely on the basis of the business record rule.[62] These decisions either explicitly or implicitly take the position that the broad definition of "business"

---

59. *See, e.g.*, United States v. Hayes, 861 F.2d 1225 (10th Cir. 1988); United States v. King, 613 F.2d 670 (7th Cir. 1980); United States v. Sawyer, 607 F.2d 1190 (7th Cir. 1979), *cert. denied*, 445 U.S. 943 (1980); United States v. Oates, 560 F.2d 45 (2d Cir. 1977); 2 Strong, *supra* note, § 296, at 292-94. *See also* United States v. Yakobov, 712 F.2d 20 (2d Cir. 1983).
60. Weinstein & Berger, *supra* note, § 803(6)[03], at 803-209.
61. Gentile v. County of Suffolk, 926 F.2d 142 (2d Cir. 1991); Perrin v. Anderson, 784 F.2d 1040 (10th Cir. 1986); Wilson v. Beebe, 743 F.2d 342 (6th Cir. 1984); Swietlowich v. County of Bucks, 610 F.2d 1157 (3d Cir. 1979).
62. Romano v. Howarth, 998 F.2d 101 (2d Cir. 1993) (prison psychiatric progress notes); Wheeler v. Sims, 951 F.2d 796 (7th Cir.) (prison's record of plaintiff's medical condition), *cert. denied*, 488 U.S. 1008 (1992); Dorsey v. City of Detroit, 858 F.2d 338 (6th Cir. 1988) (police report); Walker v. Wayne County, Iowa, 850 F.2d 433 (8th Cir. 1988) (criminal investigation report), *cert. denied*, 488 U.S. 1008 (1989); Stone v. Morris, 546 F.2d 730 (7th Cir. 1976) (prison correctional counselor's account of incident).

in Rule 803(6) includes governmental entities.[63] Although this seems to be correct, it also seems unusual to evaluate a hearsay issue concerning a public record as if the public records hearsay exception does not exist.[64]

The Sixth Circuit decision in *Dorsey v. City of Detroit*[65] illustrates the Rule 803(6) approach to public records in a § 1983 setting. In that case, involving the alleged use of excessive force against a fleeing misdemeanant and the arrest of his mother, the plaintiffs on appeal urged that the district court erred in admitting Sergeant Graber's investigatory report of the incident. Sergeant Graber's report summarized information of the incident that had been provided to Graber by fellow officers, and contained the following conclusion:

> The writer's investigation reveals that the officers were engaged in a lawful and proper police function. It is this writer's opinion that Officers Butucel and Robinson used no more than necessary force to effect the arrest of Mr. Dorsey. Officer Butucel appears to have been injured as a result of police action. The alleged injury to Robert Dorsey and the injury to Margaret Dorsey seem minimal under the circumstances. Investigation reveals that both parties were hostile and combative in their actions. The injuries occurred as a direct result of their hostilities towards the officers.[66]

---

63. Malek v. Federal Ins. Co., 994 F.2d 49 (2d Cir. 1993) (department of social services social worker's notes within business records rule); Wheeler v. Sims, 951 F.2d 796 (7th Cir.) (prisoner's file), *cert. denied*, 488 U.S. 1008 (1989); Dorsey v. City of Detroit, 858 F.2d 338 (6th Cir. 1988) (police report); Ward v. Arkansas State Police, 714 F.2d 62 (8th Cir. 1983) (police department investigatory report); Stone v. Morris, 546 F.2d 730 (7th Cir. 1976) (a prison is a "business" under the business record rule). *But see* Garcia v. Gloor, 618 F.2d 264, 272 (5th Cir. 1980) ("The admissibility of such official documents under the Federal Rules of Evidence is not determined by business records rules standard but by Rule 803(8), which provides for the admission of [the] reports of public agencies."), *cert. denied*, 449 U.S. 1113 (1981); United States v. American Cyanamid Co., 427 F. Supp. 859 (S.D.N.Y. 1977).
64. In Jenkins v. Whittaker Corp., 785 F.2d 720 (9th Cir.), *cert. denied*, 479 U.S. 918 (1986), the court evaluated the admissibility of a governmental report under Rule 803(6) and Rule 803(8)(C) jointly, that is, it engaged in one trustworthy evaluation under both rules.
65. 858 F.2d 338 (6th Cir. 1988).
66. *Id.* at 343.

The plaintiffs advanced three reasons why this report should not have been admitted under Rule 803(6). First, plaintiffs argued that a proper foundation for admitting the report had not been laid. The circuit court, however, found otherwise because "Officer Jones, who had worked under Sergeant Graber's supervision, testified that Sergeant Graber prepared such reports in the ordinary course of business, and Jones identified the signature on the report as Sergeant Graber's."[67] It was not necessary that Jones testify as to how Sergeant Graber prepared the report because, under Rule 803(6), the qualifying witness need only be familiar with the recordkeeping system.[68]

The plaintiffs' second argument was that the report contained information that was not within Sergeant Graber's personal knowledge. This argument was without merit because a business record can be prepared on the basis of information *supplied* by one with personal knowledge and a business duty to transmit the information; it is not necessary that the recorder have personal knowledge.[69]

Third, the plaintiffs argued that the report was not trustworthy because it contained Sergeant Graber's personal opinions. Rule 803(6), however, specifically permits opinions in business records. Although the Graber report did raise motivational problems because it appeared to have been prepared with an eye toward litigation, it was nevertheless within the district court's discretion to find the report sufficiently trustworthy.[70] Furthermore,

---

67. *Id.* at 342.
68. WEINSTEIN & BERGER, *supra* note, § 803(6)[02]; 2 STRONG, *supra* note, § 292.
69. *See supra* note.
70. By contrast, in Romano v. Howarth, 998 F.2d 101 (2d Cir. 1993), a § 1983 action in which the plaintiff prisoner alleged that correction officers used excessive force in restraining him in order to allow a nurse to administer a sedative, the Second Circuit ruled that the district court erred in allowing defendants to introduce the plaintiff's psychiatric "Progress Notes," made by a nurse at the Mental Health Unit (MHU) the day after the incident in question. The notes recorded an unidentified corrections officer's statement that Romano admitted that he hurt his hand punching a wall. It was unclear whether the corrections officer had a business duty to transmit the information to the MHU staff. More important, the notes did not satisfy the trustworthy requirement of Rule 803(6). The officer in question was one of the defendants, and the plaintiff "had threatened to blame his injuries on the officers and . . . the officers were aware of Romano's threat." *Id.* at 108. Under these circumstances, the corrections officer had a motive to "judge" what happened

although the circuit court in *Dorsey* found that the district court did not err in finding that the report met all of the requirements of the business records rule, it also found a significant reason why the report should have been excluded. The defendants' failure to produce the report during pretrial discovery deprived the plaintiffs of a fair opportunity to contest its trustworthiness at trial. For this reason the report should have been excluded.

What is most striking about the circuit court's decision in *Dorsey* is its failure even to mention the 803(8)(C) investigatory hearsay exception. After all, since the admissibility of Sergeant Graber's investigatory report was at issue, it seems reasonable to expect the court to make some reference to the specific hearsay exception that exists for governmental investigatory reports.

It is likely, however, that the court's evaluation and decision would have focused on substantially the same factors under Rule 803(8)(C) as it did under Rule 803(6). This is because trustworthiness is the most critical factor under both Rule 803(6) and Rule 803(8)(C). Further, the circuit court's reasoning that the defendants' failure to produce the report during pretrial discovery justified its exclusion, because it deprived the plaintiffs of a fair opportunity to contest its trustworthiness, should pertain equally under Rule 803(8)(C).

In *Dorsey*, the circuit court tested the admissibility of the public record solely under the business records rule. As noted above, however, when the admissibility of a public record is at issue, it is more likely that a federal court will turn at least initially to the specific Rule 803(8) hearsay exception for public records. Assuming that a court first tests the admissibility of a public record under the public records hearsay exception and finds it inadmissible, may the proponent then seek to admit it under the business records rule? Although the answer is not free from doubt, the business records rule, in theory, should be viewed as an alternative basis of admissibility. After all, the public record is hearsay because it is an out-of-court statement being offered for its truth. Thus, if the record meets *any* hearsay exception, it should be viewed as having overcome the hearsay hurdle.

Because Rule 803(8) is a rule of admissibility, public records that do not meet the requirements of that rule should be admissible if they meet

---

to Romano. *Id.* Therefore, the officer's statement recorded on the notes did not carry "the requisite degree of trustworthiness essential to the business records exception." *Id.*

the requirements of some other hearsay exception.[71] Nevertheless, some federal court decisions hold that the specific Rule 803(8) hearsay exception is the exclusive hearsay exception for public records.[72]

Although the relationship between the business and public records rules is significant in criminal cases in which the government seeks to introduce either a law enforcement officer's report based upon personal knowledge or an investigatory report against the defendant,[73] the relationship between the two rules seems to arise relatively infrequently in civil cases. This may be because the public records rule is broader and generally easier to satisfy than the business records rule:

1. Unlike the business records exception, the public records rule does not require the testimony of the custodian or other qualified witness;[74]
2. In contrast to the business record rule, Rule 803(8) does not require that a public record be created "contemporaneously" with the event in question;[75]
3. "Also, subdivisions (A) and (C) have no requirement that the record be routinely maintained";[76]
4. In contrast to the business records rule, the investigatory reports exception has no requirement that the information be recorded or furnished by an individual with personal knowledge; and
5. The most important requisite for admitting an investigatory report under Rule 803(8)(C) is its trustworthiness, a requirement of the Rule 803(6) business records exception as well. An investigatory

---

71. Emerging Problems, *supra* note, at 234.
72. Garcia v. Gloor, 618 F.2d 264, 272 (5th Cir. 1980) ("The admissibility of such official documents under the Federal Rules of Evidence is not determined by business records rules standards but by Rule 803(8), which provides for the admission of reports of public agencies."), *cert. denied*, 449 U.S. 1113 (1981); United States v. American Cyanamid Co., 427 F. Supp. 859, 867 (S.D.N.Y. 1977) ("Rule 803(6) is simply not applicable to government records and reports, which are to be admitted in accordance with the standards of Rule 803(8).").
73. *See* cases cited *supra* note.
74. Weissenberger, *supra*, § 803.41. "Official records frequently are admissible without a foundation witness because the self-authentication provisions of Rule 902 obviate the need for live foundational testimony." *Id.* at 427.
75. *Id.*
76. *Id.*

report that is not trustworthy for purposes of Rule 803(8)(C) is also not trustworthy for purposes of Rule 803(6).

When all of these factors are considered together, it is apparent that both public records in general, and investigatory reports in particular, that do not satisfy the requirements of the public records rule are exceedingly unlikely to be able to meet the requirements of the business records rule. Thus, while there is uncertainty regarding the relationship between the business and public records rules, this issue is not of particular significance in § 1983 civil rights suits. Despite the unusual Rule 803(6) approach taken by the Sixth Circuit in *Dorsey*, federal courts in § 1983 actions normally have taken the sensible approach and analyzed the issue under the specific Rule 803(8)(C) exception for investigatory reports.[77]

The Rule 803(8)(C) Hearsay Exception for Investigatory Reports

The Rule 803(8)(C) hearsay exception for investigatory reports, by its terms, encompasses "factual findings resulting from an investigation made pursuant to authority granted by law, unless the sources of information or other circumstances indicate lack of trustworthiness." Like Rule 803(8) generally, this hearsay exception pertains only to investigatory reports prepared by governmental officials.[78] Further, the investigation must be authorized by legal authority: "This requirement helps to ensure that the report is reliable."[79] The investigation, however, need only be authorized, not mandated, by law.[80]

---

77. *See, e.g.*, Montiel v. City of Los Angeles, 2 F.3d 335 (9th Cir. 1993); Gentile v. County of Suffolk, 926 F.2d 142 (2d Cir. 1991); McQuaig v. McCoy, 806 F.2d 1298 (5th Cir. 1987); Perrin v. Anderson, 784 F.2d 1040 (10th Cir. 1986); Wilson v. Beebe, 743 F.2d 342 (6th Cir. 1984), *vacated on other grounds,* 770 F.2d 578 (6th Cir. 1985); Swietlowich v. County of Bucks, 610 F.2d 1157 (3d Cir. 1979); Falk v. County of Suffolk, 781 F. Supp. 146 (E.D.N.Y. 1991); Anderson v. City of N.Y., 657 F. Supp. 1571 (S.D.N.Y. 1987).
78. *See* Marsee v. United States Tobacco Co., 866 F.2d 319 (10th Cir. 1989); Lamphere v. Brown Univ., 685 F.2d 743 (1st Cir. 1982); John McShain, Inc. v. Cessna Aircraft Co., 563 F.2d 632 (3d Cir. 1977).
79. Perrin v. Anderson, 784 F.2d 1040, 1046 (10th Cir. 1986). *See also* Keith v. Volpe, 858 F.2d 467 (9th Cir. 1988) (report was not used solely for litigation purposes), *cert. denied*, 493 U.S. 813 (1989).
80. Jenkins v. Whittaker Corp., 785 F.2d 720, 726 n.15 (9th Cir.), *cert. denied*,

In some cases, issues have been raised as to whether the governmental action was investigatory in nature. The issue has principally arisen with respect to (a) quasi-judicial administrative findings; (b) rulemaking; and (c) judicial findings. In *Chandler v. Roudebush*,[81] a Title VII suit, the Supreme Court, citing Rule 803(8)(C), stated that "[p]rior administrative findings made with respect to an employment discrimination claim may, of course, be admitted as evidence at a federal sector trial *de novo*." A recent study of the Federal Rules of Evidence concluded that "[w]ith respect to adjudicatory findings, the courts of appeals have uniformly followed *Chandler*'s lead."[82]

The *Chandler* line of decisions is of potential significance in § 1983 actions. Although the Supreme Court has resolved that § 1983 claimants are not obligated to exhaust state administrative remedies,[83] they nevertheless may at their option choose to do so.[84] Then, too, in some instances a state or local agency may institute quasi-judicial administrative proceedings against a private party, such as a license revocation proceeding.[85] Whether the agency proceeding was instituted by the private party or by the government, the administrative findings may come within Rule 803(8)(C).

No reported § 1983 cases have been located, however, in which this evidentiary issue has arisen. This is presumably because quasi-judicial administrative findings may be entitled to preclusive effect in federal court § 1983 actions as a matter of administrative res judicata.[86] Although it has

---

479 U.S. 918 (1986); Fraley v. Rockwell Int'l Corp., 470 F. Supp. 1264 (S.D. Ohio 1979).

81. 425 U.S. 840, 863 n.39 (1976).
82. EMERGING PROBLEMS, *supra* note, at 236. *See also* WEINSTEIN & BERGER, *supra* note, § 803(8)[03]. *See, e.g.*, Lloyd v. American Export Lines, Inc., 580 F.2d 1179 (3d Cir.), *cert. denied*, 439 U.S. 969 (1978); United States v. School Dist. of Ferndale, 577 F.2d 1339 (6th Cir. 1978); Colston v. Pingree, 498 F. Supp. 327 (N.D. Fla. 1980).
83. Patsy v. Board of Regents, 457 U.S. 496 (1982). *See also* Felder v. Casey, 487 U.S. 131 (1988).
84. *See* SCHWARTZ & KIRKLIN, *supra* note, § 10.4.
85. *Id.* §§ 10.4, 14.9.
86. University of Tenn. v. Elliott, 478 U.S. 788 (1986). *See* SCHWARTZ & KIRKLIN, *supra* note, § 11.10. To be entitled to preclusive effect under Elliott, the agency must act in a quasi-judicial capacity and its findings must be entitled to preclusive effect under the state law of preclusion. *See* Nelson v. Jefferson County, 863 F.2d 18 (6th Cir. 1988), *cert. denied*, 493 U.S. 820 (1989).

been claimed in a large number of federal § 1983 actions that agency findings are entitled to preclusive effect, the issue has been uniformly handled as a straight issue of preclusion law, rather than as an evidentiary issue.[87]

There is authority that Rule 803(8)(C) does not cover rulemaking proceedings, an issue analyzed carefully in *United States v. American Telephone & Telegraph Co.*[88] In that antitrust action, the court was asked to determine the admissibility of several decisions of the Federal Communications Commission. The court reasoned that proceedings that are clearly rulemaking because they are directed at the regulation of future conduct "with any fact-finding at most incidental and used primarily for predictive purposes . . . [are] not addressed to past facts . . . and . . . therefore cannot result [in] factual findings under Rule 803(8)(C)."[89] Rulemaking is thus distinguished from proceedings that are clearly adjudicatory, "that is, an investigation into disputed past acts with a view to determining whether those acts meet certain legal standards, with any prospective element being incidental—which certainly could yield 803(8)(C) findings."[90]

The difficulty, however, was that most of the materials before the court involved a mixture of agency adjudication and rulemaking, so that it was not possible "to draw a hard-and-fast distinction between rulemaking and fact-oriented adjudication."[91] The court thus found it necessary to determine whether each agency decision was *predominantly* of a rulemaking or adjudicatory nature. An agency finding is not outside of Rule 803(8)(C) "merely because it resulted from a procedure containing rulemaking elements."[92] Although this issue can arise in § 1983 actions, no reported § 1983 decisions involving this issue have been located.

Several decisions hold that Rule 803(8)(C) does not cover judicial findings. In *Trustees of University of Pennsylvania v. Lexington Insurance Co.*,[93] the Third Circuit held that Rule 803(8)(C) is limited to administrative and executive findings and does not cover judicial findings. The court articulated several persuasive reasons to support this conclusion:

87. *See* cases cited in SCHWARTZ AND KIRKLIN, *supra* note, § 11.10 & 1996 Cum. Supp. No. 1.
88. 498 F. Supp. 353 (D. D.C. 1980).
89. *Id.* at 360-61.
90. *Id.* at 360 n.19.
91. *Id.* at 361.
92. *Id.* at 367.
93. 815 F.2d 890 (3d Cir. 1987).

> Rule 803(8)(C) specifically refers to factual findings resulting from 'an investigation made pursuant to authority granted by law,' and the advisory committee's note focuses specifically on the findings of officials and agencies within the executive branch. Neither the advisory note nor the leading treatises make even the remotest reference to judicial findings. . . . Furthermore, Rule 803(8)(C) requires the district court to determine if the 'source or other circumstances indicate lack of trustworthiness.' Because a trustworthiness evaluation might involve calling the author of the fact-finding or his staff members to permit parties to impeach their work, the need for judicial confidentiality makes judicial findings unsuitable for this scrutiny. Finally, the general rule is that judicial findings are inadmissible against a party not present in the prior litigation. . . .[94]

The Fourth Circuit has provided additional reasons to support the conclusion that Rule 803(8)(C) "applies to the findings of agencies and offices of the executive branch, but does not apply to the findings of judges."[95] Not only is a judge of a court of law not an investigator, but there is also the danger that judicial findings, if admitted as evidence, would likely be given undue weight by the jury, thereby creating a danger of unfair prejudice.[96]

---

94. *Id.* at 905. *Accord* Carter v. Burch, 34 F.3d 257 (4th Cir. 1994); United States v. Jones, 29 F.3d 1549 (11th Cir. 1994); Nipper v. Snipes, 7 F.3d 415 (4th Cir. 1993); Zenith Radio Corp. v. Matsushita Elec. Indus. Co., 505 F. Supp. 1125, 1184-86 (E.D. Pa. 1980). Contra La Marca v. Turner, 662 F. Supp. 647 (S.D. Fla. 1987) (§ 1983 action: grand jury presentment concerning prison conditions admitted under Rule 803(8)(C)). It has been observed that although:

    [i]t might *see*m odd that Rule 803(8)(C) does not appear to admit judge or jury findings, although it plainly allows admission of findings that are probably less reliable[,] . . . there is a good reason for excluding judge and jury findings from the coverage of the Rule: Whenever Rule 803(8)(C) allows findings to be admitted, it leaves an opposing party free to challenge the reliability of the findings. Were judge and jury verdicts to be similarly treated, judges and juries would be subject to much more attack than at present. *See, e.g.*, Rule 606(b).

    Saltzburg et al., *supra* note, at 1426.

95. Carter v. Burch, 34 F.3d 257, 265 (4th Cir. 1994). *Accord* Nipper v. Snipes, 7 F.3d 415 (4th Cir. 1993).
96. *Carter*, 34 F.3d at 265; *Nipper*, 7 F.3d at 417-18.

As with administrative findings, prior judicial findings have usually raised purely legal preclusion issues in federal court § 1983 actions rather than evidentiary questions.[97]

Findings of Fact, Opinions, and Conclusions

Rule 803(8)(C) refers to a public records setting for the "factual findings resulting from an investigation. . . . " Following the enactment of the Federal Rules of Evidence, a conflict developed in the circuit courts of appeals over whether Rule 803(8)(C) encompasses opinions and conclusions, so-called evaluative reports.[98] The U.S. Supreme Court resolved this conflict in *Beech Aircraft Corp. v. Rainey*[99] by unanimously ruling that investigatory reports that are otherwise admissible under Rule 803(8)(C) are not rendered inadmissible merely because they state a conclusion or opinion: "As long as the conclusion is based on a factual investigation and satisfies the Rule's trustworthiness requirement, it should be admissible along with other portions of the report."[100]

Beech Aircraft Corp. was a products liability suit that arose out of the crash of a naval training aircraft which took the lives of both pilots on board. Following the accident, an investigatory report was prepared by a lieutenant commander. The report "was organized into sections labeled 'finding of fact,' opinions,' and 'recommendations.'"[101] The critical issue was the admissibility of those parts of the report containing opinions—for example, that the most "probable cause of the accident was the pilots [sic] failure to maintain proper interval."[102] The Supreme Court held that the report was admissible under Rule 803(8)(C).

In reaching this result, the Court relied upon such traditional indicia of congressional intent as the rule's language, legislative history, structure, and purpose. The language of Rule 803(8)(C) does not state that "factual findings are admissible" but that investigative "*reports* . . . setting forth . . .

---

97. *See, e.g.*, Migra v. Board of Educ., 465 U.S. 75 (1984); Allen v. McCurry, 449 U.S. 90 (1980); Schwartz & Kirklin, *supra* note 27, ch. 11.
98. *See* Beech Aircraft Corp. v. Rainey, 488 U.S. 153, 161-62 (1988) (describing conflicting circuit court decisional law).
99. 488 U.S. 153 (1988).
100. *Id.* at 170.
101. *Id.* at 157.
102. *Id.* at 158.

factual findings" are admissible.[103] Under this literal reading of Rule 803(8)(C), an investigatory report containing findings of fact may be admissible and is not rendered inadmissible because it *also* contains opinions and conclusions. On the other hand, "the requirement that reports contain factual findings bars the admission of statements not based on factual investigation."[104]

The Supreme Court found the legislative history of Rule 803(8)(C) inconclusive because the House and Senate committees took directly opposite positions concerning evaluative reports and made no effort to reconcile them.[105] The advisory committee's note to the Rule, however, strongly supported the view that it encompasses "evaluative reports."[106]

Turning to the structure of the rules, the Court found several safeguards against unreliable reports containing opinions and conclusions. Rule 803(8)(C) itself has an escape clause for untrustworthy reports, and Rule 403 requires consideration of the report's probative value and danger of

---

103. *Id.* at 164 (emphasis in original).

104. *Id.* at 169. The Court in Beech Aircraft specifically rejected the argument that because the business record rule, FED. R. EVID. 803(6), specifically authorizes "opinions" and "diagnoses," while the Rule 803(8)(C) investigatory report exception does not, opinions are not within the scope of 803(8)(C). The advisory committee's note to 803(6) made clear that opinions were expressly included in Rule 803(6) primarily to insure that medical diagnoses would be covered under the business records rule. Beech Aircraft, 488 U.S. at 163 n.8.

> While opinions were rarely found in traditional "business records," the expansion of that category to encompass documents such as medical diagnoses and test results brought with it some uncertainty in earlier versions of the Rule as to whether diagnoses and the like were admissible. . . . Since that specific concern was not present in the context of Rule 803(8)(C), the absence of identical language should not be accorded much significance. *Id.*

105. *Id.* at 164-65 (quoting H.R. REP. NO. 650, 93rd Cong., 2d Sess. 14 (1973), reprinted in 1973 U.S.C.C.A.N. 7051, 7088 and S. REP. NO. 1277, 93rd Cong., 2d Sess. 18 (1974), reprinted in 1974 U.S.C.C.A.N. 7051, 7064).

106. Beech Aircraft, 488 U.S. at 166-67. The Supreme Court has "referred often" to the advisory committee's notes "in interpreting the Rules of evidence. . . ." Williamson v. United States, 114 S. Ct. 2431, 2442 (1994) (Kennedy, J., concurring) (citing Huddleston v. United States, 485 U.S. 681, 688 (1988); United States v. Owens, 484 U.S. 554, 562 (1988); Bourjaily v. United States, 483 U.S. 171, 179 n.2 (1987); United States v. Abel, 469 U.S. 45, 51 (1984)).

unfair prejudice.[107] The "ultimate safeguard" is the opponent's right to introduce evidence attacking the validity of the conclusions in the report.[108]

The Court in *Beech Aircraft* found that a broad reading of Rule 803(8)(C) was consistent with the liberal treatment the Federal Rules afford to lay and expert opinion testimony.[109] Additionally, interpreting the rule to encompass opinions and conclusions avoids the necessity to resolve conflicts over whether a particular statement in a report is a fact or an opinion, often a frustrating and elusive endeavor.[110]

The Fifth Circuit's decision in *McQuaig v. McCoy*[111] the year before *Beech Aircraft* was decided serves to illustrate the impact of *Beech Aircraft* in § 1983 actions. *McQuaig* grew out of the arrest of the plaintiffs, Jacque and Linda McQuaig, and a complaint filed with the state police by Jacque following his arrest. The state police department's internal affairs section conducted an investigation that culminated in a report describing the events surrounding the arrest. The report was based upon interviews with the McQuaigs, with a friend who was with them at the time of the arrest, and with arresting officer McCoy. The report concluded that "McCoy was capricious and prejudicial in his arrest of McQuaig, but they could not totally substantiate the allegation of 'false arrest' and therefore did not sustain it."[112] The Fifth Circuit ruled that because Rule 803(8)(C) is limited to factual findings, the district court properly admitted only the findings of fact in the report, not the evaluative conclusions or opinions. Under *Beech Aircraft*, however, this position is no longer valid.

The Supreme Court in *Beech Aircraft* stated that it was not resolving whether the Rule 803(8)(C) hearsay exception covers legal conclusions in an investigatory report.[113] The weight of authority is that it does not.[114] In a case described the following year, the Eleventh Circuit reasoned that

107. *See infra* notes 224-37 and accompanying text.
108. *Beech Aircraft*, 488 U.S. at 168.
109. *Id.* at 169. *See also* Daubert v. Merrell Dow Pharmaceuticals, 113 S. Ct. 2786, 2794 (1993) (citing *Beech Aircraft*).
110. *Beech Aircraft,* 488 U.S. at 169.
111. 806 F.2d 1298 (5th Cir. 1987).
112. *Id.* at 1300.
113. *Beech Aircraft,* 488 U.S. at 170 n.13.
114. *See* Hines v. Brandon Steel Decks, 886 F.2d 299 (11th Cir. 1989); In re Plywood Antitrust Litig., 655 F.2d 627 (5th Cir. 1981); Zenith Radio Corp. v. Matsushita Elec. Indus. Co., 505 F. Supp. 1125, 1184 (E.D. Pa. 1980), *rev'd*

"[l]egal conclusions are inadmissible because the jury would have no way of knowing whether the preparer of the report was cognizant of the requirements underlying the legal conclusion and, if not, whether the preparer might have a higher or lower standard than the law requires."[115] At the same time, however, the Eleventh Circuit cautioned that the line between "factual" and "legal" conclusions in this context, as in others, is often "amorphous."[116]

It is also unclear whether an investigatory report containing opinions or conclusions is admissible if it does not also contain findings of fact. The report in *Beech Aircraft* contained both findings of fact and opinions. Then, too, the language of Rule 803(8)(C) refers to investigatory reports "setting forth . . . factual findings. . . . " This would seem to support the position that to be admissible, the report must contain findings of fact. Likewise, the Court's opinion in *Beech Aircraft* states that "[a]s long as the conclusion is based on a factual investigation and satisfies the Rule's trustworthiness requirement, it should be admissible *along with other portions of the report*."[117] On the other hand, the Court in *Beech Aircraft* stated at one point that Rule 803(8)(C) "does not create a distinction between 'fact' and 'opinion' contained in such [investigatory] reports"[118] and, later, that "[o]ur

---

in part on other grounds, 723 F.2d 238 (3d Cir. 1983), *rev'd on other grounds*, 475 U.S. 574 (1986); 2 STRONG, *supra* note, § 296, at 290 n.8.

115. *Hines*, 886 F.2d at 303. *See also Musselman-Brown*, *supra* note, at 983 n.59 (legal conclusions are "outside an investigator's area of expertise and therefore untrustworthy").

116. *Hines*, 886 F.2d at 303. *See generally* Miller v. Fenton, 474 U.S. 104, 113 (1985) (federal habeas corpus; referring to difficulties in determining if issue is of law, fact, or mixed question of law and fact); Pullman-Standard v. Swint, 456 U.S. 273, 288 (1982) (appellate review; Supreme Court has not formulated a "rule or principle that will unerringly distinguish a factual finding from a legal conclusion").

117. *Beech Aircraft,* 488 U.S. at 170 (emphasis added). The Sixth Circuit's decision in Miller v. Field, 35 F.3d 1088 (6th Cir. 1994), a § 1983 action, appears to support a reading of *Beech Aircraft* that the report must contain certain findings of fact. In *Miller*, the court ruled that while *Beech Aircraft* sanctions the inclusion of evaluations and opinions, the "report must first be a set of 'factual findings.'" *Id.* at 1091 (quoting Bright v. Firestone Tire & Rubber Co., 756 F.2d 19, 22 (6th Cir. 1984)). For an analysis of Miller v. Field, *see infra* notes 126-43 and accompanying text.

118. *Beech Aircraft,* 488 U.S. at 164.

conclusion that neither the language of the Rule nor the intent of its framers calls for a distinction between 'fact' and 'opinion' is strengthened by the analytical difficulty of drawing such a line."[119] These statements in the Court's opinion arguably support the conclusion that fact-based opinions and conclusions may be admissible even if the report does not actually contain findings of fact. Under this reading of *Beech Aircraft*, the opinions and conclusions need only be fact-based.

Underlying Data

Another unresolved issue is whether the Rule 803(8)(C) hearsay exception is limited to the findings, opinions, and conclusions in investigatory reports, or whether it also encompasses the underlying data, information, and other materials relied upon by the agency. The prevailing view is that the 803(8)(C) exception covers only the findings, opinions, and conclusions, not the underlying data.[120] To hold otherwise would allow a great deal of otherwise unreliable inadmissible hearsay to come before the trier of fact.

There may, however, be some other basis for admitting the underlying data, such as another hearsay exception.[121] Some commentators have sug-

---

119. *Id.* at 168.

120. Miller v. Field, 35 F.3d 1088 (6th Cir. 1994) (§ 1983 action: bulk of reports consisted of inadmissible hearsay statements of the parties); Moss v. Ole S. Real Estate, 933 F.2d 1300, 1304-10 (5th Cir. 1991); Brown v. Sierra Nevada Memorial Miners Hosp., 849 F.2d 1186, 1190 (9th Cir. 1988) (assumption that agency's findings are trustworthy "has substantially diminished force when extended to the sources outside the investigative agency from which the agency culls the information for its report"); McClure v. Mexia Indep. Sch. Dist., 750 F.2d 396 (5th Cir. 1985) (while admission of EEOC finding of probable cause was proper, trial court erred in admitting the entire EEOC report, which contained various hearsay statements including newspaper articles); McKinnon v. Skil Corp., 638 F.2d 270 (1st Cir. 1981); John McShain, Inc. v. Cessna Aircraft Co., 563 F.2d 632 (3d Cir. 1977); Zenith Radio Corp. v. Matsushita Elec. Indus. Co., 505 F. Supp. 1125 (E.D. Pa. 1980); Fraley v. Rockwell Int'l Corp., 470 F. Supp. 1264 (S.D. Ohio 1979). *See contra In re Air Crash Disaster,* 586 F. Supp. 711 (E.D. Pa. 1984), *rev'd*, 769 F.2d 115 (3d Cir. 1985), *cert. denied*, 480 U.S. 941 (1987).

121. *See* Fraley v. Rockwell Int'l. Corp., 470 F. Supp. 1264 (S.D. Ohio 1979); WEISSENBERGER, *supra* note, § 803.44, at 433. It has been suggested that much of the underlying data will be admissible on this basis because of (1) the

gested that the underlying data should be admitted if it meets the Rule 703 standard for material or data upon which an expert opinion may be based, namely that it is "of a type reasonably relied upon by experts in the particular field in forming opinions," even though inadmissible in evidence.[122]

It is worth observing that Rule 703 does not authorize the actual admission of the data and materials underlying an expert opinion, but only establishes the permissible bases of expert opinions.[123] Finally, there is authority that even if the underlying data does not meet a specific hearsay exception it may be admitted, not for its truth, but to show that its existence provided the basis for the agency's findings and conclusions.[124] Regardless of which of these theories is invoked, the district court should, under Rule 403, carefully evaluate whether the probative value of the underlying data is substantially outweighed by its danger to create unfair prejudice or to confuse or mislead the trier of fact.[125]

The Sixth Circuit dealt with the underlying data, as well as other investigatory report issues, in a § 1983 case, *Miller v. Field*.[126] In that case, Miller alleged "that while incarcerated in a Michigan penal institution, he was raped by another inmate."[127] He claimed that the defendant prison officials were deliberately indifferent to his safety because they ignored threats of assault against him.

At issue on appeal was the propriety of the district court's admission, over the plaintiff's objections, of investigatory reports of the Michigan State Police of the rape charge. The first report "consisted of a short summary of interviews by the reporting [corrections] officer of four . . . inmates who,

---

Federal Rules of Evidence expansive definition of vicarious admissions, FED. R. EVID. 801(d)(2)(c)(d); and (2) the likelihood that some other hearsay exception will, in fact, apply, such as present sense impression, statements for purposes of medical diagnosis or treatment, or declarations against interest. *See* WEINSTEIN & BERGER, *supra* note, § 803(8)[03].

122. *See* GRAHAM, *supra* note, § 803.8, at 906. *See also* WEINSTEIN & BERGER, *supra* note, at 803-48.

123. *See* GRAHAM, *supra* note, § 703.1.

124. *See* Fowler v. Blue Bell, Inc., 737 F.2d 1007 (11th Cir. 1984); *In re* Japanese Elec. Prods. Antitrust Litig., 723 F.2d 238 (3d Cir. 1983), *rev'd on other grounds*, 475 U.S. 574 (1986).

125. *See infra* notes 224-37 and accompanying text.

126. 35 F.3d 1088 (6th Cir. 1994).

127. *Id.* at 1088.

Miller alleged, had witnessed the assault."[128] All four prisoners denied any knowledge of the assault. The second report summarized the plaintiff's version of the event, while the third summarized an interview with the prosecutor. According to the record, "It contained information that the alleged perpetrators . . . would not be charged . . . because of the 'lack of credibility of the victim' and because there was no evidence available to corroborate the victim's allegations."[129]

In an opinion taking an especially negative view of investigatory reports, the circuit court ruled that most of the reports should have been excluded on hearsay grounds, and that their admission was reversible error. The court's decision is based upon three analytically distinct, though related, grounds. First, the court, while acknowledging that investigatory reports admitted under Rule 803(8)(C) may contain opinions and evaluations, ruled that they must contain factual findings.[130] Furthermore, these factual findings must "be based upon the knowledge or observations of the preparer of the report."[131] The court relied in part upon the statement in the advisory committee's note to Rule 803(8)(C) that "[p]olice reports have generally been excluded *except to the extent to which they incorporate first-hand observations of the officer*."[132] Although some of the information in the reports was based upon personal knowledge, e.g., that certain interviews took place and that the local prosecutor elected not to press charges, most of the report was not "part of any factual finding made through first-hand observation."[133] "[T]he statements of the victim, the alleged assailants, and various witnesses . . . [and] statements by the prosecutor regarding reasons for not pursuing criminal charges . . . contained hearsay information, not facts observed by the preparer of the police report."[134]

This part of the court's analysis is seriously flawed. Investigations by their nature involve the gathering of information from numerous sources, including from third persons. Further, the statement in the advisory committee's note relied upon by the *Miller* court referred to the state of the

---

128. *Id.* at 1089.
129. *Id.*
130. *See supra* notes 117-119 and accompanying text.
131. *Miller*, 35 F.3d at 1091.
132. *Id.* at 1091 (emphasis in original).
133. *Id.*
134. *Id.*

decisional law *prior* to the adoption of the Federal Rules of Evidence; it was not an indication of how Rule 803(8)(C) should be interpreted. Unlike Rule 803(8)(B), which specifically refers to "matters observed pursuant to duty imposed by law[,]" subdivision (C) requires only that the report contain "factual findings resulting from an investigation. . . . " A requirement that the preparer of an investigatory report must have personal knowledge would come close to obliterating the efficacy of Rule 803(8)(C). The Rule 803(8)(C) hearsay exception contemplates that the findings will be based upon "multiple layers of hearsay. . . . "[135]

The *Miller* court, however, also couched its ruling in trustworthiness terms. It quoted *United States v. Paducah Towing Co.* for the proposition "that factual findings, which are based on inadmissible hearsay, are not admissible under Rule 803(8)(C) because the underlying information is untrustworthy."[136] This seems far too broad.

The critical issue under Rule 803(8)(C) is not whether the factual findings are based upon admissible evidence, but whether "the sources of information or other circumstances indicate lack of trustworthiness."[137] The fact that the findings are based in part, or even largely, upon inadmissible hearsay should not *automatically* lead to the conclusion that the findings are untrustworthy. Indeed, Rule 803(8)(C) presumes that governmental investigatory reports are trustworthy and places the burden upon the party opposing admission to show otherwise.[138]

The *Miller* court was on much firmer ground when it focused upon the actual contents of the reports. It found that the "bulk" of the reports did not contain findings, conclusions, or opinions, but was "largely a recitation of statements of other individuals that fall under no other exception to the hearsay rule."[139] The statements of the victim's alleged assailant, other witnesses, and the prosecutor were "hearsay within hearsay" that should not have been placed before the jury.[140] This conclusion seems correct. Rule

135. MUELLER & KIRKPATRICK, *supra* note, § 8.47, at 976. *See* Moss v. Ole S. Real Estate, 933 F.2d 1300 (5th Cir. 1991).

136. *Miller*, 35 F.3d at 1091 (quoting United States v. Paducah Towing Co., 692 F.2d 412, 420-21 (6th Cir. 1982)).

137. FED. R. EVID. 803(8)(C).

138. *See infra* note 144 and accompanying text.

139. *Miller*, 35 F.3d at 1092.

140. *Id.*

803(8)(C) authorizes the admission of investigatory reports containing "factual findings," not otherwise inadmissible underlying data.[141]

The circuit court in *Miller* concluded that "only those portions of the reports that constituted either factual findings resulting from the firsthand knowledge of the report's preparer or opinions and conclusions derived from those facts should have been admitted into evidence."[142] Because the reports were admitted for their truth, to show that the sexual assault did not occur but was fabricated,[143] the error was prejudicial, calling for a new trial. Although some of the circuit court's reasons for finding the bulk of reports inadmissible are highly questionable, the court's ruling, that Rule 803(8)(C) does not authorize the wholesale admission of all the inadmissible data and information underlying the findings and conclusions in an investigatory report, seems correct.

Trustworthiness

In the great majority of federal court § 1983 actions where admissibility of an investigatory report is at issue, the report's trustworthiness is the single most important issue. The Rule 803(8)(C) hearsay exception has an escape hatch: even if an investigatory report satisfies the rule's requisites that it contain "factual findings" resulting from an "investigation" carried out pursuant to legal authority, the district court may exclude it when "the sources of information or other circumstances indicate lack of trustworthiness."

However, because it is assumed that public officials perform their duties properly, investigatory reports encompassed within Rule 803(8)(C) are presumed to be trustworthy. The burden is thus placed upon the party opposing the admissibility of the report to demonstrate its lack of reliabil-

---

141. The court found that the report did not satisfy the Rule 803(24) residual exception because it did not provide "equivalent circumstantial guarantees of trustworthiness" as out-of-court statements that come within a specific exception. *Id.*

142. *Id.* at 1093.

143. The court distinguished its unpublished opinion in Roland v. Johnson, 933 F.2d 1009 (6th Cir. 1991), where the police reports were not introduced for their truth but to show that the prison official knew about threats of homosexual violence.

ity.[144] The advisory committee's note to Rule 803(8)(C) sets forth a "non-exclusive list of four factors"[145] that should be considered in evaluating the report's trustworthiness:

1. the timeliness of the investigation;
2. the special skills or experience of the official;
3. whether a hearing was held and the level at which conducted; and
4. possible motivation problems suggested by *Palmer v. Hoffman.*[146]

The federal courts, both generally and in § 1983 actions specifically, place heavy reliance upon these four methodological factors in evaluating the trustworthiness of investigatory reports.[147] This makes sense, not just because these are the factors specifically articulated in the advisory committee's note, but also because these factors are highly relevant in assessing trustworthiness.

The timeliness of the investigation is highly pertinent because investigations that take place relatively close in time to the incidents in question are generally more likely to produce reports of greater reliability.[148] The

---

144. For § 1983 examples, *see* Miller v. Field, 35 F.3d 1088, 1090 (6th Cir. 1994); Montiel v. City of Los Angeles, 2 F.3d 335 (9th Cir. 1993); Gentile v. County of Suffolk, 926 F.2d 142 (2d Cir. 1991); Perrin v. Anderson, 784 F.2d 1040 (10th Cir. 1986). *See also* Johnson v. City of Pleasanton, 982 F.2d 350 (9th Cir. 1992); United States v. Versaint, 849 F.2d 827 (3d Cir. 1988); Bradford Trust Co. of Boston v. Merrill, Lynch, Pierce, Fenner & Smith, 805 F.2d 49 (2d Cir. 1986); Ellis v. International Playtex, 745 F.2d 292 (4th Cir. 1984); *In re* Japanese Elecs. Prods. Antitrust Litig., 723 F.2d 238 (3d Cir. 1983), *rev'd on other grounds*, 475 U.S. 574 (1986); *In re* Paducah Towing Co., 692 F.2d 412 (6th Cir. 1982); Robbins v. Whelan, 653 F.2d 47 (1st Cir.), *cert. denied*, 454 U.S. 1123 (1981); Fed. R. Evid. 803(8)(C) advisory committee's note.

    Because Rule 803(8)(C) presumes trustworthiness, the district court need not make an *explicit* finding of trustworthiness. Air Disaster at Lockerbie, Scotland v. Pan American World Airways, 37 F.3d 804, 827-28 (2d Cir. 1994).

145. Beech Aircraft Corp. v. Rainey, 488 U.S. 153, 167 n.11 (1988).

146. Fed. R. Evid. 803(8)(C) advisory committee's note (citations omitted). The reference to Palmer v. Hoffman, 318 U.S. 109 (1943), is discussed later in the text. *See infra* notes 155-57 and accompanying text.

147. *See infra* notes 187-210 and accompanying text (§ 1983 applications).

148. For § 1983 examples, *see* Perrin v. Anderson, 784 F.2d 1040 (10th Cir. 1986) (report prepared approximately five weeks after incident in question; report admitted); Wilson v. Beebe, 743 F.2d 342 (6th Cir. 1984) (report prepared within one week after incident; report admitted), *vacated on other grounds,*

reason for this is rather apparent. As Judge Weinstein stated in a significant § 1983 decision, "It is important to interview witnesses before memories fade and to inspect physical evidence before it is affected by the passage of time or by tampering."[149] On the other hand, where "the report is the result of a study or particularly where . . . the investigators depend heavily upon documents, the passage of time does not appreciably detract from reliability."[150]

The importance of the special skills or experience of the investigators who conducted the investigation is also self-evident. This factor requires an inquiry into the background and experience of the investigators. For example, in finding that the report issued by the New York State Temporary Commission of Investigation concerning the Suffolk County Police Department and District Attorney's Office was reliable, Judge Weinstein relied upon the facts that the commission was chaired by a former U.S. attorney for the Eastern District of New York who was presently the dean of a law school, that the other five commissioners were lawyers, and that "[k]ey members of the staff were lawyers with extensive experience in criminal law enforcement."[151]

With respect to the procedures employed, Rule 803(8)(C) does not require that a public or other hearing be held. However, whether the agency conducted a hearing as part of its investigation is a pertinent consideration in evaluating the report's trustworthiness.[152] When a hearing is held, there is no requirement that it be adjudicatory in nature.[153] Because most investigations are carried out without an evidentiary hearing, "[r]equiring that the government report of an investigation be based on an evidentiary hearing

---

770 F.2d 578 (6th Cir. 1985). *See also* Anderson v. City of N.Y., 657 F. Supp. 1571, 1578-79 (S.D.N.Y. 1987) (unclear how to evaluate timeliness factor); *see infra* notes, 205.

149. Gentile v. County of Suffolk, 129 F.R.D. 435, 450 (E.D.N.Y. 1990), *aff'd,* 926 F.2d 142 (2d Cir. 1991).

150. *Id. See also* Ellis v. International Playtex, 745 F.2d 292, 303 (4th Cir. 1984).

151. *Gentile*, 129 F.R.D. at 452. *Cf.* Anderson v. City of N.Y., 657 F. Supp. 1571, 1579 (S.D.N.Y. 1987) (special skill or experience found "problematic").

152. *See In re* Japanese Elecs. Prods. Antitrust Litig., 723 F.2d 238 (3d Cir. 1983), *rev'd on other grounds*, 475 U.S. 574 (1989); Walker v. Fairchild Indus., 554 F. Supp. 650 (D. Nev. 1982).

153. *Gentile*, 129 F.R.D. at 455.

providing an opportunity for cross-examination would rob Rule 803(8)(C) of any practical utility."[154]

The advisory committee's citation to the Supreme Court's decision in *Palmer v. Hoffman*[155] suggests that the possible motivational problems it had in mind were primarily those stemming from reports prepared in anticipation of litigation. The *Palmer* decision, which upheld the exclusion of an accident report prepared by the train engineer, is best explained on the ground that the report was prepared with an eye toward litigation.[156] Because of this, the Second Circuit in *Palmer* had found that the engineer's report was "dripping with motivations to misrepresent."[157]

There may, however, be other types of motivational problems. In some cases courts have found that political bias or motivation was a significant factor in the evaluation of trustworthiness.[158] In a § 1983 action, *Anderson v. City of New York*,[159] the district court, in excluding a congressional subcommittee report on police misconduct as untrustworthy, found that "[o]bviously the 'witnesses' at these hearings were self-interested in their testimony" and that these types of legislative hearings and reports "are frequently marred by political expediency and grandstanding." In contrast, in finding the investigatory report of the New York State Temporary Commission of Investigation on police and prosecutorial misconduct to be trustworthy, Judge Weinstein in *Gentile v. County of Suffolk*[160] relied upon "[t]he nonpartisan make-up of the Commission."

---

154. *In re* Japanese Elecs. Prods., 723 F.2d at 268.
155. 318 U.S. 109 (1943).
156. 2 Strong, *supra* note, § 288; Fed. R. Evid. 803(6) advisory committee's note.
157. Hoffman v. Palmer, 129 F.2d 976, 991 (2d Cir. 1942), *aff'd*, 318 U.S. 109 (1943), quoted in Fed. R. Evid. 803(6) advisory's committee note.
158. *See* Baker v. Firestone Tire & Rubber Co., 793 F.2d 1196, 1199 (11th Cir. 1986) (report of congressional subcommittee concerning Firestone 500 tires excluded because it did not contain "factual findings necessary to an objective investigation, but consisted of the rather heated conclusions of a politically motivated hearing"); Anderson v. City of N.Y., 657 F. Supp. 1571, 1579 (S.D.N.Y. 1987) (witnesses at subcommittee on police misconduct were "self-interested in their testimony").
159. *Anderson*, 657 F. Supp. at 1579. *See also* discussion accompanying notes 202-06.
160. 129 F.R.D. 435, 457 (E.D.N.Y. 1990), *aff'd*, 926 F.2d 142 (2d Cir. 1991). Gentile is discussed in detail in the text below.

Bias can result for other reasons as well. In a prisoner excessive force case, *Lewis v. Velez*,[161] the district court excluded an investigatory report prepared by corrections officers as untrustworthy because it incorporated statements from the corrections officers involved in the incident. These officers were obviously biased because their jobs were at stake and because they faced potential civil and criminal liability.[162] Whatever the possible source of bias, ultimately the district court must determine whether the investigatory body had "[a] neutral and objective stance. . . . "[163]

Other Trustworthiness Factors

Although the four trustworthiness factors articulated in the advisory committee's note to Rule 803(8)(C) are the most significant ones, they are not the only pertinent considerations. The advisory committee recognized this and after describing the four factors "which may be of assistance" in evaluating trustworthiness, the committee acknowledged that "[o]thers no doubt could be added."[164]

In his district court decision in *Zenith Radio Corp. v. Matsushita Electrical Co.*,[165] Judge Becker extensively analyzed the trustworthiness issue and identified seven other pertinent factors in addition to the four articulated by the advisory committee: (1) the finality of the agency's findings and the likelihood of modification or reversal; (2) the extent to which the agency findings are based upon inadmissible or biased evidence; (3) if a hearing was held, the procedural safeguards utilized; (4) "[t]he extent to which there is an ascertainable record on which the findings are based";[166] (5) the extent to which the findings represent an attempt to implement agency or other governmental policy; (6) "[t]he extent to which the findings are

---

161. 149 F.R.D. 474 (S.D.N.Y. 1993).
162. *See infra* notes 207-210 and accompanying text.
163. MUELLER & KIRKPATRICK, *supra* note, § 850, at 991.
164. FED. R. EVID. 803(8)(C) advisory committee's note. *See also* Beech Aircraft Corp. v. Rainey, 488 U.S. 153, 167 n.11 (1988) (referring to the advisory committee's "nonexclusive list of four factors" for assessing trustworthiness); *In re* Japanese Elecs. Prods. Antitrust Litig., 723 F.2d 238 (3d Cir. 1983), *rev'd on other grounds,* 475 U.S. 574 (1986).
165. 505 F. Supp. 1125, 1147 (E.D. Pa. 1980), *rev'd in part on other grounds*, 723 F.2d 238 (3d Cir. 1983), *rev'd on other grounds*, 475 U.S. 574 (1986).
166. *Id.* at 1147.

based upon findings of another investigative body or tribunal which is itself vulnerable as the result of trustworthiness evaluation";[167] and (7) where the report contains an expert opinion, "the extent to which the facts or data upon which the opinion is based are of a type reasonably relied upon by experts in the particular field."[168] However, "[a]lthough there may be many reasons for finding a report untrustworthy, it is clear that the inability of the defense to cross-examine the author on the conclusions in the report is not a reason for the exclusion."[169]

Although on appeal the Third Circuit did not actually "endorse the seven [additional] specific criteria," it did not reject them and agreed that trial courts are not "restricted to the four factors listed by the Advisory Committee."[170] Furthermore, the circuit court made several important rulings concerning the trustworthiness evaluation: (1) The court agreed with the district court that the lack of cross-examination is not a reason for exclusion. Since "[m]ost governmental investigations proceed without either evidentiary hearings or the opportunity for cross-examination," a requirement that investigatory reports be based upon an "evidentiary hearing providing an opportunity for cross-examination would rob Rule 803(8)(C) of any practical utility."[171] The court stated that "[t]he indice of reliability for the governmental investigative report is the fact that it is prepared pursuant to a duty imposed by law."[172] (2) The fact that the author of the report was absent from the hearings and relied upon the reports of other officials did not make the findings unreliable because governmental officials often must

---

167. *Id.*

168. *Id. See also* Moss v. Ole S. Real Estate, 933 F.2d 1300 (5th Cir. 1991).

The seven additional Zenith Radio factors were endorsed in Escrow Disbursement Ins. Agency v. American Title and Ins. Co., 551 F. Supp. 302 (S.D. Fla. 1982). *But see* Masemer v. Delmarva Power & Light Co., 723 F. Supp. 1019, 1021 (D. Del. 1989) (declining to apply the seven additional factors).

169. Distaff, Inc. v. Springfield Contracting Corp., 984 F.2d 108, 112 (4th Cir. 1993). *But see* WEINSTEIN & BERGER, *supra* note, § 8.03(7)[01], at 803 - 256-257 (where trustworthiness of the report is problematical, trial court may exclude report unless the reporting officer is produced for cross-examination).

170. *In re* Japanese Elecs. Prods. Antitrust Litig., 723 F.2d 238, 265 (3d Cir. 1983), *rev'd on other grounds*, 475 U.S. 574 (1989).

171. *Id.* at 268.

172. *Id.*

rely upon staff reports of the hearings.[173] (3) The court held that "[i]f the government, in conducting investigations pursuant to authority granted by law, is authorized to rely and does rely on confidential submissions in making a finding, that fact does not so impugn the trustworthiness of the finding as to make it inadmissible."[174] (4) Rule 803(8)(C) encompasses "accusatory" investigatory proceedings, according to the Third Circuit.[175] (5) The fact that an investigatory finding is subject to possible judicial review "does not support an inference that the investigation was unreliable or the finding based upon it untrustworthy."[176] Finally, the Third Cicrcuit also ruled that (6) [a] *recommended* investigatory decision may be trustworthy, even if it is superseded by a consent decree.[177]

Of the seven additional trustworthiness factors identified by the district court in *Zenith Radio*, the federal courts have paid the most attention to "finality." The prevailing view is that, although lack of finality is a pertinent consideration in evaluating the trustworthiness of the report, finality is not an absolute requisite of admissibility.[178]

---

173. *Id.* ("In the real world of governmental affairs, investigations into economic facts . . . will frequently require that the expert to whom the agency entrusts the task of making a finding rely on facts not directly observed by him."). *Accord* Moss v. Ole S. Real Estate, 933 F.2d 1300 (5th Cir. 1991).
174. 723 F.2d at 270-71.
175. *Id.* at 273.
176. *Id.* at 268-69.
177. The court stated: "That the recommended decision was superseded by the Consent Decree is irrelevant, since the Consent Decree in no sense rejects the findings in the recommended decision. The recommended decision unquestionably is sufficiently trustworthy for admission under Rule 803(8)(C). The congruence between the Recommendation, the draft recommended decision and the Consent Decree is strong circumstantial evidence that the staff investigation was thorough." *Id.* at 274.
178. *See* Ellis v. International Playtex, Inc., 745 F.2d 292 (4th Cir. 1984) (tentative findings may be admissible); *In re* Japanese Elecs. Prods. Antitrust Litig., 723 F.2d 238 (3d Cir. 1983) (lack of finality did not render report untrustworthy), *rev'd on other grounds*, 475 U.S. 574 (1986); United States v. School Dist., 577 F.2d 1339 (6th Cir. 1978) (fact that agency proceeding was not complete did not mean report was not trustworthy); Gentile v. County of Suffolk, 129 F.R.D. 435, 458 (E.D.N.Y. 1990) (finality is not a *sine qua non* because "[i]n many instances non-final reports may be extremely useful and reliable as far as they go. But certainly finality is a consideration favoring admission."), *aff'd*, 926 F.2d 142 (2d Cir. 1991).

On the other hand, a number of decisions have relied upon the lack of finality to support the conclusion that either the report does not contain "factual findings" or that, even if it does, it is untrustworthy.[179] Lack of finality should be considered a pertinent, not dispositive, trustworthiness factor. The critical inquiry should be the impact of the lack of finality upon the report's trustworthiness. There are still other important trustworthiness considerations: whether the investigatory body acted with care and sound methodology, pursued all relevant leads, interviewed all pertinent witnesses, considered all relevant information, employed "checking procedures that might catch mistakes," and subjected evaluative reports to peer review.[180]

As the above discussion demonstrates, trustworthiness focuses upon the methodology of the investigation, not on whether the findings and conclusions are complete and accurate.[181] So long as the trial judge finds that reasonable jurors could accept the findings and conclusions in the report, it

---

The fact that judicial review is available "does not support an inference that the investigation was unreliable or the finding based upon it untrustworthy." *In re* Japanese Elecs. Prods., 723 F.2d at 268-69.

179. *See* Toole v. McClintock, 999 F.2d 1430, 1434-35 (11th Cir. 1993) (report containing only "proposed findings" not within Rule 803(8)(C): "Rule 803 makes no [hearsay] exception for tentative or interim reports subject to revision and review."); United States v. Gray, 852 F.2d 136, 139 (4th Cir. 1988) (district court did not abuse its discretion in excluding report that was "only a tentative internal report not purporting to contain agency factual findings"); Plemer v. Parsons-Gilbane, 713 F.2d 1127, 1140 (5th Cir. 1983) ("If the document is not sufficiently final, it may not constitute a 'factual finding,' or may be considered untrustworthy. . . . "); City of N.Y. v. Pullman, Inc., 662 F.2d 910, 914-15 (2d Cir. 1981) ("As an interim report subject to revision and review, the report did not satisfy the express requirement of the Rule that the proffered evidence must constitute the 'findings' of an agency or official." The report's "broad language did not embody the findings of an agency, but the tentative results of an incomplete staff investigation."), *cert. denied*, 454 U.S. 1164 (1982).

In Skorupski v. County of Suffolk, 652 F. Supp. 690 (E.D.N.Y. 1987), a § 1983 case, the court held a noncompleted report inadmissible on hearsay and relevance grounds. At the time of trial, the commission had compiled data and the investigation was still ongoing. "No specifics or results, however, have been provided by plaintiff regarding either the scope or focus of this investigation . . . and, at all events, such investigation is inadmissible hearsay evidence in this case." *Id.* at 695.

180. Mueller & Kirkpatrick, *supra* note, § 850, at 992-93.

181. Moss v. Ole S. Real Estate, 933 F.2d 1300 (5th Cir. 1991).

may not be excluded on the grounds that the findings and conclusions are incomplete, inaccurate, or not credible.[182] These issues go to the weight the trier of fact may give to the report.

Given the numerous factors that may affect the trustworthiness determination, it is understandable that the district courts have broad discretion in this regard.[183] Further discretionary power to admit or exclude is found in Rule 403.[184] The Fifth Circuit has cautioned, however, that "Rule 403 should not be misused in such a way that 'would end the presumption that evaluative reports are admissible hearsay under Rule 803(8)(C).'"[185] Trustworthiness determinations are generally reviewed on appeal under the deferential abuse of discretion standard.[186]

Applications in § 1983 Actions

The trustworthiness of investigatory reports has been at issue in several reported § 1983 decisions. These reports have been proffered in some cases on the issue of personal liability and in others on municipal liability. In some cases the plaintiff sought to introduce the report, and in others the defendant.

In *Wilson v. Beebe,*[187] the plaintiff alleged that while being handcuffed he was shot by State Trooper Beebe. The Sixth Circuit ruled that the district court did not commit error in allowing the plaintiff to introduce into

---

182. *Id.*

183. *See* City of N.Y. v. Pullman, Inc., 662 F.2d 910 (2d Cir. 1981), *cert. denied*, 454 U.S. 1164 (1982).

184. *See supra* notes 211-37 and accompanying text.

185. Cortes v. Maxus Exploration Co., 977 F.2d 195, 201 (5th Cir. 1992).

186. Gentile v. County of Suffolk, 926 F.2d 142 (2d Cir. 1991); Perrin v. Anderson, 784 F.2d 1040 (10th Cir. 1986); City of N.Y. v. Pullman, Inc., 662 F.2d 910 (2d Cir. 1981), *cert. denied*, 454 U.S. 1164 (1982). In *In re* Japanese Elecs. Prods. Antitrust Litig., 723 F.2d 238 (3d Cir. 1983), *rev'd on other grounds*, 475 U.S. 564 (1986), the circuit court refined the standard of appellate review over the trustworthiness determination: (1) when the trial court makes Rule 104(a) findings of fact about the manner in which the report was prepared, the clearly erroneous standard of Fed. R. Civ. P. 52 governs on appeal; (2) if the determination of untrustworthiness was predicated on factors that are extraneous to the trustworthiness determination, this is an error of law reviewed de novo. *See also* Moss v. Ole S. Real Estate, 933 F.2d 1300 (5th Cir. 1991).

187. 743 F.2d 342 (6th Cir. 1984), *vacated on other grounds,* 770 F.2d 578 (6th Cir. 1985) (*en banc*).

evidence an investigatory report prepared by Beebe's district commander, Captain MacGregor. The report detailed the events that led to the shooting and contained a statement by Captain MacGregor that Trooper Beebe, "by attempting to handcuff [the plaintiff] while holding a cocked weapon, acted contrary to department training in weapons use and handling."[188]

It is not difficult to understand why the plaintiff wanted to introduce this report. It was highly probative on the personal liability of Officer Beebe. Relying on the four factors set forth in the advisory committee's note to Rule 803(8)(C), the circuit court found that the report was sufficiently trustworthy. It was written by Captain MacGregor within one week of the incident; it was prepared for interdepartmental use; MacGregor was previously a firearms instructor in the police department and was thus familiar with its training procedures and policies; there were no motivational problems; and no evidence was "presented which impugned the memorandum's trustworthiness."[189]

In *Perrin v. Anderson*,[190] it was the defendant officers who introduced the investigatory report into evidence. The complaint in *Perrin* alleged that two members of the State Highway Patrol killed the deceased in violation of his constitutional rights. Following the incident, a board consisting of five members of the state police was convened under the auspices of the State Department of Public Safety to investigate the matter. The board, after interviewing the two defendant police officers and their superiors, issued a report finding that there was "no doubt that [Officer Anderson] acted within the guidelines set forth in the Policies and Procedures Manual."[191] The Tenth Circuit found that the district court did not abuse its discretion in allowing the defendants to introduce the report into evidence. The fact that the report was prepared pursuant to lawful authority helped to ensure its reliability.[192] Furthermore, it was found trustworthy because it was prepared approximately five weeks after the incident and by high-ranking officers; hearings, although not adversarial, were held; and there were no motivational problems. The court refused to assume that an internal investigation is necessarily biased, stating, "That an investigation was

---

188. *Id.* at 346.
189. *Id.* at 347.
190. 784 F.2d 1040 (10th Cir. 1986).
191. *Id.* at 1046.
192. *Id.*

conducted internally should affect the weight to be given the report, not its admissibility."[193] The plaintiff in *Perrin* failed to offer "convincing evidence" that the report was not trustworthy.

While the investigatory reports in *Wilson* and *Perrin* were relevant on the issue of the defendant officers' personal liability, findings and conclusions in investigatory reports have also been introduced on the issue of municipal liability. The leading case is *Gentile v. County of Suffolk*,[194] in which the plaintiffs sought relief against individual police officers and the county. The plaintiffs alleged that the Suffolk County Police Department and District Attorney's Office were refusing to seriously investigate police and prosecutorial misconduct. Judge Weinstein's district court opinion contains a comprehensive analysis of most of the evidentiary aspects of investigatory reports, including their trustworthiness.

Ultimately, the Second Circuit upheld Judge Weinstein's admission of portions of the Report of the New York State Temporary Commission of Investigation of the Suffolk County District Attorney's Office and Police Department, the so-called SIC Report. The report concluded that these offices tolerated and ratified police and prosecutorial misconduct. In finding the SIC Report trustworthy, Judge Weinstein considered the timeliness of the investigation; the special skills, experience, and expertise of the investigators; the procedures employed; the nonpartisan makeup of the commission, which belied charges of bias; and the report's finality. Significantly, Judge Weinstein found that, given the evidentiary difficulties in proving a municipal custom or practice, admitting the report furthered the policies of § 1983:

> Avoidance of undue delay is of particular importance in civil rights cases brought against municipalities under § 1983. Were reports such as the SIC Report to be excluded, plaintiffs would be forced to introduce proof of innumerable individual incidents of police and prosecutorial misconduct in order to show that a municipal practice, policy or custom existed. This would make it difficult, if not impossible, for many deserving plaintiffs to prevail, thereby frustrating federal civil rights policy. . . . [195]

---

193. *Id.* at 1047. Cautionary instructions were given in *Perrin*. *See infra* notes 231-237 and accompanying text.
194. 129 F.R.D. 435 (E.D.N.Y 1990), *aff'd*, 926 F.2d 142 (2d Cir. 1991).
195. *Gentile*, 129 F.R.D. at 459.

This is an important point deserving amplification. There are rarely factual issues when a municipal policy is embodied in a formally promulgated ordinance, regulation, or policy statement, or the final decision of a municipal policymaker.[196] By contrast, sharp factual issues are often present when the municipal liability claim is premised upon an alleged custom or practice. The parties may well find it necessary to conduct broad discovery and their own investigations. To prove a custom or practice, the plaintiff's counsel will normally find it necessary to weave together numerous individual pieces of circumstantial evidence, including the testimony of many witnesses.[197] This can, as Judge Weinstein observed, be very time-consuming and costly.

However, if the government carried out an investigation of a systemic problem and issued an investigatory report finding that the particular unlawful practice existed, the government may, in effect, have done the factual work-up for the plaintiff. The report, if admissible, may be highly probative proof of the alleged practice. In this context, it becomes a type of "large-size economy measure."

Of course, the defendants must be protected against unfair prejudice. In *Gentile*, Judge Weinstein developed procedures specifically designed to prevent unfair prejudice to the defendants. The entire report was not introduced. Rather, each side was allowed to select a few findings to *read* to the jury. By refusing to admit the report itself into evidence, the district court limited the possible unfair prejudice from its being "taken into the jury room where it might continue to speak."[198] Further, both the parties and the district court stressed in instructions that because the SIC Report did not contain any findings with respect to the individual officer defendants, it was relevant only with respect to the municipal liability claim against the county.

On appeal, the Second Circuit found that Judge Weinstein did not abuse his discretion in admitting the portions of the SIC Report.[199] The report was relevant on the question of municipal liability because, as the district court found, it "supports plaintiffs' allegation that the police and

---

196. The Supreme Court has resolved that whether an official is a municipal policymaker is a question of law for the court. Jett v. Dallas Indep. Sch. Dist., 491 U.S. 701, 739 (1989); City of St. Louis v. Praprotnik, 485 U.S. 112 (1988); Pembaur v. City of Cincinnati, 475 U.S. 469 (1986).

197. *See* Martin A. Schwartz, Section 1983 Litigation: Federal Evidence §§ 12.4-12.5 (2d ed. 1995).

198. *Gentile*, 129 F.R.D. at 461.

199. 926 F.2d 142 (2d Cir. 1991).

the District Attorney's Office were likely because of a course of conduct to consistently ignore evidence of misconduct on the part of the defendant officers and to sanction and cover up any wrongdoing connected with the . . . investigation [involving the plaintiffs]."[200] Furthermore, the circuit court ruled that Judge Weinstein did not abuse his discretion in finding the report to be trustworthy and in finding that the defendants did not meet their burden of showing otherwise.

The defendants in *Gentile* also challenged Judge Weinstein's procedures for determining the trustworthiness of the report. They argued that the district court erred in admitting the report at trial and delaying the hearing on trustworthiness until the post-trial stage.

The circuit court rejected this contention. Although it is true that Judge Weinstein delayed the hearing on trustworthiness until the post-trial stage, he had found the SIC Report to be trustworthy before admitting it. Further, the defendants' request for an earlier hearing, made on the third day of trial, was untimely. Given the fact that a party does not have a legal right to a hearing to resolve questions of admissibility of evidence, the post-trial hearing actually gave the defendants more process than they were entitled to when contesting the evidentiary issue. Although it is somewhat unusual to admit evidence at trial and hold a post-trial hearing on its admissibility, under the particular circumstances there was no abuse of discretion.[201]

It is instructive to contrast the finding of trustworthiness in *Gentile* with the finding of untrustworthiness in *Anderson v. City of New York*.[202] In

---

200. 129 F.R.D. at 446.

201. The circuit court in Gentile also found that Judge Weinstein properly distinguished Janetka v. Dabe, 892 F.2d 187 (2d Cir. 1989), a § 1983 case in which the circuit court upheld the exclusion of the same State Temporary Commission of Investigation report on the ground that the plaintiff there failed to show its relevance to the case at hand and, indeed, neither produced a copy of the report for the district court nor made an offer of proof of its relevant portions. *See infra* notes 219-220 and accompanying text.

In a post-Gentile case, Ricciuti v. New York City Transit Auth., 941 F.2d 119 (2d Cir. 1991), the Second Circuit suggested that the hearsay problem involving the admissibility of investigatory reports might be avoided if the report was not admitted for the truth of its contents, but only for the fact that the report was made, which could be relevant on the issue of whether the municipal policymakers were on notice of repeated failures to investigate charges of police use of excessive force.

202. 657 F. Supp. 1571 (S.D.N.Y. 1987).

Anderson, the plaintiff, a black male, alleged that officers of the New York City Police Department used excessive force ("physical violence") while arresting him. He alleged that this violence, "as well as the arrest and prosecution itself, were manifestations of a [city] policy of civil rights deprivations against racial minorities. . . ."[203] In support of his motion for summary judgment, the plaintiff sought to rely upon a congressional report titled Report on Hearings in New York City on Police Misconduct by the Subcommittee on Criminal Justice. The report was based on two public hearings at which testimony was given by civilians alleging police misconduct, police officers, former New York City mayor Koch, and by the City Police Commissioner. "The [R]eport, summarizing these hearings, is an indictment of a system seen as encouraging—through failures of supervision, training and discipline—a pattern of illegal arrest, harassment, foul language and racial slurs, and brutality, aimed at minorities by white police officers."[204]

The court found that the report was not sufficiently trustworthy to meet the Rule 803(8)(C) hearsay exception for investigatory reports. Its reliability was undercut by the facts that the subcommittee members lacked personal knowledge of the events about which the witnesses testified, and, moreover, the witnesses were "self-interested in their testimony."[205] The court was generally distrustful of legislative subcommittee reports, finding them "frequently marred by political expediency and grandstanding."[206]

In *Lewis v. Velez*,[207] a prisoner excessive force case, the federal district court ruled that an investigatory report of the incident in question

---

203. *Id.* at 1572.
204. *Id.* at 1577.
205. *Id.* at 1579. The court in Anderson found that the timeliness factor was unclear because, although plaintiff's arrest occurred in 1982 and the hearings took place in 1983 and covered the period 1979-1983, the "[s]ubcommittee did not investigate or examine, in a timely manner, reports regarding the instant set of facts and how, if at all, they are related to the alleged general policy of discrimination." *Id.*
206. *Id.* The court in Anderson quoted Knight Pub. Co. v. United States Dep't of Justice, 631 F. Supp. 1175, 1178 (W.D.N.C. 1986) ("[C]ongressional committee hearings are oft time[s] conducted in a circus atmosphere, with a gracious plenty of posturing by the politicians for T.V. publicity in large part for benefit of constituents back home. . . . This 'circus' is hardly conducive to the development of facts. . . .").
207. 149 F.R.D. 474 (S.D.N.Y. 1993).

that incorporated statements from the corrections officers involved was not trustworthy. The investigator, Captain Bryan, lacked any training in investigative skills. Furthermore, the corrections officers' jobs were on the line and they faced potential criminal and civil liability.[208] The court stated that "[a] strong likelihood of improper motivation . . . can outweigh all other trustworthiness factors."[209] Indeed, the court found that most cases in which investigatory reports have been excluded present suspicions of bias.[210]

A finding that a report is trustworthy does not mean that it is admissible because it still must clear other hurdles of admissibility, including the balancing test of Rule 403, exclusionary rules such as that provided for in Federal Rule of Evidence 407 for subsequent remedial measures, and governmental privilege. These issues are discussed in the following sections. Before doing so, however, it should be stressed that the trustworthiness issue is closely related to the Rule 403 evaluation because the greater the trustworthiness of the report, the higher its probative value, and the less likely it will mislead or cause unfair prejudice.

Rule 403—Relevance and Cautionary Instructions

Even if an investigatory report satisfies the Rule 803(8)(C) hearsay exception, it must still meet the test of relevance[211] and the Rule 403 balancing test.[212] Given the broad definition of relevance,[213] and the strong

---

208. The *Lewis* court observed that "[a] longstanding awareness that correction officers may be liable under § 1983 for inmate beatings has been found [by the Seventh Circuit] to warrant the assumption that 'at least some guards write their reports on such occurrences with that possibility in mind.'" *Id.* at 489 (quoting Bracey v. Herringa, 466 F.2d 702, 704 (7th Cir. 1972)).

209. *Id.*

210. *Id. But see* Clark v. Clabaugh, 20 F.3d 1290 (3d Cir. 1994) (bias of persons interviewed did not render report inherently biased).

211. Federal Rule of Evidence 401 defines "relevant evidence" as "evidence having any tendency to make the existence of any fact that is of consequence to the determination of the action more probable or less probable than it would be without the evidence." Under Rule 402, "[e]vidence which is not relevant is not admissible."

212. Federal Rule of Evidence 403 provides that "[a]lthough relevant, evidence may be excluded if its probative value is substantially outweighed by the danger of unfair prejudice, confusion of the issues, or misleading the jury, or

presumption of admissibility under Rule 403,[214] these normally are not significant obstacles. Nevertheless, there are § 1983 cases in which investigatory reports have been excluded both as irrelevant and on Rule 403 grounds.

For example, in *Kinan v. City of Brockton*,[215] the plaintiff asserted § 1983 claims arising out of his arrest against the city and several of its police officers. On appeal, the plaintiff argued that the district court erred in excluding an internal affairs investigatory report of the incident involving the plaintiff. Two years after the incident, Police Chief Cronin ordered an in-house investigation, which concluded that the police officers had acted appropriately and that there was no wrongdoing by the police department.

Although the plaintiff argued that the report tended to "prove a policy on part of the city of ratification of civil rights abuses by the police department,"[216] the circuit court failed to see its relevance under the particular circumstances. The court found it difficult to comprehend how a report finding no wrongdoing by the police would prove a city policy of ratification of civil rights abuses. Presumably this no-fault report would become evidence of condonation of improper police behavior if the jury found, contrary to the report, that the police officers had in fact violated plaintiff's civil rights. Since the jury did not make such a finding, if there was error, it was harmless.[217]

The circuit court also rejected the "convoluted reasoning" of plaintiff's second argument, namely that excluding the investigatory report prevented him from proving the police chief's responsibility, as a policymaker, for the alleged constitutional violation. Cronin was neither the chief of police at the time of the event in question nor a city policymaker. The circuit court failed "to see how an investigation ordered by [the police chief] two years after the incident concluding that there was no police misconduct would be evidence of [the chief's] liability as a policymaker."[218]

---

by considerations of undue delay, waste of time, or needless presentation of cumulative evidence."

213. Under Federal Rules of Evidence 401, it is enough that the evidence has "any tendency" to make a fact of consequence more or less probable.

214. *See* GRAHAM, *supra* note, § 403.1, at 175-76. Under Rule 403, evidence may be excluded only if its probative value is "substantially outweighed" by one or more of the countervailing factors. *See supra* note.

215. 876 F.2d 1029 (1st Cir. 1989).

216. *Id.* at 1035.

217. *Id.*

218. *Id.*

Thus, the First Circuit upheld the district court's exclusion of the investigatory report on relevance grounds.

The Second Circuit upheld the exclusion of an investigatory report on relevance grounds in *Janetka v. Dabe*.[219] In *Janetka*, the plaintiff alleged § 1983 claims based upon the use of excessive force during his arrest and malicious prosecution. He sued the arresting officer, Darrell Dabe, and the County of Suffolk. On appeal, he contested the district court's refusal to admit an investigatory report of the New York State Temporary Commission of Investigation, the SIC Report, which concluded "that Suffolk County tolerated and approved of misconduct by individual police officers."[220] The plaintiff argued that the district court erred in failing to consider the pertinent trustworthiness factors under Rule 803(8)(C).

The circuit court, however, found that the district court properly evaluated the relevance of the report before proceeding to the Rule 803(8)(C) hearsay issue and, furthermore, that the district court properly found that the plaintiff failed to establish the relevance of the report. The plaintiff did not even produce a copy of the report for the district court or make an offer of proof as to its relevant portions. He also failed to connect Officer Dabe's conduct to a policy or practice of Suffolk County.

It will be recalled that in *Gentile v. County of Suffolk*,[221] the Second Circuit upheld the district court's determination that the very same SIC Report was relevant. Unlike *Janetka*, however, the plaintiffs in *Gentile* produced a copy of the report and demonstrated its relevance on the issue of municipal liability. The district court in *Gentile* found that [n]ot only does the SIC report tend to establish the existence of a municipal policy or practice, but it also supports plaintiffs' allegation that the police and the District Attorney's Office were likely because of a course of conduct to consistently ignore evidence of misconduct on the part of the defendant officers and to sanction and cover up any wrongdoing connected with the [plaintiffs] Gentile and Rydstrom investigation.[222]

Defendants' argument that the SIC Report lacked probative value because it did not specifically deal with the *Gentile* and *Rydstrom* cases was without merit. The report was relevant because it tended "to support an

219. 892 F.2d 187 (2d Cir. 1989).
220. *Id.* at 190.
221. 129 F.R.D. 435 (E.D.N.Y. 1990), *aff'd*, 926 F.2d 142 (2d Cir. 1991).
222. *Id.* at 446.

inference of an affirmative link between municipal policy and the *type* of individual behavior involved here."[223]

An investigatory report that meets the requirements of the Rule 803(8)(C) hearsay exception and the test of relevance is still subject to possible exclusion under Rule 403 balancing. It must be kept in mind, however, that not only does Rule 403 strongly favor admissibility, but the Rule 803(8)(C) trustworthy determination is also pertinent to the Rule 403 evaluation because the greater the trustworthiness of the report, the higher its probative value and the lower the danger to mislead or cause unfair prejudice.[224] The Fifth Circuit has cautioned "that the balancing test of Rule 403 should not be misused in such a way that 'would end the presumption that evaluative reports are admissible hearsay under Rule 803(8)(C),'" that is, that they are presumed trustworthy.[225]

Nevertheless, there are § 1983 cases in which investigatory reports were excluded under Rule 403. For one thing, the availability of alternative modes of proof may affect the probative value of an investigatory report. For example, in *Swietlowich v. County of Bucks*,[226] a § 1983 arrestee suicide case, the complaint alleged that the police officers did not comply with their duty to periodically look in on prisoners. The district court excluded a district attorney's investigatory report of alterations of the cell check log, primarily because it doubted its trustworthiness.

The circuit court found that this ruling was not error, "particularly since most of the information that [the report] contained could have been obtained from witnesses who were present in court and who contributed to the investigation."[227] Although the circuit court did not cite to Rule 403, the existence of alternative evidence is plainly pertinent to the Rule 403 probative value evaluation, as well as to such 403 goals as preventing needless cumulative evidence and waste of time.[228]

Because of the official character of investigatory reports, courts must be sensitive about the potential for unfair prejudice to the party against

---

223. *Id.* at 447 (emphasis in original).

224. *See In re* Japanese Elecs. Prods. Antitrust Litig., 723 F.2d 238 (3d Cir. 1983), *rev'd on other grounds*, 475 U.S. 574 (1986).

225. Moss v. Ole S. Real Estate, Inc., 933 F.2d 1300, 1308 (5th Cir. 1991) (quoting Cortes v. Maxus Exploration Co., 977 F.2d 195, 201 (5th Cir. 1992)).

226. 610 F.2d 1157 (3d Cir. 1979).

227. *Id.* at 1165.

228. *See* GRAHAM, *supra* note, § 403.1.

whom it is introduced.[229] Steps can be taken to minimize such prejudice. As discussed earlier, in *Gentile v. County of Suffolk*,[230] Judge Weinstein refused to admit the entire investigatory report into evidence, but instead allowed the parties to read selected portions of it to the jury. Further, Judge Weinstein gave the jury detailed limiting instructions emphasizing that the excerpts "were to be viewed with caution and considered only with regard to the case against the municipal defendant provided the jury first found that the individual defendants had violated plaintiff's constitutional rights."[231] By refusing to admit the report itself into evidence, the court limited the possible unfair prejudice from the report being "taken into the jury room where it might continue to speak."[232] Ultimately, the district court found that, especially because of its importance on the issue of municipal liability, the SIC Report was admissible under Rule 403:

> The trustworthiness and probative value of the SIC report, considered in conjunction with the limiting instruction given by the court, other protections afforded defendants and the opportunity defendants were given to produce evidence in derogation of the report, adequately protected against the risk that the excerpts read to the jury may have had an unfair prejudicial effect. Rule 403 does not require the court to exclude the best available evidence supporting plaintiff's *Monell* claim.[233]

On appeal, the Second Circuit ruled that Judge Weinstein did not abuse his discretion under Rule 403.[234]

Cautionary instructions also played an important role under Rule 403 in *Perrin v. Anderson*.[235] There, the Tenth Circuit ruled that the

---

229. *See* Lindsay v. Ortho Pharmaceutical Corp., 637 F.2d 87 (2d Cir. 1980) (report excluded because of danger of unfair prejudice); Gentile v. County of Suffolk, 129 F.R.D. 435, 460 (E.D.N.Y. 1990), *aff'd*, 926 F.2d 142 (2d Cir. 1991). *See also* United States v. MacDonald, 688 F.2d 224 (4th Cir. 1982) (exclusion of report upheld because of potential jury confusion), *cert. denied*, 459 U.S. 1103 (1983).

230. 129 F.R.D. 435 (E.D.N.Y. 1990), *aff'd,* 926 F.2d 142 (2d Cir. 1991).

231. *Id.* at 437.

232. *Id.* at 461.

233. *Id.*

234. Gentile v. County of Suffolk, 926 F.2d 142 (2d Cir. 1991).

235. 784 F.2d 1040 (10th Cir. 1986).

district court did not err in allowing the defendants to introduce an internal investigatory report finding that the police officer's use of deadly force was within police department guidelines. The district court had instructed the jury that this investigatory report resulted from "an agency hearing of its own personnel and for its own purpose and was to have no 'determinative effect on any issue in the case.'"[236] The Tenth Circuit found that "this cautionary instruction mitigated any prejudice the report may have had."[237]

Applying the Rule 407 Exclusionary Rule for Subsequent Remedial Measures

Federal Rule of Evidence 407 codifies the common law exclusionary rule for remedial measures taken by an alleged wrongdoer following an injury-producing event when the evidence is offered on the issue of liability.[238] The advisory committee's note to Rule 407 articulates the twin rationales for this exclusionary rule.

First, there is the relevance concept that taking a remedial step does not constitute an admission of prior wrongdoing; it may simply grow out of the lessons of experience or a present desire for greater care. "Or, as Baron Bromwell put it, the rule rejects the notion that 'because the world gets wiser as it gets older therefore it was foolish before.'"[239] Second, the "more impressive" rationale for the rule is the important public policy "of

---

236. *Id.* at 1047.

237. *Id.*

238. Fed. R. Evid. 407 provides:

> When, after an event, measures are taken which, if taken previously, would have made the event less likely to occur, evidence of the subsequent measures is not admissible to prove negligence or culpable conduct in connection with the event. This rule does not require the exclusion of evidence of subsequent measures when offered for another purpose, such as proving ownership, control, or feasibility of precautionary measures, if controverted, or impeachment.
>
> *Id.*

239. As the advisory committee's note to Rule 407 recognizes, however, this nonrelevance rationale alone would not support the exclusionary rule because, under the liberal definition of relevance set forth in Federal Rule of Evidence 401, an inference of fault from the remedial action taken may be permissible.

encouraging people to take, or at least not discouraging them from taking, steps in furtherance of added safety."[240]

The advisory committee's note to Rule 407 provides examples of the types of remedial measures that may fall within the rule: "[s]ubsequent repairs, installation of safety devices, changes in company rules and discharge of employees. . . . " To this may be added, as circuit courts have recognized in § 1983 suits, changes in governmental policies and priorities, and the conducting of employee disciplinary proceedings.[241] The question arises whether a governmental investigation and an investigatory report constitute remedial measures within the meaning of Rule 407.[242]

---

240. FED. R. EVID. 407 advisory committee's note. Given the rationale of promoting remedial measures, it follows that the Rule 407 exclusionary rule should be limited to voluntary measures undertaken by the party charged with wrongdoing and that are undertaken *after* the injury-producing event. Thus, the exclusionary rule does not pertain to remedial measures *compelled* by governmental authority, for in these circumstances the policy of encouraging remedial measures has no role; one cannot be encouraged to do what one is already compelled to do. *In re* Aircrash in Bali, Indonesia, 871 F.2d 812, 816 (9th Cir.), *cert. denied*, 493 U.S. 917 (1989); Herndon v. Seven Bar Flying Serv., Inc., 716 F.2d 1322 (10th Cir. 1983), *cert. denied*, 466 U.S. 958 (1984); Rozier v. Ford Motor Co., 573 F.2d 1332 (5th Cir. 1978). Additionally, the rationale behind the exclusionary rule justifies its limitation to remedial measures undertaken by the party charged with wrongdoing, not by third persons. STRONG, *supra* note, § 267, at 201; WEINSTEIN & BERGER, *supra* note, § 407[a].

241. Specht v. Jensen, 863 F.2d 700 (10th Cir. 1988) (disciplinary action); Ford v. Schmidt, 577 F.2d 408 (7th Cir.) (modification of regulations), *cert. denied*, 439 U.S. 870 (1978).

242. Before proceeding to that issue, it should be pointed out that the Rule 407 exclusionary rule applies only when evidence of the remedial measure is used to show liability ("negligence or culpable conduct"). Rule 407 provides that exclusion of the evidence is not required when it is "offered for another purpose, such as proving ownership, control, or feasibility of precautionary measures, if controverted, or impeachment." The critical distinction, then, is between evidence of a subsequent remedial measure offered to show liability, which is within the exclusionary rule, and such evidence offered for some other relevant controverted purpose "such as" ownership or control, which is not. The use of the phrase "such as" shows that the listing of potentially permissible uses of remedial measure evidence is not exclusive, but illustrative of the recurring potentially permissible uses. *See* 2 STRONG, *supra* note, § 267, at 201. When used for a

This issue has arisen in a number of lower federal court decisions, including several § 1983 actions. The weight of authority draws an important distinction: although the investigation and investigatory report are not remedial measures within Rule 407 because they would not have made the event less likely to occur,[243] investigatory report references to remedial measures that were taken by the party charged with wrongdoing are within Rule 407.[244] If a report clears the rule against hearsay, Rule 403, and other admissibility hurdles, and is offered on the issue of liability, the portions referring to the remedial measures should be redacted.[245]

---

permissible "other purpose," a limiting instruction to that effect should be given. WEISSENBERGER, *supra* note 25, § 407.4, at 111.

Offering evidence of a remedial measure on a relevant issue other than liability, however, does not insure its admission into evidence. To be admitted, the issue in question, e.g., ownership or control, must be "controverted." Thus, a concession of the issue by the party against whom the evidence is sought to be introduced (normally the defendant) effectively shields the evidence from the trier of fact. FED. R. EVID. 407 advisory committee's note. Further, even evidence of a remedial measure that is offered for a controverted nonliability purpose is subject to possible evaluation under Rule 403. FED. R. EVID. 407 advisory committee's note.

243. Prentiss & Carlisle Co. v. Koehring-Waterous Div. of Timberjack, Inc., 972 F.2d 6 (1st Cir. 1992) (non-§ 1983 case); Benitez-Allende v. Alcan Aluminio do Brasil, 857 F.2d 26 (1st Cir. 1988) (non-§ 1983; diagnostic test report), *cert. denied*, 489 U.S. 1018 (1989); Rocky Mountain Helicopters, Inc. v. Bell Helicopters Textron, 805 F.2d 907 (10th Cir. 1986) (non-§ 1983); Wilson v. Beebe, 770 F.2d 578 (6th Cir. 1985) (§ 1983 action); Westmoreland v. CBS, 601 F. Supp. 66 (S.D.N.Y. 1984) (non-§ 1983). Contra Alimenta, Inc. v. Stauffer, 598 F. Supp. 934 (N.D. Ga. 1984) (non-§ 1983). *Cf. In re* Aircrash, 871 F.2d 812 (9th Cir. 1989) (report prepared by government without voluntary participation of party charged with wrongdoing not within Rule 407). Documents prepared under government compulsion are clearly outside the scope of Rule 407. *See* Rozier v. Ford Motor Co., 573 F.2d 1332 (5th Cir. 1978) (non-§ 1983).

244. O'Dell v. Hercules, Inc., 904 F.2d 1194 (8th Cir. 1990) (non-§ 1983); Maddox v. City of Los Angeles, 792 F.2d 1408 (9th Cir. 1986) (§ 1983 action); Masemer v. Delmarva Power & Light Co., 723 F. Supp. 1019 (D. Del. 1989) (non-§ 1983).

245. O'Dell v. Hercules, Inc., 904 F.2d 1194 (8th Cir. 1990) (non-§ 1983); Masemer v. Delmarva Power & Light Co., 723 F. Supp. 1019 (D. Del. 1989) (non-§ 1983). *See also* Rocky Mountain Helicopters v. Bell Helicopters Textron, 805 F.2d 907 (10th Cir. 1986).

The Tenth Circuit in *Rocky Mountain Helicopters v. Bell Helicopters Textron*[246] gave a cogent explanation about why investigations, studies, and reports are not themselves remedial measures under Rule 407. That diversity jurisdiction case arose out of a fatal helicopter accident. The case was brought against the manufacturer of the helicopter.

In rejecting the defendant's argument that the post-helicopter accident study was a remedial measure that should have been excluded, the circuit court stated:

> It would strain the spirit of the remedial measure prohibition in Rule 407 to extend its shield to evidence contained in post-event tests or reports. It might be possible in rare situations to characterize such reports as 'measures' which, if conducted previously, would reduce the likelihood of the occurrence. Yet it is usually sounder to recognize that such tests are conducted for the purpose of investigating the occurrence to discover what might have gone wrong or right. Remedial measures are those actions taken to remedy any flaws or failures indicated by the test. In this case, the remedial measure was not the Photoelastic Study of the trunnion [i.e., the part of the helicopter connecting the mast with the rotor blades] but rather the subsequent redesign of the trunnion. . . . [R]eferences to redesign were excluded at trial.
>
> We believe that the policy considerations that underlie Rule 407, such as encouraging remedial measures, are not as vigorously implicated where investigative tests and reports are concerned. To the extent that such policy concerns are implicated, they are outweighed by . . . the danger of depriving 'injured claimants of one of the best and most accurate sources of evidence and information.'[247]

---

246. 805 F.2d 907 (10th Cir. 1986).

247. *Id.* at 918-19 (quoting Westmoreland, 601 F. Supp. at 68 (S.D.N.Y. 1984)). *Accord* Fasanaro v. Mooney Aircraft Corp., 687 F. Supp. 482, 487 (N.D. Cal. 1988) (non-§ 1983: "the policy considerations underlying Rule 407 are to some extent implicated in the context of post-event tests, but . . . it would extend the Rule beyond its intended boundaries to include such tests within its ambit. Post-event tests will not, in themselves, result in added safety. Rather, it is only if the defects revealed in those tests are remedied and changes implemented that the goal of added safety will be furthered. By its terms Rule 407 includes only the actual remedial measures themselves and not the

The Tenth Circuit in *Rocky Mountain* thus concluded that the "correct procedure" is for the results of the report to be communicated to the trier of fact without reference to their "post-event time frame, unless one of the exceptions to Rule 407 applies."[248]

In *Wilson v. Beebe*,[249] the § 1983 case arising out of a state trooper's shooting of the plaintiff, the Sixth Circuit, sitting en banc, held that the district court did not commit error in admitting a memorandum written after the shooting by the trooper's district commander detailing the events leading to the shooting, and concluding that the trooper acted contrary to his training in attempting to handcuff the suspect while holding a cocked weapon. The court reasoned that "[t]he report was an official interoffice communication required by a standing departmental order" that met the hearsay exception for public records.[250] Defendants' argument that the report should have been excluded under Rule 407 had no merit because "[t]he report did not recommend a change in procedures following the shooting; it was a report of that incident and nothing more."[251] *Wilson*, then, is consistent with the philosophy expressed in *Rocky Mountain Helicopters*.

Not all courts, however, have taken cognizance of the distinction between the investigation and investigatory report on the one hand, and the

---

initial steps toward ascertaining whether any remedial measures are called for."). The court in *Westmoreland* rejected the argument that the internal network report should be excluded because its admission would discourage "honest self-examination and self-policing." *Westmoreland*, 601 F. Supp. at 67.

248. *Rocky Mountain*, 805 F.2d at 919.

249. 770 F.2d 578 (6th Cir. 1985) (*en banc*).

250. *Id.* at 590 (referring to FED. R. EVID. 803 (8)(A) and (C)).

251. *Wilson*, 770 F.2d at 590. *See also* Bergman v. Kemp, 97 F.R.D. 413 (W.D. Mich. 1983). In *Bergman*, the plaintiff alleged that the FBI had advance knowledge of a conspiracy to assault participants in a "Freedom Ride," but failed to prevent the resulting violence. Defendants sought to exclude evidence of a Task Force Report on the activities of the FBI. Defendants argued that the report was within the "critical self-evaluation privilege," but the court found that privilege largely undefined and, moreover, not generally recognized. *See infra* notes 290-300 and accompanying text. With respect to defendants' Rule 407 argument, the court found that the report was not a remedial measure because it was not "an indicia of a change that was made to make an event less likely to occur or to correct a previous condition," and did not cause any change in FBI procedures regarding the use of informants. *Bergman*, 97 F.R.D. at 418.

resulting remedial measures on the other. In *Maddox v. City of Los Angeles*,[252] a deadly force arrest case brought under § 1983, the Ninth Circuit ruled that the district court did not err in excluding the police officer's admission, during a post-incident departmental disciplinary proceeding, that he violated city policy regarding the use of chokeholds. The circuit court found that "[t]he Internal Affairs investigation and measures taken by the defendant City were remedial measures taken after the incident. Pursuant to Federal Rule of Evidence 403, evidence of these proceedings was therefore properly excluded with respect to the City's liability."[253]

This analysis is not only conclusory, but imprecise and partially erroneous. First, the circuit court failed to spell out the remedial "measures" taken by the city. This is an important point because Rule 407 does not exclude all post-event evidence, but only that of a remedial nature. However, even assuming that the measures were remedial, the court should not have lumped the "investigation," "disciplinary proceeding," and "remedial measures" together. An investigation by itself is not remedial action. The taking of disciplinary action may be a remedial action, as might other "measures" taken as a result of an investigation.

In *Specht v. Jensen*,[254] a § 1983 action alleging an unconstitutional search, the Tenth Circuit held that a press release summarizing the result of the city's investigation of the event in question, and stating "that the officers involved exercised poor judgment in failing to read the writ of assistance thoroughly, and that appropriate disciplinary action would be taken," was properly excluded under Rule 407.[255] The circuit court found that the release "sets out remedial measures taken by the City to prevent the recurrence of the poor judgment the investigation revealed, and is therefore within the ambit of Rule 407."[256]

While the decision in *Specht* suffers from the same conclusory and imprecise vices that plagued the decision in *Maddox*, especially the lump-

252. 792 F.2d 1408 (9th Cir. 1986).

253. *Id.* at 1417. *See also* Segura v. City of Reno, 116 F.R.D. 42 (D. Nev. 1987) (following *Maddox*: recognizing that the statements of the parties given during the investigation may be used for impeachment purposes, but the portion of the report concerning disciplinary recommendations had no impeachment value).

254. 863 F.2d 700 (10th Cir. 1988).

255. *Id.* at 701.

256. *Id.*

ing together of the investigation with the resulting remedial action, the court at least indicated that it understood the significance of the distinction. It did so by citing *Maddox* for the proposition that a disciplinary proceeding was an inadmissible remedial measure, and *Bell* for the proposition that even though an investigatory report may be admissible, resulting remedial measures should be excluded on the issue of liability under Rule 407.[257]

Governmental Privileges—Applications to Investigatory Reports

An evidentiary governmental privilege may pose a substantial obstacle to the admissibility of an investigatory report in a federal § 1983 action. Federal Rule of Evidence 501 provides that in federal question cases, the evidentiary privileges "shall be governed by the principles of the common law as they may be interpreted by the courts of the United States in light of reason and experience."[258] It is clear, then, that the federal common law governs the evidentiary privileges in § 1983 actions.[259]

---

257. *But see In re* Aircrash in Bali, Indonesia, 871 F.2d 812, 816 n.2 (9th Cir.) ("We need not address the issue of whether post-accident studies generally qualify as remedial measures under Rule 407."), *cert. denied*, 439 U.S. 917 (1989).

258. FED. R. EVID. 501 in its entirety states:

> Except as otherwise required by the Constitution of the United States or provided by Act of Congress or in rules prescribed by the Supreme Court pursuant to statutory authority, the privilege of a witness, person, government, State, or political subdivision thereof shall be governed by the principles of the common law as they may be interpreted by the courts of the United States in the light of reason and experience. However, in civil actions and proceedings, with respect to an element of a claim or defense as to which State law supplies the rule of decision, the privilege of a witness, person, government, State, or political subdivision thereof shall be determined in accordance with State law.

259. *See, e.g.*, Coughlin v. Lee, 946 F.2d 1152 (5th Cir. 1991); Slakan v. Porter, 737 F.2d 368 (4th Cir. 1984), *cert. denied*, 470 U.S. 1035 (1985); American Civil Liberties Union v. Finch, 638 F.2d 1336 (5th Cir. 1981); Socialist Workers Party v. Grubisic, 619 F.2d 641 (7th Cir. 1980). Where § 1983 and pendent state law claims are asserted, most courts have applied the federal law of privileges to both claims. *See* SCHWARTZ, *supra* note, § 7.4.

As with other evidentiary privileges, governmental privileges are litigated most frequently at the discovery stage. Federal Rule of Civil Procedure 26(b)(1) defines the scope of discovery as all matter "not privileged, which

There are a number of different governmental privileges.[260] The two with the greatest potential for affecting the admissibility of investigatory reports in § 1983 actions are the privileges for law enforcement investigatory materials and, to the limited extent it has been recognized, for critical self-evaluations.

Like governmental privileges generally,[261] the governmental privilege for law enforcement investigatory materials is qualified and requires a bal-

---

is relevant to the subject matter involved in the pending action. . . ." The privileges referred to in Rule 26 are the same privileges that are assertable at trial under the Federal Rules of Evidence. 8 CHARLES A. WRIGHT & ARTHUR R. MILLER, FEDERAL PRACTICE AND PROCEDURE § 2016, at 122 (1970). Therefore, decisions resolving privilege disputes at the discovery stage are relevant precedents for privilege issues arising at trial.

Because a large proportion of discovery disputes are referred by federal district court judges to federal magistrate judges, *see* 28 U.S.C. § 636(b)(1)(A) (1994) (power to refer pretrial matters), many discovery decisions are written by the magistrate judges. It is unclear whether these decisions are entitled to the same precedential weight as decisions of the district court judges. The writer believes that although it is true that federal magistrates do not enjoy life tenure and protection against diminution of salary, as the district judges do, the precedential weight of a federal trial court decision should depend upon the strength of the analysis, not whether the decision was written by a district court judge or by a magistrate judge.

260. The governmental privileges include privileges for law enforcement investigatory materials, grand jury materials, personnel records, deliberate process materials, the legislative process, and, to the limited extent to which it has been recognized, critical self-evaluations. *See* SCHWARTZ, *supra* note, ch. 8. Governmental privileges belong to the government, not to private individuals who convey information to governmental authorities. Walker v. Huie, 142 F.R.D. 497 (D. Utah 1992) (§ 1983 action).

Courts at times refer to a "governmental," "executive," or "official information" privilege, without specifying the specific governmental privilege at issue. This may occur at least in some cases because there is an overlap with respect to some of the governmental privileges. For example, investigatory materials most directly implicate the specific privilege for law enforcement investigatory materials, but may also implicate the privilege for personnel records or the critical self-evaluation privilege. The label attached to the privilege should not control. Rather, what is critical is the identification and application of the competing pertinent interests in favor of the privilege and of disclosure.

261. *See* STRONG, *supra* note, § 110.

ancing between the private litigant's need for the information and the government's interest in nondisclosure.[262] Two decisions that are especially important for evaluating the law enforcement privilege in § 1983 actions are Judge Becker's decision in *Frankenhauser v. Rizzo*[263] and Judge Weinstein's decision in *King v. Conde*.[264] The opinions of these two well-respected, scholarly jurists provide a detailed analytical framework for resolving claims of governmental privileges in § 1983 actions.[265]

In *Frankenhauser*, a § 1983 deadly force case, the court held that law enforcement investigatory reports are covered by a qualified privilege requiring a balancing between "the public interest in the confidentiality of governmental information against the needs of a litigant to obtain data, not otherwise available to him, with which to pursue a non-frivolous cause of action."[266] In balancing these competing interests, Judge Becker detailed the following ten pertinent considerations:

> (1) the extent to which disclosure will thwart governmental processes by discouraging citizens from giving the government information; (2) the impact upon persons who have given information of having their identities disclosed; (3) the degree to which governmental self-evaluation and consequent program improvement will be chilled by disclosure; (4) whether the information sought is factual data or evaluative summary; (5) whether the party seeking the discovery is an actual or potential defendant in any criminal proceeding either pending or reasonably likely to follow from

---

262. Mueller v. Walker, 124 F.R.D. 654 (D. Or. 1989); King v. Conde, 121 F.R.D. 180 (E.D.N.Y. 1988); Kelly v. City of San Jose, 114 F.R.D. 653 (N.D. Cal. 1987); Urseth v. City of Dayton, 110 F.R.D. 245 (S.D. Ohio 1986); Skibo v. City of N.Y., 109 F.R.D. 58 (E.D.N.Y. 1985); Tyner v. City of Jackson, 105 F.R.D. 564 (S.D. Miss. 1985); Spell v. McDaniel, 591 F. Supp. 1090 (E.D.N.C. 1984); Elliot v. Webb, 98 F.R.D. 293 (D. Idaho 1983); Sirmans v. City of S. Miami, 86 F.R.D. 492 (S.D. Fla. 1980); Crawford v. Dominic, 469 F. Supp. 260 (E.D. Pa. 1979); Diamond v. City of Mobile, 86 F.R.D. 324 (S.D. Ala. 1978); Frankenhauser v. Rizzo, 59 F.R.D. 339 (E.D. Pa. 1973). *See also* Emerging Problems, *supra* note, at 103-04.

263. 59 F.R.D. 339 (E.D. Pa. 1973).

264. 121 F.R.D. 180 (E.D.N.Y. 1988).

265. *See also* Magistrate Brazil's elaborate analysis in Kelly v. San Jose, 114 F.R.D. 653 (N.D. Cal. 1987).

266. *Frankenhauser,* 59 F.R.D. at 344.

> the incident in question; (6) whether the . . . investigation has been completed; (7) whether any intradepartmental disciplinary proceedings have arisen or may arise from the investigation; (8) whether the plaintiff's suit is non-frivolous and brought in good faith; (9) whether the information sought is available through other discovery or from other sources; and (10) the importance of the information sought to the plaintiff's case.[267]

Of these considerations, several courts have stated that the plaintiff's need for the information is the most important consideration.[268]

The ten *Frankenhauser* factors have been "widely followed"[269] by the lower federal courts. The decision in *King v. Conde*,[270] building upon *Frankenhauser*, contains an even fuller analysis of the issue. At issue in *King* was the discoverability of police officer personnel files, civilian complaint records, disciplinary actions, and external investigatory materials.

Judge Weinstein established a detailed procedural framework for evaluating claims of qualified governmental privilege.[271] He then proceeded to evaluate the various factors in balancing the competing governmental and

---

267. *Id.*
268. *See* Urseth v. Dayton, 110 F.R.D. 245 (S.D. Ohio 1986); Inmates of Unit 14 v. Rebideau, 102 F.R.D. 122 (N.D.N.Y. 1984); Crawford v. Dominic, 469 F. Supp. 260 (E.D. Pa. 1979).
269. Spell v. McDaniel, 591 F. Supp. 1090, 1116 (E.D.N.C. 1984). *See, e.g.*, Coughlin v. Lee, 946 F.2d 1152 (5th Cir. 1991); Everitt v. Brezzel, 750 F. Supp. 1063 (D. Colo. 1990); Mueller v. Walker, 124 F.R.D. 654 (D. Or. 1989); Scouler v. Craig, 116 F.R.D. 494 (D.N.J. 1987); Segura v. City of Reno, 116 F.R.D. 42 (D. Nev. 1987); Urseth v. City of Dayton, 110 F.R.D. 245 (S.D. Ohio 1986); Elliott v. Webb, 98 F.R.D. 293 (D. Idaho 1983); Crawford v. Dominic, 469 F. Supp. 260 (E.D. Pa. 1979).
270. 121 F.R.D. 180 (E.D.N.Y. 1988).
271. The procedures adopted included the following:
    1. The party invoking the privilege has the burden of justifying its application. *Id.* at 189.
    2. "The police must make a 'substantial threshold showing' . . . that there are specific harms likely to accrue from disclosure of specific materials. . . ." *Id.* (quoting Kelly v. San Jose, 114 F.R.D. 653, 669 (N.D. Cal. 1987)).
    3. This showing requires the police department to submit an affidavit from a responsible official with personal knowledge explaining in non-conclusory terms "how the materials at issue have been generated or collected; how they have been kept confidential; what specific interests

private interests. Finding *Frankenhauser's* mere listing of the factors insufficient, Judge Weinstein attempted to give guidance about the general importance of the pertinent factors. The factors favoring disclosure include the following: (1) the relevance and importance of the information to the plaintiff's case; (2) the strength of the plaintiff's case; (3) the availability of the information from other sources; and (4) the important public interest in § 1983 actions. The first two factors are self-evident, while the last two require some elaboration.

With respect to the availability of the information from other sources, Judge Weinstein stressed that the district court should consider not just the availability of alternative sources of information, but also its quality. It may be that the information in the police department files is of a better quality than the alternative sources.[272] Judge Weinstein recognized,[273] as have other courts, that the special public interest in § 1983 litigation is a highly important factor in favor of disclosure.[274] As a federal district court

---

(e.g., of the police officers, of law enforcement, or of public concern) would be injured by disclosure. . . . " *Id.*

4. Plaintiff must demonstrate "how the requested material is relevant [and] how the plaintiff or the public would be injured by nondisclosure. . . . " *Id.*
5. Consideration should be given to whether sensitive information, such as the officers' home addresses, should be deleted.
6. At the discovery stage consideration should also be given to the issuance of a protective order limiting disclosure to only the plaintiff and plaintiff's attorney, or perhaps solely to plaintiff's attorney. "Such an order can mitigate many if not all of the oft-alleged injuries to the police and to law enforcement." *Id.* at 190.

In addition, because disclosure of the contested information in open court can obviously thwart a claimed privilege, *in camera* review may be appropriate. The Supreme Court has stated that "*in camera* review is a highly appropriate and useful means of dealing with claims of governmental privilege." Kerr v. United States Dist. Court for the N. Dist. of Cal., 426 U.S. 394, 406 (1976). *See, e.g.*, Castle v. Jallah, 142 F.R.D. 618 (E.D. Va. 1992) (§ 1983 action).

272. *King,* 121 F.R.D. at 195.
273. *Id.*
274. *See* ACLU v. Finch, 638 F.2d 1336 (5th Cir. 1981); Kelly v. San Jose, 114 F.R.D. 653 (N.D. Cal. 1987); Elliot v. Webb, 98 F.R.D. 293 (D. Idaho 1983); Diamond v. City of Mobile, 86 F.R.D. 324 (S.D. Ala. 1978); Lora v. Board of Educ., 74 F.R.D. 565 (E.D.N.Y. 1977); Frankenhauser v. Rizzo, 59 F.R.D. 339 (E.D. Pa. 1973); Wood v. Breier, 54 F.R.D. 7 (E.D. Wis. 1972).

stated, because § 1983 "represents a balancing feature in our governmental structure whereby individual citizens are encouraged to police those who are charged with policing us all . . . , it is of special import that suits brought under this statute be resolved by a determination of the truth rather than by a determination that the truth shall remain hidden."[275]

There are, however, a number of potential governmental interests in favor of secrecy. Judge Weinstein identified: (1) threats to an officer's safety; (2) invasion of an officer's privacy; (3) weakening of law enforcement programs; (4) chilling police investigation candor; and (5) chilling civilian complaint candor. Although these may be entitled to some weight, upon careful analysis the governmental interest usually turns out to not be sufficiently strong to justify nondisclosure, or there exists an alternative remedy short of nondisclosure. Thus, where there is a threat to an officer's safety, the district court should give careful consideration to redacting personnel information such as the officer's home address.

Judge Weinstein found that personnel records, including discharges, normally do not implicate serious privacy concerns because the information is not highly personal. However, because information concerning an officer's psychiatric history is personal, it is necessary to weigh the officer's privacy interest against the litigant's need for this information.[276]

Judge Weinstein found that although police departments frequently assert that disclosure of personnel and investigatory files will inhibit the candor of police officers in furnishing information to the department, this "argument is probably often overstated. . . . "[277]

"First, the possibility of disclosure to civil rights plaintiffs is probably not of great import to the officers at the time they file their reports," the judge stated. "Second, there is no empirical evidence of which this court is aware supporting the 'chilling' contention."[278]

In fact, there is a strong probability that the fear of disclosure will increase rather than chill police candor.[279] And, although § 1983 defendants often assert that disclosure of law enforcement materials may chill civilian complaint candor, it is most likely that disclosure of internal mate-

---

275. *Breier,* 54 F.R.D. at 11.
276. *King*, 121 F.R.D. at 191-92.
277. *Id.* at 192.
278. *Id.*
279. *Id.* at 193 (citing Mercy v. County of Suffolk, 93 F.R.D. 520 (E.D.N.Y. 1992)).

rials will have no influence on the willingness of private citizens to make complaints.[280]

One governmental interest that Judge Weinstein found was entitled to considerable weight was the potential for weakening law enforcement programs. To the extent that the disclosure of police procedural guidelines reveals police tactics to sinister elements, it "could compromise the effectiveness of law enforcement. . . ."[281] This is especially so if the § 1983 claimant is, or is likely to be, a criminal defendant as a result of the same incident that gave rise to the § 1983 action.[282]

Some courts have held that the governmental interest is greater when the investigatory materials relate to an ongoing investigation rather than to a completed one.[283] One federal court, for example, stated that "there is no avowed public policy in barring disclosure of the contents of police investigatory files that no longer have any relation to any ongoing criminal litigation. . . ."[284]

Although the balancing of competing interests can at times be difficult, the admission of investigatory reports in § 1983 actions should rarely be completely barred by governmental privilege. The strong public interest in § 1983 actions generally weighs heavily in favor of a full airing of the relevant evidence.[285]

On the other side of the equation, municipalities normally do not have sufficiently weighty interests to justify keeping investigatory reports from the trier of fact. In *Mercy v. County of Suffolk*,[286] the district court decisively rejected the argument that police officers will be less candid if they know that investigatory reports are not privileged. The court stated:

> These investigations are conducted, at taxpayer expense, to determine whether the procedures of the department or individual police officers were responsible for the complained-of incident, and

---

280. *Id.* at 193-94.

281. *Id.* at 192.

282. Judge Weinstein suggested that consideration be given to either the issuance of a protective order or delaying the § 1983 action until the completion of the criminal prosecution, before denying discovery altogether. *Id.*

283. *See, e.g.*, Frankenhauser v. Rizzo, 59 F.R.D. 339, 343 (E.D. Pa. 1973).

284. Diamond v. City of Mobile, 86 F.R.D. 324, 329 (S.D. Ala. 1978).

285. *See* Wood v. Breier, 54 F.R.D. 7 (E.D. Wis. 1972).

286. 93 F.R.D. 520 (E.D.N.Y. 1982).

> whether disciplinary or other remedial action is necessary to prevent the recurrence of similar incidents. No legitimate purpose is served by conducting the investigations under a veil of near-total secrecy. Rather, knowledge that a limited number of persons, as well as a state or federal court, may examine the file in the event of civil litigation may serve to insure that these investigations are carried out in an even-handed fashion, that the statements are carefully and accurately taken, and that the true facts come to light, whether they reflect favorably or unfavorably on the individual police officers involved or on the department as a whole. The claim of executive privilege is therefore rejected.[287]

Governmental privilege is not the only privilege that may be asserted to keep investigatory materials from the trier of fact. Some defendants have asserted attorney-client and work product privileges, although usually without success.[288] For example, in *Mercy*, the court, in rejecting the attorney-client privilege, focused upon the fact that the pertinent communications were not between the police officers and their attorneys, but between the police officers and those charged with carrying out the investigation. Further, the investigatory reports were not the "work product" of an attorney because they were prepared pursuant to standard police practice and contained primarily factual accounts of what transpired; they did not contain counsel's legal theories or analysis.[289]

In some § 1983 cases, the defendants have asserted a self-evaluation privilege against the disclosure of investigatory reports. There is a conflict

---

287. *Id.* at 522.

288. Hoptowit v. Ray, 682 F.2d 1237 (9th Cir. 1982) (work product and attorney-client privileges rejected); Kelly v. San Jose, 114 F.R.D. 653 (N.D. Cal. 1987) (work product); Mercy v. County of Suffolk, 93 F.R.D. 520 (E.D.N.Y. 1982) (work product and attorney-client); Diamond v. City of Mobile, 86 F.R.D. 324 (S.D. Ala. 1978) (attorney-client); Frankenhauser v. Rizzo, 59 F.R.D. 339 (E.D. Pa. 1973) (attorney-client).

289. *See also* Hoptowit v. Ray, 682 F.2d 1237 (9th Cir. 1982). In *Hoptowit*, the circuit court, with little analysis, concluded that an investigatory report prepared at the direction of the State Attorney General's office for one of the defendants, the Secretary of the Department of Social and Health Services, was not within the work product or attorney-client privileges. The court observed that the report was written by non-lawyers, was not for the purposes of litigation, and was eventually made public.

in the lower federal courts over whether such a privilege exists. Some federal courts regard it as "'at the most . . . largely undefined and . . . not generally . . . recognized.'"[290] One district court called into question the very existence of such a privilege.[291] Although some lower federal courts have recognized that self-evaluation materials are shielded by a qualified privilege,[292] "[t]he [U.S.] Supreme Court and the circuit courts have neither definitively denied the existence of such a privilege, nor accepted it and defined its scope."[293]

Courts that have recognized the privilege seek to justify it on the basis of the public interest in bringing about evaluations that may lead to improved operations. For example, in *Skibo v. City of New York*,[294] a § 1983 excessive force case, the district court stated that "[t]he public has a strong interest in the police department's ability to investigate its personnel and improve its procedures." On the other hand, the court ruled that the privilege is not absolute and, in the case at hand, gave way to the plaintiff's need for the material. The court further found that:

> because the government has a vital interest in upholding the civil rights of the populace, impediments to judicial fact-finding in a § 1983 case are not favored. In addition, courts have declined to apply the privilege of self-critical analysis when the proponent of the privilege fails to show that the process would be curtailed if discovery is allowed. The police department needs to continue to monitor itself to ensure that department procedures are effective and that officers are complying with these procedures.[295]

---

290. Bergman v. Kemp, 97 F.R.D. 413, 416 (W.D. Mich. 1983) (quoting Lloyd v. Cessna Aircraft Co., 74 F.R.D. 518, 522 (E.D. Tenn. 1977)).
291. Robinson v. Magovern, 83 F.R.D. 79 (W.D. Pa. 1979).
292. *See, e.g., In re* Crazy Eddie Sec. Litig., 792 F. Supp. 197 (E.D.N.Y. 1992) (non-§ 1983 action); Urseth v. City of Dayton, 653 F. Supp. 1057 (S.D. Ohio 1986) (§ 1983 action); Skibo v. City of N.Y., 109 F.R.D. 58 (E.D.N.Y 1985) (§ 1983 action). The privilege was first recognized by the federal courts in Bredice v. Doctors Hosp., Inc., 50 F.R.D. 249 (D.D.C. 1970), *aff'd*, 479 F.2d 920 (D.C. Cir. 1973).
293. Dowling v. American Haw. Cruises, 971 F.2d 423, 425 n.1 (9th Cir. 1992).
294. 109 F.R.D. 58, 63 (E.D.N.Y. 1985).
295. *Id.* at 64 (citations omitted).

The court in *Urseth v. City of Dayton*,[296] however, gave more weight to the privilege. In that § 1983 deadly force case, the district court stated:

> In order to preserve this important vehicle for self-evaluation, participating police department supervisors must be allowed to engage in the type of free-flowing exchange of ideas which can lead to honest reflection and considered re-evaluation of past practices. Accordingly, firearms hearing transcripts and summaries like those at issue herein must *not*, as a general rule, be discoverable. Requests by plaintiffs for disclosure of such materials should be evaluated on a case-by-case basis to determine whether 'exceptional circumstances' in a particular case would warrant discovery of firearms hearings documents.[297]

Nevertheless, the court found that "exceptional circumstances" in fact warranted disclosure because the plaintiff demonstrated the relevance of the requested materials to the police chief's credibility and to the municipal liability claim, and showed that there had already been public disclosure of the firearms hearing. "As there has already been public disclosure of the Firearms Hearing . . . , the chilling effect which would accompany the disclosure of *these* documents is reduced."[298]

The Ninth Circuit in *Dowling v. American Hawaii Cruises*,[299] a Jones Act case, analyzed the critical self-evaluation privilege. Assuming, *arguendo*, that such a privilege exists, the court articulated four requirements that would have to be satisfied for the privilege to come into play:

> first, the information must result from a critical self-analysis undertaken by the party seeking protection; second, the public must have a strong interest in preserving the free flow of the type of information sought; finally, the information must be of the type whose flow would be curtailed if discovery were allowed. To these requirements should be added the general proviso that no document will be accorded a privilege unless it was prepared with the

---

296. 653 F. Supp. 1057 (S.D. Ohio 1986).
297. *Id.* at 1061 (emphasis in original).
298. *Id.* at 1062 (emphasis in original).
299. 971 F.2d 423 (9th Cir. 1992).

expectation that it would be kept confidential, and has in fact been kept confidential.[300]

Although the debate over the existence of a critical self-evaluation privilege may be of significance in other contexts, this is not the case as applied to the admissibility of investigatory reports on § 1983 actions. This is because the pertinent competing private and governmental interests are already considered under the qualified privilege for investigatory materials. Given the existence of this privilege in the § 1983 investigatory report context, a critical self-evaluation privilege seems to be superfluous.

Finally, investigatory reports containing the names of confidential informers may implicate the well-established qualified privilege for the identity of confidential informants.[301] In *Roviaro v. United States*,[302] the

---

300. *Id.* at 426 (citation omitted). Applying these standards, the circuit court in Dowling ruled that the privilege did not apply to voluntary, routine pre-accident corporate safety reviews. The court did not believe that these reviews would likely be curtailed if they were subject to disclosure, and did not expect that they are always "performed with the expectation that they will be kept confidential." *Id.* The court placed great weight on the voluntary nature of the safety review. "It may be unfair for a court to require a party to turn over to an opposing litigant self-damning assessments that the government has required it to prepare. But this concern obviously does not exist when the party has engaged in the self-evaluation voluntarily." *Id.* at 426-27 (citations omitted). The court also stressed that there is an important distinction between pre-accident safety reviews and post-accident investigations. This is because a "candid analysis" of the causes of an accident or other incident that has already occurred is more likely to be chilled by disclosure than routine pre-incident safety reviews. *Id.* at 427. Pre-incident reviews are designed to prevent accidents and thus avoid litigation. It is unlikely that this type of review will be inhibited by the fear that it might be disclosed in future hypothetical litigation. The same cannot be said about a post-incident review.

301. In Roviaro v. United States, 353 U.S. 53, 59 (1957), a criminal case, the U.S. Supreme Court defined the privilege as "the Government's privilege to withhold from disclosure the identity of persons who furnish information of violations of law to officers charged with enforcement of that law." Its purpose is to preserve the informer's anonymity so that citizens will be encouraged to communicate information concerning criminal activity to law enforcement officers. *Id. See also* Holman v. Cayce, 873 F.2d 944, 946 (6th Cir. 1989) (§ 1983 action). The privilege is strictly limited to the identity of the informant. Thus, the contents of the informant's communication are not privileged and may be disclosed, so long as the contents do not reveal the identity of the informant.

Supreme Court explained that in criminal cases the qualified nature of the privilege requires a balancing between the public interest in encouraging individuals to supply information of criminal wrongdoing to the government and the criminal defendant's need for the information to prepare a defense. This balancing must be based upon the particular circumstances of each case. In criminal cases, "[w]here the disclosure of an informer's identity or of the contents of his communication is relevant and helpful to the defense of an accused, or is essential to a fair determination of a cause, the privilege must give way."[303]

Roviaro's balancing of competing public and private interests has been extended to civil cases and applied by the federal courts in several § 1983 actions.[304] In civil cases, the critical issues are "whether disclosure is *essential* to the fair determination of a party's cause,"[305] and whether "the need for disclosure outweighs the need for secrecy."[306] The availability of alternative means of obtaining the information weighs against disclosure, as does the possibility of retaliation against the informant, "particularly where he is an employee of the target of the investigation, or has been assured by a law enforcement official that his identity will not be disclosed."[307]

Roviaro, 353 U.S. at 60; GRAHAM, *supra* note, § 510.1. The privilege belongs to and thus may be raised only by the government or its officials, and not by the informant. 2 STRONG, *supra* note, § 111; Proposed Federal Rules of Evidence 510(b). *See, e.g.*, Belfeuil v. Waushara County, 675 F. Supp. 459 (E.D. Wis. 1987) (County Board of Supervisors is proper party to invoke privilege).

302. 353 U.S. 53 (1957).

303. *Id.* at 60-61. The balancing should occur *in camera*. United States v. Straughter, 950 F.2d 1223 (6th Cir. 1991), *cert. denied*, 112 S.Ct. 1238, 1505, 1601 (1992).

304. Hoffman v. Reali, 973 F.2d 980 (1st Cir. 1992); Coughlin v. Lee, 946 F.2d 1152 (5th Cir. 1991); Holman v. Cayce, 873 F.2d 944 (6th Cir. 1989); Cullen v. Margiotta, 811 F.2d 698 (2d Cir.), *cert. denied*, 483 U.S. 1021 (1987); Ghandi v. Police Dept. of City of Detroit, 747 F.2d 338 (6th Cir. 1984); Hampton v. Hanrahan, 600 F.2d 600 (7th Cir. 1979), *rev'd* on other grounds, 446 U.S. 754 (1980); Michelson v. Daly, 590 F. Supp. 261 (N.D.N.Y. 1984). *See also* Bergman v. United States, 565 F. Supp. 1353 (W.D. Mich. 1983).

305. Holman v. Cayce, 873 F.2d 944, 946 (6th Cir. 1989) (emphasis added).

306. Cullen v. Margiotta, 811 F.2d 698, 715 (2d Cir.), *cert. denied*, 483 U.S. 1021 (1987).

307. *Cullen*, 811 F.2d at 716 (citations omitted). *See also* Ghandi v. Police Dept. of City of Detroit, 747 F.2d 338 (6th Cir. 1984); Michelson v. Daly, 590 F. Supp. 261 (N.D.N.Y. 1984).

The decisional law provides guidance as to how this balancing should be weighed. The privilege is stronger and more likely to be sustained in civil than in criminal cases because the stakes of the private civil litigant are normally not as high as those of the criminal defendant.[308] The Sixth Circuit in a § 1983 action ruled that where the informant was neither a witness nor an active participant in the conduct at issue in the civil case, it will normally be very difficult to overcome the privilege.[309]

On the other hand, the Seventh Circuit in a § 1983 action stated that "[t]he assertion of informer's privilege by a law enforcement official defending against a civil suit for damages based on his own alleged official misconduct should be scrutinized closely."[310] In civil cases, the district courts have especially broad discretion to determine whether or not to order disclosure of an informer's identity; denial of disclosure will be overturned only for an abuse of discretion resulting in substantial prejudice.[311]

Conclusion

Rule 803(8)(C) raises a broad array of important, contentious evidentiary issues. It authorizes the admission of governmental investigatory re-

---

308. *In re* Search of 1638 E. 2nd Street, 993 F.2d 773 (10th Cir. 1993); Hoffman v. Reali, 973 F.2d 980 (1st Cir. 1992); Holman v. Cayce, 873 F.2d 944, 946-47 (6th Cir. 1989); Michelson v. Daly, 590 F. Supp. 261, 264-265 (N.D.N.Y. 1984); 2 Weinstein & Berger, *supra* note, § 510[05]. For examples of § 1983 cases sustaining the privilege, *see* Hoffman v. Reali, 973 F.2d 980 (1st Cir. 1992); Holman v. Cayce, 873 F.2d 944 (6th Cir. 1989); Cullen v. Margiotta, 811 F.2d 698 (2d Cir.), *cert. denied*, 483 U.S. 1021 (1987); Ghandi v. Police Dept. of City of Detroit, 747 F.2d 338 (6th Cir. 1984); Michelson v. Daly, 590 F. Supp. 261 (N.D.N.Y. 1984). For examples of § 1983 cases requiring disclosure, *see* Hampton v. Hanrahan, 600 F.2d 600 (7th Cir. 1979), *rev'd on other grounds,* 446 U.S. 754 (1980); Belfeuil v. Waushara County, 675 F. Supp. 459 (E.D. Wis. 1987).
309. Holman v. Cayce, 873 F.2d 944, 947 (6th Cir. 1989). In these circumstances the party seeking disclosure bears the "formidable burden" of making "a compelling demonstration that the information sought from the informant is likely to influence the outcome of the case or is essential to the party's preparation for trial." *Id.*
310. Hampton v. Hanrahan, 600 F.2d 600, 638 (7th Cir. 1979), *rev'd on other grounds*, 446 U.S. 754 (1980).
311. *Cullen*, 811 F.2d at 716; *Ghandi*, 747 F.2d at 354.

ports even though the investigators, the preparers of the report, and the suppliers of information are not subject to cross-examination. At the same time, governmental investigatory reports may contain highly important information for § 1983 actions. Further, because they carry the imprimatur of government, they are likely to be given great weight by the jury. The most critical evidentiary issue in § 1983 actions, as in other contexts, is the report's trustworthiness. For if the report is trustworthy, there is a great likelihood that it will not only be found to fall within the Rule 803(8)(C) hearsay exception, but also will satisfy Rule 403 and overcome asserted governmental privileges. Investigatory reports found to be trustworthy are especially likely to be admitted in § 1983 actions because of the special public interest in § 1983 civil rights actions that all of the relevant, reliable evidence be considered by the trier of fact.

Chapter Thirteen
Attorney's Fees
John W. Witt

The concept that the loser of a lawsuit should pay the winner's attorney's fees is often proposed as a solution to the perceived problem of rising litigation volume and cost. The concept itself is nothing new. Civil rights litigation as an area in which "loser pays," at least in a form, is not at all unusual.

The purpose of fee-shifting mechanisms in the civil rights area, however, is to *encourage* lawsuits, hardly the objective of "loser pays" advocates. The Civil Rights Attorney's Fees Awards Act of 1976[1] (§ 1988(b)) is the most prominent of its type.

Are the attorney's fee awards authorized by § 1988 a means to allow pursuit of worthy civil rights claims that otherwise would never be filed? Or are they an incentive to the filing of large numbers of spurious claims? The debate has raged since § 1988(b) was enacted. The answer probably is that both points of view are correct. The availability of § 1988(b) attorney's fees *does* encourage the filing of meritorious claims that wouldn't otherwise see the light of day. It also seems to encourage claims that ought *not* see the light of day.

Although the legislative branch, through tort reform proposals, touches the question peripherally, the judiciary furnishes the arena in which the worthiness of individual claims is tested. In recent years, the courts have seemed more willing than in the past to trim excessive attorney's fee bills and to punish lawyers and their clients who file bad claims, either through awards of attorney's fees to defendants or by the imposition of some form of sanction.[2]

It is important to realize that while § 1988 is federal legislation, it flows to the states in two major ways. First, in most states § 1983[3] may be

---

1. 42 U.S.C. § 1988(b).
2. *E.g.*, Fed. R. Civ. Proc., Rule 11.
3. 42 U.S.C. § 1983.

pleaded as a cause of action in state court and with it comes § 1988(b). Second, many states have adopted civil rights fee-shifting statutes of their own, along the lines of § 1988(b).[4]

To understand the implications of § 1988, one needs to know something of the historical background of fee-shifting statutes in general and of § 1988(b) in particular. After that, it is helpful to review the specific terms of the statute and to explore in general how it works. That, in turn, leads to questions of who is entitled to fees under the Act, in what amount, and for what kind of professional work.

Historical Background

In England, since 1278, the courts have been permitted to award attorney's fees to successful plaintiffs.[5] Since 1607, that authority has been extended to successful defendants.[6] Thus, in England today, the losing party in civil litigation usually bears the winner's attorney's fees for bringing the case to trial and for trying it.

In the United States, the general rule is directly opposite to its English counterpart: Attorney's fees are not ordinarily recoverable in the absence of a statute or an enforceable contract providing that the loser pays.[7] Stating it slightly differently, the California Supreme Court said, "Ordinarily, fees paid to attorneys are not recoverable from the opposing party as costs, damages or otherwise, in the absence of express statutory or contractual authority."[8]

---

4. *E.g.*, Cal. Civ. Code, § 52, ¶ (a):

   Whoever denies, aids or incites a denial, or makes any discrimination or distinction contrary to [Civil Code] Section 51 or 51.5 [Unruh Civil Rights Act], is liable for each and every offense for the actual damages, and any amount that may be determined by a jury, or a court sitting without a jury, up to a maximum of three times the amount of actual damage but in no case less than one thousand dollars ($1,000), *and any attorney's fees that may be determined by the court in addition thereto*, suffered by any person denied the rights provided in Section 51 or 51.5. [Emphasis supplied.]

   See also Abrams v. Lightolier Inc., 50 F.3d 1204 (3d Cir., 1995), involving the fee-shifting provision in the New Jersey Law Against Discrimination (NJLAD), N.J.S.A. 10:5-1 *et seq.*
5. Statute of Gloucester, 1278, 6 Edw I, c 1.
6. Statute of Westminster, 1607, 4 Jac I, c 3.
7. Fleischman Distilling Corp. v. Maier Brewing Co., 386 U.S. 715, 717 (1967).
8. LeFave v. Diamond, 46 Cal.2d 868, 870, 299 P.2d 858 (1956). *See also* Sum-

Three exceptions to the American rule have emerged. First, attorney's fees may be authorized by statute.[9] Second, they may be awarded under the so-called "overriding considerations" exception, as expressed by the U.S. Supreme Court in *Hall v. Cole*:[10]

> Although the traditional American rule ordinarily disfavors the allowance of attorney's fees in the absence of statutory or contractual authorization, federal courts, in the exercise of their equitable powers, may award attorney's fees when the interests of justice so require. Indeed, the power to award such fees 'is part of the original authority of the chancellor to do equity in a particular situation,' [citation] and federal courts do not hesitate to exercise this inherent equitable power whenever '*overriding considerations* indicate the need for such recovery.'[11] [Emphasis supplied.]

Finally, clauses are found in many contracts providing, if there is litigation to enforce the contract, the loser will pay the "reasonable" attorney's fees of the winner.

In the early 1970s, several environmental citizens' groups sued the Secretary of the Interior to prevent issuance of permits for construction of the trans-Alaska pipeline. After they won in the District of Columbia Circuit, they applied for an award to reimburse them for their litigation expenses, including attorney's fees. The Court of Appeals granted the application and remanded the case to the District Court for the setting of attorney's fees.[12] On certiorari, the Supreme Court reversed, saying:

---

mit Valley Industries v. Local 112, United Brotherhood of Carpenters, 456 U.S. 717, 721 (1982); Ruckelshaus v. Sierra Club, 463 U.S. 680, 683-686 (1983); Jordan v. U.S. Dept. of Justice, 691 F.2d 514, 523, fn. 85 (D.C. Cir., 1982); Schneider v. Dumbarton Developers, Inc., 767 F.2d 1007, 1016 (D.C. Cir., 1985).

9. *E.g.*:

   In any action commenced pursuant to this title [42 U.S.C. §§ 2000a - 2000a-6], the court, in its discretion, may allow the prevailing party, other than the United States, a reasonable attorney's fee as part of the costs, and the United States shall be liable for costs the same as a private person.

   42 U.S.C. § 2000a-3(b).

10. 412 U.S. 1 (1973).
11. 412 U.S. at 4-5.
12. Wilderness Society v. Morton, 495 F.2d 1026 (D.C.Cir., 1974).

> In the United States, the prevailing litigant is ordinarily not entitled to collect a reasonable attorneys' fee from the loser. We are asked to fashion a far-reaching exception to the 'American Rule'; but having considered its origin and development, we are convinced that it would be inappropriate for the Judiciary, without legislative guidance, to reallocate the burdens of litigation in the manner and to the extent urged. . . .[13]

The Civil Rights Attorney's Fees Award Act of 1976

Congress reacted relatively swiftly. *Alyeska* was decided on May 12, 1975. Senator John Tunney (D-Calif.) introduced S.2278 on July 31 of the same year.[14] The legislative process was completed with the October 19, 1976, adoption of the bill, which established the Civil Rights Attorney's Fees Award Act of 1976. It provides:

> (b) In any action or proceeding to enforce a provision of sections [1981, 1982, 1983, 1985, and 1986 of this title], title IX of Public Law 92-318, the Religious Freedom Restoration Act or title VI of the Civil Rights Act of 1964, the court, in its discretion, may allow the prevailing party, other than the United States, a reasonable attorney's fee as part of the costs.[15]

The Act's purpose, simply put, is to encourage the filing of civil rights suits. As the Senate Report on the bill indicated, "If private citizens are to be able to assert their civil rights, and if those who violate the Nation's fundamental laws are not to proceed with impunity, then citizens must have the opportunity to recover what it costs to vindicate these rights in court."[16] Recognizing congressional motivation, the Fourth Circuit recently observed,

---

13. Alyeska Pipeline Service Co. v. Wilderness Society, 421 U.S. 240, 247 (1975). *See also* Runyon v. McCrary, 427 U.S. 160 (1976).
14. Senate Judiciary Committee, S. Rep. No. 1011, 94th Cong., 2d Sess. (to accompany S.2278), reprinted in [1976] U.S. Code Cong. & Ad. News 5908-5914.
15. P.L. 95-559 [S.2278], 90 Stats. 2641 (Oct. 19, 1976), as amended by P.L. 96-481, 94 Stats. 2330 (Oct. 21, 1980), codified as 42 U.S.C. § 1988.
16. Senate Report 1011, p. 2. *See also* Price v. Pelka, 690 F.2d 98, 101 (6th Cir., 1982); Dowdell v. City of Apopka, 698 F.2d 1181, 1189 (11th Cir., 1983).

> . . . the underlying purpose of section 1988, which must always guide the award of fees, is to ensure effective access to the judicial process for persons with civil rights grievances without simultaneously producing windfalls for attorneys.[17]

An application for an attorney's fee award brought pursuant to the Civil Rights Act of 1964,[18] rather than under § 1988(b), should be analyzed the same way as a § 1988(b) application.[19] The same applies to Section 2412(d)(1)(A)[20] of the Equal Access to Justice Act,[21] Section 1415(e)(4)(B)[22] of the Individuals with Disabilities Act,[23] and Section 1132(g)[24] of the Employee Retirement Income and Security Act.[25]

Entitlement to Fees

The threshold question in § 1988(b) attorney's fee analysis is whether there is a prevailing party entitled to fees. If there is no prevailing party, the analysis ends. But if there is, that person should be awarded fees unless "special circumstances" would make an award unjust, a condition courts rarely find to exist.

Sometimes it is argued that even though there is a prevailing party, he or she should not be awarded fees because of the party's situation or status[26] or because the work the prevailing party's attorney performed was

---

17. Trimper v. City of Norfolk, 58 F.3d 68, 73 (4th Cir., 1995).
18. Title VII, 42 U.S.C. § 2000e-5(k).
19. Scales v. J. C. Bradford & Co., 925 F.2d 901 (6th Cir., 1991); Lyte v. Lead Lee Corp., 950 F.2d 101 (2d Cir., 1991); E.E.O.C. v. Clear Lake Dodge, 25 F.3d 265 (5th Cir., 1994).
20. 42 U.S.C. § 2412(d)(1)(A).
21. Lundin v. Mecham, 980 F.2d 1450 (D.C. Cir., 1992).
22. 20 U.S.C. § 1415(e)(4)(B).
23. Borengasser v. Arkansas State Board of Education, 996 F.2d 196 (8th Cir., 1993). It might be argued that the Second Circuit recently applied Section 1988(b) analysis for consideration of a fee award made under Title VIII of the Civil Rights Act of 1968 (Fair Housing Act), 42 U.S.C., §§ 3601 *et seq.*, and its attorney's fee provision, 42 U.S.C., § 3612(p). Cabrera v. Jakabovitz, 24 F.3d 372 (2d Cir., 1994), *cert. den.* 130 L.Ed.2d 135 (1994).
24. 29 U.S.C. § 1132(g).
25. Kayes v. Pacific Lumber Co., 51 F.3d 1449 (9th Cir., 1995).
26. *See infra*, pp. 35-40.

insignificant or otherwise unworthy of an award. Like "special circumstances" findings, awards denied on these bases are rare indeed.

The first question raised by an application for attorney's fees under § 1988(b) is whether the applicant is a "prevailing party." Disputed identification of the prevailing party usually comes under five general fact categories: 1) The plaintiff has only been partially successful, winning on some of the claims and losing on others; 2) There has been a settlement and the defendant voluntarily has accepted a consent decree; 3) The defendant has mooted the lawsuit through a voluntary extrajudicial act; 4) The plaintiff's success has only been on intermediate or "interlocutory" issues, not the main issue itself; and 5) The defendant is the winner.

Success on *something* relating to a civil rights claim is an obvious and unstated prerequisite for prevailing party status. "Success" usually is measured in terms of some relief on the merits of the claim.[27] Arguments rage, however, on what success is and how much of it is necessary.

Partial Plaintiff Success

The U.S. Supreme Court held, in *Texas State Teachers Ass'n. v. Garland Independent School Dist.*,[28] that a plaintiff may be considered a prevailing party if he or she succeeds on *any* significant issue, even though some other claims may be disallowed.[29] Success is achievement of some of the benefit sought by plaintiff in bringing the lawsuit in the first place.[30]

The basic rule reflects the fact that litigation often ends without an overall plaintiff's or defendant's victory—in some sort of "split decision,"

27. Makah Indian Tribe v. Verity, 910 F.2d 555 (9th Cir., 1990); Libby by Libby v. Illinois High School Assn., 921 F.2d 96 (7th Cir., 1990); Hendrickson v. Branstad, 934 F.2d 158 (8th Cir., 1991); Slade v. U.S. Postal Service, 952 F.2d 357 (10th Cir., 1991); Martinez v. Wilson, 32 F.3d 1415 (9th Cir., 1994).
28. 489 U.S. 782 (1989).
29. Texas State Teachers Ass'n. v. Garland Independent School Dist., *supra*, fn. 28. *See also* Ruckelshaus v. Sierra Club, 463 U.S. 680 (1983); Hensley v. Eckerhart, 461 U.S. 424 (1983), citing Nadeau v. Helgemoe, 581 F.2d 275 (1st Cir., 1978).
30. Texas State Teachers Ass'n. v. Garland Independent School Dist., *supra*, fn. 28, 489 U.S. at 791-792. Stated differently: "The general definition of the term 'prevailing party' requires that the plaintiff succeed on a significant issue in the lawsuit which achieves at least some of the benefit sought in bringing the action." Leffler v. Meer, 60 F.3d 369, 372 (7th Cir., 1995).

as it were—or some other disposition short of trial and judgment. Therefore, it is not always easy to say that a party has prevailed, particularly when the plaintiff has lost on more claims than he or she has won or, whatever the victory, it is largely Pyrrhic, even though the litigation is clearly over. It can be said somewhat authoritatively, however, that a plaintiff which loses on the merits of its federal civil rights claim is not a prevailing party, even though it is successful on related pendent state law claims.[31]

Since enactment of § 1988(b), the courts have grappled with the situation of a less than completely victorious plaintiff.[32] The conclusion appears to be that before a plaintiff can be ruled as "prevailing," he or she must have received, as a result of the claim, some part of the benefit sought in making it.[33] The fact that the victory is only partial or that some of the claims have been lost goes, as most courts analyze it, to the *amount* of the fees to be awarded.[34]

Judicial analysis in attorney's fee award cases in which the plaintiff was not completely successful has been somewhat murky, to say the least, confusing (1) the prevailing party question with that of (2) entitlement to a fee award for particular professional work. Clear separation of the two issues at the outset appears preferable to a confusing jumble of both of them. In other words, once it has been determined that the plaintiff has prevailed on *any* claim and is entitled to some kind of fee award, the court should separately determine the amount.[35]

---

31. National Organization for Women v. Operation Rescue, 37 F.3d 646 (D.C. Cir., 1994).
32. The U.S. Supreme Court decision most often cited in situations involving less than completely successful plaintiffs is Hensley v. Eckerhart, *supra*, fn. 29. A reading of the Hensley decision leads to the conclusion, however, that the issue of concern to the Court in that case was the scope of the work for which a plaintiff was entitled to fees, after already having been determined to have been a successful "prevailing party."
33. Makah Indian Tribe v. Verity, *supra*, fn. 27; Libby by Libby v. Illinois High School Assn., *supra*, fn. 27.
34. *E.g.*, Hensley v. Eckerhart, *supra*, fn. 29.
35. A particularly inept example of how the analysis can be completely confused can be found in the Fourth Circuit decision in Rum Creek Coal Sales, Inc. v. Caperton, 31 F.3d 169 (4th Cir., 1994), where the Court became bogged down in an analysis of the appropriate amount of fees before it analyzed whether there was a prevailing party in the first place, even though the parties were agreed on the subject. 31 F.3d at 175.

Success on *some* claim should be the focus of prevailing party analysis.[36] What success *is*, however, stands in the eye of the beholder. It seems somewhat clear that there must be some actual benefit to the plaintiff in terms of either money damages or a change in defendant's conduct in some fashion.[37] Plaintiffs must win some alteration of their legal relationships with defendants.[38]

The question of whether a plaintiff is a prevailing party on winning only nominal damages (specifically $1) was before the U.S. Supreme Court in *Farrar v. Hobby*.[39] The Court held, ". . . a plaintiff who wins nominal damages is a prevailing party under § 1988."[40] It then turned to a *Hensley v. Eckerhart* analysis of the amount of the fee, concluding that where monetary relief, presumably as opposed to some equitable remedy, is sought, but only nominal damages are recovered, "the only reasonable fee is usually no fee at all."[41] Whether a plaintiff who is awarded only nominal damages is nevertheless entitled to attorney's fees depends on three factors: "[1] the difference between the judgment recovered and the recovery sought, [2] the significance of the legal issue on which the plaintiff prevailed, and finally [3] the public purpose served by the litigation."[42]

---

36. Fisher v. Vassar College, 70 F.3d 1420, 1453 (2d Cir., 1995), where the Court said,

    Only a 'prevailing party' may recover attorneys' fees and costs in a civil rights action. [Citation.] Our reversal of the district court on the merits of plaintiff's suit therefore would automatically require that we vacate the award of attorneys' fees and costs.

37. In deciding who is a prevailing party it is not necessary that a party actually receive some form of judicially ordered relief. . . . Nevertheless, there must be some actual benefit to the plaintiff in terms of either monetary damages, injunctive relief, or a voluntary change in a defendant's conduct.

    Woolridge v. Marlene Industries Corp., 898 F.2d 1169, 1173-1174 (6th Cir., 1990).

    See also Rhodes v. Stewart, 488 U.S. 1 (1988).

38. Higgs v. Bland, 888 F.2d 443 (6th Cir., 1989); Crabtree v. Collins, 900 F.2d 79 (6th Cir., 1990). A mere finding in plaintiff's favor, without a resulting order of some sort, does not render her a prevailing party entitled to attorney's fees. Walker v. Anderson Electrical Connectors, 944 F.2d 841 (11th Cir., 1991).
39. 506 U.S. 566 (1992).
40. 506 U.S. at ___ [121 L.Ed.2d at 504].
41. 506 U.S. at ___ [121 L.Ed.2d at 506]. *See also* Cramblit v. Fikse, 33 F.3d 633, 635 (6th Cir., 1994).
42. Maul v. Constan, 23 F.3d 143, 145 (7th Cir., 1994), citing Cartwright v. Stamper,

Settlement and Voluntary Acceptance of Consent Decree

The plaintiff may be a prevailing party even though there has been no judgment resulting from a trial, at least where defendant has agreed to a settlement and a stipulated consent decree.[43] The consent decree, itself, may not be needed.

If plaintiffs succeed on a significant issue as the result of an agreed settlement *or* a consent decree, they prevail and are entitled to an attorney's fee award.[44] In fact, it has been held that a plaintiff is a "prevailing party" for § 1988(b) purposes, even though his § 1983 lawsuit was terminated by a court-approved stipulation, without a consent decree, so long as the suit "prompted defendants to take action to satisfy his demands."[45] But it must be noted, for a party to a settlement to be considered a "prevailing party," the party must be legally entitled to and receive redress.[46]

---

7 F.3d 106, 109 (7th Cir., 1993). *See also* Cabrera v. Jakabovitz, *supra*, fn. 23; Koopman v. Water Dist. No. 1, 41 F.3d 1417 (10th Cir., 1994), *cert. den.* 133 L.Ed.2d 337 (1995); Wilcox v. City of Reno, 42 F.3d 550 (9th Cir., 1994); Caruso v. Forslund, 47 F.3d 27 (2d Cir., 1995); Romberg v. Nichols, 48 F.3d 453 (9th Cir., 1995), *cert. den.* 133 L.Ed.2d 453 (1995); Piper v. Oliver, 69 F.3d 875, 877 (8th Cir., 1995); Stivers v. Pierce, 71 F.3d 732 753 (9th Cir., 1995).

43. That civil rights litigation ends in a consent judgment does not preclude an attorney's fee award under § 1988. Consent judgments normally involve some element of compromise, of 'benefit' to both parties, but the legislative history indicates that Congress intended that a plaintiff who obtained its objective through a consent judgment could be a 'prevailing party' within the meaning of the statute.

    Bonnes v. Long, 559 F.2d 1316, 1318 (4th Cir., 1979).

    See also Maher v. Gagne, 448 U.S. 122 (1980); Knighton v. Watkins, 616 F.2d 795 (5th Cir., 1980); Charles v. Graham, 689 F.2d 774 (8th Cir., 1982); Johnston v. Jago, 691 F.2d 283 (6th Cir., 1982); Barlow-Gresham Union High School Dist. v. Mitchell, 940 F.2d 1280 (9th Cir., 1991); Dixon v. City of Chicago, 948 F.2d 355 (7th Cir., 1991); Lyte v. Lead Lee Corp., *supra*, fn. 19. For a contrary view, *see* Rehnquist dissent in Long v. Bonnes and Kenley v. Young, 455 U.S. 961 (1982), from denial of certiorari in Bonnes v. Long, 651 F.2d 214 (4th Cir., 1981), and Young v. Kenley, 641 F.2d 192 (4th Cir., 1981), citing Nadeau v. Helgemoe, *supra*, fn. 29.

44. Haskell v. Washington Township, 864 F.2d 1266 (6th Cir., 1988).
45. Sablan v. Dept. of Finance, 856 F.2d 1317, 1325 (9th Cir., 1988), citing Harris v. McCarthy, 790 F.2d 753, 759 (9th Cir. 1986).
46. Kissinger v. Board of Trustees, 5 F.3d 177 (6th Cir., 1993).

Plaintiffs who win everything they ask for are prevailing parties regardless of whether they would have won if the case had been tried on its merits.[47] And a plaintiff may be a prevailing party, when he entered a post-trial settlement under which he achieved one of the benefits he sought through litigation, even though the judgment in his favor is subsequently reversed.[48] But a prevailing party only "is entitled to attorney's fees through the date the parties agreed on the damages but not thereafter."[49]

A stipulated attorney's fee probably should be included in a normal settlement agreement in a § 1983 case to avoid the embarrassment of having to defend an award claim after the litigation is apparently over.[50] The court may reject the fees agreement, however.[51]

Voluntary Extrajudicial Act of Defendant

After a civil rights claim is pending, the defendant sometimes takes a step which moots the claim by giving the plaintiff the relief sought. The question then becomes whether the plaintiff's claim was the "catalyst" which caused the defendant's act. If so, plaintiff is a prevailing party for § 1988(b) attorney's fee purposes.[52]

---

47. Hill v. Richardson, 7 F.3d 656 (7th Cir., 1993).
48. Clark v. Township of Falls, 890 F.2d 625 (3d Cir., 1989).
49. Alliance to End Repression v. City of Chicago, 899 F.2d 582, 583 (7th Cir., 1990); Eirhart v. Libby-Owens-Ford Co., 996 F.2d 846 (7th Cir., 1993).
50. *See* White v. New Hampshire Dept. of Employment Security, 455 U.S. 445 (1982); El Club del Barrio v. United Community Corporations, Inc., 735 F.2d 98 (3d Cir., 1984). *See also* Bell v. Schexnayder, 36 F.3d 447, 450 (5th Cir., 1994); Valley Disposal, Inc. v. Central Vermont Solid Waste Management Dist., 71 F.3d 1053 (2d Cir., 1995).
51. *See* Jones v. Amalgamated Warbasse Houses, Inc., 721 F.2d 881 (2d Cir., 1983). *Also see* Evans v. Jeff D., 475 U.S. 717 (1986), with respect to a waiver of attorney's fees, *infra*, pp. 62-63.
52. When defendants moot the suit by voluntary compliance the question becomes whether the suit was the 'catalyst' that brought about compliance by the defendants; if it was, the plaintiffs are prevailing parties for attorney's fees award purposes, despite the fact that judicial relief may no longer be necessary.

    Williams v. Miller, 620 F.2d 199, 202 (8th Cir., 1980).

    See also Texas Teachers Ass'n. v. Garland Independent School Dist., *supra*, fn. 28; Ross v. Horn, 598 F.2d 1312 (3d Cir., 1979), *cert. den.* 448 U.S. 906 (1980); Williams v. Alioto, 625 F.2d 468 (9th Cir., 1980), *cert. den.* 450 U.S. 1012 (1981); Little Rock School Dist. v. Pulaski County Special School

In *Shipman v. Missouri Dept. of Family Services,*[53] defendant won a summary judgment because amendments to pertinent state statutes had rendered plaintiff's § 1983 lawsuit moot. The court held that for the plaintiff to be a prevailing party for § 1988(b) purposes, he must prove a causal link between his lawsuit and the amendments. Once that link has been established, the burden shifts to defendant to show that its conduct was completely gratuitous.[54] The defendant's voluntary conduct which moots plaintiff's claim must be required by the Constitution or by federal law.[55]

Where, while it is on appeal, a lawsuit is settled with some defendants but not all, and the relief sought is supplied through the settlement, plaintiffs have not prevailed against the remaining defendants and are not entitled to an attorney's fee award against them. Even though the remaining defendants subsequently take steps giving plaintiffs something they wanted in the first place, it is too late because the dismissal of the case on appeal pursuant to the settlement operates to vacate the judgment. "Catalyst theory," according to the Fourth Circuit in *S-1 and S-2 v. State Board of Education of North Carolina,*[56] is therefore no longer available to render the plaintiff a prevailing party for § 1988 purposes, at least under such facts.

Some authorities read *Farrar v. Hobby*[57] to eliminate the so-called "catalyst theory" altogether,[58] however. They take the position that *Farrar* requires, for qualification as a prevailing party, either an enforceable judgment or comparable relief through a consent decree or settlement. A voluntary act of compliance, they say, without something more formal in the way of a final disposition of the plaintiff's claim, simply will not do. The Second Circuit, in *Marbley v. Bane,*[59] disagrees and supplies a list of opin-

---

Dist., No. 1, 17 F.3d 260 (8th Cir., 1994). Hewitt v. Helms, 482 U.S. 755 (1987), is frequently cited in support of the "catalyst" rule, but the court ruled in that case that plaintiff's lawsuit was not the catalyst causing defendant's change of position.

53. 877 F.2d 678 (8th Cir., 1989).
54. Pembroke v. Wood County, 981 F.2d 225 (5th Cir., 1993).
55. Goichman v. City of Aspen, 859 F.2d 1466 (10th Cir., 1988); Banchy v. Republican Party of Hamilton County, 898 F.2d 1192 (6th Cir., 1990).
56. 21 F.3d 49 (4th Cir., 1994), *cert. den.* 130 L.Ed.2d 135 (1994).
57. *Supra*, fn. 39.
58. For a discussion of the effect of Farrar on catalyst theory, *see* Cullens v. Georgia Dept. of Transportation, 29 F.3d 1489, 1494-1495 (11th Cir., 1994).
59. 57 F.3d 224 (2d Cir., 1995).

ions from nine other circuits it claims agree with it.[60] The Seventh Circuit, in *Cady v. City of Chicago*,[61] puts the subject in some effective perspective:

> '[M]oral satisfaction' alone does not bestow 'prevailing party' status on a plaintiff. [Citations.] The plaintiff must be able to point to a 'material alteration of the legal relationship of the parties' [citations], and 'no material alteration of the legal relationship between the parties occurs until the plaintiff becomes entitled to enforce a judgment, consent decree, or settlement against the defendant [citation] or success in modifying the defendant's behavior to the plaintiff's direct advantage. . . . [62]

Plaintiff Success on Interlocutory Decision

When the plaintiff has prevailed on some preliminary issue, but has not been awarded a final judgment on the civil rights claim, he or she is not a prevailing party for § 1988(b) purposes.[63] For instance, where a plaintiff sought an "interim" attorney's fee award after defendant's motion to dismiss (on the ground that it was no longer taking enforcement action against the plaintiffs) had been denied, leaving plaintiff's claim pending, the denial of neither the motion to dismiss nor of the interim fee award application was a final order for § 1988(b) purposes.[64] A prevailing party is not entitled to a § 1988(b) attorney's fee award where it has lost its status as such by reason of a decision on appeal.[65]

---

60. 57 F.3d at 234. Most circuits have grappled with the question of the effect of Farrar on the catalyst theory. For a post-Farrar opinion that blissfully ignores the question, however, *see* Doty v. County of Lassen, 37 F.3d 540 (9th Cir., 1994).
61. 43 F.3d 326 (7th Cir., 1994).
62. 43 F.3d at 330.
63. Hewitt v. Helms, *supra*, fn. 52; Hanrahan v. Hampton, 446 U.S. 754 (1980); Thomas v. Stalter, 20 F.3d 298 (7th Cir., 1994); N.A.A.C.P., Detroit Branch v. Detroit Police Officers Assn., 46 F.3d 528 (6th Cir., 1995); American Jewish Congress v. City of Beverly Hills, 65 F.3d 1539 (9th Cir., 1995).
64. Ray v. The Florida Cabinet, 845 F.2d 311 (11th Cir., 1988); Nosik v. Singe, 40 F.3d 592 (2d Cir., 1994).
65. Triad Associates, Inc. v. Chicago Housing Auth., 892 F.2d 583 (7th Cir., 1989); Dombeck v. Milwaukee Valve Co., 40 F.3d 230 (7th Cir., 1994); New York State National Organization for Women v. Terry, 41 F.3d 794 (2d Cir., 1994).

Defendant as the Prevailing Party

When, at the end of the litigation, the defendant has won, in plain English it could be said he or she "prevailed." Indeed, the defendant can be the prevailing party for § 1988(b) attorney's fee award purposes, but only under certain limited circumstances. The U.S. Supreme Court puts it this way: "[A] district court may in its discretion award attorney's fees to a prevailing defendant . . . upon a finding that the plaintiff's action was *frivolous, unreasonable, or without foundation*, even though not brought in subjective bad faith."[66]

In other words, "a prevailing defendant should not routinely be awarded attorney's fees simply because he has succeeded, but rather only where the action is found to be 'unreasonable, frivolous, meritless, or vexatious.'"[67] The reason for more stringent restrictions on defendant's fees, as opposed to plaintiff's fees, is concern for "the potential chilling effect on section 1983 plaintiffs" that defendants' fee awards might have.[68]

A defendant must *prove* the plaintiff's action was frivolous, unreasonable, or without foundation. Such proof requires judicial determination, if not by full trial on the merits, at least through a summary judgment. If a plaintiff voluntarily withdraws the complaint, there is no evidence he or she did so to avoid an unfavorable judicial determination on the merits, and defendant has not even filed a summary judgment motion, defendant is not entitled to a fee award.[69] In any event, "[a]n award of attorney's fees to a prevailing defendant . . . necessarily requires specific factual findings . . . with respect to the basis for the award."[70]

If, after a civil rights complaint is filed, controlling cases are decided which doom the suit to failure, it cannot be deemed frivolous at the outset.[71] Presumably, plaintiff's persistence in forging ahead would be grounds

---

66. Christianburg Garment Co. v. E.E.O.C., 434 U.S. 412, 421 (1978) [emphasis supplied].
67. Vernon v. City of Los Angeles, 27 F.3d 1385, 1402 (9th Cir., 1994), citing Roberts v. Spaulding, 783 F.2d 867 (9th Cir., 1986), *cert. den*. 479 U.S. 930 (1986).
68. Rounseville v. Zahl, 13 F.3d 625, 632 (2d Cir., 1994).
69. Marquart v. Lodge 827, International Ass'n. of Machinists & Aerospace Workers, 26 F.3d 842 (8th Cir., 1994).
70. Brooks v. Center Park Associates, 33 F.3d 585, 587 (6th Cir., 1994).
71. E.E.O.C. v. Elgin Teachers Ass'n., 27 F.3d 292 (7th Cir., 1994).

for an attorney's fee award to defendant for work undertaken after the controlling cases were handed down. Lack of success on appeal, standing alone, at least, does not imply that the plaintiff's position was "unreasonable" in the first place, however.[72]

To recover attorney's fees on a plaintiff's appeal, defendant must show the appeal was frivolous[73] and justification for the fee award must be clear on the record.[74] But a defendant awarded § 1988 attorney's fees is entitled to reimbursement for cost incurred in collecting the fee award.[75]

In *Fogerty v. Fantasy, Inc.*,[76] the Supreme Court ruled that the "dual standard" applied to defendants, as opposed to plaintiffs, in fee-shifting cases does not apply to Section 505 of the Copyright Act.[77] Rather, the same standard—award of fees to the prevailing party more or less as a matter of course—applies to defendants as well as plaintiffs. The *Fogerty* opinion clearly limits its application to the Copyright Act, however, and distinguishes fee-shifting statutes in civil rights legislation. So far, there is no further indication that *Fogerty* is any kind of a precursor of a general softening of the rules on defendant's attorney's fees.

Although plaintiff's case is pleaded strongly enough to survive defendant's early motion to dismiss, that does not mean it is not, in the final analysis, frivolous, unreasonable or without foundation and subject to an attorney's fee award to defendant.[78] Where a complaint, "well dressed with contractual and constitutional verbiage and adorned with a multitude of factual minutiae," is "form without substance" and is dismissed for failure to comply with discovery orders, the trial court must explain its determination not to award defendant's attorney's fees.[79]

---

72. E.E.O.C. v. Elgin Teachers Ass'n., *supra*, fn. 71.
73. Vukadinovich v. McCarthy, 59 F.3d 58 (7th Cir., 1995).
74. Casa Marie Hogar Geriatrico v. Rivera-Santos, 38 F.3d 615 (1st Cir., 1994).
75. Vukadinovich v. McCarthy, *supra*, fn. 73.
76. 510 U.S. 517 [127 L.Ed.2d 455] (1994).
77. 17 U.S.C. § 505.
78. Introcaso v. Cunningham, 857 F.2d 965 (4th Cir., 1988); O'Neal v. DeKalb County, 850 F.2d 653 (11th Cir., 1988); Mitchell v. Los Angeles Community College Dist., 861 F.2d 198 (9th Cir., 1988); Grant v. Farnsworth, 869 F.2d 1149 (8th Cir., 1989).
79. Metrocorps v. Eastern Massachusetts Jr. Drum & Bugle Corps, 912 F.2d 1 (1st Cir., 1990).

A legally groundless assertion by plaintiff of a constitutional claim based knowingly on a nonexistent property interest is frivolous as a matter of law, and defendants are entitled to § 1988 attorney's fees.[80] Pursuing a lawsuit knowing defendants are immune from suit is "unreasonable, frivolous, meritless, and vexatious," justifying an attorney's fee award to defendants.[81] Where a plaintiff should have known the claim was unreasonable after pretrial discovery, an attorney's fee award to defendant was appropriate, even though the plaintiff's case survived a summary judgment motion by defendant.[82] It is error not to award fees to a prevailing defendant where some claims, even though not all, were frivolous.[83]

Sometimes there are jurisdictional problems which preclude the award of defendant's attorney's fees. For instance, where plaintiff voluntarily dismisses the complaint before defendant has filed an answer or motion for summary judgment, the court loses jurisdiction and cannot award attorney's fees to defendant.[84] Where a complaint is dismissed for lack of subject matter jurisdiction, the defendant may not be awarded § 1988 attorney's fees.[85]

There are circumstances in which the courts are reluctant to award a defendant substantial attorney's fees or any fees at all. For instance, it has been held that a losing plaintiff's financial condition is a relevant factor in determining the amount of an award of defendant's attorney's fees, at least as an equitable factor supporting a reduction of the fees.[86] With respect to defendant's fees, there is a special application to "uncounseled prisoners," precluding awards against inmate plaintiffs.[87] Finally, to obtain defendant's fees, there must be a determination that plaintiff's suit was frivolous, even

---

80. Head v. Medford, 62 F.3d 351 (11th Cir., 1995).
81. Franceschi v. Schwartz, 57 F.3d 828 (9th Cir., 1995).
82. Flowers v. Jefferson Hospital Assn., 49 F.3d 391 (8th Cir., 1995).
83. Ward v. Hickey, 996 F.2d 448 (1st Cir., 1993).
84. Santiago v. Victim Services Agency, 753 F.2d 219 (2d Cir., 1985).
85. Keene Corp. v. Cass, 908 F.2d 293 (8th Cir., 1990); *see also* Elks National Foundation v. Weber, 942 F.2d 1480 (9th Cir., 1991).
86. Gibbs v. Clements Food Co., 949 F.2d 344 (10th Cir., 1991); Toliver v. County of Sullivan, 957 F.2d 47 (2d Cir., 1992). The record must show how the court arrived at the amount of the award of prevailing defendant's attorney's fees and the financial resources of the plaintiff should be considered. Patton v. County of Kings, 857 F.2d 1378 (9th Cir., 1988).
87. Hughes v. Rowe, 449 U.S. 5 (1980); Miller v. Los Angeles County Board of Education, 827 F.2d 617 (9th Cir., 1987).

when the plaintiff is the federal government[88] and even though it was ultimately unable to prove its case.[89]

Judicial Discretion—"Special Circumstances"

While § 1988 provides that the award of attorney's fees lies in the discretion of the trial court, a prevailing party "should ordinarily recover an attorney's fee *unless special circumstances would render an award unjust*."[90] The so-called "special circumstances" exception comes into play after it has been determined that the plaintiff is a prevailing party. The court is then asked to find that there are special circumstances which make an award to an otherwise entitled plaintiff unjust. If special circumstances are found, plaintiff is denied the award.

The burden of demonstrating the existence of special circumstances is on the defendant, however, and the exception is applicable only in unusual cases.[91] The question becomes what factors constitute special circumstances that justify judicial discretion in denying an attorney's fee award to a prevailing plaintiff.

The special circumstances language flows from a 1968 Supreme Court decision, *Newman v. Piggy Park Enterprises*,[92] interpreting the attorney's fee provision[93] of Title II of the Civil Rights Act of 1964.[94] A quote from the *Newman* case was used by the authors of § 1988 to describe the con-

88. E.E.O.C. v. Consolidated Services Systems, 30 F.3d 58 (7th Cir., 1994).
89. U.S. v. Crosby, 59 F.3d 1133 (11th Cir., 1995).
90. [Emphasis supplied.] Smith v. Robinson, 468 U.S. 992, 1006 (1984), citing Newman v. Piggy Park Enterprises, 390 U.S. 400 (1968). *See also* People of Territory of Guam v. Borja, 983 F.2d 914 (9th Cir., 1993); Topanga Press, Inc. v. City of Los Angeles, 989 F.2d 1524 (9th Cir., 1993); Martin v. Cavalier Hotel Corp., 48 F.3d 1343 (4th Cir., 1995).
91. Crosby v. Bowling, 683 F.2d 1068, 1072 (7th Cir., 1982); Herrington v. County of Sonoma, 883 F.2d 739 (9th Cir., 1989).
92. *Supra*, fn. 90.
93. "In any action commenced pursuant to this subchapter, the court, in its discretion, may allow the prevailing party, other than the United States, a reasonable attorney's fee as part of the costs, and the United States shall be liable for costs the same as a private person." 42 U.S.C. § 2000a-3(b) (1976 & Supp. 1978).
94. Pub. L. No. 88-352, 78 Stat. 244 (codified at 42 U.S.C. § 2000a-3 (1976 & Supp. 1978).

ditions under which attorney's fees would be awarded under the section.[95] In light of the legislative history of § 1988(b), then, it is not surprising that special circumstances supporting denial of an attorney's fee award are rarely found.

Some of the situations found *not* to be special circumstances are:

1. The plaintiff's judgment advances his cause only and not that of others.[96]
2. The amount of the damage award, too large or too small.[97]
3. Only nominal damages were awarded to plaintiff.[98]
4. An award of attorney's fees would be an undeserved windfall for plaintiff who was only partially successful on the merits.[99]
5. Plaintiff was awarded money damages (from which he can pay his own attorney's fees).[100]
6. Plaintiff's primary motive in bringing suit was financial gain.[101]
7. Plaintiff was "drunken, undisciplined, obnoxious and abusive . . . "[102]

---

95. "It follows that one who succeeds in obtaining an injunction under that Title should ordinarily recover an attorney's fee unless special circumstances would render such an award unjust." 390 U.S. at 402.
96. Perez v. University of Puerto Rico, 600 F.2d 1 (1st Cir., 1979); Ackerley Communications, Inc. v. City of Salem, 752 F.2d 1394 (9th Cir., 1985); Stefan v. Laurentius, 889 F.2d 363 (1st Cir., 1989).
97. Lenard v. Argento, 699 F.2d 899 (7th Cir., 1983); Coop v. City of South Bend (7th Cir., 1980).
98. Perez v. University of Puerto Rico, *supra*, fn. 96; Skoda v. Fontani, 646 F.2d 1193 (7th Cir., 1981). However, in Fast v. School Dist. of Ladue, 712 F.2d 379 (8th Cir., 1983), a plaintiff awarded $1.00 in nominal damages was ruled not to be a prevailing party. The ruling in Farrar v. Hobby, *supra*, fn. 39, probably settles the question in favor of denial of a fee award.
99. Sethy v. Alameda County Water Dist., 602 F.2d 894 (9th Cir., 1979), *cert. den.* 444 U.S. 1046 (1980). The *Sethy* court analyzed the "partial plaintiff success" argument in "special circumstances" terms, but rejected it in favor of a fee award using prevailing party analysis.
100. Sethy v. Alameda County Water Dist., *supra*, fn. 99; Herrington v. County of Sonoma, *supra*, fn. 91.
101. Ackerley Communications, Inc. v. City of Salem, *supra*, fn. 96; Herrington v. County of Sonoma, *supra*, fn. 91.
102. Hall v. Hall, 738 F.2d 718 (6th Cir., 1984).

8. Defendants believed the challenged statute was constitutional[103] or acted in good faith.[104]
9. The financial burden of payment of attorney's fees will fall on the taxpayers.[105]
10. Defendant's conduct was required by the state legislature.[106]
11. The case did not involve "invidious discrimination."[107]
12. Plaintiff is financially able to pay its own attorney's fees.[108]
13. Defendants' status as city employees rendered them "mere functionaries," carrying out the will of the city council.[109]
14. Existence of other similar cases being adjudicated in the same court.[110]
15. Plaintiff's lawyer is a legal services organization supported in part by public funds.[111]
16. Plaintiff is a publicly funded agency.[112]
17. The case is extremely simple.[113]

---

103. Johnson v. Mississippi, 606 F.2d 635 (5th Cir., 1979).
104. Love v. Mayor of Cheyenne, 620 F.2d 235 (10th Cir., 1980); Entertainment Concepts, Inc., III v. Maciejewski, 631 F.2d 497 (7th Cir., 1980), *cert. den.* 450 U.S. 919 (1981); Morscott v. City of Cleveland, 936 F.2d 271 (6th Cir., 1991). The "good faith" argument may render defendant eligible for qualified immunity under § 1983 and, therefore, from liability for § 1988(b) attorney's fees. *See* discussion *infra*, p. 49.
105. Aware Woman Clinic, Inc. v. City of Cocoa Beach, 629 F.2d 1146 (5th Cir., 1980); Ackerley Communications, Inc. v. City of Salem, *supra*, fn. 96.
106. Johnson v. Mississippi, *supra*, fn. 103.
107. Aware Woman Clinic, Inc. v. City of Cocoa Beach, *supra*, fn. 105.
108. International Society for Krishna Consciousness v. Collins, 609 F.2d 151 (5th Cir., 1980); Bills v. Hodges, 628 F.2d 844 (4th Cir., 1980); Ackerley Communications, Inc. v. City of Salem, *supra*, fn. 96; Herrington v. County of Sonoma, *supra*, fn. 91; Sable Communications of California, Inc. v. Pacific Telephone & Telegraph Co., 890 F.2d 184 (9th Cir., 1989); Hastert v. Illinois State Bd. of Election Commissioners, 28 F.3d 1430 (7th Cir., 1994).
109. International Oceanic Enterprises, Inc. v. Menton, 614 F.2d 502 (5th Cir., 1980).
110. David v. Travisono, 621 F.2d 464 (1st Cir., 1980).
111. Entertainment Concepts, Inc., III v. Maciejewski, *supra*, fn. 104; Teitelbaum v. Sorenson, 648 F.2d 1248 (9th Cir., 1981).
112. Washington v. Seattle School Dist No. 1, 458 U.S. 457, 487 (1982).
113. Staten v. Housing Auth., 638 F.2d 599 (3d Cir., 1980); A.J. by L.B. v. Kierst, 56 F.3d 849 (8th Cir., 1995).

18. When plaintiffs filed suit, defendants were already attempting to devise a substitute for the challenged plan.[114]
19. The case was one of first impression or involved a very novel claim.[115]
20. Failure to provide for attorney's fees in the written settlement agreement.[116]
21. State defendant acted pursuant to a federal regulation.[117]
22. The work done was in aid of the defense of a state court malicious prosecution case and was essentially a skirmish in that case.[118]
23. The award was based on state, rather than federal, grounds.[119]
24. Prejudice to the prevailing party caused by his own attorney.[120]

There have been a few situations in which "special circumstances" *have* been found and attorney's fees denied:

1. Where money damages have been awarded and the case, though clothed in § 1983 trappings, was really just a state law tort claim.[121]
2. Plaintiff prevailed by waiting for a controlling Supreme Court decision to be handed down.[122]
3. The defendant, a private party, did not violate plaintiff's constitutional rights nor knowingly act in concert with the government defendant that did.[123]
4. Plaintiff's attorney failed to brief the case adequately, causing the court to engage in extensive supplemental research.[124]

---

114. Ramos v. Koebig, 638 F.2d 838 (5th Cir., 1981).
115. Teitelbaum v. Sorenson, *supra*, fn. 111.
116. El Club del Barrio v. United Community Corporations, Inc., 735 F.2d 98 (3d Cir., 1984).
117. Martin v. Heckler, 773 F.2d 1145 (11th Cir., 1985).
118. Hatfield v. Hayes, 877 F.2d 717 (8th Cir., 1989).
119. Hewett v. Joyner, 940 F.2d 1561 (9th Cir., 1991).
120. Love v. Deal, 5 F.3d 1406 (11th Cir., 1993).
121. Buxton v. Patel, 595 F.2d 1182 (9th Cir., 1979); Knights of the Ku Klux Klan v. East Baton Rouge School Board, 643 F.2d 1034 (5th Cir., 1981), *vacated other grounds* 454 U.S. 1075 (1981); Riddell v. National Democratic Party, 624 F.2d 539 (5th Cir., 1980); Gagne v. Town of Enfield (2d Cir., 1984).
122. Brown v. Stackler, 612 F.2d 1057 (7th Cir., 1980).
123. Annunziato v. The Gan, Inc., 744 F.2d 244 (2d Cir., 1984).
124. Bateson v. Geisse, 857 F.2d 1300 (9th Cir., 1988).

5. Counsel for prevailing parties already had been granted $3 million, plus awards previously made in individual appeals at earlier stages of the litigation, and defendant only opposed intervenor's position in one discrete part of the case.[125]
6. "A request for attorney's fees is required to be in good faith and in reasonable compliance with judicial pronouncements, and not an opening gambit in negotiations to reach an ultimate result."[126]
7. The amount of fees requested is "so outrageously excessive as to shock the conscience of the court."[127]

In summary, a prevailing party in a § 1983 case should be awarded attorney's fees authorized by § 1988 unless special circumstances would render the award unjust. Such special circumstances are rarely found to exist, but there are a few unique situations in which denial of fee awards have been affirmed.

Status of Parties

The assertion often is made that, even though there is an identifiable prevailing party, because of his or her particular status, no attorney's fee should be awarded. The rationale of the argument usually is that the prevailing party is wealthy enough to be able to pay the attorney's fees[128] or poor enough that he or she will not have to pay them, or the prevailing party is represented without fee by a legal services organization[129] or is proceeding *pro se*.[130] The courts have generally rejected the first of these two arguments.

It appears reasonably well settled that a *pro se* plaintiff is not entitled to an attorney's fee award,[131] even when the *pro se* plaintiff is an attorney.[132] However, a *pro se* plaintiff who is not a lawyer, while not entitled to an

---

125. Little Rock School Dist. v. Arkansas State Board of Education, 928 F.2d 248 (8th Cir., 1991).
126. Lewis v. Kendrick, 944 F.2d 949, 958 (1st Cir., 1991).
127. Fair Housing Council v. Landow, 999 F.2d 92 (4th Cir., 1993).
128. Hastert v. Illinois State Bd. of Election Commissioners, *supra*, fn. 108.
129. Bills v. Hodges, *supra*, fn. 108.
130. Hughes v. Rowe, *supra*, fn. 87.
131. Rheuark v. Shaw, 628 F.2d 297 (5th Cir., 1980); Owens-El v. Robinson, 694 F.2d 941 (3d Cir., 1982); Smith v. DeBartoli, 769 F.2d 451 (7th Cir., 1985), *cert. den.* 475 U.S. 1067 (1986); Gonzalez v. Kangas, 814 F.2d 1411 (9th Cir., 1987); Coleman v. Turner, 838 F.2d 1004 (8th Cir., 1988).
132. Kay v. Ehrler, 499 U.S. 432 (1991).

attorney's fee award, is entitled to costs reasonably incurred, such as for paralegal and secretarial services, document reproduction, statutory witness fees, and photographs.[133] A prevailing plaintiff who proceeded *in forma pauperis* and was represented by court-appointed counsel is entitled to an attorney's fee award.[134]

An attorney for a prevailing party is not entitled to an attorney's fee award in the attorney's own right.[135] A fee application by an attorney has been treated as being that of a surrogate for the client, however.[136] Absent authorization by the client, a prevailing plaintiff's attorney lacks standing to appeal distribution of attorney's fees; plaintiffs have exclusive entitlement to the award.[137] It has been held, however, that a prevailing plaintiff's attorney has priority to receive the fee award portion of a judgment over a judgment lien held against all parts of the judgment.[138]

Where a public entity is the prevailing party, it is entitled to a fee award.[139] However, denial of fees to a prevailing state government is not an abuse of discretion.[140] An unincorporated association has standing to pursue an award of § 1988(b) fees.[141]

Even though plaintiff achieves prevailing party status, it is necessary to determine if the defendant is a person *liable* for § 1988(b) attorney's fees. A private party, for instance, can be liable under § 1988(b) only if it is subject to jurisdiction under § 1983. That means, though it is a private party, it has engaged in "state action" from which civil rights liability arises.[142]

A party who files a brief *amicus curiae* is a volunteer and not a party to the action, and therefore is not entitled to attorney's fees.[143] It is sometimes

---

133. Burt v. Hennessey, 929 F.2d 457 (9th Cir., 1991).
134. Starks v. George Court Co., Inc., 937 F.2d 311 (7th Cir., 1991).
135. Brown v. General Motors Corp., 722 F.2d 1009 (2d Cir., 1983); Jonas v. Stack, 758 F.2d 567 (11th Cir., 1985); Willard v. City of Los Angeles, 803 F.2d 526 (9th Cir., 1986).
136. Mayberry v. Walters, 862 F.2d 1040 (3d Cir., 1988).
137. Benitez v. Collazo-Collazo, 888 F.2d 930 (1st Cir., 1989).
138. Curtis v. City of Des Moines, 995 F.2d 125 (8th Cir., 1993).
139. Washington v. Seattle School Dist. No. 1, *supra*, fn. 112, 458 U.S. at 487, fn. 31.
140. People by Abrams v. 11 Cornwell Co., 695 F.2d 34 (2d Cir., 1982).
141. Citizens Against Tax Waste v. Westerville City School, 985 F.2d 255 (6th Cir., 1993).
142. Carroll v. Blinken, 42 F.3d 122, 131 (2d Cir., 1994).
143. Morales v. Turman, 820 F.2d 728 (5th Cir. 1987)

asserted that a prevailing party should be awarded attorney's fees for a successful repulse of an intervention. The question, somewhat obscure, becomes whether a prevailing plaintiff may be awarded attorney's fees related to the intervention from the unsuccessful intervenor or *from the defendant*. In a case not involving a claim against the intervenor, the Fourth Circuit ruled it improper "to shift intervention expenses to the losing defendant."[144]

In any event, a prevailing plaintiff is not entitled to an attorney's fee award against an unsuccessful intervenor unless the intervention was frivolous, unreasonable, or without foundation.[145] In contrast, where intervenors in behalf of successful plaintiffs were instrumental in obtaining a favorable settlement, they were entitled to an attorney's fee award, even though they did not assert any civil rights interests of their own.[146] Further, successful intervention for a limited purpose, which accomplishes everything it set out to achieve, renders the intervenor a prevailing party for § 1988 purposes.[147]

An attorney's fee award may be imposed against plaintiff's attorney *personally*.[148] Where a defense counsel, on appeal, pursued an issue admitted in the answer, charging counsel personally with attorney's fees as part of appellee cost is appropriate.[149] Defendants' attorney's fees may be awarded properly against both the plaintiff (under § 1988) and the attorney (under Federal Rule 11), jointly and severally.[150]

Scope of Work

While there is no doubt that a prevailing plaintiff is entitled to an award of attorney's fees for professional work directly related to preparation and

---

144. Rum Creek Coal Sales, Inc. v. Caperton, *supra*, fn. 35, 31 F.3d at 177, citing Independent Federation of Flight Attendants v. Zipes, 491 U.S. 754 (1989).
145. Independent Federation of Flight Attendants v. Zipes, 491 U.S. 754 (1989); Sable Communications of California, Inc. v. Pacific Telephone & Telegraph Co., 890 F.2d 184 (9th Cir., 1989); Davis v. City & County of San Francisco, 890 F.2d 1438 (9th Cir., 1989).
146. Wilder v. Bernstein, 965 F.2d 1196 (2d Cir., 1992). See also Ensley Branch, N.A.A.C.P. v. Seibels, 31 F.3d 1549 (11th Cir., 1994).
147. Hastert v. Illinois State Bd. of Election Commissioners, *supra*, fn. 107.
148. Limerick v. Greenwald, 794 F.2d 97 (1st Cir., 1984). *Cf.* Brown v. Borough of Chambersburg, 903 F.2d 274 (3d Cir., 1990).
149. Action Mfg., Inc. v. Fairhaven Textile Corp., 790 F.2d 164 (1st Cir., 1986).
150. Collins v. Walden, 834 F.2d 961 (11th Cir., 1987).

trial of a successful § 1983 claim,[151] disputes often arise about fees for work done on issues of secondary relationship to the claims themselves. For instance, it is generally held that fees should be awarded for work in support or defense of the fee award itself.[152] And a prevailing plaintiff is entitled to a fee award for work performed on appeal.[153]

However, "[a]s a general rule, a party who obtains the reversal of judgment on appeal is not a 'prevailing party' unless such reversal also resulted in entry of judgment for that party."[154] An unsuccessful plaintiff who obtains reversal of an award of defendant's attorney's fees is not entitled to an award of fees on appeal.[155] Where an eventually successful plaintiff was unsuccessful in an earlier appeal in the same case, she was not entitled to fees for work done on that appeal.[156]

The court of appeals will exercise its own discretion in determining whether to award attorney's fees on appeal.[157] A plaintiff may obtain an attorney's fee award for successful appellate defense of a trial court judgment, even though the court of appeals ordered that "each party bear its own costs," since attorney's fees are not "costs" under Federal Rule of Appellate Procedure 39.[158]

---

151. 42 U.S.C. § 1988(b).
152. Souza v. Southworth, 564 F.2d 609 (1st Cir., 1977); Weisenberger v. Huecker, 593 F.2d 49 (6th Cir., 1979), *cert. den.* 444 U.S. 880 (1979); Bagby v. Beal, 606 F.2d 411 (3d Cir., 1979); Cruz v. Hauck, 762 F.2d 1230 (5th Cir., 1985); Kurowski v. Krajewski, 848 F.2d 767 (7th Cir., 1988); McDonald v. Secretary of Health & Human Services, 884 F.2d 1468 (1st Cir., 1989); Thompson v. Gomez, 45 F.3d 1365 (9th Cir., 1995). It has been held, however, that a partially successful plaintiff was properly denied an award of fees for post-verdict retention of additional counsel to assist in the fee application. Winter v. Cerro Gordo County Conservation Bd., 925 F.2d 1069 (8th Cir., 1991). *See also* Dotson v. Chester, 937 F.2d 920 (4th Cir., 1991).
153. Hutto v. Finney, 437 U.S. 678 (1978); Brown v. Freedman Baking Co., Inc., 810 F.2d 6 (1st Cir., 1987); Asbury v. Brougham, 866 F.2d 1276 (10th Cir., 1989); Bigby v. City of Chicago, 927 F.2d 1426 (7th Cir., 1991); Cabrales v. City of Los Angeles, 935 F.2d 1050 (9th Cir., 1991); Nordhorn v. Ladish Co., Inc., 9 F.3d 1402 (9th Cir., 1993); Larez v. Holcomb, 16 F.3d 1513 (9th Cir., 1994).
154. Coral Construction Co. v. King County, 941 F.2d 910 (9th Cir., 1991).
155. Jensen v. City of San Jose, 806 F.2d 899 (9th Cir., 1986).
156. Evans v. City of Evanston, 941 F.2d 473 (7th Cir., 1991).
157. Elks National Foundation v. Weber, 942 F.2d 1480 (9th Cir., 1991).
158. McDonald v. McCarthy, 966 F.2d 112 (3d Cir., 1992).

The question of whether prevailing party status is "carried forward" from one case to a second depends on whether the second litigation was "inextricably intermingled" with the original to such an extent that plaintiffs have no choice but to litigate the second time. If plaintiffs are forced to litigate to preserve the relief originally obtained, for instance, their prevailing party status is carried forward to the second case.[159]

Considerable confusion reigns on the question of whether an award of attorney's fees is appropriate for work performed on civil rights claims which are wholly or partially unsuccessful but were joined in some fashion with successful claims. In *Hensley v. Eckerhart*,[160] the U.S. Supreme Court held that the extent of a plaintiff's success is a crucial factor in determining the amount of an attorney's fee award:

1. Where a plaintiff fails on a claim that is distinct in all respects from his successful claims, the hours spent on the unsuccessful claim should be excluded in considering the amount of the fee.
2. Where a lawsuit consists of related claims, a plaintiff who wins substantial relief should not have his attorney's fee award reduced simply because the District Court did not adopt every contention raised.
3. But, where plaintiff achieves only limited success, the District Court should award only that amount of fees which is reasonable in relation to the results obtained.[161]

---

159. Arvinger v. Mayor & City Council of Baltimore, 31 F.3d 196 (4th Cir., 1994).
160. *Supra*, fn. 29. On the effect of an award of nominal damages on the amount of attorney's fees to be awarded, *see* discussion, *supra*, p. 14.
161. 461 U.S. at 440. *See also* Northcross v. Board of Education, 611 F.2d 624 (6th Cir., 1979); Abshire v. Walls, 830 F.2d 1277 (4th Cir., 1987); Davis v. Southeastern Pennsylvania Transportation Auth., 924 F.2d 51 (3d Cir., 1991); Winter v. Cerro Gordo Conservation Bd., *supra*, fn. 151; Davis v. Locke, 936 F.2d 1208 (11th Cir., 1991); Nanetti v. University of Illinois at Chicago, 944 F.2d 1416 (7th Cir., 1991); Jermosen v. Smith, 945 F.2d 547 (2d Cir., 1991); U.S. v. Drabeck, 946 F.2d 630 (9th Cir., 1991); Nydam v. Lennerton, 948 F.2d 808 (1st Cir., 1991); Wallace v. Mulholland, 957 F.2d 333 (7th Cir., 1992); George Hyman Const. Co. v. Brooks, 963 F.2d 1532 (D.C. Cir., 1992); Grant v. Martinez, 973 F.2d 97 (2d Cir., 1992); Anthony v. Sullivan, 982 F.2d 586 (D.C. Cir., 1993); Phetosomphone v. Allison Reed Group, Inc., 984 F.2d 4 (1st Cir., 1993); Durant v. Ind. School Dist. No. 16, 990 F.2d 560 (10th Cir., 1993); Outdoor Systems, Inc. v. City of Mesa, 997 F.2d 604 (9th Cir., 1993).

However, where several claims are "alternate road[s] to the same result," a prevailing plaintiff's fee award should not be reduced merely because the court considered only one of the claims.[162]

HENSLEY v. ECKERHART HOLDING

DEGREE OF SUCCESS	AMOUNT OF FEE
Failure to prevail on separate claim	No fees for work on that claim
Substantial relief on related claims	Fees for all work, including related, incidental, unsuccessful claims
Limited success on some claims	Fees reasonable in relation to results obtained

The Court, in *Thorne v. City of El Segundo*,[163] put the *Hensley* rule in somewhat different language:

> First, the court asks whether the claims upon which the plaintiff failed to prevail were related to the plaintiff's successful claims. If unrelated, the final fee award may not include time expended on the unsuccessful claims. If the unsuccessful and successful claims are related, then the court must apply the second part of the analysis, in which the court evaluates the 'significance of the overall relief obtained by the plaintiff in relation to the hours reasonably expended on the litigation.' If the plaintiff obtained 'excellent results,' full compensation may be appropriate, but if only partial or limited success was obtained, full compensation may be excessive.[164]

---

162. Carston v. County of Cook, 962 F.2d 749 (7th Cir., 1992).
163. 802 F.2d 1131 (9th Cir., 1986).
164. 802 F.2d at 1141. The *Thorne* decision was recently cited with approval in O'Neal v. City of Seattle, 66 F.3d 1064, 1068-1069 (9th Cir., 1995). *See also* Spellan v. Bd. of Education for Dist. 111, 59 F.3d 642, 645-646 (7th Cir., 1995).

A plaintiff who succeeds in court is not entitled to fees for work done on parallel administrative proceedings, if § 1983 does not compel pursuit of state administrative remedies before commencing a federal action and the state proceeding is unnecessary to the federal suit.[165] However, a prevailing plaintiff may be awarded attorney's fees for work done in a prior administrative proceeding where the work was both useful and necessary to advance subsequent civil rights litigation.[166] If plaintiffs are entitled to relief under state law and it is unnecessary to consider federal claims, they are not entitled to a § 1988 attorney's fee award.[167]

The question of whether a prevailing party should be awarded fees for work that was unnecessary or duplicative of the work of another party's attorney was addressed in *E.E.O.C. v. Clear Lake Dodge*,[168] where the plaintiff's interest was fully and successfully prosecuted by the Equal Employment Opportunity Commission. Nevertheless, plaintiff hired private counsel to plow the same ground. The Fifth Circuit held most of the hours worked by plaintiff's private counsel were redundant and not subject to award of § 2000e-5(k) attorney's fees.

Fees may not be awarded for work on a successful claim in a federal administrative proceeding by way of subsequent independent litigation to recover attorney's fees.[169] Nor may fees be awarded for work on a § 1983 claim which is based on another statute, when the latter provides a "comprehensive enforcement scheme."[170]

Hours that were not reasonably expended should be excluded from calculation of the fee.[171] "The unreasonable expenditure of time includes 'hours that are excessive, redundant, or otherwise unnecessary. . . .'"[172]

---

165. Webb v. County Board of Education, 471 U.S. 234 (1985). *See also* Pennsylvania v. Delaware Valley Citizens' Council, 478 U.S. 546 (1986); Spell v. McDaniel, 852 F.2d 762 (4th Cir., 1988).
166. Cullen v. Fliegner, 18 F.3d 96 (2d Cir., 1994).
167. Smith v. Robinson, 468 U.S. 992 (1984); National Private Truck Council, Inc. v. Oklahoma Tax Commission, 515 U.S. 582 [132 L.Ed.2d 509] (1995); Clients' Council v. Pierce, 778 F.2d 518 (8th Cir., 1985).
168. E.E.O.C. v. Clear Lake Dodge, *supra*, fn. 19.
169. North Carolina Dept. of Transportation v. Crest Street Community Council, Inc., 479 U.S. 6 (1986).
170. Teresa Diane P. v. Alief Ind. School Dist., 744 F.2d 484 (5th Cir., 1984).
171. Sands v. Runyon, 28 F.3d 1323 (2d Cir., 1994).
172. Sands v. Runyon, *supra*, fn. 171, 28 F.3d at 1333, citing Hensley v. Eckerhart, *supra*, fn. 29, 461 U.S. at 434.

A prevailing plaintiff is entitled to a fee award for work done before any actual plaintiff was identified and for work which was partially duplicative,[173] but not for work done after the case is settled.[174] Fees may be awarded for work performed in monitoring a consent decree,[175] including for securing a contempt citation for failure to obey a decree,[176] but not for work performed in obtaining an extension of time and seeking a continuance.[177]

Time spent educating clients in conferences on political considerations in a redistricting case is not compensable.[178] Work performed in connection with tax levy elections conducted in compliance with a court order in a § 1983 case is reimbursable through a § 1988(b) attorney's fee award.[179]

A prevailing plaintiff is not entitled to fees for work done by lawyers as corporate officers, rather than as attorneys.[180] Work done by paralegals may properly be included in a § 1988(b) attorney's fee award, however.[181] Section 1988(b) does not authorize award of expert witness fees in excess of an otherwise applicable statutory cap on such fees.[182]

It is not an abuse of discretion for the trial court to strike a prevailing plaintiff's petition for attorney's fees as untimely under the court's local rules.[183] Where intervenors filed a late fees petition under local rules, it was not abuse of discretion for the court to refuse to reopen the question of attorney's fees.[184]

---

173. Dowdell v. City of Apopka, 698 F.2d 1181 (11th Cir., 1983).
174. Alliance to End Repression v. City of Chicago, *supra*, fn. 49.
175. Keith v. Volpe, 833 F.2d 850 (9th Cir., 1987); Duran v. Carruthers, 885 F.2d 1492 (10th Cir., 1989); Jeff D. v. Andrus, 888 F.2d 617 (9th Cir., 1989); Glover v. Johnson, 934 F.2d 703 (6th Cir., 1991); Diaz v. Romer, 961 F.2d 1508 (10th Cir., 1992); Joseph A. v. New Mexico Dept. of Human Services, 28 F.3d 1056 (10th Cir., 1994); Gates v. Rowland, 39 F.3d 1439 (9th Cir., 1994).
176. Halderman v. Pennhurst State School & Hospital, 49 F.3d 939 (3d Cir., 1995).
177. Steele v. Van Buren Public School Dist., 845 F.2d 1492 (8th Cir., 1988).
178. Daggett v. Kimmelman, 864 F.2d 1122 (3d Cir., 1989).
179. Jenkins by Agyei v. State of Missouri, 862 F.2d 677 (8th Cir., 1988).
180. Culebras Enterprises Corp. v. Rivera-Rios, 846 F.2d 94 (1st Cir., 1988).
181. Missouri v. Jenkins by Agyei, 491 U.S. 274 (1989); United Steelworkers v. Phelps Dodge Corp., 896 F.2d 403 (9th Cir., 1990).
182. West Virginia University Hospitals, Inc. v. Casey, 499 U.S. 83 (1991); Davis v. Mason County, 927 F.2d 1473 (9th Cir., 1991).
183. Quick v. Peoples Bank of Cullman County, 993 F.2d 793 (11th Cir., 1993).
184. Witty v. Dukakis, 3 F.3d 517 (1st Cir., 1993).

Amount of Fees

Once it is determined that there is a prevailing party entitled to a fee award, the next question is the amount of the award. It is the function of the district court to determine the attorney's fees to be awarded under § 1988(b).[185] An evidentiary hearing is not required, however, before the court awards attorney's fees, even though the amount awarded is substantial.[186]

The district court nevertheless is required to articulate the basis for its award.[187] The proper standard on review of a § 1988 attorney's fee award is for abuse of discretion only.[188] Where the losing defendant has failed to provide convincing evidence or persuasive argument in support of its position on fees, it is not up to the court to do so.[189] Although appellate review of attorney's fees awards is limited to a highly deferential abuse of discretion standard,[190] where the market rate used is arbitrary, the trial court abuses its discretion.[191]

"Reasonable Fees" Defined

The amount of "reasonable fees" is calculated by reference to the prevailing market rates in the community in question, not by the actual cost of

---

185. O'Rourke v. City of Norman, 875 F.2d 1465 (10th Cir., 1989).
186. Walz v. Town of Smithtown, 46 F.3d 162 (2d Cir., 1995). Contra, *see* Sockwell v. Phelps, 20 F.3d 187, 193 (5th Cir., 1994).
187. Norris v. Hartmarx Specialty Stores, Inc., 913 F.2d 253 (5th Cir., 1990); Smith v. Village of Maywood, 970 F.2d 397 (7th Cir., 1992); Gates v. Deukmejian, 987 F.2d 1392 (9th Cir., 1993); Stewart v. Gates, 987 F.2d 1450 (9th Cir., 1993); Deary v. City of Gloucester, 9 F.3d 191 (1st Cir., 1993).
188. Associated Builders & Contractors of Louisiana, Inc. v. Orleans Parish School Dist., 919 F.2d 374 (5th Cir., 1990); Ruggiero v. Krzeminski, 928 F.2d 558 (2d Cir., 1991); Carter v. Sedgwick County, 929 F.2d 1501 (10th Cir., 1991); U.S. v. Washington, 935 F.2d 1059 (9th Cir., 1991); Zuchel v. City & County of Denver, 997 F.2d 730 (10th Cir., 1993); Cullens v. Georgia Dept. of Transportation, *supra*, fn. 58.
189. Foley v. City of Lowell, 948 F.2d 10 (1st Cir., 1991).
190. Joseph A. v. New Mexico Dept. of Human Services, *supra*, fn. 175. "[T]he deferential review ordinarily inherent in [the abuse of discretion] standard is modified when the appropriate criteria that are established for a fee award are in question." Rum Creek Coal Sales, Inc. v. Caperton, *supra*, fn. 35, 31 F.3d at 174.
191. Eddleman v. Switchcraft, Inc., 965 F.2d 422 (7th Cir., 1992).

providing legal services. In other words, the fact that the prevailing party's attorney is employed by a nonprofit legal services organization is irrelevant. The fee is calculated on the basis of the market rate for legal services in the private sector.[192]

In a case tried in Mobile, Alabama, the Eleventh Circuit observed that the hourly rate selected should be "the market rate for attorneys of similar skill representing similar clients in similar cases in the Mobile area."[193] But a difficulty may arise in choosing the appropriate market from which to extract the rate when the case involves more than one venue, such as where it is filed in one place but tried in another, or some or all the attorneys come from a different place.

For instance, the Fourth Circuit holds "[t]he relevant market for determining the prevailing rate is ordinarily the community in which the court where the action is prosecuted sits."[194] But where the case was filed in one place and tried in another, the Eleventh Circuit held the reasonable rate to be applied is that of the place where the case is *filed*.[195] The Tenth Circuit

---

192. Blum v. Stenson, 465 U.S. 886, 894-900 (1984). An appropriate manner of arriving at a reasonable rate would be to do so "on the basis of affidavits of other attorneys in the area describing their level of experience and the fees they usually charge." Sloman v. Tadlock, 21 F.3d 1462, 1477 (9th Cir., 1994).

193. Perkins v. Mobile Housing Bd., 847 F.2d 735 (11th Cir., 1988), citing, for a statement of "the present state of the law of attorney's fees," Norman v. Housing Auth. of City of Montgomery, 836 F.2d 1292 (11th Cir., 1988). *See also* Lucero v. City of Trinidad, 815 F.2d 1384 (10th Cir., 1987); McDonald v. Armontrout, 860 F.2d 1456 (8th Cir., 1988); Bordanaro v. McLeod, 871 F.2d 1151 (1st Cir., 1989); Buffington v. Baltimore County, 913 F.2d 113 (4th Cir., 1990); Associated Builders & Contractors of Louisiana, Inc. v. Orleans Parish School Bd., 919 F.2d 374 (5th Cir., 1990); Davis v. Mason County, 927 F.2d 1473 (9th Cir., 1991); Davis v. Locke, 936 F.2d 1208 (11th Cir., 1991); Hessel v. O'Hearn, 977 F.2d 299 (7th Cir., 1992); Gates v. Deukmejian, 987 F.2d 1392 (9th Cir., 1993); Stewart v. Gates, 987 F.2d 1450 (9th Cir., 1993); Brooks v. Georgia State Board of Elections, 997 F.2d 857 (11th Cir., 1993).

194. Rum Creek Coal Sales, Inc. v. Caperton, *supra*, fn. 35. The foregoing observation did not stop the Fourth Circuit from accepting higher, out-of-town rates, rationalizing hometown lawyers needed out-of-town help to protect against all powerful government defendants, out-of-town lawyers were retained by plaintiffs in due course anyway, and the whole thing would end up in out-of-town counsel's venue, because that is where the Fourth Circuit sits.

195. Cullens v. Georgia Dept. of Transportation, *supra*, fn. 58.

added another twist: the local rate prevails "unless the subject of the litigation is 'so unusual or requires such special skills' that only an out-of-state lawyer possesses. . . . "[196] When attorney's fees are sought for an out-of-town specialist, the trial court must determine "(1) whether hiring the out-of-town specialist was reasonable in the first instance, and (2) whether the rates sought by the out-of-town specialist are reasonable for an attorney of his or her degree of skill, experience, and reputation."[197]

The "reasonable fee" awarded may be less than the actual fee the prevailing party's lawyer charges.[198] On the other hand, attorneys who normally charge reduced fees to poor clients may be awarded fees at the market rate, but they must prove what the appropriate market rate is.[199]

"Lodestar" Rule

The "lodestar," originally used almost exclusively in the Third Circuit, is calculated by determining the number of hours to be credited to a prevailing party's attorneys for their work in preparation and trial of the case and the hourly rate by which they are to be compensated.[200] After the "lodestar" has been determined, it may be adjusted upward or downward in light of two other factors: the contingent nature of the case and the quality of the work performed.[201]

---

196. Jane L. v. Bangerter, 61 F.3d 1505, 1510 (10th Cir., 1995). *See also* Planned Parenthood, Sioux Falls Clinic v. Miller, 70 F.3d 517 (8th Cir., 1995).
197. Hadix v. Johnson, 65 F.3d 532, 535 (6th Cir., 1995).
198. Corder v. Gates, 947 F.2d 374 (9th Cir., 1991).
199. Covington v. District of Columbia, 57 F.3d 1101 (D.C. Cir., 1995).
200. To determine a reasonable attorney's fee, the district court must arrive at a "lodestar" figure by multiplying the hours plaintiffs' counsel reasonably spent on the litigation by a reasonable hourly rate.

     Jane L. v. Bangerter, *supra*, fn. 196, 61 F.3d at 1509, citing Blum v. Stenson, 465 U.S. 886, 888 (1984), and Hensley v. Eckerhart, *supra*, fn. 29, 461 U.S. at 433.
201. Hughes v. Repko, 578 F.2d 483 (3d Cir., 1978). The development of the "lodestar" rule in the Third Circuit in non-§ 1988 cases is outlined in Siberman v. Bogle, 683 F.2d 62 (3d Cir., 1982). *See also* Hall v. Borough of Roselle, 747 F.2d 838 (3d Cir., 1984); Spell v. McDaniel, 824 F.2d 1380 (4th Cir., 1987); Quesada v. Thomason, 850 F.2d 537 (9th Cir., 1988); Gilmere v. City of Atlanta, 864 F.2d 734 (11th Cir., 1989); Watkins v. Fordice, 7 F.3d 453 (5th Cir., 1993); Trimper v. City of Norfolk, *supra*, fn. 17.

Johnson Guidelines

Until recently, at least, in determining the appropriate amount of the attorney's fees awarded, federal appellate courts have generally followed the guidelines set forth in *Johnson v. Georgia Highway Express, Inc.*[202] The courts provide that in assessing attorney's fees, the trial court should consider the *Johnson* factors, but not necessarily all of them.[203] However, "failure to consider the appropriate factors in determining the reasonableness of an award of attorney's fees is an abuse of discretion."[204]

The *Johnson* factors or guidelines are:

- Time and labor required
- Novelty and difficulty of the questions
- Skill required to perform the legal service properly
- Preclusion of other employment by the attorney due to acceptance of the case
- Customary fee
- Whether the fee is fixed or contingent
- Time limitations imposed by the client or the circumstances
- Amount involved and results obtained
- Experience, reputation, and ability of the attorneys in question
- Undesirability of the case
- Nature and length of the professional relationship with the client
- Awards in similar cases[205]

---

202. 488 F.2d 714 (5th Cir., 1974).

203. *See* Bhandari v. First National Bank of Commerce, 808 F.2d 1082 (5th Cir., 1987).

204. Wood v. Sunn, 852 F.2d 1205, 1213 (9th Cir., 1988).

205. Identical standards were set forth in Kerr v. Screen Extras Guild, Inc., 526 F.2d 67 (9th Cir., 1975), *cert. den.* 425 U.S. 951 (1976). "In 'rare' and 'exceptional' cases, an upward adjustment of the lodestar may be justified, but the relevant factors in *Kerr* . . . must be analyzed." Wood v. Sunn, *supra*, fn. 201, 852 F.3d at 1213. *See also* discussing the so-called *Kerr* factors, McGrath v. County of Nevada, 67 F.3d 248, 252, fn. 4 (9th Cir., 1995).

"Hybrid" Approach

As the Ninth Circuit said, in *Jordan v. Multnomah County*,[206] "[The hybrid] approach combines elements of the *Johnson* 12-factor analysis and the lodestar method of calculation developed by the Third Circuit . . . [citation]. The lodestar has emerged as the predominant element of the analysis." In *Clark v. Butler*,[207] the Fifth Circuit went into greater detail:

> The trial court should consider the twelve *Johnson* factors in light of the following framework: it should (1) ascertain the nature and extent of the services supplied by the attorney; (2) determine the value of the services according to the customary fee and the quality of the legal work; and, (3) adjust the compensation on the basis of the other *Johnson* factors that may be of significance in the petitioner's case. [Citations.] The product of the first two steps is the 'lodestar.' [Citation.] After calculating the lodestar amount, the district court must then apply the remaining *Johnson* factors to determine if the lodestar should be adjusted. . . . The district court must be careful not to 'double count' a *Johnson* factor already considered in calculating the lodestar when it determines the necessary adjustments under part three of the 'framework.' [Citation.] The district court, however, should pay 'special heed' to *Johnson* criteria numbers '(1) the time and labor involved, (5) the customary fee, (8) the amount involved and the results obtained, and (9) the experience, reputation, and ability of counsel.'[208]

Upward Adjustment

In *Blum v. Stenson*, the U.S. Supreme Court ruled there may be an "upward adjustment" of the reasonable attorney's fee "in some cases of

---

206. 815 F.2d 1258 (9th Cir., 1987). Accord: Lilly v. Harris-Teeter Supermarket, 842 F.2d 1496 (4th Cir., 1988); Cabrales v. County of Los Angeles, 864 F.2d 1454 (9th Cir., 1988); Cunningham v. County of Los Angeles, 879 F.2d 481 (9th Cir., 1989); Davis v. Mason County, 927 F.2d 1473 (9th Cir., 1991). *See also* Corder v. Gates, *supra*, fn. 198.

207. 916 F.2d 255 (5th Cir., 1990).

208. 916 F.2d at 258. *See also* Caban-Wheeler v. Elsea, 71 F.3d 837, 844-45 (11th Cir., 1995).

exceptional success. . . . "[209] It cited *Hensley v. Eckerhart*,[210] which also stands for the proposition that "where the plaintiff achieved only limited success, the district court should award only that amount of fees that is reasonable in relation to the results obtained."[211]

Upward adjustment, however, according to most federal appellate courts, is only appropriate in certain exceptional cases, "those in which there is a substantial risk of not prevailing, or in which the issues are so novel or complex that the lodestar amount awarded would not provide a reasonable fee that would adequately reflect the quality of the representation."[212] If a trial court decides to enhance the lodestar amount, it must make specific findings explaining the need for the enhancement.[213] Finally, it has been held that upward adjustment is necessary when an appellate court reverses and remands on a significant issue.[214]

Downward Adjustment

The amount of the fee award may be reduced in light of the limited success of the action.[215] Stating it in greater detail, one court ruled there may be a downward adjustment of the requested fee where (1) the only issue on which plaintiff prevailed was not complex, (2) the plaintiff received only nominal damages, and (3) plaintiff's attorneys failed to provide concrete information distinguishing time spent on the prevailing issue from that spent on other issues.[216] A fee reduction under *Hensley*[217] prin-

---

209. *Supra*, fn. 192, 465 U.S. at 897.
210. *Supra*, fn. 29, 461 U.S. at 435 (1983).
211. 461 U.S. at 440.
212. Clark v. Butler, 916 F.2d 255, 260 (5th Cir., 1990). Contra: King v. Palmer, 950 F.2d 771 (D.C. Cir., 1991).
213. Johnson v. Hardin County, 908 F.2d 1280 (6th Cir., 1990).
214. Carrero v. New York Housing Auth., 890 F.2d 569 (2d Cir., 1989).
215. Harris v. Marhoefer, 24 F.3d 16 (9th Cir., 1994). *See also* Smith v. Freeman, 921 F.2d 1120 (10th Cir., 1990); Wedemeier v. City of Ballwin, 931 F.2d 24 (8th Cir., 1991); Corder v. Gates, *supra*, fn. 198; Alexander v. Mayor and Council, 953 F.2d 160 (4th Cir., 1991); Sanders v. Brewer, 972 F.2d 920 (8th Cir., 1992); Loggins v. Delo, 999 F.2d 364 (8th Cir., 1993); LeMaire v. Maass, 2 F.3d 851 (9th Cir., 1993); Standley v. Chilhowee R-IV School Dist., 5 F.3d 319 (8th Cir., 1993).
216. Rogers v. Kelly, 866 F.2d 997 (8th Cir., 1989).
217. *Supra*, fn. 29.

ciples for limited success may be applied to post-judgment monitoring work, as well as to fees generated prior to judgment.[218]

Where a corporation made an all-out effort to gain victory through appeal of an adverse decision, without considering financial constraints and choosing to switch its representation on appeal to a more expensive out-of-state law firm, which spent excessive time researching issues already addressed in the trial, a reduction of the fees requested was appropriate.[219] It has been held that the lodestar may be adjusted with reference to factors not subsumed in its calculation, but it is error, however, after the lodestar has been determined, to lower fees based on the simplicity of the issues, since that factor should have been included in the lodestar calculation in the first place.[220]

A downward adjustment of the lodestar must not be a mere "arithmetical exercise." Rather, it must be based on proper standards, presumably using those set out, however obscurely, by the Court in *Hensley*.[221]

Delayed Fees

Fees unpaid until after a considerable lapse of time since the services were rendered require an adjustment for the delay.[222] There are two methods of compensation:

1. "[T]o calculate the fee award using the attorney's current rates," or
2. "[T]o 'base the award on the rates the lawyer charged when they rendered the services to the [client] and to add interest on that amount to the present.'"[223]

Plaintiff's Fee Arrangements

When the actual fee owed by a prevailing party to his or her attorney is determined by contract or on a contingency basis, rather than by an hourly

---

218. Joseph A. v. New Mexico Dept. of Human Services, *supra*, fn. 175.
219. Ackerley Communications v. City of Somerville, 901 F.2d 170 (1st Cir., 1990).
220. Cooper v. State of Utah, 894 F.2d 1169 (10th Cir., 1990).
221. Cullens v. Georgia Dept. of Transportation, *supra*, fn. 58.
222. Smith v. Village of Maywood, *supra*, fn. 187.
223. Smith v. Village of Maywood, *supra*, fn. 187, 17 F.3d at 221. *See* Corder v. Brown, 25 F.3d 833, 838 (9th Cir., 1994), where the court held "a delay in payment occasioned by appeal is redressable solely by an award of interest."

rate, the question is whether the § 1988 fee award must comport with the fee agreement and, if not, what happens when they differ? The answer to the first question is that an attorney's fee allowed under § 1988 is not limited to the amount provided in the plaintiff's contingent fee arrangement with the lawyer.[224] If the § 1988 award is greater than the contingent or contract fee, the award will be credited to fees owing under the contract and any excess will go to the attorney.[225] But plaintiff's attorney is entitled to payment of the full amount of the contingent fee, even though the § 1988 award is for less.[226]

It is not an abuse of discretion, however, to base a fee award on counsel's fee agreement with the prevailing party.[227] But where a fee agreement is entered *after* the court's expense determination was made, the agreement is unenforceable.[228] "[R]isk of nonpayment for work in a contingent fee case is not an acceptable justification for fee enhancement," one court ruled.[229]

Fee Waivers

When plaintiff's lawyer waives his or her fee, the question becomes whether the waiver has any effect on the § 1988 fee award. In general, "[a]n award of attorney's fees to a successful plaintiff is not contingent upon an

---

224. Blanchard v. Bergeron, 489 U.S. 87 (1989); Quesada v. Thomason, 850 F.2d 537 (9th Cir., 1988); Iqbal v. Golf Course Superintendents Assn., 900 F.2d 227 (10th Cir., 1990); Goodwin v. Metts, 973 F.2d 378 (4th Cir., 1992).
225. Lenard v. Argento, *supra*, fn. 97. *See also* Pennsylvania v. Delaware Valley Citizens' Council for Clean Air, 483 U.S. 711 (1987); Hamner v. Rios, 769 F.2d 1404 (9th Cir., 1985); Sears v. Atchison, Topeka & Santa Fe Ry. Co., 779 F.2d 1450 (10th Cir., 1985); Hagge v. Bauer, 827 F.2d 101 (7th Cir., 1987); Conklin v. Lovely, 834 F.2d 543 (6th Cir., 1987).
226. Venegas v. Mitchell, 495 U.S. 82 (1990); Drennan v. General Motors Corp., 977 F.2d 246 (6th Cir., 1992).
227. Winter v. Cerro Gordo County Conservation Bd., *supra*, fn. 152.
228. Alexander v. Chicago Park Dist., 927 F.2d 1014 (7th Cir., 1991).
229. Ways v. City of Lincoln, 871 F.2d 750, 758 (8th Cir., 1989), citing Pennsylvania v. Delaware Valley Citizens' Council for Clean Air, *supra*, fn. 225. As sort of an aside, it is interesting to note that an Indian tribe was not allowed to subvert the terms of its compact with a state that it bear its own attorney's fees by including a Section 1983 claim in its suit against the state on the compact's terms. Forest County Potawatomi Community v. Norquist, 45 F.3d 1079 (7th Cir., 1995).

obligation to pay an attorney and is not affected by the fact that no fee was charged."[230]

A district court has the power, however, in its discretion, to approve plaintiff's waiver of § 1988 attorney's fees, and there is no abuse of that discretion absent a showing defendant had adopted a statute, policy, or practice requiring a waiver as a condition of settlement or that defendants' request for a waiver was a "vindictive effort" to deter attorneys from representing plaintiffs in civil rights cases against the government.[231] Even if a fee waiver is objectionable, the court's options are to accept the settlement, reject it in hope another will be forthcoming, or proceed to trial.[232] The parties' intent that there be a fee waiver should be reflected in the language of the settlement agreement or release.[233]

Where issues on appeal are separate from the settlement of the underlying litigation, the fee waiver does not apply to fees for work done on those separate issues.[234] Where defendant's offer of judgment, without mention of attorney's fees, is accepted and plaintiff contends entitlement to attorney's fees above the amount of the offer, the offer may not be rescinded and plaintiff is entitled to an award of reasonable attorney's fees.[235]

Fees Paid by Someone Else and Voluntarily Reduced Rate Fees

Fees should be calculated at the market rate rather than at cost plus overhead, even though the prevailing plaintiff was represented by a salaried union attorney.[236] Attorney's fees awarded to a prevailing plaintiff should be based on the prevailing market method, even though the attorneys were members of a quasi-public interest law firm practicing for a profit, but reducing rates for noneconomic motives.[237]

---

230. Martin v. Heckler, *supra*, fn. 117. There the Court ruled that where a plaintiff's counsel arguably waived his fee by signing the form required for special admission to practice before the District Court, a fee award was appropriate anyway.
231. Evans v. Jeff D., *supra*, fn. 51.
232. Phillips v. Allegheny County, 869 F.2d 234 (3d Cir., 1989).
233. Muckleshoot Tribe v. Puget Sound Power & Light Co., 875 F.2d 695 (9th Cir., 1989).
234. Jeff D. v. Andrus, 899 F.2d 753 (9th Cir., 1990).
235. Erdman v. Cochise County, 926 F.2d 877 (9th Cir., 1991).
236. Kean v. Stone, 966 F.2d 119 (3d Cir., 1992).
237. Save Our Cumberland Mountains, Inc. v. Hodel, 857 F.2d 1516 (D.C. Cir., 1988).

A nonsettling defendant is entitled to offset attorney's fees owed by the amount already paid by settling co-defendants. A prevailing plaintiff's lawyer is entitled only to a "reasonable" fee under § 1988. If an offset is denied where settling co-defendants have already paid for some of the work needed to produce the favorable result, full payment by a nonsettling defendant would be a windfall, which would be "manifestly unreasonable."[238]

Expenses and Recordkeeping

The term "attorney's fee" in § 1988(b) "includes out-of-pocket expenses in preparation for trial."[239] The fee award may include an amount for an attorney's travel time, but it may not always be awarded at the full hourly rate.[240]

But, "the reasonable costs that can be awarded pursuant to § 1988 are only those related to plaintiffs' successful claims."[241] Section 1988 does not provide statutory authority for the awarding of compensation for nonlegal experts.[242] It is appropriate for the trial court to refuse to compensate nonlawyers for doing lawyers' work.[243] Expenses for "public relations efforts" will be excluded.[244]

The prevailing plaintiff has the burden of proving the reasonableness of the number of hours expended on the claim. "This burden does not shift

---

238. Corder v. Brown, *supra*, fn. 223, 25 F.3d at 840.
239. Henry v. Webermeier, 738 F.2d 188, 192 (7th Cir., 1984); Heiar v. Crawford County, 746 F.2d 1190 (7th Cir., 1984); Davis v. Mason County, 927 F.2d 1473 (9th Cir., 1991). The costs to be included in an attorney's fee award (specifically, under 42 U.S.C. § 2000e-5(k)) are those spelled out in 28 U.S.C. § 1920. Cullens v. Georgia Dept. of Transportation, *supra*, fn. 58. For a discussion of attorney's fees treated as "costs" under CERCLA (42 U.S.C. § 9601 et seq.), *see* Key Tronic Corp. v. U.S., 511 U.S. ___ [128 L.Ed.2d 797] (1994).
240. McDonald v. Armontrout, 860 F.2d 1456 (8th Cir., 1988). *See also* Smith v. Freeman, 921 F.2d 1120 (10th Cir., 1990); Davis v. City & County of San Francisco, 976 F.2d 1536 (9th Cir., 1992); Estate of Borst v. O'Brien, 979 F.2d 511 (7th Cir., 1992).
241. Culebras Enterprises Corp. v. Rivera-Rios, 846 F.2d 94, 103 (1st Cir., 1988); Woods v. Graphic Communications, 925 F.2d 1195 (9th Cir., 1991).
242. Sevigny v. Dicksey, 846 F.2d 953 (4th Cir., 1988).
243. Davis v. Southeastern Pennsylvania Transportation Auth., 924 F.2d 51 (3d Cir., 1991). *See also* West Virginia University Hospitals, Inc. v. Casey, 499 U.S. 83 (1991).
244. Rum Creek Coal Sales, Inc. v. Caperton, *supra*, fn. 35.

to the opposing party merely because that party does not show that the hours are unreasonable or that it did not make specific objections to the hours claimed. . . . Part of the applicant's ability to meet his burden includes maintaining billing time records that would enable the reviewing court to identify each distinct claim."[245]

Moreover, one court has ruled the burden is on the fee applicant to establish the overall reasonableness of the application.[246] In fact, a prevailing party has a duty to mitigate fees by promptly disposing of baseless claims through use of summary procedures.[247]

> Counsel for the prevailing party must exercise "billing judgment"; that is, he must act as he would under the ethical and market restraints that constrain a private sector attorney's behavior in billing his own clients.[248]

As distasteful as it may be, it is necessary for the court to undertake "a conscientious and detailed inquiry" into the accuracy of the prevailing party's attorney's records of the number of hours and relevancy of time spent on the case.[249]

"'[E]xcessive, redundant, or otherwise unnecessary' hours should be excluded . . . This means that hours excluded are those that would be unreasonable to bill a client. . . ."[250] Contemporaneous time records are helpful but not indispensable, however.[251] With a proper foundation, computer time records are admissible to support an application for attorney's fees.[252]

---

245. Clark v. Butler, 916 F.2d 255, 259 (5th Cir., 1990). *See also* Watkins v. Fordice, 7 F.3d 453 (5th Cir., 1993); Deary v. City of Gloucester, 9 F.3d 191 (1st Cir., 1993); Jane L. v. Bangerter, *supra*, fn. 196.
246. Smith v. Freeman, 921 F.2d 1120 (10th Cir., 1990).
247. Leffler v. Meer, 936 F.2d 981 (7th Cir., 1991).
248. Lunday v. City of Albany, 42 F.3d 131, 133 (2d Cir., 1994).
249. Lunday v. City of Albany, *supra*, fn. 248.
250. Martin v. University of South Alabama, 911 F.2d 604 (11th Cir., 1990).
251. Dennis v. Warren, 779 F.2d 245 (5th Cir., 1985); Lightfoot v. Walker, 826 F.2d 516 (7th Cir., 1987); Carter v. Sedgwick County, 929 F.2d 1501 (10th Cir., 1991). For further comment on prevailing attorney's recordkeeping, reasonableness of time spent and hourly rates, *see* Grendel's Den, Inc. v. Larkin, 749 F.2d 945 (1st Cir., 1984).
252. Kennedy v. Los Angeles Police Department, 901 F.2d 702 (9th Cir., 1989). *Compare*: Standley v. Chilhowee R-IV School Dist., 5 F.3d 319 (8th Cir., 1993).

In the final analysis, however, "[i]t is the burden of the party applying for attorney fees to establish the extent and reasonableness of the request, supporting the claim with 'meticulous, contemporary time records.'"[253]

Miscellaneous

In a 1986 case, the Eighth Circuit left the determination of miscellaneous issues up to the district court's discretion, stating:

> Because of its singular viewpoint, the district court is best equipped to determine whether hours were reasonably expended, whether the attorneys' hourly rates are within the general rates charged for a particular service in the relevant community, whether the prevailing party achieved a level of success justifying the hours spent, and whether the risk of the case not prevailing calls for an enhancement of the lodestar fee. . . . The appellate court's lack of knowledge concerning local fees and practices renders necessary the district court's wide discretion in the award of attorney's fees.[254]

The district court must provide a "concise and clear" explanation of factors utilized in arriving at an attorney's fee award,[255] but its findings do not have to be "excruciatingly explicit."[256] The district court's interpretation of its own timeliness standards for filing of claims for attorney's fees is acceptable when it establishes certainty as to timeliness requirements.[257]

Section 1988 permits prevailing plaintiffs to recover expert witness fees.[258] It was not an abuse of discretion, however, to deny an application

---

253. Mann v. Reynolds, 46 F.3d 1055, 1062 (10th Cir., 1995).
254. Moore v. City of Des Moines, 766 F.2d 343, 346 (8th Cir., 1985), *cert. den.* 474 U.S. 1060 (1986).
255. McGrath v. County of Nevada, *supra*, fn. 205.
256. Blanchard v. Bergeron, 893 F.2d 87 (5th Cir., 1990). *See also* Rode v. Dellarciprete, 892 F.2d 1177 (3d Cir., 1990); Gilmere v. City of Atlanta, 931 F.2d 811 (11th Cir., 1991); Morscott, Inc. v. City of Cleveland, 936 F.2d 271 (6th Cir., 1991); Foster v. Mydas Associates, Inc., 943 F.2d 139 (1st Cir., 1991).
257. Pitts v. Freeman, 755 F.2d 897 (11th Cir., 1985).
258. Friedrich v. City of Chicago, 888 F.2d 511 (7th Cir., 1989); West Virginia University Hospitals, Inc. v. Casey, 499 U.S. 83 (1991); Gates v. Deukmejian, *supra*, fn. 187.

for expert witness fees where plaintiff failed to provide a declaration that the costs were "accurate, necessary and actually incurred" and adequate documentation to assess the reasonableness of the claimed amounts.[259] The Fifth Circuit determined that "[T]he expenses reasonably incurred by a prevailing plaintiff's attorney in hiring special counsel to assist in the prosecution of the fee claim are fully compensable under § 1988."[260]

A prevailing plaintiff is entitled to interest on the attorney's fee award from the date the award was entered, rather than from the date the court quantified the fees.[261] It is not necessary that interest be requested in the original fee petition.[262]

Excessive Fees

The question, sometimes termed "proportionality,"[263] of whether a district court's award of $243,343.75 in attorney's fees was excessive where the jury awarded damages of only $33,350 was before the U.S. Supreme Court in *City of Riverside v. Rivera*.[264] The Court, splitting almost evenly on the question, affirmed the award, four justices holding the award to be reasonable, one justice holding the award may have been excessive but the trial judge did not commit an abuse of discretion in making it, and four justices finding the award to be excessive.[265]

---

259. Cabrales v. County of Los Angeles, 864 F.2d 1454 (9th Cir., 1988).
260. Alberti v. Klevenhagen, 896 F.2d 917 (5th Cir., 1990).
261. Jenkins by Agyei v. Missouri, 931 F.2d 1273 (8th Cir., 1991). *See also* Davis v. City & County of San Francisco, 976 F.2d 1536 (9th Cir., 1992).
262. Fleming v. County of Kane, 898 F.2d 553 (7th Cir., 1990); Foley v. City of Lowell, 948 F.2d 10 (1st Cir., 1991); Friend v. Kolodzieczak, 65 F.3d 1514 (9th Cir., 1995).
263. *See* Cunningham v. City of McKeesport, 807 F.2d 49 (3d Cir., 1986).
264. 477 U.S. 561 (1986).
265. *See also* Nephew v. City of Aurora, 830 F.2d 1547 (10th Cir., 1987); Hernandez v. Hill Country Telephone Coop., 849 F.2d 139 (5th Cir., 1988); Quesada v. Thomason, 850 F.2d 763 (9th Cir., 1988); Parker v. Williams, 855 F.2d 763 (11th Cir., 1988); Jackson v. Crews, 873 F.2d 1105 (8th Cir., 1989); McHenry v. Chadwick, 896 F.2d 184 (6th Cir., 1990); Davis v. Southeastern Pennsylvania Transportation Auth., 924 F.2d 51 (3d Cir., 1991); Cowan v. Prudential Ins. Co. of America, 935 F.2d 522 (2d Cir., 1991); Starks v. George Court Co., Inc., 937 F.2d 311 (7th Cir., 1991); Estate of Borst v. O'Brien, 979 F.2d 511 (7th Cir., 1992); Alexander v. Gerhardt Enterprises, Inc., 40 F.3d 187 (7th Cir., 1994).

Defendant's Fees

An additional attorney's fee was awarded to a prevailing defendant where "there was no factual or legal basis for [the] appeal. . . . "[266] One court has ruled that a fee substantially less than the lodestar is permissible in fixing a prevailing defendant's fee award.[267]

Apportionment of Award

Apportionment of fees between defendants in a settlement agreement did not preclude a county from being liable for the entire amount when its co-defendant did not pay.[268] The district court is not required to apportion among defendants in accordance with the relative liability of each.[269]

Immunity

States (and presumably their political subdivisions) and their employees are not necessarily immune from § 1988 attorney's fees under the Eleventh Amendment.[270] But where state officials are successfully sued in their *personal* capacities, as opposed to their *official* capacities, § 1988 attorney's fees may not be recovered from their governmental employer.[271] Attorney's fees may be awarded against an official entitled to qualified immunity from personal liability where he is sued in his official capacity.[272]

An enhancement of plaintiff's attorney's fees granted for delay in their recovery is not unconstitutional under the Eleventh Amendment because (1) the award is ancillary to a grant of prospective relief and is therefore

---

266. Fidelity Guarantee Mortgage Co. v. Reben, 809 F.2d 931 (1st Cir., 1987).
267. Eastway Construction Corp. v. City of New York, 821 F.2d 121 (2d Cir., 1987).
268. Dotson v. Chester, 937 F.2d 920 (4th Cir., 1991).
269. Corder v. Gates, 947 F.2d 374 (9th Cir., 1991).
270. Hutto v. Finney, 437 U.S. 678 (1978); Crane v. Texas, 759 F.2d 412 (5th Cir., 1985), *cert.den.sub.nom.* Dallas County v. Crane, 474 U.S. 1020 (1985); Rose v. Nebraska, 748 F.2d 1258 (8th Cir., 1984), *cert.den.sub.nom* Lutjeharms v. Rose, 474 U.S. 817 (1985), *rehg.den.* 474 U.S. 1014 (1985); Spain v. Mountanos, 690 F.2d 742 (9th Cir., 1982).
271. Kentucky v. Graham, 473 U.S. 159 (1985). *See also* Glover v. Alabama Dept. of Corrections, 734 F.2d 691 (11th Cir., 1984), *judgm.vac. & remand.* 474 U.S. 806 (1985); Stevens v. Gay, 864 F.2d 113 (11th Cir., 1988); Scott v. Flowers, 910 F.2d 201 (5th Cir., 1990).
272. Jackson v. Galan, 868 F.2d 165 (5th Cir., 1989).

not subject to the strictures of the Eleventh Amendment, (2) the question of how a "reasonable attorney's fee" is to be calculated is also beyond the reach of the Eleventh Amendment, and (3) an appropriate adjustment for delay in payment is within the contemplation of § 1988(b).[273]

Where a judge is entitled to absolute judicial immunity against a plaintiff's civil rights claim, the plaintiff cannot be a prevailing party and is not entitled to § 1988 attorney's fees.[274] Although a § 1983 monetary damage award against a state magistrate is prohibited by judicial immunity, injunctive relief is not similarly prohibited, and the plaintiff who obtains injunctive relief under § 1983 against the magistrate is entitled to a § 1988(b) attorney's fee award.[275] The same rule applies with respect to prosecutorial immunity.[276]

When a private defendant is entitled to good faith immunity against monetary liability for civil enforcement of rights under a statute subsequently ruled unconstitutional, the defendant is also entitled to immunity from liability for § 1988(b) attorney's fees. The immunity is independent of any claim of immunity which may be asserted by government co-defendants sued in their official capacity.[277] Awards of costs, litigation expenses, and attorney's fees from defendants in their personal capacity are barred when the defendant's conduct meets the objective good faith standard encompassed by the qualified immunity doctrine.[278]

Federal Rules of Civil Procedure

Pleadings and other documents filed in federal court must be signed by an attorney or pro se party. The signature certifies that the signer has read the document, to his or her best knowledge it is factual and warranted or there is a good faith argument for the legal principles it asserts, and it is not filed for any "improper purpose," such as harassment or delay. If it is filed in violation of the rule, the court is authorized to

273. Missouri v. Jenkins by Agyei, 491 U.S. 274 (1989).
274. Cameron v. Seitz, 38 F.3d 264 (6th Cir., 1994).
275. Pulliam v. Allen, 466 U.S. 522 (1984).
276. Wilson v. Stocker, 819 F.2d 943 (10th Cir., 1987), *see also* Kurowski v. Krajewski, 848 F.2d 767 (7th Cir., 1988).
277. Wyatt v. Cole, 928 F.2d 718 (5th Cir., 1991).
278. D'Aguanno v. Gallagher, 50 F.3d 877, 882 (11th Cir., 1995).

impose sanctions, which may include attorney's fees and other expenses incurred because of the filing.[279]

There is an obvious philosophical relationship between Rule 11 sanctions and the so-called *Christianburg*[280] standards for award of § 1988 attorney's fees to defendants. In the appropriate case, in fact, there may be

---

279. Fed. Rules Civ. Proc., Rule 11. The rule provides in pertinent part:

(a) Signature. Every pleading, written motion, and other paper shall be signed by at least one attorney of record in the attorney's individual name, or, if the party is not represented by an attorney, shall be signed by the party. . . .

(b) Representations to Court. By presenting to the court (whether by signing, filing, submitting, or later advocating) a pleading, written motion, or other paper, an attorney or unrepresented party is certifying that to the best of the person's knowledge, information, and belief, formed after an inquiry reasonable under the circumstances, . . .

(1) it is not being presented for any improper purpose, such as to harass or to cause unnecessary delay or needless increase in the cost of litigation;

(2) the claims, defenses, and other legal contentions therein are warranted by existing law or by a nonfrivolous argument for the extension, modification, or reversal of existing law or the establishment of new law;

(3) the allegations and other factual contentions have evidentiary support or, if specifically so identified, are likely to have evidentiary support after a reasonable opportunity for further investigation or discovery; and

(4) the denials of factual contentions are warranted on the evidence or, if specifically so identified, are reasonably based on a lack of information or belief.

(c) Sanctions. If, after notice and a reasonable opportunity to respond, the court determines that subdivision (b) has been violated, the court may . . . impose an appropriate sanction upon the attorneys, law firms, or parties that have violated subdivision (b) or are responsible for the violation.

(1) How Initiated.

(A) By Motion. . . . (B) On Court's Initiative. . . .

(2) Nature of Sanction; Limitations. A sanction imposed for violation of this rule shall be limited to what is sufficient to deter repetition of such conduct or comparable conduct by others similarly situated. . . . [T]he sanction may consist of, or include, directives of a nonmonetary nature, an order to pay a penalty into court, or, if imposed on motion and warranted for effective deterrence, an order directing payment to the movant of some or all of the reasonable attorneys' fees and other expenses incurred as a direct result of the violation. . . .

280. Christianburg Garment Co. v. E.E.O.C., *supra*, fn. 66.

"no distinction between the standard applicable to assessing attorney's fees under Rule 11 and assessing them under *Christianburg*."[281]

In determining Rule 11 sanctions, the court must examine two issues: (1) whether there was "good faith," meaning no intention to harass, and (2) whether the filing was objectively warranted by existing law or good faith argument that the law should be modified and the lawyer filing it believed it "well grounded in fact."[282] The standard to be applied is "objective reasonableness."[283] Abuse of discretion is the standard for appellate review of imposition of Rule 11 sanctions.[284] But, "all doubts are to be resolved in favor of the signer of the document that is the basis of Rule 11 sanctions."[285]

Rule 11 sanctions obviously may not be imposed for all actions taken in the course of litigation, but are limited to those connected with the signing of a pleading or other paper.[286] The offending papers must have been interposed for an improper purpose or in bad faith.[287]

Rule 11 sanctions should not be imposed in response to a pleading "that makes a 'good faith argument for the extension, modification, or reversal of existing law, and that is not interposed for any improper purpose.'"[288] Courts "must exercise extreme caution in sanctioning attorneys under Rule 11, *particularly* where such sanctions emerge from an attorney's efforts to secure the court's recognition of new rights."[289]

A voluntary dismissal of a frivolous complaint does not terminate the district court's jurisdiction to impose Rule 11 sanctions, but on unsuccessful appeal of their imposition, the respondent (appellee) is not entitled to its attorney's fees on an appeal.[290] Even though the court has no power to

---

281. Simons v. Southwest Petro-Chem, Inc., 28 F.3d 1029, 1033 (10th Cir., 1994).
282. Tabrizi v. Village of Glen Ellyn, 883 F.2d 587 (7th Cir., 1989).
283. Pulaski County Republican Committee v. Board of Commissioners, 956 F.2d 172 (8th Cir., 1992).
284. Leffler v. Mear, 936 F.2d 981 (7th Cir., 1991).
285. Rounseville v. Zahl, *supra*, fn. 68.
286. Introcaso v. Cunningham, 857 F.2d 965 (4th Cir., 1988); Cunningham v. County of Los Angeles, 879 F.2d 473 (9th Cir., 1989).
287. Lawshe v. Simpson, 16 F.3d 1475, 1484 (7th Cir., 1994).
288. Larez v. Holcomb, *supra*, fn. 153, 16 F.3d at 1522.
289. Larez v. Holcomb, *supra*, fn. 153, 16 F.3d at 1522.
290. Cooter & Gell v. Hartmarx Corp., 496 U.S. 384 (1990). *See also* Szabo Food Service, Inc. v. Canteen Corp., 823 F.2d 1073 (7th Cir., 1987).

award § 1988(b) attorney's fees due to lack of subject-matter jurisdiction over a civil rights claim, it is not precluded from imposing Rule 11 sanctions for the filing of a frivolous complaint in the first place.[291]

Under Rule 11, an award is *required* if a paper which is frivolous is filed.[292] Rule 11 sanctions may be awarded on the ground that complaint allegations were advanced without benefit of adequate factual investigation.[293]

A plaintiff's attorney who applies for an attorney's fee award without disclosing the client's fee waiver as part of a settlement is subject to imposition of Rule 11 sanctions.[294] Where an attorney repeatedly fails to file a complete, sufficient supersedeas bond in compliance with Federal Rule of Civil Procedure 62(d), the trial court's imposition of Rule 11 sanctions is not an abuse of discretion.[295]

Although an attorney's fee award may not be ordered against a losing Title VII plaintiff's lawyer, the court may consider an alternative, such as Rule 11 sanctions.[296] But where a plaintiff has been awarded § 1988(b) attorney's fees, he or she is not entitled to Rule 11 sanctions.[297]

A trial court's decision not to impose Rule 11 sanctions does not preclude imposition of monetary sanctions against an attorney under Section 1927 of Title 28 of the U.S. Code,[298] however. Although the trial court finds no objectively unreasonable behavior in the papers filed in the case, other conduct in the course of litigation may be found as evidence of subjective bad faith supporting imposition of Section 1927 sanctions.[299]

---

291. Branson v. Nott, 62 F.3d 287 (9th Cir., 1995).
292. Price v. Hawaii, 939 F.2d 702 (9th Cir., 1991).
293. Triad Associates, Inc. v. Chicago Housing Auth., 892 F.2d 583 (7th Cir., 1989).
294. Blackwell v. Dept. of Offender Rehabilitation, 807 F.2d 914 (11th Cir., 1987).
295. E.E.O.C. v. Clear Lake Dodge, *supra*, fn. 19.
296. Quiroga v. Hasbro, Inc., 934 F.2d 497 (3d Cir., 1991).
297. Hatfield v. Hayes, 877 F.2d 717 (8th Cir., 1989).
298. Any attorney or other person admitted to conduct cases in any court of the United States or any Territory thereof who so multiplies the proceedings in any case unreasonably and vexatiously may be required by the court to satisfy personally the excess costs, expenses, and attorneys' fees reasonably incurred because of such conduct.

     28 U.S.C. § 1927.
299. Salstrom v. Citicorp Credit Services, Inc., 74 F.3d 183 (9th Cir., 1996).

Rule 68 Offer of Settlement

The defendant is not liable for the attorney's fees incurred by a prevailing plaintiff after the defendant's rejected offer of settlement under Federal Rule 68,[300] when the recovery is less than the amount of the offer. Where an offer of settlement under Rule 68 does not include attorney's fees, the amount of a reasonable fee should be added to the offer for purposes of determining whether the recovery exceeded the offer.[301] The plaintiff is liable for defendant's costs incurred after the rejected offer was made, but not for defendant's attorney's fees.[302]

When a Rule 68 offer is accepted, the accepting plaintiff is entitled to attorney's fees accrued at the time of offer,[303] and liability for post-settlement attorney's fees may be affected by the terms of the offer. Where the plain language of the offer of judgment unambiguously limits fees and costs to those incurred prior to the date of offer, however, plaintiffs are not entitled to recover attorney's fees incurred after acceptance of the offer.[304]

To be effective, a Rule 68 offer of settlement must be a "formal" offer. That is, it must be a *written* offer made by defendant and served on plaintiff after the legal action has been commenced.[305]

Conclusion

It is clear that the federal courts believe a prevailing plaintiff should recover attorney's fees in all but an insignificant few § 1983 cases. Despite use of the term "prevailing *party*" in the statute, prevailing defen-

---

300. Fed. Rules Civ. Proc., Rule 68 (1987). The operating words in Rule 68 are: "If the judgment finally obtained by the offeree is not more favorable than the offer, the offeree must pay the costs incurred after the making of the offer." Section 1988(b) attorney's fees are "costs" for Rule 68 purposes. Marek v. Chesny, 473 U.S. 1 (1985); Erdman v. Cochise County, 926 F.2d 877 (9th Cir., 1991).
301. O'Brien v. City of Greers Ferry, 873 F.2d 1115 (9th Cir., 1989).
302. Crossman v. Marcoccio, 806 F.2d 329 (1st Cir., 1986); Hopper v. Euclid Manor Nursing Home, Inc., 867 F.2d 291 (6th Cir., 1989).
303. Holland v. Roeser, 37 F.3d 501 (9th Cir., 1994).
304. Guerrero v. Cummings, 70 F.3d 1111 (9th Cir., 1995).
305. Clark v. Sims, 28 F.3d 420 (4th Cir., 1994).

dants have been excluded except in cases where the plaintiff's claim is so ludicrous as to constitute a clear abuse of the judicial process.

The result is the single most expensive item involved in vulnerability of public entities to § 1983 claims. The plaintiff's attorney's fees in many cases will far surpass any damages which might be ordered.

In light of the fact that full litigation of a § 1983 claim is not a prerequisite to an attorney's fee award, it is imperative that counsel for prospective defendants advise their clients to take steps to limit exposure to potential § 1983 liability and, after a claim has been made, to assist defendants in bringing proceedings to a conclusion as quickly as possible.

Table of Cases

Hunter v. Bryant (1991)
Hunter v. Carbondale Area School Dist. (1993)
Hutto v. Finney (1978)
Hyland v. Wonder (1992, 1993)
Imbler v. Pachtman (1976)
Immediato v. Rye Neck School Dist. (1996)
Independent Federation of Flight Attendants v. Zipes (1989)
Ingraham v. Wright (1977)
Inmates of Unit 14 v. Rebideau (1984)
Int'l Ass'n of Machinists v. Affleck (1986)
Int'l Board of Electrical Workers v. Hawaiian Tel. Co. (1986)
Int'l Oceanic Enterprises, Inc. v. Menton (1980)
Int'l Primate Protection League v. Administrators of Tulane Educ. Fund (1991)
Int'l Soc. for Krishna Consciousness v. City of Evanston (1980, 1981)
Int'l Soc. for Krishna Consciousness v. Colorado State Fair and Indus. Exposition Commission (1983)
Int'l Soc. for Krishna Consciousness v. Collins (1980)
Introcaso v. Cunningham (1988)
Iqbal v. Golf Course Superintendents Assn. (1990)
J.O. v. Alton Community United School Dist. 11 (1990)
Jackson v. Crews (1989)
Jackson v. Galan (1989)
Jackson v. Inhabitants of the Town of Searsport (1983)
Jackson v. Metropolitan Edison Co. (1974)
Jackson v. Ward (1978)
Jacobsen v. City of Seattle (1983)
Jacobson v. Rose (1978)
Jaggers v. Zolliecoffer (1986)
James v. City of Chester (1994)
Janda v. City of Detroit (1989)
Jane L. v. Bangerter (1995)
Janetka v. Dabe (1989)
Janusaitis v. Middleburg Volunteer Fire Dep't (1979)
Japanese Elecs. Prods. Antitrust Litig. (1983)
Jeanine B. v. Thompson (1995)
Jeff D. v. Andrus (1989)
Jeff D. v. Andrus (1990)
Jefferson v. Ambroz (1996)
Jeffries v. Harleston (1995)
Jeglin v. San Jacinto Unified School Dist. (1993)
Jenkins by Agyei v. Missouri (1991)
Jenkins by Agyei v. State of Missouri (1988)
Jenkins v. Whittaker Corp. (1986)
Jensen v. City of San Jose (1986)
Jermosen v. Smith (1991)
Jett v. Dallas Independent School Dist. (1986, 1989)
John McShain, Inc. v. Cessna Aircraft Co. (1977)
John v. Barron (1990)
Johnson v. Blum (1983)
Johnson v. City of Pleasanton (1992)
Johnson v. Dallas Independent School Dist. (1994)
Johnson v. Dep't of Public Safety & Correctional Services (1995)
Johnson v. Fankell (1996)
Johnson v. Georgia Highway Express, Inc. (1974)
Johnson v. Hardin County (1990)
Johnson v. Jones (1995)
Johnson v. Lutz (1930)
Johnson v. Martin (1991)
Johnson v. Miller (1982)
Johnson v. Mississippi (1979)
Johnson v. Multnomah County, Oregon (1995)
Johnson v. Rhode Island Parole Board Members (1987)